express
power
yoga
U0856268
1
with
Ankie Beilke
貝安琪
親身演繹
新世代瑜伽
ANKIE LAU
LAUFILM INTERNATIONAL
劉氏國際影業公司
DVD
VIDEO
DELTAMAC

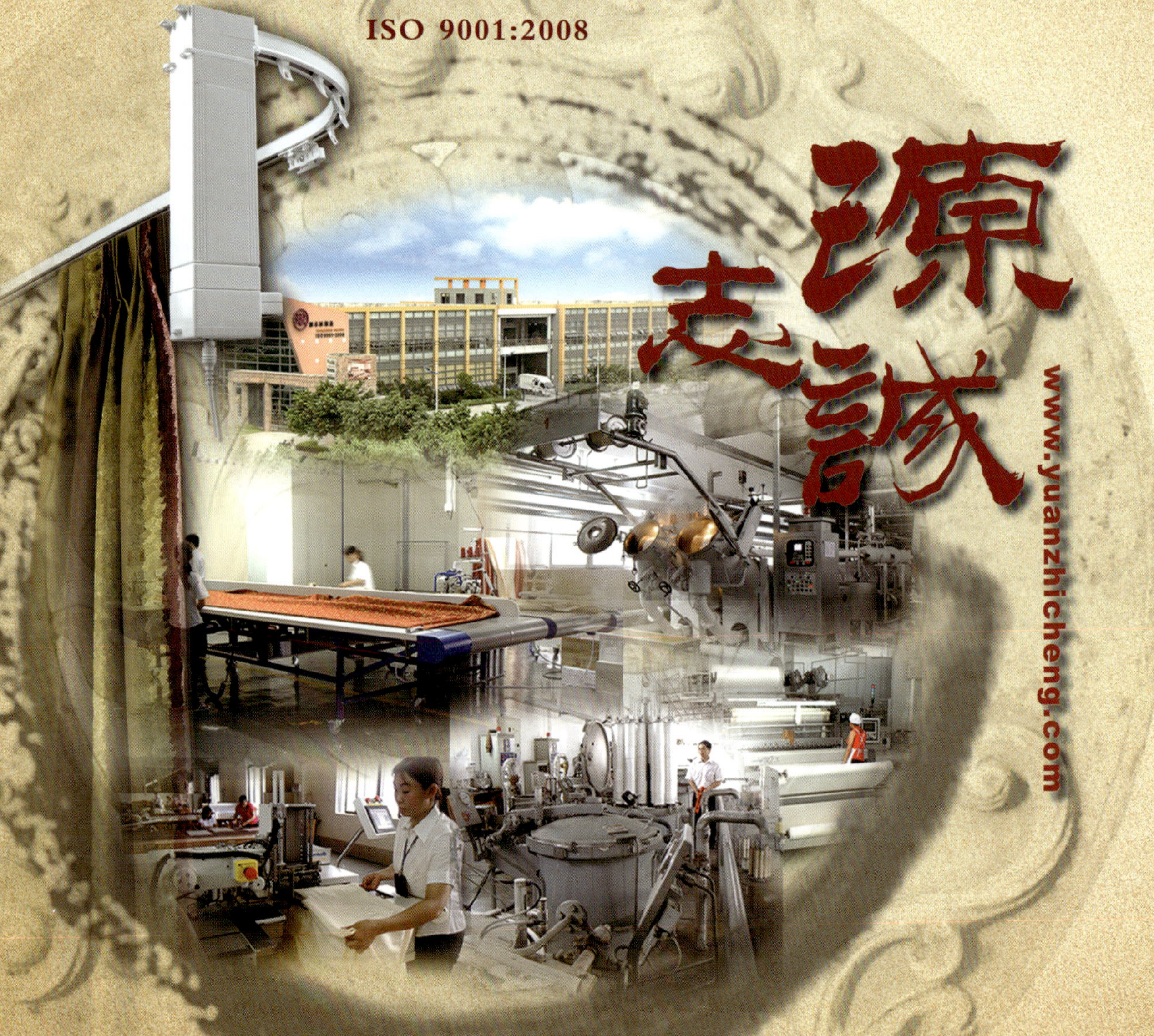

2011/2012 EDITION

上海元瑞文化传播有限公司
Shanghai Join and Joy Communications Co., Ltd

上 海 辞 书 出 版 社

慕思 GLOBAL HEALTHY SLEEP RESOURCE COLLECTOR
全球健康睡眠资源整合者
慕思睡眠系统，整合全球健康睡眠资源精华，
——科学、科技、工艺、技术、原料……
修护睡眠、修整心灵、绝佳呈现“生命中三分之一”！
dR®
de RUCCI 慕思

HRCHINA

A Directory for Hotel, Restaurant and Catering Products & Services

中国酒店工程与餐饮采购指南

2011/2012 EDITION

一本直面当今星级酒店、餐厅、餐饮业、开发商、采购及厨师的行业指南

一本汇集众多知名品牌、供应商的采购手册

一个包罗万象、囊括全球的全方位信息平台

一本业内人士必备的参考大全

在这里，你可以纵览全新的行业动态

在这里，你可以第一时间掌握业内潮流信息

精美装帧，每年一刊，发行覆盖内陆及港澳地区

我们的读者来自世界各地

以全面的资讯助推您的商业发展

为您提供充足、完善的资源后盾

An industrial directory for the stars hotels, restaurants, food & beverage industry, developers, purchasers, and chefs.

A purchasing hand book, which gathers a lot of well-known brands and suppliers.

A platform with informations of all varieties from all around the world.

A compulsory reference book, which the insiders of the industry must have.

Here, you have an overview of the brand new activities of the industry.

Here, you can obtain the latest trends of the industry.

It is a fine produced directory, which is only published once per year.

It will be distributed in mainland China, Hong Kong and Macau.

Our readers are from all over the world.

With all round information, the directory can help you to develop your business, provide you with adequate and perfect resources.

上海元瑞文化传播有限公司
Shanghai Join and Joy Communications Co., Ltd

支持单位：中国建筑文化中心
Support: China Architectural Culture Center

上海泰时广告有限公司
Shanghai TAISHI Advertisement Co., Ltd.

上海 Shanghai
上海市宜山路 439 号七建大厦 707 室
Rm 707 QiJian Building NO.439 YiShan Road,Shanghai
电话(Tel):021-54248571/72/73
传真(Fax):021-54248576
Email: shanghai@joinjoy.com

香港代表处 Hongkong Representative Office
香港九龙油塘茶果岭道 428 号荣山工业大厦四楼 D 室
4D wing shan Industrial Building,428 Cha Kwo Ling Road, YanTong,Kowloon,Hong Kong
电话(Tel)：+852-28154488
传真(Fax)：+852-28157766
Email: hongkong@joinjoy.com

北京代表处 Beijing Representative Office
北京市海淀区安宁庄东路18号4号办公室403室
Rm 403, 4 Office, NO.18 An Ning Zhuang (E)Road, Beijing
电话(Tel): 010-51617458
传真(Fax): 010-62942175
Email: beijing@joinjoy.com

德国代表处 Germany Representative Office
Neuenhausplatz 66, 40699 Erkrath-Unterfeldhaus Germany
电话(Tel)：+49 (0)211-54357309
传真(Fax)：+49 (0)211-54357715
Email: germany@joinjoy.com

广州代表处 Guangzhou Representative Office
广州市广利路75号东洲大厦B座506室
Rm 506, B NO.75 Guang Li Road, Guangzhou
电话(Tel): 020-85594979
传真(Fax): 020-85592065
Email: guangzhou@joinjoy.com

意大利代表处 Italy Representative Office
Via XXV Aprile 19, 40057 Granarolo,Dell'Emilia(Bo),Italy
电话(Tel): + 39 (0)51-763388
传真(Fax): + 39 (0)51-763190
Email: italy@joinjoy.com

图书在版编目（CIP）数据
中国酒店工程与餐饮采购指南. 2011~2012/高诗云编著. 上海：上海辞书出版社，2011.6
ISBN 978-7-5326-3432-3

I. ①中… II. ①高… III.①饮食业—采购—中国—2011~2012指南
IV. ①F719.3-62

中国版本图书馆CIP数据核字（2011）第114016号

书名：中国酒店工程与餐饮采购指南（2011~2012）
采编：高诗雲 Shanghai Join and Joy Communications Co., Ltd
责任编辑：吴雅仙 韦娜
助理编辑：Joanna Chen
视觉总监：Tai Tai
出版、发行：上海世纪出版股份有限公司
上海辞书出版社
www.ewen.cc
www.cishu.com.cn

地址：上海市陕西北路457号
邮编：200040
电话：021-62472088 62568566
传真：021-62568566

开本：625 x 880 1/8
印张：25.5
字数：500,000
版次：2011年6月第1版 2011年6月第1次印刷
ISBN 978-7-5326-3432-3/T.150
定价：398.00元
广告经营许可证号：3100620050023

目录 Contents

HRC CHINA

贺词 Congratulations

The Ladies and Gentlemen of The Ritz-Carlton Beijing, Financial Street and I would like to congratulate HRC China on another successful publication, the HRC China 2011/2012 edition. Furthermore, HRC China has an outstanding Directory with a high quantity of professional information which brings in many updated important messages every year, we are giving our strong support and wish to see continued success of HRC China.

The issue comes at an opportune time when The Ritz-Carlton Beijing, Financial Street celebrates its fifth anniversary. We are extremely proud and delighted to have received numerous international accolades and recognition from around the world such as TRAVEL + LEISURE (U.S.A.) "2011 T + L 500 World's Best Hotels" ranked No. 1 in mainland China for consecutive 2 years. Indeed it is testimony to our commitment to unique experiences and dedicated service, we will continue to set a new benchmark and deliver memorable experiences through our devoted ladies and gentlemen.

The hotel's contemporary design of glass and chrome with Oriental influences distinguishes our hotel in Beijing's newly emerging financial district. Upon arrival, guests find a sense of place steeped in harmony, comfort and good fortune. Guest rooms offer the utmost level of spacious and luxury accommodations. Our guest rooms are amongst the largest in the capital city. Discerning guests that prefer more convenience and privacy of a "hotel within a hotel" will find their haven staying in a Ritz-Carlton Club accommodation that also features many special services and privileges.

For pure luxury outside of our accommodations, the hotel's 1,500-square-meter, full-scale lifestyle spa ensures the ultimate in pampering.

For dining, prepare your senses for a culinary experience like no other as you savor the selection of our three signature restaurants, Cépe, our award-winning Italian Dining Room. Qi, Chinese restaurant offers exquisite Cantonese cuisine including favorite dishes from Sichuan and Beijing. Greenfish, offers all-day continental dining. Our Crystal Bar & Lounge serves the signature Ritz-Carlton afternoon tea with a selection of more than 88 selections of world teas. Please also join us in Crystal Bar for a nice evening to enjoy your favorite cocktail or a glass of champagne!

Above all, however, you will discover that our luxury hotel is a place where the genuine care and comfort of our guests is our highest mission.

We look forward to welcoming you to The Ritz-Carlton Beijing, Financial Street in the near future.

Yours sincerely,

Mark Lettenbichler

Regional Vice President & General Manager
The Ritz-Carlton Beijing, Financial Street

Mark Lettenbichler oversees Japan, Korea and South East Asia for The Ritz-Carlton Hotel Company, L.L.C. He has 25 years of experience in the hospitality industry. In his tenure of 21 years with The Ritz-Carlton Hotel Company, his appointments have brought him to a number of Ritz-Carlton landmark properties in cities and resorts in the United States, Asia and China. He is an active member in the Beijing and Hong Kong community serving as Chairman of the Hong Kong Hotels Association (2000 – 2010) and also a Board Member for the Hong Kong Tourism Board (2002 - 2008).

我谨代表北京金融街丽思卡尔顿酒店的全体绅士淑女们向《中国酒店工程与餐饮采购指南》的2011/2012版的成功发行表示衷心的祝贺！《中国酒店工程与餐饮采购指南》是一个高端而全面的信息平台，为我们酒店行业的发展带来了新的信息渠道，这是一本非常出色的指南，我们支持并希望他越办越好！

MARK LETTENBICHLER

此书出版的时候正值北京金融街丽思卡尔顿酒店开业五周年庆典，开业五年以来，酒店荣获了来自全球及全中国的众多奖项，为此我们深感荣幸和自豪，这是对我们多年来致力于为客人提供真诚关怀和舒适款待的认可和嘉奖，我们全体绅士淑女们将齐心协力设定一个新的里程碑目标，致力于为客人提供最完善的个性化服务及难忘的奢华体验而继续努力。

酒店赋予浓郁的现代设计，完美融合轻钢玻璃和铬合金结构外观；室内设计在沿用奢华典雅的同时，更对中国博大精深的传统文化进行完美的提炼和诠释，两者结合营造出低调而奢华的氛围。屹立于北京最新崛起的金融街，绽放出高雅内敛的气度。宽敞的客房为客人提供最大程度奢华体验，即使是最基本房型面积也达到50平米以上。酒店设计融入风水学艺术特色，为各方宾客营造一个汇聚财富、愉悦、祥和的旅途之家。喜欢更私密和便捷的客人可选择行政楼层，无论是细微服务还是特色餐饮，尊贵特权由您掌握。

酒店拥有三间风格迥异的餐厅为您提供卓越的全日创意美食、意大利及中华美味，满足您最挑剔的味蕾。全日餐厅Greenfish（四季汇），提供健康绿色饮食。屡获殊荣的意大利餐厅Cépe（意味轩），为您奉献最地道的意大利美食。特色中餐厅Qi（金阁），邀您体验纯正的精品粤菜。大堂酒廊和水晶吧每日献上经典丽思尔顿下午茶，来自世界各地共88种精选上等茶叶加之传统考究的茶道， 定会令您倍感心旷神怡。而酒店闻闻遐迩的1500平方米丽思水疗中心，让您真正体验奢华至尊享受。

总而言之，在金融街丽思卡尔顿酒店你会发现，让宾客获得真诚关怀和舒适款待是我们全体绅士淑女的最高使命，这里会是你最贴心的家。

为您服务是我们的荣幸！我们期待您光临北京金融街丽思卡尔顿酒店！

李敦白

集团区域副总裁

北京金融街丽思卡尔顿酒店总经理

李敦白先生负责丽思卡尔顿酒店管理集团日本，韩国和东南亚地区的经营管理。拥有25年酒店管理行业资深管理经验，在丽思卡尔顿集团任职的21年中，带领团队为丽思卡尔顿集团在美国、亚洲和中国地区的发展开拓了一个又一个新的里程碑。李敦白先生热衷于参加北京和香港地区的社团组织，2000年-2010年期间任香港酒店协会主席，2002年-2008年期间为香港旅游局董事会成员。

北京金融街丽思卡尔顿酒店　中国北京市西城区金城坊东街1号　邮编：100140

1 Jin Cheng Fang Street East, Financial Street, Xicheng District, Beijing 100140, China

Tel: (86 10) 6601 6666　Fax: (86 10) 6601 6029　www.ritzcarlton.com

THE RITZ-CARLTON®
BEIJING, FINANCIAL STREET

贺词 Congratulations

Dear Ladies and Gentlemen,

Warm greetings from The Ritz-Carlton, Beijing! I am honored to take this opportunity to introduce this useful edition of HRC China with all of you.

The Ritz-Carlton, Beijing, is centrally situated in one of Beijing's most thriving business area – China Central Place, within the heart of the city's central business district, the hotel is 30 minutes away from the Beijing Capital International Airport and offers easy access to the city's historical and cultural landmarks.

Blending English country manor style with contemporary luxury touches scattered rhythmic gloss of fine marble floor tiles captures the imagination as you make your way through the richly appointed lobby. Behold The Ritz-Carlton, Beijing, architecture and décor classically inspired. Whether from the full-bodied taste of Ritz-Carlton traditional afternoon tea or a refreshing spa treatment, your senses are entranced by experience. Choose from 305 guest rooms, including 38 suites and 61 Ritz-Carlton Club Level rooms, all with a standard of service that has made the Ritz-Carlton name synonymous with luxury.

Joining The Ritz-Carlton Company in 2002 and moving to Beijing in 2009 as the general manager has been a wonderful experience and having the opportunity to lead our Ladies & Gentlemen in providing our guests with the service that is expected of us has been a great privilege.

With Best Personal Regards,

David Wilson

General Manager
The Ritz-Carlton, Beijing

各位绅士和淑女们：

大家好！很高兴有机会向大家介绍《中国酒店工程与餐饮采购指南》这本十分具有参考价值的书籍。

北京丽思卡尔顿酒店位于CBD商业核心区，距北京首都国际机场仅30分钟车程，名胜古迹和文化地标皆近在咫尺。酒店共拥有305间豪华客房，包括38间套房和61间丽思卡尔顿会所级客房。

经典英式庄园设计风格，高标准的个性化服务，使北京丽思卡尔顿成为奢华的代名词。品味丽思卡尔顿经典下午茶，体验特色美食文化，沉迷独特芳香水疗，尊享丽思卡尔顿传奇服务！

我于2002年加入丽思卡尔顿酒店集团，在2009年来到北京丽思卡尔顿酒店担任总经理一职，致力于带领酒店的绅士、淑女们为客人提供最完善的个性化服务及完美的入住体验。

DAVID WILSON

威尔森

总经理

北京丽思卡尔顿酒店

I would like to congratulate on the successful launch of HRC China 2011. In its second year running, not only has this directory become an excellent platform for practitioners to exchange information, but also has proven to be a widely recognized and indispensable reference for hoteliers to learn more about the trends and best practices of the hotel industry.

The Peninsula Shanghai, which opened in October 2009, is the first new building to be constructed on the historic Bund in over 60 years. Offering the best of Peninsula traditions and a range of signature services and facilities, including Shanghai's largest guestrooms and the city's highest staff-to-guest ratio, The Peninsula also heralds the return of parent company, The Hongkong and Shanghai Hotels, Limited, to Shanghai where it owned and operated four of the city's premier hotels in the 1920s to 1940s - The Kalee, The Astor House, The Palace and The Majestic.

Located along the historic Bund with spectacular views of the Bund, Huangpu River, Pudong and former British Consulate gardens, The Peninsula Shanghai perfectly blends with the historic architecture of its landmark neighbours. It's 235 guestrooms (including 44 suites) are amongst the largest in Shanghai. The rooms are elegantly designed to provide luxurious comfort and features, with Art Deco-inspired interiors seamlessly blending traditional Peninsula standards of comfort and state-of-the-art technology with elements of Chinese heritage. The Peninsula Shanghai features a collection of five eclectic restaurants and bars offering a variety of cuisines and ambiences - The Lobby, Yi Long Court Chinese Restaurant, Sir Elly's Rooftop Restaurant, Bar & Terrace, the nautical-themed Compass Bar and Salon de Ning. The Peninsula Spa by ESPA offers a city retreat permeated by indulgence and deep relaxation. Seven treatment rooms and two VIP suites, heat experiences, highly-trained therapists and ESPA products combine and provide luxurious bespoke treatments for body and mind.

I wish HRC China every success in the coming years!

Joseph W.Y. Chong

General Manager of The Peninsula Shanghai

Joseph joined The Peninsula Hotels in 2000 as Director of Rooms at The Peninsula Beijing. In 2005, he was promoted to be Executive Assistant Manager, Rooms and soon after that, he was transferred to The Peninsula Bangkok as Resident Manager. In early 2009, he joined the pre-opening team of The Peninsula Shanghai as Hotel Manager and played an instrumental role in the opening of the hotel in October 2009. Joseph is currently a member of The Institute of Hospitality (UK). From April 2011, he has assumed General Manager of The Peninsula Shanghai.

祝贺《中国酒店工程与餐饮采购指南》2011年版出版成功。在过去一年中，此书为广大业内人士提供了酒店行业的发展趋势和颇具价值的参考信息，为酒店工程和餐饮采购创造了一座桥梁，是一个包罗万象、囊括全球的全方位信息平台，是一本酒店经理人必备的参考大全。

2009年10月隆重启业的上海半岛酒店，是六十年来外滩第一座新落成的建筑物，亦是继承半岛酒店集团的优良传统、顶级服务及完善设施的新典范，客房面积、服务人员与客人比率皆为上海之冠。上海半岛酒店母公司——香港上海大酒店有限公司早于上世纪二十至四十年代已在当地经营The Kalee、礼查(The Astor House)、大华(The Majestic)及汇中(The Palace)四家顶级酒店，上海半岛酒店盛大开幕亦见证了母公司光荣回归黄埔江畔。

上海半岛酒店雄据外滩，坐拥外滩黄浦江、浦东及前英国领事馆花园景观，酒店大楼的古典外观设计与四周的历史建筑和谐并存。上海半岛酒店的235间客房（包括44间套间）都位于上海的最大客房之列。房间设计优雅，艺术装饰风格的内饰将半岛酒店传统的舒适标准及先进科技与中国元素完美揉合，为宾客带来极致奢华的舒适感受。拥有五间风格迥异的餐厅和酒吧，上海半岛酒店更呈献舒适奢华、高水平的的餐饮选择，包括大堂茶座、逸龙阁中餐厅、艾利爵士顶层餐厅、酒吧和露台、以航海为主题的引航酒吧和玲珑酒廊。除此之外，由国际知名的水疗顾问ESPA公司设计开发的上海半岛酒店水疗中心亦为贵客打造独一无二的奢华理疗体验。

在此，我衷心祝愿《中国酒店工程与餐饮采购指南》越办越好，能够有更长远的发展。

张荣耀

上海半岛酒店总经理

张荣耀先生于2000年加入半岛集团担任北京王府半岛酒店房务总监一职。2005年，他出任房务部行政副经理。2007年，张先生调任曼谷半岛酒店驻店经理一职。2009年初，他加入上海半岛酒店开业筹备组担任酒店经理，为上海半岛酒店2009年10月的成功开业起到了关键的作用。张先生是酒店协会会员（英国），于2010年4月起升任上海半岛酒店总经理。

THE PENINSULA

SHANGHAI

上海半岛酒店

贺词 Congratulations

On behalf of Conrad Sanya Haitang Bay and Doubletree Resort by Hilton Sanya Haitang Bay, we are delighted to congratulate HRC China on Publishing HRC China 2011/2012 Edition.

Conrad Sanya Haitang Bay and Doubletree Resort by Hilton Sanya Haitang Bay opened in December 28, 2010, which are the first hotels open in Haitang Bay, Sanya, Hainan. HRC China is a comprehensive and useful directory which can help us to find more about the latest available products and makes us doing business a little easier during our pre-opening.

I sincerely wish HRC China have a successful and prosperous future!

Gerd Knaust

Cluster General Manager
Conrad Sanya Haitang Bay &
Doubletree Resort by Hilton Sanya Haitang Bay

我谨代表三亚海棠湾康莱德酒店及万达三亚海棠湾希尔顿逸林度假酒店，诚挚地祝贺《中国酒店工程与餐饮采购指南》2011/2012成功发行。

三亚海棠湾康莱德酒店及万达三亚海棠湾希尔顿逸林度假酒店于2010年12月28日开业，是海南三亚海棠湾国家旅游度假区首批开业酒店。《中国酒店工程与餐饮采购指南》是一本全面的咨询信息类刊物，开业期间让我们轻松寻找时下最新的各类产品，让我们的业务工作变得更加轻松自如。

衷心祝愿《中国酒店工程与餐饮采购指南》未来更加成功及美好！

GERD KNAUST

贺冠达

总经理

三亚海棠湾康莱德酒店

万达三亚海棠湾希尔顿逸林度假酒店

贺词 Congratulations

Dear valued reader and professional industry friend:

I am honored to write this congratulation words for HRC China. This is the guidebook for purchasing managers and other department heads alike which was especially important for The Westin Nanjing during the pre-opening stage. Being able to find any kind of reliable supplier for all kinds of equipment instantly saved us a lot of time and made us able to concentrate on the essentials.

The Westin Nanjing is strategically located in the Hunan Road central business district, on top of the Nanjing International Center, and offering a retreat and each room over looking the scenic Xuanwu Lake.

Our Westin Heavenly® Bed in each of our 234 guest rooms and suites offers an indulgent respite from the usual demands of the day. Find comfort from the sumptuous and stylish all-white bed, consisting of a custom designed high quality linen. Hotel has Seasonal Tastes all-day dining venue with open kitchen that features both buffet and a la carte selections; Five Zen5es Chinese restaurant features new-look Huaiyang fare and Chinese dishes prepared using authentic methods.

After work you can feel rejuvenated with a dip in our 25-meter indoor heated swimming pool, or a session at Westin WORKOUT®, our WORKOUT center offering the latest in cardio equipment and weights. On the service part, hotel will deliver personal and instinctive service to our guest and make guest renewal and Fell Better than They Arrived.

Lastly, I sincerely wish to HRC China and all colleagues and readers a Prosperous and Successful 2011.

Best regards.

Richard Deutl

General Manager
The Westin Nanjing

尊敬的读者及业内伙伴：

我很荣幸能够为《中国酒店工程与餐饮采购指南》写2011年的贺词。这本指南对于酒店的采购部及其他部门都提供了非常有用的采购信息，特别是在南京威斯汀大酒店的开业筹备阶段，我们将此指南作为我们的工具书籍，从而节省了许多的时间和精力。

RICHARD DEUTL

南京威斯汀大酒店的地理位置十分优越，坐落于湖南路商业中心，南京国际购物广场南楼，为您提供了一个舒适的场所，每间客房均可饱览美丽的玄武湖景色。

234间豪华湖景房和套房均配有威斯汀天梦®之床，让您体验活力焕发的每一天。威斯汀独有的豪华床垫和豪华睡枕带您进入甜蜜梦乡。知味全日餐厅内设有开放式厨房，提供西式自助餐及零点服务；中国元素中餐厅使用道地的烹饪手法，为您提供全新的淮扬佳肴。

结束一天的工作之后，在酒店25米的室内恒温泳池惬意舒展，或是在WestinWORKOUT®健身中心挥汗如雨，重塑您的身心活力。酒店的健身中心提供时下最先进的跑步机及重量机械。在酒店服务方面，我们将为宾客提供个性化和直觉灵动的服务，让宾客感到活力焕发，带着比到达时更为欣喜的心情离开酒店。

最后，我诚挚地祝愿《中国酒店工程与餐饮采购指南》、酒店同行以及各位读者，在2011年里工作顺利，万事如意！

真诚的祝福！

杜德瑞

总经理

南京威斯汀大酒店

THE WESTIN

NANJING

南京威斯汀大酒店

XU XIAO DONG

我由衷地祝贺这本《中国酒店工程与餐饮采购指南》。

感谢你的团队专注的投入与发展，使得我们餐饮采购的行业者们通过一套各种各样的产品分类中可以获得非常精细及可靠的信息资源。当处理每日的工作挑战时我们可以从中参考，我深有感受。

我祝《中国酒店工程与餐饮采购指南》明年更领先！

徐晓冬

亚洲区物资采购及全球资源总监
雅高酒店集团

My sincere congratulations on this wonderful directory.

Thanks to the solid works you and your colleagues have been devoted to in developing this directory, we hospitality procurement professionals can have a very detailed and reliable information source that covers a good variety of product categories and we can reference it when dealing with our daily challenges. I am very impressed.

I wish HRC China another great year ahead!

Xu Xiao Dong

Director of Procurement & Global Sourcing
ACCOR Hospitality

LI YU

谨代表绿地集团对《中国酒店工程与餐饮采购指南》的成功出版发行表示热烈的祝贺。

《中国酒店工程与餐饮采购指南》为中国酒店行业的高速发展提供了一个高效的信息平台，具有极高的实用性。

绿地集团将充分发挥综合性地产开发优势，以超高层标志性项目和现代服务业聚集区为重要载体，加快高端酒店的开发力度，并将携手《中国酒店工程与餐饮采购指南》继续为推动中国酒店行业的发展作出积极的贡献。

李煜

绿地集团酒店研究与发展中心 总经理
国家一级注册建筑师

On behalf of Greenland Group, we'd like to offer our sincere congratulations to the success of the HRC China's publication.

HRC China provides a high efficient and practical platform for the rapid development of Chinese hospitality industry.

Greenland Group will give full play to its advantage of comprehensive real estate development so as to accelerate the development of upmarket hotels with its iconic super high-rise landmark project and modern hospitality intensive area as an important carrier. At the same time, Greenland Group will joint hands with HRC China to make positive contribution to Chinese hospitality industry

Li Yu

General Manager
Hotel Research & Development Center
Registered Architect

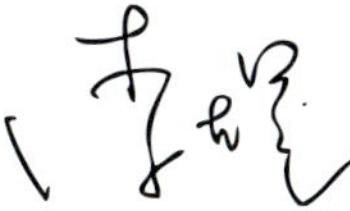

ZHU JUN FU

《中国酒店工程与餐饮采购指南》作为一本较为完善的汇集星级酒店、餐饮、厨师团队等实用信息咨询类参考指南，集中了各种具有影响力的知名企业品牌，囊括了不同产品领域的丰富资讯，对于业内人士极具参考价值，而对于客户而言也是个非常全面的展示平台，是当今的酒店与餐饮业的贸易中不可或缺的工具书！

美国波士顿国际设计集团成立于2004年，延续了美国史塔宾建筑事务所国际最高水准的设计声誉。我们一直致力于把项目的规划设计与业主的要求最大限度的保持一致。每当接受一项设计委托后，我们就会和业主一起反复研究、磨合，以确保每一座新建筑能够成为一座独特的、难忘的成功作品。

在此谨代表美国波士顿国际设计集团热烈祝贺《中国酒店工程与餐饮采购指南》2011版的发行，并衷心祝愿它有着更灿烂的明天，为行业发展及贸易推广创造更好的平台。

朱儁夫

董事长&首席设计师
美国波士顿国际设计集团

As a comprehensive reference guideline including hotels, restaurants, chefs and other useful information, HRC China has collected a variety of influential companies and amount of information in different fields of products, so it has great value for some in industry, and it is also a very comprehensive display platform for customers. HRC China is an essential book for the hotel and catering industry nowadays.

Boston International Design Group was set up in 2004. It continued the highest international standard design reputation of the Stubbins Associates of American. BIDG has been committed to matching project planning and designing with requirements of customers as much as it could. Every time we accepted a design commission, we discuss and adjust with customers over and over again to ensure that every new building can be a unique and unforgettable one.

On behalf of the Boston International Design Group, we are delighted to congratulate HRC China on publishing HRC China 2011. I extend my best wishes that HRC China would have a glorious and resplendent future, and create a better place for sector development and trade promotion.

Zhu Jun Fu

Chairman of Board,President & Chief Designer
Boston International Design Group

KEITH SCHNELLER

在完成了广州、台北一行后，我现在来到了上海，对于《中国酒店工程与餐饮采购指南》的发现令我印象深刻，我很乐意推荐其2011/2012的最新版本。我的职责就是要充当中美两国公司发展的纽带。《中国酒店工程与餐饮采购指南》也扮演着这样的角色！过去十年来中国酒店业及餐饮业发展之迅猛令人耳目一新；而在高端场合驻入高品质的国产及进口商品从而使其运作更具可取性、营利性，这也是在该《中国酒店工程与餐饮采购指南》促使下由难变易的，亦是振奋人心的！我在《中国酒店工程与餐饮采购指南》上看到了许多我所熟知的进口商和经销商，并且我也希望将来能与《中国酒店工程与餐饮采购指南》合作，收录更多美国公司以便购进高质量的美国餐饮产品。加油!!!

Keith Schneller

农业领事
美国驻沪总领事馆农业贸易处

After a tour in Guangzhou, Taipei, and now Shanghai, I was very impressed to discover the HRC China Directory and am pleased to endorse the 2011/2012 edition. My job is to act as a bridge between American companies and Chinese companies. HRC China plays a similar role! It is refreshing to see how quickly China's hospitality and culinary industry has grown in recent 10 years and that the HRC China Directory makes it even easier for upscale venues to locate high quality domestic and imported products to make their operations more desirable and profitable. I recognize many of the importers and distributors listed in the HRC China Directory and hope to cooperate with HRC China in the future to include even more companies to make it easier to source high quality, American food and beverage products. Cheers!!!

Keith Schneller

Director
Agricultural Trade Office US Consulate General Shanghai

LYLIAN FU

《中国酒店工程与餐饮采购指南》是一本很实用的信息咨询类期刊，在我们的业务活动中起着非常重要的作用。透过这份杂志，我们可以直接面对成千上万的客户，从中找到你想要的合作伙伴。《中国酒店工程与餐饮采购指南》构架了一座商贸往来的桥梁，它传播的不单是中国，甚至还有亚洲及世界各地的商业讯息。

阿拉贡是西班牙一个重要的农业食品产区。得益于《中国酒店工程与餐饮采购指南》，现在阿拉贡农业食品在中国市场的知名度日益增加。我相信，这份杂志对每个酒店与餐饮业的贸易伙伴都很有用，是贸易商手中不可或缺的工具书。我很高兴在最近的几年中有这本指南陪伴在我身边。

衷心祝愿《中国酒店工程与餐饮采购指南》能为中外客商带来无限的商机和美好的明天！

付丽

西班牙阿拉贡自治区对外局
北京代表处首席代表

HRC China es una revista muy práctica, que desempeña un papel importante en nuestras actividades. A través de esta revista, podemos enfrentar a miles de clientes y encontrar el socio de cooperación deseado. HRC China se consiste en un puente de negocios, que no sólo difunde información comercial de China, sino de toda Asia e incluso de todo el mundo.

Aragón es una zona potente de producción de agroalimentos de España. Gracias a HRC China, los productos agroalimentarios aragoneses están cada día más conocidos en el mercado chino. Creo que HRC China sirve mucho para todo el sector de hostelería y es un instrumento imprescindible para las empresas comerciales. Me alegra mucho tener el acompañamiento de HRC China durante los últimos años.

¡Deseo que HRC China traiga a los clientes chinos y extranjeros ilimitadas oportunidades comerciales y un futuro más próspero!

Lylian Fu

Representante Jefa
Oficina Representativa de Aragón Exterior en Pekín

DU HE

《中国酒店工程与餐饮采购指南》是一本具有很强市场价值、商业价值、实用价值的信息咨询类刊物。经过几年不断扩充内容、创新改版和科学分类，已经成为深受业内欢迎、每年期盼的必备的业务书籍。

2010年中国食品工业实现总产值57363亿元，同比增长25.4%，成为中国经济扩大内需的主体，同时食品工业也处在了最重要的向自主创新型发展模式转变的转型期。

希望贵刊能为更多业内企业机构提供更多商业和服务机会，创造更多价值。为促进行业发展，做出更大贡献！

杜荷

副秘书长
中国食品工业协会

The HRC China directory is an information consultation publication with competitive market value, commercial value and practical value. With continuous expansion of content, innovation and reformation of version, and scientific classification for several years, it has been greatly popular in the field, an indispensable operational book expected every year as well.

In 2010, China's food industry has achieved the gross output of RMB 5736.3 billion, which attained a year-on-year growth of 25.4%, becoming the main part of expanding domestic demand of China's economy. At the same time, the food industry is going through a period of the most important transformation towards innovation-based self-reliant development model.

It is anticipated that the publication may provide more commerce and service opportunities, and may create more value for more enterprises in the field. Wish a greater contribution to motivating the development of the industry!

Du He

Vice secretary-general
of China National Food Industry Association

HRC CHINA

ANDREAS MULLER

我们很高兴代表香港厨师协会，祝贺《中国酒店工程与餐饮采购指南》2011版的发行，它是关于亚洲酒店餐饮业在中国的商业信息。

该指南为酒店、餐饮业提供产品和供应商的信息。

香港厨师协会于1991年成立，积极参加促进、支持和号召要素饮食推广活动，以及慈善活动、国内外赛事、基础培训、社会和教育活动等。

作为世界厨师联合会的一员，我协会积极参与各大烹饪赛事、教育课程，并取得了全面的提高。与此同时，我们还与其他成员一起分享专业知识和经验。

为了对我们这个大家族中的每一个成员扶持、培养并使其持续发展这一永不停息的目标，我们怀揣着同样的追求相聚在一起。这卓越的进步表现在了我协会对外关系的扩展，和对整个香港及其他国内外市场的影响。

任何一个满怀激情追求职业理想的人往往乐于与同事们共享成就。正因如此，我愿借此良机，代表香港厨师协会，为成功出版《中国酒店工程与餐饮采购指南》2011版表示祝贺。

Andreas Muller

会长
香港厨师协会

On behalf of the Hong Kong Chefs Association, we are delighted to congratulate HRC China on publishing HRC China 2011 Edition, China's commercial information for the Hotel, Restaurant and Catering Industry throughout Asia.

The guide provides information on products and suppliers for the Hospitality, Hotel and Food & Beverage industry.

The Hong Kong Chef Association was established in 1991 and takes an active role in promoting, supporting and soliciting essential food promotions and activities such as charity events, local and international competitions, fundamental training and social and educational events.

As a member of the World Association of Chefs Society, (WACS), the Association strongly participates in culinary contests and educational programs and has globally advanced and shares its professional knowledge and experience with its members.

The continuous aims to feed, nourish and sustain life to all members of our society have enabled us to come together and cherish our common goal. This evidence of distinct progress expands our association's relations and influence on national and international market throughout Hong Kong and beyond.

Anyone who pursues his profession with passion is usually also interested in sharing with colleagues. As such, on behalf of the Hong Kong Chefs Association I would like to take this opportunity to personally congratulate HRC China on the successful publication of HRC China 2011.

Andreas Muller

President
Hong Kong Chefs Association

RAIMUND PICHLMAIER

热烈祝贺《中国酒店工程与餐饮采购指南》2011版的正式出版！

一直以来，《中国酒店工程与餐饮采购指南》为澳门厨艺协会会员起到了很好的引导作用。

澳门厨艺协会拥有约100家行业主导品牌及酒店的新老合作会员。《中国酒店工程与餐饮采购指南》能提供货真价实的资深专业信息，使我们寻找到最佳工作伙伴。

请接受我们衷心的祝贺，并祝愿你们再创佳绩。

彼基米亚

澳门厨艺协会会长

Congratulations on the launch of the HRC China in 2011!

In the past HRC China was a good guidance for Macau Culinary Association members.

Our Macau Culinary Association boasts around 100 senior and new cooperated members from the leading industry brands and hotels and this directory can really provide us with professional and experienced information to find our best working partners.

Please accept our heartiest congratulations and best wishes for your continued success.

Raimund Pichlmaier

Associação Culinária de Macau

MATTHEW N HELM

我们谨代表埃科菲国际厨师协会中国澳门分会，非常高兴祝贺2011/2012版《中国酒店工程与餐饮采购指南》的出版。

《中国酒店工程与餐饮采购指南》为亚洲地区的酒店、餐厅和饮食业提供了简明有效的指导。

《中国酒店工程与餐饮采购指南》里资源丰富，对中国快速发展的餐饮业很有参考价值。翻开书本即可找到商品供应商。

我们相信这本书能满足你的餐饮业要求。为每个会员提供一个健康的网络和美好的将来。

我们祝愿《中国酒店工程与餐饮采购指南》团队勇创佳绩。

贺文汉

副总裁
公关及媒介部

On behalf of The Disciples Escoffier, Greater China Sub-Delegation Macau, we are delighted to congratulate HRC China on there 2011/2012 directory publication.

This guide provides simple and efficient references for the Hotel, Restaurant and Catering Industries throughout Asia.

The HRC China directory is a resourceful reference for China's rapid growing hospitality sector. They provide the answers of preparation and procurement supplies at the work of a finger tip.

We trust that this book can assist you with your hospitality requirements; providing a healthy network and better future for everyone.

We wish the HRC China team the very best.

Matthew N Helm

Vice President
Public Relations and Media

HRC CHINA

贺词 Congratulations

CHRIS BUSSCHAERT

在过去的几年中，《中国酒店工程与餐饮采购指南》对华尔道夫酒店的开业筹备起到了至关重要的作用。

它对我们认识上海乃至中国范围内的供销商给予了极大的帮助。

我之所以喜欢这本指南书，是因为我轻而易举就能找到我想要的，在这里只有最实用的信息，毫无华而不实之处。这是一本十分出色的指南书，用途广泛，涵盖了厨房、餐饮部和采购部所有需要的信息。

之前在新加坡和上海我都有幸赏读此书，我必须说这本指南的影响力将会与日俱增。
我对这本指南的连续成功出版表示美好祝愿，并为能成为其中一份子而深感骄傲。

克里斯

饼房厨师长
上海外滩华尔道夫酒店

HRC China has been a key tool for preopening for Waldorf Astoria for the past year.

It has helped us extremely with meeting up with top suppliers and distributors in Shanghai and China.

What I like about the HRC China magazine is what you need is easy to find and there is only very helpful information and no fuss information.

This extremely very great guide has been very useful and covers most of all needs to find the right tools and for kitchens and culinary departments, including purchasing and food and beverage departments.

I also have experience in reading the HRC China in Singapore and in Shanghai and I must say that year by year the magazine is becoming phenomenal.

I extend my best wishes for the continuous success of your publication and I am very proud to be part of your publishing HRC China magazine.

Chris Busschaert

Executive Pastry Chef
Waldorf Astoria Shanghai

DAVID LARIS

《中国酒店工程与餐饮采购指南》的表现卓尔不群，对于采购餐饮相关设备的人士来说，这本书给出了十分适合的选择及参考。

对于餐饮业这个不断发展的行业来说，拥有这样一本能够持续为业界人士提供丰富选择的刊物是至关重要的。有了它的帮助，采购不再是一件让人头疼的工作。

衷心祝愿新一期指南再续辉煌！

David Laris

DLC CEO & 创始人

Through great effort from the HRC China, it continues to be a wonderful reference for finding hospitality related equipment.

It is so important that a publication like this continue to provide an ever-growing industry with a choice that makes doing business a little easier.

My best wishes and good luck with the new guide!

David Laris

CEO & Founder

DAVID LARIS CREATES (DLC) LIMITED

贺词 Congratulations

DIETMAR SPITZER

我谨代表上海浦东丽思卡尔顿酒店的全体绅士淑女们，向2011年《中国酒店工程与餐饮采购指南》致以最诚挚的祝贺！

这是一本涵盖酒店专业服务内容的指南书，有关资讯对行业读者来说是尤为重要。

在过去的一年中，上海浦东丽思卡尔顿酒店成功开业，绽放魅力，我作为这家酒店开业的领航员之一，感到非常自豪！

在此，我衷心祝愿贵刊在2011年再获成功！

史迪马

行政总厨
上海浦东丽思卡尔顿酒店

The Ladies and Gentlemen of The Ritz-Carlton Shanghai, Pudong would like to express our sincere and heartfelt congratulations to the HRC China 2011!

It is a great directory for all hotel professionals in the service industry. It is very important to have access to relevant and updated information in our fast paced world.

In the year 2010, we have opened the most beautiful hotel in Shanghai — The Ritz-Carlton Shanghai, Pudong and I am proud to have led our Ladies and Gentlemen through this intriguing journey.

We wish HRC China a successful year of 2011.

Dietmar Spitzer

Executive Chef
The Ritz-Carlton Shanghai, Pudong

Dietmar Spitzer

THE RITZ-CARLTON®
SHANGHAI, PUDONG

KRISTOFFER LUCZAK

我衷心地祝贺2011年版《中国酒店工程与餐饮采购指南》发行成功！

这本指南如同前几年一样，是一本以中国酒店业为基准的服务指南，在洞悉酒店服务业的世界里为读者提供最新及全面的技术和信息。我很欣赏《中国酒店工程与餐饮采购指南》在过去几年里的坚持与努力，它的确是一本很领先的业界指南，对酒店业的先锋者有很大的作用。

在此我要再次祝贺《中国酒店工程与餐饮采购指南》2011年版发行成功并获得更好的成绩！

Kristoffer Luczak

餐饮部副总裁
新濠博亚娱乐

I'd like to express my heartfelt congratulations on the successful publication of HRC China 2011!

The directory, just like in the past years, is a service guide based on Chinese hospitality industry, which provides readers with the updated and overall technologies and information. I greatly appreciate the persistence and efforts made by HRC China in the past few years. It is definitely a leading guide in the hospitality industry, providing a great help for the pioneers in the industry.

Congratulate again on the successful publication and wish a finer prospect of HRC China 2011!

Kristoffer Luczak

Vice President, Food and Beverage
Melco Crown Entertainment

THOMAS GEBLER

谨代表上海外滩华尔道夫酒店，恭贺《中国酒店工程与餐饮采购指南》2011年版的发行。该指南收录国内外众多酒店设计、用品及食品供应商介绍，为业内人士提供了全面的产品采购平台。

上海外滩华尔道夫酒店于2011年盛大开幕，拥有三座餐厅、两间休息廊以及一个酒吧，从原汁原味的中式佳肴到风靡全球的纽约时尚特色菜式，为顾客提供了高档饮食和时尚社交的绝佳场所。

真诚祝贺《中国酒店工程与餐饮采购指南》在未来取得更好的成就。

托马斯·盖伯乐

餐饮总监
上海外滩华尔道夫酒店

On behalf of the Waldorf Astoria Shanghai on the Bund, we are delighted to offer our congratulations to HRC China for the launch of HRC China 2011 Edition. The book is a comprehensive directory that provides a wide range of information covering domestic and international hotel design, products and catering services.

Waldorf Astoria Shanghai on the Bund just celebrated its grand opening in April 2011. The hotel offers an array of amenities including three restaurants, two lounges and a bar, bringing the epitome of fine dining together with chic social spaces. Authentic Chinese and New York-style specialities are available all day long, and the extraordinary variety found at our restaurants is suitable for every palate.

We would like to take this opportunity to extend our sincere congratulations to HRC China, and our best wishes for a prosperous future.

Thomas Gebler

Director of Food and Beverage
Waldorf Astoria Shanghai on the Bund

YEUNG KOON YAT

首先对于《中国酒店工程与餐饮采购指南》2011年版发行再次表示祝贺！

在我几十年的厨艺生涯里，深知选材最为关键，除了对食材的选择之外厨具和餐具的选用也很关键，自从几年前拿到《中国酒店工程与餐饮采购指南》这本书之后，不论开新店还是老店这本指南已经成为了我参考选材的好工具，这些年来我看着这本指南的发展是如此之快，国内包括香港澳门很多新酒店和餐厅的信息也如此及时的更新，让我得到了不同方位的讯息，感谢它对酒店及餐饮行业作出的贡献！

我会继续每年收集保存这本指南，希望它一直保持行业领先的地位！

杨贯一

阿一鲍鱼创始人
董事总经理
世界御厨驻港大使

First of all, I'd like to express my congratulations on the publication of HRC China 2011 once more!

In my several decades career as a chef, I have been fully aware that selecting material is the most essential, not only the food, but also the kitchen ware and the table ware. Since a few years ago, when I got HRC China, the directory has been my great reference to select material, no matter for new restaurants or old ones. For these years, I have witnessed the amazing development of the directory, noticing that in our country, including Hong Kong and Macao area, many new hotels and restaurants update their information so rapidly, which enable me to obtain message from all dimensions. I appreciate its contributions to hotels and restaurants!

I will collect this directory year by year, and wish it a lead in the field!

Yeung Koon Yat

Founder or Ah Yat Abalone

公司简介

上海畅高酒店用品有限公司是由旅游教育、旅游科研系统人员创建的酒店用品专业配套公司，致力于酒店筹建、开业期间的预算制作、软环境设计、酒店用品的配套与集成。1998年成立，十余年间已为近150家高星级酒店提供服务，现已成为多家著名酒店管理公司的合作供应商。

上海畅高酒店用品有限公司

Shanghai Charn-go Hotel Utensils Co., Ltd.

地址：上海万航渡路623弄85号建华大厦6楼

Add: 6F Jianhua Building NO85 Lane623 Wanhangdu Road Jing'an District

邮编/Zip：200042

电话/Tel：021-62301823 62301831 62491575

传真/Fax：021-62497960

电邮/E-mail：charn-go@126.com

Aftertaste

美饌令人不斷回味，美好的餐具亦是。

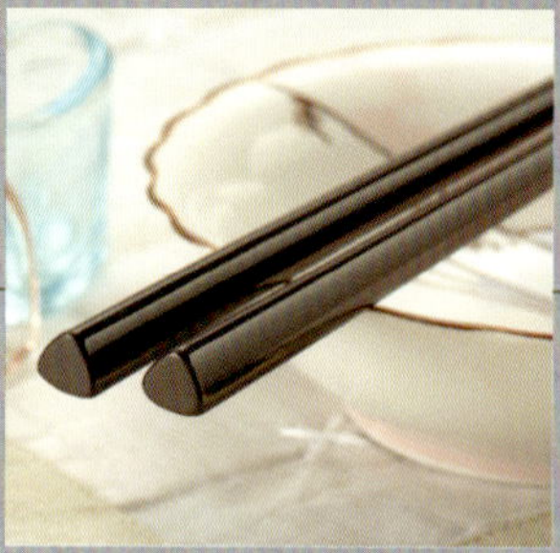

www.shunta.com

For more information please visit our website.

美耐皿第一品牌

Melamine Tableware First Brand

Dongguan ShunTa Melamine Products Co., Ltd. was built in the latter half of 1996 which is invested by the King Shun Dal Enterprise Co., Ltd. Taiwan that founded over 30 years ago.

As one of the leading melamine products manufacturer, our R & D team continually increases our large collection of melamine ware for household, catering, children wares, kitchen tools, restaurant use and gift purposes.

To guarantee that our products meet the standards for the top quality and sanitary requirements, we have found the inspection room in which we can take synchronous chemical test for our products. Not only the modern production facilities but also more than 15 years of manufacturing experience enable us to offer strict quality and efficient service. Every one of our products meets FDA and EN standards.

Our goal is to provide best products at competitive price with timely delivery to our customers.

東莞順大美耐皿制品有限公司成立於1996年下半年，為台灣金順代企業有限公司（成立於1976年）投資設立，攜台灣本土30年來不斷提升的生產技術，專業生產高品質美耐皿餐具，在多年發展下成為全系列多品種美耐皿日用產品生產高端品牌企業。

順大(Shunta)公司為確保產品的質量和安全，生產環節嚴格按照國家相關生產技術最高標準，同時為進一步確保產品的質量和安全，在行業內率先斥資設立了獨立檢驗室進行同步檢測，要求所有產品100%符合國家相關技術和安全衛生標準。通過多年來努力，企業通過國家質量檢測檢疫總局審核，獲得國內QS品質認證（編號：QS44-10301-00645）；國際上通過了美國FDA認證。由此受到國內外諸多知名品牌公司的信賴，成為其指定專屬配合的制造廠商及產品供應商。

www.shunta.com

Fore more information please visit our website.

欲知更詳細的資料，請瀏覽我們的網站！

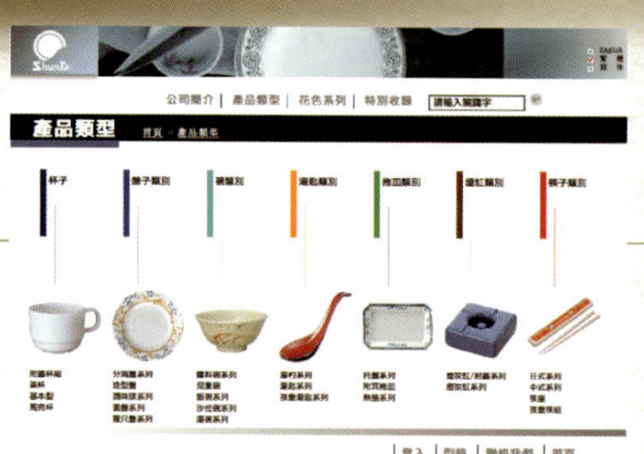

順 大
美耐皿有限公司

burgess

RCR
CRISTALLERIA ITALIANA
意大利制造
NIKKO
SINCE 1908
日本制造

特别介绍
SPECIAL INTRODUCTIONS

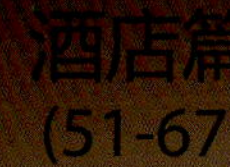

Hotel
酒店篇
(51-67)

钓鱼台美高梅酒店管理有限公司
Diaoyutai MGM Hospitality,Ltd.

澳门威尼斯人-度假村-酒店
The Venetian Macao-Resort-Hotel

澳门银河综合度假城
Galaxy Macau

上海浦东丽思卡尔顿酒店
The Ritz-Carlton Shanghai,Pudong

北京丽思卡尔顿酒店
The Ritz-Carlton,Beijing

北京金融街丽思卡尔顿酒店
The Ritz-Carlton Beijing, Financial Street

上海朗廷扬子精品酒店
The Langham Yangtze Boutique

上海半岛酒店
The Peninsula Shanghai

广州卡丽酒店
Guangzhou Carat Hotel & Spa

厨师篇Chef (70-79)

Chris Busschaert

David Laris

Dietmar Spitzer

Kristoffer Luczak

Thomas Geble

Yeung Koon Yat

餐厅篇Dine (80-82)

莫尔顿牛排坊
Morton's Of Chicago,
The Steakhouse In Shanghai

龙皇酒家
Dragon King Restaurant

协会篇Association (68-69)

Disciples Escoffier
Delegation Macau
Association pour la transmission et l'èvolution de la cuisine
www.escoffier-asia.org www.diciples-escoffier.com

埃科菲国际厨师协会
O.I.D.A.E (Displaines Escoffier)

北京钓鱼台雍和酒店
Diaoyutai Hotel Beijing, Lama Temple
开业（Opening）2011

三亚美高梅金殿度假酒店
MGM Grand Sanya
开业（Opening）2011

天津美高梅金殿酒店
天津Skylofts酒店
MGM Grand Tianjin
Skylofts at MGM Grand Tianjin
开业（Opening）2014

成都美高梅金殿酒店
成都Skylofts酒店
MGM Grand Chengdu
Skylofts at MGM Grand Chengdu
开业（Opening）2014

钓鱼台美高梅酒店管理有限公司

钓鱼台美高梅酒店管理有限公司由钓鱼台国宾馆携手美国美高梅国际度假集团合资成立，是中国最高规格的外事接待机构与世界顶级的豪华酒店集团共同打造的高端酒店管理平台。公司致力于整合双方品牌优势，实现资源最佳配置，创造独具特色的优质产品，在全世界开发和管理豪华五星级酒店和度假胜地。

Diaoyutai MGM Hospitality, Ltd.

Diaoyutai MGM Hospitality, Ltd. is a joint venture between Diaoyutai State Guesthouse of China, the highest standard service venue for hosting foreign heads of state, and MGM Resorts International, the top global luxury hotel group. The company is committed to combining the brand advantages of its parent companies, to optimizing the resource allocation, and to developing and operating luxury 5-star hotels and resorts around the world.

地址：北京市东城区东长安街1号东方经贸城C2座808室　邮编：100738
Address: Oriental Plaza, Tower C2, Suite 808, Dongcheng District, Beijing, 100738 P.R.China
电话 Tel: +86 10 58116100　传真 Fax: +86 10 58116200
www.dytmgm.com

钓鱼台美高梅酒店管理有限公司
Diaoyutai MGM Hospitality, Ltd.

澳门威尼斯人®-度假村-酒店

酒店简介

亚洲最大型的度假村酒店——澳门威尼斯人®-度假村-酒店于 2007 年开幕，标志着澳门路氹金光大道™的大型发展项目正式展开。这个高瞻远瞩的崭新发展项目，创作灵感源自美国拉斯维加斯商业区，既有气派不凡并提供各种消闲娱乐体验的综合度假村，亦有周全完备的商务设施。

度假村

澳门威尼斯人®-度假村-酒店自开业以来，已成为创新思维、超卓服务及完善设施的代名词。这个设有 3000 间豪华套房的综合度假村，以意大利威尼斯水乡风貌为建筑蓝本，并参考著名的拉斯维加斯威尼斯人度假村酒店设计，是一座超级大型的度假酒店。澳门威尼斯人®-度假村-酒店的规模更是拉斯维加斯威尼斯人度假村酒店的两倍，设施包括具威尼斯色彩的大运河购物中心、国际著名食府、太阳剧团剧院、可容纳 15000 名观众的金光综艺馆，以及亚洲区最大型的会议展览设施。

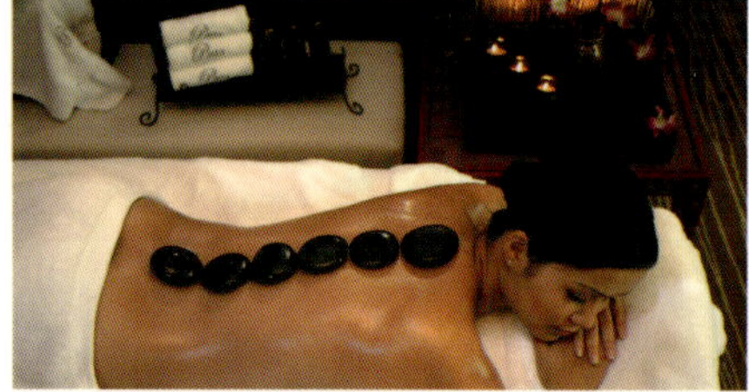

设施

澳门威尼斯人®-度假村-酒店的会议展览中心占地逾 12 万平方米，适合举办各类型的会议、展览及奖励旅游（MICE）。设有 15000 座位的金光综艺馆™，专为举办各类世界级体育赛事以及文娱活动而设。至于特别为世界闻名的太阳剧团表演 —— ZAIA™ 建造的剧院，则可容纳 1800 位观众。旅客亦可在度假村的 30 间高级特色餐厅品尝环球美馔；到马泷综合康健医疗中心，或到大运河购物中心的 330 多个商户享受购物乐趣。此外，度假村特设贡多拉之旅、精彩的街头表演 Streetmosphere™ 娱乐、历险Q立方儿童游乐场、亚洲首个足球互动地带 —— 体验曼联、游泳池及君度小型高尔夫球场，让旅客尽享家庭乐。

住宿

宽敞豪华的套房每间面积达 70 平方米或以上，设有豪华寝室、云石浴室以及舒适的客厅。每间套房更设有传真机／复印机／打印机以及高速互联网等设备，方便商务旅客处理公务。

大运河购物中心

运河上唱着醉人情歌的贡多拉船夫、色彩缤纷的威尼斯建筑及景色，都是大运河购物中心的特色。购物中心总面积达10万平方米，330多间商户汇聚国际知名品牌。
源自纽约、巴黎及米兰的世界顶尖时装店，现在已经登陆澳门！

贡多拉船河

在船夫的美妙歌声中，旅客悠然乘坐贡多拉船在大运河上漫游，感受威尼斯的独特魅力。

特色街头表演

大运河购物中心每小时会有精彩的Streetmosphere™街头表演，为旅客带来无限惊喜。踩高跷表演者、真人雕塑、魔术师、音乐家等，让旅客恍如置身威尼斯的街道上。

设施

- 超过330间特色商店
- 超过30间高级餐厅
- 1000个座位的国际美食广场
- 三道各长150米的运河
- 户外人工湖（容量相等于11个奥林匹克标准泳池）
- 由唱着醉人情歌的船夫掌舵的51艘贡多拉船

金光综艺馆™

设有15000个座位的金光综艺馆™自投入服务以来，已多次举办世界级体育赛事和音乐会。多位来自亚洲和世界各地的国际巨星先后踏上金光综艺馆的舞台，包括郭富城、张惠妹、Rain、容祖儿、Lady Gaga、Linkin Park、the Police及Beyoncé等。

金光综艺馆设有世界级广播和视像设备，包括4部巨型室内影像屏幕、高质素电视广播灯光配套、无线和光纤功能、中央悬挂式大型电子记分牌以及先进音响灯光设备等。

金光综艺馆内的地面可按不同类型体育项目的需要而铺上不同物料，包括NBA篮球赛、世界级拳击赛、溜冰、极限运动、网球，甚至是电单车障碍赛等。

金光综艺馆刚获美国权威音乐杂志《Pollstar》选为世界最顶尖的100个综艺馆之一。

澳门威尼斯人®-度假村-酒店将致力把更多体育和娱乐盛事带到澳门，协助澳门发展成为游客首选的亚洲娱乐旅游目的地。

地址：澳门氹仔望德圣母湾大马路
电话：+853 2882 8888
网址：www.venetianmacao.com/zh/

会议展览设施

终极会展中心

澳门威尼斯人特别为会议及展览的主办单位打造崭新的设施，配合其屡获殊荣的专业团队，令每一项企业活动都能成功举行。

设于澳门威尼斯人内的金光会展™提供 75000 平方米展览场地，是亚洲区内最大的展览中心之一。展馆更附设占地 6500 平方米的无柱宴会厅，以及总面积达 18500 平方米的 108 间会议室，灵活配合不同类型的会议及活动。金光综艺馆可容纳 15000 位宾客，是筹办企业活动或产品推广的理想地点。

金光会展曾主办区内重点行业最大型的展览会，如汽车、酒店、珠宝、制造业及电讯等，每年招待超过 25 万名到访澳门的买家。

澳门威尼斯人的专业展览团队与主办单位紧密合作，务求从整体活动规划到访客宣传、市场营销、旅游服务、物流、会议管理及技术支持等细节，都能巨细无遗。

澳门威尼斯人糅合最先进的设施、最瞩目的娱乐表演及经验丰富的 MICE 专业人才，务求每项活动都获得空前成功。

2003 年，中国接待了 6000 万名会议代表。2005 年，美国拉斯维加斯接待了 620 万位代表。商贸展览和企业会议的需求已远超预期，而坐落于中国南端澳门特别行政区的澳门威尼斯人，在会议、展览及奖励旅游方面的业务发展潜力毋容置疑。

宴会厅

宴会厅设在三个不同楼层，邻近展览馆，所有宴会厅均可分隔成更小的会议室和小组会议房。另外，底层还设有 4 个会议室。

地下一层

3 个小宴会厅，楼层高达 3.5 米，可分为 36 个会议室，同时举办不同的会议。

- 卡布里厅：1420 平方米
- 都灵厅及维罗纳厅：各 932 平方米

底层

4 个小宴会厅，楼层高达 6 米，可分为 56 个会议室，同时举办不同的会议。

- 米兰厅、佛罗伦斯厅、西西里厅、那不勒斯厅：各 1306 平方米
- 4 个会议室：达芬奇厅、卡萨诺瓦厅、伽利略厅、马可勃罗厅各 63 平方米，各设有一张固定的大型会议桌。

上层

- 6577 平方米、楼层高达 8.3 米的威尼斯人宴会厅是举办最盛大主题活动的理想场所，可分为 12 个会议室，同时举办不同的会议。

展览场地

展览场地分为两层，每层展馆相邻，可举办不同规模和类型的展览。

底层

A 馆：13775 平方米

B 馆：9318 平方米

C 馆：14222 平方米

A、B、C 馆能合并起来，提供合共 37315 平方米的展览空间

上层

D 馆：13465 平方米

E 馆：9090 平方米

F 馆：14812 平方米

D、E、F 馆能合并起来，提供合共 37367 平方米的展览空间

所有展馆的面积合共：74682 平方米

展位数目：2404（底层），2352（上层）

万有胜地 缔造传奇

不管您将策划的商旅活动构思是否仿如天马行空，澳门威尼斯人必定全力达成。想飞身意大利享受下午茶？想忙碌之后，走进太阳剧团的魅幻世界，暂离现实？还是……想到富特色的天台高尔夫球场，藉一场刺激比赛，加强团队精神？这里，都能为您一一实现！凭着我们多姿多彩的娱乐节目、世界一级场地、尊尚购物享受，以及型格酒吧和顶尖食府，当然，还有我们出色的活动筹划专业团队，肯定能助您冲破极限。唯一的挑战或会是您那无限的丰富想象力！您想的，我们必定全力达成。

忘我工作、忘我玩乐！

哪怕短短数天的紧凑活动行程，我们都要给您忙里偷闲，让您尽情工作、休息、享乐，再工作，体现真正生命！在澳门威尼斯人，教您舒展松弛之地，皆举步可达。忙过之后，踱步至享负盛名与口碑，一室怡人幽香的MALO CLINIC Spa，将绷紧的身心交予专业水疗按摩师……又或到户外泳池一洗疲惫，或沐浴于日光浴之中……脑力与体力又重新得力！另一边厢，我们的曼联旗盘店和18洞迷你高尔夫球场，助您寓建立团队精神于玩乐。逛尽大运河购物中心逾330家国际名店，再让四季・名店的160个尊崇品牌，尊贵地奖励您过去的努力，不然，在威尼斯的蔚蓝天幕下徜徉闲逛，或乘坐贡多拉船畅游运河，让船夫的深情歌声洗涤心灵，亦是一大乐事！

划一套房式设计 全贵宾式款待

只因澳门威尼斯人，视每位宾客如VIP，所以，3000间面积傲领全亚洲，宽敞达70平方米（755平方英尺）之贵宾套房，均以华丽为大前提，不但拥有充裕空间，足以进行小型会议，独特的分层式布局设计，亦尽显不凡气派；当然，您想到的，如意大利云石铺砌的浴室、无线互联网连接，以至一系列尊贵设备……更自不待言，应有尽有！

荟萃寰宇美馔

逾30家珍馐荟萃的寰宇食府，独具特色与品位，绝对是各类型活动最富新鲜创意之理想地；而箇中云集之世界级厨艺高手，不单全天候为您及您的团队，巧制纷陈佳肴选择，更能度身烹调拿手地道美馔，教色、香与味尽贴心！

当中的「碧涛意式渔乡」－露天池畔环境，恬然雅致，阳光与微风作伴，细味正宗意大利菜，或举行多至1,200人之酒会派对。另外，还有数不尽的酒吧、咖啡店和面馆等，悉随心情与时间挑选；而遐迩享誉之精致中菜，亦肯定令您喜出望外；不得不提的，还数我们诚聘自中国、印度、欧洲及亚洲各地的获奖名厨，他们都绞尽心思，准备为您筹划的大型盛宴，或温馨晚膳，缔造惊喜，动人更动心！

每夜，触动宾客心灵……

澳门威尼斯人，拥有逾150人之庞大表演队伍，当中有能歌善唱的贡多拉船夫，有魔术师、杂耍员、百老汇演员、器乐演奏家，还把摇滚之神——猫王活现眼前……每位演出者，都尽施绝艺，每夜，就如走进台上表演着的曼妙世界，活动与会议，固然精彩；眼前璀璨，却最是难忘。

欣赏过太阳剧团驻场剧目 ZAIA™（译音：萨雅），个中演艺奇才的舞蹈，又或出神入化的空中特技，依然萦系脑际？何不考虑邀请他们做您的席上表演嘉宾，与宾客细赏细味！

地址：澳门氹仔望德圣母湾大马路

电话：+853 2882 8888

网址：www.venetianmacao.com/zh/

「澳門銀河™」综合度假城

「澳門銀河™」夜景

银河娱乐集团有限公司(下称「银娱」)斥资128亿元人民币，在澳门特别行政区打造一个独一无二、瞩目耀眼、提供五星级亚洲式度假风情的综合度假城——「澳門銀河™」(Galaxy Macau ™)。

「澳門銀河™」综合度假城以"傲视世界　情系亚洲"为宗旨，竭诚为宾客提供一个世界级度假悠闲设施及亚洲式细腻体贴的服务。银娱为「澳門銀河™」引入两家享誉国际的亚洲品牌，包括以细腻服务遐迩闻名的悦榕庄（Banyan Tree Hotels and Resorts）与享誉日本的大仓饭店集团（Okura Hotels & Resorts），加上银娱自家五星级「銀河酒店™」(Galaxy Hotel ™)，务求为来自世界各地追求至尊品位的旅客带来远离繁嚣的难忘之旅。

于2011年初揭幕的「澳門銀河」，坐落于路氹城，占地550000平方米，为宾客提供休闲及娱乐体验。

傲视世界　情系亚洲

「傲视世界　情系亚洲」是「澳門銀河」的定位，贯彻着整个度假城的外观设计与建设，以及令每一位员工引以为荣的超凡服务标准。银娱相信，一般的亚洲式服务与「贴心」的亚洲式服务是有差异的，「澳門銀河」所推崇的，是诚心诚意、力求热情细致的待客之道，将心比心地了解及满足宾客的需要，配合度假城的独特设施、汇聚亚洲顶级美食，旨在为每一位宾客带来无可比拟的度假体验，暂将俗世烦嚣的工作生活抛诸脑后。

百分百亚洲风情的非凡体验

「澳門銀河」与银娱定意打造一个洋溢着百分百亚洲风情的综合度假城。「澳門銀河」汇聚了三家在亚洲区内享负盛名、植根亚洲的世界级酒店品牌——澳门大仓酒店、澳门悦榕庄及「銀河酒店」。

澳门大仓酒店将会贯彻大仓饭店集团一贯的质量要求，为「澳門銀河」带来500间设计时尚的客房及套房，每一间都巧妙地融合了日式优雅、和谐的设计，加上日式殷勤款客服务，为商务及休闲旅客提供舒适的环境。澳门大仓酒店附设享誉全球的日本料理——山里日本餐厅，宾客可一边欣赏日本园林景致，一边享受地道怀石料理、鲜制寿司、烧烤美食等。

澳门悦榕庄

澳门悦榕庄设有一间总统套房及250间套房，套房面积一律由逾100平方米起，房内的按摩池坐拥欣赏一望无际的天际美景。10间水上别墅坐落于「澳門銀河」备受瞩目的人造沙滩旁，专为喜爱宁静的宾客而设。此外，另有8间设计独特的池畔小屋，由房间直接连接到超豪华的悦榕庄泳池。澳门悦榕庄将可满足任何一位追求高尚生活品位的宾客的要求。

澳门大仓酒店

銀河酒店

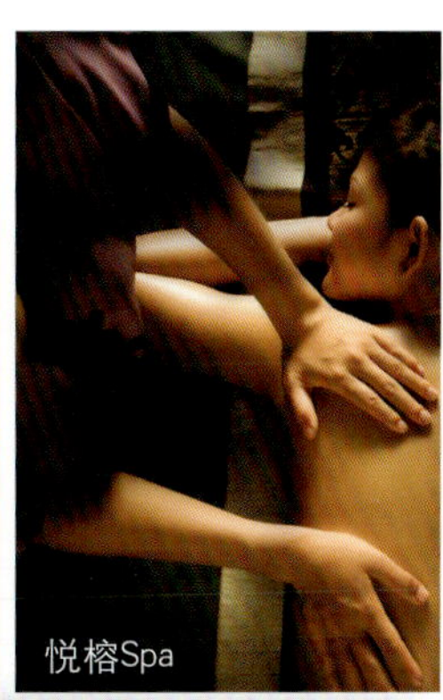
悦榕Spa

首次进驻澳门的悦榕Spa占地超过2800平方米及拥有21间水疗室，为宾客提供百分百亚洲传统特色的护理和水疗服务，带来全面感官享受。宾客更可尽享酒店内贝隆蚝吧及扒房及其他著名美食。澳门悦榕庄内餐饮环境气氛亲切、格调浪漫，体现酒店设计特色和自然风光的无比魅力。

最后是「銀河酒店™」(Galaxy Hotel ™)，它延续着银娱优质接待与服务的传统，以获奖无数的「星际酒店」之成功营运模式作为蓝本，在度假城提供1500间客房，极致的优秀服务必令大家感受到亚洲心的真与诚。「銀河酒店」亦拥有户外雅座的庭园地中海餐厅供应南欧美食与各式美酒，展现动人的地中海风情，并备有私人贵宾房。

「澳門銀河™」(Galaxy Macau ™)不仅要向世界展现亚洲人的自豪，更要向世界各地的旅客呈现「澳門銀河」超凡独特的亚洲色彩与魅力。

让宾客尊享不同类型的会议设施

「澳門銀河」亦设有宴会厅及会议室，可举办不同类型的会议。

■ 于澳门大仓酒店之宴会厅:

宴会厅
兰花厅 1: 84 平方米　兰花厅 2: 84 平方米　兰花厅 3: 84 平方米
1、2、3 宴会厅合并可提供合共 260 平方米的空间

百合厅 1: 84 平方米　百合厅 2: 84 平方米
1、2 宴会厅合并可提供合共 170 平方米的空间

莲花厅: 可提供合共 120 平方米的空间

■ 于澳门悦榕庄之宴会厅及会议室:

宴会厅: 可提供合共 1330 平方米的空间

会议室
会议室1: 165 平方米　会议室2: 165 平方米
会议室3: 165 平方米　会议室4: 165 平方米
1、2、3、4会议室合并可提供合共660平方米的空间

银娱一直致力协助促进澳门的旅游业发展，在多方面作出重大贡献，除了创造就业机会和履行企业公民的社会责任外，还创建别具特式的度假旅游胜地，提升澳门的多元化发展，吸引游客和延长其访澳时间，带动经济发展。银娱深信，通过这项最新和规模最大的发展项目，加上与举世知名的酒店伙伴合作，「澳門銀河™」(Galaxy Macau ™)综合度假城，势必成为世界各地游客在澳门的必游热点。

地址：「澳門銀河™」综合度假城，澳门路氹城
电话：853 2888 0888　　网址：galaxymacau.com

山里日本餐厅

「澳門銀河」为澳门的娱乐生活注入新活力

红伶(CHINA ROUGE, Private Members Club)——全澳门唯一顶级娱乐私人会所，定会带来无比惊艳。一个将中国繁华盛世年代所独有的艺术为设计蓝本的会所，势必轰动澳门全城。会所出自香港著名设计师陈幼坚手笔，概念源自20世纪30年代大上海，让旅客重温昔日老上海的典雅醉迷情怀。红伶设有酒廊及精心设计的华丽舞台，顶尖的餐饮及娱乐体验应有尽有。

叫味蕾充满惊喜，让飨客「满载而归」

「澳門銀河」将提供多元化、独具特色的亚洲美食。美食是内地旅客旅行计划中的一个重要元素。银娱富有卓越的餐饮经验，「澳門銀河」将在这基础上重点发扬及推广亚洲美食，整个餐饮体验的范围涵盖广泛，从快捷的美味快餐到最顶级的亚洲美食一应俱全。

贝隆蚝吧及扒房

上海浦东丽思卡尔顿酒店
The Ritz-Carlton Shanghai, Pudong

位于酒店58层的Flair顶层餐厅酒吧由日本的Super Potato精心设计，为中国最高的户外用餐环境。宾客在Flair可以享用地道亚洲小吃、寿司和海鲜；Flair已成为国际时尚人士流连的热门地点。

Designed by Super Potato, Flair Rooftop Restaurant & Bar at Level 58 offers the highest al fresco dining and wining venue in China. Featuring Asian tapas, sushi and seafood bar, Flair is where movers and shakers of the city entertain.

Scena意大利餐厅位于酒店52层，装潢精心时尚 -- 开放式厨房和随意中空设计的部分天花板和铜墙，让客人置身于活泼温馨的用餐氛围中；餐厅提供早、午、晚餐。

Located at Level 52, modern décor by Super Potato with open kitchen and exceptional lighting effects of Scena Italian Restaurant create a stylish yet causal all-day dining environment.

位于酒店52层的Aura酒廊及爵士酒吧提供香茗、咖啡、简餐和著名英式下午茶，是与亲朋相聚和与商务客人洽谈的理想场所。

Aura Lounge and Jazz Bar at Level 52 is ideal for relaxing rendezvous with friends or meetings with business acquaintances over light meals and drinks.

Aroma位处酒店一层，为您提供便捷美食和饮料。无论您需要在外出前快速用餐，或与朋友或商务客人简短交流，Aroma都是您的至佳选址。

Aroma at Level 1 is the fast-service yet friendly food and drink corner of the hotel. Whether you would like to have a quick bite on your way out or a brief encounter with contacts, it is the place to be.

酒店53层的金轩提供精致中式佳肴，拱形天花板豪华开阔，中层设计独特雅致。中餐厅同时提供主厅和8个私密包间。

Jin Xuan Chinese Restaurant at Level 53 showcases refined Chinese cuisine at a spectacular location with its high "vaulted" ceilings and a mezzanine level. On top of the main dining area, there are also 8 private dining rooms.

酒店会议室和宴会活动空间位于3楼，由蜚声国际的设计师Richard Farnell先生精心设计，面积超过2500平方米，其中包括一个面积达1135平方米的大宴会厅，此宴会厅可容纳最多800位宾客同时聚餐。

整个大宴会厅可根据宾客不同的需求，划分成三个独立的沙龙空间。另外，这里有三个多功能会议室、董事会议室和商务会议室。

宾客们在此可享用世界顶尖会议技术和设施以及酒店专业服务团队精致美善的服务。

Designed by world-famous Richard Farnell, the meeting and banquet facilities onLevel 3 of the hotel features more than 2,500 square meters of area including a 1,135-square-metre Grand Ballroom which can accommodate sit-down banquets with maximum capacity of 800 participants.

In addition, there are three multi-purpose meeting rooms, The Board Room and The Traders Room.

At The Ritz-Carlton Shanghai, Pudong, guests will be treated to world-class technology and facilities underscored by effective yet discreet services dedicated by our Ladies and Gentlemen.

THE RITZ-CARLTON®
SHANGHAI, PUDONG

北京丽思卡尔顿酒店
中国时尚之都的经典奢华之作

北京丽思卡尔顿酒店位于北京 CBD 的中心地带，是华贸中心建筑群中的重要组成部分。距北京首都国际机场 30 分钟车程，名胜古迹和文化地标皆近在咫尺。酒店拥有 305 间客房，包括 38 间套房和 61 间丽思卡尔顿行政客房，高标准的个性化服务，使丽思卡尔顿成为奢华的代名词。品味丽思卡尔顿经典下午茶，体验特色美食文化，沉迷独特芳香水疗，尊享丽思卡尔顿传奇服务！

酒店更有多种美味可供选择，客人足不出户，即可感受来自香溢餐厅、巴罗洛意大利餐厅、玉餐厅、大堂酒廊、丽思卡尔顿酒吧、大卫杜夫会所提供的世界各地的美食。

酒店拥有总面积为 14000 平方英尺的会议区域，其中包括一个大宴会厅，6 个多功能厅，一个董事会议厅，三个独立会议室和北京唯一的婚礼堂。婚礼当天，婚礼堂还有一间筹备间，新郎新娘独立休息室，户外玫瑰花园可举办鸡尾酒会。之后在大宴会厅举办华丽个性的婚宴。酒店提供一站式婚礼服务，和美容，礼服，摄影，花艺，珠宝等多家机构合作，定将为新人带来一生的完美回忆。

位于酒店顶层，丽思卡尔顿 SPA 水疗中心共 2500 平方米。Spa 设计时尚现代，并且为绅士和淑女们准备了独立的放松休闲区域。共有 10 个理疗间，其中包括 6 个独立理疗室；1 个双人理疗室，内置巴厘式按摩床和多彩泡浴；美甲室；维希浴室和 Aqua 理疗室。整个区域采用浅蓝色调，男士休息区设计为简约的皮质棕色，女士则采用温暖的橙色调。理疗菜单中包括一系列促进全身心的健康的美容疗法，所有理疗均是传统和现代手法的结合。

在同一楼层，丽思卡尔顿水疗中心还拥有高科技的健身中心，以及室内恒温泳池。

丽思卡尔顿集团的座右铭是：我们以绅士淑女的态度为绅士淑女们忠诚服务。这种卓越的服务理念在客人踏入酒店，被礼宾部热情问候的那一刻即可深刻感受。个性化的购物体验，无与伦比的美食感受，吸引人的会议场所，精致的婚礼体验，在北京丽思卡尔顿酒店，客人将感受到最完美的奢华感受。

The Ritz-Carlton, Beijing
Timeless Elegance In China's Vibrant Capital

The Ritz-Carlton, Beijing, is centrally situated in one of Beijing's most thriving business area – China Central Place, within the heart of the city's central business district, the hotel is 30 minutes away from the Beijing Capital International Airport and offers easy access to the city's historical and cultural landmarks.

Blending English country manor style with contemporary luxury touches scattered rhythmic gloss of fine marble floor tiles captures the imagination as you make your way through the richly appointed lobby. Behold The Ritz-Carlton, Beijing, architecture and décor classically inspired. Whether from the full-bodied taste of Ritz-Carlton traditional afternoon tea or a refreshing spa treatment, your senses are entranced by experience. Choose from 305 guest rooms, including 38 suites and 61 Ritz-Carlton Club Level rooms, all with a standard of service that has made the Ritz-Carlton name synonymous with luxury.

Guests are spoilt with exceptional culinary choices and will truly experience the best of both East and West gastronomic cultures in the hotel from Aroma, Barolo, Yu, The Lounge, The Ritz-Carlton Bar, Davidoff Lounge.

The hotel features more than 11,400 square feet of meeting and conference space, including a Grand Ballroom, six function rooms, three meeting rooms, one boardroom and the only wedding chapel within the hotel in Beijing. The wedding experience at the hotel is all-encompassing; the Chapel features a preparation room, separate resting rooms for the bride and groom, an outdoor Rose garden where wedding cocktails can be held. An opulent and personalized wedding can be staged in the Grand Ballroom. The hotel offers a one-stop-shop service by partnering with some of Beijing's premier wedding service providers including beauty stylists, wedding gown couturiers, photographers, floral designers and jewelers.

Located on the top floor of the hotel, The Ritz-Carlton Spa is spread over a spacious area of 2,500 square metres. The Spa is contemporary, yet designed with comfort and relaxation in mind with separate resting rooms for the Ladies and Gentlemen. It features ten treatment rooms that including six single lavish treatment rooms, one Couples Suite that comes complete with Balinese massage bed and a color hydrotherapy bathtub, a Nail Bar, one Vichy Shower room and an Aqua Bed room. The colors of the suite are aqua blue, earthly tone paired with leather in the men's salon and a warm persimmon shade for the women's salon. The treatment menu contains comprehensive health and beauty therapies with an overall goal of enhancing wellness. Treatments are a synergetic blend of ancient rituals with a modern scientific basis.

On the same level of The Ritz-Carlton Spa features a cozy, yet fully equipped with cutting edge facilities fitness centre, as well as an indoor pool.

The Ritz-Carlton's motto is "We are Ladies and Gentlemen serving Ladies and Gentlemen" – this excellence of service standard is immediately felt as guests step into the hotel and greeted by the hotel's concierges. From tailor-made shopping experiences, exceptional culinary experiences, attentive eyes to meeting and wedding requirements, guests will always be ensured to experience the most luxurious stay and personalized service with The Ritz-Carlton, Beijing.

北京金融街丽思卡尔顿酒店

北京金融街丽思卡尔顿酒店是迅速崛起的金融街之焦点，距离首都国际机场和天安门广场分别为三十五分钟和十分钟车程。地理位置得天独厚，方便商旅及休闲度假客人通往繁荣的长安街和故宫等众多著名的历史文化古迹。酒店赋予浓郁的现代设计与轻钢玻璃及铬合金结构外观完美融合，内部高贵典雅极具东方风情。拥有100多年历史的知名奢华酒店品牌丽思卡尔顿，在金融街延续着其在奢华酒店服务领域的声望和传统，为宾客提供最完善的个人服务及设施。

拥有253间融合东方特色的客房均以50平方米起，环境舒适且配置卓越，无线上网等便利的高科技设施应有尽有。客厅和卫浴均配有超薄液晶电视，提供各种节目频道供客人选择。入住丽思卡尔顿行政楼层的客人们可在酒店专属的行政酒廊享用全天免费餐饮。精通多国语言的礼宾为您带来无微不至的服务。

酒店拥有三间风格卓越的餐厅及大堂酒廊和酒吧为您提供全日创意美食、意大利及中华美味。位于酒店大堂，以绚丽彩色玻璃及马赛克砖为装饰主题的全日美食餐厅名为Greenfish（四季汇），提供绿色健康美味的“弹性素食”，“周末的饕餮海鲜自助”更是您决不能错过的美食体验。Cépe（意味轩），屡获殊荣意大利餐厅——精选地道的意大利北部佳肴，包括味道浓郁的特级牛肝菌。餐厅设计独特的蘑菇贮藏盒，无论是干蘑亦或鲜蘑都可用来烹调出各种意大利饭、面食和地道的美味佳肴。特色中餐厅Qi（金阁），邀您在典雅舒适的环境中体验纯正的精品粤菜，这里有独特文化设计的宽敞大厅和各具特色的包间，无论是商务宴请、私人聚会，还是四至十五人的中小型派对，这里诠释现代美食文化的美食体验都将是您最难忘的记忆。

水晶吧&大堂酒廊独特的中式木雕屏风配以天窗设计，自然的光线透过天花板营造置身于自然的亲近感。客人可在如此优雅惬意的环境下享用著名的中式及丽思卡尔顿下午茶、全天零点，甜品及鸡尾酒。独特的香茶展示格，陈列来自世界各地共88种精选上等茶叶加之传统考究的茶道，使您倍感心旷神怡。晚餐之后，相约三五好友来这里享用优良的雪茄和陈年波特酒。聆听水晶乐队的优雅爵士乐，让充满诱惑的水晶吧点亮您的夜晚。

The Ritz-Carlton Beijing, Financial Street

The award-winning Ritz-Carlton Beijing, Financial Street is an icon in the city's financial hub. A contemporary design of glass and chrome combined with neo-classical Chinese aesthetics, the hotel is located 35 minutes from the airport and 10 minutes from the city center. Business and leisure travelers have easy access to Chang' an Avenue, the renowned Forbidden City (4 kilometers away) as well as numerous cultural landmarks. The hotel is also adjacent to the luxurious Seasons Place Shopping Center and within 10 minutes walk to Xidan, a shopping hub.

The hotel's 253 guest rooms and suites are well appointed with luxurious amenities and technological conveniences. The deluxe rooms from 50-square meters are one of the most spacious in Beijing's luxury hotels. Dining options include three restaurants featuring Chinese, Italian and all-day cuisines as well as a lounge and bar. Cépe, our award-winning Italian Dining Room, features haute Italian style cuisine with a selection of more than 2,000 wines while Qi, Chinese restaurant offers exquisite Cantonese cuisine including favorite dishes from Sichuan and Beijing in an elegant surrounding. Greenfish, the all-day dining restaurant highlights international cuisine and features weekly "Seafood Extravaganza". The signature Ritz-Carlton afternoon tea is served at Crystal Bar & Lounge. In the evenings, this place transforms to an exclusive venue to enjoy your favorite cocktail or a glass of champagne.

A dedicated 1,500-square-meter spa features 11 treatment rooms with an extensive health club equipped with a heated swimming pool, plunge pools, steam and sauna rooms to help you relax and rejuvenate. Spacious function rooms and a divisible grand ballroom complemented by seamless conference services ensure successful meetings.

北京金融街丽思卡尔顿酒店　中国北京市西城区金城坊东街1号　邮编:100140
1 Jin Cheng Fang Street East, Financial Street, Xicheng District, Beijing 100140, China
Tel: (86 10) 6601 6666　Fax: (86 10) 6601 6029　www.ritzcarlton.com

上海朗廷扬子精品酒店
优雅传奇

上海朗廷扬子精品酒店为朗廷国际酒店集团下的首家精品酒店，受任以源自 1865 年的英国经典豪华「朗廷」品牌管理，为您再现旧上海传奇历史。上海朗廷扬子精品酒店坐落于市中心最优越地段——南京路步行街旁，位于市中心商务区内，与人民广场、大剧院、市政府、外滩等著名景点近在咫尺。

朗廷扬子精品酒店原是一栋 70 多年的历史建筑，由留法建筑师李蟠设计，在当年以设计新颖成为倍受注目的建筑地标之一，更获得「远东第三大饭店」美誉，名噪一时。酒店原汁原味地保留了当时装饰艺术的精髓和风采，鲜明的色彩和装饰图案为宾客奉上源于老上海黄金年代的独特体验。

酒店共有 96 间客房及套房，贯彻装饰艺术设计风格，完美结合了典雅与奢华。部分客房拥有独立阳台或平台，让客人在喧嚣的城市中享受悠然静谧的空间。客房设有特大浴室，约占客房三分之一面积，并内置电视及音响，客人可一边浸浴、放松身心，一边享受视听娱乐。

酒店提供多个餐饮概念，演绎完美味觉之旅。唐阁以其经典的粤菜珍馐和无可挑剔的服务为您打造极致美味。设计优雅的「巧」意带您仿佛进入了正宗意大利地中海美食的天堂。置身于「窗」居酒屋可以品尝到种类繁多的传统日本美食。入座于廷廊则可享受朗廷引以为傲的经典下午茶。而蝶吧则是一个以装饰艺术风格为特色的鸡尾酒吧，供应琳琅满目的鸡尾酒，葡萄酒，香槟和威士忌。

酒店顶层设有一个可容纳 250 人的宴会厅——「珍珠厅」(Pearl Room)。「珍珠厅」采用无柱式设计，并透过一排硕大的玻璃窗引入自然日光和最佳视野，营造出宽敞无限的宴会空间。加上朗廷恰到好处的专业服务，挥洒出让人屏息的华丽梦幻。

屡获殊荣的「川」水疗中心散发宁静私密的气质，与热闹的城市形成鲜明对比。其水疗疗程全部基于中国传统医学的支柱——五行、阴阳和经络。专业理疗师透过一系列的自然疗法，舒缓及修复客人的身心健康。

The Langham, Yangtze Boutique, Shanghai
A legacy of elegance

The first boutique hotel of Langham Hotels International reflects a legendary hotel heritage dating back to 1865 when the flagship The Langham, London originally opened. The Langham, Yangtze Boutique, Shanghai enjoys the best location in the heart of the Shanghai' s central business district adjacent to Nanjing Road. The property is also just a stone' s throw from the city' s major cultural and entertainment highlights including The People' s Square, Shanghai Grand Theatre, Shanghai Municipal Government building and The Bund.

The Langham, Yangtze Boutique opened as an art deco masterpiece in the 1930s and was touted as "The Third Largest Hotel in the Far East" by the renowned architect, Li Pan. This enchanting boutique hotel has been faithfully restored with an intense combination of colours and pattern, the striking Art Deco design offers a unique experience dating back to the Golden Years of Shanghai.

The hotel features 96 art-deco rooms and suites, some with private balconies overlooking the vibrant city. Oversized bathrooms taking up one third of the spacious guestroom area are luxuriously designed, allowing guests to indulge in ultimate relaxation with built-in TV and sound system.

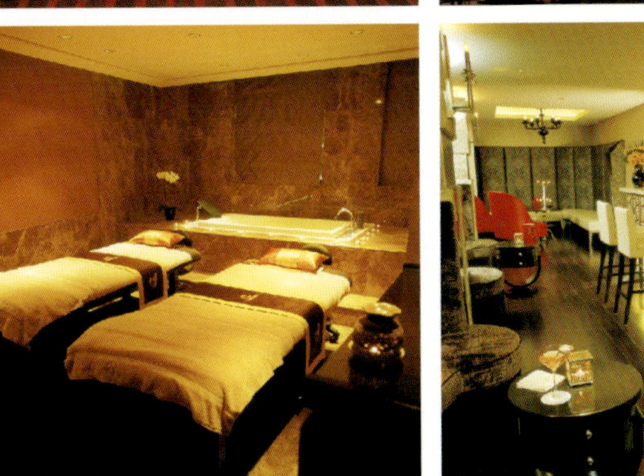

Five restaurants and bars offer a range of experiences. Find impeccable service, exquisite décor and exceptional Cantonese cuisine at T' ang Court. Authentic Mediterranean flavours at Ciao Italian Dining Room and Ciao Bambino, Mado Isakaya a convivial, stylish Japanese establishment, the Palm Court for refreshments and tempting treats or The Bar for rare and vintage beverages, served in rare, vintage surrounds.

The glamorous column-free Pearl Room on the top floor hosts up to 250 persons, paired with personalised Langham service and state-of-the-art facilities the venue adds a sense of magnificence to all luxury events. Natural light also floods the city' s beautiful art deco ballroom offering uninterrupted panoramic views of the city that add a touch of enchantment.

The award-winning Chuan Spa is based around Traditional Chinese Medicine (TCM) and the balancing the five Wu Xing elements. Chuan Spa is a serene haven where healing hands will pamper, soothe and reinvigorate guests with a wide array of natural treatments.

740 Hankou Road, Shanghai, China 中国上海市汉口路 740 号
T 电话 (86) 21 6080 0800 yangtzeboutique.langhamhotels.com

上海半岛酒店
一颗最新的外滩明珠

上海半岛酒店是半岛酒店集团旗下第九家酒店，于2009年年底正式开幕营业。酒店坐落于上海中心区域历史悠久的外滩，紧邻黄浦江畔，地理位置极为优越，不但拥有上海市以及花园景致，更呈献奢华的舒适、高水平的餐饮选择，以及半岛酒店声名远扬的优良服务，为贵客缔造独特而难忘的盛宴。

上海以其美丽的艺术装修风格建筑而闻名于世，上海半岛酒店则参考并借鉴了上世纪二、三十年代历史建筑的特点，巧妙地将酒店的设计主题与外滩建筑群和谐融合。在装修设计方面重现了上海在上世纪二、三十年代被誉为"东方巴黎"的黄金时期的风貌，同时还融入了最新的尖端科技、服务和娱乐设施。

上海半岛酒店的235间客房（包括44间套间）都位于上海的最大客房之列。标准豪华客房面积为55平方米（600平方尺），大多坐拥浦东、黄浦江、外滩和前英国领事馆花园的美景。室内设计除了大量运用深浅不一的青瓷色或象牙色外，还大量运用了各种上世纪二十年代风行上海的传统材料——桃木和黑檀木的家具和木制品以及制造出强烈对比的圣劳芝黑和圣塔利奥白石头等等。地毯是100%纯羊毛的手工制作。

上海半岛酒店拥有五间风格迥异的餐厅和酒吧，为您带来多种特色美食与情调享受，包括大堂茶座、逸龙阁中餐厅、艾利爵士顶层餐厅、酒吧和露台、以航海为主题的引航酒吧和玲珑酒廊。另外设有各类会议厅、主题场所和大宴会厅玫瑰厅。整个酒店的设计以艺术装饰风格贯穿，各餐厅都体现了上海在二、三十年代时所拥有的时尚和商业中心的杰出地位。酒店会务系统极尽尊贵完备，从可容纳1000人参加鸡尾酒会或是可容纳450人参加宴席的大宴会厅玫瑰厅，到主题酒吧，配以精心烹饪的美食和专享私人化服务，这一切都将令宾客们流连忘返。

半岛水疗中心占地1250平方米（13455平方尺），在繁忙的都市里为您提供一处忘却尘嚣的空间。水疗中心设有七间理疗室、两间私人水疗套间，配合热能设施房、技艺娴熟的理疗师，以及ESPA产品，为您的身心带来前所未有的舒畅体验。酒店内另有长25米（80尺）的室内游泳池和健身中心，共同组成了呵护身心健康的舒适空间。

The Peninsula Shanghai
The Newest Jewel On The Bund

Opened in late 2009, the ninth property in The Peninsula Hotels' portfolio fronts the historic Bund with spectacular views of the Bund, Huangpu River, Pudong and the gardens of the former British Consulate, and blends with the historic architecture of its landmark neighbours along the Bund. The Peninsula Shanghai offers commanding city and garden views, luxurious comfort, sophisticated facilities, extraordinary dining options and the legendary Peninsula service.

A homage to Shanghai in the 1920s and 1930s, The Peninsula Shanghai recreates the look and feel of this glamorous era when Shanghai was fêted as "The Paris of the East", yet also offers the latest in state-of-the-art technology, services and amenities.

The Peninsula Shanghai' s 235 guestrooms (including 44 suites) are amongst the largest in Shanghai, with a typical Deluxe Guestroom being 55 sq m (600 sq ft), and most featuring stunning views of Pudong, the Huangpu River, the Bund or the gardens of the former British Consulate. In tones of celadon or cerulean blue and ivory, the interior design incorporates a number of traditional materials used in Shanghai in the 1920s – the rich figures of mahogany and ebony for the loose furniture and millwork, and the dramatic contrasts of black Noir St Laurent and off-white St Talino stones. Carpets are 100% wool and hand-tufted.

The Peninsula Shanghai features a collection of five eclectic restaurants and bars offering a variety of cuisines and ambiences - The Lobby, Yi Long Court Chinese Restaurant, Sir Elly' s Rooftop Restaurant, Bar & Terrace, the nautical-themed Compass Bar and Salon de Ning – together with a range of meeting rooms, unique theme and terrace venues and The Rose Ballroom. Underlining the Art Deco-inspired décor throughout the hotel, a number of the outlets pay tribute to Shanghai' s celebrated position as a centre of style and commerce in the 1930s –Prestigious settings ranging from a grand ballroom for up to 1,000 for cocktails or 450 for a banquet, to themed lounges, gourmet cuisine and exceptional personalized service will combine for a function to remember.

Occupying 1,250 sq m (13,455 sq ft), The Peninsula Spa by ESPA offers a city retreat permeated by indulgence and deep relaxation. Seven treatment rooms and two VIP suites, heat experiences, highly-trained therapists and ESPA products combine and provide luxurious bespoke treatments for body and mind. With a décor inspired by F. Scott Fitzgerald' s novel "The Great Gatsby", a 25 m (80 ft) indoor swimming pool and Fitness Centre complement The Peninsula Shanghai' s innovative approach to health and rejuvenation.

THE PENINSULA
SHANGHAI
上海半岛酒店

广州卡丽酒店

广州卡丽酒店是按五星级标准设计，集商务、宴会、休闲等配套服务为一体的摩登酒店。酒店设有多类型客房 302 间，会议设施一应俱全，拥有最先进的 WIFI 无线高速网络，适合各种大小类型的会议、宴会、展览等活动的举办，另有新派粤菜食府、法国籍厨师主理的开放式西餐厅，还有新加坡管理层主理的玉 SPA，由新加坡旅游局五届授予“Best SPA Destination Award Winner”的 SPA Botanica 培训的专业水疗师，绝对是您放松身心的好去处。广州卡丽酒店是境内外游客以及五十岁以下活力人群的首选之“宿”！

广州卡丽酒店作为广州首家以摩登定位的酒店，自 2010 年初试业至今，获得不少亮眼的成绩。

广州卡丽酒店自成立之初，一直不断提高自身服务的品质优势，更荣获“2010 粤港澳最具摩登魅力酒店”、《新周刊》2010 酒店魅力排行榜的“最佳舒适卧室酒店”等奖项。不少政商娱乐界名人选择下榻广州卡丽酒店，先后成为《2010 花田喜事》、《叶问 2》、《守望者：罪恶迷途》等新闻发布会，“李健 2010 广州浅唱会”、“吉卜赛小提琴之王罗比拉•卡托斯小提琴炫技音乐会”、“音乐先锋榜 2010 颁奖典礼”等活动指定接待酒店。

在 2010 年广州艺博会举办期间，广州卡丽酒店作为第 15 届艺博会极力推荐的最具艺术气质酒店，为广大艺博会客商们提供热情而优质的服务。

广州卡丽酒店在试业短短一年的时间，承办各类型大小活动，随着玉 SPA 在 2011 年 4 月试业，酒店的摩登形象将继续深刻地留在不同国籍、区域的顾客心中！

广州市卡丽酒店有限公司
荣获第十五届广州国际艺术博览会
最具艺术气质酒店
第十五届广州国际艺术博览会组委会颁发
2010年12月13日

Guangzhou Carat Hotel & Spa

Our 5-star modern hotel features 302 tastefully renovated guests rooms and suites to cater to your Needs. Each of our guest rooms and suites features a designer look and dressed with luxurious linens bedding and feather Pillows to give the rooms a fresh modern look. Whether in pursuit of business or pleasure, you will be delighted with our Various selections and choices available. Carat Hotel has been a choice of accommodation for modern travellers Under 50 with a whole new experience as a home away from home.

YU Spa

2010粤港澳最具摩登魅力酒店
The Most Modern and Charming Hotels 2010
Guangdong, HongKong, Macau

YU Spa (managed by Singapore Hotel Team) with 40 treatment rooms is located in the central business district between Tianhe and Baiyun district. YU Spa therapists are professionally trained under Spa Botanica, Sentosa–Best Destination Spa award winner nominated by Singapore Tourism Board, Singapore. YU in Chinese means Jade. it symbolise petite, strong, beautiful and luster. Set to dazzle guests with spa facilities designed to exude Asian rejuvenation, you can look forward to an extensive menu featuring YU Spa Signature therapy treatment experience, to loosen tight muscles whilst stimulating your senses.

Guangzhou Carat Hotel being one of the most sought after Modern Hotel in Guangzhou since its establishment in 2010 has made concerted effort with careful planning to incorporate modern art into the decor as a modern business hotel surrounded by stunning achievements and much patronized by government offices and celebrities.

Since its inception, Guangzhou Carat Hotel has continuously strive to improve the service quality and management process and has won a number of awards such as the "2010 Guangdong, Hong Kong's Most Attractive Modern Hotel", voted "Most Comfortable Hotel" by News Weekly magazine and has since gained its recognition within the industry.

Over the year, Guangzhou Carat Hotel has been privileged to be the Official Host for movies like "2010 Alls Well Ends Well Too", "Yip Man 2" and "The Man behind the Courtyard House 2011" press conferences events. The Hotel was also appointed as the host for celebrities like "Li Jian Concert 2010" and "Roby Lakatos Gypsy Music Appreciation Concert" as well as the up-coming "Guangdong Music Awards Ceremony 2010".

In the recent 15th year Guangzhou Art Fair, Guangzhou Carat Hotel was voted "The Most Artistic Hotel" providing both leisure and business travelers a delightful and memorable guest experience. YU Spa which is scheduled to open in April is set to dazzle guests with its beautifully designed facilities to exude Asian rejuvenation in a nothing less than a luxurious state of ease and renewal.

广州市广园中路 388 号 388 Guang Yuan Zhong Road, Guangzhou, Guangdong, P.R.C 电话 /Tel：（8620）8396 6866 微博 /Weibo：www.weibo.com/moderncarat 酒店网址 /Web：www.moderncarat.com

HRCHINA

埃科菲国际厨师协会

埃科菲国际厨师协会代表广大厨师，竭力维护食品的质量和口感，在保证烹饪纯正传统的前提下促进专业技术的进步，分享经验和方法、革新技术。

埃科菲国际厨师协会

埃科菲国际厨师协会致力于让成员们获得愉快的经历和埃科菲先生美食精神的熏陶，为厨师提供更为专业的训练，为创造完美餐饮艺术添上更加瑰丽的色彩。

作为烹饪界的主要协会，埃科菲国际厨师协会（O.I.D.A.E） 现已入驻澳门——世界上独具特色的亚洲美食胜地之一。

Auguste Escoffier

Auguste Escoffier生于1846年10月28日，卢贝新城， 一个尼斯附近的普罗旺斯小村庄。 卒于1935年2月12日，蒙特卡洛， 终年89岁。 终其一生， 享有辉煌的事业生涯。他最初是一名厨师， 然后成为了一家著名酒店的餐厅经理， 之后开始了写作生涯。一言以蔽之，他是一位“非常杰出的人”。

突出贡献

埃科菲始终关注烹调术和人们饮食习惯的革命性变化， 从未间断对其餐饮简化这一理念的完善。

埃科菲先生以旧时的方式简化菜单，把菜名按照上菜的顺序罗列。他同时也是开发单点（a la carte）菜单的第一人。

他不再以面粉层作为调料，而首创了新式的肉酱和糖浆来取而代之。

他推动成立专业厨师队伍， 并分成不同等级的厨师：副厨师长、厨师主管、助理厨师等。他的写作才华是公认的，所著文章和书籍成为经典。时至今日，埃科菲先生（Escoffier）仍是现代烹饪业首要的理论家。

Orde International des Disciples d'Auguste Escoffier

Disciples Escoffier represents chefs eager to commit themselves to safeguarding and supporting quality and flavour in food products, promoting professional expertise, and developing and fostering the sharing of experiences, ideas and new technology, in keeping with culinary traditions.

Orde International des Disciples d'Auguste Escoffier

O.I.D.A.E (Displaines Escoffier) is contributed to provide opportunities for its members delight and edification, to further develop the professional training of chefs, and also to generate gains in the perfection of the art of fine dining.

As a major association in the culinary world, O.I.D.A.E has now brought its step into Macau - one of Asia's unique culinary scenes of the world.

Auguste Escoffier

Auguste Escoffier was born in Villeneuve-Loubet, a small Provencal village near Nice, on October 28, 1846 and died in Monte Carlo February 12, 1935 at the age of 89. During his entire life he had a prestigious career, first as a chef, then as Director of the restaurants of eminent hotels, as a writer, and simply as a "very noble man".

Great Contributions

Escoffier had a constant concern for the revolutionary changes in the cookery of art and peoples food habits, and never ceased to make generous contributions to his gastronomic philosophy of refines simplicity in dining.

He simplified the menu as it had been, writing the dishes down in the order in which they would be served (Service a la Rusee). He also developed the first al a carte menu.

He eliminated flour from sauce and invented new meat stocks and glaces.

He instigated the organization of professional kitchen brigades and divided the staff into different sections of chefs: sous chef, chef de parties, commis etc. His talent was also recognized as a writer, his great articles and books have since become classics. Escoffier remains today the first and foremost theoretician of modern cookery.

Chris Busschaert

克里斯

上海外滩华尔道夫酒店饼房厨师长

我来自比利时这样一个糕饼艺术出神入化的国度，我在那儿迈出了我糕饼师生涯的第一步。当时的经历造就了如今这个每天满怀激情，竭力创新，做到最好的糕点大厨。我的顾客与雇主们也被我出色的技艺和时刻积极的态度打动。

十四岁时，我在Kortrijk的一家叫Patisserie Francaise的法式糕饼店得到了第一份工作，在那儿我学到了基本的技巧，为我将来的职业生涯奠定了基础。这家店的店主兼大厨Bernard Devos是我的贵人，在最初的三年中给了我很大的帮助。

2004年，我有幸受邀出席了世界美食峰会，与这些来自世界各地的米其林星级厨师在新加坡齐聚一堂，真是一种曼妙的体验啊！同年，我亦有幸于新加坡获得年度三大顶级糕饼师的提名。

在那儿，我负责供应850名宾客的点心店等。作为这家顶尖酒店的一员，我们已经为它斩获了12个世界奖项。

我现在的职务是上海华尔道夫饭店这样一个在中国享有盛名的地标式酒店的行政糕点总厨。

美食为我所爱，烹饪是我激情所在。

工作经历：

1.Patisserie Francaise的法式糕饼店
2.普吉岛希尔顿酒店
3.Marquette Marke-Kortrijk酒店
4.曼谷希尔顿酒店
5.上海希尔顿酒店
6.新加坡港丽酒店
7.海南岛三亚丽兹卡尔顿酒店
8.上海外滩华尔道夫酒店

获得奖项：

1.拿到了比利时The Green Gate Bruges颁发的学位，其中包括巧克力和甜点专业课程。
2.2004年在新加坡获得年度三大顶级糕饼师的提名
3.在上海获得了"国家巧克力大师竞赛"金奖

Chris Busschaert

Executive Pastry Chef,Waldorf Astoria Shanghai on the Bund

Coming from a country as Belgium where pastry art is set to high standards and where I got the chance to build up my first steps as a pastry cook and develop myself to become what I am now a true pastry chef with the passion and hard to create and give every day the best of me so guest and employers can enjoy my great work and positive expression day in and out.

Started at the age off 14 years at my first pastry job in a French pastry shop Patisserie Francaise in Kortrijk where I learned the basic's witch was fundamental for my total future career.The owner and pastry chef Bernard Devos was my great figure where I look up to for the whole first 3 years that I have worked there.

Also at that time been part of the World Gourmet Summit was a fabulous experience cause you have al these Michelin Star's chefs from around the world coming to Singapore. At the same year 2004 I was nominated the top 3 pastry chefs off the year at Singapore.

Having found my new challenge at China with Ritz Carlton Sanya located at Hainan Island and better know for the Chinese and Hong Kong people as there Chinese Hawaii.Working at Ritz Carlton is really the cherry on the cake for a pastry chef and something that every pastry chef is dreaming off to work for one of the most World wide famous hotel industry.

There I was in charge for all pastries bakeries for 6 outlets witch include daily breakfast up to 850 guest and all desserts a la carte and boutique pastry shop. Been part of such a great performing hotel we have won more then 12 World Wide awards.

Now as Executive pastry chef now at the helm off the pre opening team for the Waldorf Astoria Shanghai a Legendary Landmark hotel for China.

"Food is my love…Cooking is my Passion…"

Work Experience

1. in a French pastry shop Patisserie Francaise in Kortrijk
2. At Hilton Phuket
3. At Hotel Restautant Marquette Marke-Kortrijk
4. At the Hilton Bangkok
5. Shanghai with Hilton
6. At Conrad Singapore
7. At China with Ritz Carlton Sanya
8. The Waldorf Astoria Shanghai

Won Prizes

1. My degree issued by The Green Gate Bruges –Belgium including special course as chocolate and sugar art work.
2. At the same year 2004 I was nominated the top 3 pastry chefs off the year at Singapore.
3. At Hilton Shanghai I pull out the Gold Medal for the Chocolate Masters National competition at Shanghai

David Laris

David Laris
概念品牌

12 Chairs
12 Chairs是David Laris先生最新的高端餐厅力作。私密的空间，豪华的设计，让您置身于全方位的美食之旅。多样化的菜单选择、新鲜的食材设计，使您可独享12 Chairs的私密空间。这里有上海最顶尖的葡萄酒酒单，您可从中选择适合的美酒搭配美食。

The Fat Olive
David Laris打造出的欧立威餐厅融合了红酒和希腊美食完美的搭配，灵感来自于 David Laris曾在希腊度过的快乐童年时光。他不仅仅想和大家分享至爱的希腊美食，更想和大家一起分享地中海美妙情愫的精髓。在这为客户营造的轻松自在的氛围里，享用着配料新鲜简洁的正宗希腊菜肴和世界精选美酒，是您午餐或下班后或深夜寻找欢乐时光的绝佳选择。

Yucca
Yucca是一个充满惊喜的地方。2010年，第一家门店在世博村绚丽登场。推出了一系列充满特色的菜单和鸡尾酒单。现在，在思南公馆你将看到全新的迷你型演绎。性感的服务、另类的鸡尾酒和mordiscos（我们全新演绎的quesadilla），这个私密的空间将带给你无限的惊喜及感官震撼。

David Laris Concepts

12 Chairs

12 Chairs is the new premium dining experience by David Laris. In the most intimate of settings, you will embark on a culinary journey. A multiple-course degustation menu freshly prepared and presented to you from your private 12 Chairs kitchen. One of the most exclusive wine lists in Shanghai to select just the right vintage to pair with each course.

The Fat Olive

The Fat Olive is a wine and mezze bar concept by David Laris. Inspired by his childhood in Greece, David wanted to create a warm & chic space reminiscent of the Mediterranean lifestyle. Guests can sample a variety of signature Greek dishes and international wines. Linger over lunch, after work for happy hour or late into the evening.

Yucca

Yucca is a place where the most unexpected things happen. The original restaurant opened in 2010 at Expo Village with a full menu and specialty cocktails list. The latest incarnation is the vibrant micro-lounge at Sinan Mansions. Serving sexy, alternative cocktails and indulgent Yucca mordiscos (our twist on the quesadilla), this intimate space will surprise and tantalize the senses.

Kristoffer Luczak

Kristoffer Luczak

新濠博亚娱乐餐饮部副总裁

Kristoffer Luczak先生是新濠博亚娱乐餐饮部的副总裁。新濠博亚娱乐是纳斯达克全球精选的上市公司（纳斯达克：MPEL），现已发展为澳门高级热门必游的综合娱乐度假胜地。

Luczak先生负责新濠锋和新濠天地的餐饮运作和体制，它包括在皇冠度假酒店，Hard Rock酒店和新濠锋的餐饮服务。另外他还负责员工的餐饮服务。

他还是一名1200多员工的领导者，包括策划、指导和协调，管理着新濠天地和新濠锋两家酒店的整个餐饮运作，包括开发业务策划和市场策略，健康卫生和认证规范，资金和经营开支的预算和控制。

Luczak先生曾经是厨房运作和餐饮策划的地区经理，负责新濠天地和新濠锋厨房部的运作。他以前当过新濠锋厨房部的经理，这个职位是于2006年12月任职的。在那儿，他赢得了促进最佳亚洲食品和提倡供给时令有机营养食物菜单的荣誉。

他出生在瑞典的Stockholm，享有在亚洲、欧洲、中东和美国20年的职业生涯，他在有些世界著名酒店集团包括The Ritz Carlton，The Peninsula 及 The Oberoi，担任着领导的职位。他在加入新濠锋以前，在新加坡世界闻名的Raffles酒店担任执行厨师。

Kristoffer Luczak

Vice President, Food and Beverage, Melco Crown Entertainment

Mr. Kristoffer Luczak is the Vice President, Food and Beverage of Melco Crown Entertainment, (NASDAQ: MPEL) ("Melco Crown Entertainment"), a company listed on the NASDAQ Global Select Market owning one of only six gaming concessions and subconcessions to operate gaming business in Macau through its Macau subsidiary.

Mr. Luczak is responsible for overseeing the Food and Beverage operations and systems of both City of Dreams and Altria Macau, which include the F&B services within Crown Towers, Hard Rock Hotel and Altria Macau; His responsibilities also cover employee dining services.

Mr. Luczak heads a workforce of over 1,200 employees and he involves planning, directing and coordinating a strategic approach to managing the entire City of Dreams and Altira Macau food and beverage operation, including developing business plans and marketing strategies; health & safety and licensing regulations; and budgeting and control of capital and operating expenditures.

Mr. Luczak previously held the position of Regional Director of Culinary Operations and F&B Strategy with responsibility for the oversight of Culinary Operations at both City of Dreams and Altira. Mr. Luczak formerly served as Director of Kitchens at Altira Macau (formerly Crown Macau), a position he took in December 2006, where he earned a reputation for promoting the best of Asian foods and advocating menus offering the best-of-season organic nutritional foods.

Born in Stockholm Sweden, Mr. Luczak has enjoyed a prestigious 20-year career having worked extensively in Asia, Europe, the Middle East and the USA where he has taken leading roles at some of the world's finest hotels groups including The Ritz Carlton, The Peninsula and The Oberoi. Before joining Altira, Mr. Luczak was an award winning Executive Chef at the world-renowned Raffles Hotel in Singapore.

Thomas Gebler

托马斯・盖伯乐

上海外滩华尔道夫酒店餐饮总监

上海外滩华尔道夫酒店坐落于举世闻名的上海外滩核心地带并坐拥浦江盛世美景。酒店由一栋全套房的百年历史建筑楼——华尔道夫会所（曾经的上海总会）以及一座新近落成的附属建筑—华尔道夫酒店组合而成，它将浓厚的文化气息与二十一世纪温文尔雅的情调完美融合。露天庭院连接着两栋楼宇，与经典华尔道夫品牌代表—纽约华尔道夫酒店“连字号相会”走廊如出一辙。酒店拥有着272间客房以及套房，同时设有六个餐厅、典雅高贵的临江上海总会宴会厅以及十个大小不一的多功能厅，健身中心，国际水疗中心等。更值得关注的是，上海外滩华尔道夫酒店的成长与进步得到了许多生活品位鉴赏家以及行业内资深人士的认同与赞赏。

托马斯•盖伯乐先生于2011年加入上海外滩华尔道夫酒店，担任餐饮总监一职，掌管该酒店三座餐厅（百味园，Pelham's纽约餐厅和蔚景阁）、两间休息廊（浦江汇和羿庭）以及一个酒吧（廊吧）的餐饮服务，为顾客提供从原汁原味的中式佳肴到风靡全球的纽约时尚菜式的华贵餐饮。

盖伯乐先生拥有丰富的餐饮服务及酒店运营经验，曾在世界多个国家及市场工作。加入上海外滩华尔道夫之前，他在欧洲Rocco Forte酒店连锁品牌旗下的圣彼得堡Astoria Hotel担任餐饮总监一职，服务两年后被晋升为酒店营运总监。加入Astoria Hotel之前，盖伯乐先生在慕尼黑卡宾斯基酒店担任宴会及餐饮部经理。此外，他先后在精致游轮（Celebrity Cruises）和荷美游轮（Holland America）担任餐饮助理经理一职。盖伯乐先生的职业生涯开始于法兰克福洲际酒店，担任包括宴会部门主管在内的多个职位。

盖伯乐先生来自德国，拥有德国工业及商业协会颁发的国际调酒师认证，熟练德语、英语和俄语三种语言。

Thomas Gebler

Director of Food and Beverage, Waldorf Astoria Shanghai on the Bund

Located at the heart of the celebrated Shanghai Bund, a waterfront boulevard which runs alongside the Huangpu River and one of the most photographed postcard scenes of the city, Waldorf Astoria Shanghai on the Bund is a two-building hotel complex with a century-old heritage building dubbed the "Waldorf Astoria Club" (in remembrance of the building's original 1911 historical identity as the Shanghai Club), and the Waldorf Astoria Tower, a newly-built annex building that rises to elevated vantage of the Huang Pu River. An outdoor courtyard joins the two buildings much like the famed "meet-me-at-the-hyphen" corridor that joins the two towers of the brand's icon – the Waldorf Astoria New York. The hotel comprises 272 rooms and suites, 6 outlets, the spectacular Shanghai Club ballroom with breathtaking river view, 10 event venues, fitness facilities, an international spa and more.

Thomas Gebler joined Waldorf Astoria Shanghai on the Bund as Director of Food and Beverage (F&B) in 2011, in charge of the catering service from an array of three restaurants (Grand Brasserie, Pelham's and Wei Jing Ge), two lounges (Salon de Ville and Peacock Alley) and a bar (Long Bar). He leads the team to bring together the epitome of fine dining and chic socializing to guests, from all-day dining and authentic Chinese to New York style specialties.

Mr. Gebler worked at different countries and markets around the world and gains extensive experience in catering and hotel operation. Prior to his role at Waldorf Astoria Shanghai on the Bund, he was Director of Operation at Astoria Hotel in St. Petersburg, which is under Rocco Forte collection, one of the finest Hotel chains in Europe. He joined Astoria Hotel in 2007 as Director of F&B and promoted to Director of Operation in 2009. Previously, Mr. Gebler was appointed as Banquet and Catering Manager at Kempinski Hotel in Munich. In addition to hotel experience, Mr. Gebler also worked at Celebrity Cruises and Holland America Cruise Line to deepen his expertise at F&B service. Mr. Gebler started his career at InterContinental Hotel in Frankfurt, where he took various roles including Banquet Supervisor.

Mr. Gebler is from Germany. He holds the degree as International Bar Master from the German Industry and Chamber of Commerce (IHK). He is fluent in German, English and Russian.

Yeung Koon Yat

杨贯一

阿一鲍鱼创始人

1992 President of Asian Region of Eurotoques, Belgium

欧洲名厨联盟亚洲区荣誉会长

1995 Member of Club des Chefs des Chefs

世界御厨协会会员

Awarded Medaille d'Honneur de Vermeil

荣获法国厨艺大师最高荣誉白金奖

1999 Knight of the Order of the Agriculture Merite

Chevalier de l'Ordre du Merite Agricole

荣获法国农业部最高荣誉勋奖

The American Academy of Hospitality Sciences 1999

Five Star Diamond Award

荣获美国五星钻石奖

2000 The Gold Medal of Club des Chefs des Chefs

By Gilles Bragard in Paris

荣获世界御厨蓝带四星奖

Mr. T. Dana Presented Yeung Koon Yat

with the Elysee Momento on behalf of French President

荣获代法国总统颁赠银碗奖

2002 The World Master of Culinary Arts

荣获世界厨艺精英奖

2008 Academie Culinaire de France

世界御厨杨贯一荣获法国烹饪学院奖

2009 To impulse the remand for lifetine achievement

of development of Cantonese food

推动粤菜发展终身成就奖

The World Master of Culinary Arts
荣获世界厨艺精英奖

To impulse the remand for lifetine achievement
of development of Cantonese food
推动粤菜发展终身成就奖

世界御厨杨贯一
荣获
Academie Culinaire de France

世界御厨杨贯一
荣获
Academie Culinaire de France

世界御厨协会主席Mr.Bragard
亲临富临饭店与杨贯一合影

世界御厨杨贯一先生于 2008 年 12 月 30 日荣获饮食界的荣誉 Academie Culinaire de France 勋章。由法国驻港副领事颁奖。他是首位中国人获此殊荣。

Academie Culinaire de France

Academie Culinaire de France 由 Universal Dictionary of Cooking 的作者 Joseph Favre 在 1883 年 2 月 18 日创立。

成员皆是法国饮食业翘楚。学院的目标是：开发法国烹饪艺术，促进 haute cuisine（法国烹饪最崇高境界）技艺，倡护烹饪行业的声望，并且为法国食谱推陈出新。多年来学院的声望享誉全国。在国外亦甚负盛名，扮演着行业大使的重要角色。在法国以外获选为成员定当地饮食业一等一的精英。Antonin Careme 乃拿破仑御厨，有近代法国烹饪之父的崇高称誉。标记由月桂冠图案及 16 星尖团拢，代表 haute cuisine 技艺中的 16 个分支，其中包括酱汁、浓汤、烧烤、冷盘、糕点、糖果及甜品等。

香港铜锣湾骆克道485号
485 Lockhart Rd. Causeway Bay, H.K.
Tel:852-2891-2555 / 852-2891-2516
Fax:852-2893-0756

上海莫尔顿牛排坊

上海莫尔顿牛排坊是世界上最大的莫尔顿餐厅，拥有400多个座位，餐厅另还设9个包房，可容纳4至60名客人，是公司宴请和家庭聚会的绝佳地点。这些多功能包房亦配备顶级的影音设施，适合举办各种活动。

餐厅的菜单汇集各款饕餮美食，其一大特色就是为客人提供上海滩最好的谷物喂养的顶级牛排。招牌菜包括上等T骨牛排和带骨肉眼牛排，以及烤波士顿龙虾和智利鲈鱼等名贵海鲜。

餐厅还为雪茄和葡萄酒行家特设了两个贵宾房，提供顶级年份葡萄酒和上等雪茄，这里的布置舒适宜人，客人在此可以欣赏上海瑰丽的夜景。

餐厅还提供多款清新美味的配菜，如煮珍宝芦笋及炒鲜菠菜和蘑菇等不胜枚举。餐厅的缤纷美式甜点，如纽约芝士蛋糕、经典莫尔顿传奇热巧克力蛋糕和莫尔顿传奇圣代等，一款款精美绝伦，让人食指大动，不容错过。

别具特色的"经典牛排"套餐备有两道佳肴。头盘为特色沙拉，以新鲜球生菜、鸡蛋丁、番茄及培根粒炮制而成，配以莫尔顿蓝纹奶酪汁或千岛汁。主菜则可选择双份牛柳或纽约西冷牛排，并伴以一系列星级配菜如珍宝芦笋、奶油菠菜、烤珍宝土豆，以及土豆泥等。

上海莫尔顿牛排坊位于中国上海浦东世纪大道8号上海国金中心商场4楼15-16商铺。
预订电话：(86 21) 6075 8888。
营业时间：周日至周四上午11:30至晚上 10:00；
周五及周六上午11:30至晚上11:00 。

关于莫尔顿

莫尔顿餐厅集团（Morton's Restaurant Group, Inc.）是世界最大的高级牛排餐厅拥有者及经营者。集团旗下的牛排餐厅一贯秉承创始人当初的远见，即恪守严格标准，烹饪顶级美食，确保真材足量，提供优质服务，让客人在舒适的环境中享用美食。

公司拥有并经营77家莫尔顿牛排餐厅，遍布美国27个州的65座城市以及海外7个城市和地区（墨西哥城、波多黎各、多伦多、新加坡、香港、澳门和上海）。

Morton's of Chicago, Shanghai

With seating for more than 400 guests, Morton's Shanghai is the largest Morton's in the world and also offers nine private dining suites styled like elegant lounge rooms - perfect for corporate entertaining and family celebrations for between 4 and 60 guests. These multifunctional rooms are also equipped with audio-visual facilities catering to a range of private functions.

The mouth-watering menu features signature dishes such as Porterhouse and Bone-In Ribeye Steak, plus fresh premium seafood – such as the Whole Baked Maine Lobster and Chilean Sea Bass.

Two additional private rooms are reserved for Cigar and Wine connoisseurs, offering the finest vintage wines and cigars in a lounge setting looking out across the night lights of Shanghai.

These are complemented with tantalising side dishes, such as Steamed Fresh Jumbo Asparagus and Sautéed Fresh Spinach & Button Mushrooms. Diners should save room for the decadent American desserts too, such as New York Cheesecake, Morton's Legendary Hot Chocolate Cake and Morton's Legendary Sundae.

The two course special menu starts with a Centre Cut Iceberg Salad served with chopped egg, tomato, bacon bits and either Morton's Blue Cheese Dressing or Thousand Island Dressing. Main course is a choice of Double Cut Filet with Béarnaise Sauce or New York Strip Steak served with a selection of signature side dishes including Jumbo Asparagus, Creamed Spinach, Jumbo Baked Potato and Mashed Potatoes.

Morton's of Chicago, The Steakhouse in Shanghai is located at Shop 15-16, 4/F, Shanghai IFC Mall, 8 Century Avenue, Pudong, Shanghai, PR China. Reservations can be made at (86 21) 6075 8888.

Regular Opening Hours: Sunday to Thursday 11:30 am to 10:00 pm; Friday and Saturday 11:30 am to 11:00 pm.

About Morton's

Morton's Restaurant Group, Inc. is the world's largest operator of company-owned upscale steakhouses. Morton's steakhouses have remained true to its founders' original vision of combining generous portions of high quality food prepared to exacting standards with exceptional service in an enjoyable dining environment.

The Company owns and operates 77 Morton's steakhouses located in 65 cities across 27 states in the USA, as well as seven international locations (Mexico City, Puerto Rico, Toronto, Singapore, Hong Kong, Macau and Shanghai).

位于十六铺的龙皇旗舰店于2009年年底开张

位于沙巴的渔场，为龙皇提供高质海鲜

九趸是龙皇招牌菜之一，
每一条都由帜哥悉心搜罗

龙皇酒家六星级的美味享受

由中国十大名厨之一——黄永帜先生主理的龙皇酒家饮食集团，以鲍翅燕参肚为主，尤以海鲜称霸。帜哥曾获多个国际性饮食奖项，包括法国厨皇会的状元奖、白金奖，近年亦主持多个电视节目，包括《厨神走天崖》、《鲜入为煮》等。帜哥特意到世界各地搜罗最优质的海产，在马来西亚沙巴州开设渔场，到印尼泗水合营燕窝场，确保材料的高品质，为大众提供优质的美食。

帜哥精心设计珍馐百味

在龙皇吃到的菜式，均由帜哥精心设计，从选材到烹调，都尽显功力与特色，可谓色香味俱全，像帜哥特别研制一系列由百年龙趸不同部位烹调的原创菜式，如蒸龙趸球、燉龙趸眼、燉龙趸骨等，肉甜味美，仅此一家，加上帜哥利用各种珍菌药材入馔，令菜式添上补身功效。

旗舰店登陆上海

龙皇酒家至今开了四间，在香港得到一众食家认同，包括铜锣湾世贸店、观塘源成中心店、湾仔皇悦酒店店及油麻地碧街店。2009年更积极进军内地市场，于上海十六铺开设旗舰店。十六铺是上海最富代表性的地标，外滩风景美丽，吸引本地及中外游客观光消费。据帜哥所言，这间新的旗舰店走高档食府路线，不但贯彻龙皇的优质美食观念，在制作上也不断求变，创作出更多姿多彩的“型格菜”。此外，在外观方面，还特意聘请著名设计师，预算投资人民币二千万装修，务求“以五星级的价格提供六星级的服务”，让客人可在最好的环境品尝龙皇的特色美食。

Contents

德国米技 炉具专家
German Miji Cooking System

总目录

源自德国,专用商业炉,安全节能、环保耐用

烹饪大师的最佳选择

创造地油烟"冷静"的烹饪环境

- 德国EGO尖端商用VARIO ATICS模块
- 采用304不锈钢制造，关键部分厚度达到2mm
- 功率范围广，覆盖到3.5KW~20KW，功率都是采用线性调节输出

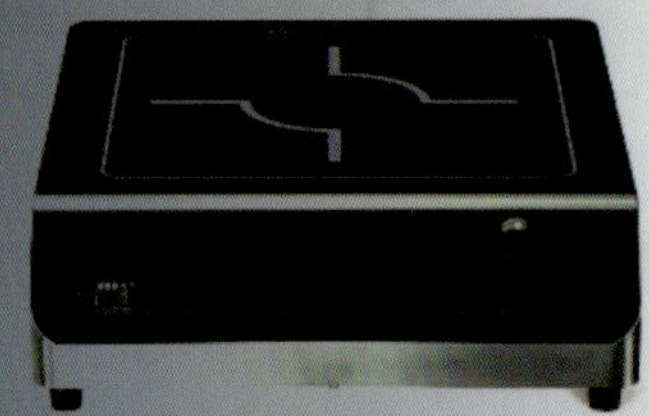

Miji Profi IEI 3500 FI(BABY)
商用平底单灶内置旋钮台式电磁感应炉
外观尺寸（L*W*H):300*471*100mm
人机操作优化系统控制

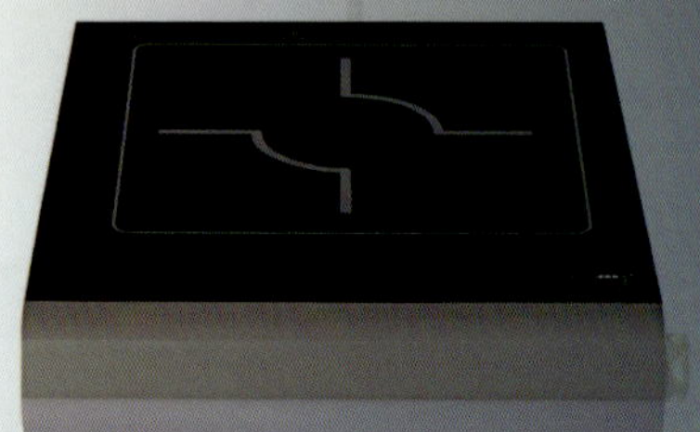

Miji Profi IEI 2200 FI
商用平底单灶内置旋钮台式电磁感应炉
外观尺寸（L*W*H):367*400*80mm
人机操作优化系统控制

ADA
Cosmetics International

afehc

air aroma

AISTIA 精致
爱斯提亚 餐具
生活新主张

ALISEO GmbH
GERMANY

Amain 雅棉

AMMEX 爱马斯

angelo po

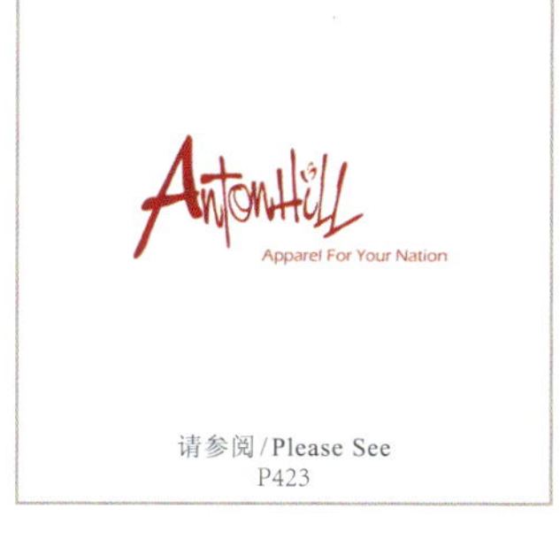
AntonHill
Apparel For Your Nation

Arcoroc
PROFESSIONAL

Armaii
德國酒店衛浴第一品牌

ATEJA
INTERIOR FABRIC INTERNATIONAL STANDARD

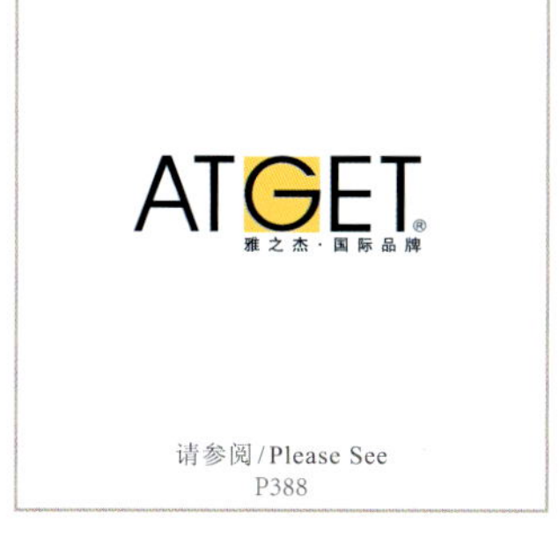
ATGET
雅之杰·国际品牌

ATHENA
Lincolnshire, UK

Aristo Party
——贵族Party

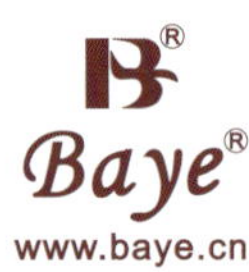

Baye
www.baye.cn
请参阅 / Please See
P409、酒店工程及用品书隔页面页

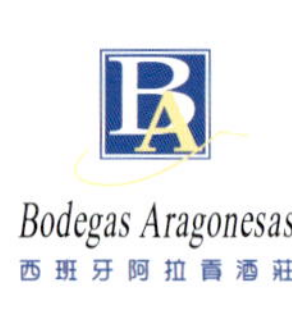

Bodegas Aragonesas
西班牙阿拉贡酒莊
请参阅 / Please See
P159

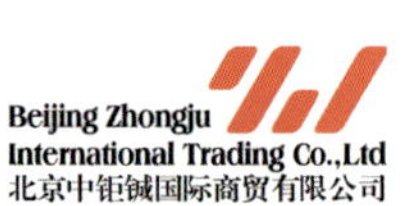

Beijing Zhongju International Trading Co.,Ltd
北京中钜诚国际商贸有限公司
请参阅 / Please See
P244

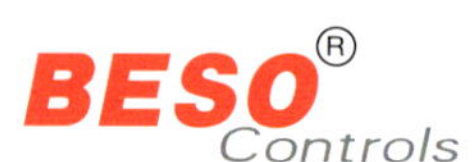

BESO Controls
请参阅 / Please See
P369

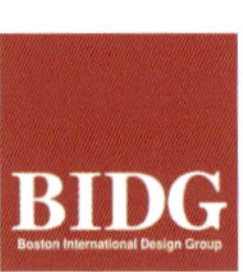

BIDG
Boston International Design Group
请参阅 / Please See
P258、P259

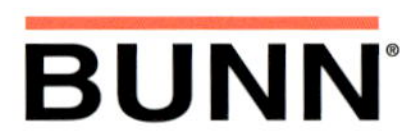

BUNN
请参阅 / Please See
P118、P119、P120

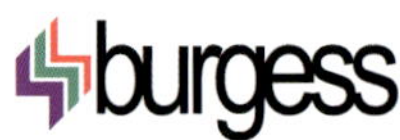

burgess
请参阅 / Please See
P48、P49

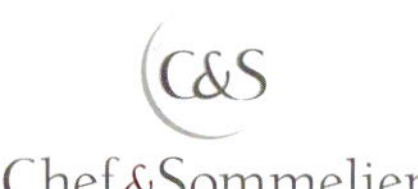

C&S
Chef&Sommelier
请参阅 / Please See
P232、P233、P236、P237

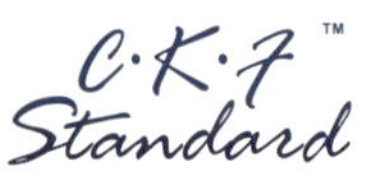

C·K·F Standard
请参阅 / Please See
P180

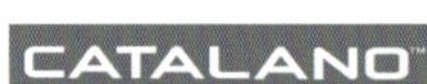

CATALANO
请参阅 / Please See
P317

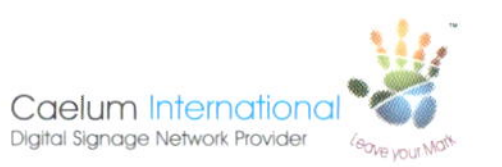

Caelum International
Digital Signage Network Provider
请参阅 / Please See
P375

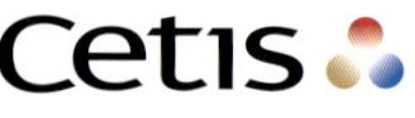

Cetis
请参阅 / Please See
P383、酒店工程及用品书隔页底页

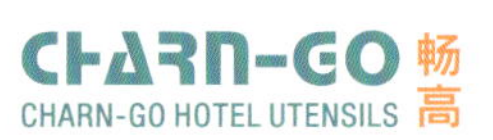

CHARN-GO 畅高
CHARN-GO HOTEL UTENSILS
请参阅 / Please See
P37

cms
请参阅 / Please See
P182

ConAgra Foods
Food you love
请参阅 / Please See
P127

Daeden 戴德
请参阅 / Please See
P207

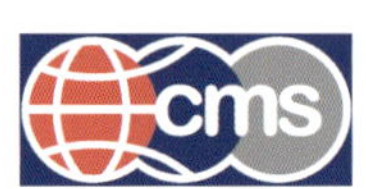

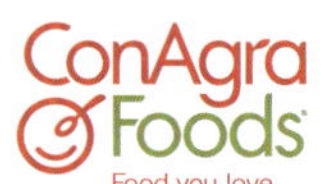

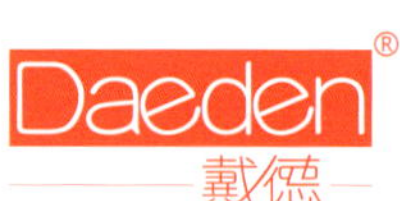

请参阅/Please See
P138、P139、P141

请参阅/Please See
P394、P395

请参阅/Please See
P4、P5、P392、P393

请参阅/Please See
P308

请参阅/Please See
P220

请参阅/Please See
P417

请参阅/Please See
P38

请参阅/Please See
P414

请参阅/Please See
P138、P139、P141

Thinking of you
Electrolux

请参阅/Please See
P168

请参阅/Please See
P397、封底

请参阅/Please See
P419

请参阅/Please See
P230、P231

请参阅/Please See
P288、P289

请参阅/Please See
P236、P237

请参阅/Please See
P422

聚河 Forward 国际

FSB

Galleon
朗進國際有限公司
Galleon International Ltd.

Ganbor
感博

GLORY
CATERING EQUIPMENT

Passion for better life

granoro
il Primo

greencook

GROHE
SPA

GUSTOSIA

goodwell

Halton

Hatco

HBA

HKCG
香記咖啡集團
HIANG KIE COFFEE GROUP

homestyle®

请参阅/Please See
P358、P359、P360、P361

请参阅/Please See
P198

请参阅/Please See
P127

亨特道格拉斯
HunterDouglasHospitality
Integrated Solution Provider of Hospitality Window Covering & Textile
酒店窗飾用品整體方案提供商

请参阅/Please See
P274、P275、P276、P277、P278、P279

请参阅/Please See
P197

请参阅/Please See
P381

请参阅/Please See
P116、P117

请参阅/Please See
P122

请参阅/Please See
P178

请参阅/Please See
P143

请参阅/Please See
P404、P405、封面格

库诗 | KENAS®

请参阅/Please See
P297

请参阅/Please See
P225

请参阅/Please See
P208、P209、封面里

请参阅/Please See
P109、P153、食品及饮料书隔页前页

请参阅/Please See
P126

LA CIMBALI

LADETINA

LAVAZZA
ITALY'S FAVOURITE COFFEE

LEVEL

Life Fitness
WHAT WE LIVE FOR

LIQIAO

LORENCE & COMPANY
義 生 洋 行
ITALIAN FINE FOOD AND WINE

幸运金银器
LUCKY SILVER & GOLDEN PLATED

Luigi Bormioli
ITALY

Luzerne

Manitowoc

marburg
WALLCOVERINGS
德国玛堡壁纸

MARCAFÈ
Gran Caffè

MEC3
Ingredients for gelato and pastry

MENGSHEN
MATTRESS
梦神床垫

Mida's

请参阅/Please See
P42

POLYTEK
保得工程
请参阅/Please See
P268、P269、封面格

请参阅/Please See
P112、P113

请参阅/Please See
P40、P41

请参阅/Please See
P180

请参阅/Please See
P178

请参阅/Please See
P112、P113

请参阅/Please See
P129、P135、P145

请参阅/Please See
P334、P335

请参阅/Please See
P169

请参阅/Please See
P308

请参阅/Please See
P48、P49、P230、P231

请参阅/Please See
P292

请参阅/Please See
P236、P237

SANEI
请参阅/Please See
P326、P327

请参阅/Please See
总目录书隔页面页

请参阅/Please See
P406

请参阅/Please See
P163

请参阅/Please See
P299

请参阅/Please See
P411、封底里

请参阅/Please See
P39

请参阅/Please See
P250、P251

请参阅/Please See
P121、书脊上

请参阅/Please See
P202、P203

请参阅/Please See
P129、P135、P145

请参阅/Please See
P318、P319

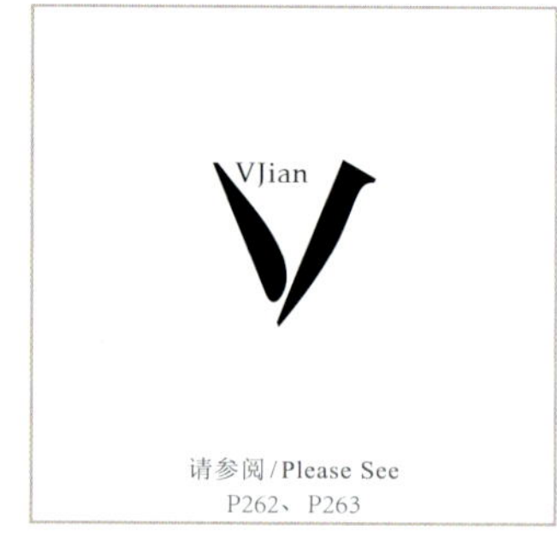

请参阅/Please See
P262、P263

请参阅/Please See
P127

请参阅/Please See
P124

请参阅/Please See
P120

请参阅/Please See
P271

请参阅/Please See
P221

请参阅/Please See
P129、P135、P145

winterhalter

请参阅/Please See
P187、展览会书隔页面页

请参阅/Please See
P219

请参阅/Please See
P293

请参阅/Please See
P201

请参阅/Please See
P376

请参阅/Please See
P312

请参阅/Please See
P291

请参阅/Please See
P2、P282、P283

请参阅/Please See
展览会书隔页底页

请参阅/Please See
P133、食品及饮料书隔页底页

请参阅/Please See
P309

请参阅/Please See
P410

请参阅/Please See
P298

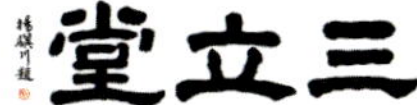

请参阅/Please See
P314、P315

请参阅/Please See
P156

食品及饮料
Food & Beverages

食 品
Food

饮　料
Beverages

厨房、餐厅及酒吧设备
Kitchen, Restaurant & Bar Equipment

厨房设备
Kitchen Equipment

餐厅、酒吧设备
Restaurant & Bar Equipment

酒店工程及用品
Hotel Project & Supplies

设计及装修
Design & Decorator

装饰及家具陈列品
Décor & Furnishings

工程及保安
Engineering & Security

管家及客房供应
Housekeeping & Guestroom Supplies

服务
Services

N

O

p

R

S

Z

其他

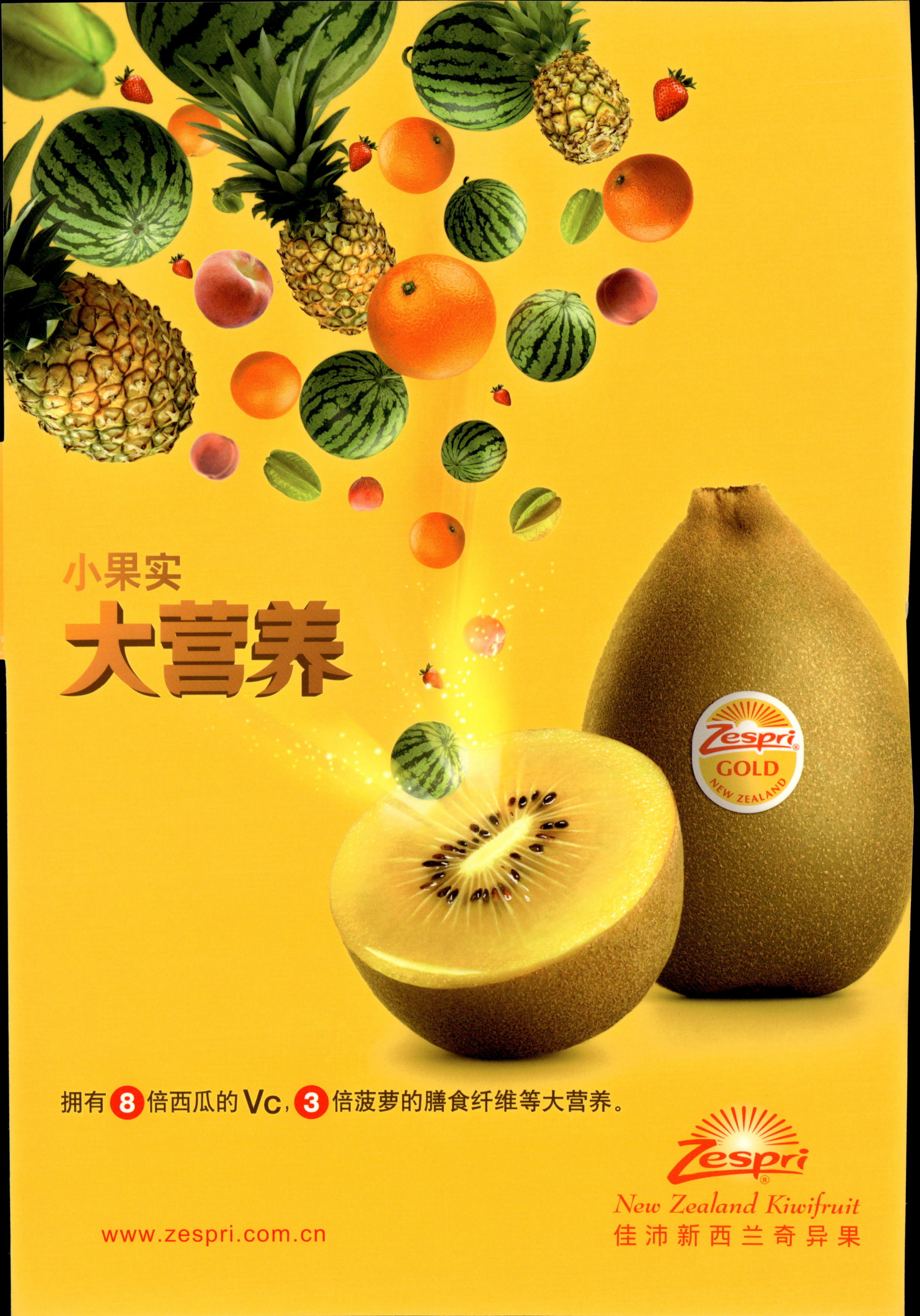
小果实
大营养
Zespri
GOLD
NEW ZEALAND
拥有8倍西瓜的Vc，3倍菠萝的膳食纤维等大营养。
Zespri®
New Zealand Kiwifruit
佳沛新西兰奇异果
www.zespri.com.cn

食品及饮料
Food & Beverages

鲍鱼
Abalones

Dalian Yuhan Trde Co., Ltd.
大连宇瀚商贸有限公司
辽宁省大连市甘井子区新星绿城5号
邮编：116031
电话：0411-8632 5518
传真：0411-8674 8819
网址：www.hs0411.com.cn

Good Plenty Industrial Co., Ltd.
好得壮实业股份有限公司
台湾省台北市大同区大龙街149号
电话：+886(2)-2591 2211
传真：+886(2)-2591 6348
电邮：goodfin@ms43.hinet.net
网址：www.good-plenty.com.tw

Lonimar Australia Pty Ltd.
6 Fink Street, Kensington, 3031, VIC Australia
电话：+61(3)-9376 5000
传真：+61(3)-9372 1198
电邮：websales@lonimar.com.au
网址：www.lonimar.com

Rongcheng Haixing Aquatic Products Co., Ltd.
荣成海兴水产有限公司
山东省荣成市俚岛镇俚岛路395号
电话：0631-766 3235
传真：0631-766 1110
电邮：songhongze@126.com
网址：www.rongyang.com

Yiqi Industrial & Trading Co., Ltd.
许榕滽心干鲍商贸（北京）有限公司
北京市丰台区大红门
京深海鲜批发市场主楼二层A19-1号
邮编：100075
电话：010-8786 6105
网址：www.1stclass.com.au

大连市双兴综合批发市场鸿梅商行
辽宁省大连市西岗区兴业街9号
邮编：116000
电话：0411-3967 2439
传真：0411-3967 2439
网址：www.hmhc717.com.cn

广州市元道贸易发展有限公司
广州市一德路369号山海城大厦5楼A5室
邮编：510120
电话：020-8130 8887
传真：020-8130 8889
电邮：gzyymy@126.com
网址：www.gz-yymy.com.cn

温州市圣王食品有限公司
温州市瓯海区潘桥镇仙门村民新路8-2号
邮编：325000
电话：0577-8861 7788
传真：0577-8862 9595
网址：www.wzswfood.com

新惠鲍翅行
上海市斜土路2570号东影大楼508室
电话：021-5283 3358
传真：021-5283 3358
电邮：332626907@qq.com
网址：www.52833358.com

面包糕点供应
Bakery/Pastry Supplies

Eastsign Foods (Quzhou) Co., Ltd.
易晓食品（衢州）有限公司
深圳市福田区深南中路6009号
绿景广场C座28楼I室
电话：0755-8296 8117
传真：0755-8296 8504
电邮：china@eastsign.com
网址：www.eastsign.cn

La Brioche Food Production (Zhangjiagang) Ltd.
拉普利奥食品（张家港）有限公司
江苏省张家港市凤凰双龙工业园
邮编：215614
电话：0512-5842 1840
传真：0512-5842 1198
电邮：customer2@la-brioche.com
网址：www.la-brioche.com

Shandong Kangquan Food Co., Ltd.
山东康泉食品有限公司
济宁市327国道与105国道交会处向西800米路南
电话：0537-211 8858
传真：0537-211 8858
电邮：kqsp188@188.com
网址：www.kqsp.cn

Shanghai Christine Foodstuff Co., Ltd.
上海克莉丝汀食品有限公司
上海市普陀区金沙江路33号
邮编：200062
电话：021-6286 8861
传真：021-6436 1188
网址：www.christine.com.cn

Shenzhen Miluga Food Co., Ltd.
深圳市麦路嘉食品有限公司
深圳市观澜镇高新产业园民爱中心4-5楼
邮编：518110
电话：0755-2752 1156
传真：0755-8310 4836
网址：www.miluga.com.cn

Sichuan Minshan Gigi Food Co., Ltd.
四川岷山芝芝食品有限公司
成都市人民南路二段55号岷山饭店
邮编：610000
电话：028-8559 9668
传真：028-8558 5588
电邮：office@scgigi.cn
网址：www.gigi.com.cn

Weihai JK Foods Co., Ltd.
威海佳康食品有限公司
山东省威海市经济技术开发区齐鲁大道53号
邮编：264205
电话：0631-592 5966
传真：0631-592 5356
网址：www.jktrade.com.cn

江苏沪耀粮油制品有限公司
江苏丹阳市麦溪芳草经济园
邮编：212300
电话：0511-8576 0777
传真：0511-8689 5333
电邮：huyao69939@126.com
网址：www.huyao.cn

燕窝
Bird's Nests

FuYuan Yang's Food (Shanghai) Co., Ltd.
馥园杨姐食品（上海）有限公司
上海市莲花南路2165弄109号
邮编：201108
电话：021-6458 7999
传真：021-3451 1886
电邮：fuyuan@fyyj.com.cn
网址：www.fyyj.com.cn

Good Plenty Industrial Co., Ltd.
好得壮实业股份有限公司
台湾省台北市大同区大龙街149号
电话：+886(2)-2591 2211
传真：+886(2)-2591 6348
电邮：goodfin@ms43.hinet.net
网址：www.good-plenty.com.tw

Istana Walet Wong Coco
龙情燕窝
江苏省南京市中山北路285号
电话：025-8347 0077
传真：025-8347 2707
电邮：chinawongcoco@gmail.com
网址：www.wongcoco.com.cn

Kinge Shanghai Nest Worldbird's Nest Product Co., Ltd.
康基上海巢天地燕窝制品有限公司
上海市徐汇区漕宝路401号2号楼6楼
电话：021-5489 3558
传真：021-5489 2166
电邮：nestworld2008@126.com
网址：www.nestworld.net

ShangHai Cave Bird Food Co., Ltd.
上海洞燕食品销售有限公司
上海市长宁区延安西路1599号怡翔大厦304-308室
邮编：200050
电话：400 888 1268
传真：021-5238 9871
电邮：yc1268@gmail.com
网址：www.eushengdang.com

Thailand Bird's Nest Ltd.
泰国燕窝莊有限公司
香港永乐街12号永昇商业中心地下B铺
电话：+852-2850 7351
传真：+852-2850 7370
电邮：info@chanloyi.com.hk
网址：www.chanloyi.com.hk

广州市元道贸易发展有限公司
广州市一德路369号山海城大厦5楼A5室
邮编：510120
电话：020-8130 8887
传真：020-8130 8889
电邮：gzyymy@126.com
网址：www.gz-yymy.com.cn

▼燕窝
Bird's Nests

杭州福燕临门保健品有限公司
杭州市建国北路709号（星汇大厦）
邮编：310006
电话：0571-8577 2887
传真：0571-8577 0398
网址：www.yanwo99.com

厦门燕之屋实业有限公司
厦门市思明区
观音山国际商务营运中心11号楼19层
电话：0592-520 9678
传真：0592-520 9808
电邮：yanzhiwu@yanzhiwu.com
网址：www.yanzhiwu.com

温州市圣王食品有限公司
温州市瓯海区潘桥镇仙门村民新路8-2号
邮编：325000
电话：0577-8861 7788
传真：0577-8862 9595
网址：www.wzswfood.com

燕尔（福州）燕窝珍品有限公司
福州市五四路155号
邮编：350001
电话：0591-8394 4568
传真：0591-8781 9608
电邮：yaner@fz-yaner.com
网址：www.fz-yaner.com

罐头食品 Canned Foods

Carl Kuehne KG (GmbH & Co.)
德国冠利有限公司
北京市海淀区太阳园9-0111室
邮编：100098
电话：010-8211 2460
传真：010-8211 2461
电邮：info@kuehne.com.cn
网址：www.kuehne.com.cn
请参阅第126页

Goodwell China Marketing Service Co., Ltd.
大昌三昶（上海）商贸有限公司
上海市梅园路228号企业广场1901室
邮编：200070
电话：021-6487 6287
传真：021-6487 6159
网址：www.goodwellchina.com
请参阅第107页、封面

Goodwell Sam Cheong Grocery Co., Ltd.
香港三昌好好办馆有限公司
香港黄竹坑道12号香华工业大厦15楼B座
电话：+852-3972 8901
传真：+852-3972 8900
电邮：info@goodwell-hk.com
网址：www.goodwell-hk.com
请参阅第138、139、141页

Haitong Food Group Co., Ltd.
海通食品集团股份有限公司
浙江省慈溪市海通路528号
邮编：315300
电话：0574-6303 9988
传真：0574-6303 9898
电邮：kaiz@kaiz.com
网址：www.kaiz.com

Kopek
Koylora Imatheias Veroia Greece
电话：+30-233 204 3237
电邮：kopek@delcof.gr
网址：www.delcof.gr

Longhai Guangfa Foods Co., Ltd.
龙海市广发食品有限公司
福建省龙海市江东旧桥头
邮编：363100
电话：0596-657 0566
传真：0596-657 0588
电邮：gfafoodcoltd@tom.com
网址：www.guangfafood.com

Oriental Foods Expert Ltd.
万福亚洲食品有限公司
香港柴湾新业街9号新业工业大厦9楼C及D室
电话：+852-2965 8828
传真：+852-3106 0211
电邮：sales@asiacurry.com
网址：www.asiacurry.com

Shanghai Kingfood's Condiment Co., Ltd.
上海津丰食品有限公司
上海市黄浦区东街123号8楼
电话：021-6330 1867
传真：021-6330 1869
电邮：kingfoods@kingfoods.com.cn
网址：www.kingfoods.com.cn

Shanghai Kuichun Industry Co., Ltd.
上海魁春实业有限公司
上海市长寿路652号10号楼308室
邮编：200060
电话：021-5186 3006
传真：021-5101 2046
电邮：kuichun@kuichun.com
网址：www.pinlivefoods.com

Shanghai SO Dragon Food Co., Ltd.
上海首龙食品有限公司
上海市闵行区罗阳路168号A座301室
电话：021-2428 3488
传真：021-2428 3484
网址：www.jydragon.com

Sino-Everygreen Foodstuff Co., Ltd.
山东润鼎食品有限公司
山东省临沂市平邑县工业园
邮编：273300
电话：0539-423 5999
传真：0539-497 0555
电邮：info@sino-everygreen.com
网址：www.sino-everygreen.com

Sinodis (Shanghai) Co., Ltd.
西诺迪斯食品（上海）有限公司
上海市金钟路658号4号楼1、2层
邮编：200335
电话：021-6128 1820
传真：021-3360 0070
电邮：info@sinodis.com.cn
网址：www.sinodis.com.cn

Strong Harbour Ltd.
昌港有限公司
香港九龙茶果岭道428号荣山工业大厦4楼G室
电话：+852-2544 6433
传真：+852-2850 6002
电邮：info@strongharbour.com
网址：www.strongharbour.com

Suqian Cannery & Food Corp Ltd.
宿迁市罐头食品有限责任公司
江苏省宿迁市经济开发区太行山路1号
邮编：223800
电话：0527-8445 0005
传真：0527-8445 0002
电邮：sqljc@163.com
网址：www.knine.cn

Tianjin Widecareer International Trade Co., Ltd.
天津广仕国际贸易有限公司
天津市河西区友谊北路
罗马花园2期戊座一栋1101室
邮编：300204
电话：022-2328 3382
传真：022-2324 4092
电邮：postmaster@widecareer.com
网址：www.widecareer.com

Yan Sheung Kee (Ming Kee) Coconut & Spices Co Ltd.
甄想记（明记）椰子香料有限公司
香港新界屯门青扬街1号
世纪城市工业大厦9楼A-D室
电话：+852-2468 2220
传真：+852-2436 1511
电邮：coconutboy@ysk-mk.com
网址：www.ysk-mk.cm
请参阅第109、153页、食品及饮料书隔页面页

Yongxiang Canned Food Co., Ltd.
永祥罐头食品有限公司
福建省晋江市安海镇西门永祥工业区
电话：0595-8570 6868
传真：0595-8570 5882
电邮：yongxiancan@163.com
网址：www.yongxiangcan.com

巧克力 Chocolates

Barry Callebaut (Suzhou) Chocolate Co., Ltd.
百乐嘉利宝（苏州）可可有限公司
苏州市工业园区方中街138号
邮编：215024
电话：0512-6289 0008
传真：0512-6289 0178
网址：www.callebaut.com

Fragata
帆船牌
——来自橄榄之乡西班牙安达卢西亚
Fragata
SPANISH
Olives
WHOLE GREEN
Fragata
SPANISH
Olives
PITTED GREEN
Fragata
SPANISH
PITTED BLACK
Fragata
SPANISH
Olives
Ideal for PIZZAS and SALADS
SLICED BLACK
上海市梅园路228号企业广场1901室
ROOM 1901, NO. 228 MEI YUAN ROAD, ENTERPRISES SQUARE, SHANGHAI CHINA
电话/Tel: 021-6487 6287
传真/Fax: 021-6487 6159
邮编/PC: 200070
Passion for better life
大昌三昶(上海)商贸有限公司
www.goodwellchina.com
Goodwell China Marketing Service Co. Ltd.

▼巧克力 Chocolates

COFCO Le Conte Food (Shenzhen) Co., Ltd.
中粮金帝食品（深圳）有限公司
深圳市北环路梅林工业区梅秀路1号
邮编：518049
电话：0755-8311 5214
传真：0755-8310 3189
电邮：leconte@leconte.com.cn
网址：www.leconte.com.cn

DKSH (China) Co., Ltd.
大昌华嘉商业（中国）有限公司
上海市浦东东方路710号汤臣金融大厦3楼
邮编：200122
电话：021-5830 0518
传真：021-5830 0519
网址：www.dksh.com

Henry Lambertz GmbH & Co. KG
Borchersstr. 18, D-52072 Aachen
电话：+49(0)-2418 9050
传真：+49(0)-241 890 5270
电邮：info@lambertz.de
网址：www.lambertz.de

Import Trade Co., Ltd.
英波特贸易有限公司
广东省佛山市禅城区华远东路13号
发展大厦11楼E单元
邮编：528000
电话：0757-8330 8018
传真：0757-8330 8017
电邮：web@fsipt.com
网址：www.fsipt.com

Shanghai Hamp Import & Export Trading Co., Ltd.
上海瀚普进出口贸易有限公司
上海市定西路1281号兆仪大厦1404室
邮编：200336
电话：021-5238 9957
传真：021-6240 0599
电邮：jane.yan@kellen-hamp.com.cn
网址：www.kellen-hamp.com.cn

Shanghai Kuichun Industry Co., Ltd.
上海魁春实业有限公司
上海市长寿路652号10号楼308室
邮编：200060
电话：021-5186 3006
传真：021-5101 2046
电邮：kuichun@kuichun.com
网址：www.pinlivefoods.com

Shanghai Sunny Life Enterprise Co., Ltd.
上海山隆实业有限公司
上海市常德路1265号兴运大厦6楼
邮编：200060
电话：021-5252 7733
传真：021-5252 7555
电邮：shsunlife@shsunlife.com
网址：www.shsunlife.cn

Shanghai Sun Way Business Development Co., Ltd.
上海商威商务发展有限公司
上海市中山西路800弄55号23楼A座（紫云大厦）
邮编：200051
电话：021-6228 3670
传真：021-5253 0168
电邮：shangwei_0011@163.com
网址：www.sun-way.net.cn

Shanghai Yicheng Food Co., Ltd.
上海亿成食品有限公司
上海市青浦区白鹤镇鹤祥路22号
（白鹤工业园A区）
电话：021-5974 0788
传真：021-5974 5787
电邮：shanghai@shdaifei.com
网址：www.shdaifei.com

Shanghai Yuanyi Import & Export Co., Ltd.
上海远怡进出口有限公司
上海市浦东新区秀沿路1168弄3支弄230号
邮编：201315
电话：021-6819 6304
传真：021-6819 5007
电邮：yuanyi5588@163.com
网址：www.importfood.com.cn

Tianjin Heijingang Food Co., Ltd.
天津黑金刚食品有限公司
天津市大港区太平镇大道口
邮编：300282
电话：022-6314 8674
传真：022-6314 5972
电邮：hjg8674@126.com
网址：www.loveebays.com

Tianjin Widecareer International Trade Co., Ltd.
天津广仕国际贸易有限公司
天津市河西区友谊北路
罗马花园2期戊座一栋1101室
邮编：300204
电话：022-2328 3382
传真：022-2324 4092
电邮：postmaster@widecareer.com
网址：www.widecareer.com

大昌行集团有限公司
香港九龙湾启祥道20号大昌行集团大厦8楼
电话：+852-2768 3388
传真：+852-2796 8838
电邮：dch@dch.com.hk
网址：www.dch.com.hk

椰子及椰子制品 Coconut & Coconut Products

Haikou Darun Industry & Trade Co., Ltd.
海口大润工贸有限公司
海南省海口市龙昆南路富人阁小区B11栋
邮编：570206
电话：0898-6679 5838
传真：0898-6679 5838
网址：www.dadarun.cn.alibaba.com

Hainan Cocoboy Food Co., Ltd.
海南椰子郎食品有限公司
海南省海口市盐灶一横路2号
邮编：570105
电话：0898-6672 3805
网址：www.cocoboyfood.com

Hainan Yeguo Foods Co., Ltd.
海南椰国食品有限公司
海口市秀英区白水塘省扶贫开发区
邮编：570311
电话：0898-6866 2059
传真：0898-6865 2659
电邮：yeguofood@126.com
网址：www.yeguo.com

Linaco Group
林纳果集团
Wisma Linaco, Lintang Sg. Keramat 2B, 12, Klang, 42100, Selangor, Malaysia
电话：+60(0)-332 914 589
传真：+60(0)-332 914 588
电邮：linaco@linaco.com.my
网址：www.linaco.com.my

Oriental Foods Expert Ltd.
万福亚洲食品有限公司
香港柴湾新业街9号新业工业大厦9楼C及D室
电话：+852-2965 8828
传真：+852-3106 0211
电邮：sales@asiacurry.com
网址：www.asiacurry.com

Thai Mei Wei International Trading Co., Ltd.
北京泰美味国际贸易有限公司
北京市朝阳区黄杉木店路188号阿曼商街底商8-1
邮编：100123
电话：010-5863 6214
传真：010-5863 6214
电邮：taimeiwei@qq.com
网址：www.thaimeiwei.com

Wenchang Hongbao Food Co., Ltd.
文昌市东郊椰利来食品厂
海南文昌东郊镇新村场
邮编：571334
电话：0898-6352 8955
传真：0898-6352 8533
网址：www.yelilaifood.cn.nowec.com

Xiamen Gold Coconut King Co., Ltd.
厦门金椰王贸易有限公司
厦门市体育路43号华夏工业中心2号楼2层
邮编：361012
电话：0592-239 0998
传真：0592-239 0599
电邮：cocoxm@163.com
网址：www.cocomas.cn

Yan Sheung Kee (Ming Kee) Coconut & Spices Co Ltd.
甄想记（明记）椰子香料有限公司
香港新界屯门青扬街1号
世纪城市工业大厦9楼A-D室
电话：+852-2468 2220
传真：+852-2436 1511
电邮：coconutboy@ysk-mk.com
网址：www.ysk-mk.cm
请参阅第109、153页、食品及饮料书隔页面页

广州市越海椰子商行
广州市增埗路江南果菜市场一马路3档
邮编：510435
电话：020-8176 0909
传真：020-8176 0909
网址：www.yhyezi.cn

上海椰申实业有限公司
上海市松江区新桥镇新庙三北路1108号新鸿企业园
邮编：201612
电话：021-5768 1133
传真：021-5768 1137
网址：www.shwangke.com

咖啡制品
Coffee

Beijing G.E.O. Coffee Co., Ltd.
北京吉意欧咖啡有限公司
北京市经济技术开发区东区经海三路1号
邮编：100023
电话：010-6789 2199
传真：010-6789 2198
电邮：myb@geocoffee.com.cn
网址：www.geocoffee.com.cn

Blue Mountain Food Corporation
东莞市蓝山食品有限公司
广东省东莞市南城区亨美水濂彭洞工业B区
邮编：523947
电话：0769-3889 7668
传真：0769-3889 7669
电邮：bmcafe@bmcafe.net
网址：www.bmcafe.net

Boncafe (Guangzhou) Trading Company Limited
邦恩咖啡（广州）贸易有限公司
广州保税区广保大道44号304室
邮编：510730
电话：020-8220 8526
传真：020-3207 0780
电邮：sales@boncafe.com.cn
网址：www.boncafe.com.cn

Bridge Shine Coffee Equipment (Shanghai) Co., Ltd.
桥升咖啡设备（上海）有限公司
上海市闵行区吴中路1000号
邮编：201103
电话：021-6401 5383
传真：021-6401 5442
电邮：gourmetcoffee@china.com
网址：www.bridgeshine.com.cn

Changzhou Super Food Co., Ltd.
常州超级食品有限公司
江苏省常州市戚墅堰区东方东路158号
邮编：213025
电话：0519-8840 0277
传真：0519-8840 0582
网址：www.czsf.com.cn

DKSH (China) Co., Ltd.
大昌华嘉商业（中国）有限公司
上海市浦东东方路710号汤臣金融大厦3楼
邮编：200122
电话：021-5830 0518
传真：021-5830 0519
网址：www.dksh.com

Frappessa Food And Beverage Management Co., Ltd.
广州市啡贝诗餐饮管理有限公司
广州市越秀区盘福路朱紫后街越心苑309
邮编：510310
电话：020-3971 6819
传真：020-8354 0054
电邮：info@frappessa.com
网址：www.frappessa.com

Guangzhou Meidu Coffee Food Co., Ltd.
广州美度咖啡食品有限公司
广州市增槎路178号三一国际咖啡城215-216档
邮编：510660
电话：020-8198 1523
传真：020-8198 1705
电邮：meiducoffee@163.com
网址：www.meiducoffee.com

Hangzhou BoDuo Industrial Co., Ltd.
杭州博多工贸有限公司
浙江省杭州市勾运路16号2号楼
邮编：310015
电话：0571-8808 8122
传真：0571-8526 5639
网址：www.boduogongmao.com

Hiangkie Coffee Group Limited
香记咖啡集团有限公司
香港九龙新蒲岗三祝街12-14号
荣森工业第二大厦3楼
电话：+852-3769 2345
传真：+852-2545 8917
电邮：enquiry@hiangkie.com.hk
网址：www.hiangkie.com.hk
请参阅第118、119页

Italian Coffee Company
美商义式企业
上海市合川路3152号北楼2楼
邮编：201103
电话：021-6405 0475
传真：021-6405 0467
网址：www.italian-coffee-company.com

Milan Gold Coffee Co., Ltd.
北京金米兰咖啡有限公司
北京市朝阳区东三环中路55号
富力双子座B座2605室
邮编：100022
电话：010-5862 2228
传真：010-5876 8622
电邮：info@milangold.com.cn
网址：www.milangold.com.cn

Popstar International Trading Co., Ltd.
亮奎・建奎国际贸易（上海）有限公司
上海市曹杨路450号绿地和创大厦510室
邮编：200063
电话：021-5235 7712
传真：021-6240 1376
电邮：hank.lin@qpopstar.com
网址：www.qpopstar.com
请参阅第112、113页

Q's Coffee
邱公馆食品（云南）有限公司
上海市浦东大道138号永华大厦10楼
邮编：200120
电话：021-6887 5008
传真：021-6887 5193
网址：www.qs-coffee.com

Render Coffee (Shanghai) Co., Ltd.
源铭咖啡（上海）有限公司
上海市松江洞泾工业开发区洞库路B1号
邮编：201619
电话：021-5767 0577
传真：021-5767 0771
电邮：sales@rendercoffee.com
网址：www.rendercoffee.com

Season Food Co., Ltd.
四季工坊有限公司
台湾省台中县雾峰乡中正路565巷17号
电话：+886(4)-2333 4468
传真：+886(4)-2333 4612
电邮：season9@ms48.hinet.net
网址：www.season-coffee.com.tw

Seng Pan Food Co., Ltd.
江门市诚品食品有限公司
广东省江门市新会区古井镇古泗村
邮编：529100
电话：0750-697 1188
传真：0750-697 1122
电邮：info@spcoffee.com
网址：www.spcoffee.com

Shanghai Carmo Foods Co., Ltd.
上海珈露梦食品有限公司
上海市闵行区万源路2759弄G幢
电话：021-6406 5998
传真：021-6406 5993
电邮：coffee.carmo@carmo.com.cn
网址：www.carmo.com.cn

Shanghai Forward Tarding Co., Ltd.
聚河贸易（上海）有限公司
上海市长宁区天山路600弄思创大厦4号28楼C座
邮编：200051
电话：021-6229 0630
传真：021-6229 0629
电邮：shforward@163.com
网址：www.shforward.cn
请参阅第111页

Shanghai Hake Foods Co., ltd.
上海哈克商贸有限公司
上海市古美路1471号319室
电话：021-5493 9393
传真：021-5493 4441
电邮：z-hake@126.com
网址：www.shhake.com

Shanghai Hamp Import & Export Trading Co., Ltd.
上海瀚普进出口贸易有限公司
上海市定西路1281号兆仪大厦1404室
邮编：200336
电话：021-5238 9957
传真：021-6240 0599
电邮：jane.yan@kellen-hamp.com.cn
网址：www.kellen-hamp.com.cn

Shanghai Walton Concepts Economic & Trading Co., Ltd.
上海和沁经贸有限公司
上海市闵行区虹许路731号3号楼3楼
邮编：201103
电话：021-6401 6449
传真：021-6401 3103
网址：www.waltonconcepts.com
请参阅第120页

Shanghai Yuanyi Import & Export Co., Ltd.
上海远怡进出口有限公司
上海市浦东新区秀沿路1168弄3支弄230号
邮编：201315
电话：021-6819 6304
传真：021-6819 5007
电邮：yuanyi5588@163.com
网址：www.importfood.com.cn

Shenzhen Sun Tin Shing Coffee Co., Ltd.
深圳市新天成贸易有限公司
深圳市龙岗区布吉镇沙湾兴华路10号3楼
电话：0755-2852 0123
传真：0755-2852 0689
电邮：info@stscoffee.com
网址：www.stscoffee.com

冷饮、热饮杯
透明杯
双层杯、瓦楞杯
冰淇淋杯
爆米花桶
汤杯
电影套餐
蛋糕盒
纸袋组合

▼咖啡制品
Coffee

SwissCoffeer Holding AG
瑞士咖啡人控股有限公司
北京市朝阳区东三环南路17号京瑞大厦B座20层
邮编：100021
电话：010-8766 5450
传真：010-8766 3081
电邮：sales@swisscoffeer.com
网址：www.swisscoffeer.com

Torrefazione Adriatica S.p.A.
Via Ripoli snc, 64021 Giulianova (TE) Italy
电话：+39(085)-807 2141
传真：+39(085)-806 1928
电邮：info@marcafe.it
网址：www.marcafe.it
请参阅第123页

Tsit Wing International Holdings Limited
捷荣国际控股有限公司
Flats F-J, 11/F., Block 3, Kwai Tak Ind. Centre, Kwai Tak St., Kwai Chung, N.T., Hong Kong
电话：+852-2429 0585
传真：+852-2480 6996
网址：www.twcoffee.com

UCC Ueshima Coffee (Shanghai) Co., Ltd.
悠诗诗上岛咖啡（上海）有限公司
上海市徐汇区漕溪路250号银海大楼A701室
邮编：200235
电话：021-6483 6036
传真：021-6408 6540
网址：www.ucc-coffee.com.cn
请参阅第121页、书脊上

YL Coffee & Tea Ltd.
云岭咖啡茶叶有限公司
云南省昆明市西山区海埂路310号
邮编：650228
电话：0871-457 9519
传真：0871-457 9816
电邮：info@ylcoffeetea.com
网址：www.ylcoffeetea.com

咖啡豆
Coffee Beans

1919 Italian Coffee Company
义久义久食品贸易（上海）有限公司
上海市闵行区合川路3152号北2楼
电话：021-6405 0475
传真：021-6405 0467
网址：www.italian-coffee-company.com

Beijing Kingtai Tenhong Trade Co., Ltd.
北京市京泰天宏经贸有限责任公司
北京市朝阳区利泽中二路2号
望京科技创业园E座405C
邮编：100102
电话：010-8795 2371
传真：010-8795 2380
电邮：info@mycafe.com.cn
网址：www.mycafe.com.cn

Beijing Prettly International Trading Co., Ltd.
北京佰特莱国际贸易有限公司
北京市朝阳区建国路88号
SOHO现代城2号楼2703室
邮编：100022
电话：010-8589 6792
传真：010-8589 5984
电邮：info@cafevip.com
网址：www.cafevip.com

Beijing Wonder Zhong's Coffee Equipment Sales Co., Ltd.
北京旺达钟记咖啡设备销售有限公司
北京市东城区灯市口大街33号国中大厦302室
邮编：100006
电话：010-6522 3500
传真：010-6522 3519
电邮：zhongs_cafe@yahoo.com.cn
网址：www.zhongs-coffee.com

Blue Mountain Food Corporation
东莞市蓝山食品有限公司
广东省东莞市南城区亨美水濂澎洞工业B区
邮编：523947
电话：0769-3889 7668
传真：0769-3889 7669
电邮：bmcafe@bmcafe.net
网址：www.bmcafe.net

Bridge Shine Coffee Equipment (Shanghai) Co., Ltd.
桥升咖啡设备（上海）有限公司
上海市闵行区吴中路1000号
邮编：201103
电话：021-6401 5383
传真：021-6401 5442
电邮：gourmetcoffee@china.com
网址：www.bridgeshine.com.cn

Coffee Secret Company Limited
咖啡秘密有限公司
广东省广州市越秀区东山龟岗一马路20号
电话：020-3762 4902
传真：020-3762 4896
电邮：info@coffeesecret.cn
网址：www.acoffee.cn

Hangzhou 4C Cafe Catering Management Ltd.
杭州氏熙餐饮管理有限公司
浙江省杭州市中山北路415号天主教堂旁
电话：0571-8604 3800
传真：0571-8724 5082
电邮：4ccafe@4ccafe.cn
网址：www.4ccafe.com.cn

Hiangkie Coffee Group Limited
香记咖啡集团有限公司
香港九龙新蒲岗三祝街12-14号
荣森工业第二大厦3楼
电话：+852-3769 2345
传真：+852-2545 8917
电邮：enquiry@hiangkie.com.hk
网址：www.hiangkie.com.hk
请参阅第118、119页

Italian Coffee Company
美商 义式企业
上海市合川路3152号北楼2楼
邮编：201103
电话：021-6405 0475
传真：021-6405 0467
网址：www.italian-coffee-company.com

Jascaffe China Co., Ltd.
王力咖啡贸易（上海）有限公司
上海市松江区九亭镇盛龙路751号
邮编：201615
电话：021-3352 2299
传真：021-5206 8338
电邮：marketing@jascaffechina.com
网址：www.jascaffechina.com

Jess (Shanghai) Trading Co., Ltd.
上海吉晟贸易有限公司
上海市虹口区物华路58号物华大楼1102-1108室
邮编：200086
电话：021-6512 7239
传真：021-6512 3629
电邮：service@jespresso.com
网址：www.jespresso.com

Luigi Lavazza SpA
Corso Novara 59, 10154 Torno, Italy
电话：+39 011 2398/1
电邮：info@lavazza.it
网址：www.lavazza.it
公司介绍：
Lavazza, founded in Turin, Italy, in 1895 has been family-owned and managed for four generations. It's one of the world's largest coffee manufacturers and market leader in Italy. Lavazza operates 11 direct international subsidiaries and its products are marketed in 90 countries. A great Italian story of a company that has come to symbolize coffee, sophisticated taste and pleasure, worldwide.
With 4,000 employees, the company operates globally in the Home and Out-of-Home markets, with a 20-year history in the manufacturing and marketing of single-serve espresso systems and products. Cafes, restaurants, hotels. For over 100 years, Lavazza coffee is served at the best establishments, in Italy and abroad. Lavazza has developed specialist products and services, with a view to boosting the value of professionalism.The result is a unique experience at each coffee break, whether in business premises or public places.
LAVAZZA
THE REAL ITALIAN ESPRESSO EXPERIENCE
欲知更多详情，请联系：
中国大陆
电话：400-820-8990 / 800-820-8990
电邮：sale@jespresso.com
香港
电话：+852-2868 0362
电邮：cshk@metadesign-group.com
新加坡
电话：+65-6841 3910
电邮：admin@dankoff.com.sg
台湾
电话：+886(2)-2503 7687*735
电邮：nickchen@eslite.com.tw
请参阅第115页、书签

Machado Coffee
南京玛卡多商贸有限公司
南京市白下区光华东街6号世界之窗18幢2楼
电话：025-8465 0722
传真：025-8463 5492
电邮：jewellery@machado-coffee.com
网址：www.machado-coffee.com

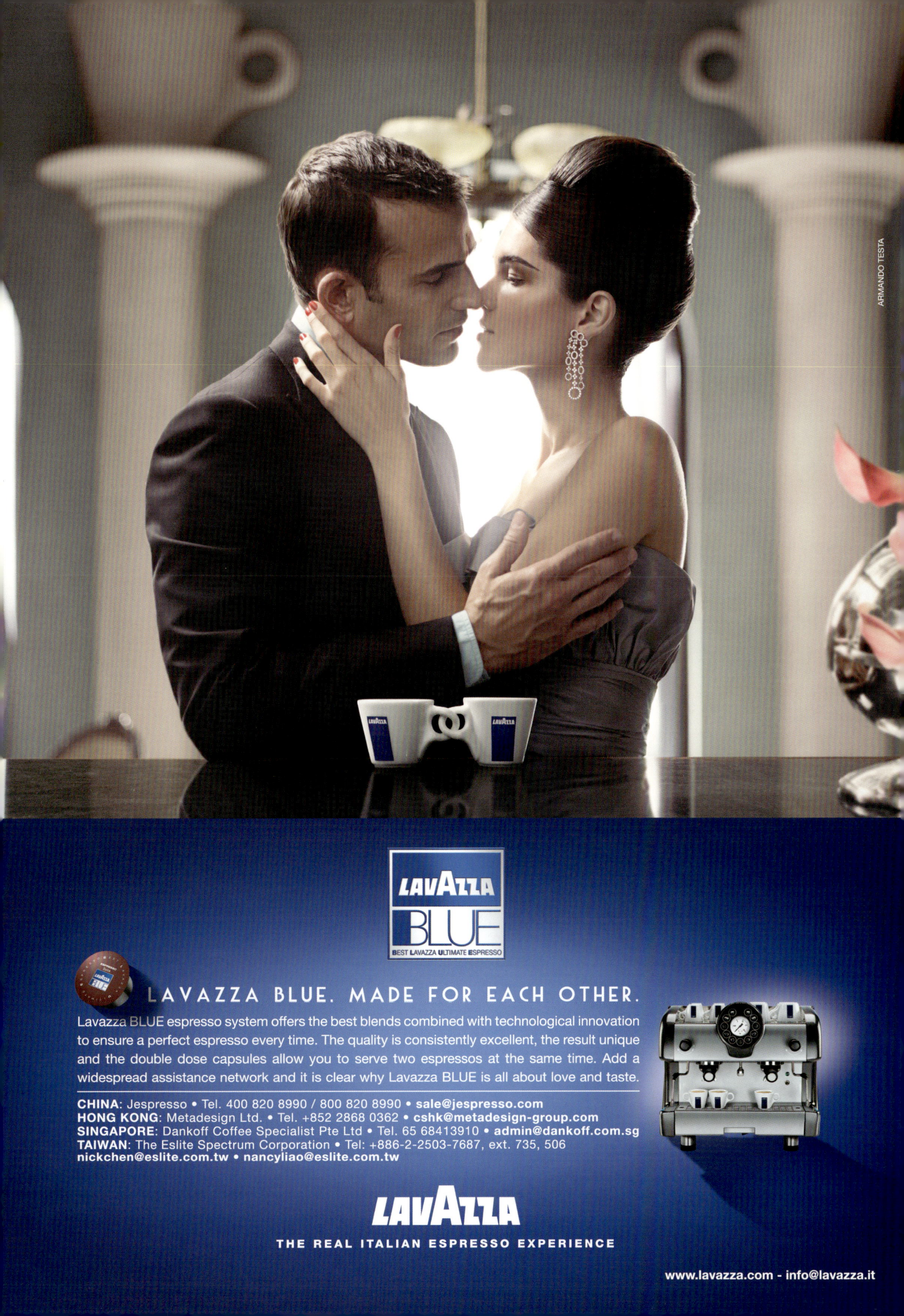
ARMANDO TESTA
LAVAZZA
BLUE
BEST LAVAZZA ULTIMATE ESPRESSO
LAVAZZA BLUE. MADE FOR EACH OTHER.
Lavazza BLUE espresso system offers the best blends combined with technological innovation to ensure a perfect espresso every time. The quality is consistently excellent, the result unique and the double dose capsules allow you to serve two espressos at the same time. Add a widespread assistance network and it is clear why Lavazza BLUE is all about love and taste.
CHINA: Jespresso • Tel. 400 820 8990 / 800 820 8990 • sale@jespresso.com
HONG KONG: Metadesign Ltd. • Tel. +852 2868 0362 • cshk@metadesign-group.com
SINGAPORE: Dankoff Coffee Specialist Pte Ltd • Tel. 65 68413910 • admin@dankoff.com.sg
TAIWAN: The Eslite Spectrum Corporation • Tel: +886-2-2503-7687, ext. 735, 506
nickchen@eslite.com.tw • nancyliao@eslite.com.tw
LAVAZZA
THE REAL ITALIAN ESPRESSO EXPERIENCE
www.lavazza.com - info@lavazza.it

LA CIMBALI 意大利第一品牌商用咖啡机

M39系列

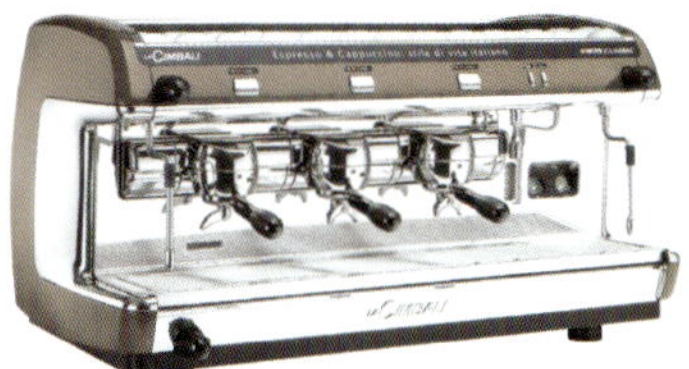
M39 CLASSIC（双头、三头、四头）

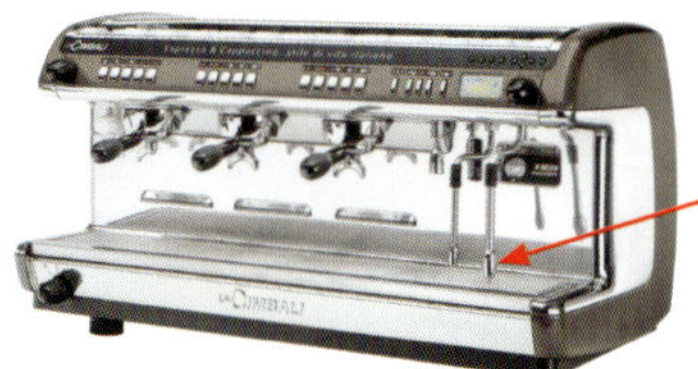
"Turbosteam"
牛奶发泡专利
增压式蒸汽头

M39 DOSATRON（双头、三头、四头）

M29系列

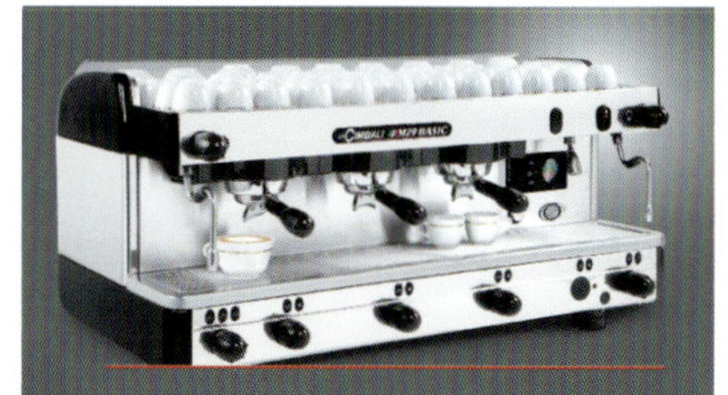
M29 BASIC（双头、三头、四头）

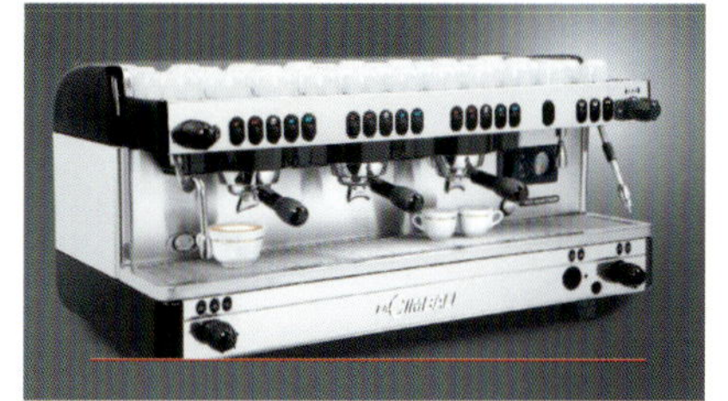
M29 SELECTRON（双头、三头、四头）

jura 瑞士进口全自动咖啡机

X7s

Xs90 OTC

M27 2008 Edition系列

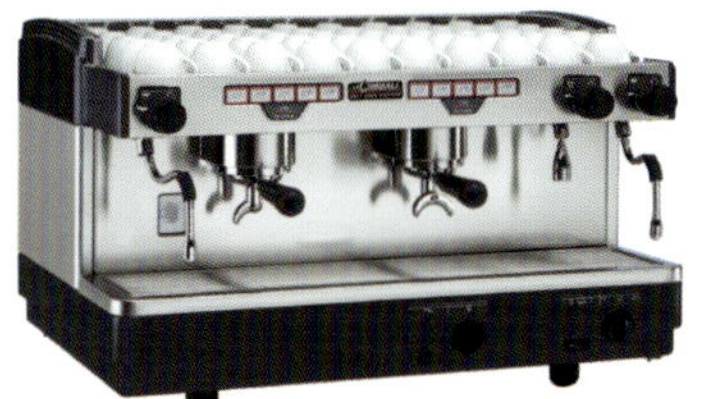
M27 A2（双头）

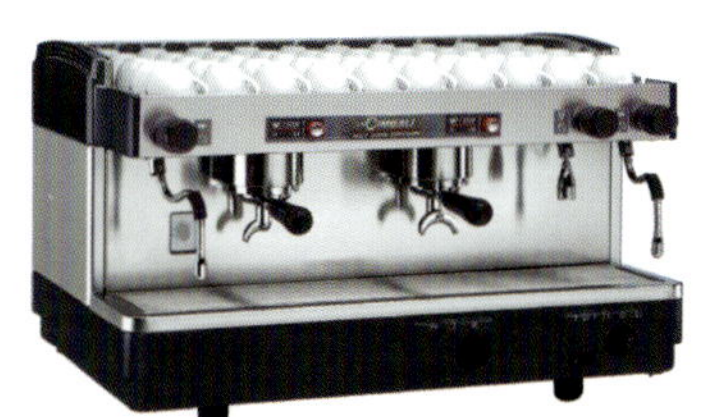
M27 S2（双头）

M1系列 M1 BARSYSTEM

MilkPS Version

（另有两款选择：
S Version,
Turbosteam Version）

LA MARZOCCO 意大利顶级商用咖啡机

世界著名咖啡连锁店——星巴克(STARBUCKS)指定使用咖啡机

LINEA(双头、三头、四头)

GB5（双头、三头、四头）

FB80（双头、三头、四头）

GS3 Lite(单头)

I-Espresso 咖啡胶囊系列

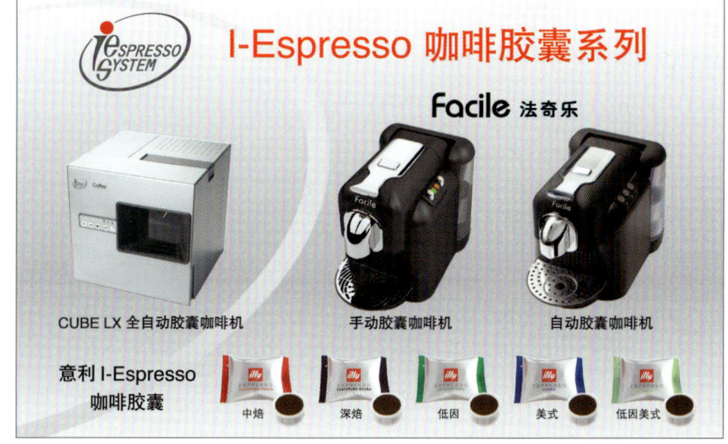

CUBE LX 全自动胶囊咖啡机

手动胶囊咖啡机

自动胶囊咖啡机

意利 I-Espresso
咖啡胶囊

Iperespresso 咖啡胶囊系列

FrancisFrancis!
X7咖啡机

意利 Iperespresso
咖啡胶囊

MÖVENPICK
OF SWITZERLAND
Premium Coffee
MÖVENPICK
OF SWITZERLAND
RICH &
SEDUCTIVE
Espresso
GROUND COFFEE
MÖVENPICK
OF SWITZERLAND
AROMATIC &
WELL-BALANCED
Heavenly
GROUND COFFEE
100% Arabica
HKCG
香記咖啡集團
HIANG KIE COFFEE GROUP

香记咖啡集团不断为您带来创新饮料的惊喜！凭着我们多年的烘培及拼配经验，除了为客户提供不同特点的咖啡，我们还亲自从斯里兰卡进口优质红茶。配合其他各种的冲调设备与各式饮料的原料，定能为您提供一站式餐饮方案。

咖啡机 ： Thermoplan、Nuova Simonelli、BUNN
磨豆机 ： Ditting
咖啡 ： MÖVENPICK、JWP、公平贸易咖啡、有机咖啡
茶/茶包 ： JWP、茶皇、兰卡象、Numi 有机茶包、Zesta 茶包
其他原料 ： 达芬奇果露、Monbana 法国朱古力

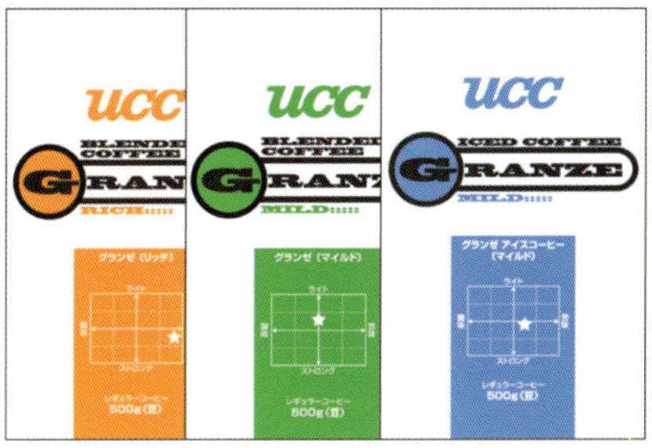

▼咖啡豆
Coffee Beans

Meseta Shanghai Co., Ltd.
美瑟达上海阔意商贸有限公司
上海市徐汇区肇嘉浜路608号联业大厦1603室
邮编：200031
电话：021-6433 3982
传真：021-6433 3982
电邮：infomeseta@yahoo.cn
网址：www.meseta.cn

Q's Coffee
邱公馆食品（云南）有限公司
上海市浦东大道138号永华大厦10楼
邮编：200120
电话：021-6887 5008
传真：021-6887 5193
网址：www.qs-coffee.com

Shanghai Carmo Foods Co., Ltd.
上海珈露梦食品有限公司
上海市闵行区万源路2759弄G幢
电话：021-6406 5998
传真：021-6406 5993
电邮：coffee.carmo@carmo.com.cn
网址：www.carmo.com.cn

Shanghai Chao Ma Import & Export Co., Ltd.
上海超玛进口有限公司
上海市浦东新区沪南路2591弄1号901室
邮编：201318
电话：021-6804 6377
传真：021-6804 6378
网址：www.zicaffe.com

Shanghai Creation Trading Co., Ltd.
上海开展贸易有限公司
上海市闵行区虹井路355号
邮编：201103
电话：021-3431 5789
传真：021-3431 1239
网址：www.creation-foods.com.cn

Shanghai Pinzhen Foodstuff Co., Ltd.
上海品珍食品有限公司
上海市青浦区华新镇华徐公路3029弄63号
邮编：201705
电话：021-3987 3795
传真：021-3987 3478
电邮：chlin278@msn.com
网址：www.phcafe.cn

Shanghai UBT International Trade Co., Ltd.
上海沃伦芬国际贸易有限公司
上海市虹口区四平路778号盛业大厦1506室
邮编：200086
电话：021-6507 6520
传真：021-6142 1912
网址：www.wallenfordblue.com.cn
请参阅本页

Shanghai Vernal Coffee Trade Co., Ltd.
上海满庭芳咖啡贸易有限公司
上海市申滨路1058弄67号702室(近天山西路)
邮编：201101
电话：021-3453 6550
传真：021-5102 6565
电邮：mantingfang@yahoo.com.cn
网址：www.office-coffee.com.cn

Shanghai Walton Concepts Economic & Trading Co., Ltd.
上海和沁经贸有限公司
上海市闵行区虹许路731号3号楼3楼
邮编：201103
电话：021-6401 6449
传真：021-6401 3103
网址：www.waltonconcepts.com
业务范围：
上海和沁经贸有限公司秉承多年的餐饮服务经验，与深圳、广州、北京的销售公司共同组合成为一个致力于为中国餐饮界提供前沿的饮品资讯和务实的一站式饮品推广服务的专业团队。是众多海外食品和饮料及相关设备知名品牌在中国市场的战略合作伙伴。
在中国独家代理的原物料品牌有：法国MONIN糖浆、意大利VERGNANO咖啡豆、美国MIGHTY LEAF丝质茶包和散茶、美国CAFFE D'AMORE顶级冰饮调和粉。设备有意大利金巴利、圣马可半自动咖啡机、瑞士FRANKE全自动咖啡机、美国BUNN饮品设备、美国EVERPURE专业水处理设备系列产品。
并特别推出了量身定做的加工产品，为连锁客户提供特别定制饮品的专业服务。
请参阅第120页

Shanghai Yujia Trading Co., Ltd.
上海郁佳贸易有限公司
上海市田东路258弄2号302室
邮编：200235
电话：021-6468 0030
传真：021-6468 0029
电邮：yuchang@pellini.com.cn
网址：www.pellini.com.cn

Shenzhen Sen Run Jia Trading Co., Ltd.
深圳市森润佳贸易有限公司
深圳市福田区新闻路华丰大厦802-803室
邮编：518034
电话：0755-6130 5660
传真：0755-8318 7402
电邮：srj@srjcoffee.com
网址：www.srjcoffee.com

Shenzhen Starhouse Coffee Food Co., Ltd.
深圳德维咖啡食品有限公司
深圳横岗镇安良三角龙工业区安平街12号D栋4楼
邮编：518115
电话：0755-8248 1015
传真：0755-8248 1027
电邮：frankseng66@hotmail.com
网址：www.starhousecoffee.com.cn

Shenzhen Sun Tin Shing Coffee Co., Ltd.
深圳市新天成贸易有限公司
深圳市龙岗区布吉镇沙湾兴华路10号3楼
电话：0755-2852 0123
传真：0755-2852 0689
电邮：info@stscoffee.com
网址：www.stscoffee.com

Torrefazione Adriatica S.p.A.
Via Ripoli snc, 64021 Giulianova (TE) Italy
电话：+39(085)-807 2141
传真：+39(085)-806 1928
电邮：info@marcafe.it
网址：www.marcafe.it
请参阅第123页

Tsit Wing International Holdings Limited
捷荣国际控股有限公司
Flats F-J, 11/F., Block 3, Kwai Tak Ind. Centre, Kwai Tak St., Kwai Chung, N.T., Hong Kong
电话：+852-2429 0585
传真：+852-2480 6996
网址：www.twcoffee.com

▼咖啡豆
Coffee Beans

UCC Ueshima Coffee (Shanghai) Co., Ltd.
悠诗诗上岛咖啡（上海）有限公司
上海市徐汇区漕溪路250号银海大楼A701室
邮编：200235
电话：021-6483 6036
传真：021-6408 6540
网址：www.ucc-coffee.com.cn
请参阅第121页、书脊上

illycaffe Shanghai Co., Ltd.
意利咖啡商贸（上海）有限公司
上海市铜仁路258号九安广场银座7楼B、D室
邮编：200040
电话：021-6279 1979
传真：021-6279 2905
电邮：illy@illychina.cn
网址：www.illychina.com
www.illyeshop.cn
请参阅第116、117页

iMOcafe
逸摩咖啡中国有限公司
上海市徐汇区零陵路899号飞洲国际大厦30楼D座
邮编：200030
电话：021-6427 9900
传真：021-6427 9917
网址：www.imocafe.com
业务范围：
逸摩咖啡中国有限公司由Temple集团创建于中国澳门，鼎鑫国际为其第二大股东。拥有总面积超过2100平方米的咖啡工厂，选用优质阿拉比卡咖啡豆，采用专业流水线和严格的质检系统生产咖啡产品。
“逸摩咖啡”是专门从事咖啡产品的研发、生产和销售以及提供相关服务的专业咖啡贸易公司。并与中国百联集团就在拓展中国的咖啡事业上开展全面的合作并签署了战略框架协议。
业务范围包括逸摩咖啡吧、家庭和办公室咖啡、咖啡豆、咖啡粉、咖啡包、咖啡机等产品。
客服电话：400-618-8948
团购邮箱：tuangou@imocafe.com
投诉建议：kefu@imocafe.com
客服服务：service@imocafe.com
请参阅第122页

北京豪克咖啡物料配送中心
北京东郊市场酒店咖啡用品一条街13号
邮编：100023
电话：010-5135 9097
电邮：kadeiwu123456@163.com
网址：www.hawkcoffee.com

北京凯乐伯商贸有限公司
北京市朝阳区东三环南路13号乐游饭店南楼二层
邮编：100021
电话：010-8771 4971
传真：010-8771 4787
网址：www.5icafe.com.cn

上海爱可咖啡有限公司
上海市古浪路415弄2号楼301
电话：021-5284 4672
传真：021-5284 4573
电邮：act@act-coffee.com
网址：www.act-coffee.com

调味品
Condiments

Ajishima Foods Co., Ltd.
味岛食品（上海）工业有限公司
上海市浦东新区南汇工业园区汇城路788号
邮编：201300
电话：021-6801 6890
传真：021-6801 6515
电邮：lu@ajishima.net
网址：www.ajishima.net

Beijing MeiQuan Food Co., Ltd.
北京美全食品有限公司
北京市大兴区庞各庄工业区田园路3号
邮编：102601
电话：010-8928 2133
传真：010-8928 2127
电邮：meiquan@meiquan.com
网址：www.meiquan.com

Carl Kuehne KG (GmbH & Co.)
德国冠利有限公司
北京市海淀区太阳园9-0111室
邮编：100098
电话：010-8211 2460
传真：010-8211 2461
电邮：info@kuehne.com.cn
网址：www.kuehne.com.cn
业务范围：
冠利：高品质承诺的代名词——德国知名食品品牌。
传统和创新是冠利历史的标记。冠利的历史可以追溯到大约300年以前，丰富的经验和卓越的创造力使得这个有着悠久历史的古老家族公司仍然如设立的第一天那样充满活力。
冠利的产品销往世界各地，美味果醋、爽脆青瓜、清爽腌菜、浓香芥末、百味沙拉酱以及更多美味也已在十二年前进入了众多中国家庭。
凭借高质量的美味产品，无论在德国还是中国冠利都是最知名最受消费者欢迎的品牌之一。
请参阅第126页

Excellence Food Biochemical Co., Ltd.
特好食品生化股份有限公司
台湾省竹北市凤冈路三段398号
电话：+886(3)-556 1666
传真：+886(3)-556 1889
电邮：a5561666@ms45.hinet.net
网址：www.shih-chuan.com.tw

Food Blessing (1988) Co., Ltd.
布莱斯食品有限公司
22 Soi Panichkul, Sukhumvit 71Rd., Prakanongnua, Wattana Bangkok 10110, Thailand
电话：+662-391 2505
传真：+662-381 2386
电邮：goldenspoon@foodblessing.co.th
网址：www.foodblessing.com

Master Sauce Co., Ltd.
状元酱油股份有限公司
台中县大肚乡沙田路一段388巷35-9号
电话：+886(04)-2693 0306
传真：+886(04)-2693 0309
电邮：service@master-sauce.com.tw
网址：www.master-sauce.com.tw

Newly Weds Foods (Beijing) Ltd.
纽利味食品（北京）有限公司
北京市怀柔区雁栖工业开发区雁栖北2街11号
邮编：101407
电话：010-6166 6868
传真：010-6166 6888
电邮：sales@newlywedsfoods.cn
网址：www.newlywedsfoods.cn

Nguan Soon Group
83/4 Mu.5 Soi. Suksawad 2, Suksawad Road, Jomtong, Bangkok 10150
电话：+66(2)-468 5611
传真：+66(2)-460 0901
电邮：spice@nguansoon.com
网址：www.nguansoon.com

Oriental Foods Expert Ltd.
万福亚洲食品有限公司
香港柴湾新业街9号新业工业大厦9楼C及D室
电话：+852-2965 8828
传真：+852-3106 0211
电邮：sales@asiacurry.com
网址：www.asiacurry.com

Qingdao Chunming Condiment Co., Ltd.
青岛春明调味品有限公司
山东青岛胶州胶西镇民营经济区
电话：0532-8522 1118
传真：0532-8522 0056
电邮：info@qdcm.com
网址：www.qdcm.com

Shanghai Chuanqi Food Co., Ltd.
上海川崎食品有限公司
上海浦东新区建陆路96号
邮编：200137
电话：021-5848 1782
传真：021-5848 3115
电邮：cqfood@cqfood.com.cn
网址：www.cqfood.com.cn

Shanghai Hake Foods Co., ltd.
上海哈克商贸有限公司
上海市古美路1471号319室
电话：021-5493 9393
传真：021-5493 4441
电邮：z-hake@126.com
网址：www.shhake.com

Shanghai Kingfood's Condiment Co., Ltd.
上海津丰食品有限公司
上海市黄浦区东街123号8楼
电话：021-6330 1867
传真：021-6330 1869
电邮：kingfoods@kingfoods.com.cn
网址：www.kingfoods.com.cn

Shanghai Mccormick Foods Co., Ltd.
上海味好美食品有限公司
上海市虹梅南路701号
邮编：200237
电话：021-6476 0859
传真：021-6479 1620
网址：www.mccormick.com.cn

Shanghai New Pacific Ocean Foodstuff Empolder
上海新太平洋食品开发有限公司
上海市嘉定区浏翔公路6501号
邮编：201811
电话：021-5997 4595
传真：021-5997 4795
电邮：sales@hsintpy.com
网址：www.newpacific.com.cn

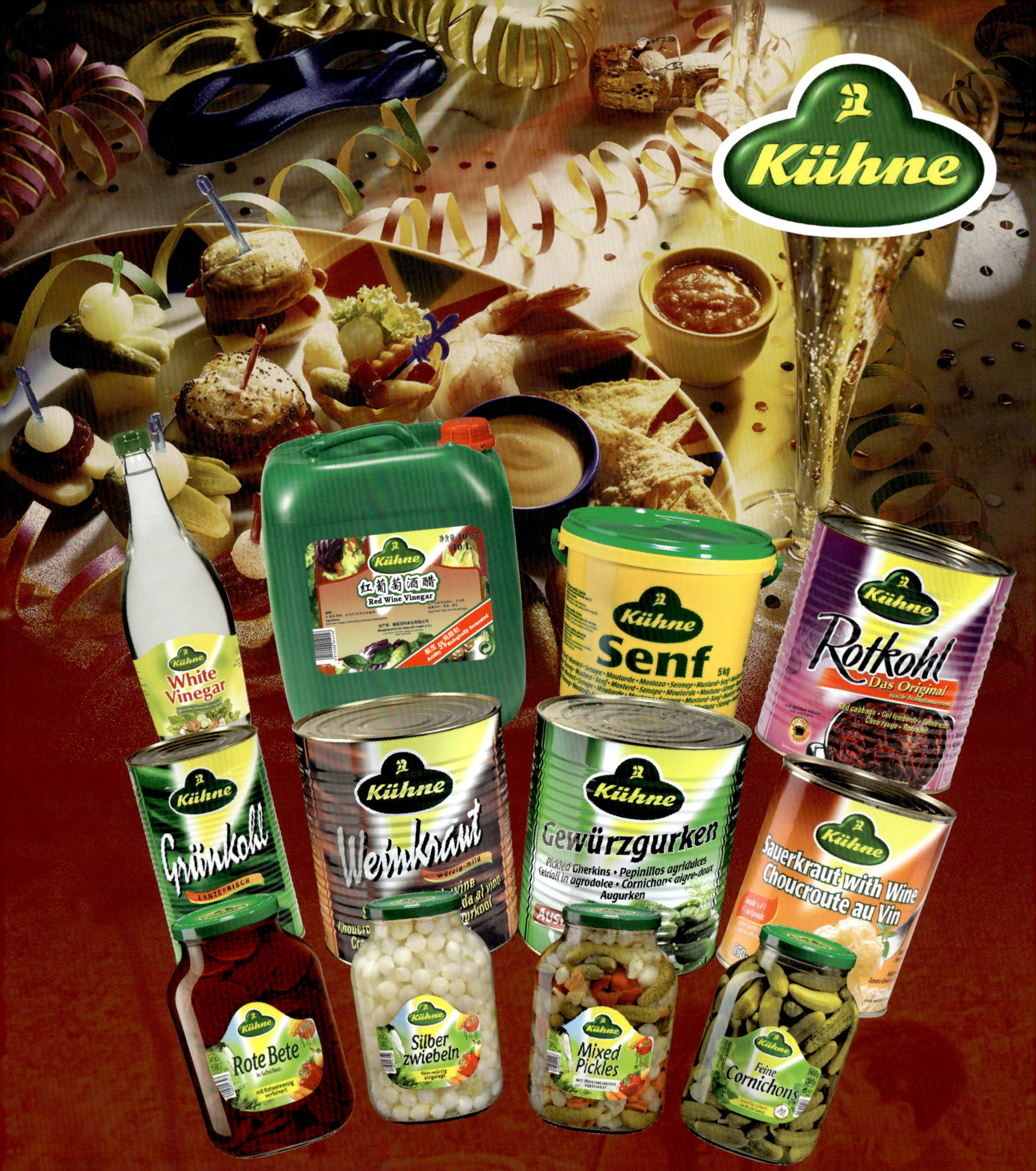
Kühne
Red Wine Vinegar
White Vinegar
Senf
Rotkohl
Das Original
Grünkohl
Weinkraut
Gewürzgurken
Pickled Gherkins • Pepinillos agridulces
Sauerkraut with Wine
Choucroute au Vin
Rote Bete
Silber zwiebeln
Mixed Pickles
Feine Cornichons

▼调味品
Condiments

Shanghai Yilin Foodstuff Co., Ltd.
上海忆霖食品有限公司
上海市闵行区七宝镇新龙路2号
邮编：201101
电话：021-6479 9731
传真：021-6419 0845
网址：www.shyilinfood.com

Shanxi Qinweijia Seasoning Food Co., Ltd.
陕西秦味佳调味食品有限公司
陕西省三原县大李村东口
电话：029-3259 1627
传真：029-3259 1627
电邮：wangxinhai1208@163.com
网址：www.qwjtw.com.cn

Sinodis (Shanghai) Co., Ltd.
西诺迪斯食品（上海）有限公司
上海市金钟路658号4号楼1、2层
邮编：200335
电话：021-6128 1820
传真：021-3360 0070
电邮：info@sinodis.com.cn
网址：www.sinodis.com.cn

TRI-Global International Co., Ltd.
上海怡缘实业有限公司
上海市瑞金南路345弄裕兴大厦1号12A2-B2
邮编：200023
电话：021-6305 1124
传真：021-6305 4355
电邮：nzshab@online.sh.cn
网址：www.triglobal-int.com

Thai Mei Wei International Trading Co., Ltd.
北京泰美味国际贸易有限公司
北京市朝阳区黄杉木店路188号阿曼商街底商8-1
邮编：100123
电话：010-5863 6214
传真：010-5863 6214
电邮：taimeiwei@qq.com
网址：www.thaimeiwei.com

Tianjin Jinwei Foodstuff Seasoning Factory
天津市津味食品调料厂
天津市河北区何兴庄北里18号
邮编：300240
电话：022-2615 0858
传真：022-2615 0878
电邮：jinweifood@263.net
网址：www.jinweifood.cn

Tianjin Widecareer International Trade Co., Ltd.
天津广仕国际贸易有限公司
天津市河西区友谊北路
罗马花园2期戊座一栋1101室
邮编：300204
电话：022-2328 3382
传真：022-2324 4092
电邮：postmaster@widecareer.com
网址：www.widecareer.com

Wencouver Foods Co., Ltd.
上海温科华食品有限公司
上海市宝山区沪太支路1107弄18号
邮编：200436
电话：021-6651 2627
传真：021-5250 0988
电邮：wencvfoods@wencouver.com
网址：www.wencouver.com

Xiamen Taohua Datong Condiment Co., Ltd.
厦门淘化调味品有限公司
福建省厦门市同安西柯西福路88号
同安西柯食品工业园
邮编：361100
电话：0592-317 3128
电邮：yxb@china-sauce.com
网址：www.china-sauce.com

多梦奈一商贸（上海）有限公司
上海市长宁区仙霞路317号
远东国际广场B栋706室
邮编：200051
电话：021-6235 0106
传真：021-6235 0665
网址：www.tamanoi.co.jp

广州万香园食品厂
广州市白云区增槎路738号
三一食品批发市场1001-1002
电话：020-8175 1472
传真：020-3658 1964
电邮：kingspicery@yahoo.com.cn
网址：www.kingspice.com

鸡泽县英达调味品有限公司
河北省鸡泽县辣椒工贸城东3号
邮编：57350
电话：0310-752 3177
传真：0310-752 3177
电邮：lajiao@ydtwp.com
网址：www.ydtwp.com

美国康家食品公司
上海市红宝石路500号东银中心A座1003室
邮编：201103
网址：www.conagrafoods.com
业务范围：
美国康家食品公司为美国第四大食品生产公司。现总部设在美国内布拉斯加的奥马哈市。年营业额超过120亿美元。公司业务范围覆盖零售，餐饮和工业用品，从调味品，零食，冷冻，冷藏以至工业原材料样样俱全。中国主打品牌包括蓝威薯类产品，汉斯番茄产品，瑞士小姐巧克力冲饮，威臣食用油和 ACT II爆米花等。
请参阅第127页

上海豪美佳（调味）食品有限公司
上海市金沙江路1060号C座1405室
邮编：200062
电话：021-6265 2268
传真：021-6265 2262
网址：www.homega.com.cn

鲜大王企业股份有限公司
台湾省桃园县平镇市关爷东路35号
电话：+886(3)-468 8999
电邮：plussun@ms15.hinet.net
网址：www.freshking.com.tw

乳制品
Dairy Products

BSI (Tianjin) Foods
邦士（天津）食品有限公司
上海市长宁区仙霞路317号
远东国际广场B栋706室
邮编：200051
电话：021-6235 0106
传真：021-6235 0665
网址：www.tamanoi.co.jp

Beijing Jikang Food Co., Ltd.
北京吉康食品有限公司
北京市昌平区崔村镇西辛峰工业区8区6号
邮编：102212
电话：010-6072 4247
传真：010-6072 4234
电邮：beijingjikang@yahoo.com.cn
网址：www.bjjikang.com

Bright Dairy & Food Co., Ltd.
光明乳业股份有限公司
上海市吴中路578号
邮编：200103
电话：021-5458 4520
传真：021-6465 4538
电邮：brightdairy@brightdairy.com
网址：www.brightdairy.com

Bright View Shanghai Ltd.
上海易觉商贸有限公司
上海市江宁路420号和一大厦27层B座
邮编：200041
电话：021-6253 0090
传真：021-6253 0127
网址：www.chefonline.com.cn

Century Intl Trading Ltd.
大连保税区倍嘉国际贸易有限公司
大连市中山区港湾街2号深业大厦14层H座
电话：0411-8271 4762
传真：0411-8271 4952
电邮：beijia@century-intl.com
网址：www.century-intl.com

Cortti Food (Shanghai) Ltd.
上海可迪食品有限公司
上海市闵行区三鲁路3585号浦江工业园区A3B幢
电话：021-5433 5400
传真：021-5433 5438
电邮：eric@cortti.com
网址：www.cortti.com

Goodwell China Marketing Service Co., Ltd.
大昌三昶（上海）商贸有限公司
上海市梅园路228号企业广场1901室
邮编：200070
电话：021-6487 6287
传真：021-6487 6159
网址：www.goodwellchina.com
请参阅第107页、封面

Inner Mongolia Mengniu Dairy (Group) Co., Ltd.
内蒙古蒙牛乳业（集团）股份有限公司
内蒙古呼和浩特和林格尔盛乐经济园区
邮编：011500
电话：0471-739 2222
网址：www.mengniu.com.cn

Shanghai Bright Cheese & Butter Co., Ltd.
上海光明奶酪黄油有限公司
上海市吴中路580号
邮编：201103
电话：021-5458 4520
传真：021-5458 0279
电邮：buttercheese@brightdairy.com
网址：www.brightcheese.com

Shanghai Gaofu Longhui Foods Co., Ltd.
上海高夫龙惠食品有限公司
上海市东方路971号钱江大厦9E
邮编：200122
电话：021-6876 7719
传真：021-5820 3466
电邮：suki@public.sta.net.cn
网址：www.gaofufoods.com

▼乳制品
Dairy Products

Silco International Ltd.
Unit B, 4/F., Freder Centre, 3 Mok Cheong Street, To Kwa Wan, Kowloon, Hong Kong
电话：+852-2764 3632
传真：+852-2764 0209
电邮：finefood@silco.com.hk
网址：www.silco.com.hk

Sinodis (Shanghai) Co., Ltd.
西诺迪斯食品（上海）有限公司
上海市金钟路658号4号楼1、2层
邮编：200335
电话：021-6128 1820
传真：021-3360 0070
电邮：info@sinodis.com.cn
网址：www.sinodis.com.cn

TRI-Global International Co., Ltd.
上海怡缘实业有限公司
上海市瑞金南路345弄裕兴大厦1号12A2-B2
邮编：200023
电话：021-6305 1124
传真：021-6305 4355
电邮：nzshab@online.sh.cn
网址：www.triglobal-int.com

广州白云区松洲长宏食品原料商行
广州市白云区松洲增槎路槎头路段
新源粮油批发市场D233、234号
邮编：510430
电话：020-8198 6973
传真：020-8198 6109
网址：www.summer8829.cn

山东巨强生物食品有限公司
山东省临沂市莒南县城西环路南段
邮编：276000
电话：0539-723 3588
传真：0539-791 9166
电邮：juqiang@juqiangfood.com
网址：www.juqiangfood.com

上海熙尚商贸有限公司
上海市军工路1486号318室
邮编：200433
电话：021-5578 0277
传真：021-5578 0277
网址：www.xishangtrade.com

甜品及点心
Desserts & Dim Sum

Barry Callebaut (Suzhou) Chocolate Co., Ltd.
百乐嘉利宝（苏州）可可有限公司
苏州市工业园区方中街138号
邮编：215024
电话：0512-6289 0008
传真：0512-6289 0178
网址：www.callebaut.com

Beijing Just Business & Trading Co., Ltd.
北京嘉思特商贸有限责任公司
北京市海淀区紫竹院路
人济山庄A栋（3号楼）104室
邮编：100048
电话：010-8855 6332
传真：010-8855 6307
电邮：just@just-mart.com
网址：www.just-mart.com

Croissants de France (CDF)
可颂国际集团
上海市中山南二路440号中粮大厦5楼
电话：021-5496 2660
传真：021-5496 2661
网址：www.cdf-group.com

GUSTOSIA Per Dessert
S.Clemente (RN) – Italy
电话：+39-054 185 9416
传真：+39-054 185 9430
电邮：info@gustosia.com
网址：www.gustosia.com
请参阅第137页

Ningbo Caohu Food Co., Ltd.
宁波草湖食品有限公司
浙江省宁波市宁海县金山二路16号
邮编：315600
电话：0574-8355 0115
传真：0574-8355 0116
电邮：nbchsp@163.com
网址：www.chfood.com

Oriental Foods Expert Ltd.
万福亚洲食品有限公司
香港柴湾新业街9号新业工业大厦9楼C及D室
电话：+852-2965 8828
传真：+852-3106 0211
电邮：sales@asiacurry.com
网址：www.asiacurry.com

Q's Coffee
邱公馆食品（云南）有限公司
上海市浦东大道138号永华大厦10楼
邮编：200120
电话：021-6887 5008
传真：021-6887 5193
网址：www.qs-coffee.com

▼甜品及点心
Desserts & Dim Sum

TRI-Global International Co., Ltd.
上海怡缘实业有限公司
上海市瑞金南路345弄裕兴大厦1号12A2-B2
邮编：200023
电话：021-6305 1124
传真：021-6305 4355
电邮：nzshab@online.sh.cn
网址：www.triglobal-int.com

Weihai JK Foods Co., Ltd.
威海佳康食品有限公司
山东省威海市经济技术开发区齐鲁大道53号
邮编：264205
电话：0631-592 5966
传真：0631-592 5356
网址：www.jktrade.com.cn

Well Ocean Foods (Shanghai) Co., Ltd.
威洋食品（上海）有限公司
上海市闸北区恒丰路218号
现代交通大厦东楼2311室
邮编：200070
电话：021-5160 3421
电邮：wilsonfd@wilsonfoods.com.hk
网址：www.wilsonfoods.com.hk
请参阅第129、135、145页

风干食品
Dried Foods

Beijing Westerm Style Food Co., Ltd.
北京西餐食品有限公司
北京市怀柔区庙城镇郑重庄村东630号
邮编：101400
电话：010-6069 7765
传真：010-6069 7824
电邮：bw.sf@hotmail.com
网址：www.bwsf.com.cn

Macao Yue Man Foods Trading Company Limited
澳门裕民食品贸易有限公司
澳门台山华大新村第二街7号地下
电话：+853-2843 9697
传真：+853-2843 9697
请参阅第159页

Neimeng Duyijia Shipin Co., Ltd.
内蒙古赤峰独伊佳食品有限公司
内蒙古赤峰市钢铁街中段独伊佳大厦五楼
电话：0476-838 0939
传真：0476-838 0805
电邮：pub@nmdyj.com
网址：www.nmdyj.com

连州市东陂林泉食品有限公司
广东省连州市东陂镇经济开发区
邮编：513423
电话：0763-626 9320
传真：0763-626 9109
电邮：16269320@126.com
网址：www.lqqy.com

南漳荆山食品有限责任公司
湖北省南漳县武安镇安集洪山路289号
邮编：441512
电话：0710-543 1801
传真：0710-543 1801
电邮：lijun5431801@163.com
网址：www.jsfgsp.com

鱼类及海鲜
Fish & Seafood

AJC International, Inc.
上海市淮海中路93号上海时代广场1306室
邮编：200021
电话：021-5116 7488
传真：021-5116 7498
电邮：ajcsh@ajcfood.com
网址：www.ajcfood.com

Dalian Zhanhai Seafood Co., Ltd.
大连湛海水产有限公司
大连市虎滩新区碧浪园10号楼1楼
电话：0411-8267 1111
传真：0411-8286 4244
电邮：1568@zhanhai.net
网址：www.zhanhai.net

Fish Union International Trading Limited
上海鱼盟国际贸易有限公司
上海市梅园路228号企业广场2101室
邮编：200070
电话：021-6381 6656
传真：021-6381 6768
电邮：information@shfishunion.cn
网址：www.shfishunion.cn

Guangdong Foodstuffs Import & Export (Group) Corporation
广东食品进出口集团公司
广东省广州市东湖西路2号金湖大厦
邮编：510100
电话：020-8385 4888
传真：020-8385 6823
电邮：gdf@china-gdf.com
网址：www.china-gdf.com

Hofung Frozen Food ltd.
荷丰冷冻食品有限公司
上海市延安东路175号旺角广场1311室
邮编：200002
电话：021-6326 9861
传真：021-6326 9863
电邮：food@hofung-global.com
网址：www.hofung-global.com

Jinjun Marine Product & Food Co., Ltd.
上海金君水产食品有限公司
江苏省昆山市花桥镇莲青路888号9幢D座
电话：0512-8617 2555
传真：0512-8617 2333
电邮：sales@junmaoseafood.com
网址：www.junmaoseafood.com

Ninghai Tanglong Seafood Refrigeration Co.,Ltd.
宁海县唐龙食品有限公司
浙江省宁波市宁海经济开发区科九南路6号
邮编：315600
电话：0574-6558 7303
传真：0574-6522 6703
电邮：nbtanglonghx@126.com
网址：www.nbtlhx.cn

Qingdao Hanzhou Foods Co., Ltd.
青岛韩洲食品有限公司
青岛市莱西威海东路1号
邮编：266600
电话：0532-8849 8066
传真：0532-8849 7899
电邮：office@hanzhoufoods.com
网址：www.wuzhoufoods.com

Qingdao Moon Seafood Products Co., Ltd.
青岛文氏水产食品有限公司
山东省青岛市城阳区惜福镇后庄
邮编：266106
电话：0532-8788 6387
传真：0532-8788 9779
网址：www.moonseafood.com.cn

Qingdao Xiyuan Refrigerate Food Co., Ltd.
青岛西苑冷冻食品有限公司
青岛市即墨通济街道办事处西元庄村
电话：0532-8252 3366
传真：0532-8252 3366
电邮：info@qd-xiyuan.com
网址：www.qd-xiyuan.com

Rongcheng Haixing Aquatic Products Co., Ltd.
荣成海兴水产有限公司
山东省荣成市俚岛镇俚岛路395号
电话：0631-766 3235
传真：0631-766 1110
电邮：songhongze@126.com
网址：www.rongyang.com

Shanghai New Fishport International
上海新鱼港国际贸易有限公司
上海市军工路2866号3幢55-56号
邮编：200438
电话：021-3381 6638
传真：021-3381 6635
电邮：newfpi@gmail.com
网址：www.newfpi.com

Silco International Ltd.
Unit B, 4/F., Freder Centre, 3 Mok Cheong Street, To Kwa Wan, Kowloon, Hong Kong
电话：+852-2764 3632
传真：+852-2764 0209
电邮：finefood@silco.com.hk
网址：www.silco.com.hk

Yantai New Ocean Food Processing Factory
烟台新大洋食品加工厂
山东省烟台市福山高科技术产业区永达街761号
邮编：265500
电话：0535-630 0592
传真：0535-630 0594
网址：www.goldenhover.com

大昌行集团有限公司
香港九龙湾启祥道20号大昌行集团大厦8楼
电话：+852-2768 3388
传真：+852-2796 8838
电邮：dch@dch.com.hk
网址：www.dch.com.hk

福建省裕记水产食品有限公司
宁德市蕉城区飞鸾镇二都上村
邮编：352100
电话：0593-259 6988
传真：0593-259 7222
电邮：ndyuji@163.com
网址：http://zhangyugeng70.b2b.hc360.com/

宁波市陆龙兄弟海产食品有限公司
宁波市老外滩人民路65号（金港大厦）
邮编：315020
电话：0574-8735 6565
传真：0574-8766 3807
电邮：lulong@nbip.net
网址：www.lulong-brother.com

温州市圣王食品有限公司
温州市瓯海区潘桥镇仙门村民新路8-2号
邮编：325000
电话：0577-8861 7788
传真：0577-8862 9595
网址：www.wzswfood.com

面粉
Flour

Anhui Fengming Flour Co., Ltd.
安徽凤鸣面粉有限责任公司
安徽省凤台县顾桥镇华东面粉基地
邮编：232100
电话：0554-839 1858
传真：0554-839 1858
电邮：fengming858@126.com
网址：www.fming.com

FaDa Flour Group
发达面粉集团
山东省夏津县发达工业园
邮编：253216
电话：0534-355 0805
电邮：fdjt@fdmf.com
网址：www.fdmf.com

Guangzhou Runfon Flour Co., Ltd.
广州市南方面粉股份有限公司
广东省广州市天河区员村二横路21号
邮编：510655
电话：020-8568 0417
传真：020-8568 0845
电邮：runfon@runfon.com
网址：www.runfon.com.cn

Hangzhou Hengtian Flour Group Co., Ltd.
杭州恒天面粉集团有限公司
浙江省萧山经济技术开发区金一路1号
邮编：311215
电话：0571-8283 5739
传真：0571-8283 5790
电邮：zjht@hengtian.net
网址：www.hengtian.net

Jinan Mintian Flour Co., Ltd.
济南民天面粉有限责任公司
济南市机床二厂路3号
邮编：250000
电话：0531-8719 2509
传真：0531-8719 2508
网址：www.china-mt.com

Orangerie (Shanghai) Food Ingredients Pte. Ltd.
上海欧润吉食品有限公司
上海市嘉唐公路888号
邮编：201807
电话：021-5954 8622
传真：021-5954 2882
电邮：orangerie@orangerie.org
网址：www.orangerie.org

Xuchang Huxue Flour Co., Ltd.
许昌湖雪面粉有限公司
河南省许昌市湖徐工业区
邮编：461102
电话：0374-576 5168
传真：0374-576 5555
电邮：huxueoffice@126.com
网址：www.huxue.cn

大名县复兴面粉有限公司
河北省大名县金滩镇
邮编：056903
电话：0310-645 6335
传真：0310-645 7835
网址：www.fxmf.com

食品添加剂及调味品
Food Additives & Flavourings

Beijing North Sunlight Food Additive Co., Ltd.
北京北方霞光食品添加剂有限公司
北京市丰台区黄土岗马家楼119号
邮编：100070
电话：010-6393 8523
传真：010-6393 8618
电邮：membermaster@bfxg-fas.com
网址：www.bfxg-fas.com

Carl Kuehne KG (GmbH & Co.)
德国冠利有限公司
北京市海淀区太阳园9-0111室
邮编：100098
电话：010-8211 2460
传真：010-8211 2461
电邮：info@kuehne.com.cn
网址：www.kuehne.com.cn
请参阅第126页

GangYang Flavor-chemistry Co., Ltd.
港阳香化企业有限公司
阳江市吉祥西路3号
邮编：529500
电话：0662-321 3296
传真：0662-323 8363
电邮：gygs@public.yangjiang.gd.cn
网址：www.gyxh.com.cn

Guangzhou Kingwell Biotechnology Compant
广州市仟壹生物技术有限公司
广东省广州市海珠区荔福路68号三楼
邮编：510250
电话：020-8443 2538
传真：020-8437 8798
电邮：kingwelltech@163.com
网址：www.kingwell.com.cn

Guangzhou Leizhinuo Food Industrial Co., Ltd.
广州市雷之诺食品实业有限公司
广州市白云区黄边二横路70号
邮编：510435
电话：020-3708 5178
传真：020-3708 5411
网址：www.wy-88.com

Guangzhou Yue-Based Food Co., Ltd.
广州市乐基食品有限公司
广州市白云区龙归园夏龙腾工业区
邮编：510410
电话：020-8814 8838
传真：020-8620 9389
电邮：yashengda@163.com
网址：www.yashengda.net

Ping Shen Enterprise Company Limited
屏山企业有限公司
香港上环干诺道西21-24号海景商业大厦2字楼
电话：+852-2858 9999
传真：+852-2858 1452
电邮：info@pingshan.com.hk
网址：www.pingshan.com.hk

Right Height Co., Ltd.
广州市人禾食品科技发展有限公司
广州市越秀区文德南路33号爱家园商务中心302室
电话：020-8600 6063
传真：020-8323 0882
网址：www.gz-renhe.com

San Da Food Factory
三大食品厂
广东省惠州市惠城区水口镇龙津工业区
邮编：516008
电话：0752-230 8226
传真：0752-202 8808
电邮：hzsdzznc@163.com
网址：www.sdzznc.com

Shanghai Dongsuo Trading Company Limited
上海东索贸易有限公司
上海市嘉定区曹安公路12号桥金园四路501号
邮编：201812
电话：021-3955 9324
传真：021-3955 9947
电邮：mang.guo@tohkin.com
网址：www.dongsuo.net

Shanghai Sainfoin International Trading Co., Ltd.
上海雪丰国际贸易有限公司
上海市普陀区常和路100号1号楼3楼
邮编：200331
电话：021-5107 7717
传真：021-5107 7767
电邮：market@sainfoin.com.cn
网址：www.sainfoin.com.cn

昆山大甫食品科技有限公司
江苏省昆山市经济开发区青阳中路255号
电话：0512-5771 6650
传真：0512-5771 6652
网址：www.ksdafu-food.com

深圳市汇高泰富贸易有限公司
深圳市罗湖区深南东路5002号
信兴广场地王商业中心4905-07室
电话：0755-8238 9510
传真：0755-8238 9050
请参阅第40、41页

食品及饮料模型
Food & Beverage Model

A2A
上海市定西路1016号
银统大厦北楼1601/1602/1610/1611室
电话：021-5531 6406
传真：021-5531 2047*1011
电邮：marketing@mail.atoa.cc
网址：www.atoa.cc

Beijing Xihualang Food Model Technology Center
北京喜花郎仿真模型科技中心
北京市海淀区阜石路69号锦绣大地物流港F2B-01
邮编：100049
电话：010-8820 8639
传真：010-8820 8639
电邮：xhlmx163@163.com
网址：www.xihualang.cn

Iwai Sample (Shanghai) Co., Ltd.
上海岩井食品模型有限公司
上海市浦东新区高科西路1908号C栋东3楼
电话：021-5873 7494
传真：021-5873 0794
电邮：iwai@samplfood.com
网址：www.samplefood.com.cn

Maruso Food Sample Co., Ltd.
广州丸创食品模型有限公司
广州市荔湾区白鹤洞鹤盛路258号A座三楼
邮编：510380
电话：020-8165 0187
传真：020-8165 0374
电邮：sales@maruso-cn.com
网址：www.maruso-cn.com

▼食品及饮料模型
Food & Beverage Model

Shanghai Haoxiang Foodmodel Co., Ltd.
上海好祥食品模型有限公司
上海市浦东新区上南路4560弄32号
邮编：200125
电话：021-6830 0059
传真：021-5082 9793
网址：www.ebisusample.com

Superb Food Model Co., Ltd. Shanghai China
上海先卓模具制造有限公司
上海市普陀区真北路3199号
星云经济园区33号二楼
邮编：200033
电话：021-6363 5828
传真：021-6284 1699
网址：www.shxzfz.cn

Yiwu ZhanGao Craft Products Co., Ltd.
义乌市展高工艺品厂
浙江省义乌市荷叶塘工业开发区8号
邮编：322000
电话：0579-8595 4216
传真：0579-8595 4210
电邮：ywzhangao@163.com
网址：www.ywzhangao.com

青岛土大力模型有限公司
青岛市市北区洛阳路33号
邮编：266051
电话：0532-8996 6539
传真：0532-8875 6356
电邮：tudali@tudali.cn
网址：www.tudali.cn

上海上善食品模型有限公司
上海市三鲁公路1301号
电话：021-3462 3711
传真：021-3462 3711
电邮：weixiaobao3246@163.com
网址：www.onex.cn

天津上善仿真食品模型工贸有限公司
天津市红桥区咸阳北路桃香园25号
邮编：300000
电话：022-2634 3881
传真：022-2634 3881
电邮：spmoxing@sina.com
网址：www.tjspmx.cn

冷冻食品
Frozen Foods

Dongguan Snowboby Co., Ltd.
东莞雪波比冷冻食品有限公司
东莞市茶山镇京山区
邮编：523399
电话：0769-8664 9120
传真：0769-8664 5093
电邮：boby1001@126.com
网址：www.china-snowboby.com

Guangdong Doumen Aquatic Products Imp. and Exp. Corp
广东斗门水产进出口公司
广东省珠海市斗门区井岸镇沿江北路201号
邮编：519100
电话：0756-552 2786
传真：0756-555 9982
电邮：dmaquatic@163.com
网址：www.zhaquatic.com

Hofung Frozen Food ltd.
荷丰冷冻食品有限公司
上海市延安东路175号旺角广场1311室
邮编：200002
电话：021-6326 9861
传真：021-6326 9863
电邮：food@hofung-global.com
网址：www.hofung-global.com

La Brioche Food Production (Zhangjiagang) Ltd.
拉普利奥食品（张家港）有限公司
江苏省张家港市凤凰双龙工业园
邮编：215614
电话：0512-5842 1840
传真：0512-5842 1198
电邮：customer2@la-brioche.com
网址：www.la-brioche.com

Ningbo Nanlian Frozen Food Co., Ltd.
宁波南联冷冻食品有限公司
浙江省宁波市鄞州区姜山镇周韩工业区
电话：0574-8846 4108
传真：0574-8846 3919
电邮：wzfeng88@163.com
网址：www.nanlianfoods.com

Qingdao Hanzhou Foods Co., Ltd.
青岛韩洲食品有限公司
青岛市莱西威海东路1号
邮编：266600
电话：0532-8849 8066
传真：0532-8849 7899
电邮：office@hanzhoufoods.com
网址：www.wuzhoufoods.com

Qingdao Xiyuan Refrigerate Food Co., Ltd.
青岛西苑冷冻食品有限公司
青岛市即墨通济街道办事处西元庄村
电话：0532-8252 3366
传真：0532-8252 3366
电邮：info@qd-xiyuan.com
网址：www.qd-xiyuan.com

Rich Products (Suzhou) Co., Ltd.
维益食品（苏州）有限公司
苏州工业园区苏虹西路75号
邮编：215021
电话：0512-6252 6636
传真：0512-6761 1656
网址：www.richs.cn

Simplot (Beijing) Co., Ltd.
辛普劳（北京）商贸有限公司
北京市朝阳区霞光里9号中电发展大厦B座3层
邮编：100016
电话：010-8468 1100
传真：010-8468 1101
电邮：info@simplot.com.cn
网址：www.simplot.com.cn

Weihai Weidongri Comprehensive Foodstuff Co., Ltd.
威海威东日综合食品有限公司
威海市经济技术开发区香港路15号
邮编：264205
电话：0631-592 5921
传真：0631-592 5021
电邮：wdr@public.whptt.sd.cn
网址：www.weidongri.com.cn

Well Ocean Foods (Shanghai) Co., Ltd.
威洋食品（上海）有限公司
上海市闸北区恒丰路218号
现代交通大厦东楼2311室
邮编：200070
电话：021-5160 3421
电邮：wilsonfd@wilsonfoods.com.hk
网址：www.wilsonfoods.com.hk
请参阅第129、135、145页

Xiamen Chongma Imp. & Exp. Co., Ltd.
厦门中马进出口有限公司
厦门市莲前西路157号水务大厦4楼
邮编：361008
电话：0592-598 7678
传真：0592-519 0788
网址：www.chongma.cn

Zhenzhou Synear Food Co., Ltd.
郑州思念食品有限公司
河南省郑州市金水区西沙路东侧
邮编：450011
电话：0371-6569 3000
传真：0371-6569 3838
电邮：synear@synear.com
网址：www.synear.cn

大昌行集团有限公司
香港九龙湾启祥道20号大昌行集团大厦8楼
电话：+852-2768 3388
传真：+852-2796 8838
电邮：dch@dch.com.hk
网址：www.dch.com.hk

水果及蔬菜
Fruits & Vegetables

AJC International, Inc.
上海市淮海中路93号上海时代广场1306室
邮编：200021
电话：021-5116 7488
传真：021-5116 7498
电邮：ajcsh@ajcfood.com
网址：www.ajcfood.com

Aafud Ingredients (Jiangsu) Co., Ltd.
江苏正兴源食品有限公司
江苏省新沂市323省道草桥段南侧
邮编：221431
电话：0516-8892 3620
传真：0516-8893 5068
电邮：xyzkf@vip.163.com
网址：www.zhengkangfood.com

Asia Leisurely Foods (Nanjing) Co., Ltd.
亚细亚休闲食品（南靖）有限公司
福建省南靖县龙山镇马山
邮编：363602
电话：0596-758 1808
传真：0596-758 1774
电邮：49115353@qq.com

Guangzhou Jinshan Fruit
广州金山鲜果行
广州市增槎路江南果菜批发市场
水果商务区A座16号
邮编：510430
电话：020-8199 0229
传真：020-8198 2676
电邮：sales@janbaofruit.com
网址：www.janbaofruit.com

▼水果及蔬菜
Fruits & Vegetables

Haitong Food Group Co., Ltd.
海通食品集团股份有限公司
浙江省慈溪市海通路528号
邮编：315300
电话：0574-6303 9988
传真：0574-6303 9898
电邮：kaiz@kaiz.com
网址：www.kaiz.com

Kangfulai Group (H.K.) Co., Ltd.
香港康福莱集团有限公司
青岛市东海西路43号凯旋大厦西塔20层
邮编：266071
电话：0532-8597 2306
传真：0532-8597 2338
电邮：info@kflgroup.com
网址：www.kflgroup.com

Kopek
Koylora Imatheias Veroia Greece
电话：+30-233 204 3237
电邮：kopek@delcof.gr
网址：www.delcof.gr

Laizhou Tiancibao Produce Co., Ltd.
莱州天赐宝物产有限公司
山东省莱州市北郊
邮编：261437
电话：0535-241 8968
传真：0535-241 8022
电邮：office@tiancibao.cn
网址：www.tiancibao.com

Longkou Oriental Food Storage Co., Ltd.
龙口市东方食品冷藏有限公司
山东省龙口市龙口开发区电厂西路929号
邮编：265700
电话：0535-884 7090
传真：0535-884 7099
网址：www.lkdongfang.cn

Shanghai Cheerful Import and Export Co., Ltd.
上海祺沃出口有限公司
上海市龙吴路3188号165座
邮编：201108
电话：021-6434 1508
传真：021-6434 1509
电邮：cheerful@shcheerful.com
网址：www.shcheerful.com

Shanghai Zhenhai International Trade Co., Ltd.
上海圳海国际贸易有限公司
上海市浦东新区金豫路100号
禹州金桥国际2期1号楼316室
邮编：201206
电话：021-6876 7199
传真：021-6875 2556
电邮：julie.yi@163.com
网址：www.shzhenhai.com

Silco International Ltd.
Unit B, 4/F., Freder Centre, 3 Mok Cheong Street,
To Kwa Wan, Kowloon, Hong Kong
电话：+852-2764 3632
传真：+852-2764 0209
电邮：finefood@silco.com.hk
网址：www.silco.com.hk

大昌行集团有限公司
香港九龙湾启祥道20号大昌行集团大厦8楼
电话：+852-2768 3388
传真：+852-2796 8838
电邮：dch@dch.com.hk
网址：www.dch.com.hk

新西兰奇异果国际行销公司
上海市肇嘉浜路1065号飞雕国际大厦1703室
电话：021-3368 7528
传真：021-3368 7533
网址：www.zespri.com.cn
请参阅第133页、食品及饮料书隔页底页

食品杂货
Groceries

Beijing Just Business & Trading Co., Ltd.
北京嘉思特商贸有限责任公司
北京市海淀区紫竹院路
人济山庄A栋（3号楼）104室
邮编：100048
电话：010-8855 6332
传真：010-8855 6307
电邮：just@just-mart.com
网址：www.just-mart.com

Goodwell China Marketing Service Co., Ltd.
大昌三昶（上海）商贸有限公司
上海市梅园路228号企业广场1901室
邮编：200070
电话：021-6487 6287
传真：021-6487 6159
网址：www.goodwellchina.com
请参阅第107页、封面

Goodwell Sam Cheong Grocery Co., Ltd.
香港三昌好好办馆有限公司
香港黄竹坑道12号香华工业大厦15楼B座
电话：+852-3972 8901
传真：+852-3972 8900
电邮：info@goodwell-hk.com
网址：www.goodwell-hk.com
业务范围：
自1840年，费洛芥茉磨坊已是勃根地其中一间独立的家族企业。
纵有完善的生产设备，仍保留芥茉工艺师专业的技术，以石头辗磨芥茉籽以保存原味。坊间有无数产品以“芥茉”自居，但成分及制作各异，亦有未符命名标准的产物滥竽充数。
费洛牌有三种主要产品：第戎芥茉酱，传统第戎芥茉酱及风味芥茉酱。费洛像一位伟大的厨师般，喜欢以各样最好的材料与芥茉结合，研发成新产品。
请参阅第138、139、141页

JLG (Shanghai) Imp. & Exp. Co., Ltd.
集龙冠联（上海）贸易有限公司
上海市长宁区遵义路107号安泰大厦1804A室
电话：021-6237 5558
传真：021-6237 5308
网址：www.jlgl.cn

Macao Yue Man Foods Trading Company Limited
澳门裕民食品贸易有限公司
澳门台山华大新村第二街7号地下
电话：+853-2843 9697
传真：+853-2843 9697
请参阅第159页

Oriental Foods Expert Ltd.
万福亚洲食品有限公司
香港柴湾新业街9号新业工业大厦9楼C及D室
电话：+852-2965 8828
传真：+852-3106 0211
电邮：sales@asiacurry.com
网址：www.asiacurry.com

Shanghai Hengyi Trading Co., Ltd.
上海衡毅商贸有限公司
上海市绥德路2弄33号3楼
邮编：200062
电话：021-6608 0276
传真：021-6291 7538
电邮：hengyi@shhengyi.com.cn
网址：www.shhengyi.com.cn

Shanghai Yizhiding Food Co., Ltd.
上海一只鼎食品有限公司
上海市瞿溪路897号4F、5F
邮编：200023
电话：021-6301 6699
传真：021-5301 6178
电邮：tingtop@tingtop.com
网址：www.tingtop.com

Shenzhen Giant Faith Marketing Co., Ltd.
深圳市隆信宝商贸有限公司
深圳市龙岗区平湖镇白泥坑麻布路1号
宝盛工业B区3B栋2楼
邮编：518023
电话：0755-8226 9177
传真：0755-8226 9105
电邮：info@giantfaith.com
网址：www.szgfm.com.cn

Sinodis (Shanghai) Co., Ltd.
西诺迪斯食品（上海）有限公司
上海市金钟路658号4号楼1、2层
邮编：200335
电话：021-6128 1820
传真：021-3360 0070
电邮：info@sinodis.com.cn
网址：www.sinodis.com.cn

Strong Harbour Ltd.
昌港有限公司
香港九龙茶果岭道428号荣山工业大厦4楼G室
电话：+852-2544 6433
传真：+852-2850 6002
电邮：info@strongharbour.com
网址：www.strongharbour.com

TRI-Global International Co., Ltd.
上海怡缘实业有限公司
上海市瑞金南路345弄裕兴大厦1号12A2-B2
邮编：200023
电话：021-6305 1124
传真：021-6305 4355
电邮：nzshab@online.sh.cn
网址：www.triglobal-int.com

大昌行集团有限公司
香港九龙湾启祥道20号大昌行集团大厦8楼
电话：+852-2768 3388
传真：+852-2796 8838
电邮：dch@dch.com.hk
网址：www.dch.com.hk

健康食品
Health Foods

Hangzhou Bodylong Healthfood Co., Ltd.
杭州博浪健康食品有限公司
浙江省杭州市文二路207号文欣大厦1202室
邮编：310012
电话：0571-8825 9435
传真：0571-8825 9438*810
电邮：info@bodylong.com.cn
网址：www.bodylong.com.cn

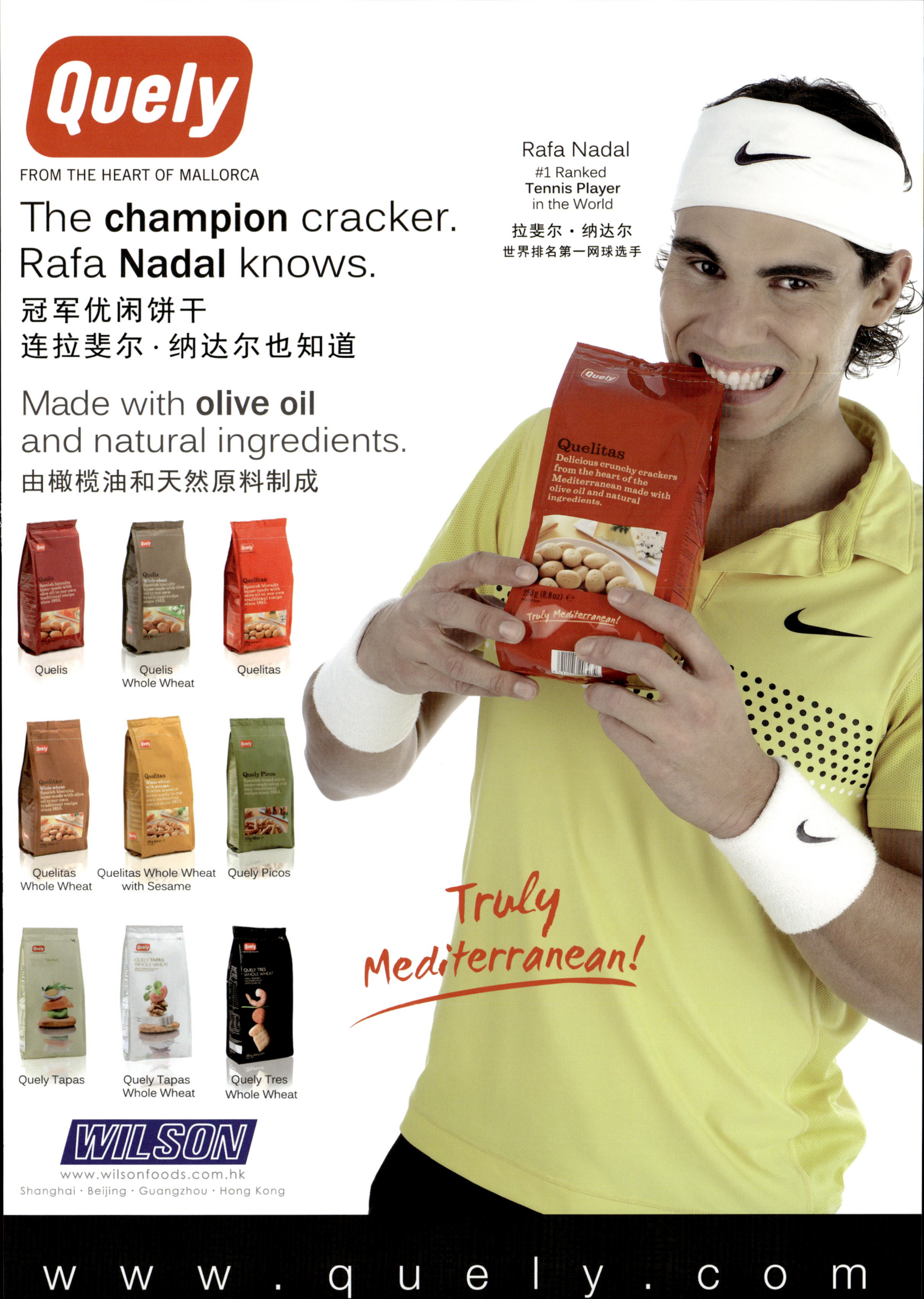
Quely
FROM THE HEART OF MALLORCA
The champion cracker.
Rafa Nadal knows.
冠军优闲饼干
连拉斐尔·纳达尔也知道
Made with olive oil
and natural ingredients.
由橄榄油和天然原料制成
Rafa Nadal
#1 Ranked
Tennis Player
in the World
拉斐尔·纳达尔
世界排名第一网球选手
Quely
Quelitas
Delicious crunchy crackers from the heart of the Mediterranean made with olive oil and natural ingredients.
250g (8.8oz)
Truly Mediterranean!
Quelis
Quelis Whole Wheat
Quelitas
Quelitas Whole Wheat
Quelitas Whole Wheat with Sesame
Quely Picos
Quely Tapas
Quely Tapas Whole Wheat
Quely Tres Whole Wheat
Truly Mediterranean!
WILSON
www.wilsonfoods.com.hk
Shanghai · Beijing · Guangzhou · Hong Kong
www.quely.com

▼健康食品
Health Foods

Hubei Shendan Healthy Food Co., Ltd.
湖北神丹健康食品有限公司
湖北省武汉市洪山区珞狮南路517号农业科技园7F
邮编：430070
电话：027-8739 8088
传真：027-8739 6141
电邮：china-shendan@vip.163.com
网址：www.shendan.com.cn

Macao Yue Man Foods Trading Company Limited
澳门裕民食品贸易有限公司
澳门台山华大新村第二街7号地下
电话：+853-2843 9697
传真：+853-2843 9697
请参阅第159页

Simplot (Beijing) Co., Ltd.
辛普劳（北京）商贸有限公司
北京市朝阳区霞光里9号中电发展大厦B座3层
邮编：100016
电话：010-8468 1100
传真：010-8468 1101
电邮：info@simplot.com.cn
网址：www.simplot.com.cn

Tianjin Widecareer International Trade Co., Ltd.
天津广仕国际贸易有限公司
天津市河西区友谊北路
罗马花园2期戊座一栋1101室
邮编：300204
电话：022-2328 3382
传真：022-2324 4092
电邮：postmaster@widecareer.com
网址：www.widecareer.com

Well Ocean Foods (Shanghai) Co., Ltd.
威洋食品（上海）有限公司
上海市闸北区恒丰路218号
现代交通大厦东楼2311室
邮编：200070
电话：021-5160 3421
电邮：wilsonfd@wilsonfoods.com.hk
网址：www.wilsonfoods.com.hk
请参阅第129、135、145页

Zhongshan Juxiangyuan Food Co., Ltd.
中山市咀香园食品有限公司
广东省中山市火炬开发区沿江东二路13号
（国家健康基地）
电话：0760-8828 2188
传真：0760-8828 2368
电邮：market@juxiangyuan.com
网址：www.juxiangyuan.com

冰淇淋
Ice Cream

Aurora International Trade Co., Ltd.
祥佑国际贸易有限公司
北京市朝阳区东大桥路8号SOHO尚都南塔1703室
电话：010-5869 6163
传真：010-5869 6187
电邮：sales@gptinternational.com
网址：www.elenkasicilia.com

Coffee Secret Company Limited
咖啡秘密有限公司
广东省广州市越秀区东山龟岗一马路20号
电话：020-3762 4902
传真：020-3762 4896
电邮：info@coffeesecret.cn
网址：www.acoffee.cn

Guangzhou Dandy Don's American Ice Cream
广州丹廸噹雪糕厂
广东省广州市荔湾区黄沙大道169号
邮编：510150
电话：020-8193 6601
传真：020-8193 7033
电邮：sale@dandydons.com.cn
网址：www.dandydons.com.cn

Mec3 Food Product Trading (Shanghai) Co., Ltd.
曼凯雪食品贸易（上海）有限公司
上海市延安东路588号东海商业中心5楼D室
邮编：200001
电话：021-6350 7169
传真：021-6350 3105
网址：www.mec3.com
业务范围：
Mec3 is an Italian company leader in the world for the production of ingredients for artisan gelato and pastry-making.
An effective marketing mix together with the image of "premium factory" have taken Mec3 along an unrestrainable growth path with no geographical limits.
At the moment Mec3 is active in more than 80 countries, directly or through trading partners and selected distributors, all of them in line with Mec3 company culture.
15.000 metres of the most advanced centre technology and systems, also including a customer centre and an gelato and pastry-making school where experts, managers and artisans meet, united by the common passion for "artisan gelato".
A workshop of ideas and enthusiasm which gave birth to a real "culture of artisan gelato", it is with satisfaction, conviction and with no false modesty that today we can proudly say "WE KNOW MORE ABOUT GELATO".
请参阅第137页

Shanghai Firenzi Co., Ltd.
上海翡冷翠食品有限公司
上海市宝山区宝祁路611号9号楼
邮编：200050
电话：021-5102 9910
传真：021-5106 2230
电邮：firenzi@firenzi-gelato.com
网址：www.firenzi-gelato.com

Tip-Top Precision Industry Co., Ltd.
江门市裕莹精密工业有限公司
广东省江门市杜阮北三路58号
邮编：529075
电话：0750-365 5888
传真：0750-365 5833
电邮：yy@yuyinggroup.com.cn
网址：www.yuyinggroup.com.cn

意式食品
Italian Foods

Beijing Jikang Food Co., Ltd.
北京吉康食品有限公司
北京市昌平区崔村镇西辛峰工业区8区6号
邮编：102212
电话：010-6072 4247
传真：010-6072 4234
电邮：beijingjikang@yahoo.com.cn
网址：www.bjjikang.com

Beijing Just Business & Trading Co., Ltd.
北京嘉思特商贸有限责任公司
北京市海淀区紫竹院路
人济山庄A栋（3号楼）104室
邮编：100048
电话：010-8855 6332
传真：010-8855 6307
电邮：just@just-mart.com
网址：www.just-mart.com

Bright View Shanghai Ltd.
上海易觉商贸有限公司
上海市江宁路420号和一大厦27层B座
邮编：200041
电话：021-6253 0090
传真：021-6253 0127
网址：www.chefonline.com.cn

Cortti Food (Shanghai) Ltd.
上海可迪食品有限公司
上海市闵行区三鲁路3585号浦江工业园区A3B幢
电话：021-5433 5400
传真：021-5433 5438
电邮：eric@cortti.com
网址：www.cortti.com

GUSTOSIA Per Dessert
S.Clemente (RN) - Italy
电话：+39-054 185 9416
传真：+39-054 185 9430
电邮：info@gustosia.com
网址：www.gustosia.com
请参阅第137页

Goodwell China Marketing Service Co., Ltd.
大昌三昶（上海）商贸有限公司
上海市梅园路228号企业广场1901室
邮编：200070
电话：021-6487 6287
传真：021-6487 6159
网址：www.goodwellchina.com
请参阅第107页、封面

Goodwell Sam Cheong Grocery Co., Ltd.
香港三昌好好办馆有限公司
香港黄竹坑道12号香华工业大厦15楼B座
电话：+852-3972 8901
传真：+852-3972 8900
电邮：info@goodwell-hk.com
网址：www.goodwell-hk.com
请参阅第138、139、141页

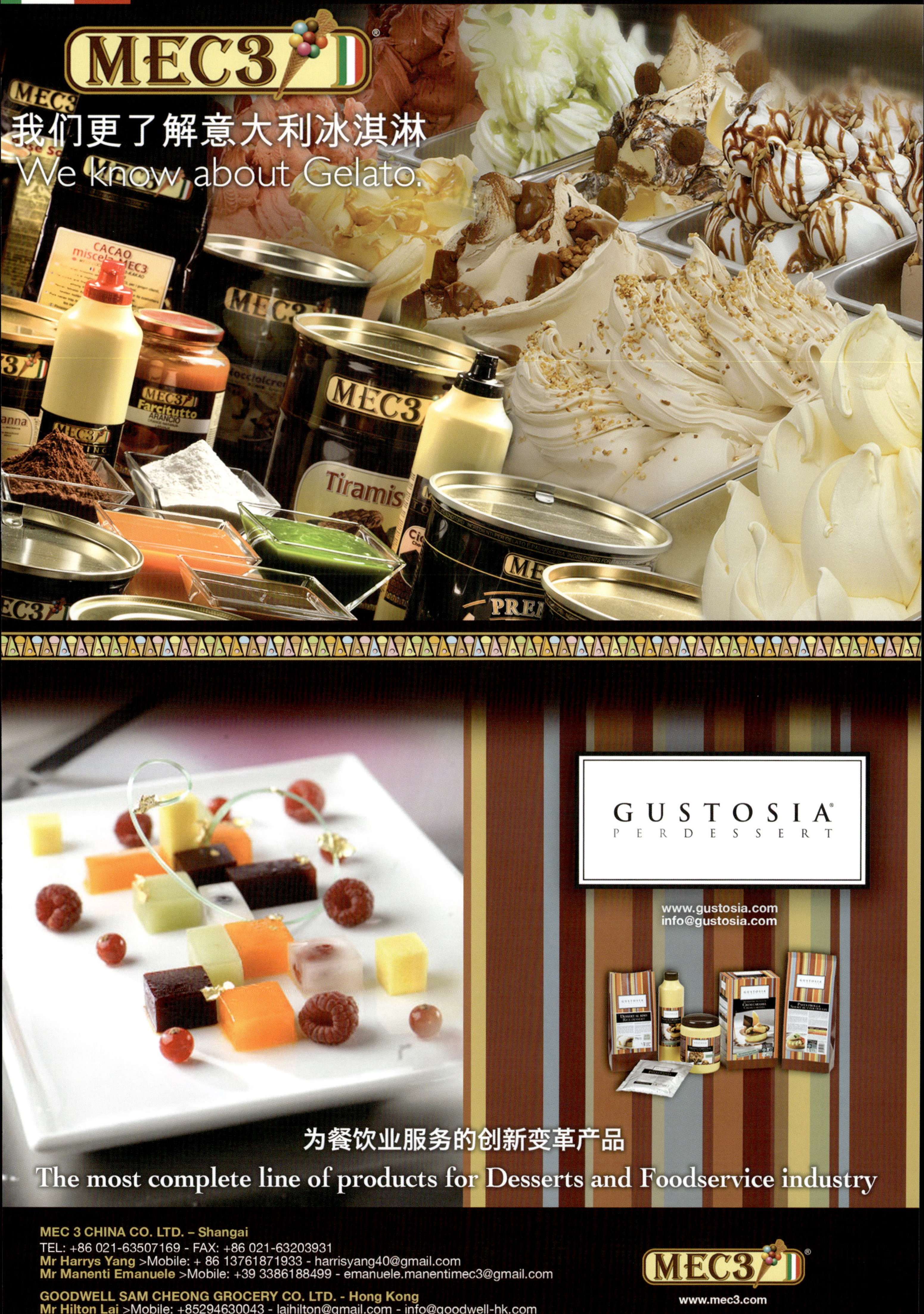
MEC3
我们更了解意大利冰淇淋
We know about Gelato.
GUSTOSIA
PER DESSERT
www.gustosia.com
info@gustosia.com
为餐饮业服务的创新变革产品
The most complete line of products for Desserts and Foodservice industry
MEC 3 CHINA CO. LTD. – Shangai
TEL: +86 021-63507169 - FAX: +86 021-63203931
Mr Harrys Yang >Mobile: + 86 13761871933 - harrisyang40@gmail.com
Mr Manenti Emanuele >Mobile: +39 3386188499 - emanuele.manentimec3@gmail.com
GOODWELL SAM CHEONG GROCERY CO. LTD. - Hong Kong
Mr Hilton Lai >Mobile: +85294630043 - laihilton@gmail.com - info@goodwell-hk.com
MEC3
www.mec3.com

THE WORLD
d'arbo
PODIUM
La Sevillana
black olives
pitted black olives
Teisseire
PELAM
真正
青柠汁
Lime Juice
ANGOSTURA
GRENADINE SYRUP
广东启丰贸易行
地址：广东省佛山市沙坪镇东升小园251号302室
电话：(0750) 8833621
传真：(0750) 8961116

▼意式食品
Italian Foods

Ping Shen Enterprise Company Limited
屏山企业有限公司
香港上环干诺道西21-24号海景商业大厦2字楼
电话：+852-2858 9999
传真：+852-2858 1452
电邮：info@pingshan.com.hk
网址：www.pingshan.com.hk

Shaanxi Italuck Trading Company Ltd.
陕西意生贸易有限责任公司
陕西省西安市新城区西一路138号
中贸国际大厦8楼D座
电话：021-3616 0856
传真：021-3616 2281
电邮：italuck@gmail.com
网址：www.lorence.hk
请参阅第143页

Shanghai Hengyi Trading Co., Ltd.
上海衡毅商贸有限公司
上海市绥德路2弄33号3楼
邮编：200062
电话：021-6608 0276
传真：021-6291 7538
电邮：hengyi@shhengyi.com.cn
网址：www.shhengyi.com.cn

Shanghai Kuichun Industry Co., Ltd.
上海魁春实业有限公司
上海市长寿路652号10号楼308室
邮编：200060
电话：021-5186 3006
传真：021-5101 2046
电邮：kuichun@kuichun.com
网址：www.pinlivefoods.com

Sinodis (Shanghai) Co., Ltd.
西诺迪斯食品（上海）有限公司
上海市金钟路658号4号楼1、2层
邮编：200335
电话：021-6128 1820
传真：021-3360 0070
电邮：info@sinodis.com.cn
网址：www.sinodis.com.cn

Tianjin Widecareer International Trade Co., Ltd.
天津广仕国际贸易有限公司
天津市河西区友谊北路
罗马花园2期戊座一栋1101室
邮编：300204
电话：022-2328 3382
传真：022-2324 4092
电邮：postmaster@widecareer.com
网址：www.widecareer.com

果酱
Jams

Awana Trading Co., Ltd.
东莞市阿瓦娜商贸有限公司
东莞市长安镇一环路中惠新城A区115号
电话：0769-8584 5575
传真：0769-8188 5859
电邮：info@awanacafe.com
网址：www.awanacafe.com

Baoding Minghua Food Co., Ltd.
保定市明花食品有限公司
河北省保定市满城满韩路立交桥西侧
邮编：072150
电话：0312-706 2057
传真：0312-707 8388
网址：www.minghuafood.com

Cortti Food (Shanghai) Ltd.
上海可迪食品有限公司
上海市闵行区三鲁路3585号浦江工业园区A3B幢
电话：021-5433 5400
传真：021-5433 5438
电邮：eric@cortti.com
网址：www.cortti.com

DKSH (China) Co., Ltd.
大昌华嘉商业（中国）有限公司
上海市浦东东方路710号汤臣金融大厦3楼
邮编：200122
电话：021-5830 0518
传真：021-5830 0519
网址：www.dksh.com

Darbo AG
Dornau 18, A-6135 Stans Tyrol, Austria
电话：+43-524 269 5145
传真：+43-524 269 5172
网址：www.darbo.com

Goodwell Sam Cheong Grocery Co., Ltd.
香港三昌好好办馆有限公司
香港黄竹坑道12号香华工业大厦15楼B座
电话：+852-3972 8901
传真：+852-3972 8900
电邮：info@goodwell-hk.com
网址：www.goodwell-hk.com
请参阅第138、139、141页

Mau Lin Food Co., Ltd.
茂霖食品股份有限公司
台湾台南市安南区科技五路157号（科技工业区）
电话：+886(6)-510 0599
传真：+886(6)-510 0598
电邮：linbio@ms28.hinet.net
网址：www.maulin.com.tw

Tianjin Widecareer International Trade Co., Ltd.
天津广仕国际贸易有限公司
天津市河西区友谊北路
罗马花园2期戊座一栋1101室
邮编：300204
电话：022-2328 3382
传真：022-2324 4092
电邮：postmaster@widecareer.com
网址：www.widecareer.com

日式食品
Japanese Foods

Fujiya (Hangzhou) Food Co., Ltd.
不二家（杭州）食品有限公司
浙江省杭州市萧山临港工业园区
邮编：311241
电话：0571-8353 1100
传真：0571-8353 1111
电邮：market@fujiya.cn
网址：www.fujiya.cn

Shanghai Guangyang Foods Co., Ltd.
上海冠洋水产食品公司
上海市长宁区仙霞西路501弄9号102室
邮编：201105
电话：021-5220 2358
传真：021-5217 4112
电邮：klbb1999@126.com
网址：www.shguanyang.com

Shanghai Riyuan Food Co., Ltd.
上海日源食品有限公司
上海市曹杨路1258弄44号
邮编：200062
电话：021-6243 2818
传真：021-6216 2446

Shenzhen Yidu Food Co., Ltd.
深圳市伊都食品有限公司
深圳市宝安区沙井民主西部工业园
E区二期B栋厂房
邮编：518104
电话：0755-2744 7012
传真：0755-2744 7011
网址：www.yidufood.com

Shibata Trading Co., Ltd.
1-Chome, 35-31 Oosu
Naka-ku Nagoya
Aichi, Japan
电话：+81(0)-5220 20638
传真：+81(0)-5220 40098
电邮：contact@confectinery.jp
网址：www.confectionery.jp

Weihai Kaneta Food Co., Ltd.
威海佳乃德食品有限公司
山东省荣成市天鹅湖经济技术开发区
邮编：264319
电话：0631-782 7766
传真：0631-782 7799
电邮：jianaide@kaneta21.com
网址：www.kaneta21.com

韩式食品
Korean Foods

Beijing Biyale Trade Co., Ltd.
北京比亚乐商贸有限公司
北京市朝阳区双桥南路西侧金卫路3号楼208室
邮编：100024
电话：010-8536 3854
传真：010-8536 6629
电邮：zhai6530@126.com
网址：www.biyale.com.cn

Haiyang Douyuan Food Co., Ltd.
海阳斗源食品有限公司
山东省海阳市经济开发区烟台街16号
邮编：265100
电话：0535-320 0806
传真：0535-320 3806
网址：www.doowonfood.com.cn

Hosan Co., Ltd.
141 Danchen-ri, Hobub-Myeon Icheon
Gyeonggi-Do 467-821 Korea
电话：+82(31)-631 9941~2
传真：+82(31)-631 9926
电邮：hosan@koreanproducts.net
网址：www.koreanproducts.net

▼韩式食品
Korean Foods

Shanghai Yidian Commerce Co., Ltd.
上海一典商贸有限公司
上海市普陀区新村路423弄23号504室
电话：021-6266 9790
传真：021-5635 3769
电邮：shyd-23023@163.com
网址：www.yidian.sh.cn

Sino International Foods
信美达国际食品
深圳市福田区八卦路31号众鑫科技大厦901室
电话：0755-2588 7894
传真：0755-2588 7823
网址：www.sinoifoods.com

青岛宝嘉仕贸易有限公司
山东省青岛市李沧区虎山路中段
电话：0532-8888 7448
传真：0532-8286 0372
电邮：koreafood@126.com
网址：www.korfood.cn

威海贤明贸易有限公司
威海市新威路128号尚城国际49号门市
邮编：264200
电话：0631-518 9997
传真：0631-521 5000
电邮：webmaster@weihaifood.com
网址：www.weihaifood.com

延边朴大姐韩式食品厂
吉林省敦化市经济开发区
邮编：133700
电话：0433-634 1165
传真：0433-634 0245
电邮：pdjsp@pdjsp.com
网址：www.pdjsp.com

肉类及肉制品
Meat & Meat Products

Advance Marketing Limited
2/27 Bath Street
PO BOX 37160, Parnell
Auckland, New Zealand
电话：+64(09)-307 3115
传真：+64(09)-377 3141
电邮：timharrison@advancemarketing.co.nz
网址：www.advancemarketing.co.nz

China Yurun Food Group Limited
中国雨润食品集团有限公司
南京市建邺区雨润路10号
邮编：210041
电话：025-6663 8888
电邮：ir@yurun.com.hk
网址：www.yurun.com.hk

Galleon International Ltd.
朗进国际有限公司
香港九龙新蒲岗三祝街12-14号
荣森工业第二大厦三楼
电话：+852-3769 2378
传真：+852-2322 6035
电邮：galleon@galleon-intl.com
网址：www.galleon-intl.com.hk
业务范围：
朗进国际有限公司乃香港主要高级食材进口商之一，从世界各地入口优质急冻或冰鲜牛肉，猪肉，羊肉，家禽，海产及加工食品，客户遍布港澳地区及中国大陆。
公司于2008年成立，负责人于行内拥有逾30年经验，具有丰富的产品知识及人际网络。公司同时开拓高级食品专门店业务，全资经营"DeliFans"。(www.delifans.com.hk)，专售各国优质食材，深受美食爱好者喜爱。

Han Wei Frozen Foods Ltd.
翰威荷德贸易（上海）有限公司
上海市闵行区紫东路689号
邮编：201111
电话：021-2416 1600
传真：021-6409 9912
电邮：sales@hanwei.com.cn
网址：www.hanwei.com.cn

Linyi Xincheng Jinluo Meat Products Group Co., Ltd.
临沂新程金锣肉制品集团有限公司
山东临沂兰山区半程镇金锣科技园
邮编：276036
电话：0539-297 7399
电邮：jinluo@jinluo.com.cn
网址：www.jinluo.com.cn

Macao Yue Man Foods Trading Company Limited
澳门裕民食品贸易有限公司
澳门台山华大新村第二街7号地下
电话：+853-2843 9697
传真：+853-2843 9697
请参阅第159页

Parker Migliorini International
百佑佳食品贸易（上海）有限公司
上海市闸北区天目西路218号
嘉里不夜城一座1607室
邮编：200070
电话：021-6353 5060
传真：021-6353 5061
电邮：sha@pmifoods.com
网址：www.pmifoods.com

Shaanxi Italuck Trading Company Ltd.
陕西意生贸易有限责任公司
陕西省西安市新城区西一路138号
中贸国际大厦8楼D座
电话：021-3616 0856
传真：021-3616 2281
电邮：italuck@gmail.com
网址：www.lorence.hk
请参阅第143页

Shanghai Hormel Foods Co., Ltd.
上海荷美尔食品有限公司
上海市宝山区南大路30号内
邮编：200436
电话：021-5650 0878
传真：021-5668 7086
电邮：webmaster@hormel.com.cn
网址：www.hormel.com.cn

Shuanghui Group
双汇集团
河南省漯河市双汇路一号双汇大厦
邮编：462000
电话：0395-262 2616
传真：0395-262 3398
网址：www.shuanghui.net

Well Ocean Foods (Shanghai) Co., Ltd.
威洋食品（上海）有限公司
上海市闸北区恒丰路218号
现代交通大厦东楼2311室
邮编：200070
电话：021-5160 3421
电邮：wilsonfd@wilsonfoods.com.hk
网址：www.wilsonfoods.com.hk
请参阅第129、135、145页

Zhejiang Zongsu Food Co., Ltd.
浙江宗苏食品有限公司
浙江省东阳市南马工业区
邮编：322121
电话：0579-8667 7666
传真：0579-8628 4688
网址：www.zongsu.com

大昌行集团有限公司
香港九龙湾启祥道20号大昌行集团大厦8楼
电话：+852-2768 3388
传真：+852-2796 8838
电邮：dch@dch.com.hk
网址：www.dch.com.hk

墨西哥食品
Mexican Foods

Grupo Michel
Andres Quintana Roo #1611. C.P. 44260. Col. Guadalupana, Guadalajara, Jalisco, México
电话：+52(33)-3682 0440
传真：+52(33)-3682 1292
网址：www.michel.com.mx

Hidroponia Maya, S.A. DE C.V.
Carretera Felipe Carrillo Puetro-Merida KM. 4, C.P. 77200 R.F.C. HMA-041125-IH9, Felipe Carrillo Puetro, Quintana Roo, Mexico
电话：+52(983)-834 0842
传真：+52(983)-834 0842
网址：www.invernaderomaya.com

Kangfulai Group (H.K.) Co., Ltd.
香港康福莱集团有限公司
青岛市东海西路43号凯旋大厦西塔20层
邮编：266071
电话：0532-8597 2306
传真：0532-8597 2338
电邮：info@kflgroup.com
网址：www.kflgroup.com

La Cazuela Mexicana Sl
Spain Madrid Madrid C, Velazquez 86b-PB
电话：+34(91)-432 1415
传真：+34(91)-578 2797

煮食用油
Oils-Edible/Cooking

Cortti Food (Shanghai) Ltd.
上海可迪食品有限公司
上海市闵行区三鲁路3585号浦江工业园区A3B幢
电话：021-5433 5400
传真：021-5433 5438
电邮：eric@cortti.com
网址：www.cortti.com

Eastocean oils & Grains Industries (Zhangjiagang) Co., Ltd.
东海粮油工业（张家港）有限公司
江苏省张家港市金港镇
邮编：215634
电话：0512-5838 1018
传真：0512-5838 0755
网址：www.eogi.com.cn

Goodwell China Marketing Service Co., Ltd.
大昌三昶（上海）商贸有限公司
上海市梅园路228号企业广场1901室
邮编：200070
电话：021-6487 6287
传真：021-6487 6159
网址：www.goodwellchina.com
请参阅第107页、封面

Goodwell Sam Cheong Grocery Co., Ltd.
香港三昌好好办馆有限公司
香港黄竹坑道12号香华工业大厦15楼B座
电话：+852-3972 8901
传真：+852-3972 8900
电邮：info@goodwell-hk.com
网址：www.goodwell-hk.com
请参阅第138、139、141页

Import Trade Co., Ltd.
英波特贸易有限公司
广东省佛山市禅城区华远东路13号
发展大厦11楼E单元
邮编：528000
电话：0757-8330 8018
传真：0757-8330 8017
电邮：web@fsipt.com
网址：www.fsipt.com

Longjiangfu Edible Oil Co., Ltd.
黑龙江龙江福粮油公司
哈尔滨开发区哈平路集中区渤海东路6号
邮编：150069
电话：0451-8678 7575
传真：0451-8678 7575
电邮：0451-86787569@163.com
网址：www.longjf.com

Macao Yue Man Foods Trading Company Limited
澳门裕民食品贸易有限公司
澳门台山华大新村第二街7号地下
电话：+853-2843 9697
传真：+853-2843 9697
请参阅第159页

Shandong Yuhuang Grain & Oil Food Co., Ltd.
山东玉皇粮油食品有限公司
山东省莒南县城南环路中段
邮编：276600
电话：0539-721 2955
传真：0539-721 0203
电邮：yh@chinayuhuang.com
网址：www.chinayuhuang.com

Shanghai Kuichun Industry Co., Ltd.
上海魁春实业有限公司
上海市长寿路652号10号楼308室
邮编：200060
电话：021-5186 3006
传真：021-5101 2046
电邮：kuichun@kuichun.com
网址：www.pinlivefoods.com

Shanghai Liangyou Haishi Oils & Fats Industrial Co., Ltd.
上海良友海狮油脂实业有限公司
上海市龙吴路2080号
邮编：200231
电话：021-6496 7800
传真：021-6496 5735
电邮：sales@shoils.cn
网址：www.shoils.cn

Shanghai YDF Co., Ltd.
上海一担坊食品有限公司
上海市浦东新区张江高科技园区松涛路489号B3
邮编：201203
电话：021-5027 3575
传真：021-5027 3628
电邮：cheng@jh21.com
网址：www.oil-workshop.com

Shanghai Yuanyi Import & Export Co., Ltd.
上海远怡进出口有限公司
上海市浦东新区秀沿路1168弄3支弄230号
邮编：201315
电话：021-6819 6304
传真：021-6819 5007
电邮：yuanyi5588@163.com
网址：www.importfood.com.cn

Sinodis (Shanghai) Co., Ltd.
西诺迪斯食品（上海）有限公司
上海市金钟路658号4号楼1、2层
邮编：200335
电话：021-6128 1820
传真：021-3360 0070
电邮：info@sinodis.com.cn
网址：www.sinodis.com.cn

Tianjin Widecareer International Trade Co., Ltd.
天津广仕国际贸易有限公司
天津市河西区友谊北路
罗马花园2期戊座一栋1101室
邮编：300204
电话：022-2328 3382
传真：022-2324 4092
电邮：postmaster@widecareer.com
网址：www.widecareer.com

Well Ocean Foods (Shanghai) Co., Ltd.
威洋食品（上海）有限公司
上海市闸北区恒丰路218号
现代交通大厦东楼2311室
邮编：200070
电话：021-5160 3421
电邮：wilsonfd@wilsonfoods.com.hk
网址：www.wilsonfoods.com.hk
请参阅第129、135、145页

Yihai Kerry Oils & Grains (Shenzhen) Co., Ltd.
益海嘉里粮油（深圳）有限公司
深圳市南山区后海滨海德三道海岸大厦西座25F
邮编：518054
电话：0755-8628 9600
传真：0755-8628 9775
电邮：info@wilmar-intl.com
网址：www.arawana.com.cn

有机食物
Organic Foods

Shanghai Aobird Trade Co., Ltd.
上海聚鸟树贸易有限公司
上海市闵行区莘朱东路426号
邮编：201100
电话：021-6476 8117
传真：021-5430 6355
电邮：aobird2008@yahoo.com.cn
网址：www.aobird.com

Shanxi Tianren Organic Food Co., Ltd.
陕西天人有机食品股份有限公司
西安市高新技术产业开发区高新一路2号
国家开发银行大厦16层
邮编：710075
电话：029-8837 7001
传真：029-8837 7295
电邮：sxtr@skypeoplejuice.com
网址：www.sxtr.com.cn

Shenzhen Ruililai Industry Co., Ltd.
深圳瑞利来实业有限公司
深圳市福田区八卦四路414栋9楼南
邮编：518029
电话：0755-8240 8531
传真：0755-8240 0602
电邮：szrll@yahoo.cn
网址：www.ruililai.com

家禽及蛋
Poultry & Eggs

Green and Lush Birds, Beasts and Eggs'Food Co., Ltd. An'Qing
安庆市绿油油禽蛋食品有限公司
安徽省安庆市枞阳县连城工业区
邮编：246738
电话：0556-283 0899
传真：0556-283 0799
电邮：lyy@aqlyy.com
网址：www.aqlyy.com

Hebei Huayu Poultry Breeding Co., Ltd.
河北华裕家禽育种有限公司
河北省邯郸市永年县南沿村镇
邮编：057151
电话：0310-699 8888
传真：0310-699 7968
电邮：huayu145@126.com
网址：www.huayuzhongqin.com

Hubei Jiuzhu Egg Industry Co., Ltd.
湖北九珠蛋业有限公司
湖北省仙桃市仙源大道12号
邮编：433000
电话：0728-323 6377
传真：0728-320 2139
电邮：xtyys@263.com
网址：www.hbjz.com

Jilin Jinyi Egg Products Co., Ltd.
吉林金翼蛋品有限公司
吉林省辽源经济开发区
邮编：136200
电话：0437-509 0007
传真：0437-317 0255
电邮：jy_xiaoshou@163.com
网址：www.jljinyi.cn

▼家禽及蛋
Poultry & Eggs

Ningbo Jinluan Fowl Egg Food Co., Ltd.
宁波金銮禽蛋食品有限公司
浙江省余姚市泗门镇振华路2号
邮编：315471
电话：0574-6215 4039
传真：0574-6215 4083
电邮：xie@eggprocess.com
网址：www.eggprocess.com

Parker Migliorini International
百佑佳食品贸易（上海）有限公司
上海市闸北区天目西路218号
嘉里不夜城一座1607室
邮编：200070
电话：021-6353 5060
传真：021-6353 5061
电邮：sha@pmifoods.com
网址：www.pmifoods.com

Ping Shen Enterprise Company Limited
屏山企业有限公司
香港上环干诺道西21-24号海景商业大厦2字楼
电话：+852-2858 9999
传真：+852-2858 1452
电邮：info@pingshan.com.hk
网址：www.pingshan.com.hk

大昌行集团有限公司
香港九龙湾启祥道20号大昌行集团大厦8楼
电话：+852-2768 3388
传真：+852-2796 8838
电邮：dch@dch.com.hk
网址：www.dch.com.hk

广东温氏食品集团有限公司
广东省云浮市新兴县新竹镇榄根温氏集团
邮编：527439
电话：0766-229 1142
传真：0766-229 1159
电邮：jcs@wens.com.cn
网址：www.wens.com.cn

杭州萧山玉泉家禽有限公司
浙江省杭州市萧山新塘街道新丰村
邮编：311201
电话：0571-8279 1200
传真：0571-8279 0102
电邮：agriculture.168@163.com
网址：www.yqjq.net

开平市旭日蛋品有限公司
广东省开平市赤坎镇中庙村委会上登学校
邮编：529300
电话：0750-262 0388
传真：0750-262 0777
网址：www.kpxuri.com.cn

加工食品
Processed Foods

Fujian Changtai Fuxiang Foods Processing Factory
福建长泰县福翔食品加工厂
福建省长泰县官山工业区
邮编：363990
电话：0596-831 3280
传真：0596-831 2889
电邮：zlz@fxfoods.com
网址：www.fxfoods.com

Oriental Foods Expert Ltd.
万福亚洲食品有限公司
香港柴湾新业街9号新业工业大厦9楼C及D室
电话：+852-2965 8828
传真：+852-3106 0211
电邮：sales@asiacurry.com
网址：www.asiacurry.com

米及面制品
Rice & Noodles

Asiarice Biotech Inc.
亚洲瑞思生物科技
台北市建国北路二段127号3楼
电话：+886(2)-2506 9119
传真：+886(2)-2506 8098
网址：www.asiarice.com.tw

Guangdong Foodstuffs Import & Export (Group) Corporation
广东食品进出口集团公司
广东省广州市东湖西路2号金湖大厦
邮编：510100
电话：020-8385 4888
传真：020-8385 6823
电邮：gdf@china-gdf.com
网址：www.china-gdf.com

Hangzhou Wellong Food Co., Ltd.
展旺（杭州）食品有限公司
浙江省杭州市萧山区瓜沥镇临港工业园区
邮编：311241
电话：0571-8250 7359
传真：0571-8250 7386
网址：www.wellong.net.cn

Shouguang Tiancheng Hongli Food Co., Ltd.
寿光市天成宏利食品有限公司
山东省寿光市开发区工业园金光街东首
邮编：262700
电话：0536-519 6296
传真：0536-510 9909
电邮：lisawu@tianchengfood.cn
网址：www.tianchengfood.cn

Xuzhou Jvefoo Foods Co., Ltd.
徐州京味福食品有限公司
江苏省徐州市丰县解放中路79号
邮编：221700
电话：0516-8635 2222
传真：0516-8921 2322
网址：www.jingweifu.cn

辽宁盘锦绿也米业有限责任公司
辽宁省盘锦市大洼县榆树农场
邮编：124213
电话：0427-883 4567
传真：0427-780 2515
电邮：pjlvye@163.com
网址：www.lvye9.com

酱汁
Sauces

Carl Kuehne KG (GmbH & Co.)
德国冠利有限公司
北京市海淀区太阳园9-0111室
邮编：100098
电话：010-8211 2460
传真：010-8211 2461
电邮：info@kuehne.com.cn
网址：www.kuehne.com.cn
请参阅第126页

Cortti Food (Shanghai) Ltd.
上海可迪食品有限公司
上海市闵行区三鲁路3585号浦江工业园区A3B幢
电话：021-5433 5400
传真：021-5433 5438
电邮：eric@cortti.com
网址：www.cortti.com

Fujian Yaokee Foodsfull Co., Ltd.
福建尧记食品有限公司
福建省惠安县辋川玉溪工业区
邮编：362103
电话：0595-8726 0888
传真：0595-8726 6999
电邮：yaokee@pub2.qz.fj.cn
网址：www.yaokee.com.cn

Global Export Maketing Company
450 7th Ave, Suite 2200, New York, 10123, United States of America
电话：+1(0)-2122 689930
传真：+1(0)-2122 689935
电邮：bob@globalxport.com
网址：www.globalxport.com

Guangdong Foodstuffs Import & Export (Group) Corporation
广东食品进出口集团公司
广东省广州市东湖西路2号金湖大厦
邮编：510100
电话：020-8385 4888
传真：020-8385 6823
电邮：gdf@china-gdf.com
网址：www.china-gdf.com

Koon Yick Foods Factory (Wah Kee)
香港冠益华记食品厂
香港九龙西贡蠔涌鹿尾村26号339-340地段
电话：+852-2719 5502
传真：+852-2358 2159
电邮：contactus@koonyick.com
网址：www.koonyick.com

Lee Kum Kee
李锦记（中国）销售有限公司
上海市漕溪北路398号
汇智大厦23楼
电话：021-6090 6777
传真：021-6090 4334
网址：www.lkk.com

ShingKee Foods Industry Co., Ltd.
盛记食品工业有限公司
福建省龙海市角美开发区第11号区
邮编：363107
电话：0596-676 6370
传真：0596-676 6371
网址：www.shingkee.com

Sinodis (Shanghai) Co., Ltd.
西诺迪斯食品（上海）有限公司
上海市金钟路658号4号楼1、2层
邮编：200335
电话：021-6128 1820
传真：021-3360 0070
电邮：info@sinodis.com.cn
网址：www.sinodis.com.cn

Well Ocean Foods (Shanghai) Co., Ltd.
威洋食品（上海）有限公司
上海市闸北区恒丰路218号
现代交通大厦东楼2311室
邮编：200070
电话：021-5160 3421
电邮：wilsonfd@wilsonfoods.com.hk
网址：www.wilsonfoods.com.hk
请参阅第129、135、145页

▼酱汁
Sauces

Yummy House International Ltd.
美味栈国际有限公司
香港干诺道西144-151号成基商业中心1楼109室
电话：+852-2803 0833
传真：+852-3528 0580
电邮：info@yum.com.hk
网址：www.yum.com.hk

广州蒸烩煮食品有限公司
广州市白云区太和镇大源村
南坑四社第八工业区A栋
邮编：510540
电话：020-8743 6660
传真：020-8743 6711
电邮：zhenghuizhu2006@163.com
网址：www.zhenghuizhu.com

石家庄市鼎鑫酿造食品科学研究所
河北省石家庄市长安区北宋戏楼胡同20号
邮编：050031
电话：0311-8506 1709
传真：0311-8506 1709
电邮：dingxin@heinfo.net
网址：www.dxfood.com

鱼翅
Shark's Fins

FuYuan Yang's Food (Shanghai) Co., Ltd.
馥园杨姐食品（上海）有限公司
上海市莲花南路2165弄109号
邮编：201108
电话：021-6458 7999
传真：021-3451 1886
电邮：fuyuan@fyyj.com.cn
网址：www.fyyj.com.cn

广州市元道贸易发展有限公司
广州市一德路369号山海城大厦5楼A5室
邮编：510120
电话：020-8130 8887
传真：020-8130 8889
电邮：gzyymy@126.com
网址：www.gz-yymy.com.cn

零食
Snack Foods

American Ocean Holy Add Company
美国美洋圣加（国际）有限公司
内蒙古包头市九原区开发区1号
邮编：014060
电话：0472-716 2916
网址：www.mysjcn.net

COFCO Le Conte Food (Shenzhen) Co., Ltd.
中粮金帝食品（深圳）有限公司
深圳市北环路梅林工业区梅秀路1号
邮编：518049
电话：0755-8311 5214
传真：0755-8310 3189
电邮：leconte@leconte.com.cn
网址：www.leconte.com.cn

Guangdong Zhongtan Investment Co., Ltd.
广东中田投资有限公司
广州市寺右马路111号五羊新城广场1919-1923室
邮编：510600
电话：020-8738 0248
传真：020-8738 0243
网址：www.zt1919.com

Import Trade Co., Ltd.
英波特贸易有限公司
广东省佛山市禅城区华远东路13号
发展大厦11楼E单元
邮编：528000
电话：0757-8330 8018
传真：0757-8330 8017
电邮：web@fsipt.com
网址：www.fsipt.com

Popstar International Trading Co., Ltd.
亮奎·建奎国际贸易（上海）有限公司
上海市曹杨路450号绿地和创大厦510室
邮编：200063
电话：021-5235 7712
传真：021-6240 1376
电邮：hank.lin@qpopstar.com
网址：www.qpopstar.com
请参阅第112、113页

Shanghai Hamp Import & Export Trading Co., Ltd.
上海瀚普进出口贸易有限公司
上海市定西路1281号兆仪大厦1404室
邮编：200336
电话：021-5238 9957
传真：021-6240 0599
电邮：jane.yan@kellen-hamp.com.cn
网址：www.kellen-hamp.com.cn

Shanghai Sunny Life Enterprise Co., Ltd.
上海山隆实业有限公司
上海市常德路1265号兴运大厦6楼
邮编：200060
电话：021-5252 7733
传真：021-5252 7555
电邮：shsunlife@shsunlife.com
网址：www.shsunlife.cn

Shanghai Yuanyi Import & Export Co., Ltd.
上海远怡进出口有限公司
上海市浦东新区秀沿路1168弄3支弄230号
邮编：201315
电话：021-6819 6304
传真：021-6819 5007
电邮：yuanyi5588@163.com
网址：www.importfood.com.cn

Tianjin Buyus International Incorporation
天津佰乐美商贸有限公司
天津新技术产业园区华苑产业区华天道8号海泰信息广场F座南楼819室
邮编：300384
电话：022-2370 7382
传真：022-2370 8982
电邮：newtrans@newtransgroup.com
网址：www.buyus.com.cn

Urashima Nori Food (Shanghai) Co., Ltd.
浦岛海苔食品（上海）有限公司
上海市松江区玉佳路77号
邮编：201600
电话：021-6772 8333
传真：021-6772 8624
电邮：sales@urashima.com.cn
网址：www.urashima.com.cn

Weihai Kaneta Food Co., Ltd.
威海佳乃德食品有限公司
山东省荣成市天鹅湖经济技术开发区
邮编：264319
电话：0631-782 7766
传真：0631-782 7799
电邮：jianaide@kaneta21.com
网址：www.kaneta21.com

黄豆制品
Soya Bean Products

广州番禺区市桥沙头统易豆业厂
广东省广州市番禺区沙头街小平工业区
邮编：511400
电话：020-6198 9811
传真：020-6198 9812
网址：www.pytongyi.cn

珠海保税区西尾食品有限公司
珠海市湾仔珠海保税区第三区域
邮编：519030
电话：0756-868 7188
传真：0756-868 7500
网址：www.nishiofoods.com.cn

香料
Spices

Goodwell Sam Cheong Grocery Co., Ltd.
香港三昌好好办馆有限公司
香港黄竹坑道12号香华工业大厦15楼B座
电话：+852-3972 8901
传真：+852-3972 8900
电邮：info@goodwell-hk.com
网址：www.goodwell-hk.com
业务范围：
妙多建立于1928年，最初只以家庭模式经营，其后发展成为印度主要的食品加工公司。
拥有先进的设备，妙多生产出高质素的印度食品，如：节喱、酸果、咖喱粉、香料酱、印度薄饼、即食包等，更出口至东南亚、中东、美洲及欧洲等地。
妙多是一间百分百的出口型企业，荣获ISO 9001: 2000, HACCP等食物安全认证，质量毋容置疑。
请参阅第138、139、141页

Shanghai Hongyu Essence & Flavor Co., Ltd.
上海宏宇香精香料有限公司
上海市静安区康定路1268弄静鼎安邦2号601室
邮编：200042
电话：021-6266 8181
传真：021-6266 8383
电邮：info@hongyultd.com
网址：www.hongyultd.com

Shantou Huaxin Flavor Co., Ltd.
汕头市华馨香料有限公司
广东省汕头市升业路35号
电话：0754-8842 6511
传真：0754-8897 8651
电邮：info@jinnan.net
网址：www.hxst.com.cn

Yan Sheung Kee (Ming Kee) Coconut & Spices Co Ltd.
甄想记（明记）椰子香料有限公司
香港新界屯门青扬街1号
世纪城市工业大厦9楼A-D室
电话：+852-2468 2220
传真：+852-2436 1511
电邮：coconutboy@ysk-mk.com
网址：www.ysk-mk.com
请参阅第109、153页、食品及饮料书隔页面页

▼香料
Spices

天津市国源食品有限公司
天津市红桥区西青道65号
金兴科技大厦23层01-06室
邮编：300122
电话：022-2771 8222
传真：022-2772 2555
网址：www.guoyuan.cn

万香源调味品公司
陕西省西安市蓝田工业园迎宾路北段18号
邮编：710500
电话：029-8273 3000
传真：029-8273 2638
网址：www.xianwxy.cn

糖
Sugar

Fujian Yake Food Co., Ltd.
福建雅客食品有限公司
福建省晋江市罗山社店工业区
邮编：362200
电话：0595-8818 3088
传真：0595-8818 6808
电邮：dongpo@yakefood.com
网址：www.yakefood.com

Fujiya (Hangzhou) Food Co., Ltd.
不二家（杭州）食品有限公司
浙江省杭州市萧山临港工业园区
邮编：311241
电话：0571-8353 1100
传真：0571-8353 1111
电邮：market@fujiya.cn
网址：www.fujiya.cn

Guan Sheng Yuan (Group) Co., Ltd.
冠生园（集团）有限公司
上海市新闸路1418号
邮编：200040
电话：021-6271 5276
传真：021-6272 7500
网址：www.gsygroup.com

Guangzhou Gotra Trading Co., Ltd.
广州冠众贸易有限公司
广州市环市东路450号华信中心11楼
邮编：510075
电话：020-3761 0310
传真：020-3761 0299
电邮：wservice@gotra.com.cn
网址：www.gotra.com.cn

Honey Candy-House Co., Ltd.
糖坊食品有限公司
5F, No.501-12, Chung Chen Road, Hsin-Tien City, Taipei County, 231-41, Taiwan
电话：+886(2)-8219 1006
传真：+886(2)-8219 1008
电邮：sales@candy-house.com.tw
网址：www.candy-house.com.tw

Inner Mongolia Drambor Food Co., Ltd.
内蒙古正北食品有限公司
内蒙古包头市东河区南门外21号
邮编：014040
电话：0472-414 3566
传真：0472-412 4035
电邮：nn-drambor@zhengbei.com
网址：www.zhengbei.com

Nanning Sugar Industry Co., Ltd.
南宁糖业股份有限公司
广西省南宁市亭洪路48号
电话：0771-491 1323
传真：0771-491 2771
电邮：nnty@nnsugar.com
网址：www.nnsugar.com

Shanghai Kangzhou Fungi Extract Co., Ltd.
上海康舟真菌多糖有限公司
上海市浦东大道1525号中国石化大厦东楼14楼
邮编：200135
电话：021-5851 2636
传真：021-5028 2226
电邮：yzy@fungi-extract.com
网址：www.fungi-extract.com

太古taikoo

Taikoo (Guangzhou) Sugar Limited
太古（广州）糖业有限公司
广州市经济技术开发区锦绣路
明华一街穗兴工业大厦6号4楼
邮编：510730
电话：020-8364 9050
传真：020-8364 9051
电邮：info@taikoosugar.com
网址：www.taikoosugar.com.cn
业务范围：
太古炼糖厂有限公司于1881年在香港注册成立，1884年，炼糖厂正式投入生产。秉承市场先驱的百年传统，太古糖业一直力求创新，致力为顾客提供最高质素及多元化的糖类产品。产品包括方糖、中式糖、糖水、糖浆、烘焙类用糖、餐饮小包糖等，更可为客户设计产品包装，提供定牌糖包等产品，通行全国。
请参阅第149、155页

Wuhu Qinshi Tangye Co., Ltd.
芜湖市秦氏糖业有限公司
安徽省芜湖市三山区绿色食品经济开发区
邮编：241203
电话：0553-747 7608
传真：0553-747 7615
电邮：michael@glucose.com.cn
网址：www.maltose.cn

深圳市汇高泰富贸易有限公司
深圳市罗湖区深南东路5002号
信兴广场地王商业中心4905-07室
电话：0755-8238 9510
传真：0755-8238 9050
请参阅第40、41页

泰国食品
Thailand Foods

Beijing Hengrun Huatai Trade Co., Ltd.
北京恒润华泰商贸有限公司
北京市朝阳区王四营乡王四营桥
东南侧368号北楼2门
邮编：100023
电话：010-8739 0696
传真：010-8739 0728
网址：www.hrht123.com.cn

Longmore (Hangzhou) Commercial Co., Ltd.
杭州郎多贸易有限公司
杭州市湖墅南路247号广电大楼307室
邮编：310011
电话：0571-8882 6937
传真：0571-8880 2083
电邮：xyding77@126.com
网址：www.longmore99.com

Shantou Chunyuan Trade Co., Ltd.
汕头市春园贸易有限公司
广东省汕头市跃进路23号
利鸿基中心大厦写字楼A栋15层1509
邮编：515031
电话：0754-8898 7918
传真：0754-8898 7913
电邮：stcyco@163.com
网址：www.chunyuan.cn

Sino Sunshine Co., Ltd.
佛山市泰扬恒升贸易有限公司
佛山市季华五路33号B座29楼07室
邮编：528000
电话：0757-8399 2501
传真：0757-8399 2500
电邮：sunshine0757@163.net
网址：www.sinosunshine.com.cn

素食品
Vegetarian Foods

Fujian Minqing Jindefu Food Co., Ltd.
闽清金德福食品有限公司
福建省闽清县城关西大路王大河工业区549号
邮编：350800
电话：0591-2237 3588
传真：0591-2237 5772
电邮：jindefu@163.com
网址：www.jindefu.com.cn

Godly Vegetable Diet Food Co., Ltd.
上海功德林素食品营销有限公司
上海市南京西路445号
邮编：200003
电话：021-3310 0700
传真：021-6372 0803
电邮：service@shgodly.com
网址：www.shgodly.com

Hung Yang Foods Co., Ltd.
弘阳食品股份有限公司
台湾省云林县四湖乡鹿场村下鹿场98号
电话：+886(5)-787 7779
传真：+886(5)-787 7000
电邮：tvp@hungyang.com.tw
网址：www.hungyang.com.tw

Tian-Su Food
天素食品
台湾省台中县清水镇秀水里海滨路178-33号
电话：+886(4)-2626 6296
传真：+886(4)-2627 7713
电邮：service@tiansu.com.tw
网址：www.tiansu.com.tw

上海齐善食品有限公司
上海市绥德路2弄7号甲
电话：021-6271 1454
传真：021-6608 0495
电邮：wqcywb@126.com
网址：www.shqsss.com

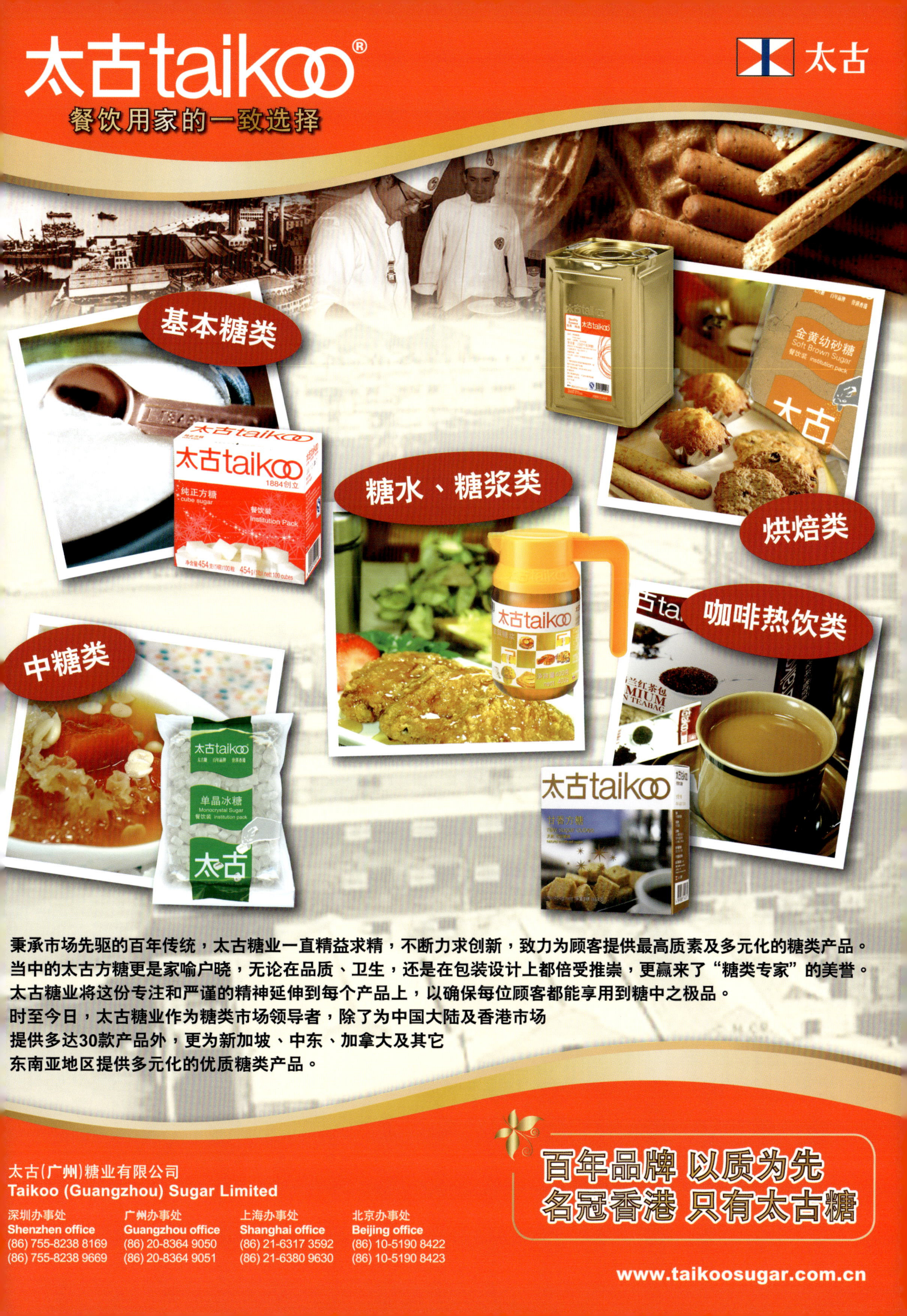

太古taikoo®
餐饮用家的一致选择
太古
基本糖类
太古taikoo
1884创立
纯正方糖
cube sugar
餐饮装
Institution Pack
糖水、糖浆类
烘焙类
金黄幼砂糖
Soft Brown Sugar
餐饮装 institution pack
咖啡热饮类
中糖类
单晶冰糖
Monocrystal Sugar
餐饮装 institution pack
秉承市场先驱的百年传统，太古糖业一直精益求精，不断力求创新，致力为顾客提供最高质素及多元化的糖类产品。
当中的太古方糖更是家喻户晓，无论在品质、卫生，还是在包装设计上都倍受推崇，更赢来了“糖类专家”的美誉。
太古糖业将这份专注和严谨的精神延伸到每个产品上，以确保每位顾客都能享用到糖中之极品。
时至今日，太古糖业作为糖类市场领导者，除了为中国大陆及香港市场
提供多达30款产品外，更为新加坡、中东、加拿大及其它
东南亚地区提供多元化的优质糖类产品。
太古(广州)糖业有限公司
Taikoo (Guangzhou) Sugar Limited
深圳办事处
Shenzhen office
(86) 755-8238 8169
(86) 755-8238 9669
广州办事处
Guangzhou office
(86) 20-8364 9050
(86) 20-8364 9051
上海办事处
Shanghai office
(86) 21-6317 3592
(86) 21-6380 9630
北京办事处
Beijing office
(86) 10-5190 8422
(86) 10-5190 8423
百年品牌 以质为先
名冠香港 只有太古糖
www.taikoosugar.com.cn

啤酒
Beer

Beijing Beer Asahi Co., Ltd.
北京啤酒朝日有限公司
北京市朝阳区建国路128号
中航工业大厦附楼三层301室
邮编：100022
电话：010-6567 7001
传真：010-6566 6885
电邮：beijingbeer2007@yahoo.com.cn
网址：www.beijingbeer.com.cn

Beijing Just Business & Trading Co., Ltd.
北京嘉思特商贸有限责任公司
北京市海淀区紫竹院路
人济山庄A栋（3号楼）104室
邮编：100048
电话：010-8855 6332
传真：010-8855 6307
电邮：just@just-mart.com
网址：www.just-mart.com

Beijing Yanjing Group Co., Ltd.
北京燕京啤酒集团公司
北京市顺义区双河路9号
邮编：101300
电话：010-8949 5588
传真：010-8949 5578
网址：www.yanjing.com.cn

Brief Introduction of Beijing Dewei Trade Co., Ltd.
北京德威贸易有限责任公司
北京市丰台区蒲方路9号院7号楼808室
邮编：100078
电话：010-5807 1741
传真：010-5807 1742
电邮：dwtd@163.com
网址：www.bjdewei.com.cn

China Resources Snow Breweries
华润雪花啤酒（中国）有限公司
北京市东城区建国门北大街8号华润大厦306室
邮编：100005
电话：010-6517 9898
网址：www.snowbeer.com.cn

Dewei Weimai Beer Trade (Beijing) Co., Ltd.
北京德威威麦啤酒销售有限公司
北京市丰台区方庄蒲方路9号院7号楼805/902室
邮编：100078
电话：010-5807 1788
传真：010-5807 1718
电邮：dewei_beer@163.com
网址：www.dwbeer.com

Jiangsu Grand Fortune Trade Co., Ltd.
江苏国富锦贸易有限公司
江苏省扬州市江阳中路433号
金天城国际商务中心6楼608室
电话：0514-8798 5738
传真：0514-8798 5385
网址：www.grandfortune.com

Shanghai Goldenage Internatinal Trade Co., Ltd.
上海锐雪国际贸易有限公司
上海市徐汇区斜土路1480弄33号706室
邮编：200032
电话：021-6418 0056
传真：021-6418 0247
电邮：info@goldenagechina.com

Shanghai Vineteria International Trading Co., Ltd.
上海维黎西国际贸易有限公司
上海市松江区文诚路358弄6号
嘉和商务中心1111室
电话：021-6775 2048
传真：021-6775 2048
电邮：xuemlee@gmail.com
网址：www.vineteria.cn

Shenzhen Yong Sheng Tai Business Co., Ltd.
深圳永盛泰商贸有限公司
深圳市深南东路2001号鸿昌广场1408室
电话：0755-2563 7079
传真：0755-2563 0494
电邮：oettinger-beer@163.com
网址：www.oettinger-beer.com.cn

Tsingtao Brewery Co., Ltd.
青岛啤酒松江有限公司
青岛香港中路五四广场青岛啤酒大厦
邮编：266071
电话：0532-8571 1119
传真：0532-8571 4719
电邮：info@tsingtao.com.cn
网址：www.tsingtao.com.cn

冷热饮品
Beverages-Hot & Cold

Hiangkie Coffee Group Limited
香记咖啡集团有限公司
香港九龙新蒲岗三祝街12-14号
荣森工业第二大厦3楼
电话：+852-3769 2345
传真：+852-2545 8917
电邮：enquiry@hiangkie.com.hk
网址：www.hiangkie.com.hk
请参阅第118、119页

Italian Coffee Company
美商 义式企业
上海市合川路3152号北楼2楼
邮编：201103
电话：021-6405 0475
传真：021-6405 0467
网址：www.italian-coffee-company.com

Oriental Foods Expert Ltd.
万福亚洲食品有限公司
香港柴湾新业街9号新业工业大厦9楼C及D室
电话：+852-2965 8828
传真：+852-3106 0211
电邮：sales@asiacurry.com
网址：www.asiacurry.com

Shanghai Wellgo Trading Co., Ltd.
源国贸易（上海）有限公司
上海市长宁区天山路600弄
思创大厦4号楼28楼C座
邮编：200051
电话：021-6233 5689
传真：021-6229 0629
电邮：sh_wellgo@126.com
网址：www.dilmahchina.com
请参阅第156页

Seng Pan Food Co., Ltd.
江门市诚品食品有限公司
广东省江门市新会区古井镇古泗村
邮编：529100
电话：0750-697 1188
传真：0750-697 1122
电邮：info@spcoffee.com
网址：www.spcoffee.com

Shanghai Walton Concepts Economic & Trading Co., Ltd.
上海和沁经贸有限公司
上海市闵行区虹许路731号3号楼3楼
邮编：201103
电话：021-6401 6449
传真：021-6401 3103
网址：www.waltonconcepts.com
请参阅第120页

果汁及糖浆
Fruit Juices & Syrups

1919 Italian Coffee Company
义久义久食品贸易（上海）有限公司
上海市闵行区合川路3152号北2楼
电话：021-6405 0475
传真：021-6405 0467
网址：www.italian-coffee-company.com

Awana Trading Co., Ltd.
东莞市阿瓦娜商贸有限公司
东莞市长安镇一环路中惠新城A区115号
电话：0769-8584 5575
传真：0769-8188 5859
电邮：info@awanacafe.com
网址：www.awanacafe.com

Beijing Fortunroad Limited Company
北京富臣路贸易有限公司
北京市朝阳区建国路88号
SOHO现代城6号楼3006室
电话：010-8580 8116
传真：010-8580 6215
电邮：fortuneroad@163.com
网址：www.fortuneroad.net

Beijing Huiyuan Beverage And Food Group Co., Ltd.
北京汇源饮料食品集团有限公司
北京市顺义区北小营镇汇源路
邮编：101305
电话：010-6048 3388
传真：010-6048 3366
电邮：hyweb@huiyuan.com.cn
网址：www.huiyuan.com.cn

▼果汁及糖浆
Fruit Juices & Syrups

Beijing Kingtai Tenhong Trade Co., Ltd.
北京市京泰天宏经贸有限责任公司
北京市朝阳区利泽中二路2号
望京科技创业园E座405C
邮编：100102
电话：010-8795 2371
传真：010-8795 2380
电邮：info@mycafe.com.cn
网址：www.mycafe.com.cn

Breakpoint Brands
北京市朝阳区东三环北路3号幸福大厦B座1320室
邮编：100027
电话：010-6465 4706
传真：010-6460 3881
电邮：info@breakpointbrands.com
网址：www.breakpointbrands.com

Darbo AG
Dornau 18, A-6135 Stans Tyrol, Austria
电话：+43-524 269 5145
传真：+43-524 269 5172
网址：www.darbo.com

Fresh Life (Kunshan) Foods Industry Co., Ltd.
鲜活实业（昆山）食品工业有限公司
江苏省昆山市玉山经济开发区鹿城路201号
邮编：215300
电话：0512-5751 5501
传真：0512-5751 5503
网址：www.sunjuice.com.cn

Greenjuice
格瑞果汁工业（天津）有限公司
天津市华苑产业园区（环外）海泰发展一路3号
邮编：300384
电话：022-8392 2891
传真：022-8392 2861
电邮：gj@juicegreen.com
网址：www.juicegreen.com

Guangdong Zhongtan Investment Co., Ltd.
广东中田投资有限公司
广州市寺右马路111号五羊新城广场1919-1923室
邮编：510600
电话：020-8738 0248
传真：020-8738 0243
网址：www.zt1919.com

Haitong Food Group Co., Ltd.
海通食品集团股份有限公司
浙江省慈溪市海通路528号
邮编：315300
电话：0574-6303 9988
传真：0574-6303 9898
电邮：kaiz@kaiz.com
网址：www.kaiz.com

Hiangkie Coffee Group Limited
香记咖啡集团有限公司
香港九龙新蒲岗三祝街12-14号
荣森工业第二大厦3楼
电话：+852-3769 2345
传真：+852-2545 8917
电邮：enquiry@hiangkie.com.hk
网址：www.hiangkie.com.hk
请参阅第118、119页

Italian Coffee Company
美商 义式企业
上海市合川路3152号北楼2楼
邮编：201103
电话：021-6405 0475
传真：021-6405 0467
网址：www.italian-coffee-company.com

Jiangsu Huaian Honest Food Co.
江苏淮安奥斯忒食品有限公司
江苏省淮安市楚州经济开发区山阳大道38号
电话：0517-8537 2158
传真：0517-8537 2198
网址：www.honestfood.net

Lingbao Xinyuan Fruit Industry Co., Ltd.
灵宝鑫源果业有限责任公司
河南省灵宝市北区工业园区振兴路中段
邮编：472500
电话：0398-863 9919
传真：0398-863 9916
电邮：lbfruit@126.com
网址：www.xyfruit.com

Mau Lin Food Co., Ltd.
茂霖食品股份有限公司
台湾台南市安南区科技五路157号（科技工业区）
电话：+886(6)-510 0599
传真：+886(6)-510 0598
电邮：linbio@ms28.hinet.net
网址：www.maulin.com.tw

Nongfu Spring
农夫山泉有限公司
浙江省杭州市曙光路148号
邮编：310007
电话：0571-8763 1888
传真：0571-8763 1218
网址：www.nongfuspring.com

Shandong Pomo Punica Juice Co., Ltd.
山东珀默珀尼卡果汁有限公司
山东省枣庄市峄城经济开发区福兴中路3号
电话：0632-518 6999
传真：0632-528 9966
网址：www.pomopunica.com

Shanghai Aobird Trade Co., Ltd.
上海聚鸟树贸易有限公司
上海市闵行区莘朱东路426号
邮编：201100
电话：021-6476 8117
传真：021-5430 6355
电邮：aobird2008@yahoo.com.cn
网址：www.aobird.com

Shanghai Creation Trading Co., Ltd.
上海开展贸易有限公司
上海市闵行区虹井路355号
邮编：201103
电话：021-3431 5789
传真：021-3431 1239
网址：www.creation-foods.com.cn

Shanghai Delthin Beverage Co., Ltd.
上海德馨饮品有限公司
上海市申南路59号泰弘研发园1号楼505室
电话：021-2281 8048
传真：021-2281 7843
网址：www.doehler.com.cn

Shanghai Lilian's Trading Company Limited
上海莲涟商贸有限公司
上海市长宁区天山支路201号703B室
电话：021-5206 8217
传真：021-5206 8217
网址：www.lilians.com.cn

Shanghai Walton Concepts Economic & Trading Co., Ltd.
上海和沁经贸有限公司
上海市闵行区虹许路731号3号楼3楼
邮编：201103
电话：021-6401 6449
传真：021-6401 3103
网址：www.waltonconcepts.com
请参阅第120页

Shenzhen Jin Jia Feng Trading Co., Ltd.
深圳市金嘉丰贸易有限公司
广东省深圳市福田区八卦四路5号
索泰克大厦4楼P区
邮编：518029
电话：0755-8247 0669
传真：0755-8205 5798
电邮：sales@milegacoffee.com
网址：www.cnjjf.com

Sino International Foods
信美达国际食品
深圳市福田区八卦路31号众鑫科技大厦901室
电话：0755-2588 7894
传真：0755-2588 7823
网址：www.sinoifoods.com

Tianjin Buyus International Incorporation
天津佰乐美商贸有限公司
天津新技术产业园区华苑产业区华天道8号
海泰信息广场F座南楼819室
邮编：300384
电话：022-2370 7382
传真：022-2370 8982
电邮：newtrans@newtransgroup.com
网址：www.buyus.com.cn

Tianjin Widecareer International Trade Co., Ltd.
天津广仕国际贸易有限公司
天津市河西区友谊北路
罗马花园2期戊座一栋1101室
邮编：300204
电话：022-2328 3382
传真：022-2324 4092
电邮：postmaster@widecareer.com
网址：www.widecareer.com

Young & Young International Beverages Ltd.
上海扬雅国际贸易有限公司
上海市石门二路333弄3号恒安大厦15楼A室
邮编：200041
电话：021-6255 0056
传真：021-6258 7187
电邮：jks@young-young.com.cn
网址：www.young-young.com.cn

大溪地诺丽饮料（中国）有限公司
上海市静安区南京西路819号1009室
邮编：200041
电话：021-6253 1199
传真：021-6253 6100
电邮：noni@cn.tni.com
网址：www.tahitiannoni.com.cn

▼果汁及糖浆
Fruit Juices & Syrups

康师傅控股有限公司
天津市经济技术开发区第三大街15号
电话：022-6686 8888
传真：022-6529 8080
电邮：info@tinghsin.com.cn
网址：www.masterkong.com.cn

上海茗晟食品有限公司
上海市松江区富荣经济区叶榭镇富园路5号
邮编：201609
电话：021-5780 3789
传真：021-5780 3620
网址：www.shmssp.com

奶类制品
Milk & Milk Products

Beijing Jikang Food Co., Ltd.
北京吉康食品有限公司
北京市昌平区崔村镇西辛峰工业区8区6号
邮编：102212
电话：010-6072 4247
传真：010-6072 4234
电邮：beijingjikang@yahoo.com.cn
网址：www.bjjikang.com

Beijing Sanyuan Foods Co., Ltd.
北京三元食品股份有限公司
北京市海淀区西二旗中路29号
邮编：100085
电话：010-6291 2266
传真：010-8241 3213
网址：www.sanyuan.com.cn

Bright Dairy & Food Co., Ltd.
光明乳业股份有限公司
上海市吴中路578号
邮编：200103
电话：021-5458 4520
传真：021-6465 4538
电邮：brightdairy@brightdairy.com
网址：www.brightdairy.com

Century Intl Trading Ltd.
大连保税区倍嘉国际贸易有限公司
大连市中山区港湾街2号深业大厦14层H座
电话：0411-8271 4762
传真：0411-8271 4952
电邮：beijia@century-intl.com
网址：www.century-intl.com

Fonterra Commercial Trading (Shanghai) Co., Ltd.
恒天然商贸（上海）有限公司
上海市卢湾区淮海中路300号
香港新世界大厦1502-03室
邮编：200021
电话：021-6133 5999
传真：021-6335 3966
电邮：albert.chen@fonterra.com
网址：www.fonterra.com

Guangdong Zhongtan Investment Co., Ltd.
广东中田投资有限公司
广州市寺右马路111号五羊新城广场1919-1923室
邮编：510600
电话：020-8738 0248
传真：020-8738 0243
网址：www.zt1919.com

Kangfulai Group (H.K.) Co., Ltd.
香港康福莱集团有限公司
青岛市东海西路43号凯旋大厦西塔20层
邮编：266071
电话：0532-8597 2306
传真：0532-8597 2338
电邮：info@kflgroup.com
网址：www.kflgroup.com

Suzhou Jiahe Foods Industry Co., Ltd.
苏州市佳禾食品工业有限公司
江苏省吴江市松陵友谊工业区五方路
邮编：215222
电话：0512-6349 7711
传真：0512-6349 7733
网址：www.kingflower.com

Tianjin Yayi Industrial Co., Ltd.
天津亚亿实业有限公司
天津市西青区中北工业园北园星光路9号
邮编：300384
电话：022-2798 4033
网址：www.milkgoat.com.cn

Want Want China Holdings Limited
中国旺旺控股有限公司
上海市红松东路1088号
邮编：201103
电话：021-6115 1111
传真：021-6115 1777
电邮：enquiry@want-want.com
网址：www.wantwant.com.cn

Yan Sheung Kee (Ming Kee) Coconut & Spices Co Ltd.
甄想记（明记）椰子香料有限公司
香港新界屯门青扬街1号
世纪城市工业大厦9楼A-D室
电话：+852-2468 2220
传真：+852-2436 1511
电邮：coconutboy@ysk-mk.com
网址：www.ysk-mk.cm
请参阅第109、153页、食品及饮料书隔页面页

大昌行集团有限公司
香港九龙湾启祥道20号大昌行集团大厦8楼
电话：+852-2768 3388
传真：+852-2796 8838
电邮：dch@dch.com.hk
网址：www.dch.com.hk

广东多乐乳业有限公司
广东省潮安县潮安大道西多乐工业城
邮编：515638
电话：0768-588 1377
传真：0768-588 3000
电邮：sales@gd-duole.com
网址：www.gd-duole.com

矿泉水
Mineral Water

Beijing Fortunroad Limited Company
北京富臣路贸易有限公司
北京市朝阳区建国路88号
SOHO现代城6号楼3006室
电话：010-8580 8116
传真：010-8580 6215
电邮：fortuneroad@163.com
网址：www.fortuneroad.net

Blue Sword Drink & Food Holding Co., Ltd.
蓝剑饮品集团
四川什邡蓝剑大道
邮编：618400
电话：028-8200 0099
传真：028-8782 5757
电邮：webmaster@bluesword.cn
网址：www.bluesword.cn

East Life Biotech Gorp.
东润水资源生技股份有限公司
台北市松江路237号12楼
电话：+886(2)-2516 2133
传真：+886(2)-2517 3380
电邮：service710m@dsw.com.tw
网址：www.dsw.com.tw

Fonte Sole Srl
Via Garibaldi, 1/A, Nuvolento, 25080, Brescia, Italy
电话：+39(0)-3068 98195
传真：+39(0)-3068 98193
电邮：export@solewater.it
网址：www.solewater.com

Goodwell China Marketing Service Co., Ltd.
大昌三昶（上海）商贸有限公司
上海市梅园路228号企业广场1901室
邮编：200070
电话：021-6487 6287
传真：021-6487 6159
网址：www.goodwellchina.com
请参阅第107页、封面

Guangzhou Fuen Chain Management Co., Ltd.
广州富恩企业管理有限公司
广州市珠江新城华强路3号
富丽盈利大厦南塔2216室
电话：020-3829 6002
传真：020-3829 6036
电邮：corrine_lam@139.com

Jebsen & Co. (Shanghai) Ltd.
捷成（中国）贸易有限公司上海分公司
上海市延安东路618号16楼
邮编：200001
电话：021-2306 4888
传真：021-2306 4999
网址：www.jebsenfinewines.com

Nongfu Spring
农夫山泉有限公司
浙江省杭州市曙光路148号
邮编：310007
电话：0571-8763 1888
传真：0571-8763 1218
网址：www.nongfuspring.com

Qingdao Laoshan Mineral Water Co., Ltd.
青岛崂山矿泉水有限公司
山东省青岛市东海西路15号英德隆大厦17层
邮编：266071
电话：0532-8386 4526
传真：0532-8387 3476
网址：www.laoshan.com.cn

金牌高达植脂淡奶
Evaporated Filled Milk

甄想記®

金牌高达罐装水果
Canned Fruits

甄想记(明记)椰子香料有限公司
Yan Sheung Kee(Ming Kee)Coconut & Spices Co Ltd.
香港新界屯门青扬街1号世纪城市工业大厦9楼A–D室
Flat A-D,9/F.,Century Industrial Building,No.1 Tsing Yeung Circuit,Tuen Mun,N.T.,Hong Kong
电话：852－24682220　传真：852－24361511
电邮：coconutboy@ysk-mk.com　网址：www.ysk-mk.com
国内免费咨询热线：8008 765 400

▼矿泉水
Mineral Water

Tianjin Widecareer International Trade Co., Ltd.
天津广仕国际贸易有限公司
天津市河西区友谊北路
罗马花园2期戊座一栋1101室
邮编：300204
电话：022-2328 3382
传真：022-2324 4092
电邮：postmaster@widecareer.com
网址：www.widecareer.com

康师傅控股有限公司
天津市经济技术开发区第三大街15号
电话：022-6686 8888
传真：022-6529 8080
电邮：info@tinghsin.com.cn
网址：www.masterkong.com.cn

米酒
Rice Wine

Huangshi Zhenzhuguo Food & Drink Co., Ltd.
黄石珍珠果食品饮料有限公司
湖北省黄石市洋浦路1号
邮编：435002
电话：0714-651 2668
传真：0714-652 2023
电邮：hszhenzhuguo@126.com
网址：www.zhenzhuguo.com

Hubei Xiaogan Sesame Chips & Rice Beverage Co., Ltd.
湖北孝感麻糖米酒有限责任公司
湖北省孝感市城隍潭9号
邮编：432100
电话：0712-282 2582
传真：0712-282 2582
电邮：mtmj@xgmtmj.com
网址：www.xgmtmj.com

Tonghua Tianze Rice Wine Brewsthe Co., Ltd.
通化天泽米酒酿造有限公司
吉林省通化县快大茂镇
邮编：134100
电话：0435-521 6161
传真：0435-521 6163
网址：www.thtzmj.com.cn

Zhuhuan black rice wine Co., Ltd.
陕西朱鹮黑米酒业有限公司
陕西省洋县纺织路1号
邮编：723300
电话：0916-821 9056
传真：0916-821 0969
电邮：web@chinahmj.com
网址：www.chinahmj.com

软饮料
Soft Drinks

Eastsign Foods (Quzhou) Co., Ltd.
易晓食品（衢州）有限公司
深圳市福田区深南中路6009号
绿景广场C座28楼I室
电话：0755-8296 8117
传真：0755-8296 8504
电邮：china@eastsign.com
网址：www.eastsign.cn

Shanghai Kingfood's Condiment Co., Ltd.
上海津丰食品有限公司
上海市黄浦区东街123号8楼
电话：021-6330 1867
传真：021-6330 1869
电邮：kingfoods@kingfoods.com.cn
网址：www.kingfoods.com.cn

Shanghai Wellgo Trading Co., Ltd.
源国贸易（上海）有限公司
上海市长宁区天山路600弄
思创大厦4号楼28楼C座
邮编：200051
电话：021-6233 5689
传真：021-6229 0629
电邮：sh_wellgo@126.com
网址：www.dilmahchina.com
请参阅第156页

Zhejiang Juicetown Drink Co., Ltd.
浙江聚仙庄饮品有限公司
浙江省仙居西炉杨梅基地
邮编：317300
电话：0576-8791 0666
电邮：sales@jxzwine.com
网址：www.jxzwine.com

茶
Tea

Awana Trading Co., Ltd.
东莞市阿瓦娜商贸有限公司
东莞市长安镇一环路中惠新城A区115号
电话：0769-8584 5575
传真：0769-8188 5859
电邮：info@awanacafe.com
网址：www.awanacafe.com

DKSH (China) Co., Ltd.
大昌华嘉商业（中国）有限公司
上海市浦东东方路710号汤臣金融大厦3楼
邮编：200122
电话：021-5830 0518
传真：021-5830 0519
网址：www.dksh.com

Eastsign Foods (Quzhou) Co., Ltd.
易晓食品（衢州）有限公司
深圳市福田区深南中路6009号
绿景广场C座28楼I室
电话：0755-8296 8117
传真：0755-8296 8504
电邮：china@eastsign.com
网址：www.eastsign.cn

Guangzhou Shang Dao Food Co., Ltd.
广州上岛食品有限公司
广州省广州市白云大道南荔枝园北路11号
电话：020-8619 5600
传真：020-8619 5260
网址：www.gzshangdao.com.cn

Hiangkie Coffee Group Limited
香记咖啡集团有限公司
香港九龙新蒲岗三祝街12-14号
荣森工业第二大厦3楼
电话：+852-3769 2345
传真：+852-2545 8917
电邮：enquiry@hiangkie.com.hk
网址：www.hiangkie.com.hk
请参阅第118、119页

Ho Fung Food Limited
浩丰食品有限公司
香港九龙新蒲岗大有街2号旺景工业大楼5楼D室
电话：+852-2353 0089
传真：+852-2325 2771
电邮：info@hofungtrading.com
网址：http://hofungtrading.com

Italian Coffee Company
美商 义式企业
上海市合川路3152号北楼2楼
邮编：201103
电话：021-6405 0475
传真：021-6405 0467
网址：www.italian-coffee-company.com

Jascaffe China Co., Ltd.
王力咖啡贸易（上海）有限公司
上海市松江区九亭镇盛龙路751号
邮编：201615
电话：021-3352 2299
传真：021-5206 8338
电邮：marketing@jascaffechina.com
网址：www.jascaffechina.com

Kanboo Agriculture (Zhangzhou) Co., Ltd.
康宝农业漳州有限公司
福建省龙海市角美镇龙江村口
电话：0596-677 8388
传真：0596-677 8389
网址：www.kanboo.com.cn

Rich Leend International Trade (Shanghai) Co., Ltd.
馥奇国际贸易（上海）有限公司
上海市徐汇区虹桥路808号加华商务中心D110室
电话：021-6448 1688
传真：021-6447 9055
电邮：services@goodteacoffee.com
网址：www.goodteacoffee.com

Shanghai Hamp Import & Export Trading Co., Ltd.
上海瀚普进出口贸易有限公司
上海市定西路1281号兆仪大厦1404室
邮编：200336
电话：021-5238 9957
传真：021-6240 0599
电邮：jane.yan@kellen-hamp.com.cn
网址：www.kellen-hamp.com.cn

Shanghai Walton Concepts Economic & Trading Co., Ltd.
上海和沁经贸有限公司
上海市闵行区虹许路731号3号楼3楼
邮编：201103
电话：021-6401 6449
传真：021-6401 3103
网址：www.waltonconcepts.com
请参阅第120页

Shanghai Wellgo Trading Co., Ltd.
源国贸易（上海）有限公司
上海市长宁区天山路600弄
思创大厦4号楼28楼C座
邮编：200051
电话：021-6233 5689
传真：021-6229 0629
电邮：sh_wellgo@126.com
网址：www.dilmahchina.com
请参阅第156页

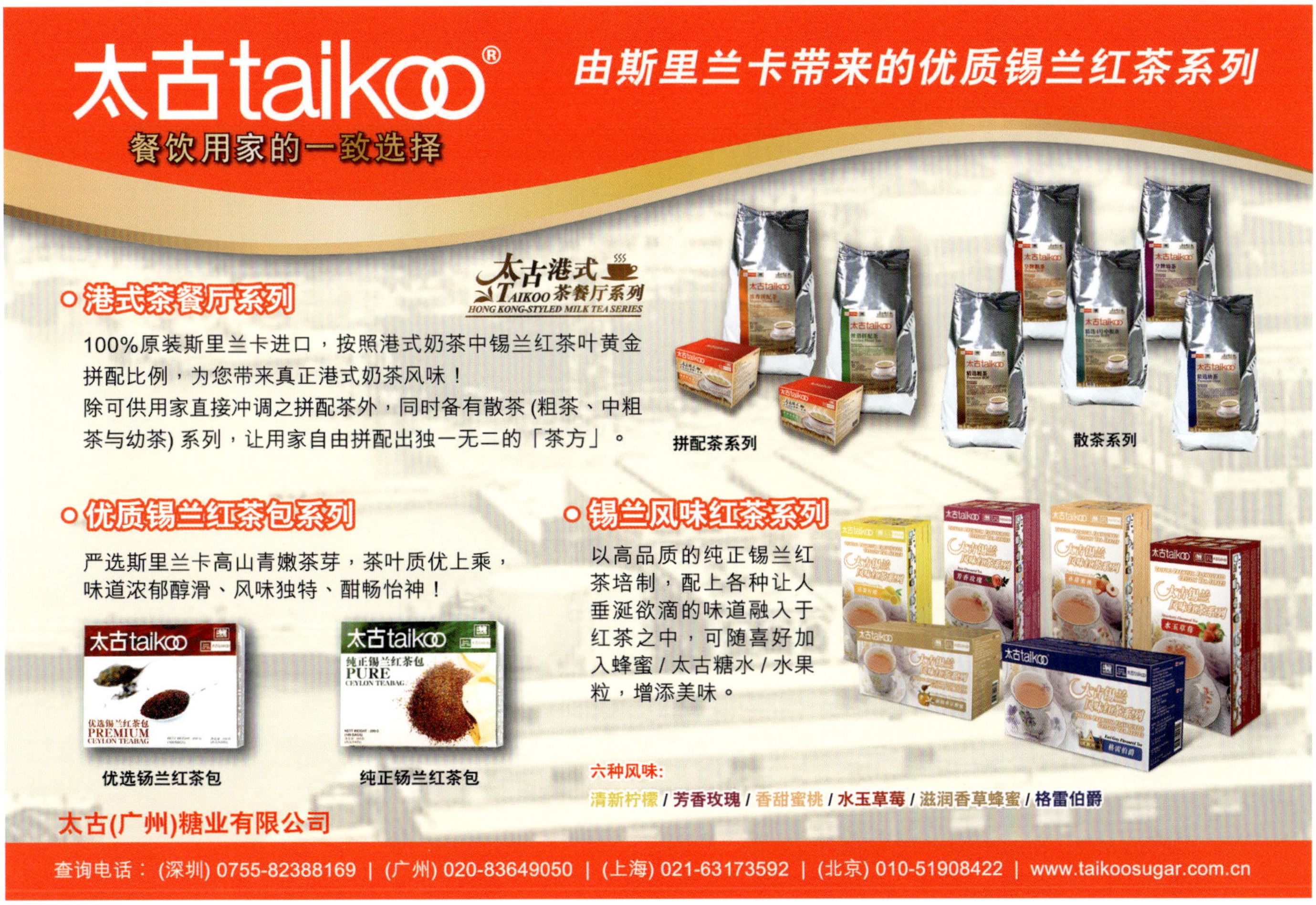

▼茶

Tea

Shanghai YongQiFeng Trading Co., Ltd.
上海永圻丰经贸有限公司
上海市静安区昌平路990号6号楼203室
电话：021-6232 2220
传真：021-6232 2216
电邮：lifehouse@lifehouse.com.cn
网址：www.lifehouse.com.cn

Shanghai Yuanyi Import & Export Co., Ltd.
上海远怡进出口有限公司
上海市浦东新区秀沿路1168弄3支弄230号
邮编：201315
电话：021-6819 6304
传真：021-6819 5007
电邮：yuanyi5588@163.com
网址：www.importfood.com.cn

Shenzhen Sun Tin Shing Coffee Co., Ltd.
深圳市新天成贸易有限公司
深圳市龙岗区布吉镇沙湾兴华路10号3楼
电话：0755-2852 0123
传真：0755-2852 0689
电邮：info@stscoffee.com
网址：www.stscoffee.com

Sino International Foods
信美达国际食品
深圳市福田区八卦路31号众鑫科技大厦901室
电话：0755-2588 7894
传真：0755-2588 7823
网址：www.sinoifoods.com

太古taikoo®

Taikoo (Guangzhou) Sugar Limited
太古（广州）糖业有限公司
广州市经济技术开发区锦绣路
明华一街穗兴工业大厦6号4楼
邮编：510730
电话：020-8364 9050
传真：020-8364 9051
电邮：info@taikoosugar.com
网址：www.taikoosugar.com.cn
业务范围：
太古（广州）糖业有限公司，母公司于1884年在香港成立，是国内有名的糖类供应商。为配合国内餐饮用家对优质茶类的需要，太古由斯里兰卡进口质优上乘的锡兰红茶，产品包括锡兰红茶包、锡兰风味红茶包（果味茶），以及为用家带来真正港式奶茶风味的“太古港式茶餐厅系列”除备有供用家直接冲调之拼配茶，还包括散茶（粗茶、中粗茶与幼茶）让用家自由拼配。太古更提供多款中国茶茶包，切合不同用家需要。
请参阅第149、155页

Tea Concepts Ltd.
Unit E, 11/F Kwong Ga Factory Building, 64 Victoria Road, Kennedy Town, Hong Kong SAR, China
电话：+852-2858 8973
传真：+852-2858 2044
电邮：info@tea-concepts.com
网址：www.tea-concepts.com

Wei-Ting Trading (Shanghai) Limited
上海香茵贸易有限公司
上海市闵行区颛兴东路745号2幢1楼
邮编：201108
电话：021-3462 5085
传真：021-3462 5087
网址：www.magnet.com.tw

广州均乾贸易有限公司
广州市海珠区福场路5号
B栋商务中心1902室
电话：020-3446 6097
传真：020-3446 6496
网址：www.gzjunqian.com

广州市白云区新市金棕榈咖啡贸易商行
广州市白云区增槎路969号
国鑫大厦508室
邮编：510000
电话：020-6119 0330
传真：020-6119 0331
网址：www.jinzonglv.com

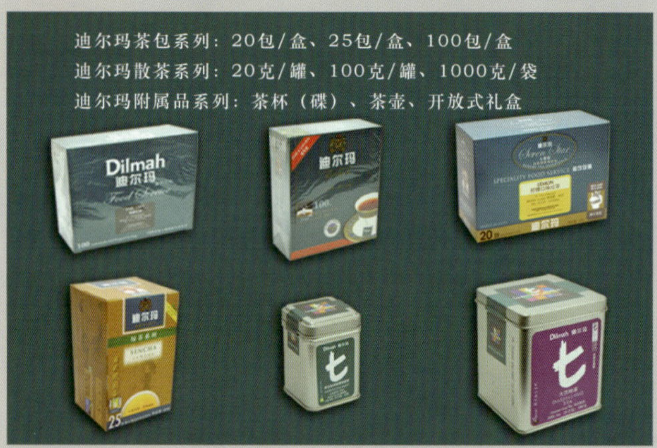

产品品质（QUALITY）

迪尔玛在各个方面都显示了自身的产品品质,从提供给客户的茶叶，到用来维持行业生产领军头衔的设备，到茶叶包装，到茶叶展会等。同时也是斯里兰卡第一家拥有HACCP认证的企业。

Every aspects of Dilmah is a manifestation of quality;beginning with the teas we offer our consumers, and extending to the equipment we use to maintain an industry-leading standard of manufacturing excellence, to our packaging, and presentation of our teas. We were the first company in Sri Lanka to receive HACCP certification.

传统（TRADITION）

迪尔玛拥有令人尊敬的悠久传统，作为饮料生产商，它的茶品已经有5000年的历史了。我们提供的茶是按照传统方法正规制作的。我们的子孙后代一直不断地完善着制茶工序。在迪尔玛，创新传统是值得尊敬的。此外，迪尔玛致力于保护这些传统，并通过公司的行业服务计划和MJF慈善机构将这些传统散播到世界各地。为了茶消费者的利益，迪尔玛公司一直寻求如何将自身发展成为锡兰最好的茶叶生产商。

Dilmah is respectful of the traditions of an industry that is centuries old, and of a beverage with a 5000 year history. The teas we offer are traditional and orthodox, made using a process perfected over generations. Innovations at Dilmah are respectful of these traditions and embody authenticity.

Dilmah is respectful of the traditions of an industry that is centuries old, and of a beverage with a 5000 year history. The teas we offer are traditional and orthodox, made using a process perfected over generations. Innovation at Dilmah are respectful of these traditions and embody authenticity.

道德（ETHICS）

迪尔玛是心存良知的品牌企业。作为天生的先锋者，迪尔玛在茶叶的世界里寻求公正，并通过自身的成功在锡兰茶行业领域为工人和其他相关人员带来利益。迪尔玛的成功促使MJF慈善机构为员工和社区带来笑容和欢乐。迪尔玛尊重自己的客户，遵循与客户相同的道德规范。我们与客户的交流是诚实和透明的。

Dilmah is a brand with a conscience, born a pioneer in seeking fairness in the world of tea, and benefiting the workers and others in the Ceylon Tea industry through its success. The activities of the MJF Charitable Foundatic in bringing a smile to the faces of our workers and the community are mad possible by Dilmah' s success. Dilmah applies the same ethics in respect o its customers. Customer communication is honest and transparent.

中国总代理

源国贸易（上海）有限公司

地址：上海市长宁区天山路600弄思创大厦四号楼28楼C座

电话：（86）21-62335689 62335699

传真：（86）21-62290629　邮编：200051

Email: sh_wellgo@126.com　网址：www.dilmahchina.com www.dilmahtea.com

酒
Wine

Andrew Barr
PO Box 1043, St Kilda South Victoria 3478, Australia
电话：+61(3)-9525 6715
传真：+61(3)-9531 3803
电邮：andrew@abwine.com.au
网址：www.abwine.com.au

Beijing Gold Luis Winery Co., Ltd.
北京金路易酒业有限公司
北京市东城区新中街18号阳光都市4号楼1106室
邮编：100027
电话：010-6415 3926
传真：010-6415 3926*805
电邮：goldenluis_wine@126.com
网址：www.goldenluis-wine.com

Hengshui Wolongquan Jiuye Youxian Gongsi
衡水卧龙泉酒业有限公司
河北省衡水市阜城县西环路168号
邮编：053700
电话：0318-466 9150
传真：0318-466 9599
电邮：wolongquan@vip.163.com
网址：www.wolongquan.com

Kinmen Kaoliang Liquor (Xiamen) Trading Co., Ltd.
金门酒厂（厦门）贸易有限公司
福建省厦门市湖滨南路90号立信广场1205室
电话：0592-559 4848
传真：0592-550 2554
网址：www.kkl.net.cn

Shanghai Kingfood's Condiment Co., Ltd.
上海津丰食品有限公司
上海市黄浦区东街123号8楼
电话：021-6330 1867
传真：021-6330 1869
电邮：kingfoods@kingfoods.com.cn
网址：www.kingfoods.com.cn

Shanghai Linghua Trading Co., Ltd.
上海领华贸易有限公司
上海市长宁区武夷路491弄14号201室
邮编：200050
电话：021-5239 4609
传真：021-5239 4608
网址：www.stuartwinesco.com.cn

Shanghai Terroir Wine Sales Co., Ltd.
上海泰勒瓦酒类销售有限公司
上海市浦东新区梅花路999弄24号
邮编：200127
电话：021-3876 2185
电邮：info@terroir.com.cn
网址：www.terroir.com.cn

Tibet Zangyuan Brewing Company Ltd.
西藏藏缘青稞酒业有限公司
西藏拉萨市达孜工业区
电话：0891-614 3888
传真：0891-614 3999
电邮：xzqingke@163.com
网址：www.qingkejiu.com.cn

Wuliangye Group
五粮液集团
四川省宜宾市岷江西路150号
邮编：644007
电话：0831-355 3988
传真：0831-355 2624
电邮：info@wuliangye.com.cn
网址：www.wuliangye.com.cn

Zhejiang Gu Yue Long Shan Shaoxing Wine Co.,Ltd.
浙江古越龙山绍兴酒股份有限公司
浙江省绍兴市北海桥
邮编：312000
电话：0575-8515 9019
传真：0575-8515 6989
电邮：hjjt@shaoxingwine.com.cn
网址：www.shaoxingwine.com.cn

Zhejiang Juicetown Drink Co., Ltd.
浙江聚仙庄饮品有限公司
浙江省仙居西炉杨梅基地
邮编：317300
电话：0576-8791 0666
电邮：sales@jxzwine.com
网址：www.jxzwine.com

贵州青酒集团有限责任公司
贵州省镇远县青溪镇
电话：0855-582 8088
电邮：qjwebmaster@gzqj.com
网址：www.gzqj.com

泸州御酒酒业有限公司
四川省泸州市福华王朝12楼
电话：0830-228 7854
传真：0830-228 6861
电邮：lzyj@lzyj.com
网址：www.lzyj.com

上海道真国际贸易有限公司
上海市共康路996号
邮编：200436
电话：021-5648 2856
传真：021-5648 2596
电邮：inf@windischwine.com
网址：www.windischwine.com

上海金枫酒业股份有限公司
上海市浦东新区张杨路579号（三鑫大厦）6楼
邮编：200120
电话：021-5081 2727
传真：021-5081 2727
电邮：jfjy@jinfengwine.com
网址：www.jinfengwine.com

葡萄酒及烈酒
Wine & Spirits

ABC Wines Ltd.
葡萄园有限公司
香港尖沙咀金巴利道27-33号永利大厦地下20号铺
电话：+852-2368 4684
传真：+852-2721 9799
电邮：abcwines@yahoo.com.hk
网址：www.abcwines.com.hk

Andrew Barr
PO Box 1043, St Kilda South Victoria 3478, Australia
电话：+61(3)-9525 6715
传真：+61(3)-9531 3803
电邮：andrew@abwine.com.au
网址：www.abwine.com.au

Aulon Wine Co., Ltd.
澳隆酒业（深圳）有限公司
广东省深圳市南山区
蛇口望海路南海玫瑰园32号商铺
电话：0755-2688 3381
传真：0755-2688 3380
网址：www.aulon.cn

Beijing Gold Luis Winery Co., Ltd.
北京金路易酒业有限公司
北京市东城区新中街18号阳光都市4号楼1106室
邮编：100027
电话：010-6415 3926
传真：010-6415 3926*805
电邮：goldenluis_wine@126.com
网址：www.goldenluis-wine.com

DKSH (China) Co., Ltd.
大昌华嘉商业（中国）有限公司
上海市浦东东方路710号汤臣金融大厦3楼
邮编：200122
电话：021-5830 0518
传真：021-5830 0519
网址：www.dksh.com

Jebsen & Co. (Shanghai) Ltd.
捷成（中国）贸易有限公司上海分公司
上海市延安东路618号16楼
邮编：200001
电话：021-2306 4888
传真：021-2306 4999
网址：www.jebsenfinewines.com

Jiangsu Grand Fortune Trade Co., Ltd.
江苏国富锦贸易有限公司
江苏省扬州市江阳中路433号
金天城国际商务中心6楼608室
电话：0514-8798 5738
传真：0514-8798 5385
网址：www.grandfortune.com

Macao Yue Man Foods Trading Company Limited
澳门裕民食品贸易有限公司
澳门台山华大新村第二街7号地下
电话：+853-2843 9697
传真：+853-2843 9697
请参阅第159页

Rich Leader (HK) Ltd.
领富（香港）有限公司
香港九龙长沙湾永康街29-33号
兆威工业中心12楼5室
电话：+852-2669 2148
传真：+852-2669 2149
电邮：ericwine@163.com
网址：www.richleader.hk

Shaanxi Italuck Trading Company Ltd.
陕西意生贸易有限责任公司
陕西省西安市新城区西一路138号
中贸国际大厦8楼D座
电话：021-3616 0856
传真：021-3616 2281
电邮：italuck@gmail.com
网址：www.lorence.hk
请参阅第143页

Shang Hai Sino-drink Ltd.
上海华饮贸易有限公司
上海市定西路1100号辽油大厦8楼K座
邮编：200050
电话：021-6226 7586
传真：021-6226 7583
电邮：sinodrink@gmail.com
网址：www.sino-drink.com

▼葡萄酒及烈酒

Wine & Spirits

Shanghai Chuxiao International Trade Co., Ltd.
上海楚啸贸易有限公司
上海市凯旋路1415号507-509室
邮编：200052
电话：021-6280 5580
传真：021-6280 6647
电邮：zpjiang@chuxiao.com.cn
网址：www.chuxiao.com.cn

Shanghai Ruby Red Fine Wine Co., Ltd.
上海红樽坊贸易有限公司
上海市长宁区天山路1718号
时尚园3号楼A座一层101室
电话：021-6234 2249
传真：021-6234 3031
电邮：info@rubyred.com.cn
网址：www.rubyred.com.cn

Shanghai Standard Intl Trading Inc.
上海思根达国际贸易有限公司
上海市松江区泗陈公路云顶别墅388号79幢
邮编：201601
电话：021-5761 1899
传真：021-5761 1866
电邮：sales@stdintl.com
网址：www.stdintl.com

Shanghai Touchroad International Trading Ltd.
上海达之路国际贸易有限公司
上海市浦东新区新金桥路58号银东大厦28C
电话：021-5030 7948
传真：021-5030 7947
电邮：touchroadsh@touchroad.com
网址：www.touchroad.com

Shanghai Vins Selection Co., Ltd.
上海圣地美琼葡萄酒有限公司
上海市普陀区中江路106号北岸长风I栋408室
电话：021-3255 2268
传真：021-3255 2269
电邮：marketing@vins-selection.com.cn
网址：www.vins-selection.com.cn

Shenzhen Sicao Electric Appliances Co., Ltd.
深圳市新潮电器有限公司
深圳市罗湖区嘉宾路2018号深华商业大厦13-14层
邮编：518001
电话：0755-8237 5212
传真：0755-2219 1799
网址：www.sicao.cn
请参阅第254页

Sino-French Joint-Venture Dynasty Winery Ltd.
中法合营王朝葡萄酿酒有限公司
天津市北辰区津围公路29号
邮编：300402
电话：022-2699 8888
传真：022-2699 0996
网址：www.dynasty.com.cn

The Champagne House
Room 1603 Horizon Plaza
2 Lee Wing Street, Ap Lei Chau
Hong Kong
电话：+852-2525 3899
传真：+852-2877 2131
电邮：sales@thechampagnehouse.com.hk
网址：www.thechampagnehouse.com.hk

Thiasos Trading Company Limited
广州泰亚氏贸易有限公司
广东省广州市越秀区东风西路132号之一1507房
邮编：510170
电话：020-8137 8860
传真：020-8137 8870
电邮：info@thiasosgroup.com
网址：www.thiasosgroup.com

Winpo Asia Limited
维宝亚洲有限公司
香港葵涌健康街18号恒亚中心10楼1006-7室
电话：+852-2423 8863
传真：+852-2423 3680
电邮：info@winpoasia.com
网址：www.winpoasia.com

法国S&T欧亚贸易公司
传真：+33-4133 36818
网址：www.steurochina.over-blog.com
www.la-martiniquaise.fr
请参阅本页

上海岑汇酒业有限公司
上海市虬江路1000号1304室
电话：021-3633 7106
传真：021-3633 7100
网址：www.solus-life.com.cn

上海朗克酒业有限公司
上海市中山南一路500弄1号楼丽都大厦31C座
电话：021-5301 8995
传真：021-6301 2598
电邮：mont-tauch@lengdok.com
网址：www.lengdok.com
请参阅第160页

西班牙阿拉贡酒庄

BODEGAS ARAGONESAS, S.A., SPAIN

阿拉贡Aragon是西班牙东北部的一个自治区，向北与法国相邻，向西与著名的葡萄酒产区里奥哈相邻。这里有四个DO等级法定产酒区——博尔哈田园乡Campo de Borja、卡拉塔玉德Calatayud、卡里涅纳Carinena和索蒙塔诺Somontano。

阿拉贡酒庄 Bodegas Aragonesas 属于博尔哈田园乡产区的一部分，位于比利牛斯山脉南部山脚和伊比利亚山脉北部下面的山谷，分享里奥哈与纳瓦拉产区的土地，因此土地本身的质量和气候形成种植葡萄的优势地带。

我们的葡萄酒来自3500公顷的葡萄园，年生产约1200万公斤葡萄，平均每年的酿造能力为150万升，是整个产区生产总量的65%。

我们的成功并非出于偶然，如果说，我们酿酒师和技术人员的工作非常出色，葡萄园的种植者也不例外，每天都有上百人悉心并严谨地照料着葡萄园，正是对葡萄园的精心改造和维护才使我们能生产出市场上最好的歌海娜葡萄酒。

葡萄园是我们最重要的资产，特别是那些歌海娜葡萄，就它们的古老程度、数量与质量可能是世界上独一无二的。

• 西班牙原瓶原装进口 •

中国内地、香港、澳门总代理

澳門裕民食品貿易有限公司

Macao Yue Man Foods Trading Company Limited

地址：澳門台山華大新村第二街7號地下　電話：(853)28439697

AMMEX
净手凝露

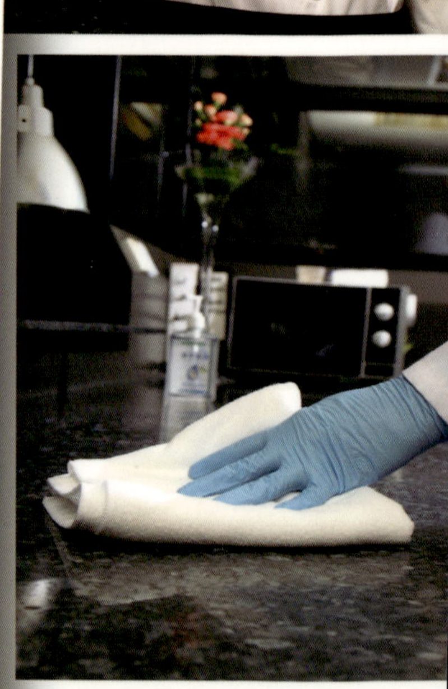

厨房、餐厅及酒吧设备
Kitchen, Restaurant & Bar Equipment

烘焙设备
Bakery Equipment

Guangzhou Baiyun District Hongtai Baking Factory
广州市白云区宏泰烘焙设备厂
广东省广州市白云区均禾街长红村双和庄工业区
邮编：510540
电话：020-8631 2128
传真：020-8631 2138
电邮：info@hongtai100.com
网址：www.hongtai100.com

Guangzhou Brandon Equipment Manufacturing Co., Ltd.
广州展卓商用设备制造有限公司
广东省广州市番禺区石基镇塱边村
企岭工业区1号D、E栋
邮编：511450
电话：020-8455 9510
传真：020-8455 6321
电邮：enquiry@brandonequipment.com
网址：www.brandonequipment.com

Guangzhou ChengGong Baking Machinery Co., Ltd.
广州市番禺成功烘焙设备有限公司
广州市番禺区石基镇文边村文坑路北侧3号
邮编：511450
电话：020-3488 2611
传真：020-8455 0862
电邮：guangzhoucg@163.com
网址：www.gzchenggong.com

Guangzhou Oongmai Baking Food Machinery Manufactur Co., Ltd.
广州市容麦烘焙食品机械制造有限公司
广州市番禺区东涌镇鱼窝头长莫工业区
邮编：511476
电话：020-3491 7123
传真：020-3491 9123
网址：www.rmachinery.net.cn

Guangzhou Sage Kitchen Equipment Co., Ltd.
广州市胜捷厨房设备有限公司
广东省广州市花都区芙蓉镇旗新村龙蚌路
邮编：510860
电话：020-8698 0468
传真：020-8698 0606
电邮：service@cn-sage.com
网址：www.cn-sage.com

Guangzhou SaiMai Food Machinert Co., Ltd.
广州赛麦机械设备有限公司
广州市黄埔区双沙工业区信华路163号
四合成协同大厦
电话：020-8239 7910
传真：020-8239 2808
网址：www.gzsaimai.com

Hangzhou Kator Foreign Trade Co., Ltd.
杭州凯特对外贸易有限公司
杭州市萧山区经济技术开发区建设四路8号
邮编：311215
电话：0571-8289 6288
传真：0571-8289 6711
电邮：sales@h-kitchen.com
网址：www.h-kitchen.com

Hebei Longmai Foodstuff Machinery Co., Ltd.
河北龙麦食品机械有限公司
河北省安平县胡林工业开发区
电话：0318-702 8578
传真：0318-786 1738
电邮：hblm@hblongmai.com
网址：www.hblongmai.com

Hong Kong Food Machinery Co., Ltd.
香港食品机械有限公司
香港柴湾祥利街18号祥达中心11楼7-8室
电话：+852-2556 0099
传真：+852-2897 3132
网址：www.hkfm.com.hk

Irinox SPA
Via Madonna Di Loreto 6/B, 31020 Corbanese Di Tarzo Treviso Italy
电话：+39-0438 5844
传真：+39-0438 5843
电邮：irinox@irinox.com
网址：www.irinox.com

JetCool Commetcial Refrigeration Company
骏宝商用设备公司
JetCool House
136 Sung Shan New Village, Yuen Long
N.T., Hong Kong
电话：+852-2442 1108
传真：+852-2442 1155
电邮：info@jetcool.com.hk
网址：www.jetcool.com.hk

JiaDe (Zhongshan) Food Machinery Co., Ltd.
佳德（中山）食品机械有限公司
广东中山市东升镇广福大道27号
邮编：528414
电话：0760-2222 3901
传真：0760-2222 3902
网址：www.jiadezs.com.cn

Kolb HK Ltd.
瑞士高比（香港）有限公司
香港九龙观塘开源道55号开联工业中心B座201室
电话：+852-2516 6093
传真：+852-2516 6518
电邮：rgeisser@kolb-hk.com
网址：www.kolb-hk.com

Linkrich Machinery Development Co., Ltd.
广州中联盈机械有限公司
广州市东风东路699号
之十三广东港澳中心3505-3506室
邮编：510080
电话：020-8760 1850
传真：020-8760 7453
电邮：info@chinalinkrich.com
网址：www.chinalinkrich.com

Middleby China Corporation
美得彼餐饮设备（上海）有限公司
上海市松江区九亭镇久富经济开发区盛高路98号
邮编：201615
电话：021-6769 0808
传真：021-6762 7640
电邮：mandyzhang@middleby.com.cn
网址：www.middleby.com
请参阅第174、175页

Shanghai Furong Industry Co., Ltd.
上海芙蓉实业有限公司
上海市闵行区浦江工业区竹园路268号
邮编：201112
电话：021-5431 1051
传真：021-5431 1052
电邮：furong@furong.com
网址：www.furong.com

Shanghai Hocres Hotel Equipment & Accessories Co., Ltd.
上海海客瑞斯酒店用品有限公司
上海市华徐公路888号
邮编：201702
电话：021-6976 5065
传真：021-5986 1696
网址：www.hocres.com

Shanghai J&C Industry Co., Ltd.
上海积创实业发展有限公司
上海市黄兴路1725号怡富商务广场1701/1706室
邮编：200433
电话：021-6587 6136
传真：021-6587 6134
网址：www.jichuang.net.cn

Shanghai JinCheng Refrigerating Equipment Co., Ltd.
上海金城制冷设备有限公司
上海市中山北路3357号
邮编：200062
电话：021-6216 8066
传真：021-6216 8070
电邮：jincheng@shkingdom.com.cn
网址：www.shkingdom.com.cn
请参阅第225页

Shanghai Unitech Food Machinery Company
上海台新食品机械有限公司
上海市万航渡路888号开开大厦26楼A座
邮编：200051
电话：021-6240 0595
电邮：unitech-sh@unitech-sh.com
网址：www.unitech-sh.com

Shenzhen Sweeda Food Equipment Co., Ltd.
深圳市斯瑞达食品设备有限公司
深圳市人民南路深房广场A座2501室
电话：0755-8229 6022
传真：0755-8229 6122
电邮：market@sweeda.com
网址：www.sweeda.com

Simplex Foodservice Equipment (Shanghai) Ltd.
新必利餐饮设备（上海）有限公司
上海市松江区九亭镇涞坊路57号
邮编：201615
电话：021-6784 1311
传真：021-6784 1331
电邮：simplex@online.sh.cn
网址：www.simplex.cn

Southstar Machinery Facilities Co., Ltd.
广州赛思达机械设备有限公司
广州市白云区竹料新广从四路88号
邮编：510545
电话：020-8748 0152
传真：020-8748 1803
电邮：master@xinnanfang.com
网址：www.southstar.cc

Sveba-Dahlen (China) Ltd.
瑞典烘焙设备（中国）有限公司
香港柴湾康民街2号康民工业中心1805室
电话：+852-2558 2293
传真：+852-2558 2089
电邮：wfy@sveba-dahlenchina.hk
网址：www.sveba-dahlenchina.com

▼烘焙设备
Bakery Equipment

THUNDERBIRD®
加拿大雷鸟牌

Thunderbird Food Machinery Co., Ltd.
德霸食品机械有限公司
上海市松江区欣玉路453弄1-5号4D
邮编：201600
电话：021-5773 6845
传真：021-5773 6093
电邮：tbfmsh@tbfmcn.com.cn
网址：www.tbfmcn.com.cn
请参阅第163页

Williams Refrigeration (Dongguan) Co., Ltd.
威廉士制冷设备（东莞）有限公司
上海市卢湾区打浦路1号金玉兰广场西峰703室
邮编：200023
电话：021-5396 0183
传真：021-5396 1335
网址：www.agafoodservice.com

Wuxi Homat Bakery Equipment Co., Ltd.
无锡好麦机械有限公司
江苏省无锡市新区梅村新泰工业园锡鸿路26号
邮编：214028
电话：0510-8855 1618
传真：0510-8855 1518
网址：www.homatbakery.cn.alibaba.com

Wuxi Shuangmai Bakery Equipment Co., Ltd.
无锡市双麦机械有限公司
无锡市锡山区私营工业园北区蓉强路2号
邮编：214192
电话：0510-8826 5977
传真：0510-8826 6877
电邮：wuxishuangmai@163.com
网址：www.wxsmjx.com

北京经开万佳国际酒店用品市场
北京市朝阳区南四环东路十八里店
南桥吕家营商业街1号
邮编：100023
电话：010-8769 8883
传真：010-8769 7773
网址：www.bjjkwj.com

久景制冷设备（上海）有限公司
上海市赵重公路1978号
电话：021-3987 6601
传真：021-3987 6501
电邮：niu@hisakage.com
网址：www.hisakage.com
请参阅第197页

烧烤设备
Barbecue Equipment

Afehc - Spanish Exporting Manufacturers Association For The Hospitality Industry
西班牙餐饮及团体用具生产及出口商协会
Rambla Catalunya 81, 5-3
08008 Barcelona
Spain
电话：+34(93)-487 3290
传真：+34(93)-487 0770
电邮：afehc@afehc.com
网址：www.afehc.com
请参阅第36页

CSPS Metal Co., Ltd.
江井金属股份有限公司
No.96, Sec.3, Yunke Road, Douliu City, Yunlin County 64064, Taiwan R.O.C
电话：+886(5)-551 0777
传真：+886(5)-551 9339
电邮：sales@cspsmetal.com
网址：www.cspsmetal.com

China Manufacturing Solutions Ltd.
中国传盛商用设备
山东省潍城经济开发区彩虹路与卧龙西街路口
电话：0536-610 5299
电邮：pan@chmans.com
网址：www.chmans.com
请参阅第182页

Fagor Industrial China
法格厨房设备（昆山）有限公司
江苏省昆山市千灯镇西班牙工业园区
邮编：215341
电话：0512-5515 5605
传真：0512-5515 5610
电邮：fagorchina@fagorindustrial.com
网址：www.fagorindustrial.cn

Fancy Industrial Technology (Kunshan) Co., Ltd.
芳成金属科技（昆山）有限公司
江苏省昆山市周市镇友谊北路92号
邮编：215313
电话：0512-5510 1818
传真：0512-5510 3111
网址：www.fancyindus.com

Foshan Nanhai Flamemax Catering Equipment Co., Ltd.
佛山市南海烽煌餐饮设备制造有限公司
广东省佛山市南海区里水镇赤山福西工业区5号
电话：0757-8561 6586
传真：0757-8561 6589
网址：www.flamemax.com

Jin Shi Kang Cookroom Equipment Co., Ltd.
深圳市金适康商厨电器有限公司
广东省深圳市罗湖区金碧路33号
电话：0755-8240 1095
传真：0755-8240 1154
电邮：ksk2008good@163.com
网址：www.ksk2008.com

Liaoning Tianhu Brewery Co., Ltd.
辽阳野田金属制品有限公司
辽宁省辽阳市宏伟区宏伟路45号
邮编：111000
电话：0419-315 9155
传真：0419-315 9255
电邮：5302710@163.com
网址：www.nodahappy.com.cn

Middleby China Corporation
美得彼餐饮设备（上海）有限公司
上海市松江区九亭镇久富经济开发区盛高路98号
邮编：201615
电话：021-6769 0808
传真：021-6762 7640
电邮：mandyzhang@middleby.com.cn
网址：www.middleby.com
请参阅第174、175页

Shanghai Chuanglv Hotel Equipment Co., Ltd.
上海创绿酒店设备有限公司
上海市浦东三灶工业园区宣春路253号
邮编：201300
电话：021-5803 8665
传真：021-5803 3433
电邮：webmaster@tiebanshao.com
网址：www.tiebanshao.com

Shanghai J&C Industry Co., Ltd.
上海积创实业发展有限公司
上海市黄兴路1725号怡富商务广场1701/1706室
邮编：200433
电话：021-6587 6136
传真：021-6587 6134
网址：www.jichuang.net.cn

Southstar Machinery Facilities Co., Ltd.
广州赛思达机械设备有限公司
广州市白云区竹料新广从四路88号
邮编：510545
电话：020-8748 0152
传真：020-8748 1803
电邮：master@xinnanfang.com
网址：www.southstar.cc

YiXi Brand Foods Stuff Processing Machineries
一喜牌食品加工机械
浙江省瑞安市飞云镇（东风）开发区友谊路2号
电话：0577-6556 2998
传真：0577-6557 3196
电邮：wzyixi@126.com
网址：www.yixi.com.cn

搅拌器
Blenders

Electrolux Professional (Shanghai) Co., Ltd.
伊莱克斯商用电器（上海）有限公司
上海市外高桥保税区爱都路390号31号楼A座
邮编：200131
电话：021-5046 0099
传真：021-5046 0077
网址：www.electrolux-professional.cn
请参阅第168页

Keepsun Electrical (Guangzhou) Co., Ltd.
广州市祈和电器有限公司
广州市番禺区大石街石北工业大道
会江村丰晟工业园C栋1-3层
电话：020-3925 2833
传真：020-3925 2116
电邮：info@keepwarm.com.cn
网址：www.keepwarm.com.cn

Oriental Engineering Company Limited
华捷洋行有限公司
香港九龙马头围道21号义达工业大厦A座二楼
电话：+852-2333 0181
传真：+852-2764 1605
电邮：sales@oriental-eng.com.hk
网址：www.oequip.com

Shunde Fontion Electrical Appliances Co., Ltd.
佛山市顺德区方胜电器实业有限公司
广东省佛山市顺德区杏棠工业区科技区10路3号
邮编：528305
电话：0757-2839 8512
传真：0757-2839 1315
电邮：ad8393212_sdb@21cn.net
网址：www.fontion.cn

▼搅拌器 Blenders

Simplex Foodservice Equipment (Shanghai) Ltd.
新必利餐饮设备（上海）有限公司
上海市松江区九亭镇涞坊路57号
邮编：201615
电话：021-6784 1311
传真：021-6784 1331
电邮：simplex@online.sh.cn
网址：www.simplex.cn

Sunny Trading Company
阳光贸易公司
香港九龙观塘兴业街16号
美兴工业大厦B座10楼11室
电话：+852-2343 2943
传真：+852-2343 4459
电邮：info@sunnytrading.com
网址：www.sunnytrading.com

Thunderbird Food Machinery Co., Ltd.
德霸食品机械有限公司
上海市松江区欣玉路453弄1-5号4D
邮编：201600
电话：021-5773 6845
传真：021-5773 6093
电邮：tbfmsh@tbfmcn.com.cn
网址：www.tbfmcn.com.cn
请参阅第163页

Zhongshan Haipan Electtical Appliances Co., Ltd.
中山市海盘电器有限公司
广东省中山市东凤镇同乐工业园
邮编：528425
电话：0760-2263 9011
传真：0760-2263 9066
电邮：shanliang88@vip.163.com
网址：www.gzshanliang.com

佛山市顺德区金日电器实业有限公司
广东省顺德区容桂华口新德路1号
电话：0757-2839 0600
传真：0757-2837 1606
电邮：caina@vip.163.com
网址：www.sdcaina.com

糕点制作设备 Cake Making Equipment

Hebei Longmai Foodstuff Machinery Co., Ltd.
河北龙麦食品机械有限公司
河北省安平县胡林工业开发区
电话：0318-702 8578
传真：0318-786 1738
电邮：hblm@hblongmai.com
网址：www.hblongmai.com

Irinox SPA
Via Madonna Di Loreto 6/B, 31020 Corbanese Di Tarzo Treviso Italy
电话：+39-0438 5844
传真：+39-0438 5843
电邮：irinox@irinox.com
网址：www.irinox.com

Shenzhen Sweeda Food Equipment Co., Ltd.
深圳市斯瑞达食品设备有限公司
深圳市人民南路深房广场A座2501室
电话：0755-8229 6022
传真：0755-8229 6122
电邮：market@sweeda.com
网址：www.sweeda.com

Southern Machine Manufacture Co., Ltd.
无锡南方机械制造有限责任公司
江苏省无锡市洛社人民南路38号
邮编：214187
电话：0510-8331 1143
传真：0510-8331 1428
电邮：sales@nfjx.com
网址：www.nfjx.com

Thunderbird Food Machinery Co., Ltd.
德霸食品机械有限公司
上海市松江区欣玉路453弄1-5号4D
邮编：201600
电话：021-5773 6845
传真：021-5773 6093
电邮：tbfmsh@tbfmcn.com.cn
网址：www.tbfmcn.com.cn
请参阅第163页

广州九阳酒店用品
广州市番禺区沙溪恒生市场北区六街19号
电话：020-3452 9551
传真：020-3452 9760
电邮：jayanmg@163.com
网址：www.jayanmg.com

糖果模具 Candy Moulds

Rifeng Hardware And Mould Making Co., Ltd.
东莞市日锋五金模具制品有限公司
广东省东莞市石碣镇黄泗围工业区
邮编：523296
电话：0769-8633 7192
传真：0769-8632 2198
电邮：ri28@ri28.com
网址：www.ri28.com

San Neng (Wuxi) Bake Ware Co., Ltd.
三能器具（无锡）有限公司
江苏省无锡市锡山经济开发区友谊北路316号
邮编：214191
电话：0510-8377 7515
传真：0510-8377 5476
电邮：yewu@wxsanneng.com
网址：www.wxsanneng.com

Shanghai Xinxings Food Mould Co., Ltd.
上海新星食品模具有限公司
上海市宁波路289号
电话：021-6322 5888
传真：021-6322 5602
电邮：mould@xinxings.com
网址：www.xinxings.com

江苏省新沂市中益糖果模具厂
江苏省新沂市郯新路186号
邮编：221000
电话：0516-8881 5292
传真：0516-8806 7486
电邮：zymjc0216@126.com
网址：www.zymjc.cn

大型厨房设备 Catering Equipment

Afehc - Spanish Exporting Manufacturers Association For The Hospitality Industry
西班牙餐饮及团体用具生产及出口商协会
Rambla Catalunya 81, 5-3
08008 Barcelona
Spain
电话：+34(93)-487 3290
传真：+34(93)-487 0770
电邮：afehc@afehc.com
网址：www.afehc.com
请参阅第 36 页

Angelo Po Trading (Shanghai)
傲桀贸易（上海）有限公司
上海市江场三路88号一楼
邮编：200436
电话：021-6094 0100
传真：021-6094 0288
电邮：info@angelopo.cn
网址：www.angelopo.it
请参阅第 167、195 页、封面

Cambro Manufacturing Company
惠州勤宝商业有限公司
广东省惠州市麦地路一号风尚国际18楼A座
邮编：516001
电话：0752-238 7033
传真：0752-238 7019
网址：www.cambro.com

China Manufacturing Solutions Ltd.
中国传盛商用设备
山东省潍城经济开发区彩虹路与卧龙西街路口
电话：0536-610 5299
电邮：pan@chmans.com
网址：www.chmans.com
请参阅第 182 页

Chinducs Technology (Ningbo) Co., Ltd.
华磁科技（宁波）有限公司
宁波市鄞州区望春工业园秋实路350号
邮编：315153
电话：0574-8826 6898
传真：0574-8844 3000
电邮：chinducs@hotmail.com
网址：www.chinducs.com.cn

SANYO

Dalian Sanyo Cold Chain Co., Ltd.
大连三洋冷链有限公司
大连经济技术开发区松岚街6号
电邮：gezhifei@163.com
网址：www.dalian-sanyo.com.cn
业务范围：
我公司2011年下半年强势推出四个系列商用厨房冷柜。分别是：
1. 专为连锁餐饮的高温高湿厨房环境开发的ES变频风冷商用冷柜，节能率达到25-35%，每台年节约电费1200-1800元
2. 为外资高端酒店开发的GN风冷系列
3. 为内资高端酒店开发的FC风冷系列
4. 为经济型用户开发的NC直冷系列产品。产品线空前丰富，专注中高端市场。给我们机会，我们为您创造商机无限！
华东营销中心 电话：021-6160 9151
华南营销中心 电话：0755-8329 9353
华北营销中心 电话：010-6418 1938
东北营销中心 电话：0411-8252 6021
请参阅总目录书隔页面页

Thinking of you
Electrolux

Electrolux Professional (Shanghai) Co., Ltd.
伊莱克斯商用电器（上海）有限公司
上海市外高桥保税区爱都路390号31号楼A座
邮编：200131
电话：021-5046 0099
传真：021-5046 0077
网址：www.electrolux-professional.cn
请参阅第 168 页

Fagor Industrial China
法格厨房设备（昆山）有限公司
江苏省昆山市千灯镇西班牙工业园区
邮编：215341
电话：0512-5515 5605
传真：0512-5515 5610
电邮：fagorchina@fagorindustrial.com
网址：www.fagorindustrial.cn

Fancy Industrial Technology (Kunshan) Co., Ltd.
芳成金属科技（昆山）有限公司
江苏省昆山市周市镇友谊北路92号
邮编：215313
电话：0512-5510 1818
传真：0512-5510 3111
网址：www.fancyindus.com

Fujimak Shanghai Corporation
福喜玛克贸易（上海）有限公司
上海市长宁区天山路18号兆益科技园东楼301室
邮编：200336
电话：021-6291 9060
传真：021-6291 9059
网址：www.fujimak.co.jp

Glory Catering Equipment Co., Ltd.
大荣厨房设备有限公司
北京市大兴区西红门镇福伟路8号
邮编：100076
电话：010-6024 5240
传真：010-6024 5370
电邮：glory@glory.org.cn
网址：www.glorycatering.com
请参阅第 172、173 页

Guangzhou New Yuehai Western Kitchen Equipment Factory
广州新粤海西厨设备厂
广东省广州市花都区花山镇华侨科技工业园
邮编：510880
电话：020-8694 9182
传真：020-8694 9123
电邮：newyuehai@newyuehai.com
网址：www.newyuehai.com

Halton Ventilation (Shanghai) Co., Ltd.
浩盾通风设备（上海）有限公司
上海市浦东新区临港新城
新元南路600号10号厂房
邮编：201306
电话：021-5868 4388
传真：021-5868 4568
电邮：sales.china@halton.com.my
网址：www.halton.com
请参阅第 176、177 页

Hatco Corporation
赫高餐饮设备（苏州）有限公司
江苏省苏州市工业园区唯新路9号
唯亭工业园区A2区1-2单元
电话：0512-6732 5199
传真：0512-6732 5092
电邮：infocn@hatcocorp.com
网址：www.hatcocorp.com
业务范围：
HATCO生产一系列的保温、加热、展示、陈列、烘烤和热水系统的专业厨房和酒店用品。我们的产品包括各种红外线保温加热设备、陈列保温保湿柜、烤面包机、红外线多功能焗炉、热水机、咖啡机、花茶机、快速电蒸炉、多功能蒸煮汤锅和汤池、仿石保温展示板、彩色红外线装饰吊灯，电力洗碗水槽加热器和嵌入式干湿两用保温槽。
HATCO值得信赖的品牌保证，绝对是您最佳的选择。HATCO产品是所有饭店，酒店，宾馆，快餐/速食店，咖啡厅，便利商店，超市，美食广场，酒吧最理想的选择。
请参阅第 179 页

Hong Kong Foodservice Equipment Co., Ltd.
香港餐饮设备有限公司
香港九龙旺角塘尾道18号嘉礼大厦3楼A至B室
电话：+852-2300 1173
传真：+852-2780 6986
电邮：info@hkfec.com.hk
网址：www.hkfec.com.hk

Hoshizaki Shanghai Co., Ltd.
星崎冷热机械（上海）有限公司
上海市恒丰路218号现代交通大厦805室
邮编：200070
电话：021-5180 1998
传真：021-5180 1947
电邮：info@hoshizaki.com.cn
网址：www.hoshizaki.com.cn
请参阅第 198 页

Huning Pallets Co.
显兴卡板有限公司
香港九龙油塘茶果岭道428号
荣山工业大厦四楼D室
电话：+852-2815 4488
传真：+852-2815 7766
请参阅第 381 页

Irinox SPA
Via Madonna Di Loreto 6/B, 31020 Corbanese Di Tarzo Treviso Italy
电话：+39-0438 5844
传真：+39-0438 5843
电邮：irinox@irinox.com
网址：www.irinox.com

Jinjiang Hotel Equipments & Utensiles Manufacture Co., Ltd.
锦江酒店设备器具制造有限公司
江苏省海门市经济技术开发区瑞江路268号
邮编：226100
电话：0513-8221 4688
传真：0513-8221 1475
电邮：jj@zx-china.net
网址：www.cn-ntjjss.com

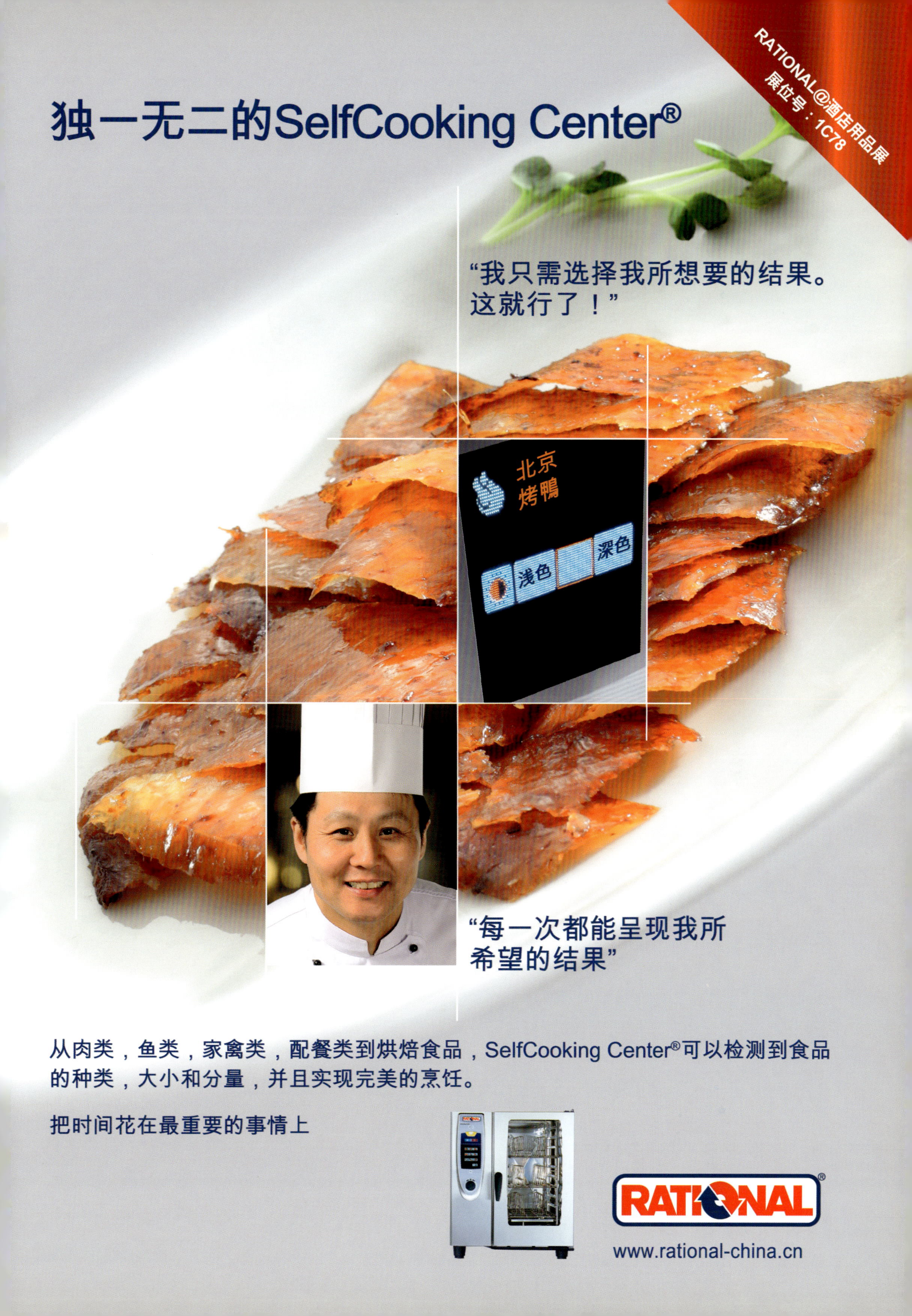
RATIONAL@酒店用品展
展位号：1C78
独一无二的SelfCooking Center®
“我只需选择我所想要的结果。
这就行了！”
北京
烤鸭
浅色
深色
“每一次都能呈现我所
希望的结果”
从肉类，鱼类，家禽类，配餐类到烘焙食品，SelfCooking Center®可以检测到食品的种类，大小和分量，并且实现完美的烹饪。
把时间花在最重要的事情上
RATIONAL®
www.rational-china.cn

Manitowoc

专业定制美式西餐炉具
Professional custom American Western Range

荣

制造厂商

3－9000

专真：（8610）60245370　邮箱：glory@glory.org.cn　网址：www.glorycatering.com

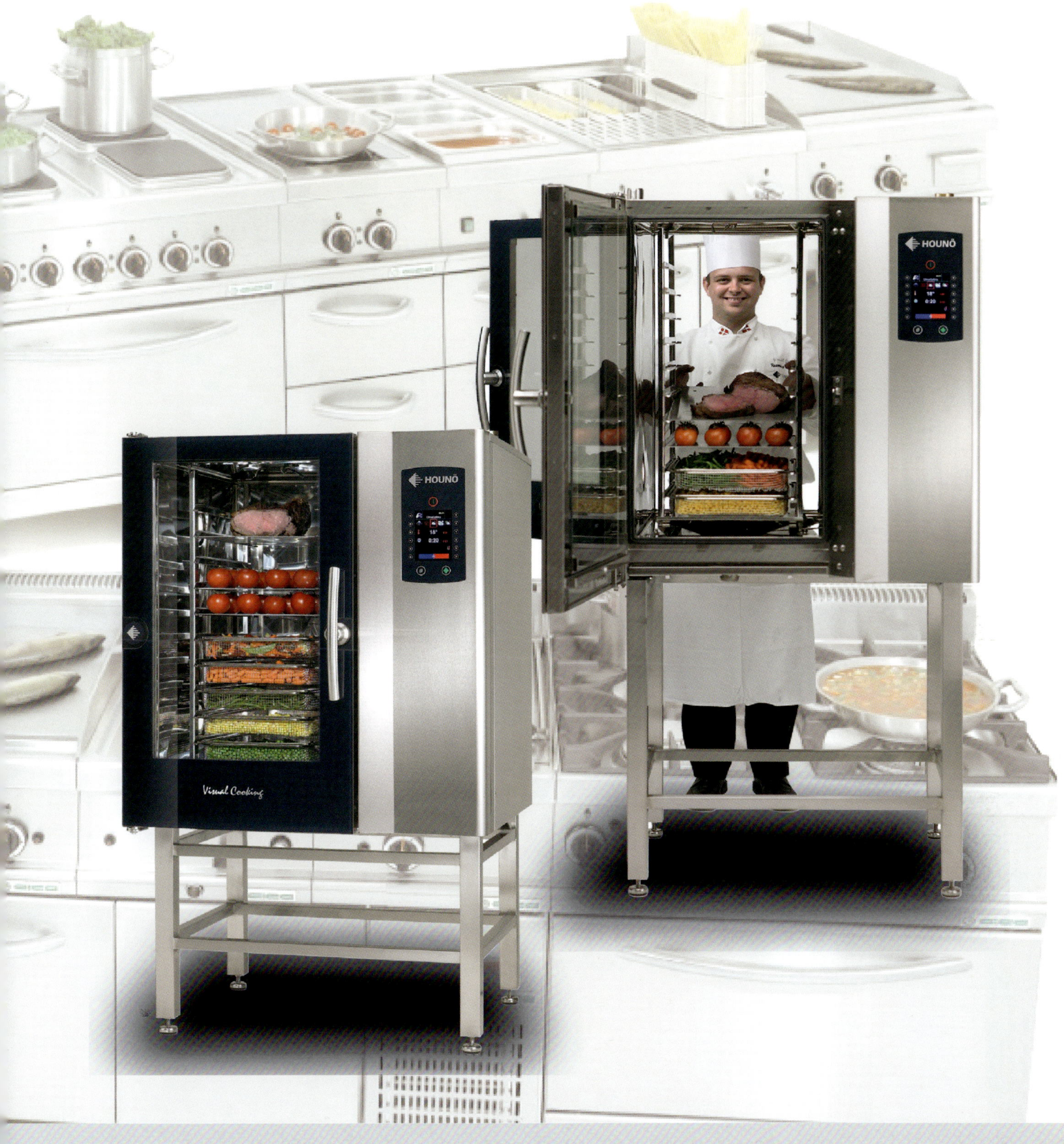

环节都力求完美，为客户提供完整而又满意的解决方案。

MIDDLEBY WORLDWIDE

PERFECT FRY COMPANY

GIGA THE MIDDLEBY CORPORATION

Holman A Star Manufacturing Company

美得彼餐饮设备（上海）有限公司

地址：上海松江九亭镇久富经济开发区盛高路98号

电话：021-67690808　传真：021-67627640

邮编：201615

Email:mandyzhang@middleby.com.cn

www.middleby.com

Capture Jet™ 烟罩

可提供高达40%的排风能源节省。

这专利的 Capture Jet™ 技术应用于浩盾烟罩上代表了最大的节能潜力。

KSA气旋式烟罩过滤油网

加强卫生和安全。

油网可过滤10微米的油粒高达95% (拥有UL, NSF和LPS 1263国际认证)。

Capture Jet™ 天花式烟罩

是灵活性和舒适性之间的最佳组合。

浩盾Capture Jet™ 天花式烟罩范围涵盖所有类型的厨房的需要。

Capture Ray™ 紫外线灯光技术

安全和降低清洗维修费用。

可以去除油脂，并减少烹饪发出的气味。

M.A.R.V.E.L. 系统 - 高效节能通风等于额外**5000***份膳食。

厨房通风通常在100%能源应用下工作整天。浩盾M.A.R.V.E.L.系统是第一个真正聪明，反应迅速，完全灵活的根据需求控制的通风系统。M.A.R.V.E.L.具有独特的能力根据厨房设备的活动来调整每一个烟罩的通风需求。这意味着一个显着的能源节省，这可能相当于一个典型餐厅额外的5000*份膳食。

*在欧洲一个典型的餐馆吃午饭，应用完全基于需求的通风系统每年可以帮助节省高达3000欧元。在平均销售利润率为4%的餐馆和每份膳食15欧元情况下,这相当于每年额外5000份膳食。

Halton Ventilation Co., LTD, Block 10, 600 Xinyuan Road, Lingang New City, Pudong
Shanghai, 201306, The People's Republic of China
Tel.: +86 (0)21 5868 4388, Fax: +86 (0)21 5868 4568, email: sales.china@halton.com.my
浩盾通风设备（上海）有限公司, 上海市浦东新区临港新城, 新元南路600号10号厂房 邮编: 201306

www.halton.com
Enabling Wellbeing

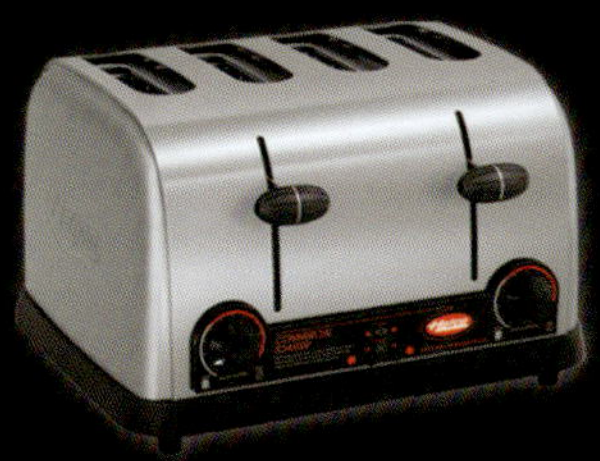

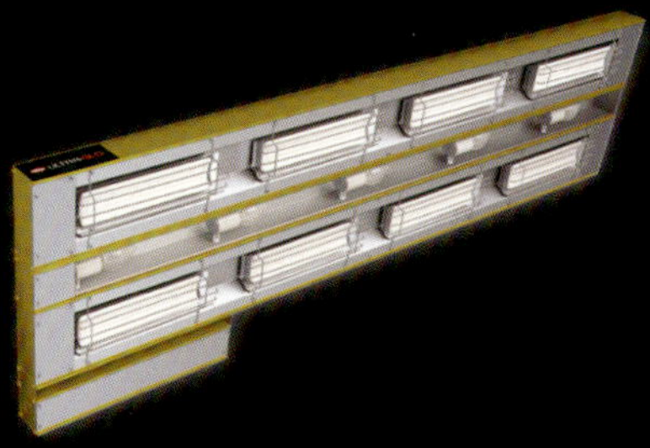

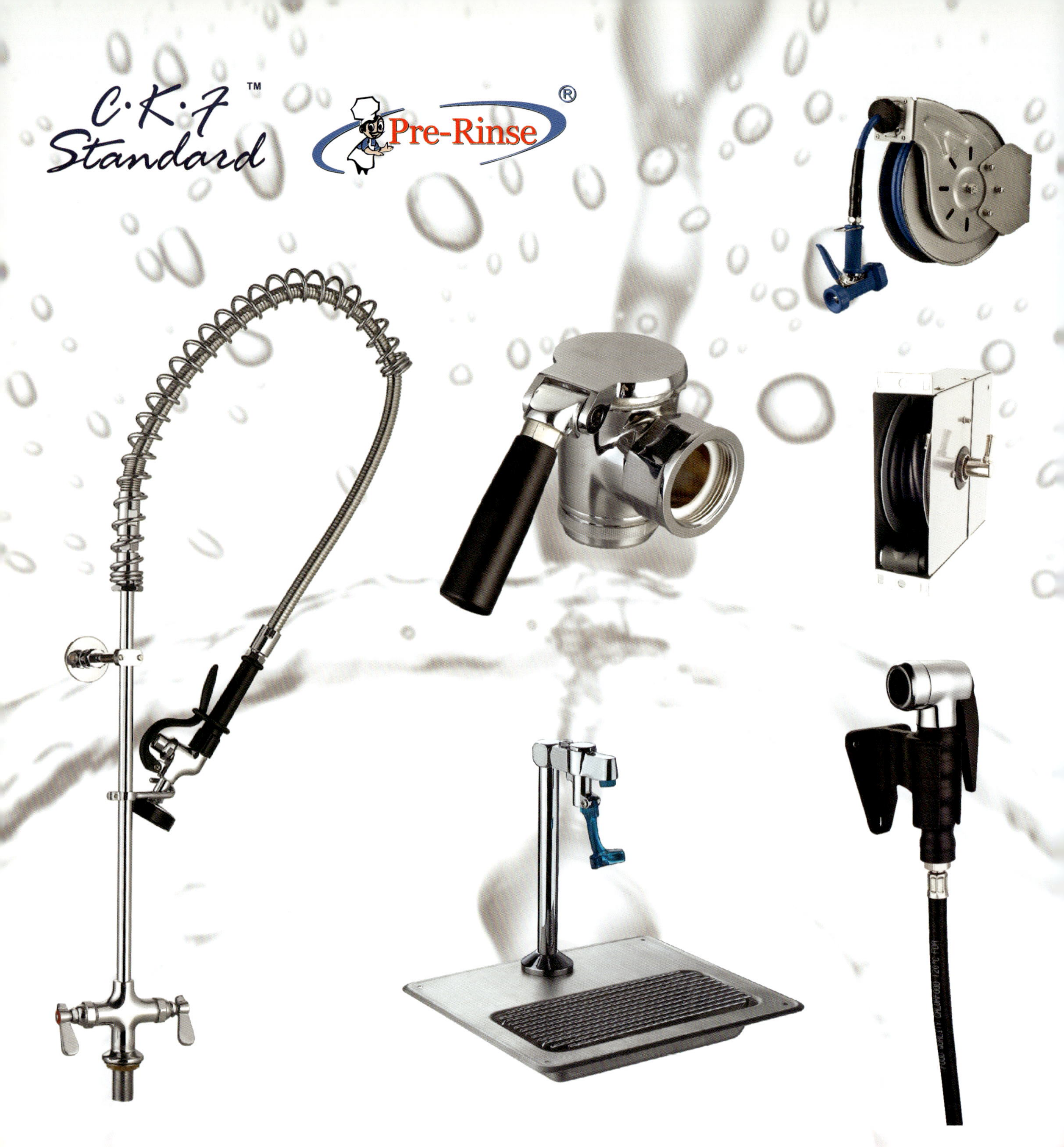

C·K·F Standard™

Pre-Rinse®

中国总代理：

无锡佑飞贸易有限公司

江苏省无锡市湖滨路655号1608室

Http://www.unifit.cn Tel: 0510-85841608/82805020

E-mail:info@unifit.cn Fax: 0510-82805357

E-mail:sales@unifit.cn

YUHUAN MEISHENG SANITARY WARE CO.,LTD.

Add:Yuanjia,Qinggang,Yuhuan,Zhejiang,China 317606

Http://www.pre-rinse.com Tel:+86-576-87121420

E-mail:info@pre-rinse.com Tel:+86-576-87121119

E-mail:young@pre-rinse.com Fax:+86-576-87121319

工程案例 UCCESSFUL PROJECT:

MERITUS
Western
Series

Combi
Steamers

Tilting
Boiling
Pan

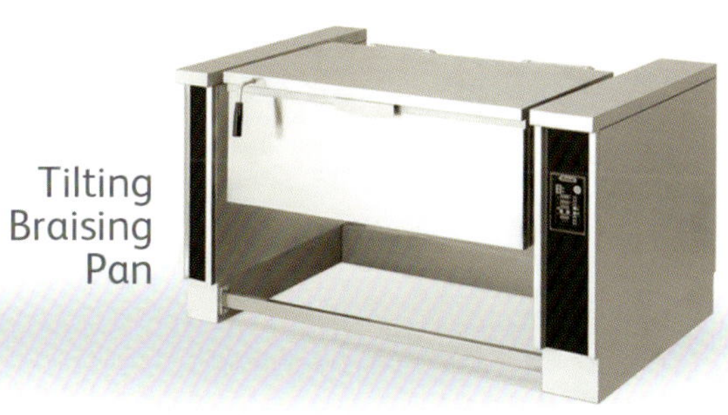

Tilting
Braising
Pan

GOURMET MASTER
Kitchen Block

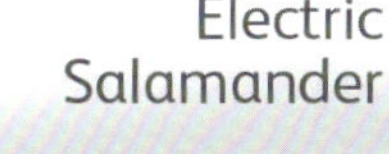

Electric
Salamander

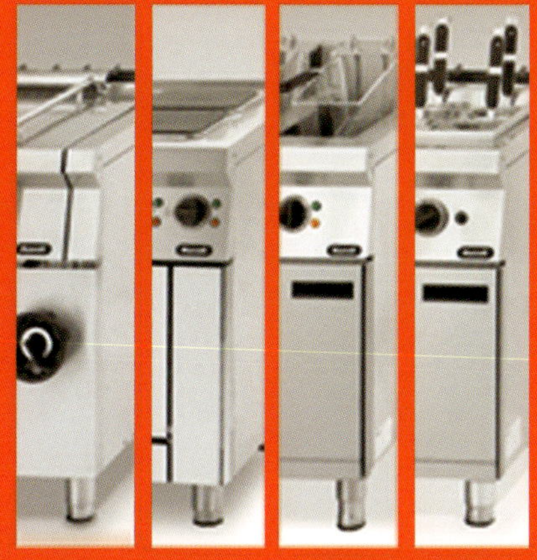

中国传盛商用设备

China Manufacturing Solutions Ltd.

The company specializes in manufacturing, processing and selling commercial hotel equipment, catering equipment and metal semi-finished products. We have our own sales office in China、UK and USA respectively. Most of the products are exported to Europe and the USA. Our main customers are international well known brands in the food service industry.Meanwhile, the company is active to develop domestic market, and have already established cooperation relations with well-known companies at home.

地址：山东潍城经济开发区彩虹路与卧龙西街路口　电话：13665362060
传真：(86) 536 6105299　邮箱：pan@chmans.com　网址：www.chmans.com

德国米技商用炉
酒店专业烹饪解决方案
Professional Front Cooking Solution

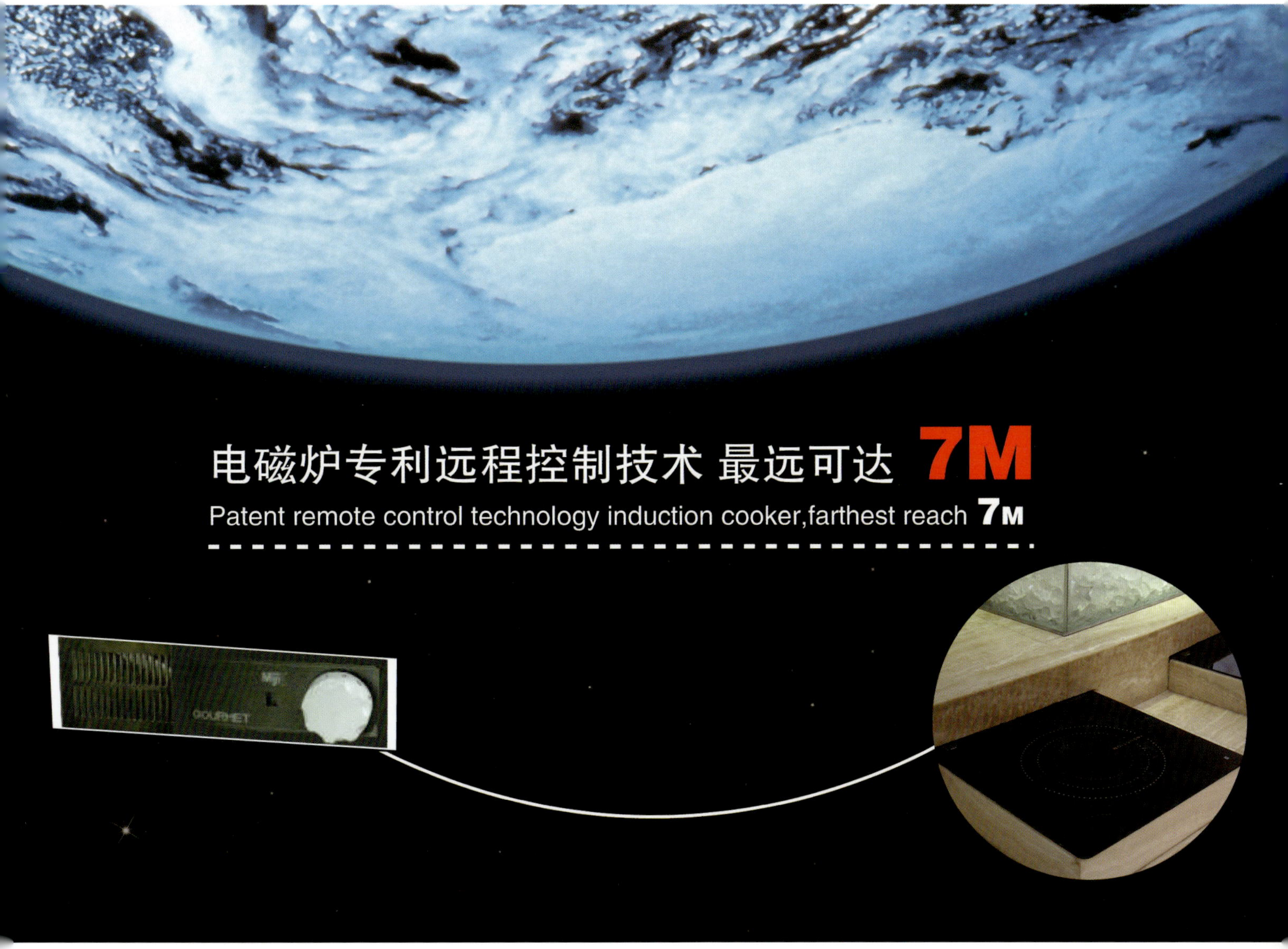

电磁炉专利远程控制技术 最远可达 7M

Patent remote control technology induction cooker,farthest reach 7M

上海东方明珠广播电视塔

上海东方明珠广播电视塔座落于上海黄浦江畔、浦东陆家嘴嘴尖，以其468米的绝对高度成为亚洲第一、世界第三之高塔。东方明珠塔卓然秀立于陆家嘴地区现代化建筑楼群，与隔江的外滩万国建筑博览群交相辉映，展现了国际大都市的壮观景色。东方明珠塔集观光餐饮、购物娱乐、浦江游览、会务会展、历史陈列、旅行代理等服务功能于一身，成为上海标志性建筑和旅游热点之一。

为了满足餐厅的美观、实用、多功能要求。我司提供了当前的经典款ITI2200II 款 嵌入式触摸式电磁炉。该款炉具设计风格简洁大气。2200w的功率，9档触摸操作可以满足保温、烹饪等所有需求。受到使用厨师的高度评价。

上海虹桥元一希尔顿大酒店

上海虹桥元一希尔顿大酒店，拥有三座大楼，四周云集各类高端时尚购物中心、娱乐设施，领馆别墅，高档住宅区。会议室设计考究，设施齐全，服务一流；拥有全日制自助式餐厅、粤式餐厅、异域氛围的大堂吧，令人饱尝寰宇的多元化风味；客房则按照希尔顿一贯的风格，装修豪华高贵、设施高端、布局合理。酒店全方位的细微服务，不仅彰显了酒店的风采，更体现了宾客的高贵。

根据希尔顿酒店的要求，我司提供了IEI2200IO型炉具 这是一款分离式控制的电磁炉，控制方便，加热速度快。是我司为酒店自助餐区 专业开发的一款炉具。为厨师提供便捷，使烹饪简单化，标准化，大气美观的造型给用餐者营造了良好的环境。

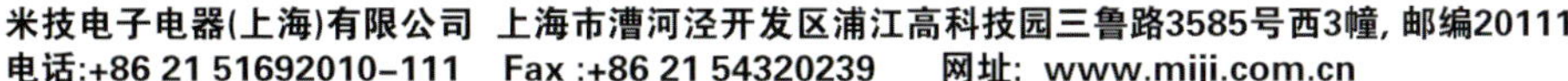

电话:+86 21 51692010-111 Fax :+86 21 54320239 网址: www.miji.com.cn

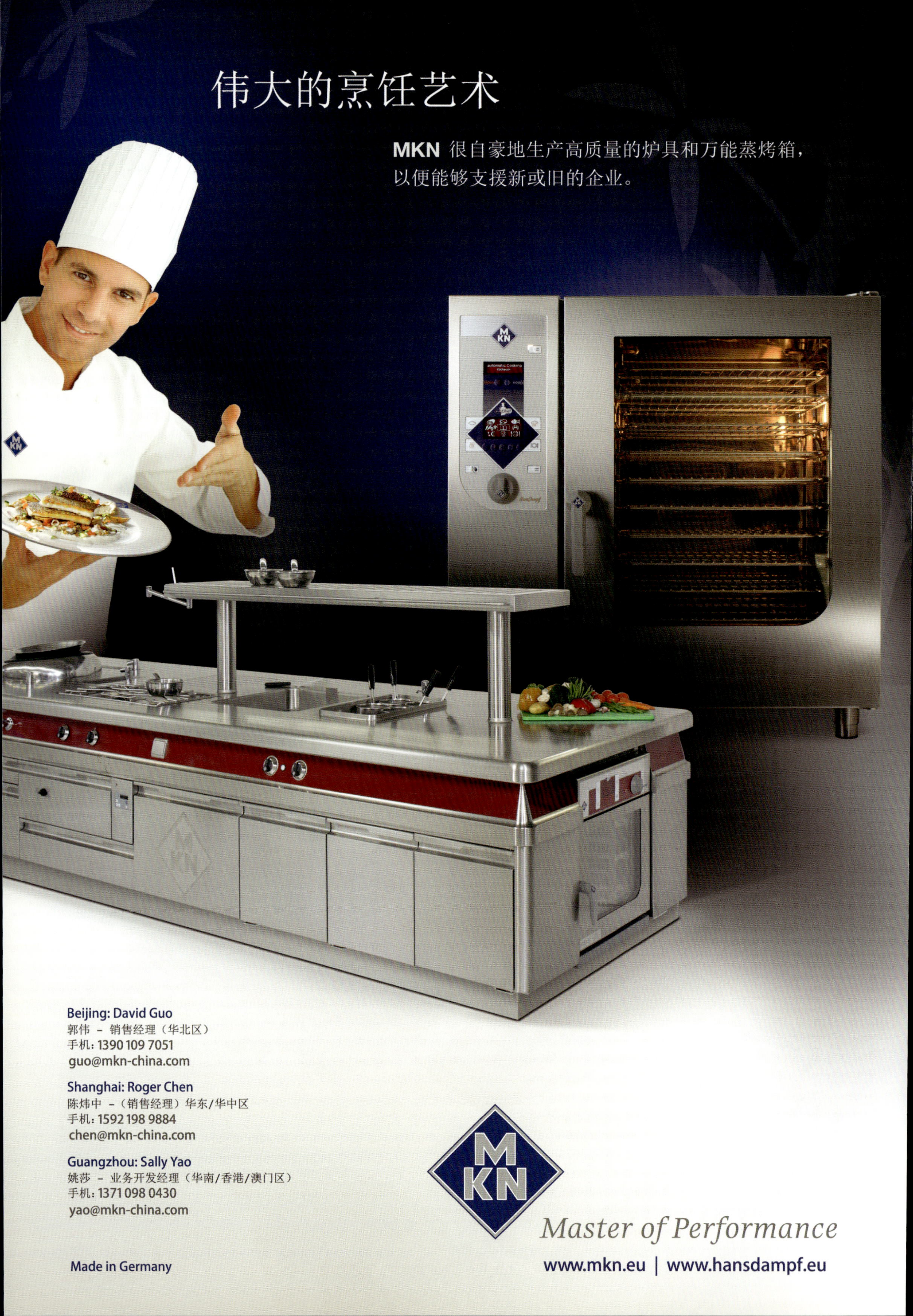
伟大的烹饪艺术
MKN 很自豪地生产高质量的炉具和万能蒸烤箱，
以便能够支援新或旧的企业。
Beijing: David Guo
郭伟 – 销售经理（华北区）
手机：1390 109 7051
guo@mkn-china.com
Shanghai: Roger Chen
陈炜中 –（销售经理）华东/华中区
手机：1592 198 9884
chen@mkn-china.com
Guangzhou: Sally Yao
姚莎 – 业务开发经理（华南/香港/澳门区）
手机：1371 098 0430
yao@mkn-china.com
Made in Germany
Master of Performance
www.mkn.eu | www.hansdampf.eu

▼大型厨房设备
Catering Equipment

Kolb HK Ltd.
瑞士高比（香港）有限公司
香港九龙观塘开源道55号开联工业中心B座201室
电话：+852-2516 6093
传真：+852-2516 6518
电邮：rgeisser@kolb-hk.com
网址：www.kolb-hk.com

Maschinenfabrik Kurt Neubauer GmbH & Co.
Halberstaedter Strasse 2a, D-38300 Wolfenbuettel, Germany
电话：+49-5331 89263
传真：+49-5331 89280
电邮：fn@mkn.de
网址：www.mkn.eu
业务范围：
MKN is the German specialist in premium thermal professional cooking technology! Thanks to the experience of more than half a century, MKN guarantees chefs and guests outstanding results. MKN's professional cooking technology is found in the best kitchens in the world and is used in demanding environments such as star rated hotels and restaurants, community catering, commercial chains, and the maritime sector. Each and every product in the extensive MKN product portfolio fulfils highest demands and inspires in particular, with high quality, durability and economic efficiency. Freely combined, multi-function and special appliances, including the innovative energy systems from MKN, melt into a highly functional integrated answer to all professional cooking needs. Whether with modern multi function cooking technology such as HansDampf Combi Cooking and Optima Express Pressure Cooking Technology, or the tailor made uniqueness of the Premium Class KUCHENMEISTER and the modular appliance range, MKN has won lots of prizes.
请参阅第184页

Middleby China Corporation
美得彼餐饮设备（上海）有限公司
上海市松江区九亭镇久富经济开发区盛富路98号
邮编：201615
电话：021-6769 0808
传真：021-6762 7640
电邮：mandyzhang@middleby.com.cn
网址：www.middleby.com
请参阅第174、175页

Miji Electronics & Appliances (Shanghai) Ltd.
米技电子电器（上海）有限公司
上海市漕河泾开发区
浦江高科技园三鲁路3585号西3幢
邮编：201114
电话：021-5169 2010*111
传真：021-5432 0239
电邮：zhouwenbing@miji.com.cn
网址：www.miji.com.cn
请参阅第183页、总目录书隔页底页

Nayati Indonesia, PT.
Jl. Raya Terboyo no.19
Kawasan Industri Terboyo Megah
Semarang - Indonesia
电话：+62(24)-658 0573
传真：+62(24)-658 0572
电邮：nayati@nayati.com
网址：www.nayati.com
请参阅第181页

New Gen Catering Equipment (HK) Ltd.
新锐餐饮设备（香港）有限公司
香港新界屯门排头路5号伟昌工业中心5字楼K室
电话：+852-2454 7711
传真：+852-2454 8833
电邮：info@newgenhk.com
网址：www.newgenhk.com

Peak Honour International Ltd.
沛鸿国际有限公司
香港北角英皇道225号国都广场13字楼1303室
电话：+852-2861 3058
传真：+852-2866 2244
电邮：headoffice@peak-honour.com
网址：www.peak-honour.com

Pioneer Catering Equipment & Engineering Limited
魄力厨具工程有限公司
香港新界葵涌葵昌路26号
豪华工业大厦16字楼B座
电话：+852-2487 1707
传真：+852-2487 1816
电邮：hpc@pcee.com
网址：www.pcee.com.hk

Pro-Fit Industrial Co., Ltd.
宝发实业有限公司
香港新界葵涌大连排道152-160号
金龙工业中心第1座25字楼C室
电话：+852-2371 2862
传真：+852-2371 2867
电邮：profit@profitind.com
网址：www.profitind.com
请参阅第178页

RATIONAL International AG Shanghai Rep. Office
乐信国际股份公司上海代表处
上海市肇嘉浜路798号201B室
邮编：200030
电话：021-6473 7473
传真：021-6473 0197
电邮：shanghai.office@rational-online.com
网址：www.rational-china.com
请参阅第169页

Saro Worldwide (Hong Kong) Ltd.
No. 4-5, G/F., 68 Lok Ku Road, Sheung Wan, H.K.
电话：+852-2581 9258
传真：+852-2581 3014
电邮：info@saro.com.hk
网址：www.saro.com.hk

Shanghai J&C Industry Co., Ltd.
上海积创实业发展有限公司
上海市黄兴路1725号怡富商务广场1701/1706室
邮编：200433
电话：021-6587 6136
传真：021-6587 6134
网址：www.jichuang.net.cn

Shanghai Qiangan Foodservice Equipment Co., Ltd.
上海强安餐饮设备有限公司
上海市松江区洞泾镇沈砖公路5599号
邮编：201619
电话：021-6786 2188
传真：021-6786 2966
网址：www.qiangan.net

Shanghai Xingjian Industry Co., Ltd.
上海星剑实业有限公司
上海市普陀区绥德路555号1号楼
邮编：200331
电话：021-6483 9061
传真：021-6482 3642
电邮：jiangfang@shxjsy.com
网址：www.shxjsy.com

Shenzhen HengXingSheng Kichen Equipment Co., Ltd.
深圳市恒兴盛厨具有限公司
深圳沙井蚝四南安科技工业园A2栋
邮编：518125
电话：0755-6116 3177
传真：0755-6116 3177
网址：www.szhxscj.com

Shenzhen Zero Carbon Technology Co., Ltd.
深圳市零碳科技有限公司
深圳市南山区高新技术产业园
科苑路坚达大厦西座4楼
电话：0755-2661 6605
传真：0755-2661 9911
网址：www.zero-carbon-tech.com
请参阅展览会书隔页底页

Sunny Trading Company
阳光贸易公司
香港九龙观塘兴业街16号
美兴工业大厦B座10楼11室
电话：+852-2343 2943
传真：+852-2343 4459
电邮：info@sunnytrading.com
网址：www.sunnytrading.com

Universal Electrical Machine Works (Shenzhen) Co., Ltd.
环球炉业（深圳）有限公司
深圳市龙岗区大鹏街道
王母第一工业区3、4号厂房
邮编：518120
电话：0755-8430 5128
传真：0755-8430 8213
电邮：cninfo@uemw.com.hk
网址：www.uemw.com.hk

WP Kitchen Equipment Manufacturing
佛山市南海振智厨房设备制造有限公司
佛山市南海区丹灶镇金沙高海工业区
邮编：538223
电话：0757-8561 1082
传真：0757-8561 1083
电邮：sales@wise-promotion.com.cn
网址：www.wise-promotion.com.cn

YongKang Bangjie Kitchen Equipment Co., Ltd.
永康市邦捷厨房设备有限公司
永康市五金城一期四街37号
邮编：321300
电话：0579-8732 1777
传真：0579-8715 9678
电邮：haote8@163.com
网址：www.bangjiechufang.com.cn

▼大型厨房设备
Catering Equipment

Yu Fu Bao Kitcheware Equipment (Shenzhen) Co., Ltd.
裕富宝厨具设备（深圳）有限公司
深圳市龙岗区坂田街道办坂田社区
大光磡工业区10号
邮编：518129
电话：0755-8471 2229
传真：0755-8471 2601
网址：www.yufubao-cn.com
Yue Po Engineering Co., Ltd.

Yuhuan Meisheng Sanitary Ware Co., Ltd.
玉环县美盛洁具有限公司
浙江省台州市玉环县清港镇袁家村
邮编：317606
电话：0576-8712 1420
传真：0576-8712 1319
电邮：info@pre-rinse.com
网址：www.pre-rinse.com
请参阅第180页

久景制冷设备（上海）有限公司
上海市赵重公路1978号
电话：021-3987 6601
传真：021-3987 6501
电邮：niu@hisakage.com
网址：www.hisakage.com
请参阅第197页

马尼托瓦克餐饮设备集团 中国
上海市凯旋路613号G号楼
电话：021-6152 6100
传真：021-6152 6030
网址：www.manitowocfoodservice.com.cn
业务范围：
一个完美的厨房需要由许多重要的元素组成。如何获得这些元素将是这个厨房组建成功与否的关键。而现在，您只要找到马尼托瓦餐饮设备集团就可以获得所有这些重要的元素。
马尼托瓦设备集团拥有一个庞大的、行业领先的品牌组合。如Cleveland, Convotherm®, Delfield®, Frymaster®, Garland®, Jackson, Kolpak®, Lincoln, Manitowoc® Ice, Merco®, Merrychef®, Multiplex®, and Servend®. 无论是烘焙还是烹饪；冷冻还是蒸烤，马尼托瓦能为您提供一系列最先进的厨房设备。此外，马尼托瓦在市场洞察、售后服务、技术支持和员工培训等方面都为您提供全方位支持和一如既往的服务。
在马尼托瓦，您能获得关于厨房设备的近乎穷尽的资源。
请参阅第170、171页

刀具
Cutlery

Afehc - Spanish Exporting Manufacturers Association For The Hospitality Industry
西班牙餐饮及团体用具生产及出口商协会
Rambla Catalunya 81, 5-3
08008 Barcelona
Spain
电话：+34(93)-487 3290
传真：+34(93)-487 0770
电邮：afehc@afehc.com
网址：www.afehc.com
请参阅第36页

Dalian Xin Jian Hai Hotel Supplies & Trade Co.
大连新建海酒店用品贸易行
大连市沙河口区星海广场B3区一品星海6-3-1
电话：0411-8480 5299
传真：0411-8480 4111
电邮：xinjianhai@hotmail.com
网址：www.china-xjh.com

Hailian Cutlrey Factory Of Yangjiang City, Guangdong. China
广东省阳江市海联五金塑料制品有限公司
广东省阳江市大令放鸡路38号
电话：0662-661 3839
传真：0662-661 2086
电邮：hl@hailiancutlery.com
网址：www.hailiancutlery.com

Liveon Industrial Co., Ltd.
阳江市力王实业有限公司
广东省阳江市阳东县工业四区裕东六路46号
电话：0662-886 9688
传真：0662-886 9688
电邮：liveon@liveon.cn
网址：www.liveon.cn

Mundial Co., Ltd.
蒙特环球有限公司
香港九龙长沙湾永康街9号19/F
电话：+852-2367 2688
传真：+852-2369 7247
电邮：mktg2@mundial.com.hk
网址：www.mundial.com.hk

Peak Honour International Ltd.
沛鸿国际有限公司
香港北角英皇道225号国都广场13字楼1303室
电话：+852-2861 3058
传真：+852-2866 2244
电邮：headoffice@peak-honour.com
网址：www.peak-honour.com

Shenzhen Pama Hotel Products Co., Ltd.
深圳市帕玛酒店用品有限公司
深圳市南山区粤海路粤海工业村
深圳动漫园4栋201室
邮编：518054
电话：0755-8605 2592
传真：0755-8605 2582
网址：www.szpama.com
请参阅第42页

Suzhou Dashye Trading Co., Ltd.
苏州市大协商贸有限公司
江苏省苏州市沧浪区盘胥路68号
城市恬园28栋108室
邮编：215007
电话：0512-6855 3015
传真：0512-6855 3227
电邮：bwenya@yahoo.com.cn
网址：www.atlanticchef.com.cn

Victorinox Hong Kong Limited
瑞士维氏钢刀香港有限公司
香港九龙观塘荣业街2号振万广场8楼801-803室
电话：+852-2345 0211
传真：+852-2341 6158
电邮：info@victorinox.com.hk
网址：www.victorinox.com.hk

Yong Ge Trading (shanghai) Co., Ltd.
上海市长宁区黄金城道676号
邮编：201103
电话：021-6308 0741
传真：021-6313 3707
电邮：wittywang@vip.163.com
网址：www.aistiashop.com
请参阅第215页

Zhejiang Yingda Cutting Tool Co., Ltd.
浙江鹰达刀具有限公司
浙江省武义县内白鹰达路8号
邮编：321200
电话：0579-8760 3438
传真：0579-8760 3188
电邮：wyyddj@mail.jhptt.zj.cn
网址：www.chinayingda.com

Zwilling J.A. Henckels Shanghai Ltd.
上海双立人亨克斯有限公司
上海市浦东新区三林路424号
邮编：200124
电话：021-3886 1343
网址：www.zwilling.com.cn

切割设备
Cutting Equipment

Anhui Hualing Kitchen Equipment Co., Ltd.
安徽华菱西厨装备股份有限公司
安徽省马鞍山市博望工业开发区
邮编：243131
电话：0555-676 9699
传真：0555-676 9511
电邮：info@fenglihua.com
网址：www.fenglihua.com

Bizerba (Shanghai) Weightech & Systems Co., Ltd.
碧彩（上海）衡器技术有限公司
上海市松江工业区东部新区茜浦路书慧置业园D-3
邮编：201611
电话：021-6760 0999
传真：021-6760 0998
网址：www.bizerba.cn

Electrolux Professional (Shanghai) Co., Ltd.
伊莱克斯商用电器（上海）有限公司
上海市外高桥保税区爱都路390号31号楼A座
邮编：200131
电话：021-5046 0099
传真：021-5046 0077
网址：www.electrolux-professional.cn
请参阅第168页

Guangzhou TeemYeah Food Machinery Co., Ltd.
广州市天烨食品机械有限公司
广东省荔湾区花地南路西塱麦村
北约55号107-108室
邮编：510385
电话：020-8141 7161
传真：020-8158 6171
电邮：ty@tianyefm.com
网址：www.tianyefm.com

渡边食品机械销售（上海）有限公司
上海市徐汇区中山西路2025号永升大厦M3室
邮编：200235
电话：021-6439 8522
传真：021-6439 8332
网址：www.watanabesh.com

洗碗碟机
Dishwashing Machines

Afehc - Spanish Exporting Manufacturers Association For The Hospitality Industry
西班牙餐饮及团体用具生产及出口商协会
Rambla Catalunya 81, 5-3
08008 Barcelona
Spain
电话：+34(93)-487 3290
传真：+34(93)-487 0770
电邮：afehc@afehc.com
网址：www.afehc.com
请参阅第36页

winterhalter

热回收装置

◆适用机型：

GS502/GS515 揭盖式洗碗机

◆工作原理：

通过热交换装置
回收洗涤区的多余蒸汽
用来加热进水(冷水)

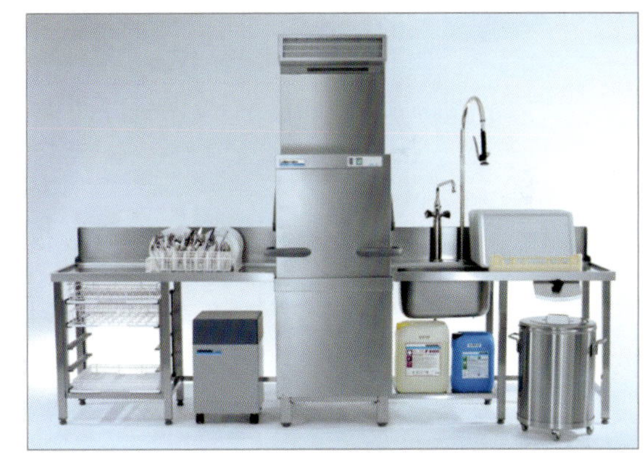

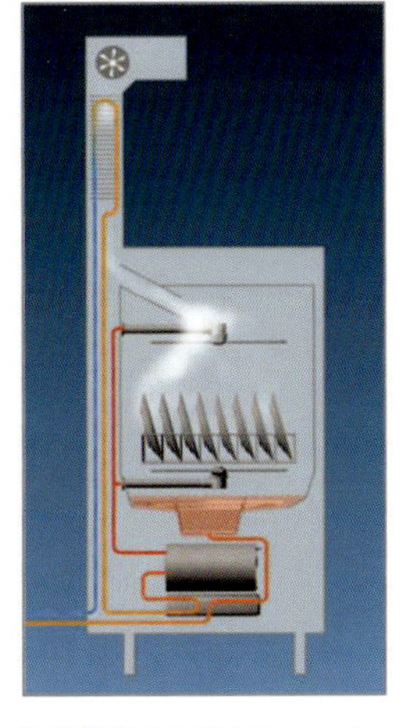

示意图是 GS 502 Energy+
热回收过程(必须是冷水接入)

优点：

◆减少总接电负荷6kW，节约电能耗。
◆除去绝大部分蒸汽，无需安装烟罩和排风。
◆大大降低厨房的温度和热度，改善厨房环境。

要求：

◆现场进水温度20℃以下

▼洗碗碟机 Dishwashing Machines

Angelo Po Trading (Shanghai)
傲桀贸易（上海）有限公司
上海市江场三路88号一楼
邮编：200436
电话：021-6094 0100
传真：021-6094 0288
电邮：info@angelopo.cn
网址：www.angelopo.it
请参阅第167、195页、封面

Beijing Harvest E & M Co., Ltd.
北京丰汇加机电设备销售有限公司
北京市宣武区建功西里1号楼天缘公寓A座2701室
邮编：100054
电话：010-8351 6972
传真：010-8351 7663
电邮：sales@bjharvest.cn
网址：www.bjharvest.cn

Century Environmental Protection Group (China) Co., Ltd.
世纪环保集团（中国）有限公司
香港中环德辅道中112-114号顺安商业大厦
电话：+852-3175 0368
传真：+852-3175 0303
网址：www.shijihuanbao.com

Champion Chemicals Ltd.
卓汇化工有限公司
香港新界元朗喜业街3号雄伟工业大厦10楼I室
电话：+852-2475 9875
传真：+852-2443 1096
电邮：sales@champion-chem.com
网址：www.champion-chem.com

Ecomax Commercial Dishwasher Co., Ltd.
广州市艺高洗碗机有限公司
广东省广州市西华路256号港丰大厦西塔四楼C座
邮编：510170
电话：020-8108 1738
传真：020-8108 1763
电邮：ecomax15@yahoo.com.cn
网址：www.ecomax.cn

Electrolux Professional (Shanghai) Co., Ltd.
伊莱克斯商用电器（上海）有限公司
上海市外高桥保税区爱都路390号31号楼A座
邮编：200131
电话：021-5046 0099
传真：021-5046 0077
网址：www.electrolux-professional.cn
请参阅第168页

Fagor Industrial China
法格厨房设备（昆山）有限公司
江苏省昆山市千灯镇西班牙工业园区
邮编：215341
电话：0512-5515 5605
传真：0512-5515 5610
电邮：fagorchina@fagorindustrial.com
网址：www.fagorindustrial.cn

Foshan Nanhai Arita Commercial Kitchen Equipment Co., Ltd.
佛山市有田商用厨房设备有限公司
广东省佛山市南海区丹灶镇金沙高海工业区
邮编：528223
电话：0757-8661 9166
传真：0757-8661 4668
电邮：manager@chujucn.com
网址：www.chujucn.com

Foshan Qing Yuan Chuju
佛山市庆源厨具
佛山市三水区南丰大道南边工业区
电话：0757-8731 8991
传真：0757-8731 1882
网址：www.gdqycj.com

Hangzhou Wiscon E.S. Equipment Co., Ltd.
杭州威士康环保卫生设备有限公司
杭州市天目山路386号龙都大厦附楼1105室
邮编：310023
电话：0571-8522 5228
传真：0571-5627 7098
电邮：wiscon@163.com
网址：www.xwjusa.com

Hobart Food Equipment Co., Ltd.
高达食品设备有限公司
上海市漕溪路222号航天宾馆601室
邮编：200235
电话：021-6482 8038
传真：021-6119 9211
网址：www.hobartchina.com

Inland Dishwasher (Shanghai) Co., Ltd.
上海伊莱德洗碗机有限公司
上海市普陀区武威路259号C3区
邮编：200444
电话：021-6153 8188
传真：021-5104 7519
电邮：xiwanji@yilaide.net
网址：www.xiwanji.com

Jackwah Hong Kong Ltd.
积华香港有限公司
Room 1221, International Trade Centre, 11-19 Sha Tsui Road, Tsuen Wan, Hong Kong
电话：+852-8209 0911
传真：+852-8209 0977
电邮：info@jackwah.com
网址：www.jackwah.com

Lee Hun Trading Co., Ltd.
香港利亨贸易行
香港九龙红磡鹤园街9-11号
凯旋工商中心第三期二楼Q室
电话：+852-2334 0873
传真：+852-2954 2181
网址：www.cpl.net.cn

Meiko Wash-Up Technologies Ltd.
迈科清洗科技（中山）有限公司
广东省中山市火炬高新技术产业开发区敬业路12号
邮编：528437
电话：0760-8531 7590
传真：0760-8531 4217
电邮：info@meikochina.com
网址：www.meikochina.com

Nanjing Lehui Light Industry Equipment Co., Ltd.
南京乐惠轻工装备制造有限公司
南京市江宁区将军南路600号
邮编：211151
电话：025-5273 3666
传真：025-5273 3600
电邮：njsales@lehui.com
网址：www.lehui.com

Ningbo Super Electrical Manufacture Co., Ltd.
宁波超胜电器制造有限公司
浙江省宁波市北仑区纬三路33号
邮编：315801
电话：0574-8622 9818
传真：0574-8622 9722
电邮：master@nb-super.com
网址：www.nbsuper.cn

Oriental Engineering (Shanghai) Co., Ltd.
港捷（上海）贸易有限公司
上海市静安区南苏州路1501号1号楼2楼
邮编：200041
电话：021-5228 6053
传真：021-6272 2738
电邮：sales@oriental-eng.com.hk
网址：www.oequip.com

Pioneer Catering Equipment & Engineering Limited
魄力厨具工程有限公司
香港新界葵涌葵昌路26号
豪华工业大厦16字楼B座
电话：+852-2487 1707
传真：+852-2487 1816
电邮：hpc@pcee.com
网址：www.pcee.com.hk

SJM China Co., Ltd.
爱思洁爱姆洗碗机（上海）贸易有限公司
上海市崧泽大道1699号左1号楼
邮编：201702
电话：021-6232 0105
传真：021-6232 0102
网址：www.sjmchina.com

Shanghai Veetsan Commercial Machinery Co., Ltd.
上海威顺商用机器有限公司
上海市奉贤区奉浦工业区远东北路1515号
龙洋工业园区20号
邮编：201401
电话：021-6710 9328
传真：021-6710 9348
电邮：sales@veetsan.com.cn
网址：www.veetsan.com.cn

Shanghai Xingjian Industry Co., Ltd.
上海星剑实业有限公司
上海市普陀区绥德路555号1号楼
邮编：200331
电话：021-6483 9061
传真：021-6482 3642
电邮：jiangfang@shxjsy.com
网址：www.shxjsy.com

Simplex Foodservice Equipment (Shanghai) Ltd.
新必利餐饮设备（上海）有限公司
上海市松江区九亭镇涞坊路57号
邮编：201615
电话：021-6784 1311
传真：021-6784 1331
电邮：simplex@online.sh.cn
网址：www.simplex.cn

Winterhalter (Shanghai) Trading Co., Ltd.
温特豪德贸易（上海）有限公司
上海市闵行区申旺路5号
邮编：201108
电话：021-5151 1310
传真：021-5151 1950
电邮：info@winterhalter.com.cn
网址：www.winterhalter.com.cn
请参阅第187页、展览会书隔页面页

YPT International Ltd.
建宏国际有限公司
香港九龙官塘鲤鱼门道2号新城工商中心1楼
电话：+852-2723 2168
传真：+852-2739 7576
电邮：ypt@techwin.com.hk
网址：www.ypt.com.hk

上海金淳酒店设备有限公司
上海市中华路235号
邮编：200010
电话：021-6311 5442
传真：021-6328 8702
电邮：kinglake@kinglake.com.cn
网址：www.kinglake.com.cn

食物搅拌机
Food Mixers

Afehc - Spanish Exporting Manufacturers Association For The Hospitality Industry
西班牙餐饮及团体用具生产及出口商协会
Rambla Catalunya 81, 5-3
08008 Barcelona
Spain
电话：+34(93)-487 3290
传真：+34(93)-487 0770
电邮：afehc@afehc.com
网址：www.afehc.com
请参阅第 36 页

Electrolux Professional (Shanghai) Co., Ltd.
伊莱克斯商用电器（上海）有限公司
上海市外高桥保税区爱都路390号31号楼A座
邮编：200131
电话：021-5046 0099
传真：021-5046 0077
网址：www.electrolux-professional.cn
请参阅第 168 页

Foshan Geuwa Electric Appliance Co., Ltd.
佛山市钜华电器有限公司
广东省佛山市南海区小塘镇东部开发区
邮编：528222
电话：0757-8666 8666
传真：0757-8666 3392
电邮：manager@geuwa.com
网址：www.geuwa.com

Guangzhou Sunmile Industries Co., Ltd.
广州新域实业有限公司
广州市体育西路103号维多利广场A座2071室
邮编：510620
电话：020-3703 8688
传真：020-3703 8188
电邮：exp@sunmile.com
网址：www.sunmile.com

Mika Electric (HK) Limited
美佳电器（香港）有限公司
广州市海珠区广州大道南448号财智大厦805室
电话：020-8421 8716
传真：020-8426 8015
电邮：hkmika@126.com
网址：www.mika.com.hk

Ningbo Eastron Electric Appliances Co., Ltd.
宁波市江北意川电器有限公司
宁波市北仑区小岗区湖芳村
电话：0574-8766 3518
传真：0574-8766 3598
电邮：eastron@eastron.net
网址：www.eastron.net

Oriental Engineering (Shanghai) Co., Ltd.
港捷（上海）贸易有限公司
上海市静安区南苏州路1501号1号楼2楼
邮编：200041
电话：021-5228 6053
传真：021-6272 2738
电邮：sales@oriental-eng.com.hk
网址：www.oequip.com

Rudong Hengyu Food Machinery Co., Ltd.
江苏如东恒宇食品机械有限公司
江苏省如东县马塘镇东工业园
邮编：226401
电话：0513-8456 5852
传真：0513-8456 5557
电邮：rdhysp@sina.com
网址：www.rdhengyu.com

Shanghai Honglian Machine Electric Appliance Co., Ltd.
上海红联机械电器制造有限公司
上海市南翔高科技园区胜辛南路185号
邮编：201802
电话：021-6917 6301
传真：021-6917 6368
电邮：honglian@sh-honglian.net
网址：www.sh-honglian.net

Shenzhen Hawkins Industrial Co., Ltd.
深圳市浩景丰实业发展有限公司
深圳市福田区北环大道7008号通业大厦南塔13层
电话：0755-8356 6221
传真：0755-8356 6227
电邮：hawkins@hawkins.com.cn
网址：www.hawkinsco.biz

Sunny Trading Company
阳光贸易公司
香港九龙观塘兴业街16号
美兴工业大厦B座10楼11室
电话：+852-2343 2943
传真：+852-2343 4459
电邮：info@sunnytrading.com
网址：www.sunnytrading.com

Sveba-Dahlen (China) Ltd.
瑞典烘焙设备（中国）有限公司
香港柴湾康民街2号康民工业中心1805室
电话：+852-2558 2293
传真：+852-2558 2089
电邮：wfy@sveba-dahlenchina.hk
网址：www.sveba-dahlenchina.com

Thunderbird Food Machinery Co., Ltd.
德霸食品机械有限公司
上海市松江区欣玉路453弄1-5号4D
邮编：201600
电话：021-5773 6845
传真：021-5773 6093
电邮：tbfmsh@tbfmcn.com.cn
网址：www.tbfmcn.com.cn
请参阅第 163 页

广东多丽食品机械有限公司
广东省佛山市南海区平洲平北工业区内
邮编：528251
电话：0757-8677 3774
传真：0757-8677 2271
电邮：duoli@gd-duoli.com
网址：www.gd-duoli.com

广州九阳酒店用品
广州市番禺区沙溪恒生市场北区六街19号
电话：020-3452 9551
传真：020-3452 9760
电邮：jayanmg@163.com
网址：www.jayanmg.com

食品加工机器
Food Processors

Anhui Hualing Kitchen Equipment Co., Ltd.
安徽华菱西厨装备股份有限公司
安徽省马鞍山市博望工业开发区
邮编：243131
电话：0555-676 9699
传真：0555-676 9511
电邮：info@fenglihua.com
网址：www.fenglihua.com

Chung Wah Kitchen Machine Limited
中华厨具设备有限公司
香港九龙红磡漆咸道436-450号富运大厦地下8号
电话：+852-2334 5411
传真：+852-2764 4249
电邮：winnie@chungwahkml.com.hk
网址：www.chungwahkml.com.hk

Electrolux Professional (Shanghai) Co., Ltd.
伊莱克斯商用电器（上海）有限公司
上海市外高桥保税区爱都路390号31号楼A座
邮编：200131
电话：021-5046 0099
传真：021-5046 0077
网址：www.electrolux-professional.cn
请参阅第 168 页

Guangzhou TeemYeah Food Machinery Co., Ltd.
广州市天烨食品机械有限公司
广东省荔湾区花地南路西塱麦村
北约55号107-108室
邮编：510385
电话：020-8141 7161
传真：020-8158 6171
电邮：ty@tianyefm.com
网址：www.tianyefm.com

Hakka Brothers Machinery Co., Ltd.
佛山市南海康莱达机电制造有限公司
广东省佛山市南海区狮山镇穆院村穆北工业区F栋
邮编：528225
电话：0757-8669 8309
传真：0757-8669 5967
电邮：sales@kanglaida.cn
网址：www.kanglaida.cn

Hangzhou Wanhe Cooker Appliance Co., Ltd.
杭州万和炊事用具有限公司
浙江省杭州市南复路59号陶瓷品市场7厅3楼28号
邮编：310003
电话：0571-8518 1486
传真：0571-8608 1218
网址：www.whcj.com

Hhangzhou Sanxin Hotel Equipment Co., Ltd.
杭州三信酒店设备有限公司
浙江省杭州市机场路277号
电话：0571-8787 5859
传真：0571-8504 6887
电邮：hzsanxin@126.com
网址：www.cn3xin.com

Irinox SPA
Via Madonna Di Loreto 6/B, 31020 Corbanese Di Tarzo Treviso Italy
电话：+39-0438 5844
传真：+39-0438 5843
电邮：irinox@irinox.com
网址：www.irinox.com

Jiangsu Changshu Nanfang Kitchen Equipment & Accessories Co., Ltd.
江苏常熟市南方厨房设备有限责任公司
江苏省常熟市东南经济开发区常昆公路288号
邮编：215542
电话：0512-5257 1555
传真：0512-5257 1516
电邮：info@china-nanchu.com
网址：www.china-nanchu.com

▼食品加工机器
Food Processors

Jiaxing Expro Stainless Steel Mechanical Engineering Co., Ltd.
嘉兴艾博不锈钢机械工程有限公司
浙江省嘉兴市二环西路2498号
电话：0571-8699 5176
传真：0571-8696 6930
电邮：exprojx@163.com
网址：www.expro.cn

Linkrich Machinery Development Co., Ltd.
广州中联盈机械有限公司
广州市东风东路699号之十三
广东港澳中心3505-3506室
邮编：510080
电话：020-8760 1850
传真：020-8760 7453
电邮：info@chinalinkrich.com
网址：www.chinalinkrich.com

Mado (Beijing) Machinery Production Co., Ltd.
马多（北京）机械制造有限公司
北京市朝阳区新源里16号世方豪庭1306室
邮编：100027
电话：010-8453 1700
传真：010-8453 1090
网址：www.mado-china.com

Pioneer Catering Equipment & Engineering Limited
魄力厨具工程有限公司
香港新界葵涌葵昌路26号
豪华工业大厦16字楼B座
电话：+852-2487 1707
传真：+852-2487 1816
电邮：hpc@pcee.com
网址：www.pcee.com.hk

Shanghai Linde Hotel Equipment Utensil Co., Ltd.
上海林德酒店设备用品配套有限公司
上海市普陀区澳门路356号1楼
邮编：200060
电话：021-5252 0630
传真：021-5252 0611
电邮：linde@lindesh.com
网址：www.lindesh.com

Sirman Spa (Consorzio Export Zafferano)
意福盟（上海）贸易有限公司
Viale Dell' Industria 9/11
Pieve Di Curtarolo (PD)
电话：+39(49)-969 8666
传真：+39(40)-969 8688
网址：www.sirman.com

Thunderbird Food Machinery Co., Ltd.
德霸食品机械有限公司
上海市松江区欣玉路453弄1-5号4D
邮编：201600
电话：021-5773 6845
传真：021-5773 6093
电邮：tbfmsh@tbfmcn.com.cn
网址：www.tbfmcn.com.cn
请参阅第163页

Yancheng China Food Machinery (Beijing) Co., Ltd.
燕诚神州食品机械（北京）有限公司
北京市西红门工业开发区福伟路甲三条5号
邮编：100076
电话：010-8771 3188
传真：010-5238 2733
网址：www.yc3333.com

上海金淳酒店设备有限公司
上海市中华路235号
邮编：200010
电话：021-6311 5442
传真：021-6328 8702
电邮：kinglake@kinglake.com.cn
网址：www.kinglake.com.cn

上海金树酒店设备有限公司
上海市普陀区府村路179号102栋3、4号门
邮编：200010
电话：021-5204 3106
传真：021-5204 3128
电邮：sales@js999.com.cn
网址：www.js999.com.cn

冰箱
Freezers

Dalian Sanyo Cold Chain Co., Ltd.
大连三洋冷链有限公司
大连经济技术开发区松岚街6号
电邮：gezhifei@163.com
网址：www.dalian-sanyo.com.cn
请参阅总目录书隔页面页

Fagor Industrial China
法格厨房设备（昆山）有限公司
江苏省昆山市千灯镇西班牙工业园区
邮编：215341
电话：0512-5515 5605
传真：0512-5515 5610
电邮：fagorchina@fagorindustrial.com
网址：www.fagorindustrial.cn

Hangzhou Meisda Electric Appliance Co., Ltd.
杭州美时达电器有限公司
杭州市西湖科技经济园振华路210号
邮编：310030
电话：0571-8830 8199
传真：0571-8830 8116
电邮：jack@meisda.com
网址：www.meisda.com

Hoshizaki Shanghai Co., Ltd.
星崎冷热机械（上海）有限公司
上海市恒丰路218号现代交通大厦805室
邮编：200070
电话：021-5180 1998
传真：021-5180 1947
电邮：info@hoshizaki.com.cn
网址：www.hoshizaki.com.cn
请参阅第198页

Jiangsu Qiaoyi Kitchen Utensils Manufacture Co., Ltd.
江苏侨谊厨房设备有限公司
江苏丹阳市丹句路28号
邮编：212300
电话：0511-8690 0071
传真：0511-8690 0029
电邮：info@jsqiaoyi.com
网址：www.jsqiaoyi.com

Nayati Indonesia, PT.
Jl. Raya Terboyo no.19
Kawasan Industri Terboyo Megah
Semarang - Indonesia
电话：+62(24)-658 0573
传真：+62(24)-658 0572
电邮：nayati@nayati.com
网址：www.nayati.com
请参阅第181页

Pro-Fit Industrial Co., Ltd.
宝发实业有限公司
香港新界葵涌大连排道152-160号
金龙工业中心第1座25字楼C室
电话：+852-2371 2862
传真：+852-2371 2867
电邮：profit@profitind.com
网址：www.profitind.com
请参阅第178页

Shandong Hongtai Electrical Appliance Co., Ltd.
山东宏泰电器有限公司
山东省莱州市宏祥经济示范区
邮编：261428
电话：0535-252 2153
传真：0535-252 2152
电邮：htdqxsb8013@126.com
网址：wwwsd-hongtai.com

Shanghai JinCheng Refrigerating Equipment Co., Ltd.
上海金城制冷设备有限公司
上海市中山北路3357号
邮编：200062
电话：021-6216 8066
传真：021-6216 8070
电邮：jincheng@shkingdom.com.cn
网址：www.shkingdom.com.cn
请参阅第225页

Shenzhen Hoowell Technology Development Co., Ltd.
深圳市弘维科技开发有限公司
深圳市南山区高新园南区深港产学研基地西座
电话：0755-8612 4495
传真：0755-8612 4495
电邮：joan@hoowell.com
网址：www.hoowell.com

Zhejiang Debao Electric Appliance Co., Ltd.
浙江德宝电器有限公司
海宁市连杭经济开发区新二路03号
邮编：310000
电话：0571-8698 8210
传真：0571-8698 8210
电邮：web@zj-debaodianqi.com
网址：www.zj-debaodianqi.com

久景制冷设备（上海）有限公司
上海市赵重公路1978号
电话：021-3987 6601
传真：021-3987 6501
电邮：niu@hisakage.com
网址：www.hisakage.com
请参阅第197页

▼冰箱 Freezers

斯科茨曼制冰系统（上海）有限公司
上海市徐虹中路20号2号楼2503室
邮编：200235
电话：021-6131 3200
传真：021-6131 3330
网址：www.scotsman-china.com
请参阅第241页

炸炉 Fryers

Electrolux Professional (Shanghai) Co., Ltd.
伊莱克斯商用电器（上海）有限公司
上海市外高桥保税区爱都路390号31号楼A座
邮编：200131
电话：021-5046 0099
传真：021-5046 0077
网址：www.electrolux-professional.cn
请参阅第168页

Fagor Industrial China
法格厨房设备（昆山）有限公司
江苏省昆山市千灯镇西班牙工业园区
邮编：215341
电话：0512-5515 5605
传真：0512-5515 5610
电邮：fagorchina@fagorindustrial.com
网址：www.fagorindustrial.cn

Foshan Nanhai Flamemax Catering Equipment Co., Ltd.
佛山市南海烽煌餐饮设备制造有限公司
广东省佛山市南海区里水镇赤山福西工业区5号
电话：0757-8561 6586
传真：0757-8561 6589
网址：www.flamemax.com

Foshan SBS Electric Appliance Co., Ltd.
佛山市思博诗电器有限公司
佛山市南海区大沥镇谢边第一工业区
电话：0757-8858 3111
传真：0757-8118 7596
电邮：fsrusy@21cn.com
网址：www.sbs-fryer.com

Gangyang Machine & Electric Equipment Co., Ltd.
佛山市南海港洋机电设备有限公司
佛山市南海区松岗镇松夏工业园日田路2号
邮编：510000
电话：0757-8520 9990
传真：0757-8520 9995
网址：www.gzverly.com

Guangzhou Haipingyang Western Kitchen Equipment Co., Ltd.
广州海平洋西厨设备有限公司
广州市白云区西槎路同德上步花园A栋北7号
电话：020-3649 7831
传真：020-3638 1831
电邮：sales@haipingyang.com
网址：www.haipingyang.com

Guangzhou Wailaan Kitchen Fixture Make Co., Ltd.
广州唯利安西厨房设备制造有限公司
广东省广州市白云区新市联边村彭上工业区
邮编：510440
电话：020-3622 0141
传真：020-3622 0723
电邮：wailaan@163.com
网址：www.wailaan.com

JetCool Commetcial Refrigeration Company
骏宝商用设备公司
JetCool House
136 Sung Shan New Village, Yuen Long
N.T., Hong Kong
电话：+852-2442 1108
传真：+852-2442 1155
电邮：info@jetcool.com.hk
网址：www.jetcool.com.hk

Maschinenfabrik Kurt Neubauer GmbH & Co.
Halberstaedter Strasse 2a, D-38300 Wolfenbuettel, Germany
电话：+49-5331 89263
传真：+49-5331 89280
电邮：fn@mkn.de
网址：www.mkn.eu
请参阅第184页

Middleby China Corporation
美得彼餐饮设备（上海）有限公司
上海市松江区九亭镇久富经济开发区盛高路98号
邮编：201615
电话：021-6769 0808
传真：021-6762 7640
电邮：mandyzhang@middleby.com.cn
网址：www.middleby.com
请参阅第174、175页

Nayati Indonesia, PT.
Jl. Raya Terboyo no.19
Kawasan Industri Terboyo Megah
Semarang - Indonesia
电话：+62(24)-658 0573
传真：+62(24)-658 0572
电邮：nayati@nayati.com
网址：www.nayati.com
请参阅第181页

Ningbo Yingfeng Metal Products Co., Ltd.
宁波英峰金属制品有限公司
宁波市鄞县大道东吴段28号
邮编：315113
电话：0574-8819 7806
传真：0574-8819 7808
电邮：info@china-yingfeng.com
网址：www.xiangying.com.cn

Shanghai De An Hang Trading Co., Ltd.
上海得安行贸易有限公司
上海市沪松公路松江高科技园区九泾路318号
邮编：201615
电话：021-6769 6703
传真：021-6763 9059
网址：www.zxcj.com.cn

Simplex Foodservice Equipment (Shanghai) Ltd.
新必利餐饮设备（上海）有限公司
上海市松江区九亭镇涞坊路57号
邮编：201615
电话：021-6784 1311
传真：021-6784 1331
电邮：simplex@online.sh.cn
网址：www.simplex.cn

Universal Electrical Machine Works (Shenzhen) Co., Ltd.
环球炉业（深圳）有限公司
深圳市龙岗区大鹏街道
王母第一工业区3、4号厂房
邮编：518120
电话：0755-8430 5128
传真：0755-8430 8213
电邮：cninfo@uemw.com.hk
网址：www.uemw.com.hk

冰雕设备 Ice Carving Equipment

Unreal Ice
PO Box 1299 Nerang, 4211, Qld Australia
电话：+61-755 749 506
电邮：info@unrealicesculptures.com
网址：www.unrealice.com

冰雕工具 Ice Sculpturing Tools

Jinnan Jin Qilin Industrial Co., Ltd.
济南金浚麒麟实业有限公司
山东省济南市市中区泺源大街229号
金龙大厦东八楼H座
邮编：250012
电话：0531-8611 9688
传真：0531-8611 5988
电邮：cnjql@126.com
网址：www.cnjql.com

厨房用品 Kitchenware

Beijing Jingguang FangYuan Kitchen Equipment Company
北京京广方园厨房设备有限责任公司
北京市宣武区建功南里3号楼一层
邮编：100054
电话：010-6354 1242
传真：010-6352 0957
电邮：zengjia0627@126.com
网址：www.jgfy.com

Boloni
博洛尼家居用品（北京）有限公司
北京市朝阳区育慧里11号
邮编：100101
电话：010-5134 8888
传真：010-5134 8810
电邮：hui@kebao.cn
网址：www.boloni.com.cn

▼厨房用品
Kitchenware

Eurochef China
欧厨专业厨房用具（北京）有限公司
北京市朝阳区酒仙桥东路1号M6座西三层B区
邮编：100016
电话：010-6438 2431
传真：010-6438 2432
网址：www.eurochefasia.com

Foshan Hefeng Electro-Chemical Works Ltd.
佛山市南海鹤峰电化厂有限公司
广东省佛山市南海区和顺镇鹤峰村
电话：0757-8511 8555
传真：0757-8511 3080
电邮：info@easycook-ware.com
网址：www.easycook-ware.com

Guangzhou San Lai Co., Ltd.
广州三莱电器有限公司
广东省广州市番禺沙溪幸福南路东南街11号2楼
电话：020-3992 8047
传真：020-3992 8049
电邮：gzzrp@126.com
网址：www.gzsamhee.com

Hangzhou Yindu Kitchen Equipment Company Limited
杭州银都餐饮设备有限公司
杭州市余杭区经济开发区星桥配套区星星路1号
邮编：311100
电话：0571-8626 0777
传真：0571-8626 0718
电邮：info@yinduchina.com
网址：www.yinduchina.com

Hotelier Service China Co., Ltd.
上海欧太黎企业管理有限公司
上海市长宁路1551号虹桥国际大厦2号楼1801室
邮编：200051
电话：021-6124 2766
传真：021-6124 2776*805
电邮：enquiry@hotelier-sc.com
网址：www.hotelier-sc.com

Huning Pallets Co.
显兴卡板有限公司
香港九龙油塘茶果岭道428号
荣山工业大厦四楼D室
电话：+852-2815 4488
传真：+852-2815 7766
请参阅第381页

Induc (Qingdao) Commercial Electrics Co., Ltd.
喜达客（青岛）商用电器有限公司
青岛市宁夏路288号青岛软件园G6楼13层
邮编：266071
电话：0532-8667 2012
传真：0532-8667 2028
电邮：info@induc.com.cn
网址：www.induc.com.cn

Jiangmen Harvest Kitchenware Co., Ltd.
江门市联丰厨具有限公司
广东省江门市西环路325号
（天朗花园）之四202室
邮编：529000
电话：0750-366 6312
传真：0750-366 6310
电邮：info@jmharvest.cn
网址：www.jmharvest.cn

Jiangmen Liantai Kitchen Equipment Co., Ltd.
江门连泰不锈钢厨具有限公司
广东省江门市荷塘镇康溪工业区
电话：0750-375 6161
传真：0750-373 5138
电邮：email@jm-liantai.com
网址：www.jm-liantai.com
上海办事处：
上海市普陀区铜川路185号
麒龙酒店用品市场A67号
电话：021-6224 8962
电邮：job@sh-liantai.com
网址：www.sh-liantai.com

King Botter Commercial Kitchen Equipment Co., Ltd.
山东金佰特商用厨具有限公司
山东省博兴县兴福工业园
邮编：256510
电话：0543-288 5888
传真：0543-216 8688
网址：www.jinbaite.com

Kinox Enterprises Ltd.
建业五金塑胶厂有限公司
香港九龙观塘鸿图道九号建业中心20楼
电话：+852-2389 6261
传真：+852-2343 2111
电邮：enquiry@kinox.com
网址：www.kinox.com

Kuntai Hotel Appliance Limited Company
广州坤泰酒店用品有限公司
广州市珠海区
南天国际酒店用品批发市场23栋32-33号
邮编：510288
电话：020-3423 3930
传真：020-3424 4830
电邮：gzkuntai@hotmail.com
网址：www.gzkuntai.com

Le Creuset (Shanghai) Co., Ltd.
酷彩法厨商贸（上海）有限公司
上海市南京西路1168号
中信泰富广场19楼1911-1912室
邮编：201200
电话：021-6372 0606
传真：021-6372 2008
网址：www.lecreuset.com

Lee Hun Trading Co., Ltd.
香港利亨贸易行
香港九龙红磡鹤园街9-11号
凯旋工商中心第三期二楼Q室
电话：+852-2334 0873
传真：+852-2954 2181
网址：www.cpl.net.cn

▼厨房用品
Kitchenware

Linkrich Machinery Development Co., Ltd.
广州中联盈机械有限公司
广州市东风东路699号之十三
广东港澳中心3505-3506室
邮编：510080
电话：020-8760 1850
传真：020-8760 7453
电邮：info@chinalinkrich.com
网址：www.chinalinkrich.com

Lucky Industrial Co., Ltd.
佛山市南海罗村联星伟仕佰日制品厂
广东省佛山市南堤路45号
河畔明珠大厦A座2107房
邮编：528000
电话：0757-8230 0447
传真：0757-8230 0445
电邮：markson@luckyco.com.tw
网址：www.luckyco.com.tw

Lui Chuen Kee.
江门吕泉记五金制品厂
广东省江门市蓬江区杜阮镇贯溪管理区新围段
邮编：529075
电话：0750-366 1211
传真：0750-366 2211
网址：www.luichuenkee.com

Pui Hing Metal Ware Factory
Blk A, 11/F., Stage 1
Tung Chun Ind. Bldg.,
9-11 Cheung Wing Road, Kwai Chung
N.T., Hong Kong
电话：+852-2423 9028
传真：+852-2420 6400
电邮：info@puihing.com.hk
网址：www.puihing.com.hk

Shanghai Baolong International Trading Co., Ltd.
上海宝隆国际贸易有限公司
上海市天潼路133号8楼
邮编：200080
电话：021-6321 2297
传真：021-6321 4385
电邮：xiex@sh-baolong.com
网址：www.sh-baolong.com

Shanghai Fang-Yuan Industial Co., Ltd.
上海方圆实业有限公司
上海市虹漕路175弄6号301室
邮编：201103
电话：021-6402 3264
传真：021-6402 0460
电邮：webmaster@sh-fangyuan.com
网址：www.sh-fangyuan.com

Shenzhen Pama Hotel Products Co., Ltd.
深圳市帕玛酒店用品有限公司
深圳市南山区粤海路粤海工业村
深圳动漫园4栋201室
邮编：518054
电话：0755-8605 2592
传真：0755-8605 2582
网址：www.szpama.com
请参阅第42页

Sunnex Metal Products (Shenzhen) Ltd.
日升五金制品（深圳）有限公司
深圳市盐田区沙头角深沙路东和工业大厦A座二楼
邮编：518081
电话：0755-2555 1458
传真：0755-2535 7498
电邮：sales@sunnexchina.com
网址：www.sunnexchina.com

Tianjin Datang Fudi Commercial Kitchen Equipment Co., Ltd.
天津市大唐富地商用厨具有限公司
天津市西青技术开发区兴华十支路6号
邮编：300385
电话：022-8832 3888
传真：022-8396 1170
电邮：sales@tj-dtfd.com
网址：www.tj-dtfd.com

Universal Electrical Machine Works (Shenzhen) Co., Ltd.
环球炉业（深圳）有限公司
深圳市龙岗区大鹏街道
王母第一工业区3、4号厂房
邮编：518120
电话：0755-8430 5128
传真：0755-8430 8213
电邮：cninfo@uemw.com.hk
网址：www.uemw.com.hk

Vollrath (Shanghai) Trading Limited
沃华夫（上海）商贸有限公司
上海市浦东新区张杨路500号
华润时代广场23楼A座
邮编：200122
电话：021-5058 9580
传真：021-5058 9581
电邮：tyeung@vollrathco.com
网址：www.vollrathco.com

Wuxi Baofeng Kitchen Set Kitchen Fitting Co., Ltd.
无锡宝丰厨配有限公司
无锡市东北塘严埭工业园
邮编：214191
电话：0510-8385 7333
传真：0510-8385 8588
电邮：wxbfcp@163.com
网址：www.wxbfcp.com

Yong Ge Trading (shanghai) Co., Ltd.
上海市长宁区黄金城道676号
邮编：201103
电话：021-6308 0741
传真：021-6313 3707
电邮：wittywang@vip.163.com
网址：www.aistiashop.com
请参阅第215页

Zhejiang WuGu Industries Co., Ltd.
浙江五谷实业有限公司
浙江省余姚市丈亭台商投资园区
电话：0574-6299 8803
传真：0574-6299 8899
电邮：sho@hwugu.com
网址：www.hwugu.com
请参阅第201页

Zhejiang Zhongbaoli Hotel Articles Co., Ltd.
浙江中宝利酒店用品有限公司
浙江省永康市松石西路899号
邮编：321300
电话：0579-8726 4178
传真：0579-8726 5278
电邮：zbl@zhongbaoli.com
网址：www.zhongbaoli.com

Zwilling J.A. Henckels Shanghai Ltd.
上海双立人亨克斯有限公司
上海市浦东新区三林路424号
邮编：200124
电话：021-3886 1343
网址：www.zwilling.com.cn

北京经开万佳国际酒店用品市场
北京市朝阳区南四环东路十八里店
南桥吕家营商业街1号
邮编：100023
电话：010-8769 8883
传真：010-8769 7773
网址：www.bjjkwj.com

模具
Moulds

Eurochef China
欧厨专业厨房用具（北京）有限公司
北京市朝阳区酒仙桥东路1号M6座西三层B区
邮编：100016
电话：010-6438 2431
传真：010-6438 2432
网址：www.eurochefasia.com

Haerbin Shengda Food Moulds Co., Ltd.
哈尔滨盛达食品模具公司
哈尔滨市道外区景阳街158号
邮编：150020
电话：0451-8832 2710
传真：0451-8834 5353
电邮：shengdamuju@163.com
网址：www.shengdamoju.com

Hotelier Service China Co., Ltd.
上海欧太黎企业管理有限公司
上海市长宁路1551号虹桥国际大厦2号楼1801室
邮编：200051
电话：021-6124 2766
传真：021-6124 2776*805
电邮：enquiry@hotelier-sc.com
网址：www.hotelier-sc.com

Jinnan Jin Qilin Industrial Co., Ltd.
济南金浚麒麟实业有限公司
山东省济南市市中区泺源大街229号
金龙大厦东八楼H座
邮编：250012
电话：0531-8611 9688
传真：0531-8611 5988
电邮：cnjql@126.com
网址：www.cnjql.com

Orangerie (Shanghai) Food Ingredients Pte. Ltd.
上海欧润吉食品有限公司
上海市嘉唐公路888号
邮编：201807
电话：021-5954 8622
传真：021-5954 2882
电邮：orangerie@orangerie.org
网址：www.orangerie.org

SHANGHAI CHANGSHUN BAKE WARE CO.,LTD
上海昌顺烘焙器具有限公司
上海市青浦区崧泽大道5345号
邮编：201706
电话：021-3987 6216
传真：021-3987 6218
电邮：cakeware@163.com
网址：www.shchangshun.com

▼模具
Moulds

Wuxi Beikeweiwe Untensil Factory
无锡贝克威尔器具厂
江苏省无锡市太湖镇梁南村
电话：0510-8507 1228
传真：0510-8507 1328
网址：www.bakeware.wjw.cn

Wuxi QianNeng Bake Ware Co., Ltd.
无锡乾能烘焙器具有限公司
江苏省无锡滨湖区太湖镇双新工业园
电话：0510-8506 6858
传真：0510-8101 7596
网址：www.qnqj.com

淮阳县新华食品机械厂
河南省淮阳县工业园区
邮编：466700
电话：0394-288 2123
传真：0394-288 2123
电邮：liu2663343@163.com
网址：www.xhmjc.com

济南磐龙冰雕模具厂
山东省济南长清区张夏工业园
邮编：250308
电话：0531-8748 3909
传真：0531-8748 3909
电邮：jnpanlong@126.com
网址：www.jnpanlong.com

周口光华食品机械厂
河南省周口市川汇区建设东路与东外环路交叉口向西80米路北（马庄）
邮编：466001
电话：0394-858 2671
传真：0394-858 8419
网址：www.zkguanghua.com

烤炉、焗炉
Ovens

Angelo Po Trading (Shanghai)
傲桀贸易（上海）有限公司
上海市江场三路88号一楼
邮编：200436
电话：021-6094 0100
传真：021-6094 0288
电邮：info@angelopo.cn
网址：www.angelopo.it
请参阅第167、195页、封面

China Manufacturing Solutions Ltd.
中国传盛商用设备
山东省潍城经济开发区彩虹路与卧龙西街路口
电话：0536-610 5299
电邮：pan@chmans.com
网址：www.chmans.com
请参阅第182页

Electrolux Professional (Shanghai) Co., Ltd.
伊莱克斯商用电器（上海）有限公司
上海市外高桥保税区爱都路390号31号楼A座
邮编：200131
电话：021-5046 0099
传真：021-5046 0077
网址：www.electrolux-professional.cn
请参阅第168页

Foshan Nanhai Flamemax Catering Equipment Co., Ltd.
佛山市南海烽煌餐饮设备制造有限公司
广东省佛山市南海区里水镇赤山福西工业区5号
电话：0757-8561 6586
传真：0757-8561 6589
网址：www.flamemax.com

Guangzhou New Yuehai Western Kitchen Equipment Factory
广州新粤海西厨设备厂
广东省广州市花都区花山镇华侨科技工业园
邮编：510880
电话：020-8694 9182
传真：020-8694 9123
电邮：newyuehai@newyuehai.com
网址：www.newyuehai.com

JetCool Commetcial Refrigeration Company
骏宝商用设备公司
JetCool House
136 Sung Shan New Village, Yuen Long
N.T., Hong Kong
电话：+852-2442 1108
传真：+852-2442 1155
电邮：info@jetcool.com.hk
网址：www.jetcool.com.hk

Jiangmen Ngan kong Kitchen Appliance Manufacturing Co., Ltd.
江门银江厨具制品有限公司
广东省江门市新会区会城镇奇榜村地苑工业区B座
邮编：529100
电话：0750-616 7080
传真：0750-616 7086
电邮：sales@ngankong.com
网址：www.ngankong.com

Maschinenfabrik Kurt Neubauer GmbH & Co.
Halberstaedter Strasse 2a, D-38300 Wolfenbuettel, Germany
电话：+49-5331 89263
传真：+49-5331 89280
电邮：fn@mkn.de
网址：www.mkn.eu
请参阅第184页

Middleby China Corporation
美得彼餐饮设备（上海）有限公司
上海市松江区九亭镇久富经济开发区盛高路98号
邮编：201615
电话：021-6769 0808
传真：021-6762 7640
电邮：mandyzhang@middleby.com.cn
网址：www.middleby.com
请参阅第174、175页

Oriental Engineering (Shanghai) Co., Ltd.
港捷（上海）贸易有限公司
上海市静安区南苏州路1501号1号楼2楼
邮编：200041
电话：021-5228 6053
传真：021-6272 2738
电邮：sales@oriental-eng.com.hk
网址：www.oequip.com

RATIONAL International AG Shanghai Rep. Office
乐信国际股份公司上海代表处
上海市肇嘉浜路798号201B室
邮编：200030
电话：021-6473 7473
传真：021-6473 0197
电邮：shanghai.office@rational-online.com
网址：www.rational-china.com
请参阅第169页

Shanghai De An Hang Trading Co., Ltd.
上海得安行贸易有限公司
上海市沪松公路松江高科技园区九泾路318号
邮编：201615
电话：021-6769 6703
传真：021-6763 9059
网址：www.zxcj.com.cn

Shanghai J&C Industry Co., Ltd.
上海积创实业发展有限公司
上海市黄兴路1725号怡富商务广场1701/1706室
邮编：200433
电话：021-6587 6136
传真：021-6587 6134
网址：www.jichuang.net.cn

Shanghai Unitech Food Machinery Company
上海台新食品机械有限公司
上海市万航渡路888号开开大厦26楼A座
邮编：200051
电话：021-6240 0595
电邮：unitech-sh@unitech-sh.com
网址：www.unitech-sh.com

Thunderbird Food Machinery Co., Ltd.
德霸食品机械有限公司
上海市松江区欣玉路453弄1-5号4D
邮编：201600
电话：021-5773 6845
传真：021-5773 6093
电邮：tbfmsh@tbfmcn.com.cn
网址：www.tbfmcn.com.cn
请参阅第163页

Universal Electrical Machine Works (Shenzhen) Co., Ltd.
环球炉业（深圳）有限公司
深圳市龙岗区大鹏街道
王母第一工业区3、4号厂房
邮编：518120
电话：0755-8430 5128
传真：0755-8430 8213
电邮：cninfo@uemw.com.hk
网址：www.uemw.com.hk

Williams Refrigeration (Dongguan) Co., Ltd.
威廉士制冷设备（东莞）有限公司
上海市卢湾区打浦路1号金玉兰广场西峰703室
邮编：200023
电话：021-5396 0183
传真：021-5396 1335
网址：www.agafoodservice.com

广东多丽食品机械有限公司
广东省佛山市南海区平洲平北工业区内
邮编：528251
电话：0757-8677 3774
传真：0757-8677 2271
电邮：duoli@gd-duoli.com
网址：www.gd-duoli.com

马尼托瓦克餐饮设备集团 中国
上海市凯旋路613号G号楼
电话：021-6152 6100
传真：021-6152 6030
网址：www.manitowocfoodservice.com.cn
请参阅第170、171页

制冷设备
Refrigerating Equipment

Beijing Harvest E&M Co., Ltd.
北京丰汇加机电设备销售有限公司
北京市宣武区建功西里1号楼天缘公寓A座2701室
邮编：100054
电话：010-8351 6972
传真：010-8351 7663
电邮：sales@bjharvest.cn
网址：www.bjharvest.cn

Beijing XuanWu Cooking Food Machine Co., Ltd.
北京市宣武炊事食品机械有限公司
北京市宣武区西便门东里甲1号
邮编：100053
电话：010-6303 1118
电邮：bxcj@bxcj.com.cn
网址：www.bxcj.com.cn

Carel Electronic (Suzhou) Co., Ltd.
卡乐电子（苏州）有限责任公司
苏州高新区鹿山路369号环保产业园26号厂房
邮编：215129
电话：0512-6662 6627
传真：0512-6662 9889
电邮：sales@carel-china.com
网址：www.carel-china.com

China Manufacturing Solutions Ltd.
中国传盛商用设备
山东省潍城经济开发区彩虹路与卧龙西街路口
电话：0536-610 5299
电邮：pan@chmans.com
网址：www.chmans.com
请参阅第182页

Dalian Sanyo Cold Chain Co., Ltd.
大连三洋冷链有限公司
大连经济技术开发区松岚街6号
电邮：gezhifei@163.com
网址：www.dalian-sanyo.com.cn
业务范围：
我公司2011年下半年强势推出四个系列商用厨房冷柜。分别是：
1. 专为连锁餐饮的高温高湿厨房环境开发的ES变频风冷商用冷柜，节能率达到25-35%，每台年节约电费1200-1800元
2. 为外资高端酒店开发的GN风冷系列
3. 为内资高端酒店开发的FC风冷系列
4. 为经济型用户开发的NC直冷系列产品。产品线空前丰富，专注中高端市场。
给我们机会，我们为您创造商机无限！
华东营销中心 电话：021-6160 9151
华南营销中心 电话：0755-8329 9353
华北营销中心 电话：010-6418 1938
东北营销中心 电话：0411-8252 6021
请参阅总目录书隔页面页

Dalian Xin Jian Hai Hotel Supplies & Trade Co.
大连新建海酒店用品贸易行
大连市沙河口区星海广场B3区一品星海6-3-1
电话：0411-8480 5299
传真：0411-8480 4111
电邮：xinjianhai@hotmail.com
网址：www.china-xjh.com

Electrolux Professional (Shanghai) Co., Ltd.
伊莱克斯商用电器（上海）有限公司
上海市外高桥保税区爱都路390号31号楼A座
邮编：200131
电话：021-5046 0099
传真：021-5046 0077
网址：www.electrolux-professional.cn
请参阅第168页

Elegance Refrigeration Corporation
昆山广腾制冷设备有限公司
江苏省昆山市友谊北路92号
邮编：215314
电话：0512-5788 9388
传真：0512-5788 9387
网址：www.neofreeze.com

Foshan Qing Yuan Chuju
佛山市庆源厨具
佛山市三水区南丰大道南边工业区
电话：0757-8731 8991
传真：0757-8731 1882
网址：www.gdqycj.com

Guangdong Xingxing Refrigeration Equipment Co., Ltd.
广东星星制冷设备有限公司
广东省佛山市三水区乐平镇
南边工业开发区南丰大道
邮编：528135
电话：0757-8732 3866
传真：0757-8732 3855
网址：www.gdxingxing.com

Guangzhou Green & Health Refrigeration Equipment Co., Ltd.
广州绿缔制冷设备制造有限公司
广东省广州市白云区龙河西路南横5路6号
电话：020-8616 6280
传真：020-8616 5579
电邮：greencooker@hotmail.com
网址：www.greencooker.com

Hangzhou Kalifon Stainless Steel Kitchen Equipment Co., Ltd.
杭州凯利不锈钢厨房设备有限公司
杭州市经济技术开发区16号大街8号
邮编：310018
电话：0571-8671 6016
传真：0571-8671 6018
网址：www.kalifon.com

Hangzhou Kator Foreign Trade Co., Ltd.
杭州凯特对外贸易有限公司
杭州市萧山区经济技术开发区建设四路8号
邮编：311215
电话：0571-8289 6288
传真：0571-8289 6711
电邮：sales@h-kitchen.com
网址：www.h-kitchen.com

Hangzhou Yindu Kitchen Equipment Company Limited
杭州银都餐饮设备有限公司
杭州市余杭区经济开发区星桥配套区星星路1号
邮编：311100
电话：0571-8626 0777
传真：0571-8626 0718
电邮：info@yinduchina.com
网址：www.yinduchina.com

Hao Da Cooling Kitchen Equipment Co., Ltd.
中山市豪达冷冻厨具设备制造有限公司
中山市石岐海景路海景工业园3-5号
威震工业楼地下
邮编：528400
电话：0760-8838 2491
传真：0760-8838 5069
电邮：fancor369647@163.com
网址：www.fancor.net

Heatcraft Worldwide Refrigeration - Asia
西克环球制冷亚洲有限公司
上海市虹桥路1号港汇广场1号楼2306室
邮编：200030
电话：021-6407 1616
传真：021-6447 7586
网址：www.heatcraft.com.cn

Hong Kong Foodservice Equipment Co., Ltd.
香港餐饮设备有限公司
香港九龙旺角塘尾道18号嘉礼大厦3楼A至B室
电话：+852-2300 1173
传真：+852-2780 6986
电邮：info@hkfec.com.hk
网址：www.hkfec.com.hk

Hoshizaki Shanghai Co., Ltd.
星崎冷热机械（上海）有限公司
上海市恒丰路218号现代交通大厦805室
邮编：200070
电话：021-5180 1998
传真：021-5180 1947
电邮：info@hoshizaki.com.cn
网址：www.hoshizaki.com.cn
请参阅第198页

Irinox SPA
Via Madonna Di Loreto 6/B, 31020 Corbanese Di Tarzo Treviso Italy
电话：+39-0438 5844
传真：+39-0438 5843
电邮：irinox@irinox.com
网址：www.irinox.com

JetCool Commetcial Refrigeration Company
骏宝商用设备公司
JetCool House
136 Sung Shan New Village, Yuen Long
N.T., Hong Kong
电话：+852-2442 1108
传真：+852-2442 1155
电邮：info@jetcool.com.hk
网址：www.jetcool.com.hk

Jiangsu Changshu Nanfang Kitchen Equipment & Accessories Co., Ltd.
江苏常熟市南方厨房设备有限责任公司
江苏省常熟市东南经济开发区常昆公路288号
邮编：215542
电话：0512-5257 1555
传真：0512-5257 1516
电邮：info@china-nanchu.com
网址：www.china-nanchu.com

HISAKAGE
REFRIGERATION SYSTEM

全球信赖的制冰系统
Global trust ice-make system

方形冰・半方形冰・圓形冰・八角冰・月形冰・鱗片冰・雪花冰・礦塊冰・自動出冰機
Cube ice・Half-cube ice・Round ice・Octagon ice・Tsukigata ice・Squamous ice・Snow ice・Irreguiar ice・Autmatic out ice-make

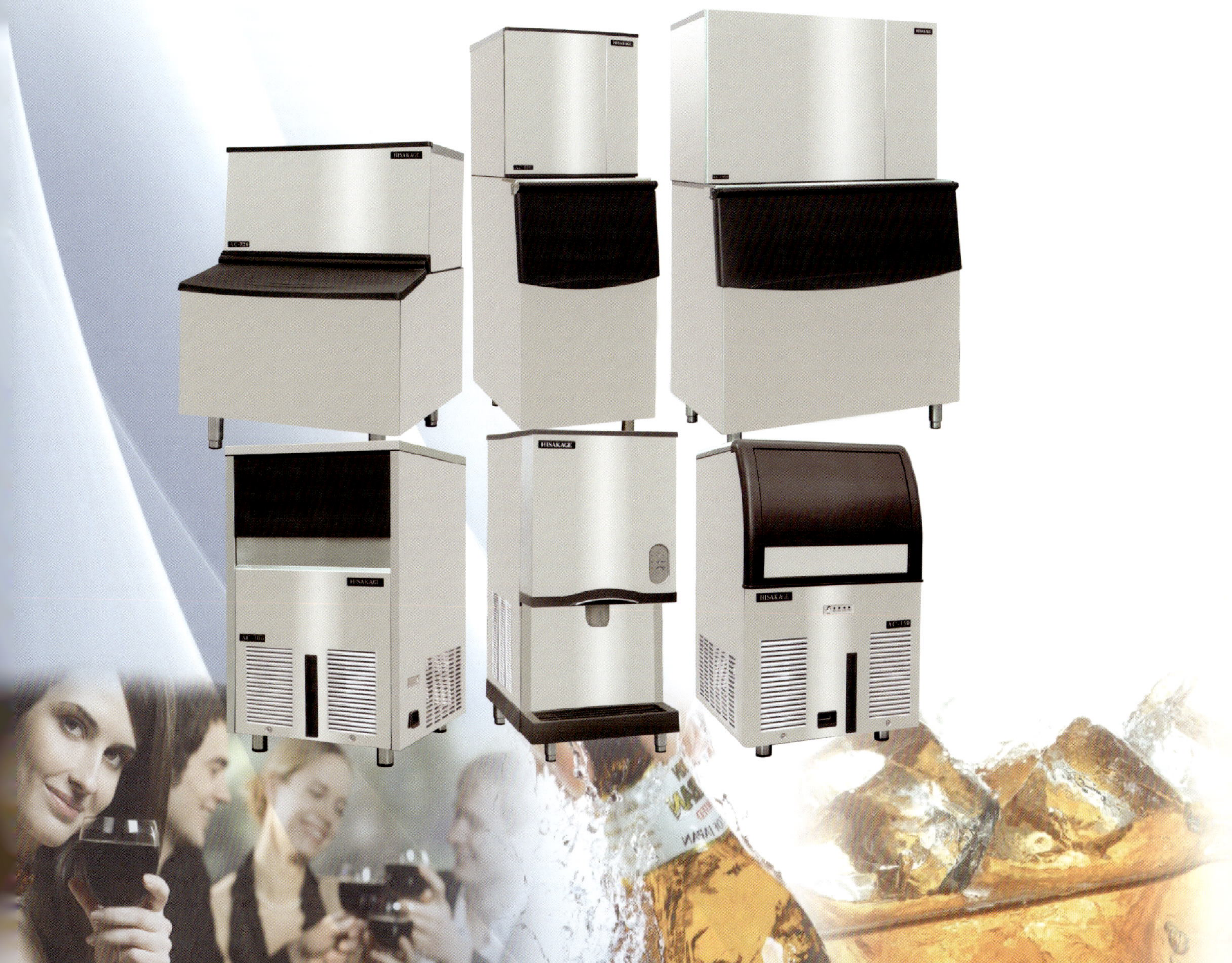

HISAKAGE是一家应用日本技术，采用全球优质部件，专业生产商用及工业用制冰设备、制冷设备的生产厂家。本公司已通过ISO9001-2000国际管理体系认证，产品已通过UL、NSF、CE等多项权威认证。现已出口全球众多国家和地区，从酒店到超市，从游轮到飞机等各大行业，HISAKAGE一直在努力提供全方位的制冰产品解决方案。

全国免费服务热线：400-820-0106

久景制冷设备（上海）有限公司
地址:上海市赵重公路1978号
Tel:86-21-39876601
Fax:86-21-39876501
Http://www.hisakage.com
Email:niu@hisakage.com

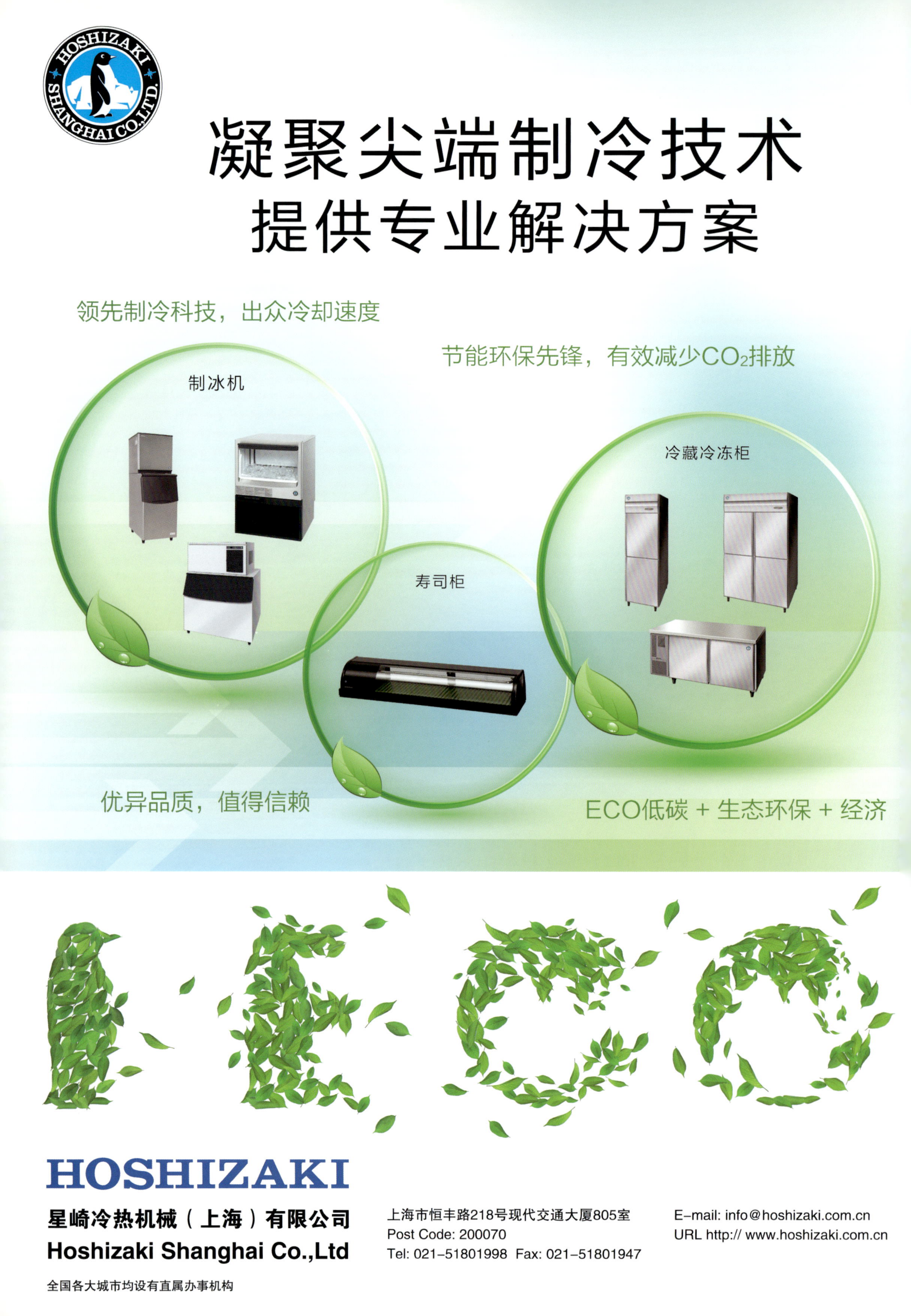

HOSHIZAKI SHANGHAI CO.,LTD.
凝聚尖端制冷技术
提供专业解决方案
领先制冷科技，出众冷却速度
节能环保先锋，有效减少CO2排放
制冰机
冷藏冷冻柜
寿司柜
优异品质，值得信赖
ECO低碳 + 生态环保 + 经济
HOSHIZAKI
星崎冷热机械（上海）有限公司
Hoshizaki Shanghai Co.,Ltd
全国各大城市均设有直属办事机构
上海市恒丰路218号现代交通大厦805室
Post Code: 200070
Tel: 021-51801998 Fax: 021-51801947
E-mail: info@hoshizaki.com.cn
URL http:// www.hoshizaki.com.cn

▼制冷设备
Refrigerating Equipment

JingLi Refrigeration Equipment Manufacturing Co., Ltd.
中山市劲力冷冻设备制造有限公司
广东省中山市东明北路民营科技园
邮编：528402
电话：0760-8870 4622
传真：0760-8870 1422
电邮：jingli@jingli.com
网址：www.jingli.com

Lee Hun Trading Co., Ltd.
香港利亨贸易行
香港九龙红磡鹤园街9-11号
凯旋工商中心第三期二楼Q室
电话：+852-2334 0873
传真：+852-2954 2181
网址：www.cpl.net.cn

Nayati Indonesia, PT.
Jl. Raya Terboyo no.19
Kawasan Industri Terboyo Megah
Semarang - Indonesia
电话：+62(24)-658 0573
传真：+62(24)-658 0572
电邮：nayati@nayati.com
网址：www.nayati.com
请参阅第181页

Professional Service Foe Commercial Kitche
上海潔城餐饮设备有限公司
上海市松江区九泾路736号2号
电话：021-6775 6410
传真：021-3373 1390
电邮：info@frinox.com.cn
网址：www.frinox.com.cn

Qingdao Dellware Electrical Appliance Co., Ltd.
青岛德莱维电器有限公司
青岛市双元路流亭国际空港工业园
邮编：266108
电话：0532-8580 2882
传真：0532-8580 2772
电邮：info@dellware.cn
网址：www.dellware.cn

Qingdao Turbo Air. Inc
青岛特博尔科技发展有限公司
青岛胶南市海滨工业园珠山路
以西海滨七路以北297号
电话：0532-8513 6600
传真：0532-8513 5638
网址：www.turboairchina.com

Rightway Asia Limited
方正亚洲有限公司
山东省青岛市城阳区春阳路167号盈国国际721室
邮编：266109
电话：0532-8110 0375
传真：0532-8796 5770
网址：www.rightwayasia.com

Saro Worldwide (Hong Kong) Ltd.
No. 4-5, G/F., 68 Lok Ku Road
Sheung Wan, H.K.
电话：+852-2581 9258
传真：+852-2581 3014
电邮：info@saro.com.hk
网址：www.saro.com.hk

Shandong Hongtai Electrical Appliance Co., Ltd.
山东宏泰电器有限公司
山东省莱州市宏祥经济示范区
邮编：261428
电话：0535-252 2153
传真：0535-252 2152
电邮：htdqxsb8013@126.com
网址：wwwsd-hongtai.com

Shanghai Bingluo Electric Machine Equipment Co., Ltd.
上海冰骆电器设备有限公司
上海市青浦区外青松公路西庆路18号3幢
邮编：201700
电话：021-6921 9086
传真：021-6921 9087
电邮：sales@shingluo.com
网址：www.shbingluo.com

Shanghai Furong Industry Co., Ltd.
上海芙蓉实业有限公司
上海市闵行区浦江工业区竹园路268号
邮编：201112
电话：021-5431 1051
传真：021-5431 1052
电邮：furong@furong.com
网址：www.furong.com

Shanghai Guodeng Refrigeration Equipment Co., Ltd.
上海国登制冷设备有限公司
上海市闵行区七宝镇华友路515号
邮编：201100
电话：021-6459 7175
传真：021-6459 7183
网址：www.guodeng.com.cn

Shanghai JinCheng Refrigerating Equipment Co., Ltd.
上海金城制冷设备有限公司
上海市中山北路3357号
邮编：200062
电话：021-6216 8066
传真：021-6216 8070
电邮：jincheng@shkingdom.com.cn
网址：www.shkingdom.com.cn
请参阅第225页

Shanghai Keshi Refrigeration Equipment Co., Ltd.
上海科式制冷设备有限公司
上海市松江区高技公路275号
邮编：201615
电话：021-5763 4410
传真：021-5763 1719
网址：www.konos.com.cn

Shanghai Xingjian Industry Co., Ltd.
上海星剑实业有限公司
上海市普陀区绥德路555号1号楼
邮编：200331
电话：021-6483 9061
传真：021-6482 3642
电邮：jiangfang@shxjsy.com
网址：www.shxjsy.com

Simplex Foodservice Equipment (Shanghai) Ltd.
新必利餐饮设备（上海）有限公司
上海市松江区九亭镇涞坊路57号
邮编：201615
电话：021-6784 1311
传真：021-6784 1331
电邮：simplex@online.sh.cn
网址：www.simplex.cn

Tornado (Beijing) Refrigeration Equipment Co., Ltd.
特耐德（北京）制冷设备有限公司
北京市朝阳区望京园601号悠乐汇E座5层505室
邮编：100102
电话：010-8478 7961
传真：010-8478 7939
电邮：tornadoworld@126.com
网址：www.tornadoworld.com.cn

Williams Refrigeration (Dongguan) Co., Ltd.
威廉士制冷设备（东莞）有限公司
上海市卢湾区打浦路1号金玉兰广场西峰703室
邮编：200023
电话：021-5396 0183
传真：021-5396 1335
网址：www.agafoodservice.com

Wuxi Gold Reached The Kitchen Sets Ccmplete Sets Of Equipment Co., Ltd.
无锡市金达成套厨房设备有限公司
无锡国家高新区坊前工业园区A区
（春阳东路6号）
邮编：214111
电话：0510-8827 7873
传真：0510-8827 7613
电邮：sale@wxjinda.com
网址：www.wxjinda.com

YPT International Ltd.
建宏国际有限公司
香港九龙官塘鲤鱼门道2号新城工商中心1楼
电话：+852-2723 2168
传真：+852-2739 7576
电邮：ypt@techwin.com.hk
网址：www.ypt.com.hk

久景制冷设备（上海）有限公司
上海市赵重公路1978号
电话：021-3987 6601
传真：021-3987 6501
电邮：niu@hisakage.com
网址：www.hisakage.com
请参阅第197页

Manitowoc

马尼托瓦克餐饮设备集团 中国
上海市凯旋路613号G号楼
电话：021-6152 6100
传真：021-6152 6030
网址：www.manitowocfoodservice.com.cn
业务范围：
一个完美的厨房需要由许多重要的元素组成。如何获得这些元素将是这个厨房组建成功与否的关键。而现在，您只要找到马尼托瓦餐饮设备集团就可以获得所有这些重要的元素。
马尼托瓦设备集团拥有一个庞大的、行业领先的品牌组合。如Cleveland, Convotherm®, Delfield®, Frymaster®, Garland®, Jackson, Kolpak®, Lincoln, Manitowoc® Ice, Merco®, Merrychef®, Multiplex®, and Servend®. 无论是烘焙还是烹饪，冷冻还是蒸烤，马尼托瓦能为您提供一系列最先进的厨房设备。此外，马尼托瓦在市场洞察、售后服务、技术支持和员工培训等方面都为您提供全方位支持和一如既往的服务。
在马尼托瓦，您能获得关于厨房设备的近乎穷尽的资源。
请参阅第170、171页

▼制冷设备
Refrigerating Equipment

山东省博兴县东方永兴厨房设备厂
山东省博兴县曹王经济开发区
邮编：256509
电话：0543-285 9718
传真：0543-285 9658
电邮：dfyx@luchuju.com
网址：www.luchuju.com

上海金淳酒店设备有限公司
上海市中华路235号
邮编：200010
电话：021-6311 5442
传真：021-6328 8702
电邮：kinglake@kinglake.com.cn
网址：www.kinglake.com.cn

斯科茨曼制冰系统（上海）有限公司
上海市徐虹中路20号2号楼2503室
邮编：200235
电话：021-6131 3200
传真：021-6131 3330
网址：www.scotsman-china.com
请参阅第241页

旋转烤箱
Rotisseries

Electrolux Professional (Shanghai) Co., Ltd.
伊莱克斯商用电器（上海）有限公司
上海市外高桥保税区爱都路390号31号楼A座
邮编：200131
电话：021-5046 0099
传真：021-5046 0077
网址：www.electrolux-professional.cn
请参阅第168页

Guangzhou Sage Kitchen Equipment Co., Ltd.
广州市胜捷厨房设备有限公司
广东省广州市花都区芙蓉镇旗新村龙蚌路
邮编：510860
电话：020-8698 0468
传真：020-8698 0606
电邮：service@cn-sage.com
网址：www.cn-sage.com

Shanghai Honglian Machine Electric Appliance Co., Ltd.
上海红联机械电器制造有限公司
上海市南翔高科技园区胜辛南路185号
邮编：201802
电话：021-6917 6301
传真：021-6917 6368
电邮：honglian@sh-honglian.net
网址：www.sh-honglian.net

Shanghai J&C Industry Co., Ltd.
上海积创实业发展有限公司
上海市黄兴路1725号怡富商务广场1701/1706室
邮编：200433
电话：021-6587 6136
传真：021-6587 6134
网址：www.jichuang.net.cn

Shenzhen Sweeda Food Equipment Co., Ltd.
深圳市斯瑞达食品设备有限公司
深圳市人民南路深房广场A座2501室
电话：0755-8229 6022
传真：0755-8229 6122
电邮：market@sweeda.com
网址：www.sweeda.com

Thunderbird Food Machinery Co., Ltd.
德霸食品机械有限公司
上海市松江区欣玉路453弄1-5号4D
邮编：201600
电话：021-5773 6845
传真：021-5773 6093
电邮：tbfmsh@tbfmcn.com.cn
网址：www.tbfmcn.com.cn
请参阅第163页

蒸炉
Steamers

Electrolux Professional (Shanghai) Co., Ltd.
伊莱克斯商用电器（上海）有限公司
上海市外高桥保税区爱都路390号31号楼A座
邮编：200131
电话：021-5046 0099
传真：021-5046 0077
网址：www.electrolux-professional.cn
请参阅第168页

Maschinenfabrik Kurt Neubauer GmbH & Co.
Halberstaedter Strasse 2a, D-38300 Wolfenbuettel, Germany
电话：+49-5331 89263
传真：+49-5331 89280
电邮：fn@mkn.de
网址：www.mkn.eu
请参阅第184页

Middleby China Corporation
美得彼餐饮设备（上海）有限公司
上海市松江区九亭镇久富经济开发区盛高路98号
邮编：201615
电话：021-6769 0808
传真：021-6762 7640
电邮：mandyzhang@middleby.com.cn
网址：www.middleby.com
请参阅第174、175页

Nayati Indonesia, PT.
Jl. Raya Terboyo no.19
Kawasan Industri Terboyo Megah
Semarang - Indonesia
电话：+62(24)-658 0573
传真：+62(24)-658 0572
电邮：nayati@nayati.com
网址：www.nayati.com
请参阅第181页

Ningbo Yingfeng Metal Products Co., Ltd.
宁波英峰金属制品有限公司
宁波市鄞县大道东吴段28号
邮编：315113
电话：0574-8819 7806
传真：0574-8819 7808
电邮：info@china-yingfeng.com
网址：www.xiangying.com.cn

Pro-Fit Industrial Co., Ltd.
宝发实业有限公司
香港新界葵涌大连排道152-160号
金龙工业中心第1座25字楼C室
电话：+852-2371 2862
传真：+852-2371 2867
电邮：profit@profitind.com
网址：www.profitind.com
请参阅第178页

Shandongsheng Ziboshi Yongwang Chufang Shebei Chang
山东省淄博市永旺厨房设备厂
山东省淄博市临淄区朱台镇
电话：0533-778 1069
电邮：yongwangchuye@163.com
网址：www.yongwangchuye.com

Shanghai De An Hang Trading Co., Ltd.
上海得安行贸易有限公司
上海市沪松公路松江高科技园区九泾路318号
邮编：201615
电话：021-6769 6703
传真：021-6763 9059
网址：www.zxcj.com.cn

Shanghai J&C Industry Co., Ltd.
上海积创实业发展有限公司
上海市黄兴路1725号怡富商务广场1701/1706室
邮编：200433
电话：021-6587 6136
传真：021-6587 6134
网址：www.jichuang.net.cn

餐具及容器
Tableware & Container

Afehc - Spanish Exporting Manufacturers Association For The Hospitality Industry
西班牙餐饮及团体用具生产及出口商协会
Rambla Catalunya 81, 5-3
08008 Barcelona
Spain
电话：+34(93)-487 3290
传真：+34(93)-487 0770
电邮：afehc@afehc.com
网址：www.afehc.com
请参阅第36页

Eatware Global Corporation
23/F, Westin Centre, 26 Hung To Road, Kwun Tong, Kowloon, Hong Kong
电话：+852-2295 1818
传真：+852-2295 1919
网址：www.eatware.com

Eurochef China
欧厨专业厨房用具（北京）有限公司
北京市朝阳区酒仙桥东路1号M6座西三层B区
邮编：100016
电话：010-6438 2431
传真：010-6438 2432
网址：www.eurochefasia.com

uma

Guangzhou XITE Hotel Supplies Co., Ltd.
广州市西特酒店用品有限公司
广州市番禺区沙溪国际酒店用品城F座2楼
电话：020-2262 0368
传真：020-2262 0638
电邮：xite1101@yahoo.cn
网址：www.gzxite.com
业务范围：
广州市西特酒店用品有限公司是一家集设计、生产和销售为一体的西餐不锈钢餐具制品有限公司。长久以来，以产品设计以及生产工艺为重心，聘请德国专业设计师，设计出一系列造型独特，观赏性与实用性兼具的西餐桌面产品；同时产品原料与生产工艺都处于顶尖水平。公司凭借精湛的工艺、先进的设备及丰富的经验，产品畅销欧美国家。广州市西特酒店用品有限公司一直专注于打造属于自己的品牌UMA。
UMA品牌主要系列有：Viner系列、Vina系列、Vink系列、Vinch系列及客房冰桶系列用品。
请参阅第202、203页

Vina维娜

崇尚极简，简约的线条以及时尚的设计。优雅与生俱来，宛如一位风姿卓越的美少女敲响了用餐的进行曲。

Advocating minimalist, clean lines and fashional design. Born with elegance, Vina is like a graceful beauty sounding the march in the dining.

Vink维克

拥有独一无二的外表与内涵，它身上同时传达出一种人生哲学：方中有圆，圆中有方；既迷人优雅，又深刻简约，无论何时都散发微妙的光与线。感悟人生，处处彰显您用餐的愉悦。

This item has a unique appearance and content. It conveys a philosophy of life: To be upright as square and to be smooth as circle. With elegance and minimalist, Vink distributes a charming light all the time, and gives you a happy feel when using it.

Vinch维奇

经典与现代共存，设计师在追求实用的同时，融入了三角形的现代设计把手，既线条鲜明又保持协调的感觉，创造出一种既现代又诗意的气氛。

The perfect mix of traditional and contemporary design. Vinch is a striking design with a beautiful triangle finish to each handle. The angular design adds originality whilst maintaining balance. Vinch will bring softness, delight and harmony to your table, creating a modern yet poetic atmosphere.

▼餐具及容器
Tableware & Container

Le Creuset (Shanghai) Co., Ltd.
酷彩法厨商贸（上海）有限公司
上海市南京西路1168号
中信泰富广场19楼1911-1912室
邮编：201200
电话：021-6372 0606
传真：021-6372 2008
网址：www.lecreuset.com

Shanghai Hocres Hotel Equipment & Accessories Co., Ltd.
上海海客瑞斯酒店用品有限公司
上海市华徐公路888号
邮编：201702
电话：021-6976 5065
传真：021-5986 1696
网址：www.hocres.com

Shenzhen Pama Hotel Products Co., Ltd.
深圳市帕玛酒店用品有限公司
深圳市南山区粤海路粤海工业村
深圳动漫园4栋201室
邮编：518054
电话：0755-8605 2592
传真：0755-8605 2582
网址：www.szpama.com
请参阅第42页

Yong Ge Trading (shanghai) Co., Ltd.
上海市长宁区黄金城道676号
上海市松江区欣玉路453弄1-5号4D
邮编：201103
电话：021-6308 0741
传真：021-6313 3707
电邮：wittywang@vip.163.com
网址：www.aistiashop.com
请参阅第215页

Zhejiang WuGu Industries Co., Ltd.
浙江五谷实业有限公司
浙江省余姚市丈亭台商投资园区
电话：0574-6299 8803
传真：0574-6299 8899
电邮：sho@hwugu.com
网址：www.hwugu.com
请参阅本第201页

Zwilling J.A. Henckels Shanghai Ltd.
上海双立人亨克斯有限公司
上海市浦东新区三林路424号
邮编：200124
电话：021-3886 1343
网址：www.zwilling.com.cn

欣创贸易（上海）有限公司
上海市静安区康定路359号502室
邮编：200040
电话：021-5867 8166
传真：021-5867 8575
网址：www.sitram.fr

温度计
Thermometers

Afehc - Spanish Exporting Manufacturers Association For The Hospitality Industry
西班牙餐饮及团体用具生产及出口商协会
Rambla Catalunya 81, 5-3
08008 Barcelona
Spain
电话：+34(93)-487 3290
传真：+34(93)-487 0770
电邮：afehc@afehc.com
网址：www.afehc.com
请参阅第36页

Dalian Xin Jian Hai Hotel Supplies & Trade Co.
大连新建海酒店用品贸易行
大连市沙河口区星海广场B3区一品星海6-3-1
电话：0411-8480 5299
传真：0411-8480 4111
电邮：xinjianhai@hotmail.com
网址：www.china-xjh.com

Eurochef China
欧厨专业厨房用具（北京）有限公司
北京市朝阳区酒仙桥东路1号M6座西三层B区
邮编：100016
电话：010-6438 2431
传真：010-6438 2432
网址：www.eurochefasia.com

Mingle Metal (Shen Zhen) Co., Ltd.
明高五金制品（深圳）有限公司
深圳市龙岗区布吉街道
甘坑社区同富裕工业园明高厂区
邮编：518112
电话：0755-336 13106
传真：0755-3361 3102
电邮：cnsales@mingle.net.cn
网址：www.mingle.net.cn

Promat (HK) Limited
宝时（香港）有限公司
香港九龙新蒲岗太子道东704号
新时代商业中心901室
电话：+852-2661 2392
传真：+852-2661 2086
电邮：info@promat.hk
网址：www.promat.hk

Shanghai Jingchuang Electronics Manufacturing Co., Ltd.
上海精创电器制造有限公司
上海市中兴路457号中宝大厦18层
电话：021-5697 0685
传真：021-5672 0256
电邮：kibnt@kibnt.com
网址：www.kibnt.net

烤面包机
Toasters

Hatco Corporation
赫高餐饮设备（苏州）有限公司
江苏省苏州市工业园区唯新路9号
唯亭工业园区A2区1-2单元
电话：0512-6732 5199
传真：0512-6732 5092
电邮：infocn@hatcocorp.com
网址：www.hatcocorp.com
请参阅第179页

Middleby China Corporation
美得彼餐饮设备（上海）有限公司
上海市松江区九亭镇久富经济开发区盛高路98号
邮编：201615
电话：021-6769 0808
传真：021-6762 7640
电邮：mandyzhang@middleby.com.cn
网址：www.middleby.com
请参阅第174、175页

Ningbo Yonghao Food Industry Co., Ltd.
宁波永豪食品工业有限公司
浙江省慈溪市周巷镇东开发区
邮编：315324
电话：0574-6330 6118
传真：0574-6330 6008
电邮：yonghao@yonghao-toaster.com
网址：www.yonghao-toaster.com

Shanghai J&C Industry Co., Ltd.
上海积创实业发展有限公司
上海市黄兴路1725号怡富商务广场1701/1706室
邮编：200433
电话：021-6587 6136
传真：021-6587 6134
网址：www.jichuang.net.cn

Thunderbird Food Machinery Co., Ltd.
德霸食品机械有限公司
上海市松江区欣玉路453弄1-5号4D
邮编：201600
电话：021-5773 6845
传真：021-5773 6093
电邮：tbfmsh@tbfmcn.com.cn
网址：www.tbfmcn.com.cn
请参阅第163页

制烘饼机
Waffle Makers

Guangzhou Xuzhong Food Machinery Co., Ltd.
广州旭众食品机械有限公司
广州市白云区龙归镇南岭龙岗路9号
邮编：510660
电话：020-2827 7160
传真：020-2827 7165
电邮：xuzhong@food-mach.com
网址：www.food-mach.com

Middleby China Corporation
美得彼餐饮设备（上海）有限公司
上海市松江区九亭镇久富经济开发区盛高路98号
邮编：201615
电话：021-6769 0808
传真：021-6762 7640
电邮：mandyzhang@middleby.com.cn
网址：www.middleby.com
请参阅第174、175页

Shanghai Qinhui Foodstuff Machinery Co., Ltd.
上海勤辉食品机械有限公司
上海市奉贤区南桥镇浦卫公路6169号
邮编：201417
电话：021-5745 9080
传真：021-5745 0421
电邮：qinhuijixie@163.com
网址：www.shqhjx.com

Thunderbird Food Machinery Co., Ltd.
德霸食品机械有限公司
上海市松江区欣玉路453弄1-5号4D
邮编：201600
电话：021-5773 6845
传真：021-5773 6093
电邮：tbfmsh@tbfmcn.com.cn
网址：www.tbfmcn.com.cn
请参阅第163页

酒吧及吧台设备 Bar Equipment

Beijing Harvest E & M Co., Ltd.
北京丰汇加机电设备销售有限公司
北京市宣武区建功西里1号楼天缘公寓A座2701室
邮编：100054
电话：010-8351 6972
传真：010-8351 7663
电邮：sales@bjharvest.cn
网址：www.bjharvest.cn

Boloni
博洛尼家居用品（北京）有限公司
北京市朝阳区育慧里11号
邮编：100101
电话：010-5134 8888
传真：010-5134 8810
电邮：hui@kebao.cn
网址：www.boloni.com.cn

Cambro Manufacturing Company
惠州勘宝商业有限公司
广东省惠州市麦地路一号风尚国际18楼A座
邮编：516001
电话：0752-238 7033
传真：0752-238 7019
网址：www.cambro.com

Dalian Xin Jian Hai Hotel Supplies & Trade Co.
大连新建海酒店用品贸易行
大连市沙河口区星海广场B3区一品星海6-3-1
电话：0411-8480 5299
传真：0411-8480 4111
电邮：xinjianhai@hotmail.com
网址：www.china-xjh.com

Foshan Nanhai YinHui Hardware Furniture Factory
佛山市南海银辉五金家具厂
广东省佛山市南海区九江镇上东奇腾路
邮编：528230
电话：0757-8650 6786
传真：0757-8650 2186
电邮：fsyinhui@tom.com
网址：www.fayinhui.com

Hangzhou Fangnan Hotel Equipment Co., Ltd.
杭州方南酒店设备有限公司
浙江省杭州市艮山西路86号
邮编：310021
电话：0571-8672 2923
传真：0571-8672 2793
电邮：mail@fangnanjd.com
网址：www.fangnanjd.com

Hong Kong Foodservice Equipment Co., Ltd.
香港餐饮设备有限公司
香港九龙旺角塘尾道18号嘉礼大厦3楼A至B室
电话：+852-2300 1173
传真：+852-2780 6986
电邮：info@hkfec.com.hk
网址：www.hkfec.com.hk

Lee Hun Trading Co., Ltd.
香港利亨贸易行
香港九龙红磡鹤园街9-11号
凯旋工商中心第三期二楼Q室
电话：+852-2334 0873
传真：+852-2954 2181
网址：www.cpl.net.cn

Nayati Indonesia, PT.
Jl. Raya Terboyo no.19
Kawasan Industri Terboyo Megah
Semarang - Indonesia
电话：+62(24)-658 0573
传真：+62(24)-658 0572
电邮：nayati@nayati.com
网址：www.nayati.com
请参阅第181页

Shanghai Hotel Equipment Co., Ltd.
上海酒店设备股份有限公司
上海市普陀区澳门路345号
邮编：200060
电话：021-6266 9988
传真：021-6276 1111
电邮：hotel@hec.com.cn
网址：www.heconline.com.cn

Shanghai JinCheng Refrigerating Equipment Co., Ltd.
上海金城制冷设备有限公司
上海市中山北路3357号
邮编：200062
电话：021-6216 8066
传真：021-6216 8070
电邮：jincheng@shkingdom.com.cn
网址：www.shkingdom.com.cn
请参阅第225页

Shanghai Linde Hotel Equipment Utensil Co., Ltd.
上海林德酒店设备用品配套有限公司
上海市普陀区澳门路356号1楼
邮编：200060
电话：021-5252 0630
传真：021-5252 0611
电邮：linde@lindesh.com
网址：www.lindesh.com

YPT International Ltd.
建宏国际有限公司
香港九龙官塘鲤鱼门道2号新城工商中心1楼
电话：+852-2723 2168
传真：+852-2739 7576
电邮：ypt@techwin.com.hk
网址：www.ypt.com.hk

Yuhuan Meisheng Sanitary Ware Co., Ltd.
玉环县美盛洁具有限公司
浙江省台州市玉环县清港镇袁家村
邮编：317606
电话：0576-8712 1420
传真：0576-8712 1319
电邮：info@pre-rinse.com
网址：www.pre-rinse.com
请参阅第180页

久景制冷设备（上海）有限公司
上海市赵重公路1978号
电话：021-3987 6601
传真：021-3987 6501
电邮：niu@hisakage.com
网址：www.hisakage.com
请参阅第197页

上海金淳酒店设备有限公司
上海市中华路235号
邮编：200010
电话：021-6311 5442
传真：021-6328 8702
电邮：kinglake@kinglake.com.cn
网址：www.kinglake.com.cn

上海金树酒店设备有限公司
上海市普陀区府村路179号102栋3、4号门
邮编：200010
电话：021-5204 3106
传真：021-5204 3128
电邮：sales@js999.com.cn
网址：www.js999.com.cn

啤酒机 Beer Dispensing Equipment

Harbin Shuncheng stainless steel product Co., Ltd.
哈尔滨市顺成不锈钢设备有限公司
哈尔滨市道里区安阳路45号
邮编：150070
电话：0451-8432 5127
传真：0451-8433 1651
电邮：shuncheng18@126.com
网址：www.hrbscview.com

Shenyang Deersen Stainless Steel Equipment Factory
沈阳德尔森不锈钢设备厂
沈阳市大东区七二四广场东侧
邮编：110042
电话：024-8667 0534
电邮：deersen@163.com
网址：www.deersen.com

北京澳格伟业酿造技术有限公司
北京朝阳区安慧东里新都市计划大厦12层1202室
电话：010-6493 3046
传真：010-6451 1505
电邮：ausgain@yahoo.com.cn
网址：www.ale168.com

北京金汉森啤酒技术开发有限责任公司
北京市大兴区瀛海镇镇政府对面
电话：010-5949 6888
传真：010-6928 1456
电邮：bjjhspj@163.com
网址：www.goldhansens.com

青岛华英啤酒设备有限公司
青岛市四方区兴隆路169号
邮编：266000
电话：0532-8606 2108
传真：0532-8872 3690
电邮：qingdao.huaying@163.com
网址：www.qingdaohuaying.com

冷热饮品机 Beverage Dispensers (Hot&Cold)

Angelhood Shanghai Co., Ltd.
上海安继行实业有限公司
上海虹梅南路4999号（新吴泾工业园区）8号楼
邮编：201109
电话：021-5169 1855
传真：021-5168 7575
电邮：shanghai@angelhood.com.cn
网址：www.angelhood.com.cn

Beijing Kingtai Tenhong Trade Co., Ltd.
北京市京泰天宏经贸有限责任公司
北京市朝阳区利泽中二路2号望京科技创业园E座405C
邮编：100102
电话：010-8795 2371
传真：010-8795 2380
电邮：info@mycafe.com.cn
网址：www.mycafe.com.cn

▼冷热饮品机
Beverage Dispensers(Hot&Cold)

Cambro Manufacturing Company
惠州勘宝商业有限公司
广东省惠州市麦地路一号风尚国际18楼A座
邮编：516001
电话：0752-238 7033
传真：0752-238 7019
网址：www.cambro.com

Hiangkie Coffee Group Limited
香记咖啡集团有限公司
香港九龙新蒲岗三祝街12-14号
荣森工业第二大厦3楼
电话：+852-3769 2345
传真：+852-2545 8917
电邮：enquiry@hiangkie.com.hk
网址：www.hiangkie.com.hk
请参阅第118、119页

IMI Cornelivs Tianjin Co., Ltd.
康富（天津）有限公司
天津市经济技术开发区欣泰街12号
邮编：300457
电话：022-2529 0858
传真：022-2529 0865
网址：www.cornelius.com.cn

Jascaffe China Co., Ltd.
王力咖啡贸易（上海）有限公司
上海市松江区九亭镇盛龙路751号
邮编：201615
电话：021-3352 2299
传真：021-5206 8338
电邮：marketing@jascaffechina.com
网址：www.jascaffechina.com

Season Food Co., Ltd.
四季工坊有限公司
台湾省台中县雾峰乡中正路565巷17号
电话：+886(4)-2333 4468
传真：+886(4)-2333 4612
电邮：season9@ms48.hinet.net
网址：www.season-coffee.com.tw

Seng Pan Food Co., Ltd.
江门市诚品食品有限公司
广东省江门市新会区古井镇古泗村
邮编：529100
电话：0750-697 1188
传真：0750-697 1122
电邮：info@spcoffee.com
网址：www.spcoffee.com

Sunny Trading Company
阳光贸易公司
香港九龙观塘兴业街16号
美兴工业大厦B座10楼11室
电话：+852-2343 2943
传真：+852-2343 4459
电邮：info@sunnytrading.com
网址：www.sunnytrading.com

广州均乾贸易有限公司
广州市海珠区福场路5号B栋商务中心1902室
电话：020-3446 6097
传真：020-3446 6496
网址：www.gzjunqian.com

自助餐设备
Buffet Equipment

Anglo-Swiss Trading Co (HK) Ltd.
英瑞贸易（香港）有限公司
香港九龙尖沙咀广东道30号
新港中心第2座1011-1012室
电话：+852-2375 1111
传真：+852-2375 3409
网址：www.angloswiss.iyp.hk

Anhui Hualing Kitchen Equipment Co., Ltd.
安徽华菱西厨装备股份有限公司
安徽省马鞍山市博望工业开发区
邮编：243131
电话：0555-676 9699
传真：0555-676 9511
电邮：info@fenglihua.com
网址：www.fenglihua.com

Beijing Jingguang Fangyuan Kitchen Equipment Company
北京京广方园厨房设备有限责任公司
北京市宣武区建功南里3号楼一层
邮编：100054
电话：010-6354 1242
传真：010-6352 0957
电邮：zengjia0627@126.com
网址：www.jgfy.com

Carlisle Foodsservice Products
卡莱森泰（上海）商贸有限公司
上海市长宁区江苏路398号舜元企业发展大厦19楼
邮编：200050
电话：021-6100 5222
传真：021-6100 5279
网址：www.carlislefsp.com

Dalian Brightland Trading Co., Ltd.
大连市辉夏贸易有限公司
大连市高新园区七贤岭爱贤街10号A座9层
电话：0411-8497 8359
传真：0411-8250 7746
电邮：info@ttxgroup.com
请参阅第250、251页

Dalian Xin Jian Hai Hotel Supplies & Trade Co.
大连新建海酒店用品贸易行
大连市沙河口区星海广场B3区一品星海6-3-1
电话：0411-8480 5299
传真：0411-8480 4111
电邮：xinjianhai@hotmail.com
网址：www.china-xjh.com

Eurochef China
欧厨专业厨房用具（北京）有限公司
北京市朝阳区酒仙桥东路1号M6座西三层B区
邮编：100016
电话：010-6438 2431
传真：010-6438 2432
网址：www.eurochefasia.com

Good-Way Tableware Manufactory Ltd.
2/F., 29 Austin Road, T.S.T.,
Kowloon, Hong Kong
电话：+852-2735 8671
传真：+852-2314 2932
电邮：export@good-way.com
网址：www.wnk-hk.com

Guangbang Kitchenware Development Co., Ltd.
广帮厨具（开发）有限公司
浙江省永康市五金科技工业园长城南路3号
邮编：321300
电话：0579-8738 6888
传真：0579-8738 6866
电邮：ykgbgs@126.com
网址：www.guangbang.com.cn

Hangzhou Fangnan Hotel Equipment Co., Ltd.
杭州方南酒店设备有限公司
浙江省杭州市艮山西路86号
邮编：310021
电话：0571-8672 2923
传真：0571-8672 2793
电邮：mail@fangnanjd.com
网址：www.fangnanjd.com

Hangzhou Yindu Kitchen Equipment Company Limited
杭州银都餐饮设备有限公司
杭州市余杭区经济开发区星桥配套区星星路1号
邮编：311100
电话：0571-8626 0777
传真：0571-8626 0718
电邮：info@yinduchina.com
网址：www.yinduchina.com

Hhangzhou Sanxin Hotel Equipment Co., Ltd.
杭州三信酒店设备有限公司
浙江省杭州市机场路277号
电话：0571-8787 5859
传真：0571-8504 6887
电邮：hzsanxin@126.com
网址：www.cn3xin.com

Hong Kong Foodservice Equipment Co., Ltd.
香港餐饮设备有限公司
香港九龙旺角塘尾道18号嘉礼大厦3楼A至B室
电话：+852-2300 1173
传真：+852-2780 6986
电邮：info@hkfec.com.hk
网址：www.hkfec.com.hk

Huizhou Futton Industrial & Trading Co., Ltd.
惠州市阜东工贸有限公司
广东省惠州市仲恺高新区惠风西二路
电话：0752-261 2688
传真：0752-261 2696
电邮：ccy@futton.com.cn
网址：www.futton.com.cn
请参阅第207页

Hyperlux International Ltd.
高领域国际有限公司
香港九龙观塘鸿图道33号王氏大厦1楼
电话：+852-2343 2081
传真：+852-2951 0629
电邮：sales@hyperlux.com.hk
网址：www.hyperlux.com.hk

Jiangmen Harvest Kitchenware Co., Ltd.
江门市联丰厨具有限公司
广东省江门市西环路325号
（天朗花园）之四202室
邮编：529000
电话：0750-366 6312
传真：0750-366 6310
电邮：info@jmharvest.cn
网址：www.jmharvest.cn

生活源于品味
lifestyle makes living

Daeden®
戴德

双连果汁鼎
Juice Dispenser/2
B10402

镀金咖啡暖鼎
Brass-plated Coffee Service
10701

双头麦片器
Cereal Dispenser/Double
10302

双头光波炉
Infrared Cooker Double
CF-3600

A款不锈钢份数盘（食物盘）
New Anti-jamming GN Pans
(Steam Table Pans)

暖汤煲
Soup Kettle
D9001-A

感应式触动圆形餐炉/钢盖/带框架
Electrical Chafer / Steel Lid / Self-openin
MD201G

专用电磁炉
Buffet Induction

方形餐炉 / 玻璃盖 / 带框架
2/3GN Chafer / Glass Lid / Electrical
D202

致臻完美　精彩无限……

可视 镀铬长方型宴会餐炉
Round Soup Station W/Chrome Legs /Show Window
S6801G-1 (单格Single)
S6801G-2 (双格Double)

可视 镀金球型宴会餐炉
Round Chafing Dish W/Gilt Legs / Show Window
S6803

触动 电动可视镀金长方型宴会汤炉
Oblong Soup Station W/Gilt Legs/Show Window/ Automatic Open
M2405

触动 电动可视镀金球型宴会汤炉
Round Soup Station W/Gilt Legs/Show Window/ Automatic Open
M2407

冷热可切换餐炉
Cold And Hot Chafing Dish
CH204

双层豪华烤牛肉车
Continental Roast Beef Service Wagon
W-0103

巧克力喷泉
Chocolate Fountain
CP-60

南洋酒店用品制造有限公司
SOUTH OCEAN HOTEL DEVICE PRODUCE CO., LTD.

电话: 0086-574-8826 6885 8826 6886 8826 6880
传真: 0086-574-8826-6882

INTERNATIONAL DEPT
Tel: 0086-574-88266887 88266997
Fax: 0086-574-88266882
网络实名: 南洋精工

广州办事处
电话: 0086-20-2262 1266　2262 1299
传真: 0086-20-2262 1318

成都办事处
电话: 0086-28-8613 0888
传真: 0086-28-8611 8966

北京办事处
电话: 0086-10-6381 6748　6381 6749
传真: 0086-10-6381 6749

武汉办事处
手机: 13036100598
传真: 0086-27-6560 2542

上海办事处
电话: 0086-21-6377 8863
传真: 0086-21-6377 8867

郑州办事处
手机: 13663860352
传真: 0086-371-6634 5553

沈阳办事处
电话: 0086-024-2386 3005
传真: 0086-024-2325 4823

昆明办事处
手机: 13888308559
传真: 0086-871-464 4300

▼自助餐设备 Buffet Equipment

Kuntai Hotel Appliance Limited Company
广州坤泰酒店用品有限公司
广州市珠海区
南天国际酒店用品批发市场23栋32-33号
邮编：510288
电话：020-3423 3930
传真：020-3424 4830
电邮：gzkuntai@hotmail.com
网址：www.gzkuntai.com

Lee Hun Trading Co., Ltd.
香港利亨贸易行
香港九龙红磡鹤园街9-11号
凯旋工商中心第三期二楼Q室
电话：+852-2334 0873
传真：+852-2954 2181
网址：www.cpl.net.cn

Lui Chuen Kee.
江门吕泉记五金制品厂
广东省江门市蓬江区杜阮镇贯溪管理区新围段
邮编：529075
电话：0750-366 1211
传真：0750-366 2211
网址：www.luichuenkee.com

Nanjing Huayi Hotel Equipment Manufacturing Engineering Co., Ltd.
南京华艺酒店设备制造工程有限公司
南京市麒麟工业园四号路
邮编：210029
电话：025-8412 1298
传真：025-8412 6041
电邮：jshy@jshy.cc
网址：www.jshy.cc

Shanghai Hotel Equipment Co., Ltd.
上海酒店设备股份有限公司
上海市普陀区澳门路345号
邮编：200060
电话：021-6266 9988
传真：021-6276 1111
电邮：hotel@hec.com.cn
网址：www.heconline.com.cn

Shanghai Jinhong Buffet Utensil & Manufacture Co., Ltd.
上海锦宏自助餐用品制造有限公司
上海市卢湾区鲁班路168弄大同花园5号101室
邮编：200023
电话：021-5302 1768
传真：021-5302 1778
电邮：jinhong9@vip.163.com
网址：www.jinhong-sh.com

Shanghai Linde Hotel Equipment Utensil Co., Ltd.
上海林德酒店设备用品配套有限公司
上海市普陀区澳门路356号1楼
邮编：200060
电话：021-5252 0630
传真：021-5252 0611
电邮：linde@lindesh.com
网址：www.lindesh.com

Shanghai Xingjian Industry Co., Ltd.
上海星剑实业有限公司
上海市普陀区绥德路555号1号楼
邮编：200331
电话：021-6483 9061
传真：021-6482 3642
电邮：jiangfang@shxjsy.com
网址：www.shxjsy.com

Shaoxing Bava Hotel Supplies Manufacture Co., Ltd.
绍兴巴菲酒店用品制造有限公司
浙江省绍兴县柯岩街道河塔村
邮编：312030
电话：0575-8438 0966
传真：0575-8438 0977
电邮：bava@188.com
网址：www.ebava.com

Shenzhen Mega-resources Hotel Supply Joint-soint-stock Co., Ltd.
深圳市兆能源酒店供应股份有限公司
深圳市龙岗区平湖镇白泥坑良白路46号
邮编：518111
电话：0755-8466 1888
传真：0755-3382 5666
电邮：zny@zny.cn
网址：www.zny.cn

South Ocean Hotel Device Produce Co., Ltd.
南洋酒店用品制造有限公司
宁波市鄞县大道后仓段
电话：0574-8826 6885
传真：0574-8826 6882
网址：www.kingo2000.com
请参阅第208、209页、封面里

Sunnex Metal Products (Shenzhen) Ltd.
日升五金制品（深圳）有限公司
深圳市盐田区沙头角深沙路东和工业大厦A座二楼
邮编：518081
电话：0755-2555 1458
传真：0755-2535 7498
电邮：sales@sunnexchina.com
网址：www.sunnexchina.com

Tianjin Samhua Internation Trade Co., Ltd.
天津三华国际贸易有限公司
天津市津南区莘庄工业园区B座
邮编：300350
电话：022-2854 8518
传真：022-2854 8519
网址：www.samhua.com

Wuxi Gold Reached The Kitchen Sets Ccmplete Sets Of Equipment Co., Ltd.
无锡市金达成套厨房设备有限公司
无锡国家高新区坊前工业园区A区
（春阳东路6号）
邮编：214111
电话：0510-8827 7873
传真：0510-8827 7613
电邮：sale@wxjinda.com
网址：www.wxjinda.com

YPT International Ltd.
建宏国际有限公司
香港九龙官塘鲤鱼门道2号新城工商中心1楼
电话：+852-2723 2168
传真：+852-2739 7576
电邮：ypt@techwin.com.hk
网址：www.ypt.com.hk

YongKang Bangjie Kitchen Equipment Co., Ltd.
永康市邦捷厨房设备有限公司
永康市五金城一期四街37号
邮编：321300
电话：0579-8732 1777
传真：0579-8715 9678
电邮：haote8@163.com
网址：www.bangjiechufang.com.cn

宁波天马股份有限公司
宁波市鄞州区横街镇桃源路陆尚书岙
邮编：315181
电话：0574-8846 2188
传真：0574-8820 9362
网址：www.china-tianma.com

上海金树酒店设备有限公司
上海市普陀区府村路179号102栋3、4号门
邮编：200010
电话：021-5204 3106
传真：021-5204 3128
电邮：sales@js999.com.cn
网址：www.js999.com.cn

深圳市惠宝隆酒店设备用品有限公司
深圳市宝安区前进二路4号
雁盟酒店文化产业园D馆6楼
邮编：518102
电话：0755-6186 1111
传真：0755-6186 0002
网址：www.vibolong.com

瓷器餐具 Chinaware

Bo Abundant Ceramic Colored Paper Co., Ltd.
博丰陶瓷花纸有限公司
淄博市博山区山头镇-道观园113号
邮编：255200
电话：0533-440 0688
传真：0533-440 0788
电邮：zbbftc@163.com
网址：www.bofengtaoci.com

Cameo China Co., Ltd.
北京佳美丽家陶瓷有限公司
北京市望京科技园爱慕大厦A501
邮编：100102
电话：010-6439 1021
传真：010-6439 1031
电邮：info@cameochina.com.cn
网址：www.cameochina.com.cn

Chaozhou Bening Ceramics Industries Co., Ltd.
潮州市伯林陶瓷实业有限公司
广东省潮州市枫溪如意路工业园5号
邮编：521031
电话：0768-292 5193
传真：0768-292 3728
电邮：bening@yahoo.com
网址：www.bening-china.com

Chaozhou Elegant Dragon Ceramics Factory
潮州市雅龙陶瓷厂
广东省潮州市浮洋工业区
电话：0768-681 0198
传真：0768-681 0883
电邮：yalongtaoci@163.com
网址：www.yalone.com

Chaozhou Fengxi Yateni Ceramics Factory
潮州市枫溪区雅特尼陶瓷制作厂
广东省潮州市枫溪区东田下东埔工业区
邮编：521031
电话：0768-298 3917
传真：0768-298 2490
电邮：yateni@tom.com
网址：www.yateni.com

Chaozhou Yayu Ceramic Co., Ltd.
潮州市雅玉陶瓷有限公司
广东省潮州市枫溪区堤头工业区
邮编：521000
电话：0768-298 5153
传真：0768-298 5495
电邮：yayuhc@126.com
网址：www.yayucn.com

ATHENA®
Lincolnshire, UK
ATHENA
中國總代理：
LP tableware
亮品
廣州市亮品餐具有限公司
LIANGPIN TABLEWARE CO.LTD, GZ
廣州市昌崗中路166號富盈大廈19樓1911室
ROOM 1911, 19/F,
FU YING INTERNATIONAL BUILDING,
166 CHANG GANG ZHONG ROAD,
HAI ZHU DISTRICT, GUANGZHOU, CHINA
TEL: 86-20-84313636 FAX: 86-20-62378332
E-mail: liangpin.gz@163.com
E-mail: info@athena-tableware.com
Website: www.athena-tableware.com

▼瓷器餐具
Chinaware

Euro Asia Shanghai Limited
上海依贵亚贸易有限公司
上海市徐汇区医学院路92号
邮编：200032
电话：021-6422 6618
传真：021-6422 6689
电邮：euroasiash@163.com
网址：www.sheuroasia.com
请参阅第230、231页

First Asia Trading Co., Ltd.
上海泛亚经贸有限公司
上海市万航渡路2452号DOHO园区A502室
电话：021-5178 6788
传真：021-5178 6758*118
电邮：firstasia99@msn.com
网址：www.firstasia-sh.com
请参阅第236、237页

Fujian Dehua Hiap Huat Koyo Toki Co., Ltd. Shanghai Branch
福建省德化协发光洋陶器有限公司上海分公司
上海市凯旋路3131号明申中心大厦2803室
邮编：200030
电话：021-5407 1201
传真：021-5407 1203
电邮：shanghai@luzerne.com
网址：www.luzerne.com
请参阅第214页

Guangdong Chaozhou HuaXing Porcelain Fty.
广东省潮州市华星瓷厂
广东省潮州市枫溪区蔡陇前街片
邮编：515300
电话：0768-293 1862
传真：0768-293 1517
电邮：info@huaxing-porcelain.com
网址：www.huaxing-porcelain.com

Guangdong Meiti Porcelain Co., Ltd.
广东美地瓷业有限公司
广州市花都区花东镇联安山前大道吉岭
邮编：510890
电话：020-8677 5555
传真：020-8677 5377
电邮：meitigz@163.net
网址：www.meiti.cn

Guangdong Songfa Ceramics Co., Ltd.
广东松发陶瓷有限公司
广东省潮州市枫溪区如意工业区
邮编：521031
电话：0768-292 0991
传真：0768-282 2362
电邮：songfa@songfa.com
网址：www.songfa.com

Guangzhou Eqichina Hotel Dishware Factory
广州市依祺瓷酒店餐具厂
广州芳村大道东31号
电话：020-8163 0300
传真：020-8163 0377
电邮：eqichina@163.net
网址：http://eqichina.163e.com.cn

Guangzhou Songfa Hotel Equipment Co., Ltd.
广州松发酒店设备用品有限公司
广州市荔湾区东沙开发区荷景路31号
电话：020-2239 9188
传真：020-2239 9132
网址：www.songfa.cn
请参阅第43页

Guangzhou United Ocean Hotel Equipment Co., Ltd.
广州汇海酒店用品有限公司
广东省广州市番禺区大石镇石北大道
电话：020-3993 0461
传真：020-3993 0460
电邮：gz_hhh@126.com
网址：www.gdhuihai.com

Irector of Zibo Huaguang Ceramics Sales Limited Liabilitu Co., Ltd.
淄博华光陶瓷营销有限责任公司
山东省淄博市张店区柳泉路8号甲1
邮编：255000
电话：0533-288 2799
传真：0533-288 8702
电邮：sd-hgyx@263.net
网址：www.taoci800.com

LiangPin Tableware Co., Ltd. GZ
广州市亮品餐具有限公司
广州市昌岗中路166号富盈大厦19楼1911室
电话：020-8431 3636
传真：020-6237 8332
电邮：liangpin.gz@163.com
网址：www.athena-tableware.com
请参阅第212页

Jiangsu Gaochun Ceramics Co., Ltd.
江苏高淳陶瓷股份有限公司
江苏省高淳经济技术开发区荆山路008号
邮编：211300
电话：025-5788 9518
传真：025-5737 7688
网址：www.gctc.cn

Jingdezhen Franz Collection Co., Ltd.
景德镇法蓝瓷实业有限公司
江西省景德镇市陶瓷科技工业园区枫林坞水库
邮编：333400
电话：0592-596 3066
传真：0592-597 5913
电邮：info@franzcollection.com.cn
网址：www.franzcollection.com.cn

Longda Bone China Co., Ltd.
隆达骨质瓷有限公司
河北省唐山开发区银河路
邮编：063020
电话：0315-317 6718
传真：0315-317 6708
电邮：gnywb@ldbonechina.com
网址：www.ldbonechina.com

Miracle Dynasty Fine Bone China (Shanghai) Co., Ltd.
玛戈隆特骨瓷（上海）有限公司
上海市南苏州路1305号B座
邮编：200003
电话：021-5375 5384
传真：021-5375 5386
网址：www.mdfbc.com

NARUMI

Narumi Shanghai Company Ltd.
鸣海（上海）商贸有限公司
上海市长宁区愚园路1258号
绿地商务大厦602-604室
邮编：200050
电话：021-5237 5038
传真：021-5237 8686
电邮：shanghai@narumi-china.com
网址：www.narumi.co.jp
业务范围：
NARUMI是世界顶级高档骨瓷餐具品牌之一；产品深受全世界各高品位人士，上海外滩华尔道夫(Waldorf Astoria Shanghai)、上海费尔蒙和平饭店(Fairmont Peace Hotel Shanghai)、四季酒店(Four-Season)、凯悦酒店(Hyatt Group)、香格里拉酒店(Shangri-La)等众多知名五星级酒店及新加坡、阿联酋等航空公司头等舱的青睐。
NARUMI骨瓷洁白细腻、通透轻巧，体薄而强度高；当之无愧地成为享受奢华生活的理想追求和绝妙选择。
请参阅第211页、封面

NIKKO
SINCE 1908

Nikko Great Time Hotel Supplies Ltd.
伟时（广州）酒店用品供应有限公司
广东省广州市天河区林和西路9号
耀中广场B座706房
电话：020-8527 0243
传真：020-8527 0347
业务范围：
我们公司主要从事进口餐具用品业务，经销品牌包括日本高级瓷器NIKKO，产品包括设计多样化的中、西式餐具；也销售水晶制品，及不锈钢餐桌用品，包括意大利水晶品牌RCR (Royal Crystal Rock)；及经营由名师设计的桌椅，如英国宴会家俱品牌BURGESS，以供高级酒店、餐厅和办工室选用。
请参阅第48、49页

Oneida (Guangzhou) Foodservice Ltd.
奥耐达（广州）餐饮用具有限公司
广州市天河区体育东路138号
金利来数码网络大厦2909-2910室
邮编：510620
电话：020-3878 0612
传真：020-3878 0613
电邮：info@oneida.cn
网址：www.foodservice.oneida.com
请参阅第249页

Patou Bonechina
上海巴度国际贸易有限公司
上海市浦东新区新声汇豪路74弄3号202室
邮编：201314
电话：021-5822 9394
传真：021-5822 9843
电邮：sophia@potouchn.com
网址：www.patouchn.com

▼瓷器餐具
Chinaware

Qidong Huatai Ceramics Industries Co., Ltd.
启东华泰陶瓷制品有限公司
江苏省启东市经济开发区南苑西路1199号
邮编：226200
电话：0513-8311 6688
传真：0513-8311 5168
电邮：sales@masalin.com.cn
网址：www.yitaifang.com

Rak Porcelain L.L.C
P.O.Box:30113, Ras Al Khaimah, United Arab Emirates
电话：+971(7)-244 7758
传真：+971(7)-244 7201
电邮：rakporcelain@rakceram.com
网址：www.rakporcelain.com

Shandong Guohua Ceramics Co., Ltd.
山东国华瓷器有限公司
山东省淄博市博山区陶琉工业园
邮编：255200
电话：0533-440 8110
传真：0533-441 5000
电邮：ghchina@vip.163.com
网址：www.ghcq.com

Shandong Institute Of Advanced Ceramics Co., Ltd.
山东硅苑新材料科技股份有限公司
山东省淄博市高新技术产业开发区
柳泉路北首286号
邮编：255086
电话：0533-358 2117
传真：0533-358 2244
电邮：sicer@sicer.com
网址：www.sicer.com

Shandong Pearlshell Porcelain Co., Ltd.
山东珍贝瓷业有限公司
山东省滨州市无棣工业园
邮编：251900
电话：0543-636 1666
传真：0543-636 1083
网址：www.seas.com.cn

Shandong Province Boshan Ceramics Research Designing Institute Co., Ltd.
博山陶瓷研究设计院有限公司
山东省淄博市博山区山头镇新博南路129号
邮编：255215
电话：0533-441 7066
传真：0533-441 7067
网址：www.tcyjy.com.cn

Shandong Province Zibo Huayang Ceramics Co., Ltd.
山东淄博华洋陶瓷有限责任公司
山东省淄博市淄川区淄城路45号
邮编：255100
电话：0533-533 6628
传真：0533-526 9331
电邮：zbhytc@vip.sina.com
网址：www.zbhytc.com

Shandong Zibo Silver Sea Ceramics Co., Ltd.
淄博银海瓷业有限公司
山东省淄博市博山区山头镇矾沟街8号
邮编：255200
电话：0533-440 0567
传真：0533-440 0555
电邮：yh@zbyhcy.com
网址：www.zbyhcy.com

Shanghai Top Bone China Co., Ltd.
上海特澳博骨质瓷有限公司
上海市汶水东路278号景明大厦2108-2116室
邮编：200434
电话：021-6561 9991
传真：021-6561 8998
电邮：topbonechina@163.com
网址：www.topbonechina.com

Steelite International PLC
Orme Street Stoke-on-Trent ST6, 3RB England
电话：+44(0)-1782 821000
传真：+44(0)-1782 819926
电邮：dlee@steelite.com
网址：www.steelite.com
业务范围：
Steelite International is a world-leading manufacturer and supplier of award-winning,inspirational tabletop ranges. The company's core chinaware products are manufactured at its Stoke-on-Trent factory. Working exclusively for the hospitality and catering industry, we have a wealth of experience and an appetite for customer satisfaction that has won us the respect of catering professionals around the world.
Steelite International's extensive tableware collections cater for all tastes, designed to offer good looks and exceptional durability. All Steelite International products provide exceptional heat retention, are fully microwave, dishwasher and freezer safe and are resistant to thermal and mechanical shock-and offer a 5 year edge chip warranty* to provide maximum confidence. Steelite International is also the exclusive supplier of the beautiful Rene Ozorio porcelain ranges and Montgatina tableware collections.
请参阅第213页

Success Hill Trading Ltd.
鸿山贸易有限公司
香港九龙官塘开源道49号创贸广场22字楼02室
电话：+852-2344 6882
传真：+852-2342 0899
电邮：succhil@netvigator.com
网址：www.successhill.biz.com.hk

Tangshan Ekaqi Ceramics Co., Ltd.
唐山市亿家亲陶瓷有限公司
河北省唐山市高新技术开发区大庆道108号
电话：0315-825 6111
传真：0315-825 6333
电邮：webmaster@ekaqi.com
网址：www.ekaqi.com

Tangshan Haina Ceramics Co., Ltd.
唐山海纳瓷业有限公司
河北省唐山市路北区天源骏景底商6号
邮编：063000
电话：0315-256 8820
传真：0315-256 9205
网址：www.hainastyle.com

The ChinaChina Homewares Co.,, Ltd.
深圳市亿采商贸发展有限公司
深圳市福田保税区市花路25号银东大厦B栋408室
邮编：518038
电话：0755-8300 2231
传真：0755-8369 5641
网址：www.thechinachina.com.cn

WMF (Shanghai) Co., Ltd.
精鸟金属制品贸易（上海）有限公司
上海市虹口区四川北路1318号
盛邦国际大厦1101-1103室
邮编：200080
电话：021-5515 5212
传真：021-5515 5220
电邮：info@wmf-china.com
网址：www.wmf-china.com
请参阅第219页

WeiYe Ceramics Co., Ltd.
伟业陶瓷有限公司
广东省潮州市枫溪如意路工业园F1
邮编：521031
电话：0768-292 3288
传真：0768-292 3338
电邮：webmaster@weiye-porcelain.com
网址：www.weiye-porcelain.com

Yong Ge Trading (Shanghai) Co., Ltd.
上海市长宁区黄金城道676号
邮编：201103
电话：021-6308 0741
传真：021-6313 3707
电邮：wittywang@vip.163.com
网址：www.aistiashop.com
业务范围：
爱斯提亚精致餐具以推动餐桌文化的理念进入餐饮界的前线，并以国内纯良的工艺结合欧洲知名设计师的美学与实用概念，精确展现餐具应有的价值，除了为饮食生活注入一股时尚感，彷佛流金岁月相映在觥筹交错间成为一则永远说不完的故事！您的选择将成就千万人对幸福感的期待，爱斯提亚同样需要您的支持！今天开始，专家与优雅的对话就在爱斯提亚！
服务专线：021-6308 0741
请参阅第215页

Zhejiang Nansong Ceramic Co., Ltd.
浙江楠宋瓷业有限公司
浙江省杭州市余杭区塘栖工业园区
邮编：311106
电话：0571-8631 8080
传真：0571-8631 8333
电邮：admin@nansongchina.com
网址：www.nansongchina.com

Zibo Futao Ceramics Industrial Co., Ltd.
淄博福陶瓷业有限公司
山东省淄博市博山区福山
邮编：255210
电话：0533-446 8118
传真：0533-446 8778
电邮：ft@ftcy.com
网址：www.ftcy.com

▼瓷器餐具
Chinaware

Zibo Zhongqiang Porcelain Co., Ltd.
淄博中强瓷业有限公司
山东省淄博市开发区万杰路95号
邮编：255086
电话：0533-358 5858
传真：0533-358 8149
电邮：zbzqcy@yahoo.com.cn
网址：www.zbzq.com

广东长城集团股份有限公司
广东省潮州市枫溪区蔡陇大道
邮编：521031
电话：0768-293 1010
传真：0768-293 1033
电邮：cctc@thegreatwall-china.com
网址：www.thegreatwall-china.com

深圳市汇高泰富贸易有限公司
深圳市罗湖区深南东路5002号
信兴广场地王商业中心4905-07室
电话：0755-8238 9510
传真：0755-8238 9050
请参阅第40、41页

唯宝贸易（上海）有限公司
上海市延安西路2299号世贸商城10A28室
邮编：200336
电话：021-6236 3281
传真：021-6236 3283
网址：www.villeroy-boch.com
请参阅第318、319页

咖啡豆搅碎机
Coffee Grinders

Hiangkie Coffee Group Limited
香记咖啡集团有限公司
香港九龙新蒲岗三祝街12-14号
荣森工业第二大厦3楼
电话：+852-3769 2345
传真：+852-2545 8917
电邮：enquiry@hiangkie.com.hk
网址：www.hiangkie.com.hk
请参阅第118、119页

Milega Hotel Equipment Supplies (Shenzhen) Co., Ltd.
麦乐嘉酒店用品（深圳）有限公司
广东省深圳市福田区八卦四路
索泰克大厦4楼S1区
邮编：518029
电话：0755-8240 8377
传真：0755-8205 5798
电邮：welcome@milegacoffee.com
网址：www.milegacoffee.com

Panasonic Corporation of China
松下电器（中国）有限公司
北京市朝阳区景华南街5号
远洋·光华国际C座5层
邮编：100020
电话：010-6562 6688
网址：www.panasonic.com.cn

上海基隆酒店用品有限公司
上海市铜川路185号
邮编：200333
电话：021-6222 8927
传真：021-6222 8936
网址：www.twjiali.com

咖啡机
Coffee Machine

Afehc - Spanish Exporting Manufacturers Association For The Hospitality Industry
西班牙餐饮及团体用具生产及出口商协会
Rambla Catalunya 81, 5-3
08008 Barcelona
Spain
电话：+34(93)-487 3290
传真：+34(93)-487 0770
电邮：afehc@afehc.com
网址：www.afehc.com
请参阅第36页

Angelhood Shanghai Co., Ltd.
上海安继行实业有限公司
上海虹梅南路4999号（新吴泾工业园区）8号楼
邮编：201109
电话：021-5169 1855
传真：021-5168 7575
电邮：shanghai@angelhood.com.cn
网址：www.angelhood.com.cn

BFC China Corporation
锟谛食品有限公司
江苏省昆山市开发区樾城路129号
邮编：215300
电话：0512-5732 6640
传真：0512-5737 8580
电邮：bfccn@163.com
网址：www.bfcsrl.it

Beijing HongYaXuan Coffee Trading Co., Ltd.
北京宏雅轩咖啡贸易有限公司
北京市朝阳区西大望路15号3号楼
外企大厦A座710室
邮编：100022
电话：010-8772 8204
传真：010-8772 9753
电邮：cj@hyxcoffee.com
网址：www.hyxcoffee.com

Beijing Kingtai Tenhong Trade Co., Ltd.
北京市京泰天宏经贸有限责任公司
北京市朝阳区利泽中二路2号
望京科技创业园E座405C
邮编：100102
电话：010-8795 2371
传真：010-8795 2380
电邮：info@mycafe.com.cn
网址：www.mycafe.com.cn

Beijing Prettly International Trading Co., Ltd.
北京佰特莱国际贸易有限公司
北京市朝阳区建国路88号
SOHO现代城2号楼2703室
邮编：100022
电话：010-8589 6792
传真：010-8589 5984
电邮：info@cafevip.com
网址：www.cafevip.com

Beijing Wonder Zhong's Coffee Equipment Sales Co., Ltd.
北京旺达钟记咖啡设备销售有限公司
北京市东城区灯市口大街33号国中大厦302室
邮编：100006
电话：010-6522 3500
传真：010-6522 3519
电邮：zhongs_cafe@yahoo.com.cn
网址：www.zhongs-coffee.com

Blue Mountain Food Corporation
东莞市蓝山食品有限公司
广东省东莞市南城区亨美水濂彭洞工业B区
邮编：523947
电话：0769-3889 7668
传真：0769-3889 7669
电邮：bmcafe@bmcafe.net
网址：www.bmcafe.net

Bravilor Bonamat B.V.
P.O. Box 188, 1700 AD Heerhugowaard, The Netherlands
电话：+31(72)-575 1751
传真：+31(72)-575 1758
电邮：sales@bravilor.com
网址：www.bravilor.com

Bridge Shine Coffee Equipment (Shanghai) Co., Ltd.
桥升咖啡设备（上海）有限公司
上海市闵行区吴中路1000号
邮编：201103
电话：021-6401 5383
传真：021-6401 5442
电邮：gourmetcoffee@china.com
网址：www.bridgeshine.com.cn

C.S. Macchine Per Caffe' Srl
Via Palladio, 11-33010 Tavagnacco (UD)-Italy
电话：+39-0432 688193
传真：+39-0432 689351
电邮：info@fiorenzatocs.com
网址：www.fiorenzatocs.com

Changzhou Pilot Electronic Co., Ltd.
常州领航电子有限公司
江苏省常州市新北区汉江路397号3号楼2楼
邮编：213022
电话：0519-8699 6761
传真：0519-8699 6791
电邮：info@bianchivendingchina.com
网址：www.lhcoffeetime.com

Crem International (Shanghai) Company Limited
群韵饮料机械（上海）有限公司
上海市浦东新区康义路521-551号A幢
电话：021-6818 7010
传真：021-6818 7020
电邮：info@coffeequeen.com.cn
网址：www.coffeequeen.com

Guangzhou Gino Trading Co., Ltd.
广州市吉诺贸易有限公司
广州市天河区林和西路167号
威尼国际10层1005-1006室
邮编：551095
电话：020-3877 6130
传真：020-3877 6133
电邮：baigdstx.555@163.com
网址：www.ginochina.com

质量始终如一
服务更胜一筹

意大利德龙公司，专业咖啡机制造商。
创立于1902年，历经百年发展，
成为全球范围的家用电器集团，
业务遍及80多个国家和地区。

拥有“IFD卡布奇诺”等多个领先技术，
奠定了在咖啡机制作方面的专家地位。

全自动意式特浓咖啡机，
整机意大利原装进口，
同样适用于办公室、餐饮连锁及商业场所，
并且拥有更胜一筹的服务：

- 始终保持统一的咖啡制作标准；
- 每小时最多可制作120杯意式特浓咖啡；
- 自购买日期起两年内10000杯咖啡保修杯量；
- 全国联保，并提供上门服务；
- 价格仅为专业机型的五分之一；

CAFFE' VENEZIA ESAM 2200.S
全自动意式特浓咖啡机

ESAM 3500 ESAM 5450 ESAM 3200 ESAM 3000.B ESAM 4000.B ESAM 2600

更多意大利德龙咖啡机请查询：
邑隆贸易（上海）有限公司（意大利德龙集团中国公司）
客户服务热线：8009881668
网址：www.delonghi-china.com

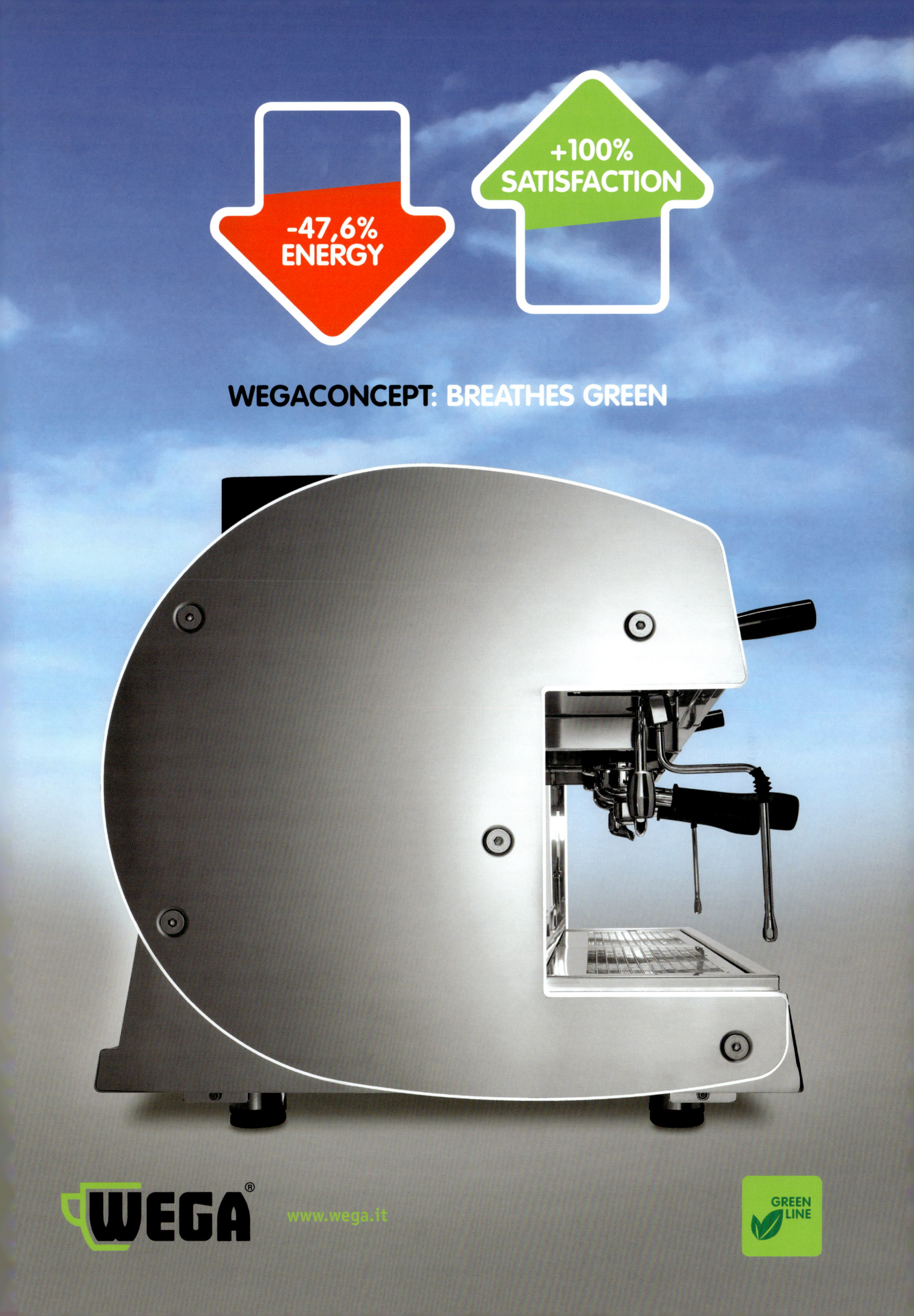
-47,6%
ENERGY
+100%
SATISFACTION
WEGACONCEPT: BREATHES GREEN
WEGA
www.wega.it
GREEN LINE

中国人自己的咖啡机

As Chinese people own the coffee machine

美耐皿高级餐具

Tiamo

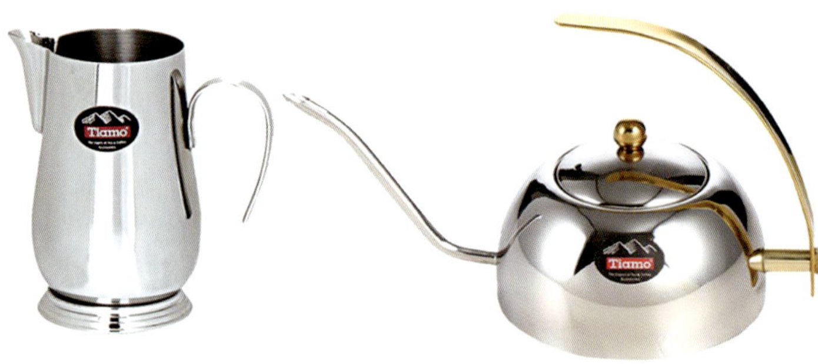

YA MI 卓越品质，定制专家

Excellent quality , Customization experts

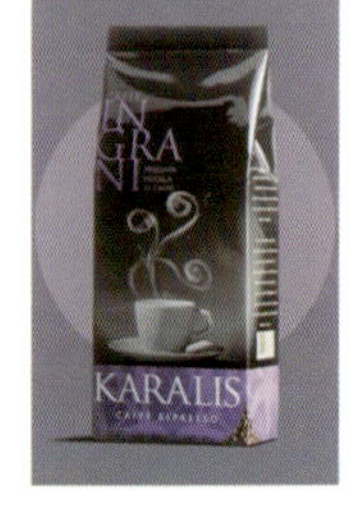

大正咖啡设备总汇
电话：400-665-8886
传真：021-64468993
网站：www.dzcj.com
上海-广州-北京

▼咖啡机
Coffee Machine

Hiangkie Coffee Group Limited
香记咖啡集团有限公司
香港九龙新蒲岗三祝街12-14号
荣森工业第二大厦3楼
电话：+852-3769 2345
传真：+852-2545 8917
电邮：enquiry@hiangkie.com.hk
网址：www.hiangkie.com.hk
请参阅第118、119页

Italian Coffee Company
美商 义式企业
上海市合川路3152号北楼2楼
邮编：201103
电话：021-6405 0475
传真：021-6405 0467
网址：www.italian-coffee-company.com

Jascaffe China Co., Ltd.
王力咖啡贸易（上海）有限公司
上海市松江区九亭镇盛龙路751号
邮编：201615
电话：021-3352 2299
传真：021-5206 8338
电邮：marketing@jascaffechina.com
网址：www.jascaffechina.com

Jess (Shanghai) Trading Co., Ltd.
上海吉晟贸易有限公司
上海市虹口区物华路58号物华大楼1102-1108室
邮编：200086
电话：021-6512 7239
传真：021-6512 3629
电邮：service@jespresso.com
网址：www.jespresso.com

Jiufu Junye (Beijing) International Trading Co., Ltd.
九福君业（北京）国际贸易有限公司
北京市朝阳区门北大街乙12号
天辰大厦2009-2010室
邮编：100020
电话：010-5129 2926
传真：010-6599 1141
电邮：coffee@china-coffee.com
网址：www.china-coffee.com

Lee Hun Trading Co., Ltd.
香港利亨贸易行
香港九龙红磡鹤园街9-11号
凯旋工商中心第三期二楼Q室
电话：+852-2334 0873
传真：+852-2954 2181
网址：www.cpl.net.cn

Meseta Shanghai Co., Ltd.
美瑟达上海阔意商贸有限公司
上海市徐汇区肇嘉浜路608号联业大厦1603室
邮编：200031
电话：021-6433 3982
传真：021-6433 3982
电邮：infomeseta@yahoo.cn
网址：www.meseta.cn

Milega Hotel Equipment Supplies (Shenzhen) Co., Ltd.
麦乐嘉酒店用品（深圳）有限公司
广东省深圳市福田区八卦四路5号
索泰克大厦4楼S1区
邮编：518029
电话：0755-8240 8377
传真：0755-8205 5798
电邮：welcome@milegacoffee.com
网址：www.milegacoffee.com

Ningbo AAA Group Electric Appliance Co., Ltd.
宁波三A集团电器有限公司
浙江省慈溪市周巷镇西工业园区9-10幢
邮编：315324
电话：0574-6333 0791
传真：0574-6332 2173
网址：www.aaacoffeemachine.com

Ningbo Bioka Coffee Equipment Department
宁波市贝欧卡咖啡设备商行
浙江省宁波市永泰花园46幢103A
邮编：315000
电话：0574-8814 5988
传真：0574-8820 4043
电邮：nb-boc@126.com
网址：www.nb-coffee.com

Nuova Ricambi
Via dei Mille 20 20061 Caarugate (Mi) Italy
电话：+39-029 253 205
传真：+39-029 215 153*838
电邮：info@nuovaricambi.it

Q's Coffee
邱公馆食品（云南）有限公司
上海市浦东大道138号永华大厦10楼
邮编：200120
电话：021-6887 5008
传真：021-6887 5193
网址：www.qs-coffee.com

Render Coffee (Shanghai) Co., Ltd.
源铭咖啡（上海）有限公司
上海市松江洞泾工业开发区洞厍路B1号
邮编：201619
电话：021-5767 0577
传真：021-5767 0771
电邮：sales@rendercoffee.com
网址：www.rendercoffee.com

Shanghai Creation Trading Co., Ltd.
上海开展贸易有限公司
上海市闵行区虹井路355号
邮编：201103
电话：021-3431 5789
传真：021-3431 1239
网址：www.creation-foods.com.cn

Shanghai Jiachun Coffee Co., Ltd.
上海佳醇咖啡有限公司
上海市嘉定区南翔镇惠平路77号一栋二楼
邮编：200333
电话：021-5279 4195
传真：021-5285 3412
电邮：sales@jccaffe.com
网址：www.shjiachun.cn

Shanghai QiJie Economic & Trade Co., Ltd.
上海齐桀经贸有限公司
上海市长宁区新华路543号1号楼3楼D室
邮编：200052
电话：021-6294 0690
传真：021-6209 9143
电邮：info@hjcoffee.com
网址：www.hjcoffee.com

Shanghai Unitech Food Machinery Company
上海台新食品机械有限公司
上海市万航渡路888号开开大厦26楼A座
邮编：200051
电话：021-6240 0595
电邮：unitech-sh@unitech-sh.com
网址：www.unitech-sh.com

Shanghai Vernal Coffee Trade Co., Ltd.
上海满庭芳咖啡贸易有限公司
上海市申滨路1058弄67号702室(近天山西路)
邮编：201101
电话：021-3453 6550
传真：021-5102 6565
电邮：mantingfang@yahoo.com.cn
网址：www.office-coffee.com.cn

Shanghai Walton Concepts Economic & Trading Co., Ltd.
上海和沁经贸有限公司
上海市闵行区虹许路731号3号楼3楼
邮编：201103
电话：021-6401 6449
传真：021-6401 3103
网址：www.waltonconcepts.com
请参阅第120页

Shanghai Yujia Trading Co., Ltd.
上海郁佳贸易有限公司
上海市田东路258弄2号302室
邮编：200235
电话：021-6468 0030
传真：021-6468 0029
电邮：yuchang@pellini.com.cn
网址：www.pellini.com.cn

Shenzhen Jin Jia Feng Trading Co., Ltd.
深圳市金嘉丰贸易有限公司
广东省深圳市福田区八卦四路5号
索泰克大厦4楼P区
邮编：518029
电话：0755-8247 0669
传真：0755-8205 5798
电邮：sales@milegacoffee.com
网址：www.cnjjf.com

Shenzhen Sen Run Jia Trading Co., Ltd.
深圳市森润佳贸易有限公司
深圳市福田区新闻路华丰大厦802-803室
邮编：518034
电话：0755-6130 5660
传真：0755-8318 7402
电邮：srj@srjcoffee.com
网址：www.srjcoffee.com

Shenzhen Starhouse Coffee Food Co., Ltd.
深圳德维咖啡食品有限公司
深圳横岗镇安良三角龙工业区安平街12号D栋4楼
邮编：518115
电话：0755-8248 1015
传真：0755-8248 1027
电邮：frankseng66@hotmail.com
网址：www.starhousecoffee.com.cn

Tsit Wing International Holdings Limited
捷荣国际控股有限公司
Flats F-J, 11/F., Block 3, Kwai Tak Ind. Centre, Kwai Tak St., Kwai Chung, N.T., Hong Kong
电话：+852-2429 0585
传真：+852-2480 6996
网址：www.twcoffee.com

▼咖啡机

Coffee Machine

WEGA S.r.l.

Via Condotti Bardini, 1

31058 Susegana (TV) – Italy

电话：+39(0438)-188 4811

传真：+39(0438)-188 4890

网址：www.wega.it

业务范围：

Wega was established in 1985, with the view to produce and supply high quality professional espresso coffee machines. In just over two decades, Wega has become a market leader throughout the world thanks to its constant search for quality, innovation and design. Wega is further represented, in 85 countries throughout the world by importers, coffee roasters and representative agents. The main line of business, is the manufacture and supply of professional espresso coffee machines, grinders and allied products. The allied products consist of ice-makers and glass-washers. In recent years, Wega has focused its research activities on products with a low environmental impact. The main objective is targeted towards energy-saving, together with increased technological innovation for improved temperature and heat stability, thus ensuring consistency in brewing and extraction. The new model "Wegaconcept" is an eco-friendly machine of the Greenline which guarantees energy savings of up to 47.6% compared to traditional machines tested over a 24 hour time period.

请参阅第 221 页

WMF (Shanghai) Co., Ltd.

精鸟金属制品贸易（上海）有限公司

上海市虹口区四川北路1318号

盛邦国际大厦1101-1103室

邮编：200080

电话：021-5515 5212

传真：021-5515 5220

电邮：info@wmf-china.com

网址：www.wmf-china.com

请参阅第 219 页

Wanshida Coffee Machine (HangZhou) Co., Ltd.

万事达（杭州）咖啡机有限公司

杭州市余杭区良渚镇勾运路69号

邮编：311112

电话：0571-8875 7688

传真：0571-8875 7796

电邮：sales@wsdcoffeemachine.com

网址：www.wsdcoffeemachine.com

illycaffe Shanghai Co., Ltd.

意利咖啡商贸（上海）有限公司

上海市铜仁路258号九安广场银座7楼B、D室

邮编：200040

电话：021-6279 1979

传真：021-6279 2905

电邮：illy@illychina.cn

网址：www.illychina.com

www.illyeshop.cn

请参阅第 116、117 页

北京凯乐伯商贸有限公司

北京市朝阳区东三环南路13号乐游饭店南楼二层

邮编：100021

电话：010-8771 4971

传真：010-8771 4787

网址：www.5icafe.com.cn

大正咖啡设备总汇

上海市闵行区合川路3136号1号楼3楼

电话：400 665 8886

传真：021-6446 8993

电邮：dzodi@163.net

网址：www.dzcj.com

业务范围：

大正企业经过十多年的努力，现已发展成中国咖啡设备与玻璃器皿行业重要的供应商，在行业内拥有良好信誉和知名度。相信在大正企业精神［质量是大正的生命 市场是大正的方向 创新是大正的使命 服务是大正的永续］的指引下，大正全体同仁将以兢兢业业工作精神、创造高标准工作效率、以高水准的服务提供高质量的商品。

请参阅第 222 页

邑隆贸易（上海）有限公司

上海市普陀区中山北路3553号伸大厦1510-1515室

邮编：200062

电话：021-5108 6098

传真：021-6245 3368

网址：www.delonghi-china.com

请参阅第 220 页

冷冻展示柜 Display Cabinets,Refrigerated

Beijing Jiade Shichuang Refrigeration Equipment Co., Ltd.

北京嘉德实创制冷设备有限公司

北京市朝阳区望京南湖东园122楼

博泰国际B座1015室

邮编：100029

电话：010-8464 4258

传真：010-8464 4261

电邮：jiadesa@sina.com

网址：www.jiadeshichuang.com

Dalian Sanyo Cold Chain Co., Ltd.

大连三洋冷链有限公司

大连经济技术开发区松岚街6号

电邮：gezhifei@163.com

网址：www.dalian-sanyo.com.cn

请参阅总目录书隔页面页

Fixwell Display System Co., Ltd.

辉和陈列设备有限公司

1401 Westlands Centre

20 Westlands Road, Quarry Bay

Hong Kong

电话：+852-2811 9381

传真：+852-2565 7094

电邮：sales@fixwell.com.hk

网址：www.fixwell.com.hk

Guangzhou Guangling Refrigeration Equipment Co., Ltd.

广菱制冷设备有限公司

广州市白云区均禾街新石路68号

邮编：510440

电话：020-3663 6092

传真：020-3664 2001

电邮：gudrun_gl@126.com

网址：www.999gl.com

Guangzhou Haipingyang Western Kitchen Equipment Co., Ltd.

广州海平洋西厨设备有限公司

广州市白云区西槎路同德上步花园A栋北7号

电话：020-3649 7831

传真：020-3638 1831

电邮：sales@haipingyang.com

网址：www.haipingyang.com

Guangzhou Ocean Refrigeration Equipment Co., Ltd.

广州远洋制冷设备有限公司

广东省广州市白云区石湖军民路大浦工业区

电话：020-6663 0391

传真：020-3742 0219

电邮：gzyuanyang888@163.com

网址：www.gzyuanyang.com.cn

Guangzhou Xidu Refrigelation Equipment Co., Ltd.

广州喜都冷冻设备有限公司

广州市番禺区钟村工业区A区

邮编：511495

电话：020-3471 9188

传真：020-3471 7288

电邮：xidu@xunfa.com

网址：www.xi-du.com

Heatcraft Worldwide Refrigeration - Asia

西克环球制冷亚洲有限公司

上海市虹桥路1号港汇广场1号楼2306室

邮编：200030

电话：021-6407 1616

传真：021-6447 7586

网址：www.heatcraft.com.cn

Keen Top Refrigerator (HK) Co., Ltd.

艺瀚冷冻设备（香港）有限公司

香港新界沙田火炭山尾街31-35号

华乐工业中心C座20楼12室

电话：+852-2409 2328

传真：+852-2614 8592

电邮：sales@keentop.com.hk

网址：www.keentop.com.hk

Oriental Engineering Company Limited

华捷洋行有限公司

香港九龙马头围道21号义达工业大厦A座二楼

电话：+852-2333 0181

传真：+852-2764 1605

电邮：sales@oriental-eng.com.hk

网址：www.oequip.com

Qingdao Enterasys Commercial Facilities Ltd.

青岛凯创商业设施有限公司

山东省青岛市城阳区寺后工业园

邮编：266109

电话：0532-8999 6379

传真：0532-8776 0070

电邮：kaichuang2006@yahoo.com.cn

网址：www.chinaqdkc.com

▼冷冻展示柜
Display Cabinets,Refrigerated

Rightway Asia Limited
方正亚洲有限公司
山东省青岛市城阳区春阳路167号盈国国际721室
邮编：266109
电话：0532-8110 0375
传真：0532-8796 5770
网址：www.rightwayasia.com

Royal-Kincool Refrigeration Equipment Co., Ltd.
中山美科冷冻设备有限公司
广东省中山市东升镇同乐佑生经济开发区
邮编：528414
电话：0760-2221 9078
传真：0760-2221 9077
网址：www.royal-kincool.com

Shanghai Guodeng Refrigeration Equipment Co., Ltd.
上海国登制冷设备有限公司
上海市闵行区七宝镇华友路515号
邮编：201100
电话：021-6459 7175
传真：021-6459 7183
网址：www.guodeng.com.cn

Shanghai JinCheng Refrigerating Equipment Co., Ltd.
上海金城制冷设备有限公司
上海市中山北路3357号
邮编：200062
电话：021-6216 8066
传真：021-6216 8070
电邮：jincheng@shkingdom.com.cn
网址：www.shkingdom.com.cn
请参阅第225页

Shanghai Shicolin Refrigeration Equipment Co., Ltd.
上海思柯林制冷设备有限公司
上海市金山区亭林镇亭卫公路9055弄55号
邮编：201505
电话：021-5723 5681
传真：021-5723 2899
电邮：info@shicolin.com
网址：www.shicolin.com

Tip-Top Precision Industry Co., Ltd.
江门市裕莹精密工业有限公司
广东省江门市杜阮北三路58号
邮编：529075
电话：0750-365 5888
传真：0750-365 5833
电邮：yy@yuyinggroup.com.cn
网址：www.yuyinggroup.com.cn

Wuxi Gold Reached The Kitchen Sets Ccmplete Sets Of Equipment Co., Ltd.
无锡市金达成套厨房设备有限公司
无锡国家高新区坊前工业园区A区
（春阳东路6号）
邮编：214111
电话：0510-8827 7873
传真：0510-8827 7613
电邮：sale@wxjinda.com
网址：www.wxjinda.com

Zhejiang Debao Electric Appliance Co., Ltd.
浙江德宝电器有限公司
海宁市连杭经济开发区新二路03号
邮编：314422
电话：0571-8698 8210
传真：0571-8698 8210
电邮：web@zj-debaodianqi.com
网址：www.zj-debaodianqi.com

Zhongshun Huaye Refrigerating Equipment Co., Ltd.
广州市中顺华业冷冻设备有限公司
广州市白云区钟落潭大纲领商业中心30号
邮编：510545
电话：020-8740 5616
传真：020-8741 7314
电邮：liriji68@126.com
网址：www.zshy888.com

余姚市圣邦制冷电器厂
浙江省余姚市新建北路151-3号
电话：0574-2266 3366
传真：0574-2266 3110
网址：www.cn-yydb.com

食品安全用品
Food Safety

Shanghai AMMEX Corporation
艾迈柯思贸易（上海）有限公司
上海市浦东新区牡丹路60号
东辰大厦9楼901-906座
邮编：201204
电话：021-6840 6006
传真：021-6840 6008
网址：www.cn.ammex.com
请参阅第227页、
厨房、餐厅及酒吧设备书隔页底页

Shanghai Soro Industrial Co., Ltd.
上海索隆劳防用品有限公司
上海市松江区新桥镇新创路385号1幢
邮编：201612
电话：021-5768 7886
传真：021-5768 7840
电邮：sales@safetyzone.com.cn
网址：www.safetyzone.com.cn

玻璃器皿
Glassware

ARC INTERNATIONAL

Arc International
法国弓箭国际实业公司
上海市延安东路175号旺角广场301室
邮编：200002
电话：021-6326 0066
传真：021-5358 0062
电邮：fscn@arc-intl.com
网址：www.arc-fs.cn
www.chefsommelier.com
www.arcoroc.com
业务范围：
法国弓箭具有超过185年的玻璃器皿制造经验，是目前世界餐桌文化的领导者。集团在世界五大洲都布有生产基地，销售网络，产品发往世界160多个国家及地区。CHEF & SOMMELIER和ARCOROC是针对餐饮市场的两个专业品牌，主要服务于星级酒店，餐厅，酒吧及酒廊等渠道。产品覆盖了高脚杯，直身杯，水壶/酒樽，餐具，各类酒吧器具等专业玻璃器皿。
创新的技术，高性价比的产品，专业的服务是法国弓箭对客户的承诺！
请参阅第232、233页

Canahot (Wuxi) Industrial Ltd.
无锡市安利酒店用品有限公司
江苏省无锡市锡山区东北塘石新路1号
邮编：214191
电话：0510-8377 2188
传真：0510-8377 2775
电邮：canahot@canahot.com.cn
网址：www.canahot.com.cn

Dalian Hantai International Trade Co., Ltd.
大连翰泰国际贸易有限公司
大连市沙河口区中山路572号星海旺座1506室
邮编：116023
电话：0411-6293 8888
传真：0411-6293 9999
电邮：office@hantai-glass.com
网址：www.table-top.cn
请参阅第234、235页

Dalian Xin Jian Hai Hotel Supplies & Trade Co.
大连新建海酒店用品贸易行
大连市沙河口区星海广场B3区一品星海6-3-1
电话：0411-8480 5299
传真：0411-8480 4111
电邮：xinjianhai@hotmail.com
网址：www.china-xjh.com

Etown China Department Co., Ltd.
厦门忆通百货有限公司
厦门市湖里区同益路50号海明大厦5层
邮编：361012
电话：0592-221 3232
传真：0592-221 6786
电邮：op@etownchina.cn
网址：www.etownchina.cn

EURO ASIA

Euro Asia Shanghai Limited
上海依贵亚贸易有限公司
上海市徐汇区医学院路92号
邮编：200032
电话：021-6422 6618
传真：021-6422 6689
电邮：euroasiash@163.com
网址：www.sheuroasia.com
业务范围：
上海依贵亚贸易有限公司专业从事酒店用品销售。
公司主要为各类客户提供专业酒杯、餐饮配件、瓷器，产品均为世界及国内知名品牌。我们的客户均为四、五星级酒店及高级餐厅。
合理的价格，良好的信誉是我们一贯坚持的目标。
请参阅第230、231页

First Asia Trading Co., Ltd.
上海泛亚经贸有限公司
上海市万航渡路2452号DOHO园区A502室
电话：021-5178 6788
传真：021-5178 6758*118
电邮：firstasia99@msn.com
网址：www.firstasia-sh.com
请参阅第236、237页

Guangzhou Songfa Hotel Equipment Co., Ltd.
广州松发酒店设备用品有限公司
广州市荔湾区东沙开发区荷景路31号
电话：020-2239 9188
传真：020-2239 9132
网址：www.songfa.cn
请参阅第43页

Guangzhou Yiyang Glass Ware Co., Ltd.
广州懿洋玻璃制品有限公司
广东省广州市番禺区
沙溪新翼国际酒店用品城2楼2B107室
电话：020-2262 0985
传真：020-2262 0985
电邮：yiyangglass@163.com
网址：www.yiyang-glass.com

Hangzhou Hongteng Trade Co., Ltd.
杭州弘腾贸易有限公司
杭州市庆春路9号长堤名苑20楼F座
邮编：310009
电话：0571-8704 0651
传真：0571-8704 0652
电邮：sales@hongteng.com.cn
网址：www.hongteng.com.cn

Hlb International Co., Ltd.
上海汇乐比玻璃工艺品有限公司
上海市松江区思贤路1129弄82号
邮编：201600
电话：021-6771 8091
传真：021-6771 8071
网址：www.hlbsh.com

Hotelier Service China Co., Ltd.
上海欧太黎企业管理有限公司
上海市长宁路1551号虹桥国际大厦2号楼1801室
邮编：200051
电话：021-6124 2766
传真：021-6124 2776*805
电邮：enquiry@hotelier-sc.com
网址：www.hotelier-sc.com

Huafu (Chengde) Glassware Co., Ltd.
承德华富玻璃器皿有限公司
河北省承德市高新技术产业开发区西区9号
邮编：067000
电话：0314-205 9103
传真：0314-205 9378
电邮：zyh@huafuglass.com
网址：www.huafuglass.com

Euro Asia Shaghai Limited

意大利
高档水晶杯

NIKKO
SINCE 1908

日本
高档骨瓷

意大利
亚克力制品

PINTINOX
MADE IN ITALY

意大利
不锈刚制品

PATRA

泰国强化瓷

NEOZ

澳大利亚
手工充电灯

西橱用品

DAVINCI CRYSTAL

意大利高级
手工水晶杯

德国水晶杯

Arzberg
MADE IN GERMANY

德国强瓷器

泰国瓷器

意大利
不锈刚制品

Luigi Bormioli
ITALY

从 2005 年起大连翰泰国际贸易有限公司非常荣幸的成为了意大利的“ Luigi Bormioli 路易治•波米奥尼”（世界玻璃制造行业前五强）品牌酒具中国区总代理。

几年来，“ Luigi Bormioli 路易治•波米奥尼”水晶酒具受到众多追求高品质生活人士和红酒品评人士的一致好评和认可。

“ Luigi Bormioli ”酒具、餐盘被选为 2008 年 8 月 8 日奥运国宴餐饮用具。人民大会堂、钓鱼台国宾馆以及众多五星级酒店和家庭都在使用我司代理的产品。

路易治•波米奥尼的学院系列（ACCADEMIA）是专业高科技的结晶，其产品代表了路易治•波米奥尼最专业的水准和世界闻名的意大利设计方式。这一系列水晶玻璃是由机器制成，它添加了特有的 SON.hyx 成分，是以高的响亮度、光泽度、透明度和持久耐用性而著称的先进科技的专有技术产品。其时尚典雅的设计可以满足专业品酒人士的需要。

路易治•波米奥尼公司研发的添加 SON.hyx 材料的珍贵无铅水晶玻璃，是绝对的透明和完全无色的，坚固，柔韧性好，撞杯声响亮、悦耳，机洗安全，经过 4000 次工业洗涤测试依然晶莹剔透。SON.hyx 水晶玻璃以其卓越的质地赢得了全世界的认同和赞誉，走在了水晶玻璃行业中的最前沿。

大连翰泰国际贸易有限公司

Dalian Hantai International Trade Co., Ltd.

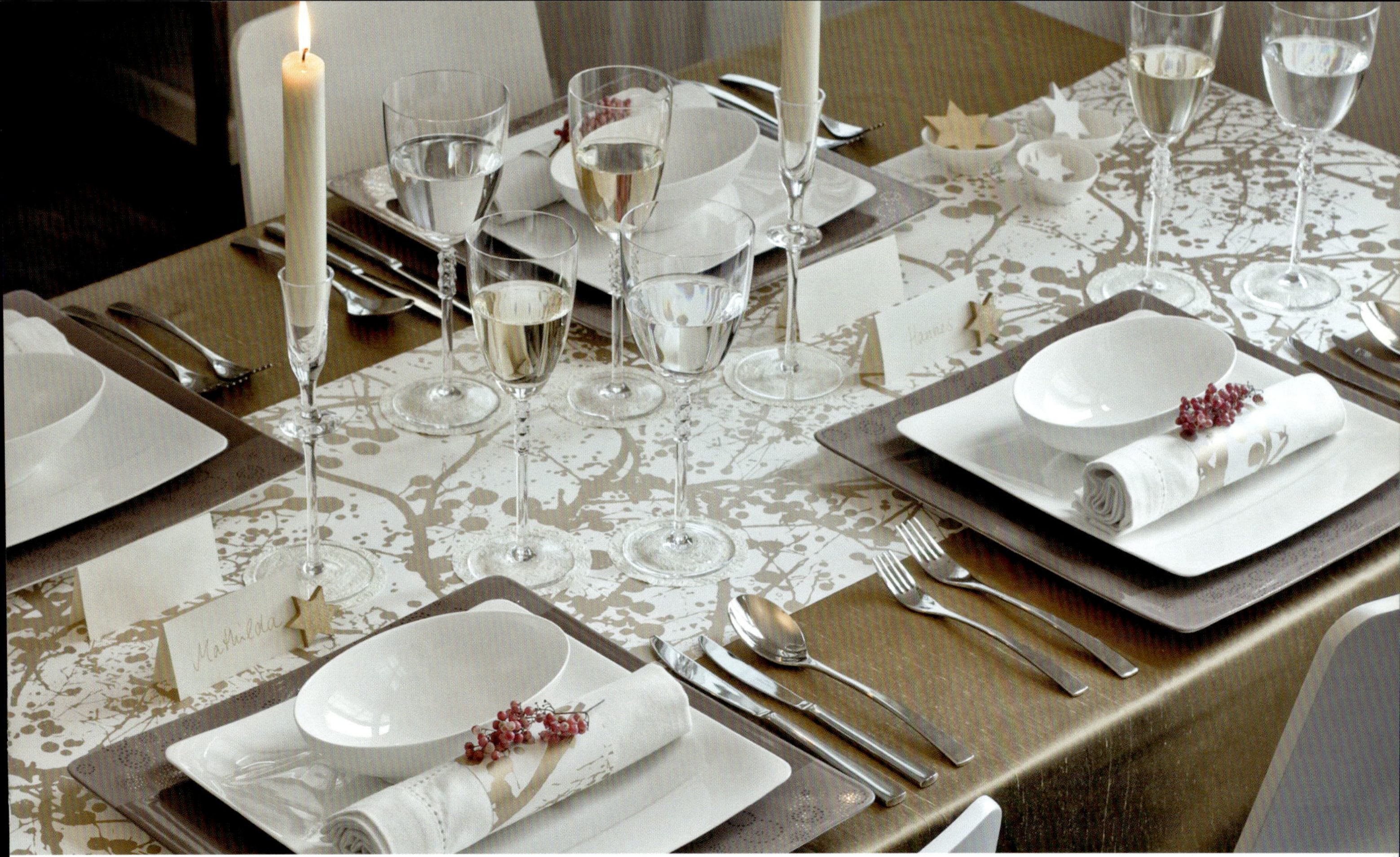

拥有250多年陶瓷制造历史的Villeroy & Boch品牌以精湛的陶瓷技术为基础，融入了设计师的超凡创意、艺术眼光及精巧工艺，使Villeroy & Boch旗下每种产品都彰显独特的个性风格。

作为世界上最大的单一陶瓷品牌制造商，Villeroy & Boch的器型和花色，从传统的典雅和精致，到田园的浪漫和随意，再到现代都市的时尚和简洁，针对各类不同品位人群设计出众多的风格。与此同时，它的瓷质更涵盖了陶器、细瓷、骨瓷、玻璃瓷，使瓷器的质地和风格更加统一。在技术和制造工艺上，Villeroy & Boch不断以创新来完善自己，将上乘的材料、精雕细琢的工艺及先进的技术融为一体，以此达到更加完美。而大量使用铜版雕刻、传统手工绘制、花纸等技艺，并将最新转印技术应用到产品图案的表达中，使陶瓷制品色彩演绎得更加丰富和润泽。

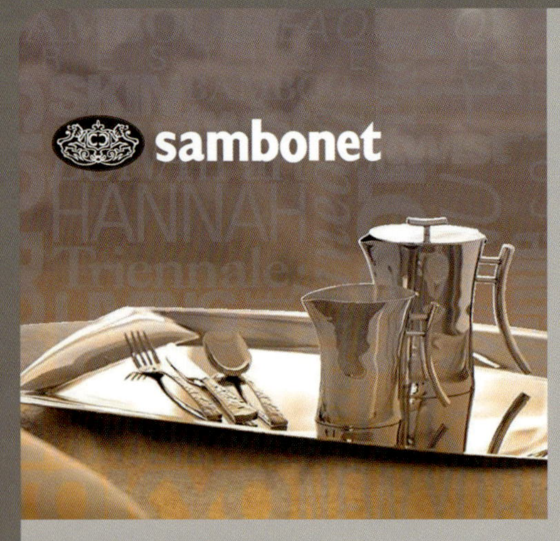

专业高级桌面用品供应服务商

专业知识 卓越服务

EGIZIA

Yalos
murano

Emile Henry
FRANCE

Robert Welch

RIEDEL
THE WINE GLASS COMPANY

alfi
Design your life

CANDOLA
Tischkultur zum Wohlfühlen

stelton

ZASSENHAUS

FIRST ASIA

▼玻璃器皿
Glassware

LiangPin Tableware Co., Ltd. GZ
广州市亮品餐具有限公司
广州市昌岗中路166号富盈大厦19楼1911室
电话：020-8431 3636
传真：020-6237 8332
电邮：liangpin.gz@163.com
网址：www.athena-tableware.com
请参阅第212页

Libbey Glassware (China) Co., Ltd.
利比玻璃制品（中国）有限公司
河北省廊坊市经济技术开发区爱民东道2211号
邮编：065001
电话：0316-606 0630
传真：0316-606 0624
电邮：sales@libbey.cn
网址：www.libbey.cn

Ocean Glass Trading (Shanghai) Co., Ltd.
翱顺玻璃贸易（上海）有限公司
上海市万航渡路83号金航大厦1502室
邮编：200040
电话：021-6135 9505
传真：021-6135 9428
电邮：eddieshchew@oceanglass.com
网址：www.ocean-professinal.com
业务范围：
Ocean Professional is the brand created exclusively for food service operators who recognize the importance of creating wining & dining pleasures for their guests. We offer portfolio of world-class quality glassware and specific drinks, outlets and occasions, to create uniqueness, style and value to guests of food service establishments of all levels.
Since the inception of our company, we have combined craftsmanship, manufacturing expertise, design innovation, with in-depth understanding of needs and demands of our customers, to deliver the best value in glassware product and service, making "Ocean" one of the most recognized names in quality glassware customers both in Thailand and worldwide.
请参阅第6、228、229页
厨房、餐厅及酒吧设备书隔页面页

Pasabahce Cam San Ve Ticas
上海黄浦区西藏南路555弄黄浦众鑫城6号503室
邮编：200050
电话：+90(212)-350 3540
传真：+90(212)-350 4540
电邮：jess.lu@dgal.hk
网址：www.pasabahce.com.tr

Rona Co., Ltd.
Schreiberova 365
020 61 Lednicke Rovne Slovak Republic
电话：+421-4246 01505
传真：+421-4246 01447
电邮：info@rona.sk
网址：www.rona.sk

Shandong Huapeng Glass Co., Ltd.
山东华鹏玻璃股份有限公司
山东省荣成市石岛龙云路468号
邮编：264309
电话：0631-738 1873
传真：0631-738 2522
电邮：info@huapengglass.com
网址：www.huapengglass.com

Shanghai Chikao Glassware Manufacture Co., Ltd.
上海奇高玻璃制品有限公司
上海市松江区九亭镇久富开发区盛高路189号
邮编：201615
电话：021-6762 6150
传真：021-6762 6155
网址：www.shanghai-chikao.cn

Shanghai First House Stores & Gifts Co., Ltd.
上海第一屋百货礼品有限公司
上海市闵行区星强街58号
邮编：201101
电话：021-6479 6760
传真：021-6478 0319
电邮：ywy@first-house.cn
网址：www.sh-first-house.com

Shanghai Richy Trading Co., Ltd.
上海睿琦贸易有限公司
上海市铜川路185号
电话：021-5224 1247
传真：021-5224 4091
网址：www.mjwy-glass.cn

Shanghai Tek Foo Enterprises Co., Ltd.
上海德孚实业有限公司
上海市零陵路791弄上影广场3号楼105室
邮编：200030
电话：021-6486 6488
传真：021-6469 2051
电邮：sales@tek-foo.com
网址：www.tek-foo.com

Skyline Hotel Supplies Limited
中山市天俊酒店物料有限公司
广东省中山市东升镇葵兴大道253号
邮编：528414
电话：0760-2221 6868
传真：0760-2221 6668
电邮：china@skylineint.cn
网址：www.skylineint.cn

Zibo Honghan Trading Co., Ltd.
淄博宏瀚贸易有限公司
山东省淄博市博山区八陡
邮编：255203
电话：0533-450 5177
传真：0533-450 5356
电邮：hongda0598@vip.sina.com
网址：www.honghangglass.com

Zwiesel Kristallglas China Co., Ltd.
水维莎（上海）贸易有限公司
上海市静安区陕西北路66号
科恩国际中心大厦2205室
电话：021-3208 0331/32
传真：021-3208 0339
网址：www.zwiesel-kristallglas.com
请参阅第238页

好璃奥（上海）商贸有限公司
Hario (Shanghai) Co., ltd.
上海市茂名南路205号瑞金大厦1510室
电话：021-6473 1333
传真：021-6473 5355
电邮：info@hario.sh.cn
网址：www.hario.sh.cn

深圳市特博威尔酒店用品供应有限公司
广州市番禺区迎宾大道
迎宾豪泰星级酒店用品城508-509号
电话：020-2868 0305
传真：020-2868 0306*666
电邮：sankie@126.com
网址：www.tbw-china.com

冰桶
Ice Buckets

Beijing Tokenism Trading Co., Ltd.
北京汤嘉今悦贸易有限公司
北京市马家堡西路32号5D902室
邮编：100068
电话：010-6754 8688/8788/8988
传真：010-8750 7596
电邮：tokenism@163.com
网址：www.tokenism.cn
请参阅第411页、封底里

Good-Way Tableware Manufactory Ltd.
2/F., 29 Austin Road, T.S.T.,
Kowloon, Hong Kong
电话：+852-2735 8671
传真：+852-2314 2932
电邮：export@good-way.com
网址：www.wnk-hk.com

Huangyan Shuangjian Plastic Co., Ltd.
黄岩南城双剑塑料制作厂
浙江省台州市黄岩区药山村一区97号
邮编：318020
电话：0576-8483 5888
传真：0576-8419 2891
网址：www.hyshuangjian.com

Shanghai Jinhong Buffet Utensil & Manufacture Co., Ltd.
上海锦宏自助餐用品制造有限公司
上海市卢湾区鲁班路168弄大同花园5号101室
邮编：200023
电话：021-5302 1768
传真：021-5302 1778
电邮：jinhong9@vip.163.com
网址：www.jinhong-sh.com

Shenzhen Pama Hotel Products Co., Ltd.
深圳市帕玛酒店用品有限公司
深圳市南山区粤海路粤海工业村
深圳动漫园4栋201室
邮编：518054
电话：0755-8605 2592
传真：0755-8605 2582
网址：www.szpama.com
请参阅第42页

Wenzhou Yinying Hotel Article and Equipment Co., Ltd.
温州银鹰酒店用品设备有限公司
温州市黎明中路283号
邮编：325000
电话：0577-8880 6600
传真：0577-8880 6622
电邮：yinying@wzyinying.com
网址：www.wzyinying.com

Wuyi Chengchi Metal Manufacturing Factory
武义诚驰金属制品有限公司
浙江省武义县白洋工业区牛背金
邮编：321200
电话：0579-8795 2696
传真：0579-8795 2699
电邮：chengchi@chengchijinshu.com
网址：www.chengchijinshu.com

▼冰桶
Ice Buckets

YPT International Ltd.
建宏国际有限公司
香港九龙官塘鲤鱼门道2号新城工商中心1楼
电话：+852-2723 2168
传真：+852-2739 7576
电邮：ypt@techwin.com.hk
网址：www.ypt.com.hk

Zhejiang WuGu Industries Co., Ltd.
浙江五谷实业有限公司
浙江省余姚市丈亭台商投资园区
电话：0574-6299 8803
传真：0574-6299 8899
电邮：sho@hwugu.com
网址：www.hwugu.com
请参阅第201页

北京庄园酒店用品有限公司
北京市昌平区天通苑西三区23号楼401室
邮编：102218
电话：010-6411 8552
传真：010-6411 9833
电邮：zhuangyuanstaff@126.com
网址：www.bjzhuangyuan.com

冰淇淋设备
Ice Cream Equipment

Beijing Harvest E & M Co., Ltd.
北京丰汇加机电设备销售有限公司
北京市宣武区建功西里1号楼天缘公寓A座2701室
邮编：100054
电话：010-8351 6972
传真：010-8351 7663
电邮：sales@bjharvest.cn
网址：www.bjharvest.cn

Carpigiani (Shanghai) Trading Limited
卡比詹尼（上海）商贸有限公司
上海市漕溪路250号银海大楼A9-11/12室
邮编：200235
电话：021-6484 6652
传真：021-6484 6659
网址：www.carpigiani.com

Dalian Sanyo Cold Chain Co., Ltd.
大连三洋冷链有限公司
大连经济技术开发区松岚街6号
电邮：gezhifei@163.com
网址：www.dalian-sanyo.com.cn
请参阅总目录书隔页面页

Guangli Machinery (Xinhui) Co., Ltd.
江门市新会区广力机械有限公司
广东省江门市新会区古井镇大园山工业区
邮编：529145
电话：0750-628 0988
传真：0750-611 9118
电邮：info@gongly.com
网址：www.gongly.com

Guangzhou Junjian Kitchen Appliances and Refrigeration Equipment Co., Ltd.
广州市钧健厨具冷冻设备公司
广州市白云区竹料良田工业园良园中路3号
邮编：510545
电话：020-6285 6006
传真：020-6285 6078
电邮：gzjunjian@126.com
网址：www.junjianchina.com

Hangzhou Fangnan Hotel Equipment Co., Ltd.
杭州方南酒店设备有限公司
浙江省杭州市艮山西路86号
邮编：310021
电话：0571-8672 2923
传真：0571-8672 2793
电邮：mail@fangnanjd.com
网址：www.fangnanjd.com

Mehen Food Machine Manufacture Co., Ltd.
南京美恒食品机械制造有限公司
南京市江宁区莱茵达路699号
邮编：211112
电话：025-6890 1892
传真：025-6890 1893
电邮：sales.cn@mehen.com
网址：www.mehen.com

Oriental Engineering Company Limited
华捷洋行有限公司
香港九龙马头围道21号义达工业大厦A座二楼
电话：+852-2333 0181
传真：+852-2764 1605
电邮：sales@oriental-eng.com.hk
网址：www.oequip.com

Shanghai Alice Import-Export Co., Ltd.
上海珈仪进出口贸易有限公司
上海市闵行区宝城路158弄38号407室
邮编：201100
电话：021-6460 7706
传真：021-6460 7709
电邮：xiong@caffeitaliano.cn
网址：www.caffeitaliano.cn

Shanghai JinCheng Refrigerating Equipment Co., Ltd.
上海金城制冷设备有限公司
上海市中山北路3357号
邮编：200062
电话：021-6216 8066
传真：021-6216 8070
电邮：jincheng@shkingdom.com.cn
网址：www.shkingdom.com.cn
请参阅第225页

Shanghai Shicolin Refrigeration Equipment Co., Ltd.
上海思柯林制冷设备有限公司
上海市金山区亭林镇亭卫公路9055弄55号
邮编：201505
电话：021-5723 5681
传真：021-5723 2899
电邮：info@shicolin.com
网址：www.shicolin.com

Simplex Foodservice Equipment (Shanghai) Ltd.
新必利餐饮设备（上海）有限公司
上海市松江区九亭镇涞坊路57号
邮编：201615
电话：021-6784 1311
传真：021-6784 1331
电邮：simplex@online.sh.cn
网址：www.simplex.cn

Taylor Foodservice Equipment Distribution (Shanghai) Co., Ltd.
泰而勒食品机械贸易（上海）有限公司
上海市闵行区沪闵路3988号43幢
邮编：201108
电话：021-3323 9898
传真：021-5483 3301
电邮：info@taylorfoodservice.com.cn
网址：www.taylorfoodservice.com.cn

Tornado (Beijing) Refrigeration Equipment Co., Ltd.
特耐德（北京）制冷设备有限公司
北京市朝阳区望京园601号悠乐汇E座5层505室
邮编：100102
电话：010-8478 7961
传真：010-8478 7939
电邮：tornadoworld@126.com
网址：www.tornadoworld.com.cn

Wuhan Sani Machinery Co., Ltd.
武汉赛林机械有限责任公司
武汉市东西湖区金山大道1369号
邮编：430040
电话：027-8324 5226
传真：027-8324 5221
电邮：chinasani@hotmail.com
网址：www.whsani.com

青岛益达制冷设备有限公司
青岛市城阳区青大工业园双元路
邮编：266109
电话：0532-8908 1199
传真：0532-8908 1177
网址：www.qdeasybest.com

制冰设备
Ice Making Equipment

Beijing XuanWu Cooking Food Machine Co., Ltd.
北京市宣武炊事食品机械有限公司
北京市宣武区西便门东里甲1号
邮编：100053
电话：010-6303 1118
电邮：bxcj@bxcj.com.cn
网址：www.bxcj.com.cn

Electrolux Professional (Shanghai) Co., Ltd.
伊莱克斯商用电器（上海）有限公司
上海市外高桥保税区爱都路390号31号楼A座
邮编：200131
电话：021-5046 0099
传真：021-5046 0077
网址：www.electrolux-professional.cn
请参阅第168页

Gelin Electric Appliance Co., Ltd.
江苏格林电器有限公司
江苏省常熟市虞山工业园汇峰路2号
邮编：215500
电话：0512-5284 7692
传真：0512-5284 8283
电邮：gldq@gelin.com.cn
网址：www.gelin.com.cn

Guangzhou Junjian Kitchen Appliances and Refrigeration Equipment Co., Ltd.
广州市钧健厨具冷冻设备公司
广州市白云区竹料良田工业园良园中路3号
邮编：510545
电话：020-6285 6006
传真：020-6285 6078
电邮：gzjunjian@126.com
网址：www.junjianchina.com

Hoshizaki Shanghai Co., Ltd.
星崎冷热机械（上海）有限公司
上海市恒丰路218号现代交通大厦805室
邮编：200070
电话：021-5180 1998
传真：021-5180 1947
电邮：info@hoshizaki.com.cn
网址：www.hoshizaki.com.cn
请参阅第198页

Iceman Corporation Chongqing China
冰人制冰系统设备（重庆）有限公司
重庆市江北区港城工业园
邮编：400026
电话：023-6710 8888
传真：023-6710 8889
电邮：info@iceman.cn
网址：www.iceman.cn

▼制冰设备
Ice Making Equipment

Ningbo Laplan Electric Appliance Co., Ltd.
宁波拉博兰电器有限公司
浙江省慈溪市宗汉街道潮塘工业区
邮编：315301
电话：0574-6300 9888
传真：0574-6322 7116
网址：www.laplan.cc

Oriental Engineering Company Limited
华捷洋行有限公司
香港九龙马头围道21号义达工业大厦A座二楼
电话：+852-2333 0181
传真：+852-2764 1605
电邮：sales@oriental-eng.com.hk
网址：www.oequip.com

Qingdao Orient Commercial Equipment Co., Ltd.
青岛澳润商用设备有限公司
山东省青岛市经济技术开发区松花江路32号
邮编：266510
电话：0532-8676 5051
传真：0532-8676 5050
电邮：icer@orien.com.cn
网址：www.orien.com.cn

Shanghai Cenlong Electric Equipment Co., Ltd.
上海市岑隆电器设备有限公司
上海市松江区九亭久富开发区
邮编：510405
电话：021-3763 8008
传真：021-6769 1182
网址：www.shcenlong.com

Shanghai Fraendcs Refrigeration Equipment Co., Ltd.
上海方兰制冷设备有限公司
上海市闵行区陈行路3998号
邮编：201114
电话：021-3468 0450
传真：021-3468 0449
电邮：fraendcs@126.com
网址：www.fraendcs.com

Shanghai Tongjia Electric Co., Ltd.
上海通佳电器有限公司
上海市松江区车墩工业区泖亭公路632号
邮编：201611
电话：021-3762 7558
传真：021-3762 7568
电邮：sales@sunice.cc
网址：www.sunice.cc

Shanghai Yinniute Refrigeration Equipment Co., Ltd.
上海因纽特制冷设备有限公司
上海市嘉定区黄渡镇春浓路732号
邮编：201804
电话：021-6959 2655
传真：021-6959 2633
电邮：ynt_ef@yinniute.com.cn
网址：www.yinniute.com.cn

Shangqiu Iberna Ice Maker Co., Ltd.
商丘依伯纳制冰机有限公司
河南省商丘市经济技术开发区
邮编：476000
电话：0370-291 0699
传真：0370-293 9978
电邮：iberna@163.com
网址：www.iberna.org.cn

Xing Ji Cold and Hot Electric Appliances Co., Ltd.
广州市星极冷热电器有限公司
广州市白云区均禾街新石路38号
邮编：510000
电话：020-3636 2918
传真：020-6264 2329
电邮：gaohan0617@126.com
网址：www.xj0001.com

Zhejiang Iceshare Refrigerating Appliance Co., Ltd.
浙江爱雪制冷电器有限公司
浙江省德清莫干山经济开发区长虹东街776号
邮编：313200
电话：0572-867 9937
传真：0572-867 9936
电邮：info@cniceshare.com
网址：www.cniceshare.com

久景制冷设备（上海）有限公司
上海市赵重公路1978号
电话：021-3987 6601
传真：021-3987 6501
电邮：niu@hisakage.com
网址：www.hisakage.com
请参阅第197页

上海博特机械设备有限公司
上海市众仁路165号
邮编：201802
电话：021-5912 0939
传真：021-5912 9949
电邮：sales@brantec.com.cn
网址：www.brantec.com.cn

Scotsman

斯科茨曼制冰系统（上海）有限公司
上海市徐虹中路20号2号楼2503室
邮编：200235
电话：021-6131 3200
传真：021-6131 3330
网址：www.scotsman-china.com
业务范围：
斯科茨曼集团旗下拥有Scotsman, Barline, Ice-O-Matic, Tecnomac等多个世界知名品牌。斯科茨曼制冰机已有60多年历史，成功源于生产全系列的制冰机及可信赖的质量，以及完善的售后服务体系。斯科茨曼制冰机能满足全球100多万用户的各种需要，提供全方位的制冰产品解决方案。斯科茨曼是世界领先的商用制冰机供应商。
服务热线：400 630 0076
请参阅第241页

日式餐具
Japanese Tableware

Guangzhou Eqichina Hotel Dishware Factory
广州市依祺瓷酒店餐具厂
广州芳村大道东31号
电话：020-8163 0300
传真：020-8163 0377
电邮：eqichina@163.net
网址：http://eqichina.163e.com.cn

Jingguan Melamine Products Co., Ltd.
晶冠美耐皿制品有限公司
广东省东莞市桥头镇邓屋工业区
电话：0769-8334 4599
传真：0769-8334 4858
电邮：melamine168@163.com
网址：www.melamineware.com.cn

Pacific China Ware
太平洋行
香港九龙大角咀洋松街64-67号
长发工业大厦4楼4室
电话：+852-3580 0680
传真：+852-3590 3384
电邮：info@china-ware.cn
网址：www.china-ware.com.cn

RuoQuan (Shanghai) Canyinyongpin Co., Ltd.
若泉上海餐饮用品有限公司
上海市徐汇区宜山路515号21C
邮编：200235
电话：021-6436 5526
传真：021-6436 5525
电邮：ruoquan_sh2@126.com
网址：www.ruoquansh.com

Shanghai Fukui Arts & Crafts Co., Ltd.
上海福井克莱福特工艺品有限公司
上海市定西路1277号305室
邮编：200050
电话：021-6211 7044
传真：021-6211 1484
电邮：info@yasuragi.com.cn
网址：www.yasuragi.com.cn

餐巾
Napkin

Damon Paper Industrial Co., Ltd.
戴盟纸业有限公司
广东省深圳市盐田区沙深路37号海滨工业区15A3
邮编：518020
电话：0755-8190 6165
传真：0755-8263 1975
电邮：china@dmtissue.com
网址：www.dmtissue.com

Foshan Nanzhuang Hengan Knitting Factory Co., Ltd.
佛山市南庄恒安制造厂有限公司
佛山市禅城区南庄镇樵乐东路79号
电话：0757-8201 6768
传真：0757-8201 6768
电邮：heng-an-sales@163.com
网址：www.hha-hoteltex.com

Huarui Paper
河北新华实业公司
河北省保定市红旗苗圃（植物园）东侧
邮编：071051
电话：0312-595 1626
传真：0312-595 1629
电邮：zp@xhzp.com
网址：www.xhzp.com

Lynn's Business Supplies Corp.
上海羚泰实业有限公司
上海市徐汇区夏城路185号
邮编：200232
电话：021-5435 7217
传真：021-5435 4905
电邮：info@lynns.cn
网址：www.lynns.cn

Shanghai Deyi Hotel Articles Manufacture Co., Ltd.
上海德义酒店用品制造有限公司
上海市民星路201号20号楼
邮编：200433
电话：021-5169 9518
传真：021-5126 2385
网址：www.sh-dy.com
请参阅第414页

▼餐巾 Napkin

Shanghai Handsome Horse Co., Ltd.
上海汉生豪斯实业有限公司
上海市浦东新区北蔡镇杨桥村西计家宅106号
邮编：201204
电话：021-6894 2694
传真：021-6892 9565
电邮：zlj@hs-hs.cn
网址：www.hs-hs.cn

Shanghai Rosegarden Commodity Co., Ltd.
上海瑞源日用品有限公司
上海市普陀区古浪路415弄2号楼2层
邮编：200331
电话：021-3633 1672
传真：021-3633 1670
网址：www.rosegarden-sh.com

纸制品 Paper Products

Beijing ZhongJu International Trading Co., Ltd.
北京中钜铖国际商贸有限公司
北京市朝阳区大郊亭中街2号院
华腾国际3号楼17AD
电话：010-8795 1433
传真：010-6772 9311
电邮：fayshi2004@126.com
网址：www.zhongjc.com.cn
请参阅第244页

Cellynne Paper Converter (Shenzhen) Co., Ltd.
西朗纸业（深圳）有限公司
广东省深圳市龙岗区龙西五联路宝鹰工业园C区
邮编：518116
电话：0755-3360 8990
传真：0755-3360 8895
网址：www.cellynne.com.cn

Hihio-Art Package Co., Ltd.
海惠沃特包装有限公司
江苏省徐州市经济开发区科技企业产业园B2幢
邮编：221004
电话：0516-8387 5283
传真：0516-8387 5283
电邮：hihioart@xzhead.com
网址：www.hihioart.com

Lynn's Business Supplies Corp.
上海羚泰实业有限公司
上海市徐汇区夏城路185号
邮编：200232
电话：021-5435 7217
传真：021-5435 4905
电邮：info@lynns.cn
网址：www.lynns.cn

OJI Kinocloth (Shanghai) Co., Ltd.
王子奇能纸业（上海）有限公司
上海市长宁区仙霞路88号太阳广场W506室
邮编：200336
电话：021-6237 5200
传真：021-6237 5600
电邮：info@kinocloth.cn
网址：www.kinocloth.cn

Pimex Paper Shanghai Ltd.
巨圆纸业（上海）有限公司
上海市松江工业区松东路368号
邮编：201613
电话：021-5774 5168
传真：021-5774 5178
电邮：pimexsj@pimex.com.cn
网址：www.pimex.com.cn

Popstar International Trading Co., Ltd.
亮奎·建奎国际贸易（上海）有限公司
上海市曹杨路450号绿地和创大厦510室
邮编：200063
电话：021-5235 7712
传真：021-6240 1376
电邮：hank.lin@qpopstar.com
网址：www.qpopstar.com
请参阅第112、113页

SCA Asia Pacific
爱生雅亚太区集团
上海市闵行区浦东南路1958号
邮编：201114
电话：021-5433 5200
传真：021-5433 3916
电邮：info@sca.com
网址：www.sca.com

Shanghai Forward Tarding Co., Ltd.
聚河贸易（上海）有限公司
上海市长宁区天山路600弄思创大厦4号28楼C座
邮编：200051
电话：021-6229 0630
传真：021-6229 0629
电邮：shforward@163.com
网址：www.shforward.cn
请参阅第111页

Shanghai Shenxin Paper Co., Ltd.
上海申馨纸业有限公司
上海市广粤支路87号
邮编：200434
电话：021-5561 0650
传真：021-6592 7111
电邮：zbzx@printinginst.com
网址：www.shsxzy.com.cn

一次性塑胶制品 Plastic Products-Disposable

Beijing ZhongJu International Trading Co., Ltd.
北京中钜铖国际商贸有限公司
北京市朝阳区大郊亭中街2号院
华腾国际3号楼17AD
电话：010-8795 1433
传真：010-6772 9311
电邮：fayshi2004@126.com
网址：www.zhongjc.com.cn
请参阅第244页

Binhui Articles For Tourism Co., Ltd.
汕头市彬辉旅游用品有限公司
广东省汕头市潮南区峡山拱上工业区
邮编：515144
电话：0754-8792 9559
传真：0754-8792 8549
电邮：binhui@stbinhui.com.cn
网址：www.stbinhui.com.cn

Good Flag Biotechnology Corporation
瑞旗生物科技有限公司
苏州市吴中区甪直镇联谊路268号
邮编：215200
电话：0512-6504 6268
传真：0512-6504 6266
电邮：reygoodflag@163.com
网址：www.goodflag.com

Hhangzhou Sanxin Hotel Equipment Co., Ltd.
杭州三信酒店设备有限公司
浙江省杭州市机场路277号
电话：0571-8787 5859
传真：0571-8504 6887
电邮：hzsanxin@126.com
网址：www.cn3xin.com

Jiaxing Zhongli Plastics Co., Ltd.
浙江省嘉兴众立塑胶有限公司
嘉兴市经济开发区塘汇工业园区正原路183号
邮编：314000
电话：0573-8220 1120
传真：0573-8221 7738
电邮：zlsj@jxzlsj.com
网址：www.jxzlsj.com

Popstar International Trading Co., Ltd.
亮奎·建奎国际贸易（上海）有限公司
上海市曹杨路450号绿地和创大厦510室
邮编：200063
电话：021-5235 7712
传真：021-6240 1376
电邮：hank.lin@qpopstar.com
网址：www.qpopstar.com
请参阅第112、113页

Shanghai Chengyu Plastic Product Co., Ltd.
上海诚宇塑料制品有限公司
上海市闵行区华江路1260弄14-16号
邮编：201106
电话：021-5218 9058
传真：021-6220 4338
电邮：shh-chengyu@126.com
网址：www.shh-chengyu.com

Shanghai Forward Tarding Co., Ltd.
聚河贸易（上海）有限公司
上海市长宁区天山路600弄思创大厦4号28楼C座
邮编：200051
电话：021-6229 0630
传真：021-6229 0629
电邮：shforward@163.com
网址：www.shforward.cn
请参阅第111页

Shanghai Hocres Hotel Equipment & Accessories Co., Ltd.
上海海客瑞斯酒店用品有限公司
上海市华徐公路888号
邮编：201702
电话：021-6976 5065
传真：021-5986 1696
网址：www.hocres.com

Shanghai Soro Industrial Co., Ltd.
上海索隆劳防用品有限公司
上海市松江区新桥镇新创路385号1幢
邮编：201612
电话：021-5768 7886
传真：021-5768 7840
电邮：sales@safetyzonne.com.cn
网址：www.safetyzone.com.cn

Shantou Yongjia Tour Things Factory
汕头市永佳旅游用品厂
广东省汕头市潮南区司马浦仙港工业区
电话：0754-8773 1766
传真：0754-8772 3428
电邮：yjst@yongjiast.com
网址：www.yongjiast.com

爆米花机 Popcorn Machines

Beijing ZhongJu International Trading Co., Ltd.
北京中钜铖国际商贸有限公司
北京市朝阳区大郊亭中街2号院
华腾国际3号楼17AD
电话：010-8795 1433
传真：010-6772 9311
电邮：fayshi2004@126.com
网址：www.zhongjc.com.cn
请参阅第244页

▼纸制品
Popcorn Machines

Guangzhou Hongxing Food Co., Ltd.
广州市宏兴食品有限公司
广州市白云区黄石西路2号福生鞋材城C101
邮编：510160
电话：020-3639 2347
传真：020-3639 2347
电邮：guangzhou.hongxing@163.com
网址：www.hx-my.com

Guangzhou Wailaan Kitchen Fixture Make Co., Ltd.
广州唯利安西厨房设备制造有限公司
广东省广州市白云区新市联边村彭上工业区
邮编：510440
电话：020-3622 0141
传真：020-3622 0723
电邮：wailaan@163.com
网址：www.wailaan.com

Shanghai Forward Tarding Co., Ltd.
聚河贸易（上海）有限公司
上海市长宁区天山路600弄思创大厦4号28楼C座
邮编：200051
电话：021-6229 0630
传真：021-6229 0629
电邮：shforward@163.com
网址：www.shforward.cn
请参阅第 111 页

Shanghai Hengfu Kitchen Co., Ltd.
上海恒富厨房设备有限公司
上海市奉浦工业区富康路34号
电话：021-3744 1245
传真：021-6710 1318
电邮：hengfu@sh-hengfu.com
网址：www.sh-hengfu.com

银器餐具
Silverware

Anglo-Swiss Trading Co (HK) Ltd.
英瑞贸易（香港）有限公司
香港九龙尖沙咀广东道30号
新港中心第2座1011-1012室
电话：+852-2375 1111
传真：+852-2375 3409
网址：www.angloswiss.iyp.hk

Euro Asia Shanghai Limited
上海依贵亚贸易有限公司
上海市徐汇区医学院路92号
邮编：200032
电话：021-6422 6618
传真：021-6422 6689
电邮：euroasiash@163.com
网址：www.sheuroasia.com
请参阅第 230、231 页

Foshan Qingyuan Chuju
广东省佛山市庆源厨房设备厂
广东省佛山市三水区南丰大道南边工业区
电话：0757-8731 8991
传真：0757-8731 1882
网址：www.gdqingyuan.com

Huaihua Stainless Steel Tableware Co., Ltd.
山东淄博怀华不锈钢餐具制品厂
山东省淄博市临淄区齐园路8号
邮编：255400
电话：0533-776 5698
传真：0533-719 9679
电邮：178@daochashao.com
网址：www.daochashao.com

Mebotableware Co., Ltd.
东莞石排美宝五金制品厂
广东省东莞市石排福隆第三工业区
邮编：523349
电话：0769-8653 0038
传真：0769-8665 2656
电邮：mebogolden@mebotableware.com
网址：www.mebotableware.com

Right Season Industrial Ltd. (Hong Kong)
顺时宝业有限公司（香港）
香港新界沙田大围成运路21-23号
群力工业大厦三楼11室
电话：+852-2489 2202
传真：+852-2489 8281
电邮：rightseason@163.com
网址：www.rightseason.com.hk

Sanshui Shunchuang Cabinet Ironware Has Factory
三水顺创五金厨具厂
广东省佛山市三水中心科技园工业区
芦苞园C区5-3号之一
邮编：528100
电话：0757-8767 2739
传真：0757-8767 7575
电邮：sales@fs-shunchuang.com
网址：www.fs-shunchuang.com

Shanghai Angneng Trade and Economic Development Co., Ltd.
上海昂能经贸发展有限公司
上海市育绿路301弄6幢109室
电话：021-6915 1065
传真：021-6915 1065
电邮：angneng001@yahoo.cn
网址：www.shjingdian.com

Shanghai Han Jia Hotel Equipment Ltd.
上海瀚嘉酒店设备有限公司
上海市徐汇区浦北路999弄1号百合苑10楼E座
邮编：200233
电话：021-5418 5651
传真：021-5418 6711
电邮：lamhingwan@163.com
网址：www.chinalkk.com

Shenzhen Pama Hotel Products Co., Ltd.
深圳市帕玛酒店用品有限公司
深圳市南山区粤海路粤海工业村
深圳动漫园4栋201室
邮编：518054
电话：0755-8605 2592
传真：0755-8605 2582
网址：www.szpama.com
请参阅第 42 页

Sunnex Metal Products (Shenzhen) Ltd.
日升五金制品（深圳）有限公司
深圳市盐田区沙头角深沙路东和工业大厦A座二楼
邮编：518081
电话：0755-2555 1458
传真：0755-2535 7498
电邮：sales@sunnexchina.com
网址：www.sunnexchina.com

Well-In Hotel Supplies Co., Ltd.
华艺酒店供应有限公司
上海市长宁区愚园路1258号绿地商务大厦908室
邮编：200050
电话：021-5239 7278
传真：021-5239 6850
电邮：wellin@wnksh.com
网址：www.wnk-hk.com

Zhangjiagang Lucky Metal Handicraft Co., Ltd.
张家港幸运金属工艺有限公司
江苏省张家港市泗港西新工业园一号
电话：0512-5858 1306
传真：0512-5858 2377
电邮：hjl@jslucky.com
网址：www.jslucky.com
请参阅第 246、247 页

幸运金银器
LUCKY SILVER & GOLDEN PLATED

【公司介绍】

“幸运”公司位于长江三角经济地带的现代繁荣港城张家港市，本公司于1986年成立，占地面积25000平方米,建筑面积18000平方米，员工200多人，是一家由中美共同出资的中外合资企业。本公司在同行业中首家通过了ISO9002国际质量认证，是国内专业生产镀金镀银餐具规模最大的企业。

本公司产品均选用优质铜材，纯金、银锭和进口化工原料，将西方先进的电镀技术融入于中国传统手工艺，在产品表面镀上99.99纯银或是24K纯金，制成一件件熠熠生辉的工艺品，完美地诠释了宫廷的豪华气派、富贵典雅，是星级宾馆酒店、高档会所品尝美味佳肴的精品餐具，更是国外皇室的御用珍品。

长期以来，本公司以优良的品质、合理的价格、可靠的信誉和完善的服务赢得了广大用户的欢迎和好评，现在，我们的新目标是巩固国内市场，进一步开拓海外市场，让产品更加国际化，让“幸运”品牌成为国际化的金银餐具品牌。

“Lucky Silver & Gold plated tableware company” is situated in the morden port city-Zhangjiagang, the interior of Jiangsu province golden Yangtse Delta economic zone. With an area of 25,000sqm including a building area of 18,000sqm. We are the largest maufacturer, which is spcialized in producing silver plated and gold plated tableware and gifts. With the advanced technology ,we supply the finest products to super hotels, restaurants and clubs. And now we are marching to the goal of making LUCKY a internationalized brand.

方格型

线条型

餐具
Tableware

Angelhood Shanghai Co., Ltd.
上海安继行实业有限公司
上海虹梅南路4999号（新吴泾工业园区）8号楼
邮编：201109
电话：021-5169 1855
传真：021-5168 7575
电邮：shanghai@angelhood.com.cn
网址：www.angelhood.com.cn

Canahot (Wuxi) Industrial Ltd.
无锡市安利酒店用品有限公司
江苏省无锡市锡山区东北塘石新路1号
邮编：214191
电话：0510-8377 2188
传真：0510-8377 2775
电邮：canahot@canahot.com.cn
网址：www.canahot.com.cn

Carlisle Foodsservice Products
卡莱森泰（上海）商贸有限公司
上海市长宁区江苏路398号舜元企业发展大厦19楼
邮编：200050
电话：021-6100 5222
传真：021-6100 5279
网址：www.carlislefsp.com

Dalian Brightland Trading Co., Ltd.
大连市辉夏贸易有限公司
大连市高新园区七贤岭爱贤街10号A座9层
电话：0411-8497 8359
传真：0411-8250 7746
电邮：info@ttxgroup.com
请参阅第250、251页

Dalian Hantai International Trade Co., Ltd.
大连翰泰国际贸易有限公司
大连市沙河口区中山路572号星海旺座1506室
邮编：116023
电话：0411-6293 8888
传真：0411-6293 9999
电邮：office@hantai-glass.com
网址：www.table-top.cn
请参阅第234、235页

Etown China Department Co., Ltd.
厦门忆通百货有限公司
厦门市湖里区同益路50号海明大厦5层
邮编：361012
电话：0592-221 3232
传真：0592-221 6786
电邮：op@etownchina.cn
网址：www.etownchina.cn

First Asia Trading Co., Ltd.
上海泛亚经贸有限公司
上海市万航渡路2452号DOHO园区A502室
电话：021-5178 6788
传真：021-5178 6758*118
电邮：firstasia99@msn.com
网址：www.firstasia-sh.com
请参阅第236、237页

Fujian Dehua Hiap Huat Koyo Toki Co., Ltd. Shanghai Branch
福建省德化协发光洋陶器有限公司上海分公司
上海市凯旋路3131号明申中心大厦2803室
邮编：200030
电话：021-5407 1201
传真：021-5407 1203
电邮：shanghai@luzerne.com
网址：www.luzerne.com
请参阅第214页

Guangzhou Lixin Hotel Supplies Co., Ltd.
广州市立信酒店设备用品有限公司
广东省广州市荔湾区芳村大道东仁厚直街26号7栋
邮编：510370
电话：020-6275 3888
传真：020-8157 0559
电邮：lx.com.gz@163.com
网址：www.gzlixin.com

Guangzhou United Ocean Hotel Equipment Co., Ltd.
广州汇海酒店用品有限公司
广东省广州市番禺区大石镇石北大道
电话：020-3993 0461
传真：020-3993 0460
电邮：gz_hhh@126.com
网址：www.gdhuihai.com

Hengxin Superior Service
苏州市恒信餐具有限公司
苏州市平江区园林路48号
邮编：215001
电话：0512-6720 0165
传真：0512-6770 1440
电邮：hxgs165@163.com
网址：www.raphael-hengxin.com

Home Base Ceramics Co., Ltd.
上海雅家时尚瓷业有限公司
上海市局门路436弄8号桥二期6号104室
邮编：200023
电话：021-6208 8629
传真：021-6280 5728
电邮：tony@inhesiongroup.com
网址：www.homebase.com.cn

Jingguan Melamine Products Co., Ltd.
晶冠美耐皿制品有限公司
广东省东莞市桥头镇邓屋工业区
电话：0769-8334 4599
传真：0769-8334 4858
电邮：melamine168@163.com
网址：www.melamineware.com.cn

Oneida (Guangzhou) Foodservice Ltd.
奥耐达（广州）餐饮用具有限公司
广州市天河区体育东路138号
金利来数码网络大厦2909-2910室
邮编：510620
电话：020-3878 0612
传真：020-3878 0613
电邮：info@oneida.cn
网址：www.foodservice.oneida.com
请参阅第249页

Only Tableware (Shanghai) Co., Ltd.
上海超凡餐具有限公司
上海市金山区廊下镇新建丰村1106号
邮编：201516
电话：021-5739 5329
传真：021-5739 4990
电邮：onlytableware@yahoo.com.cn
网址：www.onlytableware.com

Shanghai Baolong International Trading Co., Ltd.
上海宝隆国际贸易有限公司
上海市天潼路133号8楼
邮编：200080
电话：021-6321 2297
传真：021-6321 4385
电邮：xiex@sh-baolong.com
网址：www.sh-baolong.com

Shanghai Charn-go Hotel Utensils Co., Ltd.
上海畅高酒店用品有限公司
上海市万航渡路623弄85号建华大厦6楼
邮编：200042
电话：021-6230 1823
传真：021-6249 7960
电邮：charn-go@126.com
请参阅第37页

Shanghai Meiernai Melamine Wares Co., Ltd.
上海美尔耐密胺制品有限公司
上海市浦东新区金桥出口加工区
新金桥路230号2栋1楼
邮编：201206
电话：021-5899 4232
传真：021-5899 5709
电邮：58994232@163.com
网址：www.ctc1993.com

Pama

Shenzhen Pama Hotel Products Co., Ltd.
深圳市帕玛酒店用品有限公司
深圳市南山区粤海路粤海工业村
深圳动漫园4栋201室
邮编：518054
电话：0755-8605 2592
传真：0755-8605 2582
网址：www.szpama.com
业务范围：
Pama的品质，根基于20余年专业生产不锈钢餐具的丰富经验。
Pama的设计，得益于来自意大利、法国、英国等国际知名设计师组成的设计团队，产品造型打破常规而又经典实用。
Pama的愿景，是为全球星级酒店提供设计优美，制作精良的不锈钢餐具。
我们希望这一生的事业所呈现出来的作品，能全面提升您的用餐品味，带给您最舒适愉快的用餐感受。
请参阅第42页

Shunta Melamine Products Co., Ltd.
东莞顺大美耐皿制品有限公司
广东省东莞市桥头镇田新第二工业区
邮编：523533
电话：0769-8345 8733
传真：0769-8334 6777
电邮：info-china@shunta.com
网址：www.shunta.com
请参阅第44、45、46、47页

WMF (Shanghai) Co., Ltd.
精鸟金属制品贸易（上海）有限公司
上海市虹口区四川北路1318号
盛邦国际大厦1101-1103室
邮编：200080
电话：021-5515 5212
传真：021-5515 5220
电邮：info@wmf-china.com
网址：www.wmf-china.com
请参阅第219页

Wuhan Wuyang Hotel Supplies Co., Ltd.
武汉五羊酒店用品有限公司
武汉市江汉区沿江大道36号
邮编：430021
电话：027-8567 0710
传真：027-8566 9593
电邮：yang@5yang.com
网址：www.5yang.com

ONEIDA®

Designing the dining experience.™

Sola:1868年源自荷兰，全球最大的航空餐具、亚洲超豪华酒店餐具供应商，同时以精湛的工艺，优秀的品质，高雅时尚的造型受到各国客商的青睐。2011年我们成为Sola中国地区总代理，将继续以专业化、国际化为准则，传承百年经典。

TTX：1993年在德国正式成立，TTX作为专业的酒店用品供货商，声名享誉全球各地。同时TTX秉承“shaping your life”的理念，为全世界五星级酒店提供最优质的服务。

我们的产品远销美洲、欧洲、澳洲、东南亚等多个国家和地区的主要百货商店、大型超市、航空公司，并长期为喜来登等五星级酒店用品商供货。国内市场方面，与雀巢、南航、好利来均有大笔订单往来。2008年又荣幸的成为北京奥运会的指定西餐餐具供应商、2010年上海世博会指定餐具礼品供应商、2010年夏季达沃斯宴会厅餐具供应商。我们集创意设计、研发、生产、贸易于一体。2011年，我们将经营战略瞄准国内市场，发挥行业优势，争做本行业领跑者，力争为您提供最优质的服务。

▼餐具
Tableware

Yong Ge Trading (shanghai) Co., Ltd.
上海市长宁区黄金城道676号
邮编：201103
电话：021-6308 0741
传真：021-6313 3707
电邮：wittywang@vip.163.com
网址：www.aistiashop.com
请参阅第215页

Zhangjiagang Lucky Metal Handicraft Co., Ltd.
张家港幸运金属工艺有限公司
江苏省张家港市泗港西新工业园一号
电话：0512-5858 1306
传真：0512-5858 2377
电邮：hjl@jslucky.com
网址：www.jslucky.com
请参阅第246、247页

Zwilling J.A. Henckels Shanghai Ltd.
上海双立人亨克斯有限公司
上海市浦东新区三林路424号
邮编：200124
电话：021-3886 1343
网址：www.zwilling.com.cn

广州豪唯尔酒店用品有限公司
广东省广州市黄埔双岗双沙工业区C2座
电话：020-8236 2307
传真：020-8236 0612
电邮：cnhower@gmail.com
网址：www.cnhower.com

上海昂升餐具有限公司
上海市浦东大道555号裕景东楼1501室
邮编：200120
电话：021-6163 9188
传真：021-6163 9190
电邮：info@action-catering.com
网址：www.action-catering.com

深圳市惠宝隆酒店设备用品有限公司
深圳市宝安区前进二路4号
雁盟酒店文化产业园D馆6楼
邮编：518102
电话：0755-6186 1111
传真：0755-6186 0002
网址：www.vibolong.com

深圳市汇高泰富贸易有限公司
深圳市罗湖区深南东路5002号
信兴广场地王商业中心4905-07室
电话：0755-8238 9510
传真：0755-8238 9050
请参阅第40、41页

唐山陶瓷股份有限公司骨质瓷分公司
河北省唐山市唐马路中段
邮编：063000
电话：0315-328 2945
传真：0315-328 2814
电邮：wenglibin@tsrrbc.com
网址：www.tsrrbc.com

自动售货机
Vending Machines

Changzhou Pilot Electronic Co., Ltd.
常州领航电子有限公司
江苏省常州市新北区汉江路397号3号楼2楼
邮编：213022
电话：0519-8699 6761
传真：0519-8699 6791
电邮：info@bianchivendingchina.com
网址：www.lhcoffeetime.com

Dalian Fushi Bingshan Vending Machine Co., Ltd.
大连富士冰山自动售货机有限公司
辽宁省大连经济技术开发区淮河西路61号
邮编：116600
电话：0411-8730 5912
传真：0411-8730 5911
电邮：lnz@fujibingshan.com.cn
网址：www.fujibingshan.com.cn

N&W Global Vending S.p.A Shanghai Representative Office
意大利那克塔—威戈全球自动售货系统公司上海代表处
上海市肇嘉浜路1065号飞雕国际大厦2005室
邮编：200030
电话：021-3368 0570
传真：021-3368 0590
电邮：info@nwglobalvending.com
网址：www.nwglobalvending.com.cn

Ningbo Bioka Coffee Equipment Department
宁波市贝欧卡咖啡设备商行
浙江省宁波市永泰花园46幢103A
邮编：315000
电话：0574-8814 5988
传真：0574-8820 4043
电邮：nb-boc@126.com
网址：www.nb-coffee.com

Qingdao Aucma Vending Machine Co., Ltd.
青岛澳柯玛自动售货机股份有限公司
青岛经济技术开发区前湾港路315号
邮编：266510
电话：0532-8676 3616
传真：0532-8676 3602
电邮：xs-avm@aucma.com.cn
网址：www.aucmavm.com

Wuhan Openmuch Technology Development Co., Ltd.
武汉欧朋美至科技发展有限公司
武汉市江汉经济开发区欧朋科技园
邮编：430023
电话：027-8351 7266
传真：027-8351 7266*801
网址：www.opencoffee.cn

饮水机
Water Dispensers

Eco Water System (China)
美国怡口净水系统中国总部
江苏省昆山市经济技术开发区三巷路483号
邮编：215335
电话：0512-5702 6555
传真：0512-5702 6808
电邮：navy.yang@ecowater.net.cn
网址：www.ecowater.net.cn

Hatco Corporation
赫高餐饮设备（苏州）有限公司
江苏省苏州市工业园区唯新路9号
唯亭工业园区A2区1-2单元
电话：0512-6732 5199
传真：0512-6732 5092
电邮：infocn@hatcocorp.com
网址：www.hatcocorp.com
请参阅第179页

Ningbo Apple Electrical Appliances Co., Ltd.
宁波爱普电器有限公司
浙江省慈溪市附海镇花塘路83号
邮编：315332
电话：0574-6356 1508
传真：0574-6356 9098
电邮：zhou@nb-apple.com
网址：www.nb-apple.com

Qingdao Gemi Electronic Appliances Co., Ltd.
青岛吉之美电子有限公司
山东省青岛市李沧区文昌阁外资工业园2号
邮编：266101
电话：0532-8706 6123
传真：0532-8706 7070
电邮：info@gemi.com.cn
网址：www.gemi.com.cn

Shenzhen Angel EquipmentT & Technology Co., Ltd.
深圳市安吉尔设备技术有限公司
深圳市福田区车公庙
天安数码城创新科技广场B座507室
邮编：518040
电话：0755-8343 3889
传真：0755-8343 4634
电邮：info@waterdispenser.com.cn
网址：www.waterdispenser.com.cn

杭州富阳中荷电子有限公司
杭州富阳场口工业新区中荷路1号
邮编：311412
电话：0571-6351 7588
传真：0571-6351 7208
电邮：zhonghe@fuyang.com
网址：www.sinoaqua.com

葡萄酒配件
Wine Accessories

Jinhua Chenxiang Tools Manufacture Co., Ltd.
金华市晨翔工具制造有限公司
浙江省金华市工业园区美和路218号
邮编：321000
电话：0579-8226 1622
传真：0579-8226 1667
电邮：cx@chenxiangtools.com
网址：www.chenxiangtools.com

YPT International Ltd.
建宏国际有限公司
香港九龙官塘鲤鱼门道2号新城工商中心1楼
电话：+852-2723 2168
传真：+852-2739 7576
电邮：ypt@techwin.com.hk
网址：www.ypt.com.hk

Yiqi Industrial & Trading Co., Ltd.
艺奇工贸有限公司
广东省阳江市阳东县东城镇永兴二路9号
邮编：529533
电话：0662-660 8018
传真：0662-660 8293
电邮：yiqi@yjyiqi.com
网址：www.yjyiqi.com

Zhejiang Zhongxing Industry & Trade Co., Ltd.
浙江中星工贸有限公司
浙江省永康市经济开发区子政路89号
邮编：321300
电话：0579-8751 1678
传真：0579-8751 1787
电邮：ykzx@zhongxingtools.com
网址：www.cnzx.cc

Zwilling J.A. Henckels Shanghai Ltd.
上海双立人亨克斯有限公司
上海市浦东新区三林路424号
邮编：200124
电话：021-3886 1343
网址：www.zwilling.com.cn

葡萄酒柜
Wine Cabinets

Angelo Po Trading (Shanghai)
傲桀贸易（上海）有限公司
上海市江场三路88号一楼
邮编：200436
电话：021-6094 0100
传真：021-6094 0288
电邮：info@angelopo.cn
网址：www.angelopo.it
请参阅第167、195页、封面

Gelin Electric Appliance Co., Ltd.
江苏格林电器有限公司
江苏省常熟市虞山工业园汇峰路2号
邮编：215500
电话：0512-5284 7692
传真：0512-5284 8283
电邮：gldq@gelin.com.cn
网址：www.gelin.com.cn

Guangdong Fuxin Electronic Technology Co., Ltd.
广东富信电子科技有限公司
广东省佛山市顺德区容桂高黎高新区科苑3路20号
邮编：528306
电话：0757-2881 5536
传真：0757-2880 3301
电邮：info@fuxin-cn.com
网址：www.fuxin-cn.com

Hangzhou Meisda Electric Appliance Co., Ltd.
杭州美时达电器有限公司
杭州市西湖科技经济园振华路210号
邮编：310030
电话：0571-8830 8199
传真：0571-8830 8116
电邮：jack@meisda.com
网址：www.meisda.com

Ningbo Jingeao Electronics Co., Ltd.
宁波金格奥电器有限公司
浙江省慈溪市龙山工业园区金园大道2号
邮编：315311
电话：0574-6397 3723
传真：0574-6397 3722
电邮：cooler@jingeao.com
网址：www.jingeao.com

Pro-Fit Industrial Co., Ltd.
宝发实业有限公司
香港新界葵涌大连排道152-160号
金龙工业中心第1座25字楼C室
电话：+852-2371 2862
传真：+852-2371 2867
电邮：profit@profitind.com
网址：www.profitind.com
请参阅第178页

Saixin Electrical Appliance Co., Ltd.
中山市赛鑫电器有限公司
广东省中山市黄圃镇马新工业区强业南路
电话：0760-2250 6896
传真：0760-2250 6886
网址：www.gdsaixin.com

Shanghai JinCheng Refrigerating Equipment Co., Ltd.
上海金城制冷设备有限公司
上海市中山北路3357号
邮编：200062
电话：021-6216 8066
传真：021-6216 8070
电邮：jincheng@shkingdom.com.cn
网址：www.shkingdom.com.cn
请参阅第225页

Shanghai Pengxie Co., Ltd.
上海朋协实业有限公司
上海市虹莘路1955弄半岛豪门5号别墅
邮编：201100
电话：021-5417 0281
传真：021-5417 0282
电邮：webmaster@wine-town.com.cn
网址：www.wine-town.com.cn

Shanghai Shang Ling Tech Development Co., Ltd.
上海上菱科技开发有限公司
上海市浦东新区景雅路165号
邮编：201201
电话：021-5068 3575
传真：021-5068 6920
电邮：shsltech@126.com
网址：www.sltech.com.cn

Shenzhen Beauty and Harmony Electrical Co., Ltd.
深圳美和电器有限公司
广东省深圳市宝安区观澜镇四黎路东豪工业园
邮编：518110
电话：0755-3323 4333
传真：0755-3307 9333
网址：www.meihe-elec.com

Shenzhen Hoowell Technology Development Co., Ltd.
深圳市弘维科技开发有限公司
深圳市南山区高新园南区深港产学研基地西座
电话：0755-8612 4495
传真：0755-8612 4495
电邮：joan@hoowell.com
网址：www.hoowell.com

Shenzhen Raching Technology Co., Ltd.
深圳市美晶科技有限公司
深圳市深圳市宝安区观澜镇
福民富康工业区美晶工业园
邮编：518001
电话：0755-8953 9339
传真：0755-8953 9329
电邮：sales@raching.com
网址：www.raching.com

Shenzhen Sicao Electric Appliances Co., Ltd.
深圳市新潮电器有限公司
深圳市罗湖区嘉宾路2018号深华商业大厦13-14层
邮编：518001
电话：0755-8237 5212
传真：0755-2219 1799
网址：www.sicao.cn
请参阅第254页

Vsong Electronics Co., Ltd.
深圳市维颂电子有限公司
上海市洱海路（近春申路）99弄43号702室
电话：021-5499 5602
传真：021-5437 7609
网址：www.coltekproducts.com

北京酒柜酒窖专业设计制作中心
北京市大羊坊北桥东北角横街子中心
电话：13522769382
电邮：cl_8578@163.com
网址：www.shentingshengye.com

南京中瑞展示设备有限公司
江苏省南京市雨花经济开发区凤集大道20号
邮编：210006
电话：025-5226 3156
传真：025-8673 0411
电邮：njzrzs@126.com
网址：www.zrzsw.com

上海朗克酒业有限公司
上海市中山南一路500弄1号楼丽都大厦31C座
电话：021-5301 8995
传真：021-6301 2598
电邮：mont-tauch@lengdok.com
网址：www.lengdok.com
请参阅第160页

中山市越海电器有限公司
广东省中山市南头镇升辉南工业园建业路
邮编：528400
电话：0760-2383 2788
传真：0760-2313 7018
电邮：vinbo@yehos.
网址：www.yehos.com

冷酒器
Wine Coolers

Zhejiang Shengsong Industry & Trade Co., Ltd.
浙江圣松工贸有限公司
浙江省金华市武义泉溪金岩山工业区纵二路
邮编：321307
电话：0579-8706 2777
传真：0579-8784 7800
电邮：cup@angsong.com
网址：www.angsong.com

倒酒器
Wine Dispensers

High-gentle Inernational (HK) Limited
深圳市英爵斯生活用品有限公司
深圳市宝安区宝城25区
创业二路华丰商贸城四楼C20
电话：0755-2778 7397
传真：0755-2778 7355*802
网址：www.enjoy-arts.cn

Yantai Taifa Wine-Accessory Co., Ltd.
烟台泰发酒业用品有限公司
山东省烟台市经济开发区昆仑山路67号
邮编：264006
电话：0535-695 8757
传真：0535-695 8760
电邮：yt@yttaifa.com
网址：www.yttaifa.com

Zhuhai Zheshang Trading Development Co., Ltd.
珠海市浙商贸易发展有限公司
广东省珠海市香洲区紫荆路256号
邮编：519000
电话：0756-211 8007
传真：0756-213 5998
电邮：shen@zheshang.cn
网址：www.zheshang.cn

葡萄酒架
Wine Racks

Shenzhen Sicao Electric Appliances Co., Ltd.
深圳市新潮电器有限公司
深圳市罗湖区嘉宾路2018号深华商业大厦13-14层
邮编：518001
电话：0755-8237 5212
传真：0755-2219 1799
网址：www.sicao.cn
请参阅第254页

上海朗克酒业有限公司
上海市中山南一路500弄1号楼丽都大厦31C座
电话：021-5301 8995
传真：021-6301 2598
电邮：mont-tauch@lengdok.com
网址：www.lengdok.com
请参阅第160页

酒店工程及用品
Hotel Project & Supplies

浴缸翻新
Bathtub Resurfacing

Beijing Irea Trade Development Co., Ltd.
北京伊瑞商贸发展有限公司
北京市丰台区南方庄1号安富大厦801室
邮编：100078
电话：010-6765 5427
传真：010-6765 5427
电邮：irea@irea.com.cn
网址：www.irea.com.cn

Beijing Rsd Science and Technology Development Centre
北京荣盛达创业科技发展中心
北京市昌平区鼓楼东街33号金宇大厦417号
邮编：102200
电话：010-8788 2377
传真：010-8788 2377
电邮：bjrsda2008@163.com
网址：www.bjrsda.com

Caree Hotel Maintenance Engineering Ltd.
凯尔酒店保养工程有限公司
北京市朝阳区东直门幸福二村32号楼5层
邮编：100027
电话：010-6415 1201
传真：010-6415 1203
电邮：caree1818@bjcaree.com
网址：www.bjcaree.com

幕墙公司
Curtain-Wall Companies

Fujian Xishi Co., Ltd.
福建溪石股份有限公司
福建省南安市水头镇福山工业区
邮编：362300
电话：0595-8638 3948
传真：0595-8635 5068
电邮：xishi@xishigroup.com
网址：www.xishigroup.com

Fushuai Curtain Wall Science And Technology Co., Ltd.
上海富帅幕墙科技有限公司
上海市浙江中路599弄14号
电话：021-6322 6100
传真：021-5169 6148*602
电邮：fsbxg@fsmq.cn
网址：www.fsmq.cn

Jinfei
金飞企业
上海市西渡工业园区扶港路880号
电话：021-6514 3659
传真：021-6514 5977
电邮：shjf@vip.163.com
网址：www.sh-jf.com.cn

Mei Te Curtain Wall System Co., Ltd.
上海美特幕墙有限公司
上海市青浦区崧泽大道9777号
邮编：201700
电话：021-6921 3000
传真：021-6921 3019
电邮：webmaster@meitesh.com
网址：www.meitesh.com

Qingdao ILJIN Curtain Wall Co., Ltd.
青岛新日进幕墙有限公司
山东省青岛胶州市北京东路777号
电话：0532-8227 9680
传真：0532-8227 9173
电邮：xinrijin@163.com
网址：www.xinrijin.com

Qingdao Yongxin Curtain Walls Co., Ltd.
青岛永鑫幕墙有限公司
山东省青岛香港东路238-2号
邮编：266101
电话：0532-8870 2288
传真：0532-8870 2288
电邮：yongxin_bgs@126.com
网址：www.qdyxmq.cn

Shanghai Jilong Curtain Wall Building & Decoration Co., Ltd.
上海吉龙建筑装潢工程有限公司
上海市中山北二路99弄7号1501室
邮编：200090
电话：021-5580 7878
传真：021-5580 7878
电邮：shjlzzh@163.com
网址：www.shjilong.com

Shanghai Xinan Curtain Wall Building & Decoration Co., Ltd.
上海信安幕墙建筑装饰有限公司
上海市九亭伴亭东路278弄
邮编：201615
电话：021-5763 2802
传真：021-5763 1419
电邮：xinancw@163.com
网址：www.shxinan.com

Shenzhen Fucheng Science & Technology Co., Ltd.
深圳市富诚幕墙装饰工程有限公司
深圳市南山区科技园高新南一道富诚科技大厦9楼
邮编：518057
电话：0755-8602 2928
传真：0755-2698 9966
电邮：info@fucheng.com
网址：www.fucheng.com

Somfy China Co., Ltd.
尚飞中国
上海市华山路1520弄121号2楼
邮编：200052
电话：021-6280 9660
传真：021-6280 0270
网址：www.somfy.cn
请参阅第338、339页、封面

Suzhou Jinjin Curtain Wall Co., Ltd.
苏州金近幕墙有限公司
苏州市相城区元和镇蠡口万里路280号
邮编：215133
电话：0512-6545 1328
传真：0512-6545 1408
电邮：info@jinjin-cn.com
网址：www.jinjin-cn.com

Taizhou Arrowfish Curtain Wall Science and Technology Co., Ltd.
台州市旗鱼幕墙科技有限公司
浙江省温岭市泽国镇泽楚路113号
邮编：317523
电话：0576-8644 8673
传真：0576-8644 8672
电邮：info@arrowfish.cn
网址：www.arrowfish.cn

装饰公司
Decoration Companies

Boloni
博洛尼家居用品（北京）有限公司
北京市朝阳区育慧里11号
邮编：100101
电话：010-5134 8888
传真：010-5134 8810
电邮：hui@kebao.cn
网址：www.boloni.com.cn

GP Design & Decoration Co.
高宝设计工程公司
香港九龙官塘成业街6号摩登仓13楼09室
电话：+852-2790 0082
传真：+852-2372 9078
电邮：info@gpdesign.com.hk
网址：www.gpdesign.com.hk

Hangzhou Wulin Curtain Wall Co., Ltd.
杭州武林幕墙有限公司
浙江省杭州市解放路178号科技大厦
邮编：310001
电话：0571-8707 0798
传真：0571-8702 1668
电邮：web@hzwlmq.com
网址：www.hzwlmq.com

Jinhaique Decorate Design
上海金海雀建筑装饰有限公司
上海市南阳路98号
邮编：200436
电话：021-6612 1209
传真：021-6612 1206
电邮：jhqzs@sina.com
网址：www.jhqzs.com

Mas Interiors Ltd.
联艺室内设计有限公司
Flat A2, 7/F Paterson Building, 47 Paterson Street, Causeway Bay, Hong Kong
电话：+852-2576 8824
传真：+852-2576 3619
电邮：enquiry@masinteriors.com.hk
网址：www.masinteriors.com.hk

Shanghai Honghai Construction Decoration & Co., Ltd.
上海鸿海建筑装饰工程有限公司
上海市钦州路785号
电话：021-6475 1964
传真：021-6436 4490
电邮：anyedec@sina.com
网址：www.shdecoration.com

▼装饰公司
Decoration Companies

Shanghai Langyi Decoration & Design Co., Ltd.
上海朗艺装饰设计工程有限公司
上海市吴中路1029号灿虹世纪广场3F
电话：021-5108 8816
传真：021-5107 9668
电邮：langyi800@126.com
网址：www.langyi.com.cn

Shanghai Xiejin Design Decorate Co., Ltd.
上海协进室内设计装饰工程有限公司
上海市闵行区珠城路118弄7号
电话：021-6460 9637
传真：021-6414 5995
电邮：home@shxiejin.com
网址：www.shxiejin.com

Somfy China Co., Ltd.
尚飞中国
上海市华山路1520弄121号2楼
邮编：200052
电话：021-6280 9660
传真：021-6280 0270
网址：www.somfy.cn
请参阅第338、339页、封面

Wams Interior Design Ltd.
宏思室内设计有限公司
Flat 703-704 7/F Tung Wah Mansion, 199-203
Hennessy Road, Wan Chai, Hong Kong
电话：+852-2838 5822
传真：+852-2838 8640
电邮：info@wams.com.hk
网址：www.wams.com.hk

Zhengzhou Hong Wings Architectural Decoration & Design Co., Ltd.
郑州弘文建筑装饰设计有限公司
郑州市红专路128号金成宜家美景B座201室
邮编：450052
电话：0371-6563 5059
传真：0371-6578 3660
电邮：hw6060@126.com

北京龙发建筑装饰工程有限公司
北京市朝阳区东三环中路39号
建外SOHO办公楼A座8层
邮编：100022
电话：010-5869 2222
传真：010-5869 2173
电邮：dragon@longfa.com.cn
网址：www.longfa.com

设计公司
Design Companies

Boloni
博洛尼家居用品（北京）有限公司
北京市朝阳区育慧里11号
邮编：100101
电话：010-5134 8888
传真：010-5134 8810
电邮：hui@kebao.cn
网址：www.boloni.com.cn

Boston International Design Group
美国波士顿国际设计集团
上海市浦东新区福山路33号
邮编：200120
电话：021-5132 7266
传真：021-5132 7269
网址：www.bidg.com.cn
请参阅第258、259页

Dishes Sdn Bhd
No.22 Jalan Semenyih Indah 3, Taman Semenyih
Indah, 43500 Semenyih, Selangor, Malaysia
电话：+603-8723 3118
传真：+603-8723 0018
电邮：info@dishes.com.my
网址：www.dishes.com.my

GP Design & Decoration Co.
高宝设计工程公司
香港九龙官塘成业街6号摩登仓13楼09室
电话：+852-2790 0082
传真：+852-2372 9078
电邮：info@gpdesign.com.hk
网址：www.gpdesign.com.hk

Gold Mantis Construction Decoration Co., Ltd.
金螳螂建筑装饰股份有限公司
江苏省苏州市西环路888号
邮编：215004
电话：0512-6828 2740
传真：0512-6828 2741
电邮：jtl@goldmantis.com
网址：www.goldmantis.com

Hangzhou Gracetang Scene Household Co., Ltd.
杭州观唐景致家居有限公司
浙江杭州拱墅区通益路49号LOFT49
电话：0571-8809 8991
传真：0571-8819 9053
电邮：guantang168@126.com
网址：www.gracetang.com.cn
业务范围：
"观唐"景致家居是智汇堂公司原创设计的家具品牌，旨在表现中国顶级的生活形态和品味哲学。它以复兴中国传统院落生活为己任，其深厚的历史底蕴和人文气息铸就了"观唐"品牌的价值基因，原汁原味的江南古韵在"观唐"产品中再现。凭依传承与创新姿态，"观唐"家具与国际时尚理念实现完美对接，致力于向世界展示中国的家具文化与生活态度。
请参阅第309页

Hirsch Bedner Associates HongKong
Units 2604-6, 26/F COSCO, Tower
183 Queen's Road Central
Hong Kong
电话：+852-2542 2022
传真：+852-2545 2051
网址：www.hbadesign.com
请参阅第260、261页

Mas Interiors Ltd.
联艺室内设计有限公司
Flat A2, 7/F Paterson Building, 47 Paterson Street,
Causeway Bay, Hong Kong
电话：+852-2576 8824
传真：+852-2576 3619
电邮：enquiry@masinteriors.com.hk
网址：www.masinteriors.com.hk

Mei Mei (Shenzhen) Hotel Decorate and Design Ltd.
深圳市美美酒店装饰设计有限公司
深圳市南山区华侨城创意文化园F1栋03号
邮编：5180010
电话：0755-8623 2945
传真：0755-8623 2927
电邮：design@meimeihomesz.com
网址：www.meimeihomesz.com

Munich Urban Design Int'l Shanghai Co., Ltd.
慕迪建筑设计咨询（上海）有限公司
上海市光复路1号403室
邮编：200070
电话：021-6381 8852
传真：021-6381 2082
电邮：shanghai@mudi.com
网址：www.mudi.com

SLK Design Ltd.
立基设计有限公司
Unit A 12F JCG Building
10-16 Mongkok Road
Kowloon, Hong Kong
电话：+852-2116 2666
传真：+852-2116 9884
电邮：slk@slkdesign.com.hk
网址：www.slkdesign.com.hk

Shanghai Favour Engineer Design Co., Ltd.
上海泛文装饰设计工程有限公司
上海市长寿路587号
沙田大厦10楼1005-1008室
电话：021-6230 3665
电邮：favourdesign@126.com
网址：www.favourorg.com

Shanghai Haisheng Industrial & Trading Co., Ltd.
上海海圣工贸有限公司
上海市杭州路740号
邮编：200090
电话：021-6543 0686
传真：021-6543 0686*85
电邮：info@shhaisheng.com
网址：www.shhaisheng.com

Shanghai Langyi Decoration & Design Co., Ltd.
上海朗艺装饰设计工程有限公司
上海市吴中路1029号灿虹世纪广场3F
电话：021-5108 8816
传真：021-5107 9668
电邮：langyi800@126.com
网址：www.langyi.com.cn

Shanghai Sanleng Adorn Design Co., Ltd.
上海善仁室内装饰设计有限公司
上海市浦东上南路3521号宝丰商务楼2楼
电话：021-6832 8395
电邮：sxw@shr-sh.com
网址：www.shr-sh.com

Shanghai Shenyuan Buiding Decoration Engineering Co., Ltd.
上海申远建筑装饰工程有限公司
上海市杨浦区鞍山路5号杨浦商城21层
电话：021-6501 2083
传真：021-6501 1297
网址：www.sy-021.com

美国波士顿国际设计集团
BOSTON INTERNATIONAL DESIGN GROUP

波士顿国际设计成立于2004年，延续了美国史塔宾建筑事务所国际最高水准的设计声誉，总部位于美国麻省剑桥市，毗邻着著名的哈佛大学和麻省理工学院。公司的主要创始人及主要的设计人员均来自两所名校，因此波士顿国际设计有着浓郁的学院气氛。

波士顿国际设计一直致力于把项目的规划设计与业主的要求最大限度的保持一致。我们从来不局限于某一种特定的模式，而是结合分析场地、文脉、经济、社会机遇等一系列因素后，根据项目的实际情况来找寻最合适的解决方案。因此，我们的项目总是在超越在创新。

我们的设计是国际化的。我们的实践主要集中在以下几个方面：

1.城市规划和城市设计(City Planning /Urban Design)
2.大型多功能综合体(Mixed-use)
3.高端住宅(Luxury Residential)
4.酒店和度假村的建筑(Hotel/Resort)
5.校园规划和教学设施(Campus Planning/Education)
6.生态节能建筑研究(Sustainable Architecture)

北京·国子监SPA酒店

基地位于北京市国子监南侧，环境静谧高雅。由美国美高梅酒店集团与钓鱼台国宾馆联合经营，是一个集温泉SPA、高档餐饮、客房、美术馆，中医药养生于一体的休闲精品酒店。设计延续了国子监历史与文化的脉络，突出中式文化主题，通过一系列室外室内设计，将院落式的中国传统建筑精髓与现代酒店功能巧妙结合，成为京城不多见的四合院式精品酒店。

杭州·喜来登酒店

基地位于杭州市钱塘江南岸，三桥与四桥之间，是一个集酒店、办公，住宅于一体的综合体。地上总建筑面积11.1万平方米，地下总建筑面积5.48万平方米。规划布局充分利用一线临江优势，使江景房占据四分之三的比例，高品质办公空间，全江景视觉盛宴。办公独享尊贵空中接待大厅，160米高度临江俯瞰杭城全景。立面造型简洁挺拔，过目难忘，双层呼吸式玻璃幕墙开创了杭州节能建筑的新标杆。

三亚·香水湾一号

香水湾1号位于海南三亚陵水镇，项目占地39公顷。

基地拥有连绵的优质海岸线，作为度假，旅游，休闲于一体的私人别墅度假酒店，香水湾的建筑景观与室内一体化设计,注重室内外的通透性与私密性。优美的私家泳池，茂密的热带植被，简洁的石材汀步，营造出静谧的海南风情，与商周式建筑群融为一体，表达了项目大隐隐于景的中国文化意境。

湖州·长兴万豪酒店

湖州长兴万豪酒店项目位于浙江省湖州市长兴县龙山新区，西邻行政中心，南邻长兴大剧院，是长兴县重点发展的核心区域。交通便利，地理位置十分优越。以湖州飞英塔“七层八面” 为原型，根据建筑功能需求和严谨的立面比例关系，建筑立面层层拔高，逐渐收分，整体形象高峻挺拔，极具特色。精心设计的酒店屋顶细部，来自钻石切割工艺的灵感，使酒店具有强烈的可识别性，无论白天还是黑夜，都将成为长兴人民瞩目的焦点。

上海外滩英迪格酒店
Hotel Indigo Shanghai on the Bund

由享誉国际的室内设计公司Hirsch Bedner Associates（HBA）一手打造的上海外滩英迪格酒店 (Hotel Indigo Shanghai on the Bund)最近惊艳亮相上海。该酒店是洲际酒店集团旗下亚洲首家英迪格酒店，HBA的创新设计兼收并蓄而又亲切和谐，体现了上海东西交融、海纳百川、面向未来的城市精神。

负责这一项目的HBA首席设计师Andrew Moore 表示："历史上，黄浦江对于上海的商贸繁荣与沟通交流起着巨大的影响。上海外滩英迪格酒店的设计就是要体现浦江之畔上海里弄的独特风情。"
酒店的大堂入口异常绚烂瑰丽，堪称沪上一绝；既反映了酒店位于黄浦江畔的位置，还体现了品牌对自然环境、循环再用，以及生态敏感型设计的承诺。

HBA选择原钢、混凝土、外露砖及抛光石膏等富有张力的基本材料为大堂进行装潢，令人不禁联想到这一空间是从码头旁的滨江阁楼改建而来。而开放式隔室与清水混凝土天花便进一步增强这种效果，并配以全日色彩幻变的灯光。

与大堂如出一辙，客房也呈现一种自然色调：外露的上海灰砖、磨耗效果的灰色嵌板、抛光石膏墙和帆布。与之产生强烈对比效果的是色彩鲜艳跳跃的地毯。

中式灯笼、传统家具、陶瓷和古董等兼收并蓄、机巧别致的工艺品和家具带来老上海的感觉。带顶篷的睡床为原创设计，灵感源自传统中式婚礼所用的喜床，经当代手法重新演绎。

偌大的浴室设有一堵镶在抛光钢框中的玻璃墙，望向黄浦江；并设开放式湿区，当中附设配上长方形瓷面盆的简约盥洗台，营造当代风尚；而独立浴缸也同样时尚摩登。

HBA设计的这一亚洲首家英迪格酒店，使英迪格品牌雄踞上海外滩十六铺这一充满近现代历史风云的时尚新地标，并且为未来的英迪格酒店树立了一个可以借鉴的标杆。

The Langham, Yangtze Boutique, Shanghai A legacy of elegance

With the goal of transforming Hotel Indigo Shanghai on the Bund, flagship for the debut of InterContinental Hotel Group's boutique Hotel Indigo brand in Asia, global interior design firm Hirsch Bedner Associates (HBA) has stamped an innovative design onto the hotel that is at once eclectic and harmonious, a design that connects the ancient with the modern.

"Throughout, Hotel Indigo's design is about connecting the hotel to the neighbourhood – one anchored by the river and its influence on commerce and connection," said Andrew Moore, HBA's lead designer on the project.

The lobby entrance is among the most striking and dramatic in Shanghai, reflecting Hotel Indigo's position on the river and the brand's commitment to nature, recyclables and ecologically sensitive design.

HBA chose strong elemental materials to render the lobby: raw steel, concrete, exposed brick, and polished plaster – suggesting this gallery space has been repurposed from a wharf-side waterfront loft. The open cell, cast concrete ceiling enhances this effect, studded with lighting that changes colours throughout the day.

As in the lobby, the guestroom palette is the natural tone of exposed Shanghai gray brick, distressed gray paneling, and polished plaster walls, a canvas against which shines colorful and lively carpets.

The sense of an older Shanghai is in eclectic and whimsical artifacts and furniture: with Chinese lanterns, authentic furniture, ceramic pieces and antiques. The canopy bed, an original design, was inspired by traditional Chinese wedding beds, but reinterpreted though a contemporary lens.

Oversized bathrooms have a glass wall framed in polished steel, looking out onto the river. They feature an open wet area, where a minimalist vanity topped with rectangular porcelain basins gives a contemporary feel, as does the freestanding tub, which is a sleek and modern.

In helping develop the first Hotel Indigo in Asia, HBA created a design that transforms the boutique brand name into a vantage point onto the most interesting areas within the storied and dynamic city of Shanghai – creating a standard against which all future Hotel Indigo properties will be judged.

“一切从设计开始”

如何孵化一个酒店？
选址设计+投资设计+方案设计+经营设计

宋微建

上海微建建筑空间设计有限公司 董事长兼首席设计师

中国建筑学会室内设计分会 理事/专家委员会委员

中国建筑学会室内设计分会第十二专业委员会 会长

全国有成就资深室内建筑师

2005中国十佳酒店设计师

2005中国室内设计师十大年度封面人物

2008国际传媒杰出设计师

1989-2009 CIID杰出设计师

▲南通王子饭店

▲上海瑞金宾馆总统楼－太原别墅

设计 价值

20余年的专业、经验及预见性，致力于形象定位、商业规划、设计到酒店管理，整合纵横资源，全程为您提供专业顾问意见为您创造更多价值。

设计 精明

合理的空间布局，易维护的功能规划，精心每处细节，帮您节省酒店运行的庞大开支。

1987 年至今，Vjian 已为上百家本土、跨国公司提供设计服务。

由宋微建领衔的精英团队，开创了“新江南形式语言”，将民族元素与世界潮流相融，创造出杰出案例。

设计 舒适

我们不为自己工作，也不为您工作，而是为您最珍视的顾客工作。

一切设计都源自顾客最本质的需求舒适，倾注能被领会的文化和特色，引导顾客最自由的消费体验。

◀▲吴地人家红楼主题餐厅

▲张家港新世汇酒店

团队荣誉

上海微建建筑空间设计有限公司 获“2008年度中国最强的室内设计企业”

上海微建建筑空间设计有限公司 获“中国（1989-2009）二十大知名室内设计团队”

苏州老东吴食府雅都店 获“2005年中国十佳饭店”评比第一

同里湖度假大酒店 获中国饭店协会评比的“饭店室内设计一等奖”

广西贵港国际大酒店 获“最佳酒店大堂设计作品奖”

中青旅酒店 获 “中国酒店设计大师赛-最佳照明设计奖”

www.vjian.cn

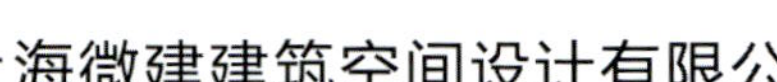

为博物馆、酒店、餐饮、办公楼、购物中心、高档别墅、会所、旧建筑改造等各类别的室内设计、建筑设计、环境设计、城区改造提供服务

地址：上海卢湾区黄陂南路751号（建国东路口）卓维创意园2号楼南楼2F-3F P.C.：200025 TEL：021-53833220 Email：vjian@vip.163.com

品鉴·传奇

高文安室内设计

APPRECIATE QUALITY

KENNETH KO DESIGNS

香港(HONG KONG)

地址（Address）：香港新界火炭坳背湾街41-43号安华大厦15楼L室
Flat L,15/F,On Wah Ind.Bldg.,41-43 Au Pui Wan Street,Fo Tan,HongKong.
电话（Tel）：852-2604 9494
传真（Fax）：852-2694 1016
电邮（E-mail）：kkdl@netvigator.com

深圳(SHEN ZHEN)

地址（Address）：深圳市南山区华侨城东部工业区F-1栋107#
Room 107#.NO.F-1,Industrial Park(East),Overseas Chinese Town,Nanshan District,Shenzhen,Guangdong Province,China PR
电话（Tel）：0755 -8299 8288
传真（Fax）：0755- 8299 8281
电邮（E-mail）：szoffice@gaowenan.com

成都(CHENG DU)

地址（Address）：成都市青羊区宽窄巷子窄巷子Z20院落
Z20 Courtyard Zhai Alleys Kuan & Zhai Alleys Cheng Du
电话（Tel）：028-8664 9494
传真（Fax）：028-8624 9494
电邮（E-mail）：cdgaowenan@126.com

上海(SHANG HAI)

地址（Address）：上海市卢湾区茂名南路56号甲西楼2楼
2/F,Jiaxi District,No.56 Maoming Nan Road,Lu Wan District,ShangHai
电话（Tel）：021-6514 9494
传真（Fax）：021-6513 4500
电邮（E-mail）：shgaowenan@126.com

▼设计公司
Design Companies

Shenzhen Best-One Ltd.
深圳丑石文化传播有限公司
广东省深圳市宝安区龙华街道办
胜立工业园丑石大厦
邮编：518000
电话：0755-8361 7831
传真：0755-8361 6068
电邮：best-one@best-one.cn
网址：www.best-one.cn

Shenzhen The Highest Sign Co., Ltd.
深圳市高度标识设计有限公司
广东省深圳市布吉镇吉华路393号
英达丰科技园2栋3楼
邮编：518000
电话：0755-8450 6067
传真：0755-8450 6285
电邮：shi-san-fa@163.com
网址：www.szgaodu.com

Shuoer Design and Decoration Limited Company of Shanghai
上海硕而装修设计工程有限公司
上海市浦东康桥路1131B
电话：021-5812 4198
传真：021-5812 4987
电邮：shuoer@shuoer.com
网址：www.shuoer.com

Som Architectural Consultants (Shanghai) Co., Ltd.
上海市卢湾区建国中路8-10号7号楼201室
邮编：200025
电话：021-5466 6888
传真：021-5465 7536
电邮：somshanghai@som.com
网址：www.som.com

Somfy China Co., Ltd.
尚飞中国
上海市华山路1520弄121号2楼
邮编：200052
电话：021-6280 9660
传真：021-6280 0270
网址：www.somfy.cn
请参阅第338、339页、封面

Vicorous Vision
北京盛世博文文化传播有限公司
北京丰台区大红门西路35号院
西马金润家园7号楼1501室
电话：010-8759 6040
电邮：ssbw@ssbwbj.com
网址：www.ssbwbj.com

Visual Language Design & Consulting Co., Ltd.
视语设计顾问有限公司
上海市漕溪路258弄23号3栋105室
邮编：200235
电话：021-6475 8851
传真：021-6475 8850

Vjian Design Institute
上海微建(Vjian)建筑空间设计有限公司
上海市卢湾区黄陂南路751号
建国东路口卓维创意园2号楼南楼2F-3F
邮编：200025
电话：021-5383 3220
传真：021-5383 3995
电邮：vjian@vip.163.com
网址：www.vjian.cn
请参阅第262、263页

Wams Interior Design Ltd.
宏思室内设计有限公司
Flat 703-704 7/F Tung Wah Mansion
199-203 Hennessy Road
Wan Chai, Hong Kong
电话：+852-2838 5822
传真：+852-2838 8640
电邮：info@wams.com.hk
网址：www.wams.com.hk

Yipin Interior Design
深圳逸品室内设计有限公司
深圳市车公庙泰然8路安华工业区6栋
邮编：518000
电话：0755-8355 5945
传真：0755-8296 4039
电邮：info@yipin.cn
网址：www.yipin.cn

朗顿设计机构
北京市朝阳区后现代城五号楼A座5层
电话：010-5165 3028
传真：010-8721 7114
电邮：svip@randodesign.com
网址：www.randodesign.com

深圳高文安设计有限公司
深圳市南山区华侨城东部工业区F-1栋107室
电话：0755-8299 8288
传真：0755-8299 8281
电邮：szoffice@gaowenan.com
请参阅第264、265页

酒店翻新改造
Hotel Renovation Transformation

ABM (HK) Co., Ltd.
立星企业（香港）有限公司
湖南省长沙市芙蓉南路中段
现代空间商务楼B座421室
电话：0731-8262 2055
传真：0731-8262 2055
电邮：abmchina@yahoo.com.cn
网址：www.abmhk.net

Caree Hotel Maintenance Engineering Ltd.
凯尔酒店保养工程有限公司
北京市朝阳区东直门幸福二村32号楼5层
邮编：100027
电话：010-6415 1201
传真：010-6415 1203
电邮：caree1818@bjcaree.com
网址：www.bjcaree.com

沈阳星耀酒店设施维护有限公司
沈阳市沈河区北站路102号
沈铁大酒店B座0830、0833室
邮编：110013
电话：024-6223 2029
传真：024-6223 1157
电邮：stonecare@163.com
网址：www.stonecarenet.com

厨房洗衣房设备安装及顾问
Kitchen & Laundry Consultation and Equipment Supply & Installation

Bei-wong Automation Equipment Installation Co., Ltd.
北京北黄自动化设备安装有限公司
北京市朝阳区曙光西里1号第三置业A座901室
邮编：100028
电话：010-5822 0071
传真：010-5822 0075
电邮：beiwong@public.ba.net.vn
网址：www.beiwong.com

Beijing Harvest E & M Co., Ltd.
北京丰汇加机电设备销售有限公司
北京市宣武区建功西里1号楼天缘公寓A座2701室
邮编：100054
电话：010-8351 6972
传真：010-8351 7663
电邮：sales@bjharvest.cn
网址：www.bjharvest.cn

Nanjing Guanghui Hotel Equipment Co., Ltd.
南京鑫广汇酒店设备工程有限公司
南京市龙蟠中路592号
邮编：210012
电话：025-5245 8598
传真：025-5245 8590

Polytek Engineering Co., Ltd.
保得工程有限公司
香港荃湾沙咀道66号大成大厦15楼
电话：+852-2807 3322
传真：+852-2806 0388
电邮：polytek@polytek.com.hk
网址：www.polytek.com.cn
请参阅第268、269页、封面

Shanghai Top bloom Kitchen Equipment Co., Ltd.
上海冠盛厨具工程有限公司
上海市陆家浜路976号富南大厦20A1
邮编：200011
电话：021-3305 0791
传真：021-6318 8086
电邮：topbloom@163.com
网址：www.topbloom.com
请参阅第39页

云石翻新及护理
Marbles,Restoration & Maintenance

Beijing Europe and Asia Valuable Clean Service Limited Company
北京欧亚洁保洁服务有限公司
北京市海淀区钢院附中
邮编：100083
电话：010-6235 0546
传真：010-6235 0546
网址：www.bjoyj.com

Beijing Oracle Building & Decoration Engineering Co., Ltd.
北京甲骨文建筑装饰工程有限公司
山东省日照市巨峰工业园金栈路7号
邮编：276800
电话：0633-836 7577
传真：0633-836 7677
电邮：bjjgw777@126.com
网址：www.jgwzs.com

Beijing Zhongke AoJie Technology Co., Ltd.
北京中科奥洁科技有限公司
北京市回龙观二拨子工业园北区西路3号院
邮编：102208
电话：010-8271 1337
传真：010-5278 8439
电邮：aojie-fx@263.net
网址：www.zkaj888.com

Dechang Nursing of Stone Material
广东云浮德昌石材护理
广东省云浮市东郊大岬杜
电话：0766-810 0908
传真：0766-810 2085
电邮：cjj@yfdechang.com
网址：www.yfdechang.com

Guangzhou Fuyuan Stone Retread Care Co., Ltd.
广州富源石材翻新护理有限公司
广州市天河区车陂东路8号东灏商业大厦406室
邮编：510660
电话：020-8231 8768
传真：020-8231 8722
电邮：service@fysrc.com
网址：www.fysrc.com

Guangzhou Jialian & Matble Care Ltd.
广州市佳廉石材护理有限公司
广东省广州市广园西路223号
电话：020-8625 9779
传真：020-8625 9037
电邮：jialian@chinajialian.com
网址：www.chinajialian.com

Polyclean Stone & Marble Care Ltd.
玛斯域云石护理有限公司
Room 808, Opulent Commercial Building, 402-406 Hennessy Road, Wanchai, Hong Kong
电话：+852-2572 3601
传真：+852-2836 0972
电邮：info@polycleancare.com
网址：www.polycleancare.com

Shanghai Lanyun Cleaning Co., Ltd.
上海蓝云保洁有限公司
上海市宝山区月罗路569号
邮编：200941
电话：021-5619 3309
传真：021-5664 9705
电邮：lybjxxbs@online.sh.cn
网址：www.lybj.com.cn

Shanghai Shengji Wenshan Cleaning Equipment Co., Ltd.
上海盛吉文善清洁设备有限公司
上海市浦东新区耀华路215号2号楼307室
邮编：200126
电话：021-5119 9703
传真：021-6089 7367
电邮：sjwsclean@126.com
网址：www.sjwsclean.com

Wuhan Keda Marble Protective Materials Co., Ltd.
武汉市科达云石护理材料有限公司
武汉市东西湖区张柏路
电话：027-8356 3963
电邮：sales@whk8.com
网址：www.whk8.com

Yantai Auya Stone Apply Technique Co., Ltd.
烟台奥亚石材应用技术有限公司
烟台市南大街211号
电话：0535-606 5378
传真：0535-651 0052
电邮：auya@yahoo.cn
网址：www.auyas.com

广州荔湾区鸿基石材护理用品商行
广东省广州市荔湾区西华路小桥涌基17号综合楼9号
邮编：510170
电话：020-8103 0536
传真：020-8103 0509
电邮：hongjicn@hc360.com.cn
网址：www.gzhongjisc.com

广州市荔湾区明伽昌石材护理用品厂
广州市芳村龙溪大道蟠龙村22号B区7栋之一
邮编：510378
电话：020-8160 8712
传真：020-8160 9155
电邮：sales@karva.cn
网址：www.karva.cn

上海利豪石材养护技术工程有限公司
上海市浦东民生路499号
电话：021-5851 7203
传真：021-5821 4137
电邮：jwfdc@sina.com
网址：www.lehostone.com

上海旭日清洗服务有限公司
上海市佳林路919弄12号101室
电话：021-5031 3045
传真：021-5031 3045
电邮：xuriqingxi@163.com
网址：www.xurish.cn

酒窖
Wine Celler

Shanghai Pengxie Co., Ltd.
上海朋协实业有限公司
上海市虹莘路1955弄半岛豪门5号别墅
邮编：201100
电话：021-5417 0281
传真：021-5417 0282
电邮：webmaster@wine-town.com.cn
网址：www.wine-town.com.cn

Shenzhen Sicao Electric Appliances Co., Ltd.
深圳市新潮电器有限公司
深圳市罗湖区嘉宾路2018号深华商业大厦13-14层
邮编：518001
电话：0755-8237 5212
传真：0755-2219 1799
网址：www.sicao.cn
请参阅第254页

北京酒柜酒窖专业设计制作中心
北京市大羊坊北桥东北角横街子中心
电话：13522769382
电邮：cl_8578@163.com
网址：www.shentingshengye.com

南京中瑞展示设备有限公司
江苏省南京市雨花经济开发区凤集大道20号
邮编：210006
电话：025-5226 3156
传真：025-8673 0411
电邮：njzrzs@126.com
网址：www.zrzsw.com

上海朗克酒业有限公司
上海市中山南一路500弄1号楼丽都大厦31C座
电话：021-5301 8995
传真：021-6301 2598
电邮：mont-tauch@lengdok.com
网址：www.lengdok.com
请参阅第160页

仿真花草树木
Artificial Plants

Beijing Coconut Preserved Palm Co., Ltd.
北京可可纳保鲜棕榈树景观艺术有限公司
北京市朝阳区观音堂文化大道
邮编：100023
电话：010-8774 4684
电邮：bjccn@bjccn.cn
网址：www.bjccn.cn

Beijing Palm Technique Development Co., Ltd.
北京棕榈树技术开发有限公司
北京市朝阳区高碑店CBD国际高尔夫球会北侧
邮编：100023
电话：010-8401 1200
传真：010-5135 2966
电邮：zonglvshu@zonglvshu.com
网址：www.zonglvshu.com

Beijing Shiji Jingbin Fangzhen Yuanlinhuahui Co., Ltd.
北京世纪京滨仿真园林花卉有限公司
北京市丰台区方庄桥往南500米路东
邮编：100078
电话：010-6765 8993
传真：010-6768 5552
电邮：sjjbgcb@163.com
网址：www.sjjb.net

Dalian Jiyuan Artificial Plant Co., Ltd.
大连市济园仿真植物有限公司
辽宁省大连市西岗区新康巷29-1号
邮编：116011
电话：0411-8378 2855
传真：0411-8378 2822
电邮：dl@fzzw.cn
网址：www.fzzw.cn

Dongguan Winda Arts Industry Co., Ltd.
东莞市荣昊工艺实业有限公司
广东省东莞市东城科技工业园
邮编：523127
电话：0769-8899 9033
传真：0769-8899 9718
电邮：winda@winda-arts.com
网址：www.winda-arts.com

Flora Bunda (Shenzhen) Ltd.
深圳市卉之源实业有限公司
深圳市深南大道6006号华丰大厦806室
邮编：518034
电话：0755-8306 7759
传真：0755-8391 6217
电邮：florabundasz@yahoo.com.cn
网址：www.florabundasz.com

Palm Sunshine Interior Landscaping Co., Ltd.
北京棕榈阳光景观艺术有限公司
北京市通州区宋庄艺术中心六合桥西
电话：010-8951 9661
传真：010-8951 9662
电邮：zlyg008@126.com
网址：www.bjzlyg.com

Ruixing Flower Art (Dongguan) Co., Ltd.
瑞兴花艺（东莞）有限公司
广东省东莞市厚街镇新围工业区
电话：0769-8588 0232
传真：0769-8588 0232
电邮：gd-ruixing@163.com
网址：www.gdruixing.com

Shanghai Czj Artistry Landscape Engineering Co., Ltd.
上海超之杰艺术景观工程有限公司
上海市浦东新区龙东大道东胜路38号A10栋
邮编：201201
电话：021-6891 8620
传真：021-6891 9193
网址：www.czjcn.com

Shanghai Fangyuan Flower Ornament Industrial Corporation
上海芳园花卉装饰实业有限公司
上海市灵石路702号（先锋工业园区43号房）
邮编：200072
电话：021-6353 9721
传真：021-6353 9752
电邮：sales@fy95.com
网址：www.fy95.com

Shanghai Surprize Artistry Landscape Engineering Co., Ltd.
上海晶雅艺术景观工程有限公司
上海市闵行区江川路1405号
邮编：200240
电话：021-6580 7900
传真：021-6580 7900*801
电邮：tosurprize@126.com
网址：www.surprize.com.cn

Shanghai Xin Yan Yi Milieu Art De Co., Ltd.
上海新演绎环境艺术有限公司
上海市浦东新区浦建路729号东方金座大厦702室
邮编：200127
电话：021-6146 4158
传真：021-6146 4159
电邮：xinyanyi@sohu.com
网址：www.shbxs.com

Yongzhou Haihong (Shanghai) Arts & Crafts Co., Ltd.
上海永州海虹工艺品有限公司
上海市闸北区场中路3135号
邮编：200436
电话：021-6650 8120
传真：021-6651 8571
电邮：yongzhouhaihong@vip.sina.com
网址：www.yzhaihong.com

工艺品
Artworks

Ariamotion (Dalian) Co., Ltd.
大连尚艺玻璃集团有限公司
辽宁省大连市中山区友好路158号友好大厦1211室
邮编：116001
电话：0411-8252 0539
传真：0411-8252 0501
电邮：info@casamotion.com
网址：www.casamotion.com

Beijing Sanlitang Cultural Media Co., Ltd.
北京三立堂文化传媒有限公司
北京市西城区西直门内金泰华云写字楼A109室
邮编：100035
电话：010-6221 8893
传真：010-6221 8893
请参阅第314、315页

Beijing Zai Xian Hui Huang Design Corp. Ltd.
北京市再现辉煌艺术设计有限公司
北京市通州区马驹桥镇郭村332号
邮编：101102
电话：010-6059 2995
电邮：zxhh@263.net
网址：www.bjzxhh.com

Dongguan Aim Decoration Factory
东莞市尔美工艺饰品厂
东莞市茶山镇卢屋工业区
邮编：523008
电话：0769-2306 7346
传真：0769-2306 1726
电邮：aim@chinaaim.com.cn
网址：www.chinaaim.com.cn

Euro-Artpainting Co., Ltd.
深圳市欧雅油画有限公司
深圳市南山区大新路金龙工业城62栋2楼
邮编：518052
电话：0755-8621 6828
传真：0755-2644 4996
电邮：ouya@sz-eapt.com
网址：www.sz-eapt.com

Glong International Trade Co., Ltd.
上海技隆国际贸易有限公司
上海市虹口区花园路128号运动创意园A栋351室
邮编：200083
电话：021-6140 9708
传真：021-6140 9706
电邮：daniel@wazalife.com
网址：www.wazalife.com

Hans Houseware Co., Ltd.
东莞市汉斯家居用品有限公司
广东省东莞市谢岗镇五星管理区
新星路28号汉斯大厦
邮编：523633
电话：0769-8779 9083
传真：0769-8779 8583
电邮：info@hanshouseware.com
网址：www.hanshouseware.com
请参阅第271页

Jingdezhen Franz Collection Co., Ltd.
景德镇法蓝瓷实业有限公司
江西省景德镇市陶瓷科技工业园区枫林坞水库
邮编：333400
电话：0592-596 3066
传真：0592-597 5913
电邮：info@franzcollection.com.cn
网址：www.franzcollection.com.cn

Mimoda Furnishing Co., Ltd.
米尚家居有限公司
广东省深圳市坂田镇吉通工业区门口
电话：0769-8588 0886
传真：0769-8588 0886
电邮：info@mimodafurn.com
网址：www.mimodafurn.com

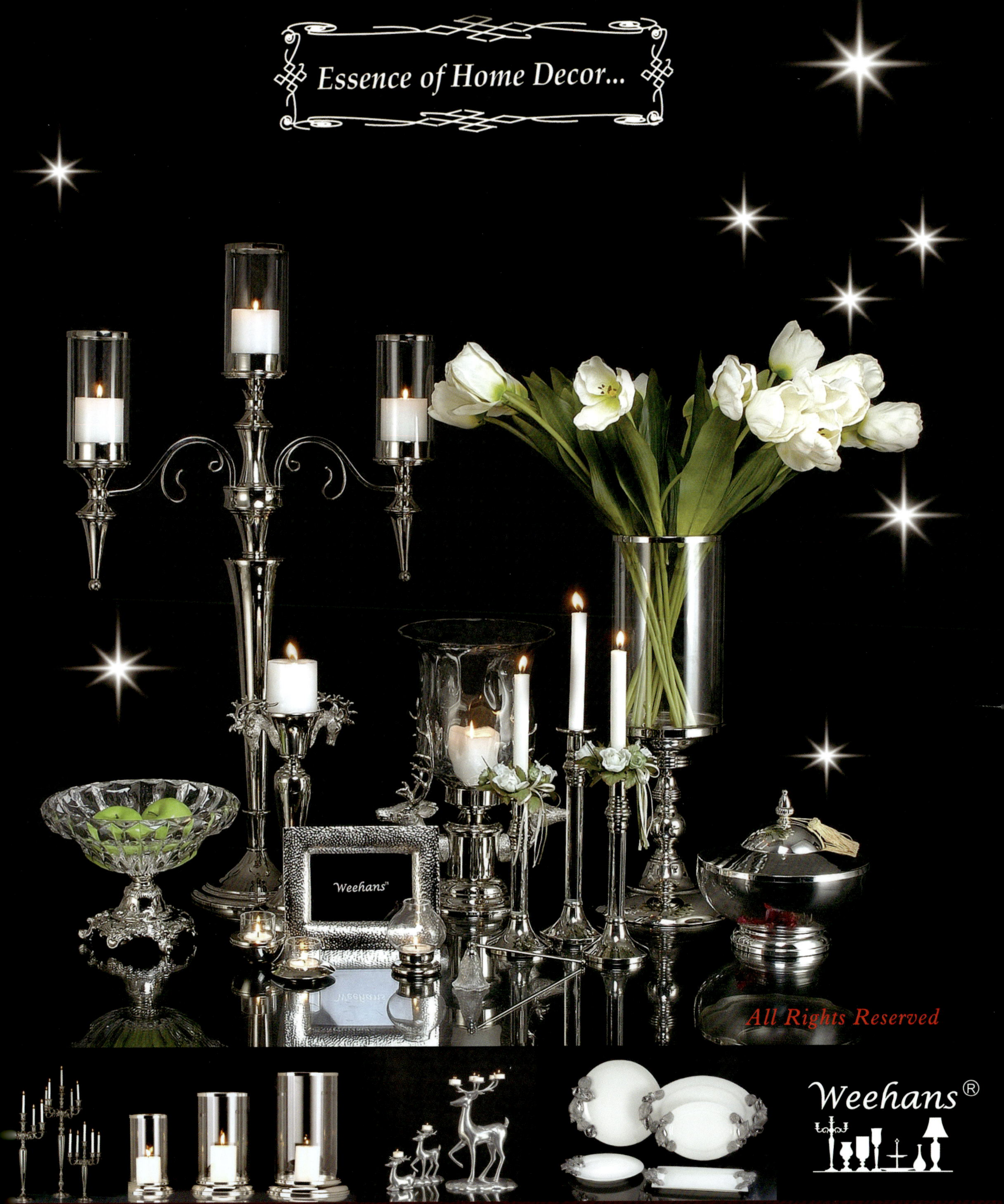

▼工艺品
Artworks

New Impression Art (Shenzhen) Workshop
深圳市新印象实业有限公司
深圳市布吉镇西环路新印象128艺术区（东升学校旁）
电话：0755-8326 1711
传真：0755-8332 7007
电邮：szxyxart@xyxart.com
网址：www.xyxart.net
请参阅本页

Nicole Schoeni
少励画廊
香港中环奥卑利街21-31号
电话：+852-2869 8802
传真：+852-2522 1528
电邮：gallery@schoeni.com.hk
网址：www.schoeni.com.hk

Pupoyan House Decoration Trading
深圳市富百年家居饰品有限公司
深圳市龙岗区同乐社区新布村128工业区
电话：0755-8964 2113
传真：0755-8964 2389
电邮：fbnjs@21cn.com
网址：www.fbnjs.com

Reappear Crafts Co., Ltd.
桂林市古之韵工艺品有限公司
桂林市育才路55号
邮编：541003
电话：0773-361 2902
传真：0773-361 2902
网址：www.reappear.com.cn

Shanghai Chuan Arts & Crafts Co., Ltd.
上海传家工艺品有限公司
上海市奉贤区青村镇奉永路399号
邮编：201414
电话：021-5756 7155
传真：021-5756 7157
电邮：chuan888@vip.163.com
网址：www.chuanstone.com

Shanghai Xin Si Lu Metal Products Co., Ltd.
上海鑫丝陆金属制品有限公司
上海市金沙江西路1555弄C1区5号楼
电话：400 820 1773
传真：021-3951 2115
电邮：xsl@xslmetalfabrics.com
网址：www.xslmetalfabrics.com
请参阅本第312页

Shenzhen Artcate Craftworks Co., Ltd.
深圳市雅尔卡迪工艺品有限公司
深圳市龙岗区坑梓街道龙田社区
龙窝工业区龙英发工业园3号厂房
邮编：518122
电话：0755-6122 0288
传真：0755-6122 0268
电邮：liyujiashi@126.ocm
网址：www.iartcate.com.cn

Shenzhen Best-One Ltd.
深圳丑石文化传播有限公司
广东省深圳市宝安区
龙华街道办胜立工业园丑石大厦
邮编：518000
电话：0755-8361 7831
传真：0755-8361 6068
电邮：best-one@best-one.cn
网址：www.best-one.cn

Shenzhen European & American Famous Painting Arts Co., Ltd.
深圳市欧美名画艺术有限公司
深圳市福田区振华路工艺大厦3楼
邮编：518031
电话：0755-8325 8226
传真：0755-8324 5839
电邮：eafpg@eafpg.com
网址：www.eafpg.com

Shenzhen Nuoqi Oil Painting Art Co., Ltd.
深圳诺奇油画工艺有限公司
东莞市石龙镇织儒街4-19号
电话：0769-8688 1400
传真：0769-8192 2977
电邮：nuoqiart82@gmail.com
网址：www.nuoqiart.com

Shenzhen Sunsister Design Co., Ltd.
深圳市太阳姐妹设计有限公司
深圳市宝安区石岩湾工业区创成大厦2栋
邮编：518108
电话：0755-2982 7611
传真：0755-2982 7300
电邮：sunsister@sunsister.com
网址：www.sunsister.com

Shenzhen Xiongshi Zhenggang Art Co., Ltd.
深圳市熊氏正刚艺术有限公司
深圳市龙岗区布吉大芬油画村大芬路22号
电话：0755-8951 2361
传真：0755-2827 4076
电邮：sale_a@xszgart.com
网址：www.xszgart.com

▼工艺品
Artworks

Shenzhen Ya Shi Art Ornaments Co., Ltd.
深圳市雅诗艺术饰品有限公司
深圳市罗湖区宝岗路269号西侧七楼
邮编：518020
电话：0755-8226 2690
传真：0755-8242 4323
网址：www.sha-arts.com

Shenzhen Yinbo Painting & Artwork Co., Ltd.
深圳市银波油画工艺有限公司
深圳市龙岗区五联社区协平路协平工业区G栋
邮编：518129
电话：0755-2879 3332
传真：0755-2879 0354
电邮：yb@yinbo-art.com
网址：www.yinbo-art.com

Yixing Sunong Ceramic Co., Ltd.
宜兴市苏农陶业有限公司
江苏省宜兴市丁山镇红星路39号
邮编：214221
电话：0510-8740 2311
传真：0510-8740 2581
网址：www.tscer.com

广东长城集团股份有限公司
广东省潮州市枫溪区蔡陇大道
邮编：521031
电话：0768-293 1010
传真：0768-293 1033
电邮：cctc@thegreatwall-china.com
网址：www.thegreatwall-china.com

惠州市惠阳区秋长顺昌工艺制品厂
广东省惠州市秋长镇维布工业区
邮编：516200
电话：0752-355 3118
传真：0752-355 6606
电邮：ken.treasures@163.com
网址：www.treasuresarts.cn

重庆恩德雕塑有限公司
重庆市巴南区李家沱工业搪瓷厂
邮编：400054
电话：023-6259 0032
电邮：office@edds.cn
网址：www.edds.cn

窗帘
Blinds

Baoli Plastics Products Co., Ltd.
浙江省瑞安市宝利塑料制品有限公司
浙江省瑞安市塘下镇上金工业区
邮编：325204
电话：0577-6535 7258
传真：0577-6535 4318
电邮：chinabaoli@163.com
网址：www.bao-li.com

Changzhou Yameite Textile Co., Ltd.
常州雅美特纺织有限公司
江苏省常州市新北区太湖中路27号5楼
邮编：213022
电话：0519-8515 2901
传真：0519-8515 2902
网址：www.yameite.cn

Changzhou Yiliyasi Textile Co., Ltd.
常州依丽雅斯纺织品有限公司
江苏省常州市新北区汉江西路118号
邮编：213125
电话：0519-8595 5733
传真：0519-8596 2987
电邮：chinagoldcock@hotmail.com
网址：www.czgoldcock.com

Chung's Carpet Development Ltd.
钟氏地毯发展有限公司
1-3/F Waitex House, 7-9 Mongkok Road, Mong Kok, Kowloon, Hong Kong
电话：+852-2770 6215
传真：+852-2770 1576
电邮：chcarpet@chungscarpet.com.hk
网址：www.chungscarpet.com.hk

Haoyan Home Supplies Co., Ltd.
浩燕竹木帘织品有限公司
浙江绍兴中国轻纺城北二区2楼499号
邮编：312030
电话：0575-8411 4106
传真：0575-8412 9423
电邮：haoyan@cnhaoyan.com
网址：www.cnhaoyan.com

Heilongjiang Changjiu Wood Co., Ltd.
黑龙江长九木业有限公司
黑龙江省通河县清河林业局
邮编：150913
电话：0451-5744 7111
传真：0451-5748 3799
电邮：wanghong0501@163.com
网址：www.hljchangjiu.com

Many Blinds Manufactory Limited
中山万利窗帘制造有限公司
广东省中山市南区振南路
邮编：528455
电话：0760-8889 1923
传真：0760-8889 3795
电邮：zhongshan@manyblinds.com.hk
网址：www.manyblinds.com.hk

Mingcheng Enterprise
名成企业
上海市松江泗泾工业区九干路289号
邮编：201601
电话：021-5762 7111
传真：021-5762 6148
电邮：market@mingcheng.com.cn
网址：www.mingcheng.com.cn
请参阅第340、341页

Molike Lives At Home The Cloth Industry Co., Ltd.
摩力克家居布业有限公司
广东省佛山市禅城区张槎纯阳道1号
邮编：528000
电话：0757-8251 8352
传真：0757-8221 8808
电邮：molik@fsmolik.com
网址：www.fsmolik.com

Nanjing Yadisi Cloth Skill Decoration Project Co., Ltd.
南京雅迪斯布艺装饰工程有限公司
江苏省南京市汉中西路298号裕康大厦11F
电话：025-8632 3609
传真：025-8653 3609
电邮：yadisi@yadisi.com
网址：www.yadisi.com

Shanghai Doma Light Textile Co., Ltd.
上海杜玛轻纺有限公司
上海市奉贤区西渡扶港路900号
邮编：201401
电话：021-6089 0666
传真：021-6089 0555
电邮：info@doma-china.com
网址：www.doma-china.com

Shanghai Mingyang Window Blinds Manufacture Co., Ltd.
上海名扬窗饰制造有限公司
上海松江佘山工业区明业路198号
邮编：201602
电话：021-5779 4330
传真：021-5779 4335
电邮：mingyang_800@163.com
网址：www.mywb.cn

Shanghai Xin Si Lu Metal Products Co., Ltd.
上海鑫丝陆金属制品有限公司
上海市金沙江西路1555弄C1区5号楼
电话：400 820 1773
传真：021-3951 2115
电邮：xsl@xslmetalfabrics.com
网址：www.xslmetalfabrics.com
请参阅第312页

Shenzhen Huake Chuangshi Co., Ltd.
深圳市华科窗饰有限公司
深圳市龙岗区中心城龙翔大道397-399号
邮编：518000
电话：0755-2898 4748
传真：0755-2898 4393
电邮：szhkcs@163.com
网址：www.szchuanglian.com

Somfy China Co., Ltd.
尚飞中国
上海市华山路1520弄121号2楼
邮编：200052
电话：021-6280 9660
传真：021-6280 0270
网址：www.somfy.cn
请参阅第338、339页、封面

Yuanzhicheng Hometextile Co., Ltd.
源志诚家纺有限公司
广东省广州市越秀区大南路62号
邮编：510115
电话：020-8330 2177
传真：020-8330 4376
电邮：yzc@yuanzhicheng.com
网址：www.yuanzhicheng.com
业务范围：
源志诚家纺有限公司成立于1994年，是一家集研发设计、生产织造、染整及成品加工、销售服务为一体的专业公司。主要生产以丝织物、仿丝织物、化纤、混纺及纯棉等为主的高密度酒店及家居室内纺织用布及布艺成品，公司自成立以来，一直以时尚的产品向广大同行提供优质服务，同时致力为国内外星级酒店研发风格化的产品及提供多元化的合作模式。
请参阅第2、282、283页

荷兰亨特道格拉斯集团始创于1919年，总部设在荷兰王国鹿特丹市，是在荷兰阿姆斯特丹上市的公共国际公司。集团是全球运用窗饰遮阳和建筑产品作为光线调节和阳光热量控制解决方案的市场领导者。其160多家独资子公司遍布全球100多个国家，集产品研发、设计加工、生产装配和机械制造于一体，是全球最大的窗饰遮阳产品生产企业。

亨特道格拉斯集团一直专注于提供高星级酒店需求的酒店布艺、窗饰产品和电动开合轨及智能控制系统等专业酒店产品，致力于高级酒店布艺和窗饰及相关配套产品的研发、生产及市场推广。我们能够满足全球各地区星级酒店对软装饰的个性化要求，为室内设计大师们追求完美风格提供理想的解决方案。而且，亨特道格拉斯不断提升产品质量和整体服务能力，我们的产品凭借着质量的可靠性、设计的创新性及服务的专业性，已成为世界各国高端酒店市场中相关产品的最优之选；成为中国高级室内软装饰的整体解决方案的专业提供商；成为酒店档次和品位的重要象征！

◎ 窗饰产品
WINDOW COVERING PRODUCTS

在酒店窗饰产品领域，亨特窗饰表现非凡，提供的产品涵盖了丝络雅，风琴帘，颖雅帘，铝合金百叶帘，实木/仿木百叶帘等，品类非常丰富。并且，亨特的各类酒店专用窗饰产品均具有极好的防火性能，具备坚实可靠的安全使用保障。

◎ 酒店布艺
HOSPITALITY TEXTILES

● 窗帘布艺
DRAPERY FABRIC

从窗帘、窗纱到遮光布，亨特拥有一整套高品位的窗帘布艺解决方案，在用料、颜色及款式上的考究，让独具匠心的亨特窗饰产品成为世界顶级酒店的青睐之选。

● 沙发装饰布
UPHOLSTERY

多达百余种的色织布系列使得亨特的沙发装饰布产品拥有了丰富多彩的自由搭配选择，而正是凭借如此强大的材质选择空间，让亨特的沙发装饰布系列产品拥有了坚实的品质保障和广泛的应用空间，沙发、休闲椅、办公桌、搁脚凳以及床板上的空间等等都是亨特沙发装饰布完美的演绎舞台！

● 床品
BEDDING

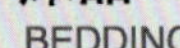

亨特道格拉斯酒店窗饰与布艺可为客户提供的床上用品包括床褥、床单、枕套、欧式抱枕及床边毯等，所有这些亨特床品同样是品质之选，它们厚实耐用，可用商用洗衣机频繁清洗，手感柔顺，缝制精良！另外，亨特还拥有全球唯一可用机洗的高端雪尼尔面料床边毯。

◎ 电动开合轨及智能控制系统
MOTORIZED DRAPERY TRACK & CONTROL SYSTEM

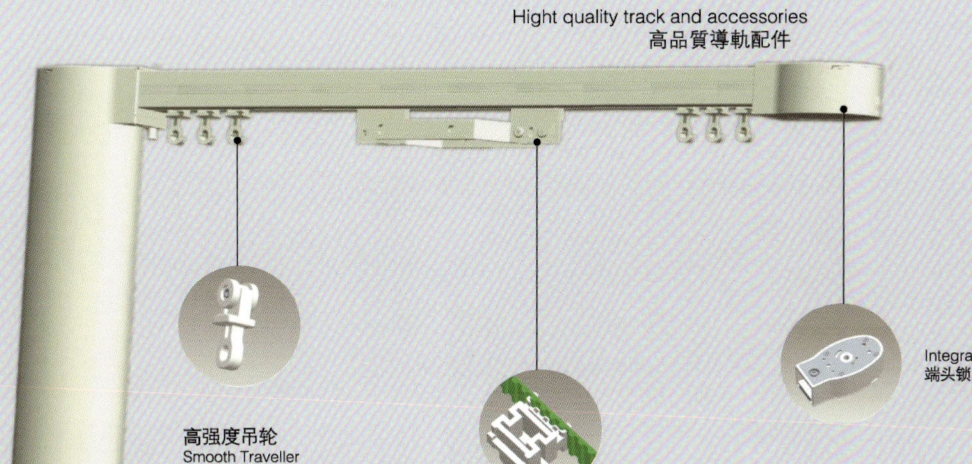

Hight quality track and accessories
高品質導軌配件

高强度吊轮
Smooth Traveller

Integrated with Loop Stop
端头锁紧耳一体化设计

Master carrier with Belt button
滑车架皮带扣一体化设计，
皮带扣吃皮带4个齿更加牢固耐用

- Powerful function with load capacity up to 50kg
  强大的功能，单机负重可达50KG
- Completely inverted and hidden motor.
  单机可倒装，电机完全可隐蔽系统美观大方
- Stable and quiet system.Noise level less than 46db "
  静音运行，轻开轻合，平稳运行，系统噪音 <46db "
- Automatically-set for gradual shutdown.
  自动设定停机点进行软停机
- Reliable remote control with FSK FM control technology.
  亨特FSK调频控制技术，无线遥控更加稳定可靠

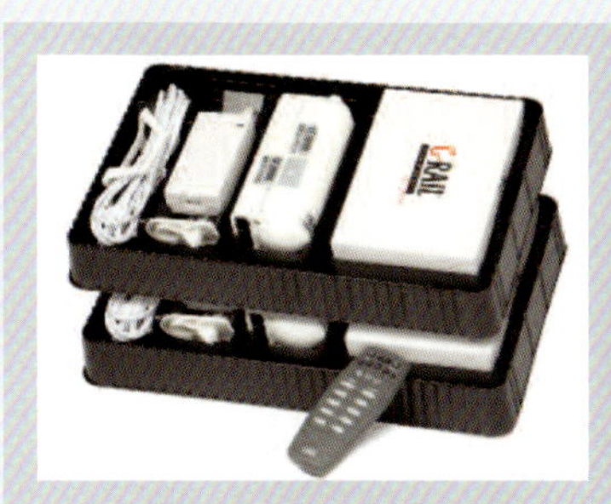

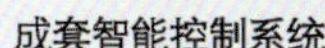

成套智能控制系统

电机设备

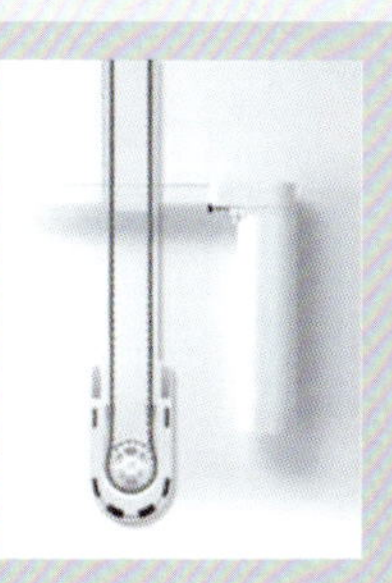

开合轨

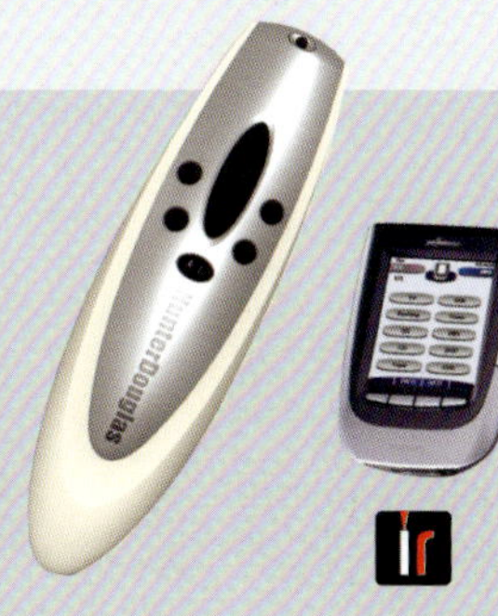

遥控设备

适用于大多数工程项目

电动开合轨可手动开合

可与所有智能控制系统匹配

亨特道格拉斯酒店窗饰与布艺通过在酒店窗饰布艺领域里20多年的专业探求，已经拥有了从窗帘布艺、耐火专业电动窗饰产品、家具沙发装饰布到各类床上用品的强大核心产品链，而除此之外，在电动开合轨及智能控制系统应用方面亨特也取得了不菲的成绩！

我们拥有专业的设计团队为您量身打造创意空间！

我们向所有的优秀设计师开放了高效的定制服务，可以根据设计师们对室内软装饰的特殊需求，在较短时间内提供最符合其心目中理想布艺的设计，同时也保证产品的一贯优异品质和可靠性。

▲ Armani Hotel Dubai
迪拜哈利法塔阿玛尼酒店

▶ Shanghai Expo Intercontinental Hotel
上海世博洲际酒店

▼ The Ritz-Carlton Shanghai, Pudong
上海浦东丽思卡尔顿酒店

SHANGHAI
亨特窗飾產品（上海）有限公司
Hunter Douglas Window Covering Products (Shanghai) Co., Ltd.
上海市閔行區光中路355號
No.355 Guangzhong Road,Minhang District Shanghai 201108, China
電話 TEL：（86-21）34717777
傳真 FAX：（86-21）34717520

SHENZHEN
亨特窗飾產品（深圳）有限公司
Hunter Douglas Window Covering Products (Shenzhen) Co., Ltd.
深圳鹽田區沙頭角保税區19棟1樓
1/F No. 19 Industrial Building, Shatoujiao Bonded Zone,Yantian District,Shenzhen
電話 TEL:（86-755）25261068
傳真 FAX:（86-755）25266661

BEIJING
亨特窗飾產品（北京）有限公司
Hunter Douglas Window Covering Products (Beijing) Co., Ltd.
北京市朝陽區姚家園路105號萬企控股大厦（觀湖國際3號樓）501/502室
Room 501/502, Vantage Holdings Plaza (Block 3 Green Lake International),No.105 Yaojiayuan Road, Chaoyang District, Beijing
電話 TEL：（86-10）59623311
傳真 FAX:（86-10）59623258

HONG KONG
亨特道格拉斯中國/香港有限公司
Hunter Douglas China / Hong Kong Ltd.
香港新界沙田安心街11號華順廣場6樓608-612室
Unit 608-612,6/F,Topasail Plaza No.11 On Sum Street Shantin, N.T. Hong Kong
電話 TEL: 852-26378111
傳真 FAX: 852-26378611

e Meridien Shimei Bay,Hainan
海南石梅湾艾美酒店

◎ 经典案例
HOTEL JOB REFERENCE

上海世博洲際酒店
上海證大喜瑪拉亞酒店
上海浦東麗思卡爾頓酒店
上海鬆江皇冠酒店
上海盛高康橋假日酒店
上海雅居樂萬豪酒店
上海萬豪酒店
上海安亭皇冠酒店
南京綠地洲際酒店
南京威斯汀酒店
杭州國會洲際酒店
千島湖喜來登酒店
温州喜來登酒店
寧波南苑酒店
青島萬麗海景酒店

北京首都機場T3希爾頓酒店
北京國貿三期香格裏拉酒店
北京威斯汀酒店
北京財富中心二期公寓
北京麗思卡爾頓酒店
北京萬豪酒店
北京千禧酒店
北京昆侖飯店
北京中國大飯店
北京麗晶酒店
天津環貿商務中心東塔樓酒店式公寓
天津水晶宫飯店
内蒙古鄂爾多斯久泰迎賓館
青海中浩酒店
合肥翡翠湖賓館

深圳JW萬豪酒店
深圳君悦酒店
深圳華强廣場酒店
廣州喜來登酒店
廣州正佳萬豪酒店
海南萬寧喜來登酒店
海南福鵬喜來登酒店
海南石梅灣艾美酒店
三亞麗思卡爾頓酒店
三亞海棠灣萬麗大酒店
廈門艾美酒店
貴陽凱悦酒店
成都信德東方賓館
温州鹿城廣場

www.hunterdouglashospitality.com.cn

▼窗帘 Blinds

北京华灵瑞博窗帘销售中心
北京市朝阳区十里河家和家美A3-26号
电话：010-8736 5459
传真：010-8736 5156

HunterDouglasHospitality

亨特制造（中国）有限公司
上海市闵行区光中路355号
邮编：201108
电话：021-3471 7777*131
传真：021-3471 7521
电邮：info@hunterdouglashospitality.com.cn
网址：www.hunterdouglashospitality.com.cn
业务范围：
作为国际知名的酒店布艺业务整体方案提供商，始创于1919年荷兰亨特道格拉斯集团一直专注于提供高星级酒店需求的酒店布艺、窗饰产品和电动轨道及智能控制系统等专业酒店产品。身为行业的领导者我们能够满足全球各地区高星级酒店对软装饰的个性化要求，为室内设计大师追求完美风格提供理想解决方案。
请参阅第274、275、276、277、278、279页

地毯 Carpets

Changzhou Around Globe Carpet Manufacture Co., Ltd.
常州环球地毯制造有限公司
江苏省常州市西门花园陈渡镇北91号
邮编：213016
电话：0519-8328 4514
传真：0519-8329 0583
电邮：czcmmc@globe-carpet.com
网址：www.aroundglobe-carpet.com

China Worldbest Group Carpet Co., Ltd.
华源集团地毯有限公司
上海市中山北路1958号华源世界广场2楼
邮编：200063
电话：021-6203 7144
传真：021-6203 6721
电邮：scb@cwcc.com.cn
网址：www.cwcc.com.cn

Chongqin Hailun Carpet Co., Ltd.
重庆市海伦地毯有限公司
重庆市江津区燕窝六路119号
邮编：402260
电话：023-4755 4308
传真：023-4755 4718
电邮：hailun@tlcarpet.com
网址：www.tlcarpet.com

Chung's Carpet Development Ltd.
钟氏地毡发展有限公司
1-3/F Waitex House, 7-9 Mongkok Road, Mong Kok, Kowloon, Hong Kong
电话：+852-2770 6215
传真：+852-2770 1576
电邮：chcarpet@chungscarpet.com.hk
网址：www.chungscarpet.com.hk

DongSheng Carpet Group
东升地毯集团
山东日照海曲西路79号
邮编：276800
电话：0633-868 8999
传真：0633-868 8901
电邮：dongsheng@dongsheng.com
网址：www.dongsheng.com

Fuhua Carpet Co., Ltd.
福华地毯有限公司
东莞市厚街镇恒锋家具博览中心后栋
电话：0769-8591 0069
传真：0769-8591 0528
电邮：fuhua@fuhuacarpet.com
网址：www.fuhuacarpet.com

Haima Group Corp
海马集团公司
山东省威海市青岛南路329号
邮编：264200
电话：0631-522 0592
传真：0631-522 6887
电邮：sale@haimacarpet.com
网址：www.haimacarpet.com

Haining Liduo Carpet Co., Ltd.
海宁利多毯业有限责任公司
浙江省海宁市中国轻纺村工业区
邮编：314422
电话：0573-8799 9688
传真：0573-8799 9689
网址：www.zjldty.com

Jackson Carpet (Qingdao) Co., Ltd.
捷成地毯（青岛）有限公司
山东省青岛即墨经济开发区黄河3路29号
邮编：266200
电话：0532-8755 2222
传真：0532-8755 2272
电邮：china@jcarpet.com
网址：www.jcarpet.com

Jiangxi Huateng Carpet Industrial Park Co., Ltd.
江西华腾地毯产业园有限公司
上海市陕西北路1438号1708室
邮编：200060
电话：021-6298 9325
传真：021-6298 8960
电邮：jennifer@cttcc.com.cn
网址：www.cttcc.com.cn

Jimei Carpet Factory
集美地毯厂
广东省东莞市沙田镇齐沙工业区集美地毯厂
邮编：523999
电话：0769-8880 8808
传真：0769-8866 3878
电邮：carpet@jimei.net
网址：www.jimei.net

Kunpeng Carpets Co., Ltd.
威海昆鹏地毯有限公司
山东省威海市尚山镇深圳路8号
电话：0631-390 9076
电邮：sales@kunpengcarpet.com.cn
网址：www.kunpengchina.com.cn

Kunshan Rongguang Carpet Co., Ltd.
昆山市荣光地毯有限公司
浙江省瑞安市马屿镇56省道边
电话：0577-8261 7110
传真：0577-6578 2775
网址：www.rgcarpet.com

Nanhai Flamboo Enterprises Co., Ltd.
广东佛山市南海通兴地毯厂
广东省佛山市南海区西樵山根工业区
邮编：528211
电话：0757-8689 8165
传真：0757-8689 8754
电邮：nanhai@flamboo.com
网址：www.flamboo.com

OFC Catering Equipment Co., Ltd.
OFC地毯有限公司
无锡市锡山区东港镇五星工业园区
邮编：214199
电话：0510-8835 1999
传真：0510-8876 4888
电邮：ofc@ofc-carpet.com
网址：www.ofc-carpet.com

Oriental Carpet Co., Ltd.
东方地毯有限公司
滨州市经济开发区渤海二十八路497号
邮编：256617
电话：0543-341 5821
传真：0543-341 5826
电邮：gs@cndfdt.com
网址：www.cndfdt.com

Shandong Hongye Carpets Group Corp
山东红叶地毯集团公司
山东省临朐县临朐镇工业园区
电话：0536-318 8887
传真：0536-318 8889
电邮：hongye@redleafcarpets.com
网址：www.hongyeditan.com

Shanghai Heya Decoration Co., Ltd.
上海赫雅装饰材料有限公司
上海市沪闵路9120号B座501室
电话：021-5448 7421
传真：021-5448 7422
电邮：heyaditan@126.com
网址：www.sh-heya.com

Shanghai Judong Tile Carpet Co., Ltd.
上海巨东方块地毯有限公司
上海市嘉定区安亭镇宝安公路4997号
邮编：201805
电话：021-5956 3033
传真：021-6957 6128
电邮：jdtc@shjdtc.com
网址：www.shjdtc.com

Shanghai Xuande Decorate Data Co., Ltd.
上海轩德装饰材料有限公司
上海市宜山路395号博雅广场2-18-1
电话：021-5437 4350
传真：021-3363 0070
电邮：xuande010@126.com
网址：www.xuandecarpet.com

▼地毯
Carpets

Suzhou Babylon Carpet Co., Ltd.
苏州巴比伦地毯有限公司
江苏省苏州市相城区澄阳路12号N栋二楼
电话：0512-6575 0024
传真：0512-6575 7907
电邮：service@regalcarpet.com.cn
网址：www.regalcarpet.com.cn

Suzhou Tuntex Fiber & Carpet Co., Ltd.
苏州东帝士纤维地毯有限公司
上海市长宁区仙霞137号盛高国际大厦2505室
邮编：200051
电话：021-6233 3488
传真：021-6259 6265
电邮：karen@tuntex-carpet.com
网址：www.tuntex-carpet.com

Wuxi Kunda Carpet Co., Ltd.
无锡昆达地毯有限责任公司
无锡市东港镇港王路
邮编：214199
电话：0510-8835 3497
传真：0510-8835 0039
网址：www.shiba.cn

Yarns Ltd.
金汇地毡建材有限公司
FlatB, 1/F, Kam Man Fung Factory Building, 6 Hong Man Street, Wan Chai, Hong Kong
电话：+852-2833 2886
传真：+852-2833 2836
电邮：info@yarns-ltd.com
网址：www.yarns-ltd.com

Zhaoqing Guanghui Carpet and Chemical Fibre Manufacturing Co., Ltd.
肇庆广惠地毯化纤制造有限公司
广东省肇庆市高新技术开发区迎宾大道
邮编：528244
电话：0758-362 5188
传真：0758-362 5182
电邮：gh@ghcarpets.com
网址：www.ghcarpets.com

Zhejiang Artistic Carpets Manufacturing Co., Ltd.
浙江美术地毯制造有限公司
杭州余杭区临平镇保障桥
邮编：311100
电话：0571-8622 4904
传真：0571-8622 6308
电邮：info@zhemeicorp.com
网址：www.zhemeicorp.com

Zhenzhou Huade Mutual Benefit Carpet Co., Ltd.
郑州华德永佳地毯有限公司
河南省巩义市紫荆路北段
邮编：451200
电话：0371-6431 9402
传真：0371-6431 9420
电邮：ehuade@126.com
网址：www.ehuade.com

圣诞饰品
Christmas Ornamental

Shanghai Surprize Artistry Landscape Engineering Co., Ltd.
上海晶雅艺术景观工程有限公司
上海市闵行区江川路1405号
邮编：200240
电话：021-6580 7900
传真：021-6580 7900*801
电邮：tosurprize@126.com
网址：www.surprize.com.cn

Shenzhen Wanmao Christmas Factory
深圳市万茂圣诞厂
深圳市龙岗镇爱联奋叶村晨光路金利街
邮编：518172
电话：0755-8991 5878
传真：0755-2898 8639
电邮：webmaster@szwanmao.com
网址：www.szwanmao.com

Worldex International Industrial Ltd.
世达国际实业有限公司
香港红磡民乐街21号富高工业中心B座9楼27室
电话：+852-2172 6178
传真：+852-2172 6890
电邮：worldexi@netvigator.com
网址：www.worldexhk.com

水晶及水晶制品
Crystals & Crystal Products

Amity Crystal Craft Factory
浦江县友好水晶工艺品厂
浙江省浦江县环城西路202号
邮编：322200
电话：0579-8808 8895
传真：0579-8808 8897
电邮：amitycrystal@vip.sina.com
网址：www.amitycrystal.com

Dongguan Kam Tat Lighting Co., Ltd.
东莞市金达照明有限公司
东莞市万江谷涌管理区
电话：0769-2228 4761
传真：0769-2227 7195
电邮：info@kamtatlighting.com
网址：www.riservalighting.com

Haitai Ornaments Co., Ltd.
浦江县海泰水晶灯饰有限公司
浙江省浦江县浦南区平安平一222号
邮编：322200
电话：0579-8424 7771
传真：0579-8424 7707
电邮：goldenhaitai@yahoo.com.cn
网址：www.goldenhaitai.com

Hangzhou Tieying Crystal Handicraft Co., Ltd.
杭州铁莹水晶工艺有限公司
杭州市滨江区西兴科技经济园聚工路23号
邮编：310051
电话：0571-8668 2959
传真：0571-8668 2869
电邮：hzty@vip.163.com
网址：www.asiacrystal.com

Huayi Crystal Goods Co., Ltd.
深圳市恒缘水晶制品有限公司
深圳市宝安区龙华街道简上村B42栋3楼
电话：0755-2978 7756
传真：0755-2978 7756
电邮：sz1408@126.com
网址：www.szhuayee.com

Pujiang Copor Crystal Handicrafts Factory
浦江县古珀水晶工艺品厂
浙江省浦江县水晶路10号
邮编：322200
电话：0579-8420 7078
传真：0579-8420 7079
电邮：copor@163.com
网址：www.copor.cn

Pujiang Jingjing Crystal Craftwork Co., Ltd.
浙江浦江县精晶水晶工艺有限公司
浙江省浦江县人民西路59号
邮编：322200
电话：0579-8413 2989
传真：0579-8413 2990
电邮：jingjing@chinajjcrystal.com
网址：www.zjsjzh.com

Shanghai Kang Yu Jie-Sen Cast Glass Artwork Co., Ltd.
上海康宇杰森水晶艺术品有限公司
上海市肇嘉浜路789号
邮编：200032
电话：021-6438 5109
传真：021-5227 1335
电邮：kycopper@kygroup.com
网址：www.kygroup.com

Yuzhou Crystal Glass Production Co., Ltd.
宇洲水晶玻璃制品有限公司
浙江省金华市浦江县白林工业区
邮编：322217
电话：0579-8410 3711
传真：0579-8410 3710
网址：www.hzyuzhou.com.cn

Zhejiang Pujiang County Tin Fung Commodity Factory
浙江浦江县天丰日用品厂
浙江省浦江县班班大道49号
邮编：322200
电话：0579-8451 7580
传真：0579-8451 7582
网址：www.ywmlrysjc.ywco.cn

Zhejiang Pujiang Yijia Crystal Product Factory
浙江省浦江艺佳水晶制品厂
浙江省金华市浦江县水晶工业园区C08-3
邮编：322200
电话：0579-8808 6815
传真：0579-8808 6816
电邮：yijia@chinacrystal.net.cn
网址：www.chinacrystal.net.cn

窗帘及布艺
Curtains & Draperies

Beijing Jinyibairong Co., Ltd.
北京金艺百荣遮阳技术有限公司
北京市大兴区金星乡志远庄工业园
邮编：100076
电话：010-6128 9811
传真：010-6128 9277
电邮：jinyibairong@126.com
网址：www.jybr.com

Jackson Law Properties & Sefas Design Ltd.
Suite 1308, 13/F, Central Bldg, 1-3 Pedder Street, Central, H.K.
电话：+852-2530 2132
传真：+852-2558 4101
电邮：amy@jldsd.com
网址：www.jacksonlawsuite.com.hk

Mingcheng Enterprise
名成企业
上海市松江泗泾工业区九干路289号
邮编：201601
电话：021-5762 7111
传真：021-5762 6148
电邮：market@mingcheng.com.cn
网址：www.mingcheng.com.cn
请参阅第340、341页

源志誠
設計研發・織造染整・成品加工・電動產品・配套安裝・一體化銷售
Product Design & Development・Fabric Waving & Dying・Product Processi
Electrical Products・Complete Installation・Integration Sales Service
【工程经验优势】
我们拥有设计、生产织造、染整、配套加工、遮阳、电动等工程配套产品销售及安装服务，提供多元化的项目合作模式；公司的产品销售网络遍布全球五大洲，同时在多年的酒店项目运作中形成了国际顶级品牌酒店客户群，其中包括喜达屋酒店管理集团、香格里拉酒店集团、假日酒店集团、万豪酒店集团、索菲特集团等，与它们的成功合作使公司在同行和客户中赢得了非常高的声誉。
We have a strong operation model in design, weaving, dye, production and service, which forms as solid foundation for hotel project work. Yuanzhicheng business has spread to all over the world,, and successfully completed hundreds of hotel projects for five star hotels, example like: Sheraton, Shangri—la, Holiday Inn, Four Season, Marriott, Sofitel and etc. Our excellent service from beginning to end, has won high reputation in the line of hotel textiles project.
Yuanzhicheng
源志誠家紡
源志誠家紡有限公司
Yuanzhicheng Home Textile CO.,LTD.
www.yuanzhicheng.com
中国广东省广州市越秀区大南路62号
62-64#, Danan Road Yuexiu District Guangzhou, Guangdong Province,China. / Post Code: 510115
Tel: 86-20-83302177 / Fax: 86-20-83304376 / E-mail: yzc@yuanzhicheng.com

【我们服务过的品牌酒店客户】
Famous brand of hotel customers we offer service ever
Hotel Curtain & Uphdstery Experts
配套专家
酒店 家私 窗簾
布
www.yuanzhicheng.com
ZiQoo
THE PALMYRA
DOUBLETREE
HOTELS·SUITES·RESORTS·CLUBS
香格里拉酒店集團
SHANGRI-LA
HOTELS and RESORTS
FOUR SEASONS
Hotels and Resorts
GRAND LISBOA
Macau
C.KONG
INTERNATIONAL HOTEL
THE RITZ-CARLTON
HOTEL COMPANY, L.L.C.
INTERCONTINENTAL
HYATT
MARCO POLO
Sheraton
HOTELS & RESORTS
CROWNE PLAZA
SANYA
東方賓館
DONG FANG
HOTEL
ROYAL
GARDEN HOTEL
SOFITEL
Hilton
WESTIN
HOTELS & RESORTS
Holiday Inn
pullman

▼窗帘及布艺
Curtains & Draperies

Nantong Jingda Textile Corporation
南通泾达纺织装饰配套用品有限公司
江苏省南通市闸西工贸园兴隆路29号
邮编：226003
电话：0513-8556 4668
传真：0513-8556 7382
网址：www.nt-jd.cn

Nantong Sidefu Textile Decoration Co., Ltd.
南通斯得福纺织装饰有限公司
江苏省南通市永兴路52号
邮编：226005
电话：0513-8356 8888
传真：0513-8356 8600
电邮：sidefu@public.nt.js.cn
网址：www.sidefu-china.com

Shanghai Eurasitex Textile Co., Ltd.
上海阖达布艺有限公司
上海市闵行区吴中路1258号
中家缘欧美经典馆1楼和2楼
电话：021-5422 0567
传真：021-5422 0575
电邮：knox@eurasitex.com.cn
网址：www.eurasitex.com.cn

Shunde Good Brother Kolok Supplies Furnishings Designed Ltd.
佛山市顺德区哥好哥乐家饰用品设计有限公司
广东省佛山市高明区沧江纺织基地古孟工业园4号
电话：0757-8362 9331
传真：0757-8362 9330
电邮：gehaogele@126.com
网址：www.gehaogele.com

Sofamark Ltd.
梳化仓
香港九龙荔枝角长沙湾道748号地下
电话：+852-2959 2929
传真：+852-2959 2924
电邮：sofa@sofamark.com
网址：www.sofamark.com

Somfy China Co., Ltd.
尚飞中国
上海市华山路1520弄121号2楼
邮编：200052
电话：021-6280 9660
传真：021-6280 0270
网址：www.somfy.cn
请参阅第338、339页、封面

Yuanzhicheng Hometextile Co., Ltd.
源志诚家纺有限公司
广东省广州市越秀区大南路62号
邮编：510115
电话：020-8330 2177
传真：020-8330 4376
电邮：yzc@yuanzhicheng.com
网址：www.yuanzhicheng.com
请参阅第2、282、283页

佛山市丰业纤维有限公司
佛山市顺德区龙江镇325国道旁十里家私城107号
邮编：528318
电话：0757-2337 5028
传真：0757-2337 6603
电邮：shirmily@tom.com
网址：www.shirmily.com

广州志达纺织装饰有限公司
广东省佛山市顺德区龙江镇广湛路199号志达大厦
电话：0757-2388 2522
传真：0757-2388 2052
电邮：zhida@zhida.com
网址：www.zhida.cc

HunterDouglasHospitality

亨特制造（中国）有限公司
上海市闵行区光中路355号
邮编：201108
电话：021-3471 7777*131
传真：021-3471 7521
电邮：info@hunterdouglashospitality.com.cn
网址：www.hunterdouglashospitality.com.cn
业务范围：
作为国际知名的酒店布艺业务整体方案提供商，始创于1919年荷兰亨特道格拉斯集团一直专注于提供高星级酒店需求的酒店布艺、窗饰产品和电动轨道及智能控制系统等专业酒店产品。身为行业的领导者我们能够满足全球各地区高星级酒店对软装饰的个性化要求，为室内设计大师追求完美风格提供理想解决方案。
请参阅第274、275、276、277、278、279页

陕西西安晨曦布艺窗帘沙发
陕西省西安市大明宫建材家居城3楼6通道36号
邮编：710016
电话：029-8811 9592
传真：029-8811 9592
电邮：chenxiby@163.com
网址：www.chenxiby.cn

地板及墙面材料
Floor & Wall Coatings

Beijing Fu Mei Lai New Tectonic Material Co., Ltd.
北京福美来新型材料有限公司
北京市通州区张家湾镇南火堡村村委会南700米
电话：010-6958 6391
传真：010-6958 6392
电邮：bjfml@bjfml.com
网址：www.bjfml.com

Beijing Wuhua Development Co., Ltd.
北京物华恒通商贸有限公司
北京市朝阳区建国门外大街24号
华侨村1号楼802室
邮编：100022
电话：010-6515 9550
传真：010-6515 9550
电邮：admin@wuhuacorp.com
网址：www.woodsward.com.cn

Changzhou Jinhai Anti-Static PVC Floor Co., Ltd.
常州金海防静电地板有限公司
江苏省常州市武进雪堰雪湖北路3号
电话：0519-8615 8467
传真：0519-8615 5203
网址：www.china-xueyan.com

Foshan Rucca Wood Co., Ltd.
佛山市鲁卡木业有限公司
佛山市禅城区季华4路33号
创意产业园12栋401-403室
邮编：528000
电话：0757-8398 7999
传真：0757-8236 3114
电邮：ruccawood@163.com
网址：www.ruccawood.com

Fujian Huatai Group Co., Ltd.
福建华泰集团有限公司
福建省晋江市磁灶镇宝洋工业区
邮编：362217
电话：0595-8583 7801
传真：0595-8583 7802
网址：www.tob.com.cn

Jiaxing Only Stone Decorative Material Co., Ltd.
嘉兴欧丽装饰材料有限公司
浙江省嘉兴市嘉善县嘉善大道2188号
邮编：314100
电话：0573-8468 1686
传真：0573-8468 1687
电邮：market@sh-only.com
网址：www.sh-only.com

Linan Ailige Decorative Material Co., Ltd.
临安市艾丽格装饰材料有限公司
浙江省临安市锦城街道长桥村8-1号
电话：0571-6370 8686
传真：0571-6371 2788
电邮：airik@cnairik.com
网址：www.cnairik.com

Penglai Huasheng Electronic Co., Ltd.
山东蓬莱华升板材有限公司
山东省蓬莱市经济开发区
电话：0535-564 4484
传真：0535-564 2493
网址：www.hec-genor.com

Power Dekor
圣象集团
上海市宜山路508号景鸿大厦18层D座
邮编：200135
电话：021-6486 5566
传真：021-5425 6500
电邮：order@powerdekorgroup.com
网址：www.powerdekor.com.cn

Shanghai Huayuan New Composite Materails Co., Ltd.
上海华源复合新材料有限公司
上海市青浦区外青松公路6085号
邮编：201700
电话：021-5973 2001
传真：021-5972 7234
电邮：huayuanfu@online.sh.cn
网址：www.huayuanfu.com

Shanghai Jiuchao Building Decoration Materials Co., Ltd.
上海久潮建筑装饰材料有限公司
上海市虹口区东宝兴路157号精武大厦2603室
邮编：200080
电话：021-6529 0122
传真：021-6592 0980
电邮：shjc999@126.com
网址：www.shjc2008.cn

▼地板及墙面材料
Floor & Wall Coatings

Tetris Shanghai Office
荷兰亮世公司上海代表处
上海市浦东大道桃林路18号环球广场A座2208室
电话：021-5028 0250
传真：021-5028 2223
电邮：info@wood-be.com
网址：www.wood-be.com

Vicwood Industry (Suzhou) Co., Ltd.
维德木业（苏州）有限公司
苏州市国家高新技术产业开发区维德工业城
邮编：215151
电话：0512-6539 3117
传真：0512-6671 1444
电邮：info@vicwoodtimber.com.cn
网址：www.vicwoodtimber.com.cn

青岛元石壁纸有限公司
青岛市崂山区苗岭路29号山东高速大厦12B05
邮编：266100
电话：0532-8606 8811
传真：0532-8896 2720
电邮：wons777@188.com
网址：www.wons.cn

家具配饰
Furniture Accessories

Atdecotek
上海市程家桥支路201弄智地大厦F07室
电话：021-6268 5137
传真：021-6268 5137
电邮：sales@artdecotek.com
网址：www.artdecotek.com

Beijing Zai Xian Hui Huang Design Corp. Ltd.
北京市再现辉煌艺术设计有限公司
北京市通州区马驹桥镇郭村332号
邮编：101102
电话：010-6059 2995
电邮：zxhh@263.net
网址：www.bjzxhh.com

Boloni
博洛尼家居用品（北京）有限公司
北京市朝阳区育慧里11号
邮编：100101
电话：010-5134 8888
传真：010-5134 8810
电邮：hui@kebao.cn
网址：www.boloni.com.cn

Como Hardware Shanghai Co., Ltd.
科莫五金（上海）有限公司
上海市金山大道398号Y-9栋
邮编：201100
电话：021-6722 2888
传真：021-6722 2100
电邮：comosh@comosh.com
网址：www.comosh.com

Dongguan Jihua Hardware Products Co., Ltd.
东莞市基华五金制品有限公司
广东省东莞市石碣镇同德路刘屋
邮编：523303
电话：0769-8638 3122
传真：0769-8663 8991
电邮：jihua@gdjihua.com
网址：www.gdjihua.com

Mimoda Furnishing Co., Ltd.
米尚家居有限公司
广东省深圳市坂田镇吉通工业区门口
电话：0769-8588 0886
传真：0769-8588 0886
电邮：info@mimodafurn.com
网址：www.mimodafurn.com

Reappear Crafts Co., Ltd.
桂林市古之韵工艺品有限公司
广西省桂林市育才路55号
邮编：541003
电话：0773-361 2902
传真：0773-361 2902
网址：www.reappear.com.cn

Sino Trend Industries Co., Ltd.
广州中展信业有限公司
广东省广州市白云区均禾街长红村第二工业区
邮编：510430
电话：020-8609 7811
传真：020-8609 7892
电邮：sitty99@sitty.com.cn
网址：www.sitty.com.cn

Sugatsune Shanghai Co., Ltd.
世嘉智尼五金配件（上海）有限公司
上海市闸北区万荣一路2号一层
邮编：200436
电话：021-3632 1858
传真：021-3632 1868
电邮：lamp@sugatsune.com.cn
网址：www.sugatsune.com.cn
请参阅第353页、书脊下

上海大盟装饰材料有限公司
上海市闵行区澄建路248号
电话：021-6434 1170
传真：021-6434 1172
电邮：md-market@163.com
网址：www.bestvim.com

宴会家具
Furniture-Banquet

Changzhou Eafo Furniture Co., Ltd.
常州市易丰家具有限公司
江苏省常州市洛阳镇工业园区创新路7号
邮编：213104
电话：0519-8879 8845
传真：0519-8852 2310
电邮：info@eafo.cn
网址：www.eafo.cn

Beijing Kingmee Hotel Supplies Manufacturing Cenier
北京金和致美酒店用品制造中心
北京市大兴区团河工业区北2路17号
邮编：100046
电话：010-6128 1047
传真：010-6128 0744
电邮：kinmee2000@163.com
网址：www.kingmee.net

Beijing Sico-Sst Hospitality Equipment Manufacturing Co., Ltd.
北京西科盛世通酒店会展设备制造有限公司
北京市顺义天竺空港工业区B区安庆大街8号
邮编：101312
电话：010-8048 1587
传真：010-8048 2510
电邮：sales@sico-sst.com
网址：www.sico-sst.com

Dalian Xin Jian Hai Hotel Supplies & Trade Co.
大连新建海酒店用品贸易行
大连市沙河口区星海广场B3区一品星海6-3-1
电话：0411-8480 5299
传真：0411-8480 4111
电邮：xinjianhai@hotmail.com
网址：www.china-xjh.com

Foshan Nanhai ZhenMei Furniture Company
九江年年好家具有限公司
佛山市南海区九江镇梅圳会龙村
邮编：528230
电话：0757-8651 8123
传真：0757-8651 8132
电邮：jinmei222@163.com
网址：www.fszhenmei.com

Foshan Shunde Wanhaomei Furniture Co., Ltd.
佛山市顺德区迈豪美家具有限公司
佛山市顺德区龙江镇仙塘宝涌工业区西区一路
邮编：528318
电话：0757-2336 9345
传真：0757-2338 5699
网址：www.wanhaomei.com

Foshan Shunde Longjiang ZhaoHui Furniture
佛山市顺德区龙江镇朝辉家具有限公司
广东省佛山市顺德区325国道龙江路段308号
邮编：528319
电话：0757-2322 0878
传真：0757-8655 0808
电邮：master@zhao-hui.com
网址：www.zhao-hui.com

Foshan Style Metal Products Co., Ltd.
佛山喜泰来金属制品有限公司
广东省佛山市顺德区勒流镇连杜大道25-1号
邮编：528300
电话：0757-2867 0299
传真：0757-2867 0028
电邮：xitailai@xitailai.com
网址：www.xitailai.com
请参阅第286页

Fushan Furniture Co., Ltd.
富山家具有限公司
广东省佛山市顺德区龙江镇龙峰大道25号
邮编：528319
电话：0757-2388 9269
传真：0757-2322 6908
网址：www.fushan.com.cn

Guangan New Furniture Co., Ltd.
广安新家具有限公司
广东省佛山市南海区西樵镇朝山工业1区
电话：0757-8681 7888
传真：0757-8681 8238
电邮：info@ga-cn.com
网址：www.ga-cn.com

Guangdong Renel Industry Development Co., Ltd.
广东如蕾尔实业发展有限公司
广东省肇庆市高新区文德三街道7号
邮编：526238
电话：0758-362 6685
传真：0758-362 6686
电邮：renel@renelcn.com
网址：www.renelcn.com

Style®

喜泰来

佛山喜泰来金属制品有限公司是一家专业生产酒店宴会以及餐厅配套的厂家，主要产品有：酒店宴会铝椅，铁椅，折叠桌，舞台，推车，椅子套以及西餐厅家具用品，产品同时也适用于婚庆和会议！

我们公司从原材料的选择到成品的生产都有一系列的管理体系严格的控制质量，近年来，我们的产品因为产品质量好，款式新颖，售后服务好在新老客户中享有很高的声誉！

在未来的日子里，我们将继续扩大努力，加大投入，生产一流品质的产品；以实惠的价格，与广大新老客户互惠互利，达到双赢，携手进步，共创辉煌。

Foshan Style Metal Products Co;Ltd (Xitailai Banquet Furniture) has been dedicated to production, development and sales of hotel banquet furniture. It has advanced manufaturing facilities and perfect production techniques for all hotel banquet aluminum chairs, steel chairs, foldable banquet tables, movable stage transport carts, dancing floors and screens, chair covers and so on. Our products are deeply loved by domestic and foreign customers, selling well throughout the world.

佛山喜泰来金属制品有限公司
广东省佛山市顺德区勒流镇连杜大道25-1号
邮编：528300
电话：0086-757-28670299 / 28670007　传真：0086-757-28670028
电子邮箱：xitailai@xitailai.com　style_xitailai@yahoo.cn
网址：http://www.xitailai.com

FOSHAN STYLE METAL PRODUCTS CO.,LTD
NO.25-1, LIANDU ROAD, LELIU TOWN, SHUNDE, FOSHAN CITY, GUANGDONG, CH
POST CODE: 528300
TEL: 0086-757-28670299 / 28670007　FAX: 0086-757-28670028
EMAIL: xitailai@xitailai.com　style_xitailai@yahoo.cn
Webpage: http://www.xitailai.com

▼宴会家具
Furniture-Banquet

Guangzhou Jingong Hotel Furnishings Co., Ltd.
广州市金宫酒店家具有限公司
广州市越秀区建设横马路2号宸宇大厦4楼409室
邮编：510060
电话：020-3741 0806
传真：020-8376 6480
电邮：china@jingong.net.cn
网址：www.jingong.net.cn

Halmey Hotel Furniture Manufrcture Co., Ltd.
广州番禺恒美酒店金属家具制造有限公司
广东省广州市番禺区大石镇河村工业区
邮编：511430
电话：020-8478 9338
传真：020-8478 7838
电邮：sales@chinahalmay.com
网址：www.chinahalmay.com

New Idea Hotel Furniture Co., Ltd.
佛山市南海新思路酒店家具制造有限公司
佛山市南海黄岐沙溪工业区涌泉路12-13号
邮编：528248
电话：0757-8591 5691
传真：0757-8591 5737
电邮：slp-newidea@126.com
网址：www.slp.com.cn

Nikko Great Time Hotel Supplies Ltd.
伟时（广州）酒店用品供应有限公司
广东省广州市天河区林和西路9号
耀中广场B座706房
电话：020-8527 0243
传真：020-8527 0347
请参阅第48、49页

Shanghai Deyi Hotel Articles Manufacture Co., Ltd.
上海德义酒店用品制造有限公司
上海市民星路201号20号楼
邮编：200433
电话：021-5169 9518
传真：021-5126 2385
网址：www.sh-dy.com
请参阅第414页

Shanghai Via-Trade Hotel Equipment Co., Ltd.
上海灏晟酒店设备用品有限公司
上海市黄浦区中山南路505号13号楼106室
邮编：200010
电话：021-6152 6733
传真：021-6152 6739
电邮：service@via-trade.com.cn
网址：www.via-trade.com.cn

Sofamark Ltd.
梳化仓
香港九龙荔枝角长沙湾道748号地下
电话：+852-2959 2929
传真：+852-2959 2924
电邮：sofa@sofamark.com
网址：www.sofamark.com

Wallyjade Hotel Appliance Factory
北京威尔金顿酒店用品厂
北京市大兴区北臧经济开发区
邮编：102609
电话：010-6125 2575
传真：010-6125 2577
电邮：bjwallyjade@163.com
网址：www.wallyjade.com

Wuxi Mingtai Plastic & Metal Products Manufacturing Co., Ltd.
无锡铭泰塑钢制造有限公司
江苏省宜兴市经济开发区屺亭镇前红村
邮编：214213
电话：0510-8782 1218
传真：0510-8782 1268
网址：www.wxmtsg.cn

Yuantai Hotel Furniture Factory
佛山市源泰酒店家具厂
广东省佛山市南海区沙头石江工业区2马路2号
电话：0757-8651 5576
传真：0757-8651 5517
电邮：fsyt10@yahoo.com.cn
网址：www.yuantaijiaju.com

Zhenmei Furniture
臻美家具
广东省佛山市南海区九江镇梅圳会龙村
邮编：528203
电话：0757-8651 8123
传真：0757-8651 8132
电邮：zm@fszhenmei.com
网址：www.fszhenmei.com

佛山市南海区永隆家具厂
佛山市南海区九龙沙头水南工业区
电话：0757-8691 4738
传真：0757-8691 0889
电邮：cnyonglong@163.com
网址：www.gdyonglong.com

家具经销商
Furniture Dealers

Atdecotek
上海市程家桥支路201弄智地大厦F07室
电话：021-6268 5137
传真：021-6268 5137
电邮：sales@artdecotek.com
网址：www.artdecotek.com

Dongguan Chang Shi Furniture Co., Ltd.
东莞市长实家具有限公司
广东省东莞市厚街镇新塘管理区
邮编：523949
电话：0769-8559 3272
传真：0769-8559 2781
电邮：chang-shi2009@163.com
网址：www.chang-shi.com

Dongguan Zhirun Furniture Co., Ltd.
东莞市志润家具有限公司
广东省东莞市谢岗镇曹乐格塘村
邮编：523590
电话：0769-8776 5301
传真：0769-8768 4309
电邮：zhirun666@163.com
网址：www.zrmuye.com

KENAS Lifestyle
库诗
上海市虹口区沙泾路10号
1933老场坊1号楼1-104室
电话：021-6513 9316
传真：021-6513 9317
电邮：shop@kenas.cn
网址：www.kenas.cn
请参阅第297页

Shanghai Yun Sheng Trading Co., Ltd.
上海允晟贸易有限公司
上海市密林路1018号901室
电话：021-5506 1481
传真：021-5506 1483
电邮：stressless@worldofcomfort.com.cn
网址：www.worldofcomfort.com.cn

Sofamark Ltd.
梳化仓
香港九龙荔枝角长沙湾道748号地下
电话：+852-2959 2929
传真：+852-2959 2924
电邮：sofa@sofamark.com
网址：www.sofamark.com

Supreme Furniture (Kunshan) Co., Ltd.
首邦家具（昆山）有限公司
昆山市经济开发区太湖支二路7号
邮编：215335
电话：0512-5763 9596
传真：0512-5763 9598
电邮：ng.soonheng@uhui.com.cn
网址：www.lorenzo-international.com

酒店家私
Furniture-Hotels

Beijing Kingmee Hotel Supplies Manufacturing Cenier
北京金和致美酒店用品制造中心
北京市大兴区团河工业区北2路17号
邮编：100046
电话：010-6128 1047
传真：010-6128 0744
电邮：kinmee2000@163.com
网址：www.kingmee.net

Beijing Zai Xian Hui Huang Design Corp. Ltd.
北京市再现辉煌艺术设计有限公司
北京市通州区马驹桥镇郭村332号
邮编：101102
电话：010-6059 2995
电邮：zxhh@263.net
网址：www.bjzxhh.com

Bigwig House Furniture Manufacturing Co., Ltd.
广东大公馆家具制造有限公司
广东省东莞市厚街镇陈屋管理区
邮编：523942
电话：0769-8589 8608
传真：0769-8589 8208
电邮：bigwig@vip.163.com
网址：www.bigwig.cn

Boloni
博洛尼家居用品（北京）有限公司
北京市朝阳区育慧里11号
邮编：100101
电话：010-5134 8888
传真：010-5134 8810
电邮：hui@kebao.cn
网址：www.boloni.com.cn

Chinart Woodware Factory
东莞市中艺木业制品厂
东莞市厚街涌口华发工业区8号
邮编：523947
电话：0769-8559 6393
传真：0769-8591 4122
电邮：business@omnitron.cc
网址：www.omnitron.cc

▼酒店家私
Furniture-Hotels

Fenabel, Lda.
Rua das Fontainhas, 162
P.O.Box32
4589-907 Rebordosa
Porto-Portugal
电话：+351-224 119 120
传真：+351-224 119 129
电邮：fenabel@fenabel.com
网址：www.fenabel.com
请参阅第 288、289 页

Fookyik Furniture Co., Ltd.
福溢家具有限公司
广东省中山市板芙镇顺景工业园
邮编：528459
电话：0760-8651 1507
传真：0760-8650 3639
电邮：akitty@fookyikfurniture.com
网址：www.fookyik.com

Foshan Artisan Furniture Co., Ltd.
佛山市艺匠家具有限公司
广东省佛山市顺德区325国道
龙江路段时代广场34号家居生活贵族馆
邮编：528319
电话：0757-2808 9228
传真：0757-2808 9223
网址：www.foshanartisan.com
请参阅第 296 页

Guangdong ZhongTai Furniture Industry Co., Ltd.
广东中泰家具实业有限公司
广东省佛山市顺德区325国道龙江路段世埠长路口
邮编：528319
电话：0757-2388 2138
传真：0757-2388 2130
网址：www.zhong-tai.net
请参阅第 293 页

Hong Kong Royal Furniture
香港皇朝家私集团有限公司
广东省增城仙村镇皇朝家私工业区
邮编：511335
电话：020-8294 6362
传真：020-8294 3725
电邮：hkroyal@public.guangzhou.gd.cn
网址：www.hkroyal.com

Housen Forniture Corporation
深圳市华源轩股份有限公司
深圳市龙岗区同乐社区水流田园新路22号
邮编：518116
电话：0755-8487 3888
传真：0755-8487 3999
电邮：xsc@cn-furniture.com
网址：www.cn-furniture.com

Hua Wei Furniture (Hong Kong) International Group Co., Ltd.
华伟家私（香港）国际集团公司
广东省东莞市厚街镇涌口华伟路16-19号
邮编：523947
电话：0769-8559 9777
传真：0769-8581 9777
电邮：market@huaweigroup.com
网址：www.huaweigroup.com

Jiang Feng Furniture Ltd.
上海江丰家具有限公司
上海市闵行区华漕镇北翟路1630弄51号
电话：021-6220 4945
传真：021-6270 7801
电邮：weber@staruss.com
yeongjin@staruss.com
网址：www.homie.cc
请参阅第 290 页

Jinan Yate Furniture Co., Ltd.
济南雅特家私有限责任公司
山东省济南市工业北路201号
邮编：250100
电话：0531-8896 6106
传真：0531-8861 0286
电邮：yate1992@yahoo.com.cn
网址：www.yatefurniture.com

KENAS Lifestyle
库诗
上海市虹口区沙泾路10号
1933老场坊1号楼1-104室
电话：021-6513 9316
传真：021-6513 9317
电邮：shop@kenas.cn
网址：www.kenas.cn
请参阅第 297 页

Maxxa International Limited
美兆国际有限公司
广东省广州市中山六路2号新宝利大厦2006-7室
邮编：510180
电话：020-8326 6222
传真：020-8326 6555
电邮：margaret@maxxa.com
网址：www.maxxa.com

Rongfeng Furniture Co., Ltd.
融峰家具有限公司
广东省东莞市厚街镇家具大道双岗村委会后
邮编：523948
电话：0769-8599 8907
传真：0769-8599 8460
电邮：rf_furniture@163.com

Shanghai Etna Furniture Co., Ltd.
上海林南家具有限公司
上海市徐汇区漕溪北路88号圣爱广场1411室
邮编：200030
电话：021-5784 5366
传真：021-5784 5377
网址：www.etna.com.cn

Shanghai Joybells Enterrise Co., Ltd.
上海淳艺家饰有限公司
上海市闵行区华翔路1195号
邮编：201106
电话：021-5227 0740
传真：021-5227 0742
电邮：frank@garden-leisure.cn
网址：www.garden-leisure.cn

Shanghai Kent Furniture Co., Ltd.
上海肯特酒店家具专业制造厂
上海市浦东新区川沙镇吴店路88号
邮编：201202
电话：021-5859 6488
传真：021-5859 8747
电邮：shkent2007@gmail.com
网址：www.shkent.com

Shanghai Pengju Furniture Co., Ltd.
帕克洛蒂
上海奉贤区奉城镇奉城工业园区奉旺路688号
邮编：201411
电话：021-5751 0583
传真：021-5755 0594
电邮：zhengzhiyun@egatt.cn
网址：www.egatt.cn

Shanghai QiYi Fumiture & Decoration Co., Ltd.
上海琦艺家具装饰有限公司
上海市松江区新浜工业园区林天路392-397号
邮编：201605
电话：021-6789 1469
传真：021-6789 1499
电邮：qiyibq@126.com
网址：www.qiyish.com
请参阅第 298 页

Shunde Meihua Furniture Manufacture Company Ltd.
顺德区美化家私制造有限公司
佛山市顺德区龙江镇华西工业区154号
邮编：528319
电话：0757-2388 0368
传真：0757-2322 3368
电邮：mh@china-meihua.com
网址：www.china-meihua.com

Stylution Int'l (China) Corp.
运时通（中国）家具有限公司
广东省东莞市大岭山镇百花洞村
厚大公路侧（百花洞工业区）
电话：0769-8335 8888
传真：0769-8563 7077
网址：www.beddingplaza.com
请参阅第 398、399 页

Tianyi Furnisings Co., Ltd.
天一·美家
东莞市厚街镇第壹城家具博览中心
电话：0769-8863 3896
传真：0769-8863 8768
网址：www.sztianyi.com

YaBo Hotel Furniture Industry Co., Ltd.
广东雅柏家具实业有限公司
广东省佛山市南海区九江镇沙咀工业园
电话：0757-8186 6999
传真：0757-8186 6000
电邮：sales@sdyabo.com
网址：www.sdyabo.com
请参阅第 291 页

Yi Mei Furniture Industrial Co., Ltd. Dongguan
东莞市意美家具实业有限公司
东莞市厚街镇家具大道22号（国际会展中心侧）
邮编：523948
电话：0769-8590 3668
传真：0769-8590 6889
电邮：yimei.163@vip.163.com
网址：www.yimeifurniture.com

▼酒店家私
Furniture-Hotels

Zhejiang Yufeng Hotel Furniture Manufacturing Co., Ltd.
浙江愈丰酒店家具制造有限公司
温州市瓯海区瓯海农业高新工业园仙门路134号
邮编：325000
电话：0577-8605 9001
传真：0577-8605 9003
电邮：wzyufeng@gmail.com
网址：www.0577yf.com

北京恒鑫雅酒店用品有限公司
北京市大兴区魏善庄开发区吴庄街
邮编：102611
电话：010-8920 4136
传真：010-8920 2963
电邮：hallsia@126.com
网址：www.hallsia.com

北京黎明文仪家具有限公司
北京市朝阳区东三环南路58号富顿B座10层
邮编：100022
电话：010-5867 2727
传真：010-5867 2976
电邮：osidea@126.com
网址：www.lmfu.com

佛山市南海区永隆家具厂
佛山市南海区九龙沙头水南工业区
电话：0757-8691 4738
传真：0757-8691 0889
电邮：cnyonglong@163.com
网址：www.gdyonglong.com

佛山市迅发德盛家具实业有限公司
佛山市顺德区北滘镇广珠路林头段
邮编：528311
电话：0757-2665 2012
传真：0757-2665 2129
网址：www.xunfajj.cn.alibaba.com

上海馨瑞家具有限公司
上海市浦东新区川六公路1018号
电话：13701710279
传真：021-5859 9297
电邮：hotel@rosa-furniture.com
请参阅第292页

家具制造商
Furniture Manufacturers

Changzhou Eafo Furniture Co., Ltd.
常州市易丰家具有限公司
江苏省常州市洛阳镇工业园区创新路7号
邮编：213104
电话：0519-8879 8845
传真：0519-8852 2310
电邮：info@eafo.cn
网址：www.eafo.cn

Alma Contract (Holdings) Limited
澳马集团有限公司
广州市番禺区洛溪新城莱茵学院410室
邮编：511431
电话：020-2287 6233
传真：020-2287 6210
电邮：info@almacontract.com
网址：www.almacontract.com

Asian Land Furniture (Shenzhen) Co., Ltd.
亚陆家具制造（深圳）有限公司
深圳市龙岗区坪地镇中心社区富民路泥陂工业区
电话：0755-8409 6606
传真：0755-8409 6639
网址：www.yalus.com

Beijing Aboss Furniture Manufacturing Co., Ltd.
北京世纪京洲家具有限责任公司
北京市大兴区生物医药产业基地天华街39号
邮编：102629
电话：010-6027 3005
传真：010-6027 0707
网址：www.iboss.cc

Bigwig House Furniture Manufacturing Co., Ltd.
广东大公馆家具制造有限公司
广东省东莞市厚街镇陈屋管理区
邮编：523942
电话：0769-8589 8608
传真：0769-8589 8208
电邮：bigwig@vip.163.com
网址：www.bigwig.cn

Boloni
博洛尼家居用品（北京）有限公司
北京市朝阳区育慧里11号
邮编：100101
电话：010-5134 8888
传真：010-5134 8810
电邮：hui@kebao.cn
网址：www.boloni.com.cn

Chinart Woodware Factory
东莞市中艺木业制品厂
东莞市厚街涌口华发工业区8号
邮编：523947
电话：0769-8559 6393
传真：0769-8591 4122
电邮：business@omnitron.cc
网址：www.omnitron.cc

Dajin Furniture Co., Ltd.
顺德达晋酒店家具有限公司
广东省佛山市顺德区龙江镇
仙塘宝涌工业区三路6号
电话：0757-2322 3433
传真：0757-2322 0289
电邮：dajin@globai-gatc.info
网址：www.dajin-f.com

Elger Furniture Group Ltd.
镇江艾格尔家居有限公司
江苏省镇江市长江路35号宾江1号商务公馆413室
邮编：212000
电话：0511-8508 0500
传真：0511-8528 5600
电邮：jackcnsh@gmail.com
网址：www.eiger.en.alibaba.com

Enlanda
爱蒙床垫
广东省惠州市大亚湾经济技术开发区
西区敏华工业城
电话：0752-528 2559
电邮：hotel-china@enlanda.com
网址：www.enlanda.com
请参阅第397页、封底

Fenabel, Lda.
Rua das Fontainhas, 162
P.O.Box32
4589-907 Rebordosa
Porto-Portugal
电话：+351-224 119 120
传真：+351-224 119 129
电邮：fenabel@fenabel.com
网址：www.fenabel.com
请参阅第288、289页

Foshan Artisan Furniture Co., Ltd.
佛山市艺匠家具有限公司
广东省佛山市顺德区325国道
龙江路段时代广场34号家居生活贵族馆
邮编：528319
电话：0757-2808 9228
传真：0757-2808 9223
网址：www.foshanartisan.com
请参阅第296页

Foshan City Shunde District, Heng Yang Hotel Furniture Factory
佛山市恒扬酒店家具有限公司
广东省佛山市顺德区龙江镇旺岗工业区联新路9号
电话：0757-2866 3608
传真：0757-2866 3609
电邮：guangdong@fs-hy.cc
网址：www.fs-hy.cc

Foshan Fushan Furniture Factory
佛山市顺德区富山家具厂
佛山市顺德区龙江镇龙峰大道25号
电话：0757-2388 9272
传真：0757-2322 6908
网址：www.fushan.com.cn

Foshan Kian China Furniture Company Limited
健（香港）有限公司
广东省佛山市南海区狮山镇
小塘新城星星工业园9号厂房
邮编：825000
电话：0757-8550 4078
传真：0757-8550 4100
电邮：waisonzhong@kain.com.cn
网址：www.kian.com

Foshan Shunde Wanhaomei Furniture Co., Ltd.
佛山市顺德区迈豪美家具有限公司
佛山市顺德区龙江镇仙塘宝涌工业区西区一路
邮编：528318
电话：0757-2336 9345
传真：0757-2338 5699
网址：www.wanhaomei.com

Foshan Shunde Shenghaomei Furniture Co., Ltd.
佛山市顺德区盛豪美家具制造有限公司
广东省佛山市顺德区龙江镇新龙工业区
邮编：528319
电话：0757-2387 0383
传真：0757-2387 0387
电邮：shenghaomei@vip.163.com
网址：www.shenghaomei.com

Guangdong Meige Furniture
广东美阁家具
广东省佛山市顺德区龙江镇涌口工业区优越路
邮编：528318
电话：0757-2322 8712
传真：0757-2387 0718
电邮：mg9988@163.com
网址：www.meige-china.com

Aristo Party®
—— 贵族Party
鼎盛傳世·奢華瀲灩

库诗 | KENAS®
EUROPEAN
LIVING
我们把温馨舒适的生活带入中国
欢迎您来我们的陈列室亲身感受
Kenas Lifestyle Furniture Store at 1933
Open 7 days a week
Monday - Sunday 10AM- 7PM
上海市虹口区上沙泾路10号 1933老场坊1号楼1-104室
Address: 1933 | 10 Shajing Road | Unit 1-104
Hongkou District | Shanghai
T: 021 6513 9316 | F: 021 6513 9317 | E: shop@kenas.cn

Trans Mart Group Ltd.

东莞市全世贸易有限公司

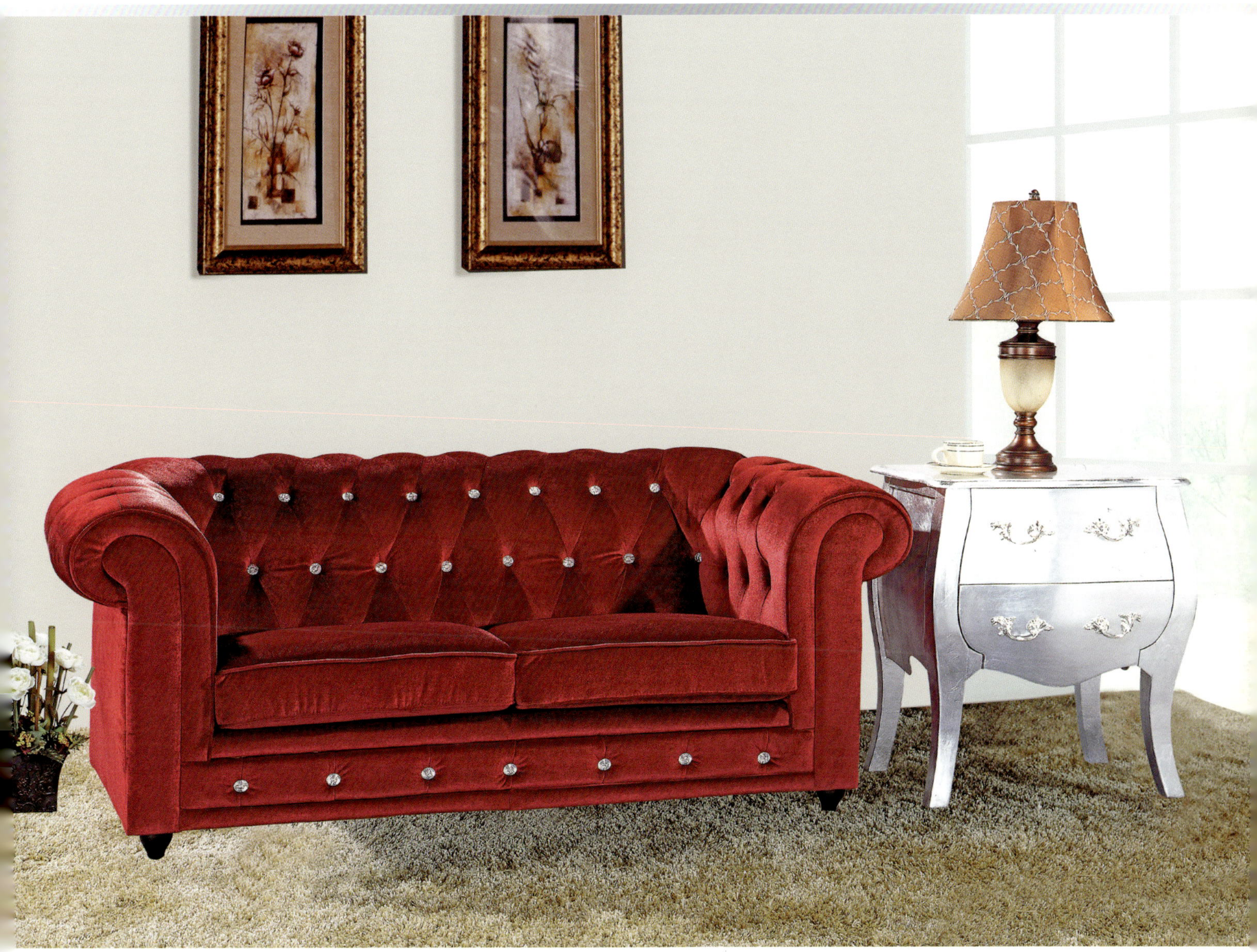

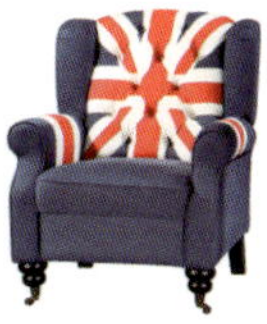

RB-644

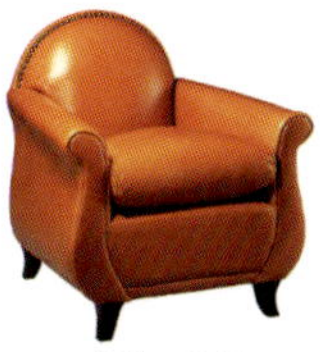

RB-940

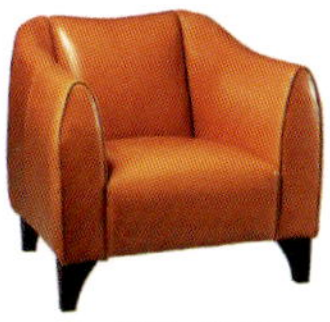

RB-939

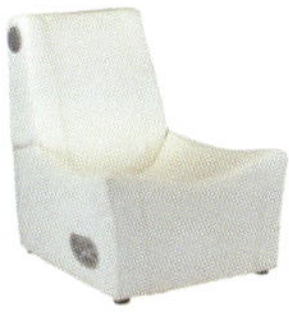

RB-1070

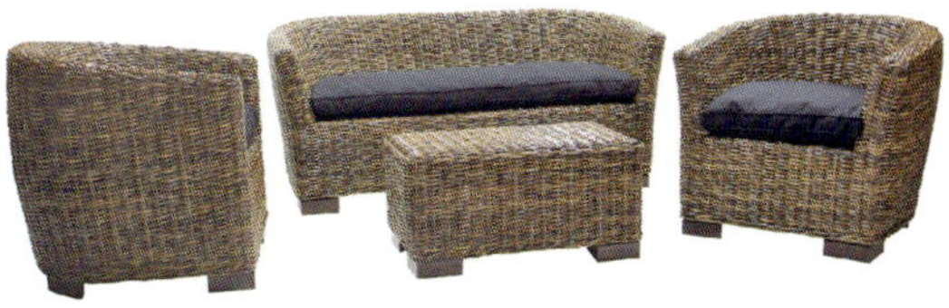

TRF-6462

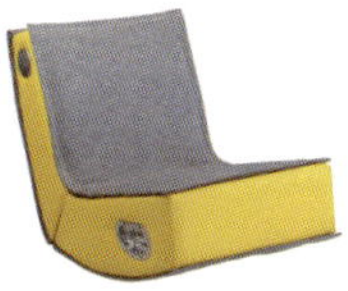

RB-1072

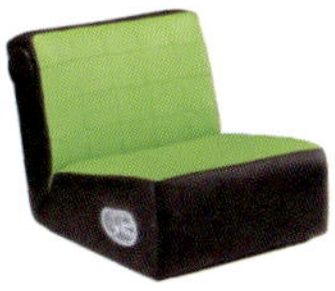

RB-1068

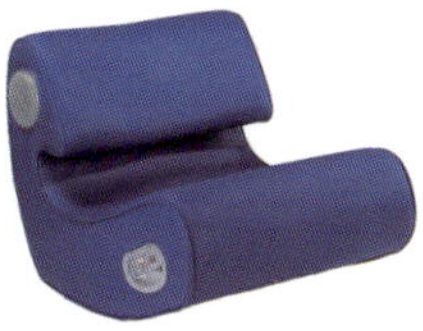

RB-1069

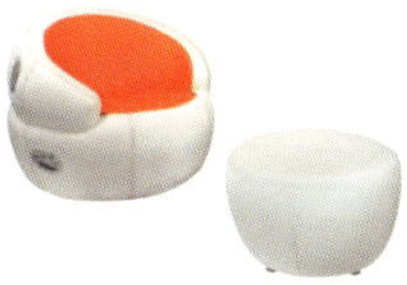

RB-1071

台湾公司
Tel：+886-3-427-2885（代表号）
Fax：+886-3-425-6350
Email：tmltwnin@ms17.hinet.net

中国公司
Tel：+86-769-86409200 （代表号）
Fax：+86-769-86409500
Email：transmart@china.com

印尼公司
Tel：+62-21-6348328（代表号）
Fax：+62-21-6348330
Email：tml@cbn.net.id

东莞贸易部地址：广东省东莞市茶山镇丽江豪园商铺，C-7 三楼　邮政编码：523399
公司网址：http://transmart.en.furnitureinchina.com

▼家具制造商
Furniture Manufacturers

Guangdong ZhongTai Furniture Industry Co., Ltd.
广东中泰家具实业有限公司
广东省佛山市顺德区325国道龙江路段世埠长路口
邮编：528319
电话：0757-2388 2138
传真：0757-2388 2130
网址：www.zhong-tai.net
请参阅第293页

Guangzhou Catering Concept Metal Hotel Euriniture Manufacture Co., Ltd.
广州市理念酒店金属家具制造有限公司
广州市番禺区大石街石北工业大道
石北工业区大维路段自编19号
邮编：511430
电话：020-8479 5444
传真：020-8479 6299
电邮：ccln@vip.sina.com
网址：www.cateringconcept.com

Guangzhou Huajin Hotel Furniture Co., Ltd.
广州华晋酒店家具有限公司
广东省广州市番禺区禺山西路大平村工贸园J座
邮编：511400
电话：020-2287 9266
传真：020-3481 7078
电邮：gzhj88@163.com
网址：www.gzhuajin.com.cn

Heshan Baihui Furniture Manufacturing Co., Ltd.
鹤山市百晖家具制造有限公司
广东省鹤山市港口路368号
邮编：527900
电话：0750-841 1991
传真：0750-841 8868
电邮：baihuijiaju@126.com
网址：www.baihuijiaju.com

Homeyoung Group
新红阳集团
广东省鹤山桃源镇富民工业区
电话：0750-877 9966
传真：0750-877 9588
网址：www.xhy.com.cn

HongKong Creation Furniture Co., Ltd.
香港创新家具有限公司
Daluosha Administrative District, Creation Furniture Industry Zone, Daojiao Town, Dongguan Ctiy, China
邮编：523170
电话：0769-8831 9888
传真：0769-8838 8228
电邮：creation168@sohu.net
网址：www.creation2000.com

Hua Wei Furniture (Hong Kong) International Group Co., Ltd.
华伟家私（香港）国际集团公司
广东省东莞市厚街镇涌口华伟路16-19号
邮编：523947
电话：0769-8559 9777
传真：0769-8581 9777
电邮：market@huaweigroup.com
网址：www.huaweigroup.com

Jackson Law Properties & Sefas Design Ltd.
Suite 1308, 13/F, Central Bldg
1-3 Pedder Street, Central, H.K.
电话：+852-2530 2132
传真：+852-2558 4101
电邮：amy@jldsd.com
网址：www.jacksonlawsuite.com.hk

Jiang Feng Furniture Ltd.
上海江丰家具有限公司
上海市闵行区华漕镇北翟路1630弄51号
电话：021-6220 4945
传真：021-6270 7801
电邮：weber@staruss.com
yeongjin@staruss.com
网址：www.homie.cc
请参阅第290页

Jilin Forest Industry Group Huaying Wood Furniture Co., Ltd.
吉林森工华英家具有限责任公司
吉林省长春市长吉北路888号
邮编：130032
电话：0431-8471 0116
传真：0431-8472 0889
电邮：huaying@hywoods.com
网址：www.hywoods.com

库诗 KENAS®

KENAS Lifestyle
库诗
上海市虹口区沙泾路10号
1933老场坊1号楼1-104室
电话：021-6513 9316
传真：021-6513 9317
电邮：shop@kenas.cn
网址：www.kenas.cn
业务范围：
KENAS—家居生活时尚引领者，创立于1995年，我们不仅是一个国际规模的家具制造商，也是多个家居展览奖项得主的家具设计公司。一直以来，KENAS以稳固的品质和不断出新的设计走在家居产业前列。KENAS拥有高效率的内部设计团队，以设计出最新的现代欧式家具，在末道漆和材料的处理上尤为独特，追求完美。
KENAS在2009年夏季首次踏入中国市场，并命名零售品牌为「库诗 - KENAS Lifestyle」，我们的第一家旗舰店开设于上海虹口区的1933老场坊内。
请参阅第297页

Kuka Techincs Sofa Manufacture Co., Ltd.
浙江顾家工艺沙发制造有限公司
杭州市下沙经济技术开发区11号大街113号
电话：0571-8675 5388
传真：0571-8675 5188
网址：www.kukasofa.com

Maxxa International Limited
美兆国际有限公司
广东省广州市中山六路2号新宝利大厦2006-7室
邮编：510180
电话：020-8326 6222
传真：020-8326 6555
电邮：margaret@maxxa.com
网址：www.maxxa.com

Mingmeixuan Furniture Industrial Co., Ltd.
名美轩实业有限公司
广东省佛山市顺德区龙江镇涌口开发区冠业路8号
邮编：528318
电话：0757-2337 0900
传真：0757-2337 0903
电邮：sdmmx1328@163.com
网址：www.mingmeixuan.com

Nasca Furniture Co., Ltd.
纳斯卡家具有限公司
苏州市相城大道1539号嘉元广场1605室
电话：400 887 5299
传真：0512-6586 6999
网址：www.nascasofa.com

New Idea Hotel Furniture Co., Ltd.
佛山市南海新思路酒店家具制造有限公司
佛山市南海黄岐沙溪工业区涌泉路12-13号
邮编：528248
电话：0757-8591 5691
传真：0757-8591 5737
电邮：slp-newidea@126.com
网址：www.slp.com.cn

Ningbo Hengsen Furniture Co., Ltd.
宁波亨森家私制造有限公司
浙江省宁波市镇海镇电西路21号
邮编：315200
电话：0574-8628 1586
传真：0574-8626 3938
电邮：info@nbhengsen.com
网址：www.nbhengsen.com

Orient Sino (GZ) Industrial Corp. Ltd.
广州东恩贸易有限公司
广州市天河北路合晖街200号御晖苑3楼
邮编：510610
电话：020-3849 2067
传真：020-3849 1362
电邮：info@orientsino.com
网址：www.orientsino.com
请参阅第305页

Rongfeng Furniture Co., Ltd.
融峰家具有限公司
广东省东莞市厚街镇家具大道双岗村委会后
邮编：523948
电话：0769-8599 8907
传真：0769-8599 8460
电邮：rf_furniture@163.com

Senyuan Furniture Group
森源家具集团
福建省南安市康美镇森源工业园森源家具
邮编：362300
电话：0595-8665 7888
传真：0595-8595 7889
网址：www.senyuan.com

Shanghai Aureole Furniture Decoration Co., Ltd.
上海澳瑞家具装饰有限公司
上海市宝山区月浦工业园区园和路217号
邮编：200941
电话：021-5692 7288
传真：021-5692 7588
电邮：aureole@aureolesh.com
网址：www.aureolesh.com

▼家具制造商
Furniture Manufacturers

Shanghai Canghai Cane Industry Co., Ltd.
上海苍海藤业有限公司
上海市青浦区外青松公路7900号
电话：021-6920 9960
传真：021-6920 9960
电邮：shchty@companyqp.com
网址：www.shchty.com

Shanghai Kent Furniture Co., Ltd.
上海肯特酒店家具专业制造厂
上海市浦东新区川沙镇吴店路88号
邮编：201202
电话：021-5859 6488
传真：021-5859 8747
电邮：shkent2007@gmail.com
网址：www.shkent.com

Shanghai QiYi Fumiture & Decoration Co., Ltd.
上海琦艺家具装饰有限公司
上海市松江区新浜工业园区林天路392-397号
邮编：201605
电话：021-6789 1469
传真：021-6789 1499
电邮：qiyibq@126.com
网址：www.qiyish.com
请参阅第298页

Shanghai Shenglin Furniture Co., Ltd.
上海升林家具有限公司
上海市宝山区沪太路6058弄
邮编：201908
电话：021-6601 1377
传真：021-6601 1377
电邮：sales@sh-shenglin.com
网址：www.sh-shenglin.com

Shanghai Ying Yue Outdoor Furniture Co., Ltd.
上海映月（户外）家具有限公司
上海市青浦区徐泾华徐公路666号
电话：021-6102 6456
传真：021-3980 7960
电邮：aufreesh@hotmail.com
网址：www.aufree.cn

Shanghai YunDian Mahogany Furniture Co., Ltd.
上海允典红木家具有限公司
上海市闵行区金都路1515号
邮编：201108
电话：021-6497 6100
传真：021-6497 2266
电邮：123433811@qq.com
网址：www.yundian.com

Shida Furniture Factory
顺德时大酒店家具厂
广东省佛山市顺德区龙江镇仙塘工业区朝阳路26号
邮编：518319
电话：0757-2338 3301
传真：0757-2338 3378
电邮：sdshida@vip.163.com
网址：www.shidajiaju.cn

Sofamark Ltd.
梳化仓
香港九龙荔枝角长沙湾道748号地下
电话：+852-2959 2929
传真：+852-2959 2924
电邮：sofa@sofamark.com
网址：www.sofamark.com

Stylution Int'l (China) Corp.
运时通（中国）家具有限公司
广东省东莞市大岭山镇百花洞村
厚大公路侧（百花洞工业区）
电话：0769-8335 8888
传真：0769-8563 7077
网址：www.beddingplaza.com
请参阅第398、399页

Tianyi Furnisings Co., Ltd.
天一·美家
东莞市厚街镇第壹城家具博览中心
电话：0769-8863 3896
传真：0769-8863 8768
网址：www.sztianyi.com

Trans Mart Group Ltd.
东莞市全世贸易有限公司
广东省东莞市茶山镇丽江豪园商铺，C-7三楼
邮编：523399
电话：0769-8640 9200
传真：0769-8640 9500
电邮：transmart@china.com
网址：http://transmart.en.furnitureinchina.com
请参阅第299页

Wegmans Furniture Industries Sdn. Bhd.
伟迈家具有限公司
12 rue de la Boissellerie 67580, Mertzwiller, France
电话：+33-3889 03107
传真：+33-3889 01985
网址：www.weberlifestyle.com

Wuxi Mingtai Plastic & Metal Products Manufacturing Co., Ltd.
无锡铭泰塑钢制造有限公司
江苏省宜兴市经济开发区屺亭镇前红村
邮编：214213
电话：0510-8782 1218
传真：0510-8782 1268
网址：www.wxmtsg.cn

Wuxi Senlong Furniture Factory Co., Ltd.
无锡市森隆家具厂
无锡市新区鸿山镇后宅东塘街
邮编：214145
电话：0510-8899 0291
传真：0510-8899 4885
网址：www.wxsljj.com

Yaubong Furniture Co., Ltd.
广东省佛山市优榜家具有限公司
广东省佛山市南海区西樵新田工业区
邮编：528211
电话：0757-8686 8638
传真：0757-8686 8330
电邮：feng@yaubong-meidi.com
网址：www.yaubong-meidi.com

Yi Mei Furniture Industrial Co., Ltd. Dongguan
东莞市意美家具实业有限公司
东莞市厚街镇家具大道22号（国际会展中心侧）
邮编：523948
电话：0769-8590 3668
传真：0769-8590 6889
电邮：yimei.163@vip.163.com
网址：www.yimeifurniture.com

Yuda Furniture Co., Ltd.
广东裕达家具有限公司
广东省佛山市南海区里水镇大冲工业管理区
电话：0757-8566 8166
传真：0757-8560 5528
电邮：nh85605528@126.com
网址：www.yudafurniture.com

Zhejiang Yufeng Hotel Furniture Manufacturing Co., Ltd.
浙江愈丰酒店家具制造有限公司
温州市瓯海区瓯海农业高新工业园仙门路134号
邮编：325000
电话：0577-8605 9001
传真：0577-8605 9003
电邮：wzyufeng@gmail.com
网址：www.0577yf.com

Zhenmei Furniture
臻美家具
广东省佛山市南海区九江镇梅圳会龙村
邮编：528203
电话：0757-8651 8123
传真：0757-8651 8132
电邮：zm@fszhenmei.com
网址：www.fszhenmei.com

Zhongyuan Wooden Furniture Co., Ltd.
中原木器有限公司
大连市保税区泰华大厦A座315、317室
电话：0411-8732 0411
传真：0411-8754 6111
电邮：hongyuan@dlzhongyuan.com
网址：www.dlzhongyuan.com

北京黎明文仪家具有限公司
北京通州区马驹桥
金桥科技产业基地景盛南四街18号
邮编：101102
电话：010-6059 8811
传真：010-6050 9177
电邮：osidea@126.com
网址：www.lmfu.com

上海朋聚家具有限公司
上海市奉贤区奉城工业园区奉旺路688号
电话：021-5755 0594
传真：021-5101 2137*0991
电邮：shpjjj@126.com
网址：www.egatt.cn

上海品至家居用品发展有限公司
上海市胜辛南路251号
邮编：201802
电话：021-3917 0606
传真：021-3917 0533
网址：www.sh-pzjj.com

上海太亿企业股份有限公司
上海市富联三路28号
邮编：201906
电话：021-3604 0022
传真：021-3604 4077
电邮：neil_taiyi@126.com
网址：www.taiye.com.cn

户外家具
Furniture-Outdoor

Alma Contract (Holdings) Limited
澳马集团有限公司
广州市番禺区洛溪新城莱茵学院410室
邮编：511431
电话：020-2287 6233
传真：020-2287 6210
电邮：info@almacontract.com
网址：www.almacontract.com

Atdecotek
上海市程家桥支路201弄智地大厦F07室
电话：021-6268 5137
传真：021-6268 5137
电邮：sales@artdecotek.com
网址：www.artdecotek.com

Ateja Tritunggal Co., Ltd.
上海雅迈隆纺织品装饰有限公司
上海市南苏州路1415号5楼
电话：021-5834 0710
传真：021-5031 2276
电邮：atejashh@sh163.net
网址：www.ateja.co.id
请参阅第302、304页

B. van Zuiden (Guangzhou) Textile Co., Ltd.
万瑞庭（广州）纺织品有限公司
广州市荔湾区芳村海南赤岗西约458号
海南工贸园C1栋二楼
邮编：510388
电话：020-8151 5224
传真：020-8151 5591
电邮：info@bvzchina.com
网址：www.bvz.com

Bazhou Hongjiang Furniture Co., Ltd.
霸州市宏江家具有限公司
河北省霸州市胜芳经济协作区
邮编：065701
电话：0316-566 9885
传真：0316-566 9886
电邮：hj@cnhjj.com
网址：www.cnhjj.com

Cardy Leisure Articles Co., Ltd.
上海卡迪休闲用品有限公司
上海市世纪大道1777号东方希望大厦11楼E座
邮编：200122
电话：021-6104 9918
传真：021-6104 9928
电邮：marketing@mail.yotrio.com
网址：www.bettergarden.com.cn

Dynamix Co., Ltd. (Shanghai)
凯裕贸易（上海）有限公司
上海市青浦区赵巷镇盛伟邦绿地国际家具村
嘉松中路5299号南区B6馆一层105号
电话：021-5975 5788
传真：021-5975 5789
网址：www.agio.com.cn

Foshan Darwin Furniture Co., Ltd.
佛山市达尔文家具有限公司
广东省佛山市顺德区北滘镇西海工业区
电话：0757-2810 5615
传真：0757-2897 8512
电邮：alex@darwincn.com
网址：www.darwincn.com

Foshan Yatai Furniture Ltd.
佛山市亚太家私有限公司
广东省佛山市南海区大沥镇盐步新城村工业区30号
邮编：528247
电话：0757-8577 0647
传真：0757-8577 6071
电邮：nhyatai@163.com
网址：www.mr-dream.com
请参阅第306、307页

Gangcai Awningequip Ment Co., Ltd.
上海港彩装饰用品有限公司
上海松江区九亭镇金马路358号
电话：021-6763 1043
传真：021-6763 1698
电邮：shgangcai@163.com
网址：www.shgangcai.com

Grupo Kettal China Office & Showroom
上海市南京西路1038号
上海梅陇镇广场21楼2109室
电话：021-5228 2275
传真：021-5228 2276
网址：www.grupokettal.com

Guangdong Gaoxiu Garden Product Co., Ltd.
广东高秀花园制品有限公司
广东省云浮市郁南县都城镇平江路G321
（德庆西江大桥右转34Km）
电话：0766-731 5019
传真：0766-731 5053
电邮：ynsnp_yfb@21cn.net
网址：www.cngarden.com

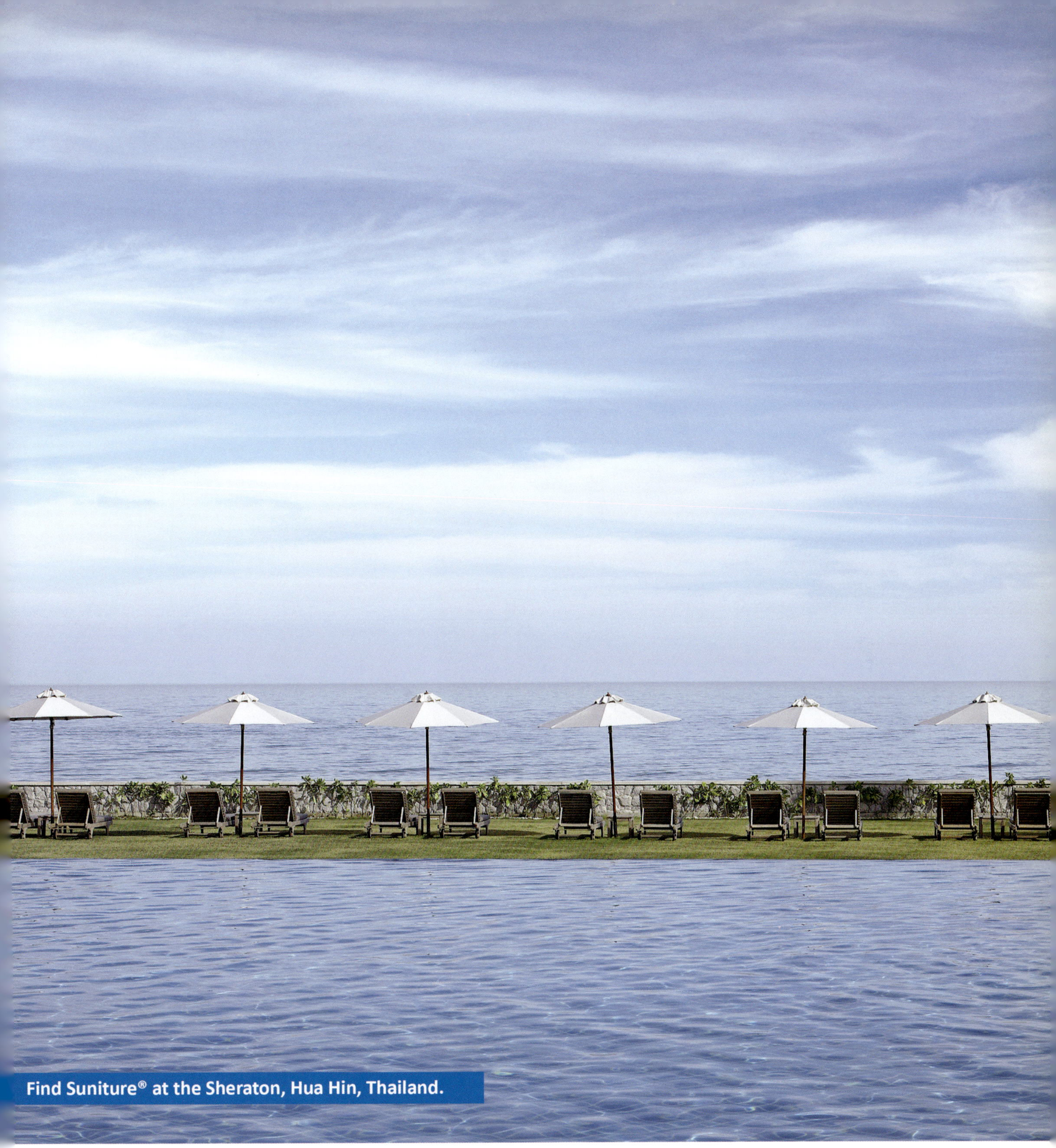

Patent No.: ZL 200530124121.9

OSMEN®
Design

Add: 3Fl,Yu-Hui-Yuan Bldg,
200 He-Hui-Jie St,Tian-He-Bei Rd,
Guangzhou,510610
China 廣州天河北路合暉街200號御暉苑3樓
Tel: +86-20-38492067/38492626
Fax: +86-20-38491362/38492771
E-mail: info@orientsino.com
orientsino@vip.163.com
www.orientsino.com / www.osmen-design.com

部分客户

Mr. Dream integrates design, art and new process, and create the furniture brand using the aspiration for and pursuit of fine life as inspiration. 米斯特.梦是以结合设计，艺术及新兴工艺，以对美好生活的向往与追求为灵感创作的家具品牌。

WWW.MR-DREAM.COM

Foshan Yatai Furniture Ltd TEL 0757-8577 0647 FAX 0757-8577 6071 Hotline工程热线 0757-8576 6668 EMAIL NHYATAI@163.COM

传 统 手 工 编 制 德 国 经 典 设

J&E FURNITURE LTD
PERFECT FURNITURE(GUANGZHOU)CO.LTD
广州派风家具有限公司

ADDRESS: No.143, Liangsha Road, Liangtian Town, Baiyun Area, Guangzhou, China
广州市白云区良田镇良沙路143号
TEL: 8620-87621400 8620-87609611 FAX: 8620-87621802
EMAIL: INFO@PERFECTFURNITURE.COM.CN INFO_JE@126.COM
WEB: WWW.PERFECTFURNITURE.COM.CN WWW.RATTANELEMENT.COM

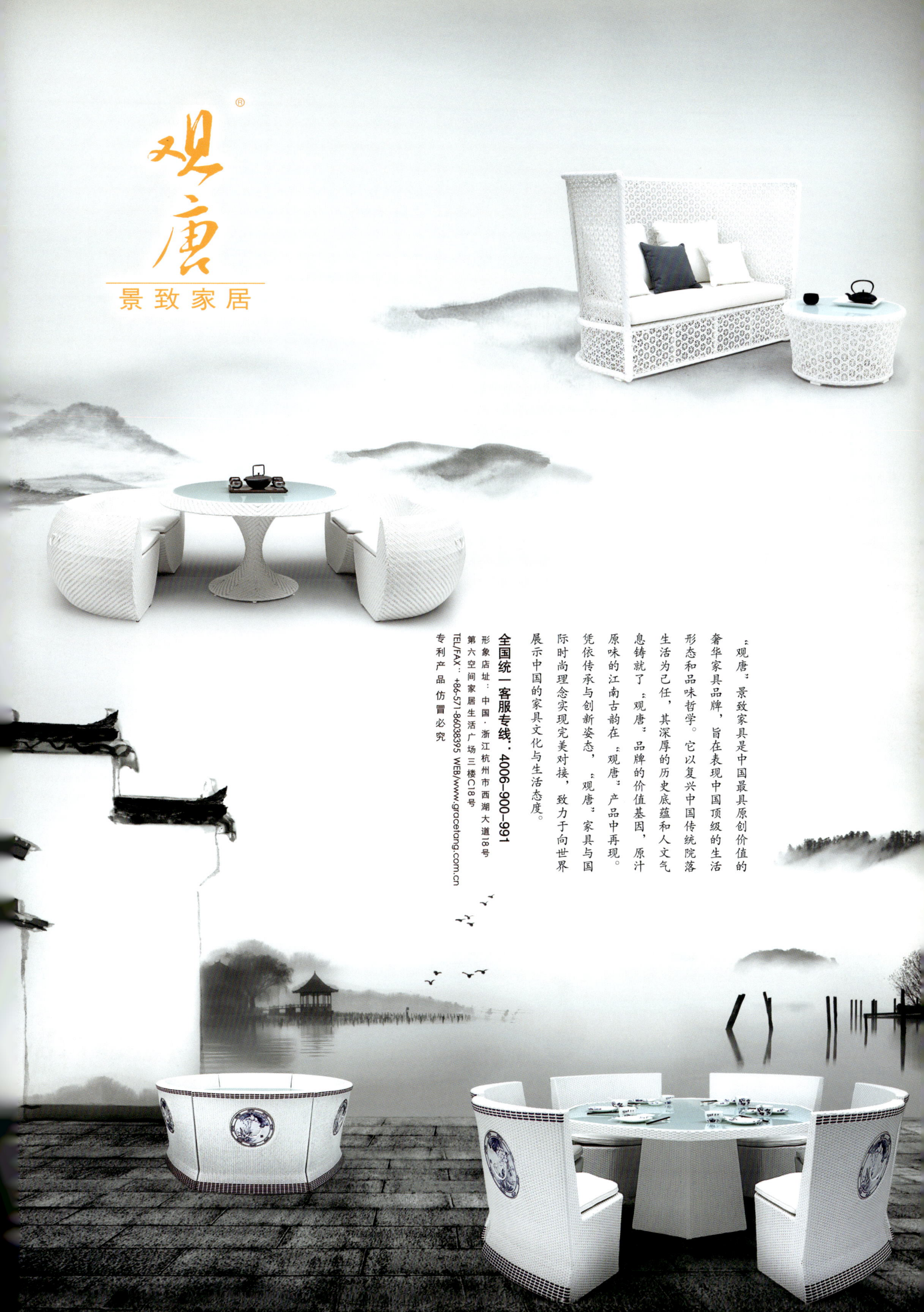
观唐®
景致家居
“观唐”景致家具是中国最具原创价值的奢华家具品牌，旨在表现中国顶级的生活形态和品味哲学。它以复兴中国传统院落生活为己任，其深厚的历史底蕴和人文气息铸就了“观唐”品牌的价值基因，原汁原味的江南古韵在“观唐”产品中再现。凭依传承与创新姿态，“观唐”家具与国际时尚理念实现完美对接，致力于向世界展示中国的家具文化与生活态度。
全国统一客服专线：4006-900-991
形象店址：中国·浙江杭州市西湖大道18号
第六空间家居生活广场三楼C18号
TEL/FAX：+86-571-86038395 WEB/www.gracetang.com.cn
专利产品 仿冒必究

▼户外家具
Furniture-Outdoor

Guangzhou Haoyuan Outdoor Furniture Co., Ltd.
广州豪园户外家具有限公司
广东省广州市番禺区大石镇河村工业区100号
邮编：511430
电话：020-3478 3811
传真：020-3479 6113
电邮：sales@haoyuanfurniture.com
网址：www.haoyuanfurniture.com

Guangzhou Jinjia Ooutdoor Furniture Factory
广州金佳户外家具厂
广州市番禺区沙湾龙湾工业区龙古路30号
邮编：511483
电话：020-8474 3496
传真：020-3487 4313
电邮：kinguid@yahoo.cn
网址：www.kinguid.com

Guangzhou Qihe Trading Company Limited
广州其和贸易有限公司
广东省广州市水荫路54号五楼
邮编：510075
电话：020-3761 2456
传真：020-3761 2450
电邮：key-all@key-all.com

Hangzhou Gracetang Scene Household Co., Ltd.
杭州观唐景致家居有限公司
浙江杭州拱墅区通益路49号LOFT49
电话：0571-8809 8991
传真：0571-8819 9053
电邮：guantang168@126.com
网址：www.gracetang.com.cn
请参阅第309页

Hings Plastic & Metal Products Mfy
兴业塑胶五金制品厂
广东省顺德市勒流镇富裕工业区
邮编：528324
电话：0757-2533 2788
传真：0757-2533 2993
电邮：hingspmp@hingsgroup.com
网址：www.hingsgroup.com

Ningbo Freestyle Enterprises Co., Ltd.
宁波保税区欧亚工贸有限公司
浙江省宁波市和意路168号万豪中心1504号
电话：0574-8725 8260
传真：0574-8725 8274
电邮：sales@freestylecasual.com
网址：www.freestylecasual.com

Orient Sino (GZ) Industrial Corp. Ltd.
广州东恩贸易有限公司
广州市天河北路合晖街200号御晖苑3楼
邮编：510610
电话：020-3849 2067
传真：020-3849 1362
电邮：info@orientsino.com
网址：www.orientsino.com
请参阅第305页

Perfect Furniture (Guangzhou) Co., Ltd.
广州派风家具有限公司
广州市白云区良田镇良沙路143号
电话：020-8762 1400
传真：020-8762 1802
电邮：info@perfectfurniture.com.cn
网址：www.perfectfurniture.com.cn
请参阅第308页

Pylon Leisure Products Co., Ltd.
安徽湃隆户外休闲用品有限公司
安徽省铜陵市金桥开发区
邮编：244100
电话：0574-8728 1106
传真：0574-8728 2072
电邮：administrator@pylonindustry.com
网址：www.pylonleisureproducts.com

Royal Garden Furnishings Inc.
上佰家贸易（上海）有限公司
上海市松江区九亭镇涞亭南路99号
电话：021-5488 9680
传真：021-5488 7010
电邮：sbj.furnishings@gmail.com
网址：www.royalgarden.net.cn

Shanghai Joybells Enterrise Co., Ltd.
上海淳艺家饰有限公司
上海市闵行区华翔路1195号
邮编：201106
电话：021-5227 0740
传真：021-5227 0742
电邮：frank@garden-leisure.cn
网址：www.garden-leisure.cn

Shanghai Violet Shine Enterprise Co., Ltd.
上海紫灿实业有限公司
上海市虹中路361号1幢1楼
邮编：201103
电话：021-6405 2223
传真：021-6405 2229
网址：www.vshinebiz.com

Shanghai Ying Yue Outdoor Furniture Co., Ltd.
上海映月（户外）家具有限公司
上海市青浦区徐泾华徐公路666号
电话：021-6102 6456
传真：021-3980 7960
电邮：aufreesh@hotmail.com
网址：www.aufree.cn

Shanghai Zian Trade & Development Co., Ltd.
上海资安贸易发展有限公司
上海市虹口区临潼路133-135号飞林商务楼3A-3B
邮编：200082
电话：021-6586 6954
传真：021-6541 7480
电邮：zian@sh163.net
网址：www.zian-sh.com

Suniture China
广州市荔湾区芳村海南赤岗西约458号
海南工贸园C1栋二楼
邮编：510388
电话：020-8151 5254
传真：020-8151 5424
电邮：info@suniture.com
网址：www.suniture.com
请参阅本第303页

Sunstyle In & Out Luxury Furniture
圣诗得顶级户内外家居
北京市朝阳区南皋路东1号
邮编：100015
电话：010-6431 0020
传真：010-6432 4648
电邮：info@sunstyle.cn
网址：www.sunstyle.cn

路易生花园家具厂
广州市番禺区沙湾镇福涌公安基地对面
邮编：511400
电话：020-8474 0052
传真：020-8473 8539
电邮：luiser@163.com
网址：www.luiser.com.cn

玻璃
Glass

Beijing All Vrilliant Technology Co., Ltd.
北京众智同辉科技有限公司
北京市丰台区张仪村50号
邮编：100166
电话：010-5166 8992
传真：010-8368 1009
电邮：sales@abtglass.com
网址：www.abtglass.com

Beijing Chenhui Hongda Glass Co., Ltd.
北京晨辉鸿达玻璃有限公司
北京大兴区西红门
（京良路除留路口西400米路北）
邮编：100076
电话：010-6020 1276
传真：010-6020 1380
电邮：lqt@chhhd.com
网址：www.chhhd.com

Beijing Zhongda Lantian Glass Company
北京中大蓝天玻璃有限公司
北京市丰台区花乡羊坊村623号
邮编：100070
电话：010-8370 2663
传真：010-8370 2828
电邮：info@bjlt-glass.com
网址：www.bjlt-glass.com

DSA Hong
迪生行
4C, Yen Men Building
98-108 Jaffe Road, Wan Chai
Hong Kong
电话：+852-2646 1498
传真：+852-2635 4689
电邮：dsaglass@163.com

Dorma Door Controls (Suzhou) Co., Ltd.
多玛门控（苏州）有限公司
苏州市工业园区同胜路101号
邮编：215126
电话：0512-6295 2596
传真：0512-6761 4582
网址：www.dorma.com

▼玻璃
Glass

Jiaxing Godenria Glass Products Co., Ltd.
嘉兴市高登利雅玻璃制品有限公司
浙江省嘉兴市建国北路
华庭街财富中心F405-407号
邮编：314000
电话：0573-8207 6111
传真：0573-8207 6111
电邮：tianxingboli@alibaba.com.cn
网址：www.godenriaglass.com

Lanshi Group (Glass)
蓝实玻璃集团
安徽省合肥市经济技术开发区锦绣大道119号
电话：0551-382 8677
传真：0551-382 8678
电邮：ahls@glass.com.cn
网址：www.lanshiglass.com

Shanghai Huayi Glass Co., Ltd.
上海华译玻璃有限公司
上海市松江区九亭镇久富开发区金马路22号
邮编：201615
电话：021-6769 1398
传真：021-6769 0730
电邮：webmaster@huayiglass.com
网址：www.huayiglass.com

Yaohua Decorative Glass Co., Ltd.
耀华建筑装饰玻璃有限公司
秦皇岛开发区孟营营宝佳花园南新房
电话：0335-856 8098
传真：0335-856 6683
网址：www.artglassyh.com

河北恒安玻璃有限公司
河北省沙河市金百家工业园区尾山路东段
邮编：054100
电话：0319-884 0566
传真：0319-884 0668
电邮：hebha@yahoo.cn
网址：www.henganglass.com

装饰板
Laminates

Alpi S.P.A
意大利阿尔卑股份有限公司
上海市普陀区陕西北路1388号银座企业中心915
邮编：200060
电话：021-5169 1913
传真：021-5169 2205
电邮：china@alpi.it
网址：www.alpi.it

Burgeree Acoustics Technology Materials (Suzhou) Co., Ltd.
佰家丽声学科技材料（苏州）有限公司
江苏省苏州市三香路1131号
电话：0512-6863 6112
传真：0512-6863 6113
电邮：bjl0512@163.com
网址：www.burgeree.com

Foshan Jihong Decoration Panel Co., Ltd.
佛山市吉弘装饰板业有限公司
南海区大沥黄岐泌冲大沙工业区东约大街1号
电话：0757-8559 9051
传真：0757-8559 1585
网址：www.fsjihong.cn.alibaba.com

Gecko Wood Co., Ltd.
壁虎木业有限公司
沈阳市铁西区兴工北街海韵广场B座1611室
邮编：110026
电话：024-2567 6300
传真：024-2567 6355
电邮：gecko@italygecko.com
网址：www.italygecko.com

Guangzhou Winnper Decorative Materials Co., Ltd.
广东市文鹏装饰材料有限公司
广东市番禺区东涌镇三沙公路18号
邮编：511453
电话：020-3490 5108
传真：020-3490 5038
网址：www.winnper.com

Hongkong Tak Ye Tat Industrial Co., Ltd.
香港德意达实业有限公司
上海市陆家浜路1398号恒升大厦B座906室
电话：021-6312 7999
传真：021-6312 8159
电邮：deyida@sina.com
网址：www.deyida.com

Nanjing Jiuding Goldfoil Technology Co., Ltd.
南京九鼎金箔工艺有限公司
江苏省南京市龙蟠家苑1栋18屋4室
邮编：210001
电话：025-8486 8306
传真：025-8427 4262
电邮：njjd001@163.com
网址：www.jdgoldleaf.com

Nanjing New Human Prefabricated House Co., Ltd.
南京新人类房屋制造有限公司
江苏省南京市江宁经济技术开发区金龙路4号
邮编：211102
电话：025-5272 3345
电邮：njxrl@njxrl.com
网址：www.njxrl.com

Shangdong Dehuilai Decoration Vitrolite Co., Ltd.
山东德惠来装饰瓷板有限公司
山东淄博高新技术开发区鲁泰大道111号
邮编：255000
电话：0533-398 3977
传真：0533-398 2698
电邮：zbdhl@126.com
网址：www.zbdhl.com

Shanghai Dingzhong Construction Material Co., Ltd.
上海鼎中建材有限公司
上海浦东大道2508号龙居大厦1202室
电话：021-5846 5315
传真：021-6850 5733
网址：www.shdzjc.cn

Shanghai QiYi Fumiture & Decoration Co., Ltd.
上海琦艺家具装饰有限公司
上海市松江区新浜工业园区林天路392-397号
邮编：201605
电话：021-6789 1469
传真：021-6789 1499
电邮：qiyibq@126.com
网址：www.qiyish.com
请参阅第298页

Shenzhen Emmy Shell Mosaic & Tiles Co., Ltd.
深圳市艾美贝类工艺品有限公司
深圳市龙岗区布吉镇沙湾沙平北路98号
邮编：518000
电话：0755-2560 5690
传真：0755-2560 8260
电邮：sales@szaimei.com
网址：www.szaimei.com

Tip-Top Limited Company
宏达建材装饰材料
深圳市福田区彩田南路海滨广场朝恒大厦2楼
电话：0755-8830 5716
传真：0755-8830 5736
电邮：wtwt@wellrich.com.hk
网址：www.tip-top.hk

Zhejiang Ling Long Aper Group
浙江玲珑纸业集团
浙江省临安市玲珑工业园区
邮编：311301
电话：0571-6376 4117
传真：0571-6376 2271
电邮：linglong@linglongpaper.com
网址：www.linglongpaper.com

四川远大新兴建筑装饰材料有限公司
成都市青羊工业发展同诚路八号B区9栋202室
邮编：610092
电话：028-8707 9856
传真：028-8707 9866
电邮：ydxxjc@ydxxjc.com
网址：www.ydxxjc.com

隔断
Partitions

Beijing Huahongyujian Trading Co., Ltd.
北京华宏宇建商贸有限公司
北京市朝阳区建东苑18号商业楼320室
电话：010-6574 3789
传真：010-6576 7797
网址：www.beijinghhyj.com

Beijing Obert Scientific Technology Co., Ltd.
北京欧波特科技有限公司
北京市大兴区旧宫镇大有庄工业三区16号
邮编：100076
电话：010-8796 9648
传真：010-8796 0323*620
网址：www.bjoubote.com

▼隔断
Partitions

Beijing Qingke Activity Partition Manufacturing Co., Ltd.
北京青科活动隔墙制造有限公司
北京市大兴区旧宫工业区军民路5号
邮编：100076
电话：010-6794 1091
传真：010-6794 0863
电邮：qkgdbj@163.com
网址：www.qkgd.com

Cellox
卡劳仕
上海市闵行区星中路25幢11号
电话：021-6478 1015
传真：021-6478 1015
电邮：sh@cellox.com.cn
网址：www.cellox.com.cn

Dorma Door Controls (Suzhou) Co., Ltd.
多玛门控（苏州）有限公司
苏州市工业园区同胜路101号
邮编：215126
电话：0512-6295 2596
传真：0512-6761 4582
网址：www.dorma.com

Guangzhou Dalai Partition Industrial Co., Ltd.
广州大来隔断实业有限公司
广东省广州市荔湾区西塱东西路工业三区12号
邮编：510385
电话：020-6113 7553
传真：020-8162 4979
电邮：drlai@drlai.com
网址：www.drlai.com

Hadlina Building Products Co., Ltd.
北京海德林纳建材有限公司
北京市通州区漷县镇漷兴四街海德林纳工业园
邮编：101109
电话：4006 506 988
传真：010-8058 2525
电邮：hadlina@sina.com
网址：www.hadlina.com

Hufcor Partition & Decoration Products (Shanghai) Co., Ltd.
赫福高隔断装饰制品（上海）有限公司
上海市梅园路228号嘉里不夜城企业广场1510室
邮编：200070
电话：021-6415 0101
传真：021-6415 2211
网址：www.hufcor.com.cn

Shanghai Deko Wall Materials Co., Ltd.
上海代高墙体材料有限公司
上海市福山路33号建工大厦24层
邮编：200120
电话：021-5169 8699
传真：021-5882 2022
电邮：bh@deko-cn.net
网址：www.deko-cn.net

Shanghai Dewan Management & Trade Co., Ltd.
上海德望经贸有限公司
上海市浦东新区西营路118号明珠花苑2102室
邮编：200126
电话：021-6858 1307
传真：021-5847 2830
电邮：sh.dewan@yahoo.com.cn
网址：www.hoehen.com

Shanghai Fuchun Rongqiang Industry Co., Ltd.
上海富春荣强实业有限公司
上海市东方路1361号3号14E
邮编：200127
电话：021-5089 4358
传真：021-5089 7476
电邮：fcrq@fcrq.com
网址：www.fcrq.com

Shanghai Xin Si Lu Metal Products Co., Ltd.
上海鑫丝陆金属制品有限公司
上海市金沙江西路1555弄C1区5号楼
电话：400 820 1773
传真：021-3951 2115
电邮：xsl@xslmetalfabrics.com
网址：www.xslmetalfabrics.com
请参阅第312页

Yokah International Ltd.
旭华国际有限公司
香港九龙长沙湾永康街79号恒龙工商中心7楼D室
电话：+852-2991 4051
传真：+852-2423 0922
电邮：ybs@yokah.com
网址：www.yokah.com

画及画框制造商
Picture & picture Frame Makers

Beijing Sanlitang Cultural Media Co., Ltd.
北京三立堂文化传媒有限公司
北京市西城区西直门内金泰华云写字楼A109室
邮编：100035
电话：010-6221 8893
传真：010-6221 8893
请参阅第314、315页

Capital D é cor Asia Limited
佳必多装饰（上海）有限公司
上海市徐汇区文定路258号
文定生活广场B区309-2
邮编：200030
电话：021-3356 2996
传真：021-3356 2997
电邮：exportdep@nedgroup.hk
网址：www.nedgroup.hk

Glong International Trade Co., Ltd.
上海技隆国际贸易有限公司
上海市虹口区花园路128号运动创意园A栋351室
邮编：200083
电话：021-6140 9708
传真：021-6140 9706
电邮：daniel@wazalife.com
网址：www.wazalife.com

Huahong Holding Group Co., Ltd.
华鸿控股集团有限公司
浙江省义乌市义南工业区大士路1号
邮编：322000
电话：0579-8998 3116
传真：0579-8998 3116
网址：www.chinaframe.com

Jiangmen Se Se Craft Work Co., Ltd.
江门市色色工艺品有限公司
广东省江门市高新技术开发区新兴路96号
邮编：529000
电话：0750-386 6701
传真：0750-386 6700
网址：www.seseframe.com

Qufu Shengmei Frame Co., Ltd.
曲阜圣美框木有限公司
山东省青岛市东海路26号浪琴园B-1
邮编：266071
电话：0532-8572 2136
传真：0532-8572 3337
电邮：sale@qufushengmei.com
网址：www.qufushengmei.cn

Shenzhen European & American Famous Painting Arts Co., Ltd.
深圳市欧美名画艺术有限公司
深圳市福田区振华路工艺大厦3楼
邮编：518031
电话：0755-8325 8226
传真：0755-8324 5839
电邮：eafpg@eafpg.com
网址：www.eafpg.com

Shenzhen Xiongshi Zhenggang Art Co., Ltd.
深圳市熊氏正刚艺术有限公司
深圳市龙岗区布吉大芬油画村大芬路22号
电话：0755-8951 2361
传真：0755-2827 4076
电邮：sale_a@xszgart.com
网址：www.xszgart.com

北京悦嘉睿智文化传播有限责任公司
北京市通州宋庄北四
电话：010-5128 6283
网址：www.bjbihua.com

上海柏轩工艺品有限公司
上海市闵行区莘浙路128号1号楼B座506室
邮编：200011
电话：021-6431 0881
传真：021-6431 0881
网址：www.boximum.com.cn

深圳播安飞天文化传播有限公司
深圳市南山区珠光村西区10号302室
电话：0755-8627 5123
传真：0755-2762 5559
电邮：cnbihua@163.com
网址：www.cnbihua.com

武汉木星彩绘有限公司
武汉市雄楚大道（图书城对面）
智源财富中心A-602室
邮编：430000
电话：400 631 6184
网址：www.mxcaihui.com

Resplendent simulation art of painting and calligraphy

璀璨的书画高仿艺术

北京三立堂文化传媒有限公司

近年来书画仿真技术在我国出版、印刷行业中迅速发展起来，北京三立堂文化传媒有限公司就是一家研究、探讨并推广中国书画高级仿真复制近十年的公司。在这块富有活力的新兴艺坛上，三立堂的作品无论在质量和信誉方面都彰显出独有的魅力和特点。

在多年的研究实践中，公司特别邀请了清华大学美术学院李燕教授作为长期的艺术顾问，并视临现场指导，大大地提高了技术人员对中国书画艺术的深层理解和认识。我们体会要想复制出高品质的富有生命力的书画作品，首先要抓住原作的灵魂，理解每位画家各种技法的运用特点，体会中国画的笔墨在山水、人物、花鸟画中的不同表现，亦如鉴定书画真迹一样，把握特点，把握细节。由此，再把对绘画艺术上的认识搭接到技术操作的范畴内，“翻译”成数字语言，将思维程序转化为电脑操作程序，并通过反复的分析和研究，把中国画的“意存笔先，画尽意在”的意境与先进的高科技技术相结合，最终达到以形写神，形神兼备。当今社会，无论从艺术欣赏和收藏的角度看，这些高仿真书画作品都具有相当的市场价值和收藏价值。

三立堂文化传媒有限公司同时代理销售艺术家书画作品。立言、立德、立人是我们的精神理念和发展动力。为了推动文化产业的发展我们将不断努力，不断进取。

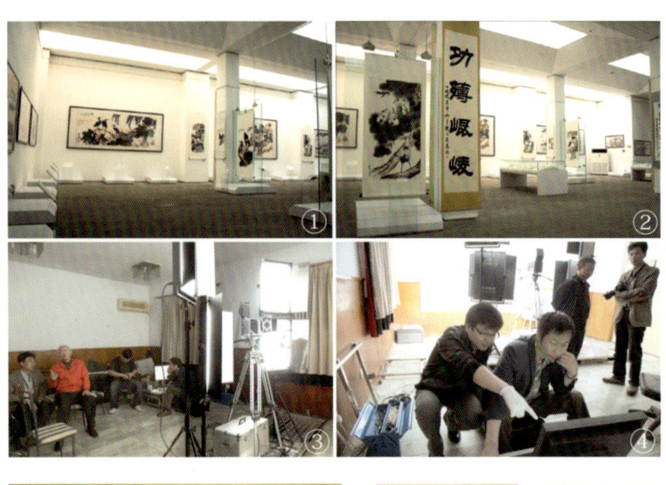

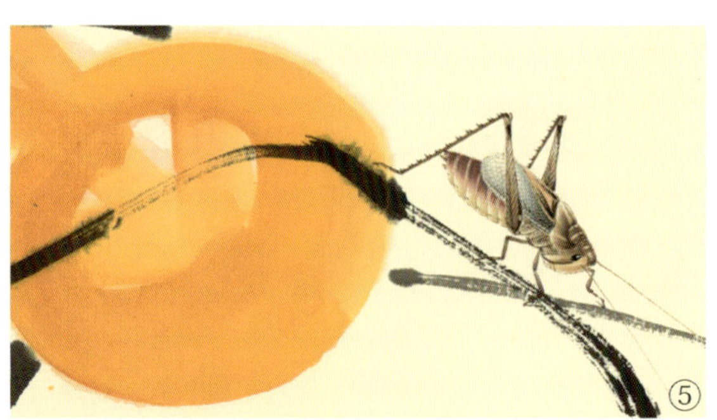

图①②为李苦禅高仿复制作品展
图③为李燕教授视临现场指导高仿复制工作
图④为三立堂技术人员正在操作照相扫描设备
图⑤为齐白石高仿复制作品之局部

作品：鹿
作者：八大山人

作品：窗清供图
作者：任伯年

作品：白菜
作者：吴昌硕

作品：柳梢栖雀图
作者：徐悲鸿

作品：山水
作者：张大千

作品：四条屏
作者：齐白石

作品：秋色图
作者：溥心畬

作品：月季花
作者：何香凝

作品：松峰雄鹰图
作者：李苦禅

作品：小孩鸽子
作者：蒋兆和

作品：赶驴图
作者：黄胄

作品：济公戏猴图
作者：李燕

洁具
Sanitary Ware

American Standard (China) Co., Ltd.
美标（中国）有限公司
上海市田林路487号宝石园24号楼
邮编：200233
电话：021-3395 2888
传真：021-3367 4255
电邮：sales@americanstandard.com.cn
网址：www.americanstandard.com.cn

Annwa Ceramic Sanitary Ware Co., Ltd.
佛山市高明安华陶瓷洁具有限公司
广东省佛山市高明沧江工业园区
邮编：528511
电话：0757-8851 0390
传真：0757-8851 0190
网址：www.annwa.com.cn

Appollo (China) Co., Ltd.
阿波罗（中国）有限公司
广州经济技术开发区永和经济区黄旗山路19号
邮编：510623
电话：020-2839 7111
传真：020-2839 7100*7101
电邮：business@appollo.cn
网址：www.china-apollo.com

Bellagio Sanitary Wares (China) Ltd.
佛山伯朗滋洁具有限公司
佛山市三水区大塘大布沙工业区
邮编：528143
电话：0757-8729 9688
传真：0757-8279 9668
电邮：info@oxo.com.cn
网址：www.oxo.com.cn

Catalano Asia Pacific Limited
卡特雷诺（亚太）有限公司
深圳市南山区华侨城OCT创意园E-6栋601-A
邮编：518053
电话：0755-8633 7106
传真：0755-8609 6149
电邮：asia-p@catalano.com.hk
网址：www.catalano.it
请参阅第317页

CRW Shower Equipment Co., Ltd.
佛山市高明英皇卫浴有限公司
广东省佛山市高明区沧江工业园
邮编：528000
电话：0757-8271 5180
传真：0757-8227 7585
网址：www.crw.com.cn

Chaozhou Yatao Ceramics Co., Ltd.
潮州市亚陶瓷业有限公司
广东省潮州市火车站北片兴工路13号
邮编：521031
电话：0768-299 3933
传真：0768-299 8230
电邮：sales@yatao.com
网址：www.yatao.com

Eago sanitary ware co., Ltd.
佛山市南海益高卫浴有限公司
广东佛山市南海区小塘狮岭工业开发区
电话：0757-8663 2966
传真：0757-8663 2278
电邮：eagocn@yahoo.com.cn
网址：www.eago.com.cn

Foshan MICAWA Ceramics Co., Ltd.
佛山美加华陶瓷有限公司
广东省佛山市三水区三水大道南82号
邮编：528131
电话：0757-8756 3886
传真：0757-8751 2305
网址：www.micawa.com

Foshan Summit Ceramic Co., Ltd.
佛山市萨米特陶瓷有限公司
佛山市禅城区南庄镇华夏陶瓷博览城
萨米特营销中心
邮编：528061
电话：0757-8539 9911
传真：0757-8539 9910
电邮：info@esummit.cn
网址：www.esummit.cn

Foshan Zunlong Sanitary Ware Co., Ltd.
佛山市尊龙洁具有限公司
佛山市石湾区雾岗路河宕陶瓷交易中心A-9-13号
邮编：528000
电话：0757-8227 7232
传真：0757-8271 9788
电邮：zunl@zunlong-bathware.com
网址：www.zunlong-bathware.com

Fuzhou Sanxie Electron Co., Ltd.
福州三协电子有限公司
福建省福州市金山工业区浦上园D区24号楼
电话：0591-8365 0378
传真：0591-8363 3528
电邮：147@china.com
网址：www.sanxie.com.cn

Gibo (Fuzhou) Induction Equipment Co., Ltd.
福州洁博利感应设备有限公司
福建省福州市浦上工业园B区54栋
邮编：350002
电话：0591-8806 6000
传真：0591-8806 5595
电邮：sales@gibo.com.cn
网址：www.gibo.com.cn

Hocheng (China) Co., Ltd.
和成（中国）有限公司
上海闸北区虬江路1538号和成大楼
邮编：200336
电话：021-6628 6111
传真：021-6628 7898
网址：www.hcg.com.cn

Ivrin Sanitary Ware Co., Ltd.
平湖市欧文洁具有限公司
浙江省平湖市洁具科技城
邮编：314211
电话：0573-8564 6222
传真：0573-8564 4261
电邮：irvin@irvin.cn
网址：www.irvin.cn

Kohler China Investment Co., Ltd.
科勒（中国）投资有限公司
上海市闸北区江场三路158号
邮编：200436
电话：021-2606 2000
传真：021-6107 8900
网址：www.kohler.com.cn

Major International (China) Company Limited
名家国际（中国）有限公司
广东省珠海市吉大光大国际贸易中心1908-1912室
邮编：519015
电话：0756-332 2001
传真：0756-332 2009
电邮：michael@major.com.cn
网址：www.major.com.cn

Monarch Sanitary Ware Co., Ltd.
四川帝王洁具有限公司
四川省成都市龙泉驿区阳光城锦绣路一段
电话：028-2792 6003
传真：028-8483 6068
电邮：xs@monarch-sw.com
网址：www.monarch-sw.com

Nanguo Ceramics Sanitary Wares Industrial Co., Ltd.
南国陶瓷洁具实业有限公司
广东省潮安县古巷镇枫一工业开发区
电话：0768-683 8953
传真：0768-683 3818
电邮：webmaster@nanguo-cn.com
网址：www.nanguo-cn.com

Ningbo Zhanying Equipment Induction Co., Ltd.
宁波展鹰感应设备有限公司
浙江省宁波市江北大道648号（洪塘）
邮编：315033
电话：0574-8784 4011
传真：0574-8787 3756
电邮：zy2001@chinazhanying.com
网址：www.chinazhanying.com

Roca (China) Ltd.
乐家（中国）有限公司
上海市徐汇区漕溪北路396号
汇智大厦裙楼503-505室
邮编：200030
电话：021-3368 8822
传真：021-3368 8299
网址：www.roca.cn

Speakman Company
美国舒波曼公司
北京市朝阳区望京西路48号
金隅国际大厦C座2105室
电话：010-8477 5228
传真：010-8477 5176
网址：www.speakmancompany.com.cn

TOTO (China) Co., Ltd.
东陶（中国）有限公司
上海市延安西路2201号上海国际贸易中心210室
邮编：200336
电话：021-6270 1010
传真：021-6270 3099
网址：www.toto.com.cn

Tangshan Huida Ceramic (Group) Co. Ltd.
唐山惠达陶瓷（集团）股份有限公司
河北省唐山市丰南区惠达陶瓷城
邮编：063307
电话：0315-852 3618
传真：0315-852 2827
电邮：huida@heinfo.net
网址：www.huidagroup.com

Wenzhou Dili Weiss Induction Sanitary Ware Co., Ltd.
温州帝威斯感应洁具有限公司
浙江省温州市龙湾海城工业区工贸路65号
电话：0577-8523 8788
传真：0577-8522 9996
电邮：office@tweis.com
网址：www.tweis.com

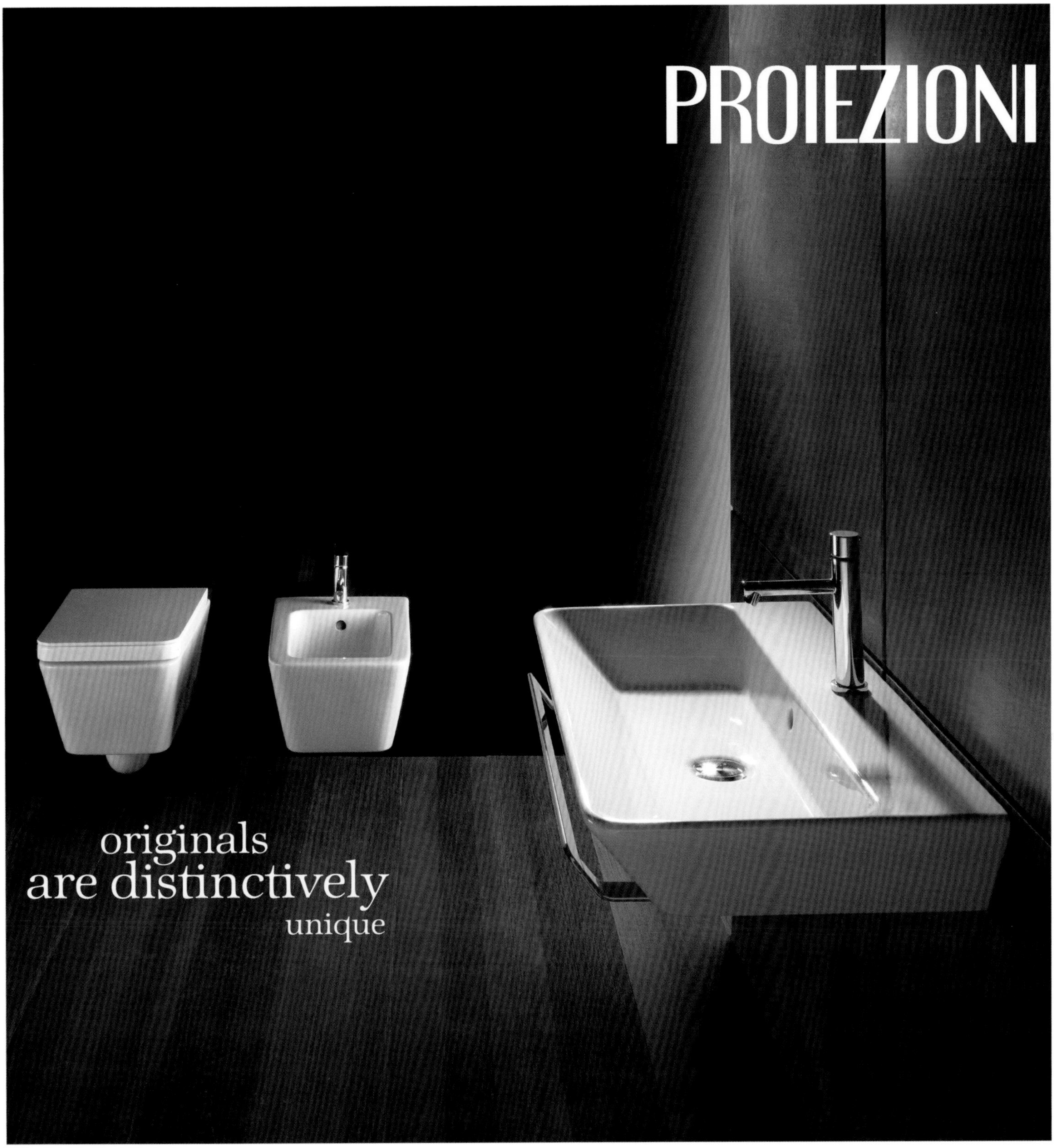

reddot design award
winner 2010

▼洁具
Sanitary Ware

Wenzhou Interhasa Sanitary Ware Co., Ltd.
温州英特汉莎洁具有限公司
浙江省温州市龙湾区海城锦泉街58号
电话：0577-8521 6517
传真：0577-8522 3517
电邮：interhasa@interhasa.com
网址：www.interhasa.com

XinLe Bathroom Products (Foshan) Co., Ltd.
新乐卫浴（佛山）有限公司
广东佛山市禅城区石湾来长岗鹰卫浴总部大楼
电话：0757-8266 2211
传真：0757-8266 2233
电邮：info@ying-sw.com
网址：www.ying-sw.com

Zhongshan Benta Building Materials Co., Ltd.
中山市宾德建材有限公司
中山市东区东裕路11号之六
电话：0760-2332 0298
传真：0760-8823 8937
电邮：sales@benta.cn
网址：www.benta.cn

东莞市卡西奥建材有限公司
广东省东莞市虎门镇虎门大道164号
电话：0769-8511 2312
传真：0769-8161 2018
电邮：marketing@casero.com.cn
网址：www.casero.com.cn

东莞市龙邦卫浴有限公司
广东省东莞市东坑镇东安路262号
邮编：523459
电话：0769-8386 3528
传真：0769-8388 4627
电邮：km@dgkamon.com
网址：www.kamon.net.cn

佛山市百田建材实业有限公司
广东省佛山市三水区乐平中心工业园基业路2号
邮编：528143
电话：0757-8736 3800
传真：0757-8736 3811
电邮：webmaster@sun-coo.com
网址：www.sun-coo.com

佛山市三水维可陶陶瓷有限公司
广东省佛山市三水区三水大道南82号
邮编：528131
电话：0757-8756 0288
传真：0757-8756 0093
电邮：victor@victorbathroom.cn
网址：www.victorbathroom.com

佛山市顺德区乐华陶瓷洁具有限公司
广东省佛山市顺德区乐从镇大墩工业区
邮编：528315
电话：0757-2618 6039
传真：0757-2868 3833
网址：www.arrowceramic.com

汇康卫浴（新会）有限公司
广东省新会市崖南工业园区1路1号
电话：0750-645 6788
传真：0750-645 6988
网址：www.arto.com.cn

唯宝贸易（上海）有限公司
上海市延安西路2299号世贸商城10A28室
邮编：200336
电话：021-6236 3281
传真：021-6236 3283
网址：www.villeroy-boch.com
请参阅第318、319页

新乐陶（亚洲）上海代表处
上海市淮海中路93号大上海时代广场1705室
邮编：200021
电话：021-6391 8190
传真：021-6391 8195
网址：www.pozzi-ginori.com

重庆四维卫浴有限公司
重庆市江津区油溪镇
邮编：402285
电话：023-6108 8699
电邮：swell@swell.com.cn
网址：www.swell.com.cn

雕塑
Sculptures

Beijing Creater Excellent Artwork Company Limited
北京创世华彩艺术装饰品有限公司
北京市朝阳区东四环CBD高尔夫球会北侧
邮编：100023
电话：010-8774 4068
传真：010-8774 3085
电邮：bjcshc@bjcshc.com
网址：www.bjcshc.com

Beijing Zai Xian Hui Huang Design Corp. Ltd.
北京市再现辉煌艺术设计有限公司
北京市通州区马驹桥镇郭村332号
邮编：101102
电话：010-6059 2995
电邮：zxhh@263.net
网址：www.bjzxhh.com

Costonrart Co., Ltd.
惠州市采岩装饰材料有限公司
广东省惠州市惠城区沥林镇埔仔工业区
邮编：516235
电话：0752-386 8108
传真：0752-386 8109
电邮：costoneart@vip.163.com
网址：www.costoneart.com

Guangzhou Chuhan Garden Sculpture Co., Ltd.
广州楚汉园林雕塑公司
广东省广州市海珠区礼岗路信和大厦10-908
邮编：510280
电话：020-3435 5836
传真：020-3405 4073
电邮：lbn@chylds.com
网址：www.chylds.com

Jinan Jing Wen Diao Su Yi Shu Co., Ltd.
济南京文雕塑艺术有限公司
山东省济南市济北开发区
电话：0531-8448 0272
传真：0531-8448 2318
电邮：liuhaibo807@163.com
网址：www.jingwendiaosu.com

Laizhou Huanqiu Stone Sculpture Co., Ltd.
莱州环球石材雕塑有限公司
山东省莱州市莱州南路八腊庙对面
邮编：261400
电话：0535-221 6184
传真：0535-226 6358
电邮：flj@huanqiu-sculpture.com
网址：www.huanqiu-sculpture.com

New Impression Art (Shenzhen) Workshop
深圳市新印象实业有限公司
深圳市布吉镇西环路新印象128艺术区（东升学校旁）
电话：0755-8326 1711
传真：0755-8332 7007
电邮：szxyxart@xyxart.com
网址：www.xyxart.net
请参阅第272页

Quyang Chuangyi Modern Sculpture Factory
河北曲阳创意现代雕塑公司
河北省曲阳县定曲公路曲阳收费站西1公里路北
邮编：073100
电话：0312-436 9118
传真：0312-436 9128
电邮：cn@cyms.cn
网址：www.cyms.cn

Quyang Huicheng Sculpture Arts Ltd.
曲阳县汇成雕塑艺术有限公司
河北省曲阳县羊平经济开发区
邮编：073102
电话：0312-431 3360
传真：0312-431 2166
电邮：sqle@heinfo.net
网址：www.sqdk.com

Rak Ceramics
P.O.Box:6679, Ras Al Khaimah, United Arab Emirates
电话：+971(7)-244 5046
传真：+971(7)-244 5062
电邮：swsales@rakceram.com
网址：www.rakceram.com

Shanghai Chuan Arts & Crafts Co., Ltd.
上海传家工艺品有限公司
上海市奉贤区青村镇奉永路399号
邮编：201414
电话：021-5756 7155
传真：021-5756 7157
电邮：chuan888@vip.163.com
网址：www.chuanstone.com

Shanghai Qishi Sculpture Art Manufactrue Co., Ltd.
上海启石雕塑艺术品制造有限公司
上海市闵行区龙吴路5295号
邮编：200241
电话：021-6450 6600
传真：021-6450 7242
电邮：qishi@cnqishi.com
网址：www.cnqishi.com

Shenzhen European & American Famous Painting Arts Co., Ltd.
深圳市欧美名画艺术有限公司
深圳市福田区振华路工艺大厦3楼
邮编：518031
电话：0755-8325 8226
传真：0755-8324 5839
电邮：eafpg@eafpg.com
网址：www.eafpg.com

Shenzhen Nuoqi Oil Painting Art Co., Ltd.
深圳诺奇油画工艺有限公司
东莞市石龙镇织儒街4-19号
电话：0769-8688 1400
传真：0769-8192 2977
电邮：nuoqiart82@gmail.com
网址：www.nuoqiart.com

▼雕塑 Sculptures

Shenzhen Yinbo Painting & Artwork Co., Ltd.
深圳市银波油画工艺有限公司
深圳市龙岗区五联社区协平路协平工业区G栋
邮编：518129
电话：0755-2879 3332
传真：0755-2879 0354
电邮：yb@yinbo-art.com
网址：www.yinbo-art.com

Shijiazhuang City Sculpture Limited
石家庄市艺苑雕塑有限公司
河北省石家庄艺术市场街205号
邮编：050061
电话：0311-8551 2650
传真：0311-8779 5582
电邮：hbyyds@126.com
网址：www.hbyyds.com

Veronese Design Company Limied
威罗尼创意有限公司
上海市延安西路2299号世贸商城8A32
邮编：200336
电话：021-6236 0991
传真：021-3228 3280
网址：www.veronesedesign.com

Zhengzhou Neolites Generation Sculptre Co., Ltd.
郑州新石代工艺雕塑有限公司
河南省郑州市西三环与厂家路交叉口
电话：0371-6809 2775
传真：0371-6809 2775
网址：www.zzxsdsy.com

Zhuhai Great Forest Sculpture
珠海大森林雕塑
广东省珠海市南屏镇北山村北街20号
邮编：519070
电话：0756-231 2192
传真：0756-231 2193
电邮：b_d888@163.com
网址：www.dsl128.com

广州亚美特艺术雕塑有限公司
广州市芳村龙溪大道花卉科技园艺林东街8号
电话：020-8141 3668
传真：020-8141 3693
电邮：ymt020@126.com
网址：www.ymt8.com

杭州亚龙雕塑艺术有限公司
杭州市上城区滨江四区在水一方2号楼9B座
邮编：310016
电话：0571-8655 0811
传真：0571-8655 0822
网址：www.yalongart.com

江苏艺林雕塑工程有限公司
江苏省无锡市梁溪路928号
邮编：214011
电话：0510-8241 8928
传真：0510-8240 0918
电邮：ylchina614@sohu.com
网址：www.ylchina.com

上海云昭雕塑装饰工程有限公司
上海市徐汇区漕溪路198号
好饰家石材街288-298和10-11号
邮编：200235
电话：021-6469 0917
传真：021-6464 7765
电邮：zhen64690917@126.com
网址：www.dingxindk.com

深圳市米兰·映象工艺品（制造厂）有限公司
深圳市龙岗区同乐同德路三颗松工业区
电话：0755-3360 8833
传真：0755-3360 1926
电邮：milan_impression@126.com
网址：www.milanimpression.com.cn

水槽 Sink

Bangsite Kitchen and Sanitary Ware Co., Ltd.
中山市德星厨卫有限公司
中山市南头镇升辉南工业区
邮编：528429
电话：0760-2322 2566
传真：0760-2251 7599
电邮：zsbangsite@yahoo.cn
网址：www.bangsite.cn

Blanco Co., Ltd. - China Rep. Office
德国铂浪高有限公司中国代表处
上海市浦东新区商城路800号斯米克大厦312室
邮编：200120
电话：021-5835 5662
传真：021-5835 5667
电邮：sales@blanco.com.cn
网址：www.blanco.com.cn

China Light Industry Hecheng Company Limited
中轻和成有限公司
福建省南安市溪美崎峰工业区
邮编：362300
电话：0595-2655 6999
传真：0595-2655 6000
电邮：hccp@hccp.cn
网址：www.hccp.cn

Franke (China) Kitchen System Co., Ltd.
弗兰卡（中国）厨房系统有限公司
上海市徐汇区零陵路899号飞洲国际广场15楼K座
邮编：200030
电话：021-5489 3126
传真：021-5489 3155
网址：www.franke.com.cn

Fuzhou Mor-Ning Kitchen Co., Ltd.
福州墨林厨具设备有限公司
福建省福州市马尾区快安科技园快洲路28号
邮编：350015
电话：0591-8397 1632
传真：0591-8397 1733
电邮：mn@mor-ning.com
网址：www.mor-ning.com

Moen Ine.
摩恩（中国）公司
上海市浦东新区银城中路168号
上海银行大厦1001室
邮编：200120
电话：021-6360 9600
传真：021-5876 4678
电邮：webmaster@moen.com
网址：www.moen.cn

Ningbo Franta Kitchenware Co., Ltd.
宁波福兰特厨具有限公司
浙江省慈溪市长河镇
邮编：315326
电话：0574-2363 6777
传真：0574-2361 2777
电邮：flt@hkfranta.com
网址：www.hkfranta.com

Oulin
欧琳
浙江省宁波市鄞州区投资创业中心祥和东路128号
邮编：315104
电话：0574-8819 6888
传真：0574-8819 6665
网址：www.oulin.com

Yehua Kitchen Equipments Co., Ltd.
宁波帕恩（POINT）厨具有限公司
浙江省慈溪市坎墩工业区永安西路529号
电话：0574-6328 4816
传真：0574-6328 9345
网址：www.point-de.com

Zhuhai Jiade Kitchenware Co., Ltd.
珠海市佳德厨卫产品有限公司
珠海市新青工业区新青六路15号
邮编：519180
电话：0756-513 6888
传真：0756-513 6866
电邮：service@gorlde.com.cn
网址：www.gorlde.com.cn

实心材料 Solid Surfacing

Tkl Development Ltd.
嘉诺发展有限公司
1302 Hung Tai Industrial Building, 37-39 Hung To Road, Kwun Tong, Kowloon, Hong Kong
电话：+852-2303 1632
传真：+852-2362 9775
电邮：info@tkldevelopment.com.hk
网址：www.vockastone.com

水龙头 Taps

American Standard (China) Co., Ltd.
美标（中国）有限公司
上海市田林路487号宝石园24号楼
邮编：200233
电话：021-3395 2888
传真：021-3367 4255
电邮：sales@americanstandard.com.cn
网址：www.americanstandard.com.cn

Armati AG (HK) Limited
德国阿玛提（香港）有限公司
香港火炭坳背湾街57-59号
利达工业中心12字楼1222室
电话：+852-6872 7458
传真：+852-2699 2776
电邮：armati@armati.hk
网址：www.armati.hk
请参阅第328页

Atget Decoration & Hardware Co., Ltd.
广州市雅之杰装饰五金有限公司
广州市荔湾区龙津西路172号之2首层、二层
邮编：510150
电话：020-8102 8098
传真：020-8103 8982
电邮：atget@atgetco.com
网址：www.atgetco.com
请参阅第388页

HOME IS WHERE
MY GROHE SPA™ IS
Transform your bathroom into a haven of relaxation with GROHE SPA™ luxury fittings.
高仪（中国）
服务热线：400-881-1698
官方网址：www.grohe.com.cn
地址：上海黄陂北路227号中区广场605-610室
电话：（021）63758878
传真：（021）63758665

GROHE
SPA
www.grohespa.com

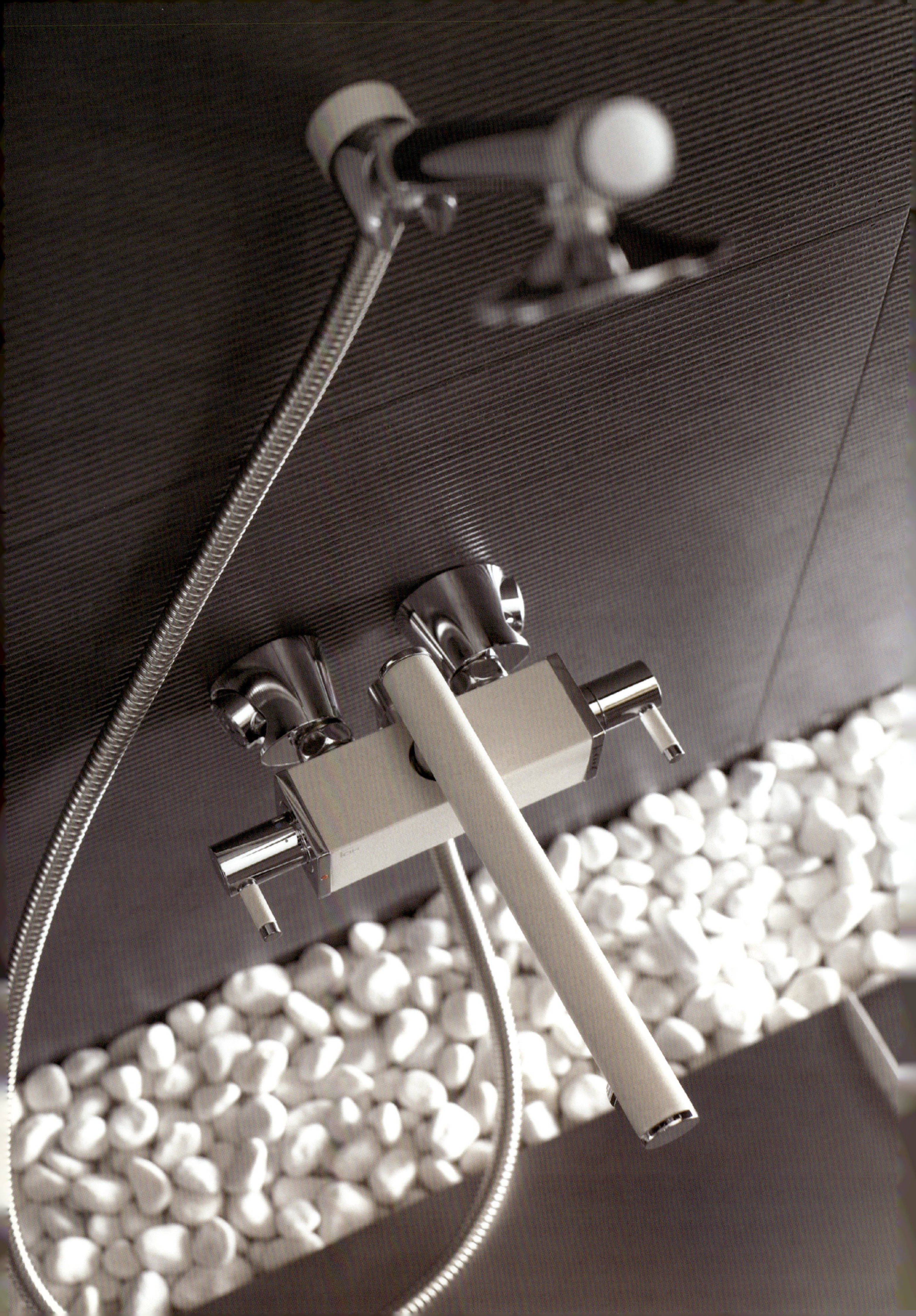

Armati®
德國酒店衛浴第一品牌
我們服務過的品牌酒店客户
Famous brand of hotel customers we offer service ever
東南亞銷售公司—德國阿瑪提（香港）有限公司 / Armati ag(hk)limited
香港火炭坳背灣街57-59號利達工業中心12字樓1222室 / No.1222.12/F.,Leader Industrial Centre,57-59 Au Pui Wan St.,Fotan,HongKong
電話（Tel）:852-6872 7458 傳真（Fax）:852-2699 2776 / Http://www.armati.hk Http://www.armati.co / E-mail:armati@armati.hk
全球唯一終身保用的龍頭品牌 Lifetime warranty is the only one brand in the world

▼水龙头
Taps

Bravat (Guangzhou) Plumbing Industrial Co., Ltd.
贝朗（广州）卫浴器材有限公司
广州市番禺区市桥镇小平工业区福平路二街6号
邮编：511490
电话：020-3480 2916
传真：020-3480 2936
电邮：bravat@bravat.com.cn
网址：www.bravat.com

CAE Sanitary Fittings Ind. Co. Ltd.
广东希恩卫浴实业有限公司
广东省开平市水口镇沙冈兴达路62-64号
邮编：529321
电话：0750-271 2668
传真：0750-271 6328
电邮：cae2@china-cae.com
网址：www.china-cae.com

Chaozhou Yatao Ceramics Co., Ltd.
潮州市亚陶瓷业有限公司
广东省潮州市火车站北片兴工路13号
邮编：521031
电话：0768-299 3933
传真：0768-299 8230
电邮：sales@yatao.com
网址：www.yatao.com

Franke (China) Kitchen System Co., Ltd.
弗兰卡（中国）厨房系统有限公司
上海市徐汇区零陵路899号飞洲国际广场15楼K座
邮编：200030
电话：021-5489 3126
传真：021-5489 3155
网址：www.franke.com.cn

Fuzhou Zhirong Reaction Equipment Co., Ltd.
福州志荣感应设备有限公司
福建省福州市金山工业区
浦上片台江园百花洲路30号
邮编：350008
电话：0591-8385 0111
传真：0591-8385 5399
电邮：zilong@zilong.com.cn
网址：www.zilong.com.cn

Globe Union
成霖集团
广州市先烈中路102号华盛大厦南塔18楼
电话：020-3766 0360
传真：020-3766 3305
网址：www.gobo.com.cn

Grohe (Shanghai) Sanitary Products Co., Ltd.
高仪（上海）卫生洁具有限公司
上海市黄陂北路227号中区广场605-610室
邮编：200003
电话：021-6375 8878
传真：021-6375 8665
网址：www.grohe.com.cn
请参阅第322、323页

Guangdong Heshan Andeli Sanitary Ware Co., Ltd.
广东鹤山市安得利卫浴有限公司
广东省鹤山市址山镇人民北路19号
邮编：529729
电话：0750-865 0888
传真：0750-865 0555
电邮：larsd@163.com
网址：www.larsd.com

Hansgrohe Sanitary Products (Shanghai) Co., Ltd.
汉斯格雅卫浴产品（上海）有限公司
上海市松江工业区东部新区申港路2999号
邮编：201611
电话：021-3774 2200
传真：021-3774 2202
电邮：info@hansgrohe.com.cn
网址：www.hansgrohe.com.cn

Heshan City Kangliyuan Sanitary Ware Industry Co., Ltd.
鹤山市康立源卫浴实业有限公司
广东省鹤山市址山镇东溪工业开发区B区
电话：0750-866 8658
传真：0750-866 6833
电邮：hjy@kly-faucet.com
网址：www.kly-faucet.com

HuiHuang Plumbing Group Co., Ltd.
辉煌水暖集团有限公司
福建省南安市仑仓辉煌工业园区
邮编：362304
电话：0595-8614 8888
传真：0595-8614 2888
电邮：hhsn@hhsn.cn
网址：www.hhsn.cn

Inax (China) Investment Co., Ltd.
伊奈（中国）投资有限公司
上海市西藏南路218号永银大厦704室
电话：021-6334 3366
传真：021-6473 2360
电邮：sales@inax.com.cn
网址：www.inax.com.cn

Joyou Group
中宇建材集团有限公司
福建省南安市仑苍镇中宇工业园
电话：0595-8618 8888
传真：0595-8614 6689
电邮：joyou@joyou.com.cn
网址：www.joyou.com.cn

Kaiping City Edea Sanitary Ware Co., Ltd.
开平市伊丹卫浴实业有限公司
广东省开平市水口镇第二工业园
邮编：529321
电话：0750-271 1901
传真：0750-271 0386
电邮：kp@edea-faucet.com
网址：www.edea-faucet.com

Kohler China Investment Co., Ltd.
科勒（中国）投资有限公司
上海市闸北区江场三路158号
邮编：200436
电话：021-2606 2000
传真：021-6107 8900
网址：www.kohler.com.cn

Madison Sanitary Fittings Co., Ltd.
开平美迪晨卫浴实业有限公司
广东省开平市水口镇外环北路工业区A24-2号
电话：0750-271 2182
传真：0750-271 9838
电邮：springsan@126.com
网址：www.hongkee.com

Moen Ine.
摩恩（中国）公司
上海市浦东新区银城中路168号
上海银行大厦1001室
邮编：200120
电话：021-6360 9600
传真：021-5876 4678
电邮：webmaster@moen.com
网址：www.moen.cn

Nanguo Ceramics Sanitary Wares Industrial Co., Ltd.
南国陶瓷洁具实业有限公司
广东省潮安县古巷镇枫一工业开发区
电话：0768-683 8953
传真：0768-683 3818
电邮：webmaster@nanguo-cn.com
网址：www.nanguo-cn.com

Ningbo Zhanying Equipment Induction Co., Ltd.
宁波展鹰感应设备有限公司
浙江省宁波市江北大道648号（洪塘）
邮编：315033
电话：0574-8784 4011
传真：0574-8787 3756
电邮：zy2001@chinazhanying.com
网址：www.chinazhanying.com

Rak Ceramics
P.O.Box:6679, Ras Al Khaimah
United Arab Emirates
电话：+971(7)-244 5046
传真：+971(7)-244 5062
电邮：swsales@rakceram.com
网址：www.rakceram.com

Roca (China) Ltd.
乐家（中国）有限公司
上海市徐汇区漕溪北路396号
汇智大厦裙楼503-505室
邮编：200030
电话：021-3368 8822
传真：021-3368 8299
网址：www.roca.cn

Shanghai Aosi Sanitary Wares Co., Ltd.
上海奥思卫浴设备有限公司
上海市漕宝路1783弄顾家塘158号
邮编：201101
电话：021-5485 8026
传真：021-6461 8883
电邮：lbqi@os-boslong.com
网址：www.os-boslong.com

Shanghai Meike Electric Co., Ltd.
上海美克电器有限公司
上海市浦东新区康桥工业区川周公路2600弄78号
邮编：200124
电话：400 711 1887
电邮：meikty@foxmail.com
网址：www.meike-gm.com

Shenluda Group Co., Ltd.
申鹭达集团公司
福建省南安市英都恒坂阀门基地申鹭达工业园
邮编：362305
电话：0595-8616 8888
传真：0595-8616 9999
电邮：shenluda@pub1.qz.fj.cn
网址：www.shenludagroup.com

▼水龙头
Taps

Sunlot Shares Co., Ltd.
申鹭达股份有限公司
福建省南安市英都恒坂阀门基地申鹭达工业园
邮编：362305
电话：0595-8616 6892
传真：0595-8616 9999
网址：www.shenludagroup.com

TOTO (China) Co., Ltd.
东陶（中国）有限公司
上海市延安西路2201号上海国际贸易中心210室
邮编：200336
电话：021-6270 1010
传真：021-6270 3099
网址：www.toto.com.cn

Tailin Sanitary Ware Industry Co., Ltd.
中国泰林卫浴实业有限公司
广东省鹤山市址山镇东溪开发区B区
邮编：529729
电话：0750-866 6681
传真：0750-866 6686
电邮：tailin@china-tailin.com
网址：www.china-tailin.com

Taizhou Yadi Water Heating Equipments Co., Ltd.
台州雅迪水暖器材有限公司
浙江省玉环县机电工业园区
邮编：317600
电话：0576-8729 8837
传真：0576-8729 8828
电邮：yader@yader.com
网址：www.yader.com

Tangshan Huida Ceramic (Group) Co. Ltd.
唐山惠达陶瓷（集团）股份有限公司
河北省唐山市丰南区惠达陶瓷城
邮编：063307
电话：0315-852 3618
传真：0315-852 2827
电邮：huida@heinfo.net
网址：www.huidagroup.com

Tianlong Sanitary Facil Industrial Co., Ltd.
天龙卫浴实业有限公司
广东省开平市水口镇外环北路A-21号
邮编：529321
电话：0750-271 1389
传真：0750-272 2807
电邮：info@tilo.com.cn
网址：www.tilo.com.cn

Yatin Bath Art Co., Ltd.
浙江雅鼎卫浴股份有限公司
杭州建德市雅鼎路777号
邮编：311607
电话：0571-6409 7766
传真：0571-6409 7799
电邮：service@yatin.com.cn
网址：www.yatin.com.cn

Zhongshan Benta Building Materials Co., Ltd.
中山市宾德建材有限公司
中山市东区东裕路11号之六
电话：0760-2332 0298
传真：0760-8823 8937
电邮：sales@benta.cn
网址：www.benta.cn

Zoje Kitchen & Bath Co., Ltd.
中捷厨卫股份有限公司
浙江省玉环大麦屿港口工业区
邮编：317604
电话：0576-8733 7976
传真：0576-8733 7999
电邮：cn@suneli.com
网址：www.suneli.com

得而达水龙头（中国）有限公司
广东省广州番禺南村镇兴南大道618号
邮编：511422
电话：020-8476 0018
传真：020-8476 0038
电邮：smpan@deltafaucet.com
网址：www.deltafaucet.com.cn

佛山辉映卫浴洁具有限公司
广东省佛山市顺德容桂镇
容边天河工业区容辉路2号
电话：0757-2831 1878
传真：0757-2881 7082
电邮：coso@coso.cn
网址：www.coso.cn

广东华艺卫浴实业有限公司
广东省开平市水口镇联竹开发区D1
电话：0750-272 6688
传真：0750-271 6688
电邮：Market@huayi-faucet.com
网址：www.huayi-faucet.com

汉莎（德国）金属制造股份公司中国代表处
上海市黄浦区延安东路222号外滩中心1830室
邮编：200002
电话：021-6132 3859
传真：021-6335 0643
网址：www.hansa.com

上海匡隆建材有限公司
上海市上肇嘉浜路201号5楼
电话：021-6422 7917
传真：021-6422 7903
网址：www.kl-king.com
请参阅第326、327、354、355页

乔登卫浴(江门)有限公司
广东省江门市二合山工业区永盛路148号
电话：0750-350 2188
传真：0750-350 2181
网址：www.joden.com.cn

厦门人水科技有限公司
厦门市海沧区中沧工业区坪埕北路1-39号
电话：0592-619 2666
传真：0592-619 2601
电邮：sales@renshui.com
网址：www.solux.com.cn
请参阅第324、325页、书签

瓷砖
Tiles

ASA Group Holdings Ltd.
上海亚细亚陶瓷有限公司
上海市闵行区虹梅南路2599号
邮编：201108
电话：021-6497 8888
传真：021-6497 0818
网址：www.asatiles.com

Beijing Minghe Jili Building Materials Co., Ltd.
北京市明禾吉利建筑材料有限公司
北京市丰台区花乡桥东白盆窑208号
邮编：100071
电话：010-8379 3688
传真：010-8379 3808
电邮：mhjl@mhjlbj.com
网址：www.mhjlbj.com

Foshan City Mango Building Material Co., Ltd.
佛山市芒果建材有限公司
佛山市中国陶瓷产业总部基地中区C座07栋
邮编：528000
电话：0757-8252 3628
传真：0757-8252 0877
网址：www.mgbm.net

Foshan City Faenza Sanitary Ware Co., Ltd.
佛山市法恩洁具有限公司
广东省佛山市高明沧江工业园
电话：0757-8862 8788
传真：0757-8851 0161
电邮：sale@faenza.com.cn
网址：www.faenza.com.cn

Foshan Handmade Ceramics Co., Ltd.
佛山市汉美陶瓷有限公司
广东省佛山市禅城区湾海口大道
邮编：528000
电话：0757-8270 2391
传真：0757-8270 2381
网址：www.arttiles.cn

Foshan Hummingbird Ceramic Co., Ltd.
佛山蜂鸟建陶有限公司
佛山市季华西路168号瓷海国际C区14座15-18号
邮编：528000
电话：0757-8253 3196
传真：0757-8253 3195
网址：www.fsfnjt.com

Foshan Lzard Ceramic Ltd.
佛山市蜥蜴陶瓷有限公司
广东省佛山市中国陶瓷城A318
电话：0757-8266 0919
传真：0757-8801 5075
网址：www.lizardceramics.com

Foshan Miclear Ceramic Technology Co., Ltd.
佛山市明可丽尔陶瓷科技有限公司
广东省佛山市禅城区石湾卫浴城
邮编：528000
电话：0757-8311 0649
传真：0757-8365 3089
电邮：miclear2006@yahoo.com.cn
网址：www.miclear.com

Foshan Ottima Ceramic Co., Ltd.
佛山市奥特玛陶瓷有限公司
佛山市禅城区季华三路奥特玛瓷旋宫
邮编：528000
电话：0757-8278 3210
传真：0757-8277 0336
网址：www.fsotm.cn

Foshan Sunny Ceramics Co., Ltd.
佛山市阳光陶瓷有限公司
佛山市南庄镇华夏陶瓷博览城
陶博一路维罗生态砖营销中心
邮编：528061
电话：0757-8539 3888
传真：0757-8539 2277
电邮：info@vero.cn
网址：www.vero.cn

▼瓷砖
Tiles

Guangdong DongPeng Ceramic Co., Ltd.
广东东鹏陶瓷股份有限公司
广东省佛山市禅城区江湾三路8号东鹏大厦
电话：0757-8272 9997
传真：0757-8227 2343
电邮：cizhuan@dongpeng.net
网址：www.dongpeng.net

Guangdong Kito Ceramics Co., Ltd.
广东金意陶陶瓷有限公司
广东佛山季华西路瓷海国际B-1金意陶思想公园
邮编：528031
电话：0757-8253 3888
传真：0757-8253 3800
电邮：kito100@126.com
网址：www.ekito.cn

Hitom Ceramics Co., Ltd.
海棠陶瓷有限公司
广东省佛山市季华四路33号佛山创意产业园14楼
邮编：528219
电话：0757-8226 5888
传真：0757-8531 5686
电邮：info@hitom-ceramics.com
网址：www.hitom-ceramics.com

Inax (China) Investment Co., Ltd.
伊奈（中国）投资有限公司
上海市西藏南路218号永银大厦704室
电话：021-6334 3366
传真：021-6473 2360
电邮：sales@inax.com.cn
网址：www.inax.com.cn

Jinduo Ceramics
佛山市金舵陶瓷有限公司
佛山市禅城区华夏陶瓷博览城会展一路12座
邮编：528000
电话：0757-8531 0888
传真：0757-8533 8822
电邮：info@jinduo.com.cn
网址：www.jinduo.com.cn

Po Tak Hong Limited
保德行有限公司
香港九龙弥敦道337-339号金满楼12楼F室
电话：+852-2375 6988
传真：+852-2375 6998
电邮：enquiry@pth.com.hk
网址：www.pth.com.hk

Roma Ceramic
罗马瓷砖有限公司
江苏省苏州市吴中区苏沪机场路888号
电话：0512-6501 0712
传真：0512-6501 0713
电邮：mysc@roma-mail.com
网址：www.romaceramic.com.cn

Shanghai Bravo Building Materials Co., Ltd.
上海巴沃建材有限公司
上海市普陀区西康路1068号
维多利广场A座8楼B室
邮编：200060
电话：021-5252 2659
传真：021-5252 2669
电邮：369000@163.com
网址：www.yagebotao.com.cn

Shanghai Cimic Tiles Co., Ltd.
上海斯米克建筑陶瓷股份有限公司
上海市闵行区浦江镇三鲁公路2121号
邮编：201112
电话：021-6411 0567
传真：021-6411 7463
网址：www.cimic.com

Zhongshan Benta Building Materials Co., Ltd.
中山市宾德建材有限公司
中山市东区东裕路11号之六
电话：0760-2332 0298
传真：0760-8823 8937
电邮：sales@benta.cn
网址：www.benta.cn

佛山市顺德区乐华陶瓷洁具有限公司
广东省佛山市顺德区乐从镇大墩工业区
邮编：528315
电话：0757-2618 6039
传真：0757-2868 3833
网址：www.arrowceramic.com

广东蒙娜丽莎陶瓷有限公司
广东省佛山市南海区西樵旅游度假区工业区
电话：0757-8682 2683
传真：0757-8682 8138
电邮：monalisa@monalisa.com.cn
网址：www.monalisa.com.cn

唯宝贸易（上海）有限公司
上海市延安西路2299号世贸商城10A28室
邮编：200336
电话：021-6236 3281
传真：021-6236 3283
网址：www.villeroy-boch.com
请参阅第318、319页

鹰牌控股有限公司
广东省佛山市禅城区大江路
邮编：528031
电话：0757-8396 2288
传真：0757-8227 1664
网址：www.eagleceramics.com

椅子套
Upholsteries

Foshan Nanhai Huaxing Sleave Weaving Factory
广东省南海华兴丝绵织厂
广东省佛山市南海区丹灶镇塱心上尧工业区
邮编：528216
电话：0757-8544 0122
传真：0757-8541 2128
电邮：weave@weave.cn
网址：www.weave.cn

Guangzhou Seechin Hotel Supplies Production Co., Ltd.
广州鑫铖酒店用品制造有限公司
广州市白云区均禾街石马村新石路16号
邮编：510430
电话：020-8661 3491
传真：020-8661 3428
电邮：seechin-008@163.com
网址：www.seechin.com.cn

Jin Yuan Decorative Articles Manufacturing Factory
大连锦源装饰用品有限公司
辽宁省大连市金州区后石工业园区
邮编：116000
电话：0411-8430 5430
传真：0411-8435 4545
电邮：bosoo@china.com
网址：www.bosoo.com.cn

Nantong Longfeng Textile Co., Ltd.
南通龙凤纺织有限公司
江苏省南通经济开发区花园港路81号
邮编：226009
电话：0513-8592 8856
传真：0513-8592 8855
网址：www.ssissi.com.cn

Nantong Minghong Home Textile Co., Ltd.
南通明宏纺织品有限公司
江苏省南通市家纺城金五路182号
电话：0513-8295 9558
传真：0513-8295 9559
网址：www.yuanzb1016.cn

Nantong Yiya Textile Co., Ltd.
南通宜雅纺织品有限公司
江苏省如皋市丁堰镇大河南6号
邮编：226521
电话：0513-8856 3618
传真：0513-8856 2898
电邮：manager@yiyatex.com
网址：www.yiyatex.com

Qingdao Weimay Textile Co., Ltd.
青岛唯美纺织有限公司
山东省青岛市市南区香港中路32号27层
邮编：266071
电话：0532-8079 3158
传真：0532-8384 7637
网址：www.wemaytextile.com

Shanghai Deyi Hotel Articles Manufacture Co., Ltd.
上海德义酒店用品制造有限公司
上海市民星路201号20号楼
邮编：200433
电话：021-5169 9518
传真：021-5126 2385
网址：www.sh-dy.com
请参阅第414页

Shanghai Diyi Hotel Supplies Maintenance Factory
上海地一酒店用品厂
上海市青浦工业园区崧复路1590号
邮编：201706
电话：021-5986 8719
传真：021-5986 8720
网址：www.shdyjd.cn

▼椅子套 Upholsteries

Weihai SiWei Textile Co., Ltd.
威海思维纺织有限公司
山东省威海羊亭玉林工业园5号
邮编：264205
电话：0631-576 9675
传真：0631-576 9677
网址：www.swtextile.com

Yixing Jinfenghuang Yarn-Dyed Tablecloth Plant
宜兴市金凤凰色织台布厂
江苏省宜兴市屺亭镇北
邮编：214213
电话：0510-8786 1834
传真：0510-8786 6834
网址：www.wx-tb.com

临安渊达布艺织造有限公司
杭州市临安太湖源镇纺织服装开发区青溪街22号
邮编：311306
电话：0571-6379 3088
传真：0571-6379 3088
网址：www.hzydby.cn

欣诚诺纺织品有限公司
北京市丰台区南苑乡赵王庄
邮编：100023
电话：010-6737 8089
传真：010-6736 3730
网址：www.zhashoufeng.diytrade.com

墙面涂料 Wall Coatings

Alligator Coatings (Shanghai) Co., Ltd.
鳄鱼制漆（上海）有限公司
上海市沪青平公路3966号
电话：021-5975 8688
传真：021-5975 8680
网址：www.alligator.cn

Auroras (HK) Ltd.
傲丽（香港）有限公司
香港沙田火炭坳背湾街45号喜利佳大厦E4号地铺
电话：+852-2884 3876
传真：+852-3020 8898
电邮：info@auro.com.hk
网址：www.auro.com.hk

Flugger Coating (Shanghai) Co., Ltd.
福侣阁涂料贸易（上海）有限公司
上海市蒲汇塘路123号1楼
邮编：200030
电话：021-5425 8626
传真：021-6487 6962
电邮：customerservice@flugger.cn
网址：www.flugger.cn

Foshan Wanlei Building Paint Co., Ltd.
佛山市南海万磊建筑涂料有限公司
佛山市南海区松岗镇万石工业区元岗市场
电话：0757-8522 7712
传真：0757-8522 5962
网址：www.fswanlei.com

Guangdong Huarun Paints Co., Ltd.
广东华润涂料有限公司
广州市顺德区高新技术开发区科技产业园
邮编：528306
电话：0757-2837 6688
传真：0757-2837 6666
网址：www.huarun.com.cn

Maoming Rihua Paint Co., Ltd.
茂名日化涂料有限公司
广东省茂名市光华北路10号外贸大厦四楼
邮编：525000
电话：0668-288 0808
传真：0668-288 0878
电邮：webmaster@rihua.com.cn
网址：www.rihua.com.cn

Shanghai DAYU Coating Co., Ltd.
上海大禹涂料有限公司
上海市卢湾区普安路189号曙光大厦8楼D座
电话：021-6385 5996
传真：021-6385 5997
网址：www.dayu818.com

Shanghai Loge Chemical & Print Co., Ltd.
上海劳格化工涂料有限公司
上海市工业综合开发区航南路2号（原北一路）
邮编：201400
电话：021-6710 2299
传真：021-6710 2255
网址：www.logepaint.com

Shanghai Shanyi Enterprise Co., Ltd.
上海三银制漆有限公司
上海市西郊经济技术开发区华徐路685号
邮编：201702
电话：021-5988 3377
传真：021-5988 4001
电邮：sy@san-yin.com
网址：www.adani.cn

Shanghai Viero Coatings Co., Ltd.
上海威罗涂料有限公司
上海市曲阳路800号商务中心2705室
邮编：200437
电话：021-5588 6711
传真：021-6552 8600
网址：www.lafarge-coatings.com.cn

Shanghai Zheng Ou Paint Factory Co., Ltd.
上海正欧涂料有限公司
上海市嘉定区宝钱公路1958号
邮编：201816
电话：021-5995 1654
传真：021-5995 1582
电邮：zong@zheng.cc
网址：www.zheng.sh.cn

广东江门市维克特涂料有限公司
广东省江门市江海区明星村业成工业区
电话：0750-395 0398
传真：0750-395 0718
电邮：jaky_1218@126.com
网址：www.diboine.com

柳州市绿环涂料有限责任公司
广西省柳州市西江路静兰工业开发区2号
邮编：545006
电话：0772-311 9113
传真：0772-311 0533
网址：www.lzlhtl.com

武汉祥和磷化涂料有限公司
武汉市汉阳区汉阳大道139号汉商大厦1506室
邮编：430050
电话：027-5940 9153
传真：027-5940 9158
电邮：limilll@163.com

云南省昆明市永华涂料厂
云南省昆明市高新开发区昌源北路
邮编：650108
电话：0871-819 2526
传真：0871-819 2526
网址：www.yahoosme.com

墙纸、壁布 Wallpapers & Wallcoverings

Beijing Topli Decorative Materials Co., Ltd.
北京特普丽装饰装帧材料有限公司
北京市房山区周口店
邮编：102451
电话：010-6930 1133
传真：010-6930 3539
电邮：topli@topli.com.cn
网址：www.topli.com.cn

Brewster Wallcovering International Trade (Shanghai) Ltd.
布鲁斯特墙纸国际贸易（上海）有限公司
上海市闵行区景联路439号2号楼1层
邮编：201108
电话：021-6497 6060
传真：021-6497 4988
电邮：kelly@brewsterchina.com
网址：www.brewsterchina.com

Changzhou Hanree Decorative Material Co., Ltd.
常州韩利装饰材料有限公司
常州市天宁区青龙街道东风民营工业园28-9号
邮编：213000
电话：0519-8556 9701
传真：0519-8556 9703
电邮：hanree@163.com
网址：www.hanree.com

Changzhou Walldec Special New Materials Co., Ltd.
常州华碧宝特种新材料有限公司
江苏省常州市新区玉龙北路501号
邮编：213002
电话：0519-8520 2768
传真：0519-8520 7053
电邮：hbb@walldec.com
网址：www.walldec.com

Chung's Carpet Development Ltd.
钟氏地毯发展有限公司
1-3/F Waitex House, 7-9 Mongkok Road, Mong Kok, Kowloon, Hong Kong
电话：+852-2770 6215
传真：+852-2770 1576
电邮：chcarpet@chungscarpet.com.hk
网址：www.chungscarpet.com.hk

Dimoon Building Materials Co., Ltd.
迪幕墙纸（上海戴莫建筑材料有限公司）
上海市长宁区天山路789号天山商厦西楼2501室
电话：021-6228 2381
传真：021-6228 2918
电邮：info@dimoon.com.cn
网址：www.dimoon.com.cn

marburg
WALLCOVERINGS
德国玛堡壁纸
舒雅室
solari
marburg
WALLCOVERINGS
德国玛堡壁纸
Nina Campbell
LORCA
OSBORNE & LITTLE
ARTE
GUY MASUREEL®
ART I INTERIORCONCEPTS
SANDBERG
Svensk Tapetkonst
GIARDINI
WALLCOVERINGS
AGENA®
pininfarina
DESIGNS OF THE TIME
INTERIOR FABRICS
Christian Fischbacher
JAKOB SCHLAEPFER
nya nordiska
donati
舒雅室
solari
www.marburg.net.cn
400-890-7698

德国朗饰墙纸　缔造健康精致生活
德国朗饰墙纸制造有限公司位于德国布拉姆舍市，公司成立于1897年，至今已有100多年生产优质壁纸的历史。现今，朗饰集团已发展成为全球规模最大的壁纸生产企业之一，5000多款不同风格的壁纸远销世界各地，出口到65个国家。2010年朗饰壁纸在中国市场占有率已跃居所有欧洲品牌之首，并荣幸地应用到北京奥运村和国家大剧院等重大项目。

rasch®
DESIGN
DESTINATIONS
德国朗饰墙纸制造有限公司上海代表处
地址 上海市成都北路333号 招商局广场南楼908室
电话 021-5298 0789 传真 021-5298 1822
网址 www.rasch.com.cn

▼墙纸、壁布
Wallpapers & Wallcoverings

Erfurt
爱尔福特
北京市朝阳区延静西里2号华商大厦503-507室
邮编：100025
电话：010-6585 0954
传真：010-6585 2128
电邮：info@denizen-online.com
网址：www.erfurrt.com.cn

Graham & Brown (Shanghai) Trading Co., Ltd.
格兰布朗（上海）商贸有限公司
上海市黄浦区黄陂北路227号中区广场602室
邮编：200003
电话：021-6375 8111
传真：021-5375 9375
电邮：sales@grahambrown-cn.com
网址：www.grahambrown.com

Guangdong Magnolia Decorative Material Co., Ltd.
广东玉兰装饰材料有限公司
广东省东莞市东城区莞龙路莞城科技园
邮编：523119
电话：0769-2265 6789
传真：0769-2267 7262
电邮：yulan@yulanwallpaper.com.cn
网址：www.yulanwallpaper.com.cn

Hangzhou BaiLun Wallpaper Co., Ltd.
杭州百伦壁纸有限公司
杭州市江干区秋涛北路120号
佳好佳居饰商城B区110室
电话：0571-8698 1352
传真：0571-2802 5083
电邮：zyscjz@163.com
网址：www.hzbibz.com

Hangzhou Girsun Decoration Material Co., Ltd.
杭州格尚装饰材料有限公司
浙江省东阳市西城工业园甑山路10号
电话：0579-8685 7571
传真：0579-8685 7574
网址：www.geshang.net

Mulan Decoratedatum Co., Ltd.
木兰装饰材料有限公司
无锡市太湖西大道1890号
太湖明珠发展大厦1703室
电话：0510-8516 4468
传真：0510-8516 4498
网址：www.mulanbizhi.com

Shanghai AS Creation Internation Trading Co., Ltd.
上海市艾仕国际贸易有限公司
上海市徐汇区漕宝路400号
明申商务广场1203-1206室
邮编：200233
电话：021-6150 8095
传真：021-6150 8094
电邮：red.zhang@as-creation-china.com
网址：www.as-creation-china.com

Shanghai Suwalper Wallpaper Co., Ltd.
上海欣旺壁纸有限公司
上海市奉贤区奉城镇洪庙工业园区兰博路298号
邮编：201411
电话：021-5713 8000
传真：021-3759 1043*44
电邮：livingstyle@livingstylechina.com.cn
网址：www.livingstylechina.com.cn

Shangmei Shijia Beijing Commerce Co., Ltd.
尚美世家（北京）贸易有限公司
北京市朝阳区东土城路8号
林达大厦B座北端1-2层
邮编：100013
电话：010-6446 6899
传真：010-6446 6674
电邮：roen@roen.com.cn
网址：www.roen.com.cn

Today Wallpaper Limited
尚翘装饰材料有限公司
香港湾仔轩尼诗道216-218号宝升中心22楼A室
电话：+852-3791 2293
传真：+852-3791 2292
电邮：today@todaywallpaper.com
网址：www.todaywallpaper.com

Zambaiti (Baoding) Wallcovering Co., Ltd.
展拜邸（保定）墙纸有限公司
河北省保定市高开区复兴中路3200号
邮编：071000
电话：0312-313 5068
传真：0312-311 1744
网址：www.zambaitichina.com

Zhejiang Kexiang Wallpaper Manufacturing Co., Ltd.
浙江科翔壁纸制造有限公司
浙江安吉塘浦工业新城经二路88号
邮编：313300
电话：0572-521 3333
传真：0572-560 8666
电邮：8888@kxbz.cn
网址：www.kxbz.cn

ZhiSheng Wallpaper & Clothart Co., Ltd.
上海致盛墙纸布艺有限公司
上海市双柏路888号1栋3楼
邮编：201100
电话：021-5187 6188
传真：021-6434 9617
电邮：sale@zhisheng-wp.com
网址：www.zhisheng-wp.com

北京美堡·饰家丽装饰材料有限公司
北京市朝阳区慈云寺
住邦2000商务楼3号楼1503室
电话：010-8586 7670
传真：010-8586 4554
网址：www.marburg.net.cn
请参阅第333页、封面

德国朗饰墙纸制造有限公司上海代表处
上海市成都北路333号招商局广场南楼908室
电话：021-5298 0789
传真：021-5298 1822
网址：www.rasch.com.cn
请参阅第334、335页

欧雅壁纸大连公司
辽宁省大连市幸福家居世界5F22号
邮编：116000
电话：0411-8458 9595
传真：0411-8458 9696
电邮：dl001@dleuroart.com
网址：www.dleuroart.com

青岛元石壁纸有限公司
青岛市崂山区苗岭路29号山东高速大厦12B05
邮编：266100
电话：0532-8606 8811
传真：0532-8896 2720
电邮：wons777@188.com
网址：www.wons.cn

窗饰及遮阳 Window Blinds & Architectural Sun-Shading

Activa Leisure Inc
宁波万汇休闲用品有限公司
浙江省宁波市鄞州投资创业园区祥和西路118号
邮编：315104
电话：0574-8824 1888
传真：0574-8824 2999
电邮：sales@activa-leisure.com
网址：www.activa-leisure.com

Gangcai Awningequip Ment Co., Ltd.
上海港彩装饰用品有限公司
上海松江区九亭镇金马路358号
电话：021-6763 1043
传真：021-6763 1698
电邮：shgangcai@163.com
网址：www.shgangcai.com

Guangzhou Greenawn Outdoor Products Co., Ltd.
广州格绿朗户外用品有限公司
广东省广州市番禺区石基镇石岗广华南路152号
电话：020-3461 0612
传真：020-3462 1991
电邮：info@greenawn.com.cn
网址：www.greenawn.com.cn

HZ Jiahuo Sun Shading Co., Ltd.
杭州家和遮阳技术有限公司
浙江省杭州市江干区秋涛北路43号315室
邮编：310020
电话：0571-8133 8390
传真：0571-2891 6872
电邮：rwj362525@tom.com
网址：www.hzjhzy.com

Huzhou Dulun Metallic Co., Ltd.
湖州都伦金属制品有限公司
湖州南浔经济开发区枯村
邮编：313009
电话：0572-308 9666
传真：0572-308 9665
电邮：info@dljscp.com
网址：www.dljscp.com

Mingcheng Enterprise
名成企业
上海市松江泗泾工业区九干路289号
邮编：201601
电话：021-5762 7111
传真：021-5762 6148
电邮：market@mingcheng.com.cn
网址：www.mingcheng.com.cn
请参阅第340、341页

Ningbo ABD Smart Window Co., Ltd.
宁波奥贝迪智能门窗科技有限公司
宁波市鄞州区望春工业园区杉杉路181-197号
电话：0574-2886 7001
传真：0574-2886 7007
电邮：sales@cnabd.net
网址：www.cnabd.net

Shanghai ChuangMing Intelligent Sunshade Technical Co., Ltd.
上海创明智能遮阳技术有限公司
上海市嘉定区高潮路168号
邮编：200000
电话：021-6911 2125
传真：021-5914 2873
网址：www.wintom.net

Shanghai Hongkai Intelligent Sun-Shading Material Co., Ltd.
上海弘凯智能遮阳材料有限公司
上海市浦东新区沪南路3097号
宾悦汽车工业园区2号楼3楼
邮编：200125
电话：021-5090 4815
传真：021-5039 6028
网址：www.sh-hanker.com

Shanghai Huajing Sun-Shading Equipment Manufacture Co., Ltd.
上海桦景遮阳设备制造有限公司
上海市中山北路198号申航大厦1703室
邮编：200071
电话：021-5698 3237
传真：021-5697 1073
电邮：sales@sh-huajing.net
网址：www.sh-huajing.net

Shanghai Jifeng Zhineng Zheyang Jishu Co., Ltd.
上海际风智能遮阳技术有限公司
上海市普陀区未来岛工业园区绥德路889号2号楼
电话：021-6640 0508
传真：021-6640 0508*8006
电邮：jifengzheyang@163.com
网址：www.jifengzheyang.cn

Shanghai Mingyang Window Blinds Manufacture Co., Ltd.
上海名扬窗饰制造有限公司
上海松江佘山工业区明业路198号
邮编：201602
电话：021-5779 4331
传真：021-5779 4335
电邮：mingyang_800@163.com
网址：www.mywb.cn

Shanghai Qing Ying Sun-Shading Technical Development Co., Ltd.
上海青鹰遮阳技术发展有限公司
上海市佘山北部工业园区勋业路251号
邮编：201602
电话：021-6501 2228
传真：021-5779 3270
电邮：sun-shading@qingying.net
网址：www.qingying.net

Shanghai San Jing Decoration Products Co., Ltd.
上海三进装潢制品有限公司
上海市闵行区七宝镇中春路7761弄78号
电话：021-6419 8801~3
传真：021-6419 8208
网址：www.sh-sanjin.com.cn

Shanghai Star Blinds Co., Ltd.
上海星芝骄遮阳系统设备有限公司
上海市漕溪北路468号14C/D室
邮编：200030
电话：021-3424 6718
传真：021-5106 2280
电邮：sales@chinablinds.com
网址：www.chinablinds.com

Shanghai Xin Si Lu Metal Products Co., Ltd.
上海鑫丝陆金属制品有限公司
上海市金沙江西路1555弄C1区5号楼
电话：400 820 1773
传真：021-3951 2115
电邮：xsl@xslmetalfabrics.com
网址：www.xslmetalfabrics.com
请参阅第312页

somfy

Somfy China Co., Ltd.
尚飞中国
上海市华山路1520弄121号2楼
邮编：200052
电话：021-6280 9660
传真：021-6280 0270
网址：www.somfy.cn
业务范围：
Somfy法国尚飞公司是全球领先的智能遮阳及门窗自动化系统的专业制造商。
Somfy成立于上世纪60年代，总部在法国，在世界53个国家和地区设有办事机构，产品销往全球100多个国家和地区。迄今为止，Somfy共获得了600多项专利技术。
尚飞解决方案致力于以下三个生态建筑的目标：自然采光，保温隔热及自然通风。
尚飞产品被广泛应用于办公楼、酒店、医院、学校、博物馆、剧院、会展中心、别墅及公寓住宅等，包括：电动开合帘、电动卷帘、电动天篷帘、电动投影幕、电动百叶帘、电动卷窗、电动卷门、电动遮阳板、电动通风开窗等。
请参阅第338、339页、封面

Yuanzhicheng Hometextile Co., Ltd.
源志诚家纺有限公司
广东省广州市越秀区大南路62号
邮编：510115
电话：020-8330 2177
传真：020-8330 4376
电邮：yzc@yuanzhicheng.com
网址：www.yuanzhicheng.com
业务范围：
源志诚家纺有限公司成立于1994年，是一家集研发设计、生产织造、染整及成品加工、销售服务为一体的专业公司。主要生产以丝织物、仿丝织物、化纤、混纺及纯棉等为主的高密度酒店及家居室内纺织用布及布艺成品，公司自成立以来，一直以时尚的产品向广大同行提供优质服务，同时致力为国内外星级酒店研发风格化的产品及提供多元化的合作模式。
请参阅第2、282、283页

HunterDouglasHospitality

亨特制造（中国）有限公司
上海市闵行区光中路355号
邮编：201108
电话：021-3471 7777*131
传真：021-3471 7521
电邮：info@hunterdouglashospitality.com.cn
网址：www.hunterdouglashospitality.com.cn
业务范围：
作为国际知名的酒店布艺业务整体方案提供商，始创于1919年荷兰亨特道格拉斯集团一直专注于提供高星级酒店需求的酒店布艺、窗饰产品和电动轨道及智能控制系统等专业酒店产品。身为行业的领导者我们能够满足全球各地区高星级酒店对软装饰的个性化要求，为室内设计大师追求完美风格提供理想解决方案。
请参阅第274、275、276、277、278、279页

尚飞酒店窗饰

A Dedicated Solution for Each Part of the Building 窗饰设计

方便安装，容易使用并与市场上的控制系统全面兼容…Somfy解决方案完全满足酒店工程的需要。你可以通过开关或遥控器控制电动窗饰产品；或者根据自动感应器（时间，光，风，雨等）及预设程序自动控制。不管是在客房，大堂，会议室，餐厅还是户外空间，Somfy系统都能根据您或客户的需要智能运行和管理。在酒店客房的窗饰搭配上，越来越多的设计师采用了混搭设计，以满足遮阳，调光，隐私各方面的综合需要，如：

- 遮光布帘＋布艺纱帘；
- 遮光布帘＋罗马纱帘；
- 遮光布帘＋调光柔纱；
- 遮光卷帘＋遮阳卷帘；
- 遮光卷帘＋调光百叶

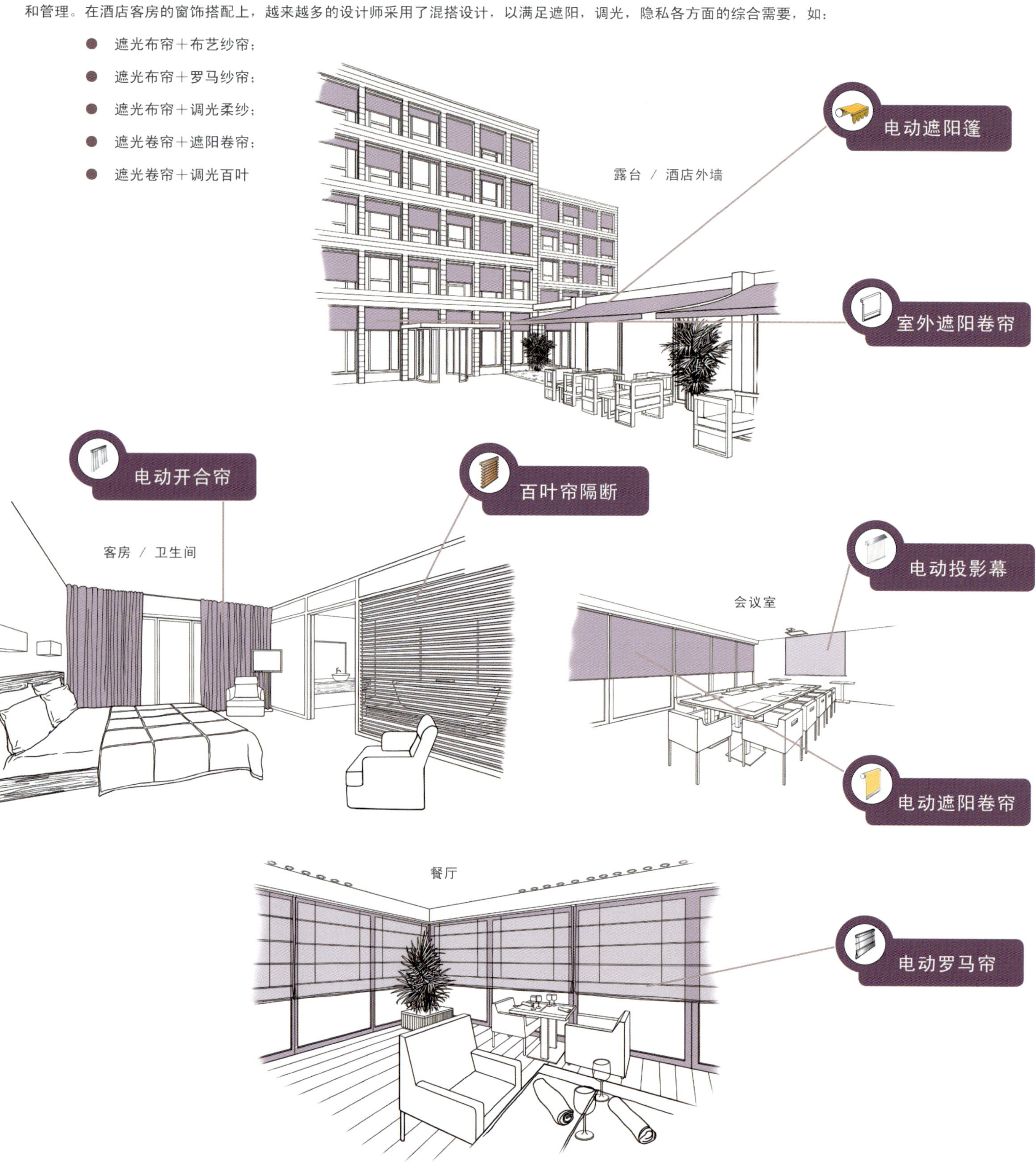

门禁设备
Access Control Equipment

Changzhou Bonwin Technology Co., Ltd.
常州市邦威电子科技有限公司
江苏省常州市高新科技园2号楼A座5楼
邮编：213022
电话：0519-8519 9118
传真：0519-8512 9611
电邮：bonwin@126.com
网址：www.bonwin.com

Changzhou Eversafe Electronic Lock Co., Ltd.
常州科新永安电子锁有限公司
江苏省常州市新北区汉江路400号
邮编：213022
电话：0519-8511 6707
传真：0519-8511 1788
电邮：eversafe@126.com
网址：www.eversafelock.com

Dongguan Visisv Electronic Technology Co., Ltd.
东莞威萨电子科技有限公司
东莞市石龙镇李屋工业园11号
电话：0769-8138 0022
传真：0769-8138 0028
电邮：visisv@126.com
网址：www.visilock.com

Eiffel Digital Image Technology Co., Ltd.
深圳市艾菲尔数字图像技术有限公司
深圳市留学人员（龙岗）创业园1园238
邮编：518172
电话：0755-8972 4869
传真：0755-8972 4648
电邮：apps@eiffeltech.com
网址：www.eiffeltech.com

Guangdong BE-Tech Security Systems Co., Ltd.
广东必达保安系统有限公司
广东省佛山市顺德高新区（容桂）
科技产业园科苑三路17号
邮编：528306
电话：0757-2830 8833
传真：0757-2830 8823
电邮：info@be-tech.com.cn
网址：www.be-tech.com.cn

Guangdong Level Intelligent Lock Industrial Co., Ltd.
广东力维智能锁业有限公司
广东省佛山市禅城区市东下路67号三层
邮编：528000
电话：0757-8399 8880
传真：0757-8399 8055
电邮：sales@cnlevellock.com
网址：www.levellock.com
请参阅第343页

Guangzhou Elite Electronic Co., Ltd.
常州市爱莱特电子有限公司
江苏省常州市钟楼开发区梅花路12-2号
邮编：213023
电话：0519-8686 7388
传真：0519-8801 1021*8020
电邮：sales@elitelock.com
网址：www.elitelock.com

Hangzhou Jinzhima Industrial Co., Ltd.
杭州金指码实业有限公司
杭州市滨江区江晖路1772号苏泊尔大厦3A楼
电话：0571-8808 0888
传真：0571-8885 8811
网址：www.ksmak.com

Ingersoll Rand (Shanghai) Trading Co., Ltd.
英格索兰（上海）贸易有限公司
上海市遵义路100号虹桥上海城B座9-10楼
邮编：200051
电话：021-2208 1288
传真：021-6237 1992
电邮：irst_marketing@ap.irco.com
网址：www.irsecurity.com.cn

Keyu Intelligence Co., Ltd.
广东江门市科裕智能科技有限公司
广东省江门市麻三平顶山科裕工业园
邮编：529000
电话：0750-386 2220
传真：0750-310 8819
网址：www.gdhnkj.com

Nanchang Aland Industrial Co., Ltd.
南昌阿兰德实业有限公司
江西省南昌市高新民营科技园民安路375号
邮编：330029
电话：0791-816 9421
传真：0791-816 9637
电邮：nc-aland@nc-aland.com
网址：www.nc-aland.com

Nanjing Easthouse Electrical Co., Ltd.
南京东屋电气有限公司
南京市大校场路5号三楼
邮编：210022
电话：025-8655 3388
传真：025-5263 8736
电邮：info@easthouse.net
网址：www.talenca.com

Ningbo Yada Safe Equipment Manufacturing Co., Ltd.
宁波亚大安全设备制造有限公司
浙江省余姚市经济开发区南区鸿运路10号
邮编：315403
电话：0574-6277 8819
传真：0574-6277 7052
电邮：market@yadasafe.com
网址：www.yadasafe.com

Obe Door Control Technology (Shanghai) Co., Ltd.
欧必翼门控科技（上海）有限公司
上海市浦东新区秀浦路聚诚工业园区30A
邮编：201319
电话：021-3825 6026
传真：021-3825 6018
电邮：obe@chinaobe.com
网址：www.worldobe.com

Shanghai Haibi Electric Echnology Co., Ltd.
上海海比电子科技有限公司
上海市闵行区沪闵路2759号
邮编：201100
电话：021-5495 2099
传真：021-5495 2199
电邮：coffee@vip.sina.com
网址：www.haibi.net

Shanghai Maxxon Enterprise Co., Ltd.
上海麦克森实业有限公司
上海市静安区愚园路546号10号楼101室
邮编：200040
电话：021-6288 4116
传真：021-6288 4119
网址：www.saflok.com

Shanghai PAD Autodoor Co., Ltd.
上海乘方自动门有限公司
上海市嘉定区华亭镇高石公路2439号
电话：021-6221 5156
传真：021-5226 0423
电邮：padsh@126.com
网址：www.autodoor.com.cn

Shenzhen Ideal Microelectronics Co., Ltd.
深圳爱迪尔电子有限公司
深圳市南山区松白路西丽南岗第二工业园A1栋
邮编：518108
电话：0755-8381 2050
传真：0755-8393 0677
电邮：service@adellock.com
网址：www.adellock.com

Shenzhen MBT Electronics Co., Ltd.
深圳市微蓝特电子有限公司
深圳市福田区益田路南方国际广场A栋2610室
邮编：518000
电话：0755-8297 2798
传真：0755-8282 3601
电邮：mbt@vip.163.com
网址：www.mbtlock.com

Shenzhen Tongchuangxinjia Science Technology Co., Ltd.
深圳市同创新佳科技有限公司
深圳市龙岗区龙岗街道办同乐社区水田路20号C栋
邮编：518116
电话：0755-2807 2722
传真：0755-2807 2922
电邮：locstar@locstar.com
网址：www.locstar.com

Shenzhen Wan Qiao Hong Science & Technology Co., Ltd.
深圳万侨鸿科技有限公司
深圳市宝安区石岩镇石头山工业区一栋
电话：0755-8179 1585
传真：0755-8179 1515
网址：www.wan-qiao.com.cn

Somfy China Co., Ltd.
尚飞中国
上海市华山路1520弄121号2楼
邮编：200052
电话：021-6280 9660
传真：021-6280 0270
网址：www.somfy.cn
请参阅第338、339页、封面

Sugatsune Shanghai Co., Ltd.
世嘉智尼五金配件（上海）有限公司
上海市闸北区万荣一路2号一层
邮编：200436
电话：021-3632 1858
传真：021-3632 1868
电邮：lamp@sugatsune.com.cn
网址：www.sugatsune.com.cn
请参阅第353页、书脊下

▼门禁设备

Access Control Equipment

Zhejiang Koachi Electronic Technology Co., Ltd.
浙江科亚启电子科技有限公司
浙江省杭州市滨江区滨盛路1777号
萧宏大厦18楼A室
电话：0571-5667 6679
传真：0571-5669 7797
网址：www.koachi.cn

安徽赛科智能技术有限公司
安徽省合肥市翠竹园中心广场2栋402室
邮编：230061
电话：0551-515 7936
传真：0551-515 3708
电邮：sayok@sayok.com.cn
网址：www.sayok.com.cn

深圳市宝迅达科技有限公司
深圳市宝安区民治街道办梅龙路
南贤商业广场B座1102A
邮编：518000
电话：0755-8366 3832
传真：0755-8366 3831*888
网址：www.xeeder.cn

深圳市超伦飞智能科技有限公司
深圳市福田区福虹路华强花园A座13E
邮编：518033
电话：0755-8374 0970
传真：0755-8374 1365
电邮：sales@szchaolun.com
网址：www.szchaolun.com

深圳银方加博科技有限公司
深圳市宝安区华龙镇民治大道
铁路桥东美大厦B栋三楼
邮编：518000
电话：0755-2516 4511
传真：0755-2553 9077
网址：www.szcanbo.com

天宇工贸集团有限公司
温州市新桥高翔工业区高风路2号
电话：0577-8841 1550
传真：0577-8841 1549
网址：www.tenyale.com.cn

胶黏剂及密封胶 Adhesives & Sealants

Bostik Findley China Co., Ltd.
波士胶芬得利（中国）粘合剂有限公司
上海市闵行区莘庄镇
莘建东路58弄2号A座1507-1509室
邮编：201100
电话：021-6413 9387
传真：021-6413 9362
网址：www.bostik.com.cn

Danyang Taiyang Chemical Industry Co., Ltd.
江苏台阳化工有限公司
江苏省丹阳市里庄镇
邮编：212363
电话：0511-8667 7168
传真：0511-8667 5518
电邮：info@taiyangchem.com
网址：www.taiyangchem.com

Hings Plastic & Metal Products Mfy
兴业塑胶五金制品厂
广东省顺德市勒流镇富裕工业区
邮编：528324
电话：0757-2533 2788
传真：0757-2533 2993
电邮：hingspmp@hingsgroup.com
网址：www.hingsgroup.com

Huzhou Goodfo Industrial Co., Ltd.
湖州固福化工有限公司
湖州市凤凰开发区计祥路256号
电话：0572-220 2557
传真：0572-220 2620
电邮：777@goodfo.net
网址：www.goodfo.net

Mapei Construction Materials (Guangzhou) Co., Ltd.
马贝建筑材料（广州）有限公司
广州市沿江中路313号
康富来国际大厦2003-2004室
电话：020-8365 3489
传真：020-8365 3481
电邮：mapei-gz@mapei.com.cn
网址：www.mapei.com.cn

Shanghai Rocky Adhesives Co., Ltd.
上海路嘉胶粘剂有限公司
上海市青浦区徐泾经济开发区华徐路566号
邮编：200030
电话：021-5976 1668
传真：021-5976 1668*204
电邮：lj1@china-rocky.com
网址：www.china-rocky.com

Shenzhen Sveck Technology Co., Ltd.
深圳市斯威克科技有限公司
深圳市光明新区公明街道楼村
凤新路新健兴科技工业园A5栋1-2楼
电话：0755-3369 9199
传真：0755-3369 9198
电邮：sveck@sveck.com.cn
网址：www.sveck.com.cn

海德堡金属配件加工厂
山东省济南市天桥区民营工业园内
邮编：250031
电话：0531-8693 9234
传真：0531-8236 7200
电邮：zhugehui88@yahoo.cn
网址：www.china-tigertools.com
请参阅本页

高空工作台 Aerial Work Platforms

Ajax Pong Group
亚积邦集团
香港新界石冈上村锦田公路641号
电话：+852-2751 7555
传真：+852-2305 2929
电邮：info@ajaxpong.com.hk
网址：www.ajaxpong.com.hk

Copyright Beijing XinYaZhong Co., Ltd.
北京欣亚中恒力科贸易有限公司
北京市朝阳区东直门外斜街小关56号
邮编：100027
电话：010-6463 8872
传真：010-6468 4926
电邮：xyz@xyz-china.com
网址：www.xyz-china.com

▼高空工作台
Aerial Work Platforms

GZ Lianyi Zhongxin Co., Ltd.
广州联谊忠信贸易有限公司
广东省广州市西华路414-416号金平大厦B1802室
邮编：510170
电话：020-8135 9310
传真：020-8135 9309
电邮：li_hjz@163.com
网址：www.lianyizhongxin.com

Guangzhou Weicheng Trade Co., Ltd.
广州维诚贸易有限公司
广州市环市东路369号友谊商业大厦1108室
邮编：510095
电话：020-8358 9049
传真：020-8358 9687
电邮：weicheng@uprightcn.com
网址：www.gz-weicheng.com

Hangzhou Sivge Aerial Work Machinery Co., Ltd.
杭州赛奇高空作业机械有限公司
杭州市拱墅区康桥工业区康贤路15号
邮编：310015
电话：0571-8804 3737
传真：0571-8804 3715
电邮：info@sivge.com
网址：www.sivge.com

Mantall (Nantong) Heavy Industry Co., Ltd.
美通（南通）重工有限公司
北京市朝阳区东辛店中街257号
电话：010-6435 6902
传真：010-8456 9735
电邮：sales@mantall.com
网址：www.mantall.com

Nanjing Gold Modern Science & Technology Industry Co., Ltd.
南京金现代科技实业有限公司
南京市鼓楼区草场门大街96号1-401
邮编：210036
电话：025-8621 0667
传真：025-8621 2868
网址：www.jxd.com.cn

Shanghai Honyee Cleanning Equipment Ltd.
上海汉英清洁机械有限公司
上海市松江区九亭镇九新公路599号（近富田路）
电话：021-5485 2222
传真：021-6270 1605
电邮：info@honyee.com.cn
网址：www.honyee.com.cn

Shanghai JF Engineering Equipment Co., Ltd.
上海捷斐工程设备有限公司
上海市虹桥路1765弄（锦苑）24号1楼
邮编：200336
电话：021-6281 8999
传真：021-6278 1188
网址：www.jf-8.com

Zhuhai Extreme High Altitude Work Facility Co., Ltd.
珠海及力高空作业设备有限公司
珠海市香洲区唐家湾镇鸡山工业区
广大学院实训基地2栋东侧（清华科技园旁）
电话：0756-331 6847
传真：0756-361 0038
电邮：jilimc@163.com
网址：www.jilimc.cn

芳香系统
Air Aroma Systems

Air Aroma 空间香氛
上海熠坤商贸有限公司
上海市零陵路585号24F
电话：021-6481 1773
传真：021-6481 1972
电邮：china@air-aroma.com
网址：www.air-aroma.com.cn
请参阅第346页

Aroma Loire
深圳市艾罗曼香料科技有限公司
深圳市罗湖区深南东路文华大厦西座26楼F
邮编：518003
电话：0755-2265 3600
传真：0755-2265 5600
电邮：info@aroma-lorie.com
网址：www.aroma-loire.com

Guangzhou Faner Aroma Product Co., Ltd.
广州凡而芳香日用品有限公司
广州市白云区均禾街新科村新东路10号
邮编：510430
电话：020-3628 0192
传真：020-3628 0200
网址：www.faner.com

空调设备
Air Conditioning Equipment

Carrier China
开利中国
上海市汉口路266号申大厦5楼
邮编：200001
电话：021-2306 3000
传真：021-2306 3024
网址：www.carrier.com.cn

Climaveneta Chat Union Refrigeration Equipment (Shanghai) Co., Ltd.
克莱门特捷联制冷设备（上海）有限公司
上海市奉贤区星火开发区白云路88号
邮编：201419
电话：021-5750 5566
传真：021-5750 5797
电邮：info@climaveneta.com.cn
网址：www.climaveneta.com.cn

Daikin (China) Investment Co., Ltd.
大金（中国）投资有限公司
北京东城区东长安街1号东方广场东三办公楼20层
邮编：100738
电话：010-8518 1117
传真：010-8518 3856
网址：www.daikin-china.com.cn

Dongguanshi Junda Kongtiao Shebei Youxian Gongsi
东莞市骏达空调设备有限公司
广东省东莞市南城宏远花园一街2号
邮编：523000
电话：0769-2241 9306
传真：0769-2241 9113
电邮：jianli@jian-li.com
网址：www.jian-li.com

Guangdong Jirong Aor-Conditioning Equipment Company
广东省吉荣空调设备公司
广东省揭阳市吉荣路
邮编：522000
电话：0663-888 8888
传真：0663-888 1916
电邮：jr@jirong.com
网址：www.jirong.com

Qingdao Tonghe Air Conditioning Equipment Co., Ltd.
青岛同和空调设备股份有限公司
山东省青岛市平度市同和街道办事处
电话：0532-8731 1108
传真：0532-8731 1135
电邮：web@tong-he.com.cn
网址：www.tong-he.com.cn

Shandong Cooling Aor-Conditioning Equipment Co., Ltd.
山东科灵空调设备有限公司
山东省潍坊市高新区创业大厦7楼
电话：0536-889 0057
传真：0536-889 0057
电邮：keling88@163.com
网址：www.sdkeling.com

Shandong Zhongli Air-Condition Co., Ltd.
山东中立空调设备有限公司
山东省德州武城滕庄开发区
电话：0534-264 9456
传真：0534-267 5008
电邮：sdzl@sdzl.cn
网址：www.sdzl.cn

Shanghai Gree Air Conditioner Sales Co., Ltd.
上海格力空调销售有限公司
上海市静安区万航渡路888号17楼E座
邮编：200042
电话：021-5237 5047
传真：021-5237 5061
电邮：gree_sh@sohu.com
网址：www.gree.com

Wuxi Shenda Air-Conditioner Equipment Co., Ltd.
无锡申达空调设备有限公司
无锡市西漳锡澄南路208号
邮编：214171
电话：0510-8375 9688
传真：0510-8375 1552
电邮：shendaac@shendaac.com
网址：www.shendaac.com

▼空调设备
Air Conditioning Equipment

Wuxi Tianxing Purification Air-Conditioner Equipment Co., Ltd.
无锡市天兴净化空调设备有限公司
江苏省宜兴市杨巷高新技术开发区
邮编：214255
电话：0510-8707 1688
传真：0510-8707 1333
电邮：cwd@jstxair.com
网址：www.jstxair.com

Yantai Ebara Air Conditioning Equipment Co., Ltd.
烟台荏原空调设备有限公司
山东省烟台市福山高新技术产业园区永达路720号
邮编：265500
电话：0535-632 2303
传真：0535-632 1196
电邮：ytebara@public.ytptt.sd.cn
网址：www.ytebara.com.cn

Zhenjing Air Conditioning Equipment Factory
靖江市振靖空调设备厂
江苏省靖江市孤山镇勇进路18号
邮编：214522
电话：0523-8455 0068
传真：0523-8455 1558
电邮：jszhenjing@163.com
网址：www.zhenjingkt.com

Zhuhai Boka Cool Source Equipment Co., Ltd.
珠海博佳冷源设备有限公司
珠海市高新区创新海岸科技5路1号
邮编：519085
电话：0756-380 3688
传真：0756-339 1668
电邮：zhuhai@boka.com.cn
网址：www.boka.com.cn

北京盾安空调设备安装有限公司
北京市朝阳区广渠路21号院
新金海国际花园5号楼2门4层
邮编：100124
电话：010-5820 2781
传真：010-5820 2782
电邮：bjdunan@vip.sina.com
网址：www.bjdunan.com

北京金万众空调制冷设备有限责任公司
北京市昌平区北七家镇金万众工业园
邮编：102290
电话：010-8178 6410
传真：010-8178 6410
电邮：gmtd@163.com
网址：www.gmtd.com.cn

德州旭日空调设备有限公司
山东省武城鲁权屯工业开发区
邮编：253308
电话：0534-638 0866
传真：0534-638 0886
电邮：xuri@dzxuri.com
网址：www.dzxuri.com

广东申菱空调设备有限公司
广东省佛山市顺德区陈村镇南涌工业区
邮编：528313
电话：0757-2383 2888
传真：0757-2335 3300
电邮：sl@shenling.com
网址：www.shenling.com

广东新雅空调设备有限公司
广东省佛山市顺德区乐从镇三乐路劳村路段
邮编：528315
电话：0757-2885 0303
传真：0757-2886 9823
电邮：webmaster@newsuper-aire.com
网址：www.newsuper-aire.com

空气净化设备
Air Purification Equipment

Beijing Great Wall Equipment & Engineering Co. For Air Purification
北京昌平长城空气净化设备工程公司
北京市昌平区沙河镇豆各庄9号
邮编：102206
电话：010-6973 1016
传真：010-6973 2603
电邮：ccjh@guwei.com
网址：www.guwei.com

Shanghai Cont Environment Protection Technology Company
上海康特环保科技发展有限公司
上海市浦东金桥出口加工区金皖路389号708室
邮编：201206
电话：021-3872 0362
传真：021-3872 0360
电邮：cont@cont.net.cn
网址：www.cont.net.cn

Suzhou Sanxing Air Clean Technology Co., Ltd.
苏州工业园区三兴净化科技有限公司
苏州市吴江临沪经济区金家坝工业园
邮编：215021
电话：0512-6562 4762
传真：0512-6211 1345
电邮：postmaster@szsanxing.com
网址：www.szsanxing.com

Wuxi Zhaier Air Depuration Equipment Co., Ltd.
无锡市寨尔空气净化设备有限公司
无锡市堰桥经济开发区
邮编：214000
电话：0510-8022 0739
传真：0510-8022 0752
电邮：sales@wxzr.com.cn
网址：www.wxzr.com.cn

Zhejiang Ruian Lvmei Air Purifying Appliances Co., Ltd.
浙江省瑞安市绿美空气净化设备有限公司
东山经济开发区集贤路388号
电话：0577-6515 7607
传真：0577-6515 7620
电邮：zjlmjh@alibaba.com.cn
网址：www.zjlmjh.cn

济南杰康净化设备厂
山东省济南市天桥区北辛工业园田黄路50-6号
邮编：250032
电话：0531-8596 7228
传真：0531-8599 1718
电邮：jnjiekang@163.com
网址：www.jnjk.com

确时环保科技（上海）有限公司
上海市江场三路76-78号103室
邮编：200436
电话：021-3632 1592
传真：021-3632 1591
电邮：sales@transep.com
网址：www.transep.com

无锡市福力空气净化设备厂
无锡市堰桥山浜路18号
邮编：214174
电话：0510-8547 1008
传真：0510-8547 1185
电邮：sales@wxfljh.com
网址：www.wxfljh.com

视听系统
Audio-Visual Systems

Amtt Digital
安美数字
北京市西城区西直门外大街1号楼(T3)20层B4-5室
邮编：100044
电话：010-5830 5488
传真：010-5830 5300
网址：www.amttgroup.com

Cabletime Asia Ltd.
启博通亚有限公司
Room2504, 25/F Westin Centre, 26 Hung To Road, Kwun Tong, Kowloon, Hong Kong
电话：+852-3101 2650
传真：+852-3101 2640
电邮：asia@cabletime.com
网址：www.cabletimeasia.com

Guangzhou Panyu Concord Trading Co., Ltd.
广州番禺合和贸易有限公司
广州市番禺区市桥富华中路富源二街18号
合和大厦2楼
邮编：511400
电话：020-8480 0168
传真：020-8480 0288
电邮：service@concord.net.cn
网址：www.concord.net.cn

Hangzhou Viais Electronic Co., Ltd.
杭州市维莱司电子有限公司
杭州市下城区朝晖路221号
中山花园秋月苑25层H座
邮编：310000
电话：0571-5688 0111
传真：0571-5688 0111
电邮：vlaiscom@163.com
网址：www.apzcn.com

Leader Radio Technologies (Shanghai) Limited
赋信（上海）贸易有限公司
上海市普陀区西康路1018号元茂金豪大厦1010室
邮编：200060
电话：021-5155 2786
传真：021-5155 2785
电邮：info@leaderradio.cn
网址：www.leaderradio.cn

▼视听系统
Audio-Visual Systems

Media-go Engineering Ltd.
美歌工程有限公司
25/F Westin Centre, 26 Hung To Road, Kwun Tong, Kowloon, Hong Kong
电话：+852-2797 8128
传真：+852-2790 5732
电邮：mediago@mediago.com.hk
网址：www.mediago.com.hk

Peoriv Technology Co., Ltd.
倍奥锐（北京）科技有限公司
北京市海淀区永泰中路25号
中关村永泰创新园B座132室
邮编：100192
电话：010-8281 7363
传真：010-8281 7363
电邮：sales-cn@peoriv.com
网址：www.peoriv.com

Philips (China) Investment Co., Ltd.
飞利浦（中国）投资有限公司
上海市嘉定区马陆镇沪宜公路1805号
邮编：201801
电话：021-5915 5149
传真：021-5915 9727
网址：www.philips.com.cn

Roland Shanghai Electronics Co., Ltd.
上海乐兰电子有限公司
上海市杨浦区平凉路1500号5F
邮编：200090
电话：021-5580 0800
传真：021-6572 7999
电邮：sales@roland.com.cn
网址：www.roland.com.cn

Shanghai Realpartner Intelligent Engineering Co., Ltd.
上海具友建设工程有限公司
上海市创智天地大学路277号7101室
邮编：200443
电话：021-5523 8929
传真：021-5523 8930
电邮：info@realpartner.com.cn
网址：www.realpartner.com.cn

Shenzhen Dnets Technology Co., Ltd.
深圳市唐诺科技有限公司
深圳市罗湖区笋岗东路百汇大厦南座11H
邮编：518010
电话：0755-2559 1128
传真：0755-2558 8008
电邮：service@dnets.com.cn
网址：www.dnets.com.cn

Shenzhen Dong Fang Audio & Visual Equipment Co., Ltd.
深圳市万年青视听设备有限公司
深圳市福田区燕南路96号格林阁苑908-910室
邮编：518028
电话：0755-8374 5621
传真：0755-3390 2868
电邮：szwnq888@vip.163.com
网址：www.szwnq.com

Somfy China Co., Ltd.
尚飞中国
上海市华山路1520弄121号2楼
邮编：200052
电话：021-6280 9660
传真：021-6280 0270
网址：www.somfy.cn
请参阅第338、339页、封面

Songya Av Equipment Co., Ltd.
松雅音响设备有限公司
广州市花都区狮岭镇杨屋工业区
邮编：514300
电话：020-6181 7732
传真：020-8696 5692
电邮：av6318@163.com
网址：www.songya-hk.com

Sony (China) Limited
索尼中国有限公司
上海市卢湾区湖滨路222号企业天地一号8楼
邮编：200021
电话：021-6121 6908
网址：www.sony.com.cn

Sound of East Audio Equipment Co., Ltd.
东方之声音响设备有限公司
广州市海珠区华洲街土华路78号2楼
电话：020-3408 3673
传真：020-3408 3679
电邮：sales@east-sound.com.cn
网址：www.east-sound.com.cn

South China House of Technology Consultants Ltd.
南中国科技顾问有限公司
Unit 1303-04， Block B,Sea View Estate， 2-14 Watson Road, North Point， Hong Kong
电话：+852-2590 6808
传真：+852-2590 6383
电邮：audiovisual@schot.com
网址：www.schot.com

TOA China Limited
提讴艾（上海）电器有限公司
上海市南京西路1038号梅龙镇广场3002室
邮编：200041
电话：021-6272 2584
传真：021-6217 6579
电邮：sales@toachina.com.cn
网址：www.toachina.com.cn

帐篷及天幕
Awnings & Canopies

Foshan Nanhai Sanli Awning Co., Ltd.
佛山市南海三力阳篷有限公司
佛山市南海区盐步穗盐路河东工业区
邮编：528247
电话：0757-8577 1487
传真：0757-8577 5761
网址：www.nhsanli.com

Gangcai Awningequip Ment Co., Ltd.
上海港彩装饰用品有限公司
上海松江区九亭镇金马路358号
电话：021-6763 1043
传真：021-6763 1698
电邮：shgangcai@163.com
网址：www.shgangcai.com

Guangzhou Area Expansion Industrial Co., Ltd.
广州朗域实业有限公司
广州市海珠区新港东路中洲中心南塔A座1801室
电话：020-8923 6700
传真：020-8923 6432*818
网址：www.m-c.cn

Hebei Wanli Stage Curtain Co., Ltd.
河北万里舞台幕布台有限公司
河北省肃宁县万里镇
邮编：062350
电话：0317-508 0409
传真：0317-508 0695
电邮：wtmubu@sina.com
网址：www.wtmubu.com

Shanghai ChuangMing Intelligent Sunshade Technical Co., Ltd.
上海创明智能遮阳技术有限公司
上海市嘉定区高潮路168号
邮编：200000
电话：021-6911 2125
传真：021-5914 2873
网址：www.wintom.net

Shanghai Lixing Hide Rrecreational Thing Co., Ltd.
上海利星遮阳休闲用品有限公司
上海市莲花路1058弄6号101室
邮编：200233
电话：021-3422 5981
传真：021-3422 5981
电邮：lixing@lixingsh.com
网址：www.lixingsh.com

Somfy China Co., Ltd.
尚飞中国
上海市华山路1520弄121号2楼
邮编：200052
电话：021-6280 9660
传真：021-6280 0270
网址：www.somfy.cn
请参阅第338、339页、封面

Taixing Jiayu Wutai Jixie Chang
泰兴市佳宇舞台机械厂
江苏省泰兴市根思周里工业园
邮编：225475
电话：0523-8775 5223
传真：0523-8296 9958
电邮：info@wtsb.cn
网址：www.wtsb.cn

锅炉
Boilers

A.O. Smit (China) Water Heater Co., Ltd.
艾欧史密斯（中国）热水器有限公司
江苏省南京市经济技术开发区尧新大道336号
邮编：210038
电话：025-8580 1000
传真：025-8580 3100
电邮：info@aosmith.com.cn
网址：www.aosmith.com.cn

Bosch Thermotechnology (Beijing) Co., Ltd.
博世热力技术（北京）有限公司
北京经济技术开发区永昌南路6号3楼
邮编：100176
电话：400 820 6017
传真：010-6782 7616
电邮：sales.tt@cn.bosch.com
网址：www.buderus.com.cn

▼锅炉
Boilers

Ferroli
法罗力中国
上海市福州路318号高腾大厦308室
邮编：200001
电话：021-6391 2098
传真：021-6391 2097
电邮：project@ferroli.com.cn
网址：www.ferroli.com.cn

Guanguo Boiler Works Co., Ltd.
东莞市莞锅热能设备有限公司
东莞市东城上桥工业区莞龙路段
电话：0769-2265 2525
传真：0769-8903 2369
电邮：dgboiler@126.com
网址：www.dgboiler.net

Guangzhou Tianlu Boiler Co., Ltd.
广州天鹿锅炉有限公司
广州市萝岗区天鹿南路26号
邮编：510520
电话：13060927049
传真：020-8709 1337
电邮：tianlugl@public.guangzhou.gd.cn
网址：www.tianlu.com

Miura Industries (Suzhou) Co., Ltd.
三浦工业设备（苏州）有限公司
江苏省江苏市苏州工业园区南前巷8号
邮编：215024
电话：0512-8816 8892
传真：0512-8816 8893
网址：www.miura-cn.com

Viessmann Heating Technology Beijing Co., Ltd.
北京菲斯曼供热技术有限公司
北京市顺义区天竺空港工业开发区
B区裕民大街26号
邮编：101318
电话：010-8049 0888
传真：010-8049 6336
电邮：info@viessmann.cn
网址：www.viessmann.cn

Yangzhou Chenguang Special Kind Equipments Co., Ltd.
扬州晨光特种设备有限公司
江苏省宝应秋秋工业园区
邮编：225800
电话：0514-8824 6666
传真：0514-8822 2365
网址：www.cgglboiler.com

美国威玛（上海）公司
上海市华山路1568号财瑞大厦2楼
邮编：200052
电话：021-2208 5690
传真：021-2208 5532
网址：www.weil-mclain.com.cn

威能（北京）供暖设备有限公司
北京市朝阳区建国门外大街
甲6号A座SK大厦17层
电话：010-6563 0667
电邮：info@vaillant.com.cn
网址：www.vaillant.com.cn

停车场系统
Carparking Systems

Beijing Dragonmen Computer System Engineering Co., Ltd.
北京龙人计算机系统工程有限公司
北京市海淀区紫竹院路31号华澳中心2-19G
邮编：100089
电话：010-6842 0866
传真：010-6842 2119
电邮：market@dragonmen.com
网址：www.dragonmen.com

Beijing Eytone Electronic Technology Co., Ltd.
北京易通伟杰电子科技有限公司
北京市丰台区科学城星火路10号A座201-208室
电话：010-5129 3001
电邮：eytone@126.com
网址：www.eytone.com

Beijing Naiweist Teconology Co., Ltd.
北京耐维思科技有限公司
北京市朝阳区北苑路13号
领地OFFICE写字楼B座301室
电话：010-5109 5808
传真：010-5109 5809
网址：www.nice-bj.com

Beijing Unispark Technology Co., Ltd.
北京紫光百会科技有限公司
北京市海淀区清华大学东门紫光大楼525室
电话：010-6271 7325
传真：010-6279 9207
电邮：baihui@unispark.com.cn
网址：www.unispark.com.cn

Faac (Shanghai) Gates and Door Automation Trading Co., Ltd.
法柯（上海）门自动系统贸易有限公司
上海市康桥工业区康桥东路1159弄51号3幢
邮编：201315
电话：021-6818 2970
传真：021-6818 2968
电邮：info@faac.com.cn
网址：www.faac.com.cn

Hings Plastic & Metal Products Mfy
兴业塑胶五金制品厂
广东省顺德市勒流镇富裕工业区
邮编：528324
电话：0757-2533 2788
传真：0757-2533 2993
电邮：hingspmp@hingsgroup.com
网址：www.hingsgroup.com

Nanjing Easthouse Electrical Co., Ltd.
南京东屋电气有限公司
南京市大校场路五号三楼
邮编：210022
电话：025-8655 3388
传真：025-5263 8736
电邮：info@easthouse.net
网址：www.talenca.com

Shenzhen Lisite Electronic and Science Co., Ltd.
深圳市利思特电子科技有限公司
深圳市南山区南海大道4050号上汽大厦1103室
邮编：518052
电话：0755-8325 0428
传真：0755-2650 4028
电邮：stoney@szlst.cn
网址：www.szlst.cn

Shenzhen Nanze Electric Co., Ltd.
深圳市南泽电子有限公司
深圳市深南中路2201号嘉麟豪庭B座1703室
邮编：518026
电话：0755-3334 1556
传真：0755-3334 0258
电邮：nanze@szonline.net
网址：www.sznanze.com

Shenzhen Wan Qiao Hong Science & Technology Co., Ltd.
深圳万侨鸿科技有限公司
深圳市宝安区石岩镇石头山工业区一栋
电话：0755-8179 1585
传真：0755-8179 1515
网址：www.wan-qiao.com.cn

北京安思达科技发展有限公司
北京市海淀区上地十街
辉煌国际中心东6号写字楼368室-369室
邮编：100085
电话：010-8274 8849
传真：010-8274 8843
电邮：bjasdkj@126.com
网址：www.bjasd.cn

深圳麦耐士科技有限公司
深圳市南山区西丽塘朗工业区B区48栋
邮编：518055
电话：0755-2699 8050
传真：0755-2699 8050
电邮：mag@magnice.com
网址：www.magnice.com

通宝停车设备有限公司（北京）
北京市朝阳区惠新东街紫光发展大厦B座3-301
邮编：100029
电话：010-6482 3939
传真：010-6482 3078
电邮：top-parking@163.com
网址：www.top-parking.com

烟台福达门业有限公司
烟台市芝罘区幸福中路162号
电话：0535-684 3645
传真：0535-680 6645
网址：www.yt-fdmy.com

收银机/销售计算系统 Cash Registers/Point-of-Sale Systems

Beijing Dragonmen Computer System Engineering Co., Ltd.
北京龙人计算机系统工程有限公司
北京市海淀区紫竹院路31号华澳中心2-19G
邮编：100089
电话：010-6842 0866
传真：010-6842 2119
电邮：market@dragonmen.com
网址：www.dragonmen.com

Beijing Dwin Technology Co., Ltd.
北京迪文科技有限公司
北京市海淀区知春路108号豪景大厦9层
邮编：100086
电话：010-6210 2630
传真：010-6255 3095
网址：www.dwin.com.cn

Bizerba (Shanghai) Weightech & Systems Co., Ltd.
碧彩（上海）衡器技术有限公司
上海市松江工业区东部新区茜浦路书慧置业园D-3
邮编：201611
电话：021-6760 0999
传真：021-6760 0998
网址：www.bizerba.cn

Chaoying Software Co., Ltd.
广州超赢信息科技有限公司
广州市天河区五山路248号金山大厦南塔3层
邮编：510630
电话：020-6101 6066
传真：020-6101 6011
电邮：sales@chaoying.com.cn
网址：www.pos.cn

Citaq Co., Ltd.
广东川田科技有限公司
汕头市龙湖区汕头高新区
科技中路六号创业大厦13楼
邮编：515041
电话：0754-884 5120
传真：0754-884 5109
网址：www.citaq.com

Guangzhou Dazhong Computer Technology Co., Ltd.
广州达众计算机科技有限公司
广东省广州市天河区棠下大片路53号
裕辉商务中心401室
邮编：510635
电话：020-3825 9302
传真：020-3825 9796
网址：www.hongdazhong.com

Guangzhou Jingjie Electronic Equipment Co., Ltd.
广州晶杰电子设备有限公司
广东省广州市天河区科韵北路大地工业区A栋3楼
电话：020-3828 9706
传真：020-3837 0076
网址：www.jingjie.cn

Guangzhou Zonerich Computer Equipments Co., Ltd.
广州市中崎电脑设备有限公司
广州市高新技术产业开发区香山路17号
优宝工业园四楼
邮编：510663
电话：020-3229 0530
传真：020-3229 0575
电邮：webmaster@zonerich.com
网址：www.zonerich.com

Partech (Shanghai) Co., Ltd.
上海帕泰电子信息技术有限公司
上海市闸北区江场三路165号101室
邮编：200436
电话：021-6139 8535
传真：021-6139 8577
电邮：tina_guo@partech.com
网址：www.partech.com

Partner Trading (Shanghai) Co., Ltd.
拍档电子科技（上海）有限公司
上海市松江区九亭镇松江高科技园区涞寅路1969号
邮编：201615
电话：021-6769 6699
传真：021-6769 6224
电邮：sales@partnertech.cm.cn
网址：www.partnertech.com.cn

Rinpak Technology (SH) Ltd.
润百计算机（上海）有限公司
上海市天山西路568号卡帝乐鳄鱼大厦A区3楼
电话：021-5219 0707
传真：021-6239 3868
电邮：sales@rinpak.com.cn
网址：www.rinpak.com.cn

Senor Tech Co., Ltd.
广州星乔计算机科技有限公司
广州市先烈中路100号
中科院广州分院9号楼西126室
电话：020-8768 7718
传真：020-8768 7719
网址：www.senortech.com

Shanghai Hantang Software Science Co., Ltd.
上海瀚唐软件科技有限公司
上海市中山北路3064号绿洲广场B座1810室
邮编：200063
电话：021-6245 5577
电邮：sales@mystery.net.cn
网址：www.mystery.net.cn

Vtop Technology
唯拓科技
广州市天河区石牌西路111号天晟明苑北座2205室
电话：020-8551 0002
传真：020-8756 4012
电邮：vtoppos@163.com
网址：www.vtoppos.net

天花 Ceilings

Baroque Ceiling Systems Ltd.
巴力天花（香港）有限公司
香港九龙尖沙咀梳利士巴利道3号星光行1502室
电话：+852-2314 1688
传真：+852-2314 0138
电邮：bcsct@126.com
网址：www.hk-baroque.com

Beijing Create Boom Space Menbrance Strcture Technology Co., Ltd.
北京创荣空间拉膜技术有限公司
北京市大兴区西红门宏大北园7-4-304
邮编：100076
电话：010-6029 6379
传真：010-6029 6379
电邮：cykj18126.com
网址：www.bjcrkj.com.cn

Beijing Dingcai Weiye Decoration Materials Technology Co., Ltd.
北京顶彩伟业装饰材料技术有限公司
北京市大兴区瀛海姜场工业园二排2号院
邮编：100076
电话：010-6927 4819
传真：010-6927 4820
电邮：dingcaiweiye@163.com
网址：www.chinaruanmo.com

Beijing Salcan Building Materials Co., Ltd.
北京圣惠凯达建筑材料有限公司
北京市西城区裕民路18号北环中心A座1211室
邮编：100029
电话：010-8225 1621
传真：010-8225 1921
电邮：deko2008@sina.com
网址：www.salcan.com.cn

Beijing Shijitianya Zhuangshisheji Ltd.
北京世纪天雅装饰设计有限公司
北京市大兴区西红门工业区25号
电话：010-8727 5451
传真：010-6128 0693
电邮：sjty_jw@126.com
网址：www.shijitianya.com

Futian Decoration Material (Shanghai) Co., Ltd.
甫天装饰材料（上海）有限公司
上海市嘉定区安亭镇
国际汽车城零部件配套工业园区园大路9号
邮编：201805
电话：021-6957 6615
传真：021-6957 6148
电邮：futian6618@hotmail.com

Guangzhou Area Expansion Industrial Co., Ltd.
广州朗域实业有限公司
广州市海珠区新港东路中洲中心南塔A座1801室
电话：020-8923 6700
传真：020-8923 6432*818
网址：www.m-c.cn

Guangzhou Daguang Aluminum Decoration Material Corp
广州大广铝业装饰材料有限公司
广东省广州市番禺区大石镇迎宾路634号
邮编：511430
电话：020-3910 2137
传真：020-3910 2290
电邮：gdzdc@yahoo.com.cn
网址：www.gzceiling.com

Jiangsu Fengshun NewMaterial Technology Co., Ltd.
江苏丰顺新材料科技有限公司
常州市武进区礼嘉镇华渡工业区
邮编：213173
电话：0519-6886 9500
传真：0519-8625 1258
电邮：mail@cnfsun.com
网址：www.cnfsun.com

▼天花 Ceilings

Mellkit Bathroom & Kitchen Technology Co., Ltd.
美尔凯特卫厨科技有限公司
嘉兴市秀洲区王店镇东西一路北侧
电话：0573-8325 5588
传真：0573-8325 1008
电邮：mellkit@126.com
网址：www.mellkit.com

Shanghai Chuan Arts & Crafts Co., Ltd.
上海传家工艺品有限公司
上海市奉贤区青村镇奉永路399号
邮编：201414
电话：021-5756 7155
传真：021-5756 7157
电邮：chuan888@vip.163.com
网址：www.chuanstone.com

Shanghai Tianyu Decoration Building Material Development Co., Ltd.
上海天宇装饰建材发展有限公司
上海市松江区新闵经济开发区
邮编：201612
电话：021-6764 8327
传真：021-6764 8108
电邮：kefu01@hos.com.cn
网址：www.tyjc88.cn

北京一海凡天装饰材料有限公司
北京市大兴区廊坊东桥亿发工业区18号
邮编：100055
电话：010-6334 0169
传真：010-6334 0168*808
电邮：bjyhft@yhft-zg.com
网址：www.yhft-zg.com

广州欧巨亚装饰工程有限公司
广州天河区华景北路113号
电话：020-8585 7388
传真：020-6102 2688
电邮：ojychina@163.com
网址：www.ojychina.cn

广州天信装饰工程公司
广州市天河区黄埔大道205号伟诚广场1201号
邮编：510655
电话：020-3868 0383
传真：020-3868 0456
电邮：tianxinhl@163.com
网址：www.gztianxin.com

清洁化学用品 Cleaning Chemicals

Polyclean Stone & Marble Care Ltd.
玛斯域云石护理有限公司
Room 808, Opulent Commercial Building, 402-406 Hennessy Road, Wanchai, Hong Kong
电话：+852-2572 3601
传真：+852-2836 0972
电邮：info@polycleancare.com
网址：www.polycleancare.com

Shenzhen HCH Chemical Ltd.
深圳市华昌化工有限公司
深圳市南山区留仙大道西丽镇南国丽城1F54号
邮编：518055
电话：0755-8615 1942
传真：0755-2651 4997
电邮：hch111@hch111.cn
网址：www.hch111.cn

Tianjin Weldmaster Technological Co., Ltd.
天津市威马科技发展有限公司
天津市北城区丁字沽3号路延长线奥林匹克花园
电话：022-5858 3088
传真：022-5858 3018
电邮：wmkj_120@163.com
网址：www.tjrhw.com

美佳精细化工股份有限公司
海南省海口市国家高新技术产业开发区A-16美佳科技工业园
邮编：570216
电话：0898-6863 8444
传真：0898-6863 9444
电邮：meijia@meijia.cc
网址：www.meijia.cc

无尘室 Cleanrooms

Beijing Beijing Kanghua Tech Co., Ltd.
北京北净康华科技有限公司
北京市大兴区旧宫西路5号407室
邮编：100076
电话：010-8797 0434
传真：010-8797 0740
电邮：84724574@163.com
网址：www.khcoo.com

ShenZhen JunXinDa Environment Control Systems Co., Ltd.
深圳市君信达环境控制系统有限公司
深圳市南山区创业路中兴工业城11栋425室
电话：0755-2640 9509
传真：0755-2640 8509
电邮：myecs@126.com
网址：www.szctecs.com

Suzhou Sanxing Air Clean Technology Co., Ltd.
苏州工业园区三兴净化科技有限公司
苏州市吴江临沪经济区金家坝工业园
邮编：215021
电话：0512-6562 4762
传真：0512-6211 1345
电邮：postmaster@szsanxing.com
网址：www.szsanxing.com

Wuxi Deyi Purify Equipment Factory
无锡市德怡净化设备厂
无锡市锡澄北路54号
邮编：214174
电话：0510-8547 1238
传真：0510-8547 1278
网址：www.wuxidy.com

弘佑净化科技有限公司
江苏省昆山市高新区娄江工业集中区长阳路69号
邮编：215316
电话：0512-5773 5583
传真：0512-5773 5681
电邮：suzhou@szhongyou.com
网址：www.szhongyou.com

防虫涂料 Coatings-Insect Repellent

Vica Fireseals (H.K) Co., Ltd.
威达（香港）创建有限公司
香港新界荃湾沙咀道11号达贸中心19楼1室
电话：+852-2412 3288
传真：+852-2739 8793
电邮：sales@vica.com.hk
网址：www.vica-uk.com

玻璃幕墙 Curtainwalls

Beijing Oracle Building & Decoration Engineering Co., Ltd.
北京甲骨文建筑装饰工程有限公司
山东省日照市巨峰工业园金栈路7号
邮编：276800
电话：0633-836 7577
传真：0633-836 7677
电邮：bjjgw777@126.com
网址：www.jgwzs.com

Foshan Lyibi Curtain Wall Glass Co., Ltd.
佛山市洛玻幕墙玻璃有限公司
佛山市南海区九江镇沙头石江工业区
邮编：528208
电话：0757-8691 6445
传真：0757-8691 6799
电邮：fsluobo@yahoo.com.cn
网址：www.fslb.com.cn

Hennan Hongge Glass Curtain Wall Decoration Co., Ltd.
河南红革玻璃幕墙装饰工程有限公司
河南省郑州市郑卞路白沙工业园区青年路
电话：0371-6236 6167
传真：0371-6236 6167
电邮：hg163@163.com
网址：www.hgmq.com

Jiangsu Longsheng Glass Engineering Co., Ltd.
江苏龙升幕墙工程有限公司
江苏省无锡市锡山区
安镇镇大成工业园东盛路999号
电话：0510-8235 5888
传真：0510-8236 1000
电邮：lsgs@lsglass.cn
网址：www.lsglass.cn

Nanjing Ruiyang Glass Walls Ltd.
南京瑞阳玻璃幕墙有限公司
江苏省南京市铁心桥大定坊工业园内18号
邮编：210012
电话：025-5235 5482
传真：025-5235 5483
电邮：bancang@bancang.com.cn
网址：www.bancang.com.cn

Shanghai Yaohua Pilkington Glass Co., Ltd.
上海耀华皮尔金顿玻璃股份有限公司
上海市浦东新区莲溪路1210号1号楼
电话：021-6163 3599
传真：021-5880 1554
电邮：office@sypglass.com
网址：www.sypglass.com

Shenyang Lixin Glass Curtain Co., Ltd.
沈阳黎新玻璃幕墙有限公司
沈阳市东陵区东陵路87号
邮编：110161
电话：024-8841 0474
传真：024-8841 6625
电邮：sylx@sylx.com
网址：www.sylx.com

▼玻璃幕墙
Curtainwalls

南京中宇玻璃幕墙制造有限公司
江苏省南京市江宁区滨江开发区翔凤路8号
电话：025-8612 9311
传真：025-8610 6916
电邮：zhongyuboli@yahoo.com.cn
网址：www.zyglass.cn

上海恒利益建装潢工程有限公司
上海市奉贤区金海公路3500号
邮编：201400
电话：021-5747 5179
传真：021-5747 4908
电邮：songyda11@163.com
网址：www.sh-zhuzong.com

门五金
Door Hardwares

Beijing Century O&T Trading Co., Ltd.
北京世纪欧度经贸有限公司
北京市丰台区木樨园南曦大厦A座1105室
电话：010-8787 5946
传真：010-8787 5846*801
电邮：odusuocheng@yeah.net
网址：www.sjot.com.cn

Beijing Toms Hardware Co., Ltd.
北京汤姆斯五金有限公司
北京市丰台区南三环中路70号1幢B-802室
邮编：100075
电话：010-8368 6099
传真：010 8368 6453
电邮：tmswj88@sina.com
网址：www.tms88.com

Dorma Door Controls (Suzhou) Co., Ltd.
多玛门控（苏州）有限公司
苏州市工业园区同胜路101号
邮编：215126
电话：0512-6295 2596
传真：0512-6761 4582
网址：www.dorma.com

FSB Asia Ltd. Shanghai Rep. Office
福适博亚洲有限公司上海代表处
上海市南京西路818号长春藤运通大厦1013室
邮编：200041
电话：021-6217 8840
传真：021-6217 8740
电邮：shanghai@fsb.de
网址：www.fsb.de

Foshan Xuanbiao Hardware Product Co., Ltd.
佛山市炫标五金制品有限公司
佛山市南海区松岗镇松石路段堪头村工业区
电话：0757-8837 0822
传真：0757-8837 0838
电邮：hy@fshy-hardware.com
网址：www.fshy-hardware.com

Geze Industries (Tianjin) Co., Ltd.
盖泽工业（天津）有限公司上海分公司
上海市徐汇区零陵路899号非洲国际广场25N
邮编：200030
电话：021-5234 0960
传真：021-6447 2007
电邮：geaesh@geze.com.cn
网址：www.geze.com.cn

Jieyang Yadidun Lock Co., Ltd.
揭阳市雅迪顿五金制品厂
广东揭阳市榕城区梅云镇梅畔工业区
邮编：522061
电话：0663-888 6689
传真：0663-888 3989
电邮：yadidun@163.com
网址：www.yadidun.com

Miwa Lock Co., Ltd. Shanghai Office.
日本美和锁业株式会社上海代表处
上海市浦东新区陆家嘴环路1000号
汇丰大厦15楼022室
电话：021-6841 1633
传真：021-6841 1622
电邮：meihe@miwa-lock.com.cn
网址：www.miwa-lock.co.jp

Shanghai Canaan Hardware Co., Ltd.
上海谢恩贸易有限公司
上海市宜山路439号七建大厦1448室
邮编：200235
电话：021-6464 1737
传真：021-6441 1472
电邮：sales@shanghaicanaan.com
网址：www.shanghaicanaan.com

Shanghai Dongguan Hardware Co., Ltd.
上海东冠五金有限公司
上海市闵行区华中路300号
邮编：201101
电话：021-5488 1910
传真：021-6479 0263
网址：www.door-lock.com.tw

Shanghai Doormax Hardware Manufacturing Co., Ltd.
上海多麦克司企业发展有限公司
上海市长宁区金钟路658号
东华大学科技园5号楼5楼
邮编：200335
电话：021-3360 1678
传真：021-3360 1318
电邮：sales@doormax.com.cn
网址：www.doormax.com.cn

Shanghai Fanle Hardware Product Co., Ltd.
上海帆乐五金制品有限公司
上海市浦东新区新坦瓦路3号
电话：021-5660 0313
电邮：mi.kailang@163.com
网址：www.miklan.cn

Shanghai Woojin Corporation
优珍贸易（上海）有限公司
上海市闵行区吴中路1050号5幢北楼807室
邮编：201103
电话：021-6465 8091
传真：021-6465 8810
电邮：admin@homeseq.com.cn
网址：www.homeseq.com.cn

Shenzhen Ducheng Electrical & Hardware Co., Ltd.
深圳市都成电器五金有限公司
深圳市石岩镇料坑第三工业区3栋
邮编：518000
电话：0755-2765 7048
传真：0755-2765 7050
网址：www.ducheng.cn

Sugatsune Shanghai Co., Ltd.
世嘉智尼五金配件（上海）有限公司
上海市闸北区万荣一路2号一层
邮编：200436
电话：021-3632 1858
传真：021-3632 1868
电邮：lamp@sugatsune.com.cn
网址：www.sugatsune.com.cn
请参阅第353页、书脊下

Torch (Xi'an) Security Technology Co., Ltd.
湘火炬（西安）安防科技有限公司
西安市高新区西部大道107号
邮编：710075
电话：029-8832 9169
传真：029-8888 0301
电邮：torchst@sina.com
网址：www.torchst.com

Wenzhou Lucheng Elegant Decoration Hardwares Plant
温州市鹿城高雅装饰五金厂
温州市鹿城区牛山北路
邮编：325000
电话：0577-8860 8516
传真：0577-8860 8517
网址：www.gaoyawj.com

Wenzhou Tilanco Industry & Trade Co., Ltd.
温州市帝朗珈工贸有限公司
温州市沿江工业区沿兴路152号四楼
电话：0577-8879 7760
传真：0577-8879 6766
电邮：tilanco.info@gmail.com
网址：www.tilanco.com

Zhongshan Deksun Spectroscopy Hardware Products Factory
中山市南区德信光学五金制造厂
中山市南区东环三路23号
邮编：528400
电话：0760-889 3886
传真：0760-8881 8260
电邮：deksun@deksun.com
网址：www.deksun.com

上海匡隆建材有限公司
上海市肇嘉浜路201号5楼
电话：021-6422 7917
传真：021-6422 7903
网址：www.kl-king.com
请参阅第326、327、354、355页

门
Doors

Beijing Big Luck Doors Co., Ltd.
北京市大运门业有限公司
北京市通州区张家湾镇工业园姚辛庄村甲23号
电话：010-6957 1744
传真：010-6957 1844
网址：www.bjdy888.cn

Beijing Longyang Xingye Metallic Products Co., Ltd.
北京珑阳兴业金属制品有限公司
北京市顺义区林河工业开发区顺和路51号
邮编：101300
电话：010-8945 1302
传真：010-8945 1303
电邮：longyangxingye@sina.com
网址：www.bjlymy.com.cn

SUGATSUNE

LAMP®

世嘉智尼是一家总部位于日本东京，其技术中心、配送仓库和工厂设立在东京和邻近的千叶县。另外还在日本全国设立了4个地区办事处。通过80多年努力，世嘉智尼已构建了全球客户网络。通过采用高效的管理系统，使世嘉智尼现代化工厂(日本千叶)的质量控制达到了最高水平。世嘉智尼在世界各地的仓库和经销机构中备有20,000种产品，可满足客户广泛的应用需求。世嘉智尼五金配件（上海）有限公司成立于2005年7月，主要销售工业和家具五金配件，主要服务区域为中国大陆地区。

• LAPCON系列

LAPCON是世嘉智尼公司为表示某些产品含有可以柔和、顺畅的控制物体运动的阻尼功能部件。由于这些阻尼功能部件具有出色的操作性和安全性，因此在阻尼支撑、挂衣架、闭门器、合页、可收藏折叠床等许多的产品都装载了这种阻尼功能部件。无论在日本国内还是在海外市场世嘉智尼的LAPCON被广泛的使用着。

• 搁板架系统

高承重可调整的整体设计，可以展现壁面的整体效果；同时可以在壁板背面布置电缆，能方便的和照明系统、音像系统进行组合。搁板可以使用木质或玻璃，自由展示和配合多样化的设计风格。

• 移门系统

移门配件以其独特的功能和优秀的品质引领行业。安装方式有外装式和隐藏式。另有隐藏固定玻璃夹式，最终形成玻璃墙体的效果。我们现在拥有双阻尼功能（即打开和关闭时都拥有阻尼功能）的移门系统，让您开闭门更安全舒适。

• 折叠门系统

公司拥有多种折叠门配件，性能上分有导轨和无导轨系列，还可提供附带阻尼关闭的功能，安装方便，提供给您多样化的选择。

• 隐形合页

安装简单，有三维可调式和无调节功能的多款产品可供选择，外观精美，门关闭时隐藏。此外还有多种小门和玻璃门用合页。

• 滑轨

拥有带反弹和阻尼功能的三节滑轨，可实现轻柔的打开和关闭，此外还拥有各种功能的不锈钢滑轨系列和高承重的滑轨系列。

世嘉智尼五金配件（上海）有限公司

SUGATSUNE SHANGHAI CO.,LTD.

上海市闸北区万荣一路2号一层　　邮编：200436

电话（Tel）：(+8621) 3632 1858　传真（Fax）：(+8621) 3632 1868

E-mail: lamp@sugatsune.com.cn　Website: www.sugatsune.com.cn

▼门
Doors

Beijing Tiger Door Co., Ltd.
北京泰戈尔门业有限公司
北京市大兴区西红门南中轴路东5号
邮编：100076
电话：010-6128 4008
传真：010-6128 4016*801
网址：www.bjtger.com

Boloni
博洛尼家居用品（北京）有限公司
北京市朝阳区育慧里11号
邮编：100101
电话：010-5134 8888
传真：010-5134 8810
电邮：hui@kebao.cn
网址：www.boloni.com.cn

Dalian E-Hamm Copper Door Manufacturing Co., Ltd.
大连一和铜门制造有限公司
辽宁省大连市甘井子区辛艺街2号
邮编：116039
电话：0411-6600 9900
传真：0411-6600 9990
电邮：ehamm@live.cn
网址：www.ehamm.com

Dorma Door Controls (Suzhou) Co., Ltd.
多玛门控（苏州）有限公司
苏州市工业园区同胜路101号
邮编：215126
电话：0512-6295 2596
传真：0512-6761 4582
网址：www.dorma.com

Forest Timber Panyu Co., Ltd.
广州番禺泰林木业有限公司
广东省广州市番禺区沙湾镇古西大围工业区
邮编：511483
电话：020-8474 7663
传真：020-8474 7667
网址：www.tlgoldboss.com.cn

Geze Industries (Tianjin) Co., Ltd.
盖泽工业（天津）有限公司上海分公司
上海市徐汇区零陵路899号非洲国际广场25N
邮编：200030
电话：021-5234 0960
传真：021-6447 2007
电邮：geaesh@geze.com.cn
网址：www.geze.com.cn

Guangzhou Luyi Door Co., Ltd.
广州鲁艺门业有限公司
广东省广州市海珠区南洲路119-2号工业区8号
邮编：510228
电话：020-6276 6219
传真：020-6276 6209
电邮：luyi@luyidoor.com
网址：www.luyidoor.com

Hangzhou Lijun Copper Door Co., Ltd.
杭州市利军铜门厂
浙江省杭州市萧山党湾镇团结村
电话：0571-8211 6348
传真：0571-8211 3348
网址：www.hzljtm.com

Hangzhou Xizhou Doors Co., Ltd.
杭州西州门业有限公司
浙江省杭州市西湖区转塘工业园
邮编：310024
电话：0571-8709 3117
传真：0571-5627 7516
电邮：xizhoudoor@xizhoudoor.cn
网址：www.xizhoudoor.cn

Hong Risheng Industry and Trade Co., Ltd.
北京红日升工贸有限公司
北京市通州区马驹桥镇工业区马村
邮编：101102
电话：010-6050 6981
传真：010-6050 6324
电邮：hrs@hrsgood.com
网址：www.hrsdoor.com

Huzhou Kaiya Wood Co., Ltd.
湖州凯雅木业有限公司
浙江省湖州市南浔富强经济开发区
邮编：313009
电话：0572-378 8585
传真：0572-378 8955
电邮：info@kaiyawood.com
网址：www.kaiyawood.com

Jiangshan Wufu Door Co., Ltd.
江山五福门业有限公司
浙江省江山市虎山路76号
邮编：324100
电话：0570-423 3006
传真：0570-422 2003
电邮：jswfmy@163.com
网址：www.jswfmy.cn

Ningbo Meibisheng Auto-Gate Factory
宁波市鄞州美必盛自动门厂
宁波市鄞州区茅山工业区
邮编：315193
电话：0574-8807 7777
传真：0574-8807 7999
网址：www.nbmbs.com

Ningbo Tyi Copper Development Co., Ltd.
宁波天益铜业发展有限公司
宁波市北仑区小港渡头董工业区创富路18号
电话：0574-8790 6400
传真：0574-8790 9400
电邮：ty87906400@126.com
网址：www.tyi.com.cn

Obe Door Control Technology (Shanghai) Co., Ltd.
欧必翼门控科技（上海）有限公司
上海市浦东新区秀浦路聚诚工业园区30A
邮编：201319
电话：021-3825 6026
传真：021-3825 6018
电邮：obe@chinaobe.com
网址：www.worldobe.com

Shanghai Dewan Management & Trade Co., Ltd.
上海德望经贸有限公司
上海市浦东新区西营路118号明珠花苑2102室
邮编：200126
电话：021-6858 1307
传真：021-5847 2830
电邮：sh.dewan@yahoo.com.cn
网址：www.hoehen.com

Shanghai Diancang Door Industry Co., Ltd.
上海典藏门业有限公司
上海市闵行区顾戴路3009号801室
邮编：201100
电话：021-3415 3957
传真：021-5488 8926
电邮：ella868@gmail.com

Shanghai Haibi Electric Echnology Co., Ltd.
上海海比电子科技有限公司
上海市闵行区沪闵路2759号
邮编：201100
电话：021-5495 2099
传真：021-5495 2199
电邮：coffee@vip.sina.com
网址：www.haibi.net

Shanghai Huijiang Doors Co., Ltd.
上海惠江门业有限公司
上海市宝山区顾北路88号厂区A厂房
邮编：200436
电话：021-6637 3714
传真：021-5643 3095
电邮：info@hjmysh.com
网址：www.hjmysh.com

Shanghai Kang Yu Jie-Sen Cast Glass Artwork Co., Ltd.
上海康宇杰森水晶艺术品有限公司
上海市肇嘉浜路789号
邮编：200032
电话：021-6438 5109
传真：021-5227 1335
电邮：kycopper@kygroup.com
网址：www.kygroup.com

Shanghai PAD Autodoor Co., Ltd.
上海乘方自动门有限公司
上海市嘉定区华亭镇高石公路2439号
电话：021-6221 5156
传真：021-5226 0423
电邮：padsh@126.com
网址：www.autodoor.com.cn

Shanghai Resun Autodoor Co., Ltd.
上海锐圣自动门有限公司
上海市宝山区大场镇化工路69弄9-10号
邮编：200463
电话：021-6616 3886
传真：021-6616 3886
网址：www.resunautodoors.com

Shanghai Taiyue Automatic Door Co., Ltd.
上海太岳自动门有限公司
上海市金沙江路1060号申汉大厦C座1506室
邮编：200062
电话：021-5282 5371
传真：021-5282 5375
电邮：sales@etautodoor.com
网址：www.etautodoor.com

Slide & Hide System (Suzhou) Co., Ltd.
新来贺隐藏门系统（苏州）有限公司
苏州工业园区东景工业园区7号楼1层
电话：0512-6930 0005
网址：www.slidehide.com

▼门
Doors

Tianjin Sowin Automatic Door Co., Ltd.
天津市双兴自动门有限公司
天津市津南区八里台工业园区（南区）
邮编：300353
电话：022-8881 0000
传真：022-8881 1806
网址：www.cnsowin.com

Zhangjiagang Tian Yi Copper Door & Copper Skill Co., Ltd.
张家港天一铜门铜艺有限公司
江苏省张家港塘桥镇刘村工业园内
电话：0512-5835 3988
传真：0512-5835 3977
电邮：tytmty@sohu.com
网址：www.tytmty.com

Zhejiang Jindi Door Co., Ltd.
浙江金迪门业有限公司
浙江省杭州市萧山区党山工业园区
邮编：311245
电话：0571-2280 9513
传真：0571-8253 3982
电邮：goldea@goldea.cn
网址：www.jindi.com

美国朗亚集团广州公司
广州天河区广利路75号东洲大厦A座2902室
电话：020-3845 6069
传真：020-8523 9919
电邮：sales@loyaliron.com
网址：www.loyalirondoors.cn

上海高藤门业发展有限公司
上海市松江区久富开发区易富路西88号
邮编：201615
电话：021-6762 6544
传真：021-6762 6370
电邮：gao-teng@gao-teng.com
网址：www.gao-teng.com

上海宇诺门窗装饰工程有限公司
上海市临夏路98弄50号902室
邮编：210000
电话：021-6911 7229
传真：021-6911 9445
网址：www.afdrautodoor.com.cn

烟台福达门业有限公司
烟台市芝罘区幸福中路162号
电话：0535-684 3645
传真：0535-680 6645
网址：www.yt-fdmy.com

防火门
Doors-Fire-Rated

Beijing Guanghua Anfuye Door & Window Co., Ltd.
北京光华安富业门窗有限公司
北京市昌平区沙河镇七里渠北村406号
电话：010-8072 1724
传真：010-8072 1725
网址：www.ghafy.com

Hangzhou Xizhou Doors Co., Ltd.
杭州西州门业有限公司
浙江省杭州市西湖区转塘工业园
邮编：310024
电话：0571-8709 3117
传真：0571-5627 7516
电邮：xizhoudoor@xizhoudoor.cn
网址：www.xizhoudoor.cn

Hoermann Beijing Door Production Co., Ltd.
霍曼（北京）门业有限公司
北京市经济技术开发区中和街13号
邮编：100176
电话：010-6788 8371
010-6788 8372
传真：010-6788 7318
电邮：sales.bj@hoermann.cn
网址：www.hoermann.com.cn
请参阅第358、359、360、361页

Huzhou Jingcheng Doord Co., Ltd.
湖州精诚门业有限公司
浙江省湖州市南浔区华侨投资区10地块
邮编：313009
电话：0572-308 7070
传真：0572-308 7083
网址：www.xydoors.com

Kunshan Nihonfunen Co., Ltd.
昆山富耐安全门有限公司
江苏省昆山开发区蓬朗大通路1088号
电话：0512-5781 5700
传真：0512-5781 5727
电邮：ksfunen@ks-funen.com.cn
网址：www.ks-funen.com.cn

Ruizhong Tianming (Beijing) Door Co., Ltd.
瑞中天明（北京）门业有限公司
北京市东城区北三环东路36号
北京环球贸易中心D座11层
邮编：100013
电话：010-5913 7188
传真：010-5913 7288
电邮：info@tianmingdoor.com
网址：www.tianmingdoor.com

Shanghai Huijiang Doors Co., Ltd.
上海惠江门业有限公司
上海市宝山区顾北路88号厂区A厂房
邮编：200436
电话：021-6637 3714
传真：021-5643 3095
电邮：info@hjmysh.com
网址：www.hjmysh.com

Taizhou Houle Industrial Co., Ltd.
台州市豪力实业有限公司
浙江省台州市路桥区金清镇环西路188号
邮编：318058
电话：0576-8287 6810
传真：0576-8287 6763
电邮：info@kalata.com.cn
网址：www.kalata.com.cn

Yokah International Ltd.
旭华国际有限公司
香港九龙长沙湾永康街79号恒龙工商中心7楼D室
电话：+852-2991 4051
传真：+852-2423 0922
电邮：ybs@yokah.com
网址：www.yokah.com

Zhao Shi Zhuang Shi
兴化市赵氏装饰制品厂
江苏省兴化市张郭镇华兴路88号
邮编：225722
电话：0523-8376 1362
传真：0523-8399 8362
电邮：zjy@zsfhb.com
网址：www.zsfhb.com

Zhejiang Tangmen Metal Structure Company
浙江唐门金属结构有限公司
浙江省义乌市机场路631号
邮编：322000
电话：0579-8542 1711
传真：0579-8542 1722
电邮：ywtangmen@public.ywptt.zj.cn
网址：www.chinatangmen.com

山东淄博中环木制家私公司
山东省桓台县田庄镇田庄村
邮编：256402
电话：0533-858 6987
传真：0533-606 2999
网址：www.zbzhonghuan.cn

上海时答门业有限公司
上海市浦东新区沪南公路4528号
邮编：201317
电话：021-5038 0366
传真：021-6814 8283
电邮：shidamenye@163.com
网址：www.shidamenye.cn

控尘地垫
Dust Control Mat

Beijing Fuyuan Shiji Trade Co., Ltd.
北京福源世纪商贸有限公司
北京市海淀区阜成路42号中裕商务花园23C-103
电话：010-8812 1841
传真：010-8812 8240
网址：www.shuidaodidian.com

Beijing Kadi Weiye Decoration Co., Ltd.
北京德雅伟业商贸有限公司
北京市朝阳区八里庄西里远洋国际D座501室
邮编：100025
电话：010-5908 1197
传真：0101-5908 1179
电邮：kd@bjkadi.com
网址：www.bjkadi.com

Changchun Maisika Carpet Co., Ltd.
长春麦斯卡地毯有限公司
吉林省长春市南关区东南湖大路788号
鸿城国际商务中心1112室
邮编：130000
电话：0431-8528 7988
传真：0431-8528 1577
网址：www.maisika.com

Fuzhou Yamazaki Industry Co., Ltd.
福州山崎实业有限公司
福州市新店镇金城民营科技工业集中区10号
电话：0591-8806 1851
传真：0591-8806 1727
网址：www.yamazakicn.com

HÖRMANN
德国霍曼

HÖRMANN

ICU 重症监护病房

作为工业门系统的权威机构
霍曼门不仅快速高效，安全可靠，
而且经济实用。

▼控尘地垫
Dust Control Mat

Meibaojie Commodity Co., Ltd.
沈阳市美宝洁日用品有限公司
沈阳市铁西区景星南街38号甲
电话：024-2564 1544
传真：024-2584 3839
电邮：meibaojie@sohu.com
网址：www.sy-3d.com

Milta Construction Materials Foshan Co., Ltd.
佛山市美而达建材有限公司
广东省佛山市南海区罗村北湖一路罗村开发区内
邮编：528226
电话：0757-8180 0383
传真：0757-8180 0331
电邮：milta@21.cn.com
网址：www.chinamilta.com

Mountvillemills China Co., Ltd.
广州市豪特商用地垫有限公司
广州市天河区天河路490号壬丰29大厦2911室
电话：020-3803 8161
传真：020-3888 6773
电邮：mmicn@mountville.com
网址：www.mountville.com.cn

Rismat International Company Limited
丽施美国际有限公司
上海市凯旋北路1299号4楼
邮编：200063
电话：021-3126 1933
传真：021-2301 0003
电邮：rismat.shanghai@rismat.net
网址：www.rismat.net

Shanghai Paaler Environmental Protecting Technology Co., Ltd.
上海派勒环保科技有限公司
上海浦东新区张杨北路497号
邮编：200129
电话：021-3876 7886
传真：021-3876 7886*18
网址：www.paalermat.com

电器开关
Electrical Switch

Dongguan Visisv Electronic Technology Co., Ltd.
东莞威萨电子科技有限公司
东莞市石龙镇李屋工业园11号
电话：0769-8138 0022
传真：0769-8138 0028
电邮：visisv@126.com
网址：www.visilock.com

Fung Yip Electrical Mfg Ltd.
丰叶电器制造厂有限公司
NO.3.14/F, Blk B.Po Yip Building, 62-70 Texaco Road, Tsuen.Wan, Hong Kong
电话：+852-2414 4989
传真：+852-2415 0934
电邮：sales@fungyip.com
网址：www.fungyip.com

Gira Giersiepen GmbH & Co. KG
德国吉徕·吉尔西本有限两合公司上海代表处
上海市天目西路218号
嘉里不夜城一座2509-2510室
邮编：200070
电话：021-6390 6670
传真：021-6353 9107
电邮：info@gira.net.cn
网址：www.gira.net.cn

Guangzhou Elite Electronic Co., Ltd.
常州市爱莱特电子有限公司
江苏省常州市钟楼开发区梅花路12-2号
邮编：213023
电话：0519-8686 7388
传真：0519-8801 1021*8020
电邮：sales@elitelock.com
网址：www.elitelock.com

Guangzhou Rishun Electronic Technology Co., Ltd.
广州日顺电子科技有限公司
广州市番禺区洛溪新城恒达工业园D2栋
邮编：511431
电话：020-8454 2845
传真：020-8454 2840
电邮：rishun@126.com
网址：www.gzrishun.com

JOBO Hotel Equipment Co., Ltd. Huizhou
惠州市尊宝酒店设备有限公司
广东省惠州市惠城区三新工业区B6栋六楼
邮编：516003
电话：0752-280 7078
传真：0752-280 7178
电邮：hzjbswb@163.com
网址：www.jobo-hotel.com

Kejin Power Supply Wires Co., Ltd.
中山市科进电源线有限公司
中山市古镇海洲东岸公路加油站
往顺德均安方向300米
邮编：528422
电话：0760-2231 7601
传真：0760-2231 6762
电邮：zskejin@vip.163.com
网址：www.zskejin.com

Oulu Electric Co., Ltd.
乐清市欧璐智能电器有限公司
浙江省乐清市柳市镇柳青北路96-98号
邮编：325604
电话：0577-6276 2060
传真：0577-6276 2065
电邮：choulu@choulu.com
网址：www.choulu.com

Schneider Electric (China) Investment Co., Ltd.
施耐德电气（中国）投资有限公司
北京市朝阳区望京东路6号施耐德大厦
邮编：100102
电话：010-8450 1130
传真：010-8434 6699
网址：www.schneider-electric.cn

Shanghai Meike Electric Co., Ltd.
上海美克电器有限公司
上海市浦东新区康桥工业区川周公路2600弄78号
邮编：200124
电话：400 711 1887
电邮：meikty@foxmail.com
网址：www.meike-gm.com

Shanghai Tianyi Electric Co., Ltd.
上海天逸电器有限公司
上海市零陵路631号爱乐大厦10楼
邮编：200030
电话：021-6486 3796
传真：021-6486 6353
电邮：sale@tianyi-electric.com
网址：www.tianyi-electric.com

Shanghai Vimar Electric and Electronic Products Co., Ltd.
上海伟迈电气电子产品有限公司
上海市嘉定区南翔镇嘉美路550号（近惠申路口）
邮编：200030
电话：021-6917 6331
传真：021-6917 6303
电邮：info@vimar.cn
网址：www.vimar.cn

Shenzhen Aureke Control System Co., Ltd.
深圳市奥立科控制系统有限公司
深圳市福田区彩田路彩福大厦嘉福阁28E
邮编：518000
电话：0755-8328 0851
传真：0755-8328 0861
电邮：sales@aureke.com
网址：www.aureke.com

Shenzhen Catry Electric Co., Ltd.
深圳市开创电器有限公司
深圳市龙岗区坂田街道办风门路
禾坪岗科技园工业区第B栋401号
邮编：518057
电话：0755-8291 4448
传真：0755-8291 4849
电邮：dlh2006921@126.com
网址：www.catry.cn

Shenzhen Permay Technology Co., Ltd.
深圳市普美科技有限公司
深圳市南山区南光路151号明舍御园A11
邮编：518059
电话：0755-8619 0780
传真：0755-8619 0780*602
电邮：service@permay.cn
网址：www.permay.cn

Zhejiang Longsheng Electric Co., Ltd.
浙江龙胜电器有限公司
浙江省温州市龙湾区海城工业区
邮编：325055
电话：0577-8522 2666
传真：0577-8522 5666
网址：www.ls-elc.com

上海匡隆建材有限公司
上海市肇嘉浜路201号5楼
电话：021-6422 7917
传真：021-6422 7903
网址：www.kl-king.com
请参阅第326、327、354、355页

电子显示系统
Electronic Display Systems

Beijing Dwin Technology Co., Ltd.
北京迪文科技有限公司
北京市海淀区知春路108号豪景大厦9层
邮编：100086
电话：010-6210 2630
传真：010-6255 3095
网址：www.dwin.com.cn

▼电子显示系统
Electronic Display Systems

Caelum International Ltd.
加隆国际有限公司
深圳市福田保税区桂花路5号西塔4层
邮编：518038
电话：0755-8358 8709
传真：0755-8358 8704
网址：www.caelumint.com
请参阅第375页

Guangdong Songtian Electronic Appliance Co., Ltd.
广东松田电子电器有限公司
广东省佛山市南海盐步广佛新干线联桂工业区
电话：0757-8839 7574
传真：0757-8579 2900
电邮：gdsongtian@163.com
网址：www.songtian.com.cn

M.L.S Electronics Co., Ltd.
中山市木林森电子有限公司
中山市城区民营科技园木林森工业区1-5号
邮编：528400
电话：0760-8871 7177
传真：0760-8871 4636
电邮：mls@zsmls.com
网址：www.zsmls.com

Media-go Engineering Ltd.
美歌工程有限公司
25/F Westin Centre, 26 Hung To Road, Kwun Tong, Kowloon, Hong Kong
电话：+852-2797 8128
传真：+852-2790 5732
电邮：mediago@mediago.com.hk
网址：www.mediago.com.hk

Shanghai Kinzon Technology Co., Ltd.
上海尖创电子科技有限公司
上海市徐汇区凯进路151号中油企业大厦四楼B座
邮编：200233
电话：021-6487 8611
传真：021-6464 3819
网址：www.kinzon.com

Shanghai Polar Vision Co., Ltd.
上海极品光电科技有限公司
上海市曹杨路1222弄8号1704室
邮编：200063
电话：021-6243 3329
传真：021-6243 3329
电邮：sales@polarvision.net
网址：www.polarvision.net

Shanghai Popular Technology Limited
上海保浦乐软件有限公司
上海市浦东新区峨山路91弄101号5号楼101室
邮编：200127
电话：021-5039 2269
传真：021-5039 3529
网址：www.shpopulartech.com

Shanghai Trufeel Technology Co., Ltd.
上海卓飞科技有限公司
上海市长宁区天山支路168号401室
邮编：200051
电话：021-6233 4791
传真：021-6274 9666
网址：www.avin.cn

Shenzhen HuiChaoDe Electronics Co., Ltd.
深圳市惠超德电子有限公司
深圳市龙岗区坂田发达路物资工业园8栋4楼东边
邮编：518129
电话：0755-2847 1651
传真：0755-8292 8367
网址：www.huicd.com

South China House of Technology Consultants Ltd.
南中国科技顾问有限公司
Unit 1303-04, Block B,Sea View Estate, 2-14 Watson Road, North Point, Hong Kong
电话：+852-2590 6808
传真：+852-2590 6383
电邮：audiovisual@schot.com
网址：www.schot.com

Sun Shine Multimedia Co., Ltd.
北京阳光视翰科技有限公司
北京市海淀区丹棱街16号海兴大厦C座901
邮编：100080
电话：010-6213 0496
电邮：vod@shinepop.com
网址：www.shinemds.com.cn

Zhengzhou Anjia Electronics Co., Ltd.
郑州安嘉电子科技有限公司
郑州市国家高新技术产业开发区须水路97号
邮编：450002
电话：0371-8605 6091
传真：0371-8605 6089*8008
电邮：anjialed6@163.com
网址：www.zzanjia.com

北京九华互联科技有限公司
北京市清华大学学研大厦B座808室
邮编：100084
电话：010-6279 0320
传真：010-6279 0310
电邮：info@99view.com
网址：www.99view.com

吉林省积石科技工程有限公司
吉林省长春市朝阳区东平大路进化街东胡同25号
邮编：130012
电话：0431-8592 6466
传真：0431-8596 4253
电邮：info@jsbworld.com
网址：www.js-tech.us

上海新联纬讯科技发展有限公司
上海市石门二路333弄3号
振安广场恒安大厦23A/B室
邮编：200041
电话：021-6255 1798
传真：021-5213 0652
电邮：ycy@newlan.cn
网址：www.newlan.com.cn

深圳市维纳光电有限公司
深圳市南山区科技园中区维用综合楼4楼
邮编：518057
电话：0755-8166 1588
传真：0755-2663 1568
电邮：pcqszled@sina.com
网址：www.shenzhenled.com

节能咨询
Energy Efficiency Consultants

Hangzhou Longsong Electronical Co., Ltd.
杭州隆松电子科技有限公司
杭州市余杭区勾运路48号
邮编：311112
电话：0571-8875 6281
传真：0571-8875 6276
网址：www.longsong.net

杭州科望企业管理咨询有限公司
杭州市绍兴路168号和平大厦11楼
邮编：310004
电话：0571-8526 1595
传真：0571-8526 1584
电邮：postmaster@qualitymaker.net
网址：www.qualitymaker.net

上海定杰电气设备有限公司
上海市松江区明中路275号226全幢（欣绿名苑）
邮编：200235
电话：021-6764 1658
传真：021-6764 1658
网址：www.shdjdq.com.cn

伊诗邦光电科技（上海）有限公司
上海市青浦区北青公路6588号D2-71
邮编：201706
电话：021-3987 8227
网址：www.espasole.com

通风及排气系统
Fans-Ventilation & Exhaust

Aereco (Beijing) Trading Co., Ltd.
爱瑞雷格（北京）贸易有限公司
北京东城区建国门内大街7号
光华长安大厦1座806室
电话：010-5911 1888
传真：010-6517 0091
电邮：contact@aereco.com.cn
网址：www.aereco.com.cn

Foshan Shunde Jinkui-Fan Co., Ltd.
佛山市顺德区金葵风机有限公司
佛山市顺德区华口聚龙工业区保民路2B号
邮编：528305
电话：0757-2881 0308
传真：0757-2881 0308
电邮：oym@jin-kui.com
网址：www.jin-kui.com

Halton Ventilation (Shanghai) Co., Ltd.
浩盾通风设备（上海）有限公司
上海市浦东新区临港新城
新元南路600号10号厂房
邮编：201306
电话：021-5868 4388
传真：021-5868 4568
电邮：sales.china@halton.com.my
网址：www.halton.com
请参阅第176、177页

▼通风及排气系统
Fans-Ventilation & Exhaust

Shanghai Fengyi Air-Condition Equipment Co., Ltd.
上海风翼空调设备有限公司
上海市凯旋路2200号3501室
邮编：200030
电话：021-6448 1863
传真：021-6448 1863*820
电邮：wang-yuqi@263.net
网址：www.airflysh.com

北京德盛行通风技术有限公司
北京市海淀区花园北路38号
邮编：100191
电话：010-8207 8768
传真：010-6235 0061
电邮：info@maico.cn
网址：www.maico.cn

北京恒捷力通风空调安装公司
北京市海淀区永丰基地
邮编：100094
电话：010-6126 8049
传真：010-6247 5210
电邮：hengjieli2006@163.com
网址：www.bjbhl.com

丹东奥特雷格科技有限公司
辽宁省丹东市振兴区汇友古玩城三楼
电话：0415-233 3336
电邮：autogyre@autogyre.com.cn
网址：www.autogyre.com.cn

嘉兴速净环保设备有限公司
上海市浦东新区浦电路400号A座1202室
邮编：200122
电话：021-5820 7159
传真：021-5081 0705
电邮：suparwy@hotmail.com
网址：www.supar.com.cn

青岛闻森科技发展有限公司
山东省青岛市海门路17号海纳尊祇2单元503室
邮编：266700
电话：0532-8202 0075
传真：0532-8202 0079
电邮：vensonchina@tom.com
网址：www.vensonchina.net

上海兰舍空气技术有限公司
上海市闵行区龙吴路3199号
邮编：201108
电话：021-5169 6733
传真：021-6434 3713
电邮：natherchina@163.com
网址：www.nather.com.cn

深圳市开来环境技术有限公司
深圳市南山区学府路8号B-26F
电话：0755-2642 2753
传真：0755-2645 4217
网址：www.szkailai.net

耐火材料
Fire Proofing Materials

Changzhou Weide Da Refractory Board Co., Ltd.
常州市威德达耐火板有限公司
江苏省常州市武进区横林镇卫星村崔卫路15号
邮编：213103
电话：0519-8850 0570
传真：0519-8823 1722
电邮：zjfbigsai@163.com
网址：www.weideda.cn

Dongtaishi Gangtai Refractory Co., Ltd.
东台市港泰耐火材料有限公司
江苏省东台市后港镇西工业园区
邮编：224213
电话：0515-8554 0726
传真：0515-8554 0127
电邮：ygg@china-gangtai.net
网址：www.china-gangtai.com

Guangzhou Winnper Decorative Materials Co., Ltd.
广东市文鹏装饰材料有限公司
广东市番禺区东涌镇三沙公路18号
邮编：511453
电话：020-3490 5108
传真：020-3490 5038
网址：www.winnper.com

Hopewell Plastics (Dongguan) Limited
合和胶板（东莞）有限公司
广东省东莞市道滘镇南阁工业区
邮编：523187
电话：0769-8838 1666
传真：0769-8838 1777
电邮：sales@hopewellplastics.com
网址：www.hopewellplastics.com

Penglai Huasheng Electronic Co., Ltd.
山东蓬莱华升板材有限公司
山东省蓬莱市经济开发区
电话：0535-564 4484
传真：0535-564 2493
网址：www.hec-genor.com

Tangshan Huifang Thermal Insulation Material Co., Ltd.
唐山市慧芳保温材料有限公司
唐山市西外环新机场路工业园区
邮编：064001
电话：0315-551 8145
传真：0315-551 8888
电邮：wwwhfbw@vip.sohu.com
网址：www.hfbw.com

Wuxi Chenguang Refractory Co., Ltd.
无锡市晨光耐火材料有限公司
江苏省宜兴市大浦镇
邮编：214226
电话：0510-8745 2999
传真：0510-8745 5999
电邮：web@cgnh.com
网址：www.cgnh.com

Yantai Monco Board Co., Ltd.
烟台盟禾板材有限公司
山东省蓬莱市东郊沙河路北首
邮编：265600
电话：0535-561 0049
传真：0535-561 1604
电邮：info@monco-board.com
网址：www.monco-board.com

YingKou TianRun Refractory Co., Ltd.
营口市天润耐火材料有限公司
辽宁省营口市老边区冶金工业园8号
邮编：115005
电话：0417-392 0188
传真：0417-392 0495
电邮：sale@refractory-fibre.com
网址：www.refractory-fibre.com

Zhangjiagang Yandao Board Factory
张家港市烟道防火板厂
张家港市鹿苑立交桥北
电话：0512-5803 3513
传真：0512-5822 7162
电邮：zjgchenyi@163.com
网址：www.zjghl.com

Zhejiang Changxing Xiangfa Refractory Co., Ltd.
浙江省长兴县翔发耐火材料有限公司
浙江省长兴县环桥
邮编：313114
电话：0572-601 1048
传真：0572-601 1283
电邮：hyx@chinarefractory.com
网址：www.chinarefractory.com

防火设备
Fire Protection Equipment

Hangzhou New Epoch Fire Protechtion Science and Technology Co., Ltd.
杭州新纪元消防科技有限公司
浙江省杭州市临平经济开发区塘宁路3号
邮编：311100
电话：0571-8918 3512
传真：0571-8918 3588
网址：www.zjfire.com

Jing Dun Fire Protection Equipment Engineering
北京京盾消防设备工程有限公司（朝阳分公司）
北京市朝阳区十八里村135号
邮编：100073
电话：010-6747 4139
传真：010-6748 0795
电邮：web@jdxfsb.com
网址：www.jdxfsb.com

Mansion Fire Services Co., Ltd.
民信消防服务有限公司
2/F On Yip Factory Building, 33 Ivy Street, Taikoktsui, Kowloon, Hong Kong
电话：+852-2907 9393
传真：+852-2907 9911
电邮：enquiry@sunmansion.com
网址：www.sunmansion.com

▼防火设备
Fire Protection Equipment

Nanjing Jiangpu Fire Control Equipment Co., Ltd.
南京江浦消防器材有限公司
江苏省南京市浦口珠江镇南门
邮编：211800
电话：025-5815 2833
传真：025-5815 2833
网址：www.njjpxf.com

Shanghai Kaiyue Fire Equipment Co., Ltd.
上海凯越安全消防器材有限公司
上海市延安西路1390弄6号202室
邮编：200052
电话：021-6282 7240
传真：021-5230 0182
电邮：sales@shkaiyuefire.com
网址：www.shkaiyuefire.com

Xingye Air Conditioning Fireproof Equipment Factory
兴业空调防火设备有限公司
佛山市大福路高新技术开发区
邮编：528041
电话：0757-8383 1247
传真：0757-8383 3028
电邮：406382504@qq.com
网址：www.fsxingye.com

北京集星创业消防设备科技有限公司
北京市房山区饶乐府市场
电话：010-5110 0763
传真：010-6938 5796
电邮：69385798@163.com
网址：www.bjstars.com

北京优迪安全系统工程有限公司
北京市丰台区草桥欣园四区八号楼一层
邮编：100067
电话：010-8750 7323
传真：010-8750 7323*801
电邮：bjut2008@126.com
网址：www.beijingyoudi.com

健身设备
Fitness Equipment

Active Lifestyle (China) Ltd.
奥力来康体设备有限公司
北京市朝阳区朝阳门北大街乙12号天辰大厦608室
邮编：100020
电话：010-6551 6098
传真：010-6551 6095
电邮：activechina@vip.sina.com
网址：www.active.cn

Amersports Shanghai
亚玛芬体育用品贸易（上海）有限公司
上海市浦东新区花园石桥路66号
东亚银行金融大厦6楼602室
邮编：200120
电话：021-5116 5288
传真：021-5116 5299
网址：www.precor.com.cn

BH China Co., Ltd.
钜劻健身器材（上海）有限公司
上海市普陀区真南路822弄455支弄68号
邮编：200331
电话：021-5284 6694
传真：021-5284 6814
电邮：info@i-bh.cn
网址：www.i-bh.cn

Fitness Solutions
上海巍得健身器材有限公司
上海市浦东新区东风路989号中达广场1003室
邮编：200122
电话：021-6867 0768
传真：021-5820 5428
电邮：sandy.yuan@fitness-solutions.com.cn
网址：www.fitness-solutions.com.cn

Jiangsu Junxia Gym Equipment Co., Ltd.
江苏军霞健身器材有限公司
江苏省邳州市奚仲路40号
邮编：221300
电话：0516-8624 1707
传真：0516-8622 4304
电邮：junxia@junxia.net
网址：www.junxia.net

Me Fitness Ltd.
2/F Olympian City One, 11 Hoi Fai Road, Tai Kok Tsui, Kowloon, Hong Kong
电话：+852-2271 4144
传真：+852-3544 7892
电邮：enquiry@mefitness.com.hk
网址：www.mefitness.com.hk

Nantong Dongli Body-Built Equipment Co., Ltd.
南通东力健身器材有限公司
江苏省如东县新店工业园区
电话：0513-8438 7888
传真：0513-8438 7103
电邮：dongli@ntdongli.com
网址：www.ntdongli.com

Shanghai D-L Enterprise Development Co., Ltd.
上海东亚利邦企业发展有限公司
上海市瑞金南路1号海兴广场15楼H座
邮编：200023
电话：021-6418 5035
传真：021-6418 5037
电邮：sales@dongyalibang.com
网址：www.dongyalibang.com

Shanghai Kondin Fitness Equipment Co., Ltd.
上海康丁健身器材有限公司
上海市虹口区大连路1079号和平商厦11楼04室
电话：021-5595 6665
传真：021-6515 9484
电邮：123@kondin.com
网址：www.kondin.com

Shanghai Yuankuang Health Engineering Equipment Co., Ltd.
上海远旷康体设备工程有限工程
上海市杨浦区黄兴路1号中通大厦1316室
邮编：200090
电话：021-5580 6108
传真：021-6543 5029
电邮：shyuankuang@126.com
网址：www.yuankuang.com.cn

Technogym (Shanghai) Int'l Trading Co., Ltd.
泰诺健（上海）国际贸易有限公司
上海市静安区延平路98号B栋101室
邮编：200042
电话：021-5175 9833
传真：021-5888 6950
电邮：sales_china@technogym.com
网址：www.technogym.com

Vision Machinery Shanghai Limited
上海遂生机电成套设备有限公司
上海市长宁区淮海西路570号红坊B区110室
电话：021-6127 0975
传真：021-6127 0961
电邮：info@lifefitnesschina.cn
网址：www.lifefitness.com
请参阅第366、367页、封面

地板采暖
Floor Heating

Anhui Anze Electrical Co., Ltd.
安徽安泽电工有限公司
安徽省宁国市经济技术开发区外环南路
邮编：242300
电话：0563-418 7588
传真：0563-418 7577
电邮：ngaz@anze.cn
网址：www.anze.cn

Beijing Beiyang Intelligence Ground Warm Science Technology Co., Ltd.
北京北阳佳业智能地暖科技有限公司
北京市朝阳区北苑路媒体村天畅园C7座2202室
邮编：100017
电话：010-8482 7017
传真：010-8482 7017
电邮：bjbeiyang@163.com
网址：www.bjbeiyang.com

Beijing Carol Roca Science Co., Ltd.
北京卡润乐佳科技发展有限公司
北京市朝阳区管庄
电话：010-6577 5578
传真：010-6577 5578
电邮：top@topwarm.com
网址：www.topwarm.com

Bosch Thermotechnology (Beijing) Co., Ltd.
博世热力技术（北京）有限公司
北京经济技术开发区永昌南路6号3楼
邮编：100176
电话：400 820 6017
传真：010-6782 7616
电邮：sales.tt@cn.bosch.com
网址：www.buderus.com.cn

DCR Union (Beijing) Electron & Equipment Co., Ltd.
狄诺合众（北京）电子设备有限公司
北京市顺义区天竺出口加工区
邮编：101312
电话：010-8041 1358
传真：010-8041 1809
电邮：dcr-china@hotmail.com
网址：www.un-dn.com

全球最新概念的加速振动训练器

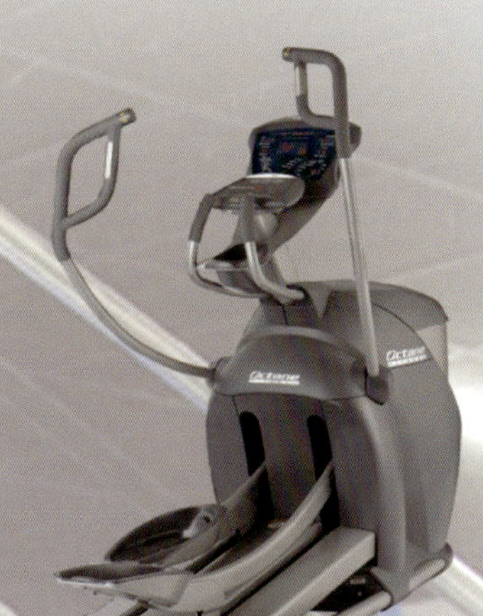

全球最流行的
有氧-力量间歇循环训练器

我们的优势：

◎对所有国内外品牌酒店的标准熟识，更参与制定多家品牌的标准；

◎全国最专业的团队，协助投资者减低成本同时提升质量；

◎全面的售前和售后服务，包括场地勘察、平面布局、3D效果、设计、工程、培训、维保等...

◎协助客户确定用户种类，提供适合的产品和服务；

◎力健中国总代理 - 始于1998年，稳定的团队拥有超过13年行业服务经验；

◎全国拥有数百家5星级酒店客户

项目展示：

◎洲际酒店旗舰店，上海世博洲际酒店；

◎索菲特酒店旗舰店，广州圣丰索菲特酒店；

◎君悦酒店旗舰店，深圳华润君悦酒店；

◎北京国贸三期香格里拉酒店；

◎上海半岛酒店

2011年力健有氧新功能：

您环保了吗?

▼地板采暖
Floor Heating

Holy Yard Enviromental Protect Construction Material Co., Ltd.
北京豪怡嘉德环保建材有限公司
北京市朝阳区首图东路5号院御景园1号楼8G室
邮编：100122
电话：010-6530 5197
传真：010-6530 5197
电邮：ouellet@126.com
网址：www.holyyard.com

Shanghai Hanchu Heating Equipment Co., Ltd.
上海瀚初暖通设备有限公司
上海市延安西路1329号10号楼901室
邮编：200051
电话：021-3319 0968
传真：021-5291 7938
电邮：hanchu@sendwarm.com
网址：www.sendwarm.com

Tyco Thermal Controls
泰科热控
上海市宜山路1009号创新大厦20楼
邮编：200233
电话：021-2412 1688
传真：021-5426 2967
网址：www.tycothermal.com

Ytwd Cold Warm Project Technology Co., Ltd.
北京亚特伟达冷暖节能工程技术有限公司
北京市朝阳区北苑路13号
领地OFFICE一号楼C座910室
邮编：100107
电话：010-5109 5077
传真：010-5109 5098
电邮：wdjz96@yeah.net
网址：www.weidagroup.cn

Yunsor Carbon Crystal Technology (Shanghai) Co., Ltd.
元硕碳晶技术（上海）有限公司
上海市浦东新区张江高科技
医疗器械园区瑞庆路528号第4号楼
邮编：201201
电话：021-5072 0266
传真：021-5072 0267
电邮：yunsor@ysccc.cn
网址：www.ysccc.cn

北京鸿威电热采暖公司
北京市朝阳区北三环中路36号603室
邮编：100029
电话：010-6445 2165
传真：010-6445 2164
电邮：bjhvdn@163.com
网址：www.bjhvdn.com

北京康运吉科贸有限责任公司
北京市丰台区万柳桥樊家村甲8号
汇丰家园7-1-202
邮编：100071
电话：010-8361 9702
传真：010-8361 9702
电邮：kangyunjidn@sina.com
网址：www.kangyunji.com

北京三恒科贸有限公司
北京市石景山区阜石路166号泽洋大厦505室
邮编：100043
电话：010-8890 9978
传真：010-8890 9982
电邮：shdn@shdn.com.cn
网址：www.shdn.com.cn

汉堡阁电热系统（上海）有限公司
上海市徐汇区田州路159号莲花大厦1002室
电话：021-6091 8996
传真：021-6091 8995
电邮：shanghai@halmburger.cn
网址：www.halmburger.cn

河南宝泰实业万家暖智能电地暖营销中心
河南省郑州市紫荆山路60号金成国贸大厦1416室
邮编：450052
电话：0371-6661 6909
电邮：wanjianuan@163.com
网址：www.wanjianuan.com

喷泉
Fountains

Daguang Fountain Engineering Co., Ltd.
大连大广喷泉工程有限公司
大连市西岗区长春路239-8号
邮编：116011
电话：0411-8368 3630
传真：0411-8368 3630
电邮：dgew@dgpq.com
网址：www.dgpq.com

Guangzhou Huarun Fountain & Sprinkler Irrigation Co., Ltd.
广州华润喷泉喷灌有限公司
广东省广州市白云区钟落潭镇金盆华润产业基地
邮编：510545
电话：020-8745 0111
传真：020-8745 0329
电邮：gzhuarun@163.com
网址：www.gzhuarun.com

Hangzhou Sanjiang Fountain Whole Set Equipment Co., Ltd.
杭州三江喷泉设备成套有限公司
浙江省杭州市西湖区袁浦镇轮渡路21号
邮编：310024
电话：0571-8764 6395
传真：0571-8764 6395
电邮：web@sjpq.com.cn
网址：www.sjpq.com.cn

Hangzhou West-Lake Fountain Whole Set Co., Ltd.
杭州西湖喷泉设备成套有限公司
浙江省杭州市西湖区三墩西湖科技经济园区
西园八路6号
邮编：310030
电话：0571-8798 6040
传真：0571-8796 2421
电邮：xihupenquan@126.com
网址：www.jl-penquan.com

Hongrun China Group Company
浙江省诸暨市宏润喷泉喷灌厂
浙江省诸暨杨梅桥开发区
邮编：311826
电话：0575-8769 8518
传真：0575-8760 6101
电邮：jpj@hongrunchina.com
网址：www.hongrunchina.com

Qingdao Huapu Fountain Technology Co., Ltd.
青岛华普喷泉科技有限公司
山东省青岛市崂山区山东头路58号盛和大厦
邮编：266061
电话：0532-8192 0118
传真：0532-8192 0117
电邮：lqhuapu@sina.com
网址：www.cnhpc.net

Shanghai Spoondrift Fountan Engineering Ltd.
上海浪花喷泉工程有限公司
上海市浦东新区桃林路18号环球广场A座24层
邮编：200135
电话：021-5108 8899
传真：021-6855 6227
电邮：info@pqsj.com
网址：www.pqsj.com

上海丽达喷泉喷灌设备有限公司
上海市宝山区月罗路1558号6号楼2楼
邮编：200436
电话：021-6612 7790
传真：021-5292 6592
电邮：sh-lida@126.com
网址：www.sh-lida.com

客房控制系统
Guest Room Management System

栢力国际
上海市松江区九亭镇淀浦河路399弄133号
邮编：201615
电话：021-6762 0633
传真：021-3373 9863
电邮：terence@parklake.cn
网址：www.parklake.cn

Guangzhou Rishun Electronic Technology Co., Ltd.
广州日顺电子科技有限公司
广州市番禺区洛溪新城恒达工业园D2栋
邮编：511431
电话：020-8454 2845
传真：020-8454 2840
电邮：rishun@126.com
网址：www.gzrishun.com

JOBO Hotel Equipment Co., Ltd. Huizhou
惠州市尊宝酒店设备有限公司
广东省惠州市惠城区三新工业区B6栋六楼
邮编：516003
电话：0752-280 7078
传真：0752-280 7178
电邮：hzjbswb@163.com
网址：www.jobo-hotel.com

▼客房控制系统
Guest Room Management System

Nanjing Puietel Intelligent Systems Co., Ltd.
南京普杰智能系统有限公司
南京市江宁区东山镇石羊路88号（章村工业园）
邮编：210000
电话：025-8618 0311
传真：025-8618 0966
网址：www.puietel.com

New Shanbang Info. & Tech. Co., Ltd. Shanghai
上海新善邦信息科技有限公司
上海市长寿路97号世纪商务大厦602室
邮编：200060
电话：021-6255 5123
传真：021-5180 1593
网址：www.shanbangchina.com

Oulu Electric Co., Ltd.
乐清市欧璐智能电器有限公司
浙江省乐清市柳市镇柳青北路96-98号
邮编：325604
电话：0577-6276 2060
传真：0577-6276 2065
电邮：choulu@choulu.com
网址：www.choulu.com

Reach Best It Co., Ltd.
至真（上海）信息技术有限公司
上海市愚园路1037号5层
邮编：200050
电话：021-6210 9048
传真：021-6210 9049
网址：www.hot-net.com.cn

Shandong Bittel Electronics Co., Ltd.
山东比特电子工业有限公司
山东省日照市日照北路1号
邮编：276800
电话：0633-221 2188
传真：0633-221 2132
电邮：sales@bittel.com.cn
网址：www.bittelcom.com

Shanghai Beso Electronic Science & Technology Co., Ltd.
上海北索电子科技有限公司
上海市闵行区金都路4299号
莘闵高科技园区综合楼3F
邮编：201108
电话：400 168 1800
传真：021-3468 1391
电邮：beso@besoasia.com
网址：www.besoasia.com
业务范围：
BESO为世界各地的酒店客户提供创新和节能的智能化解决方案，这些解决方案能够提高酒店的舒适性和安全性，并优化酒店及设施的管理，提高能源效率。全面的能源和环境解决方案，可以降低建筑的能源成本和运营成本，在保证舒适的前提下实现能源的节约。创新的建筑智能化解决方案将帮助我们一起保护绿色地球。
主要客户为国内外高星级酒店，知名酒店管理集团，系统集成商等。产品广泛用于喜达屋，豪生，卡尔森、香格里拉，洲际，恒大地产等旗下酒店。

Shanghai Sino-Vision Technology Co., Ltd.
上海慧浦神望电子科技有限公司
上海市中山西路1525号技贸大厦5楼
邮编：200030
电话：021-5187 0618
传真：021-5187 0618*855
电邮：ggliqiong@163.com
网址：www.sino-vision.cn

Shenzhen Amy letter Science and Technology Limited company
深圳市艾美信科技有限公司
深圳市宝安中心区华丰科技园A座6楼
电话：0755-2965 7482
传真：0755-2678 1272
电邮：wenjb12@163.com
网址：www.i-maisontech.com

Shenzhen International Solusoft Software Co., Ltd.
深圳万国思迅软件有限公司
广东省深圳市南山区
高新技术产业园南区W2-B栋4楼
邮编：518057
电话：0755-2652 0701
传真：0755-2652 0744
电邮：sales@siss.com.cn
网址：www.siss.com.cn

Zhuhai Holion Electronic Engineering Co., Ltd.
珠海宏利来电子工程有限公司
广东省珠海市前山双龙山工业区9号9栋5楼
邮编：519070
电话：0756-850 1218
传真：0756-850 1218*603
电邮：sales@holion.net
网址：www.holion.net

盛达英畅科技有限公司
北京市海淀区紫竹院路
赛迪大厦附座1号楼2单元2031
邮编：100040
电话：010-8846 2743
传真：010-8846 2743*607
电邮：bj-sdkj@163.com
网址：www.bj-sdkj.com

热水保温
Hot Water Temperature Maintenance

Tyco Thermal Controls
泰科热控
上海市宜山路1009号创新大厦20楼
邮编：200233
电话：021-2412 1688
传真：021-5426 2967
网址：www.tycothermal.com

厨房设备
Kitchen Systems

Beijing Sunny Kitchen Equipment Co., Ltd.
北京市新丽厨房设备有限公司
北京市朝阳区马各庄
邮编：100024
电话：010-6542 5366
传真：010-6541 8029
电邮：sales@sunny-kitchen.com
网址：www.sunny-kitchen.com

Franke (China) Kitchen System Co., Ltd.
弗兰卡（中国）厨房系统有限公司
上海市徐汇区零陵路899号飞洲国际广场15楼K座
邮编：200030
电话：021-5489 3126
传真：021-5489 3155
网址：www.franke.com.cn

Jiangsu Changshu Nanfang Kitchen Equipment & Accessories Co., Ltd.
江苏常熟市南方厨房设备有限责任公司
江苏省常熟市东南经济开发区常昆公路288号
邮编：215542
电话：0512-5257 1555
传真：0512-5257 1516
电邮：info@china-nanchu.com
网址：www.china-nanchu.com

Qingdao Turbo Air. Inc
青岛特博尔科技发展有限公司
青岛胶南市海滨工业园
珠山路以西海滨七路以北297号
电话：0532-8513 6600
传真：0532-8513 5638
网址：www.turboairchina.com

Suzhou Dongfeng Stainless Steel Products Factory
苏州市东风不锈钢制品厂
江苏省苏州市相城开发区88号
邮编：215100
电话：0512-6757 1801
传真：0512-6751 8003
电邮：szeastwlnd@126.com
网址：www.sz-eastwind.com

上海金树酒店设备有限公司
上海市普陀区府村路179号102栋3、4号门
邮编：200010
电话：021-5204 3106
传真：021-5204 3128
电邮：sales@js999.com.cn
网址：www.js999.com.cn

升降机及扶手电梯
Lifts & Escalators

Guangzhou Shen Ling Elevator Co., Ltd.
广州申菱电梯有限公司
广州市海珠区工业大道南华西第五工业区
邮编：510288
电话：020-8401 1509
传真：020-8401 1532
电邮：yes163@163.com
网址：www.espcn.cn

Mitsubishi Electric Shanghai Electric Elevator
三菱电机上海机电电梯
上海市闵行区中春路1211号
邮编：201108
电话：021-3409 3030
传真：021-3409 3053
网址：www.mese-cn.com

Qingdao Keda Elevator Co., Ltd.
青岛科达电梯有限公司
山东省青岛市市北区长山路52号甲
邮编：266012
电话：0532-8382 3587
传真：0532-8382 0587
电邮：keda@qdkeda.com
网址：www.qdkeda.com

▼升降机及扶手电梯
Lifts & Escalators

Shanghai Middiamond Elevator
上海中菱电梯
上海市中山西路1919号
电话：021-6115 9299
传真：021-6115 9211
电邮：shmd999@163.com
网址：www.shmdchina.com

Shanghai Suoyuan Tailing Elevator Co., Ltd.
上海索远台菱电梯有限公司
上海曹杨路450号绿地和创大厦1405室
邮编：200063
电话：021-5179 0663
传真：021-5179 0664
电邮：hui.zhang@suoyuandt.com
网址：www.suoyuandt.com

Shanghai Xiernuo Elevator Co., Ltd.
上海席尔诺电梯有限公司
上海市怒江北路598号1619室
邮编：200333
电话：021-6216 5490
传真：021-6216 9365
电邮：xiernuo@xiernuo.com
网址：www.xiernuo.com

Shanghai Yungtay Elevator Equipment Co., Ltd.
上海永大电梯设备有限公司
上海市松江区九亭镇九新公路99号
邮编：201615
电话：021-5763 3888
传真：021-5763 2251
电邮：yungtay@yungtay.com.cn
网址：www.yungtay.com.cn

Shanghai Zhongye Elevator Co., Ltd.
上海中业电梯有限公司
上海市浦东新区高东二路315号
邮编：200137
电话：021-5848 5835
传真：021-5848 1369
网址：www.sh-zhongye.com

Suzhou WeiErTe Aluminium Alloyelevator Co., Ltd.
苏州威尔特铝合金升降机械有限公司
苏州市相城区望亭镇机场路788号
邮编：215155
电话：0512-6538 2883
传真：0512-6670 6150
电邮：wetsjj@qq.com
网址：www.wetsjj.com

Toshiba Elevator (China) Co., Ltd.
东芝电梯（中国）有限公司
上海市宝山区蕰川路685号
邮编：201901
电话：021-5680 8888
传真：021-5680 6789
网址：www.toshiba-elevator.com.cn

北京市乾济电梯公司
北京市朝阳区光华里2号金茂公寓E-602室
邮编：100020
电话：010-6500 1312
传真：010-6500 1326
电邮：qianji_elev@163.com
网址：www.qianjielev.com

中美合资苏州华蒂电梯有限公司
苏州市桐泾北路张家浜5幢北1号
邮编：215004
电话：0512-6552 7058
传真：0512-6531 1953
电邮：dts@cn-dts.com
网址：www.cn-dts.com

灯光照明
Lightings

Aero Lightology Inc.
中山艾罗照明有限公司
广东省中山市小榄镇
菊城大道西中永第一工业区J栋
电话：0760-2255 7055
传真：0760-2255 7501
网址：www.aerolight.com.cn

Atdecotek
上海市程家桥支路201弄智地大厦F07室
电话：021-6268 5137
传真：021-6268 5137
电邮：sales@artdecotek.com
网址：www.artdecotek.com

BHL Lighting Limited
东莞市壮朗灯饰有限公司
广东省东莞虎门北栅仁中岗大道5号
邮编：523925
电话：0769-8862 8868
传真：0769-8520 6239
网址：www.bhl-lighting.com

Crasc Lighting (Zhongshan) Co., Ltd.
中山市古镇德莱通照明电器厂
中山市古镇富兴路18号（国贸车站对面）
电话：0760-2235 8555
传真：0760-2239 5887
电邮：dilate@vip.163.com
网址：www.crasc.com.cn

Dongguan Gabriel Lighting Factory
东莞嘉佰利灯饰厂
东莞市虎门镇东风工业区
电话：0769-8151 7360
传真：0769-8151 7361
电邮：wwsong88@126.com
网址：www.cnlight.net

Dongguan Kam Tat Lighting Co., Ltd.
东莞市金达照明有限公司
东莞市万江谷涌管理区
电话：0769-2228 4761
传真：0769-2227 7195
电邮：info@kamtatlighting.com
网址：www.riservalighting.com

Foloretina Company
佛罗伦蒂娜公司
深圳市罗湖区梅园路艺贸中心三楼318
电话：0755-2590 5749
传真：0755-8249 7849
电邮：szftina8888@vip.163.com
网址：www.ftina.com

Foshan Yatai Furniture Ltd.
佛山市亚太家私有限公司
广东省佛山市南海区大沥镇盐步新城村工业区30号
邮编：528247
电话：0757-8577 0647
传真：0757-8577 6071
电邮：nhyatai@163.com
网址：www.mr-dream.com
请参阅第306、307页

Media-go Engineering Ltd.
美歌工程有限公司
25/F Westin Centre, 26 Hung To Road, Kwun Tong, Kowloon, Hong Kong
电话：+852-2797 8128
传真：+852-2790 5732
电邮：mediago@mediago.com.hk
网址：www.mediago.com.hk

NVC Lighting Technology Corporation
惠州雷士光电科技有限公司
广东惠州汝湖雷士工业园
邮编：516021
电话：0752-278 6666
传真：0752-278 6689
网址：www.nvc-lighting.com.cn

Shanghai Bright Lighting Technology Co., Ltd.
上海莹辉照明科技有限公司
上海市普陀区曹杨路648号
邮编：200063
电话：021-6216 6666
传真：021-6216 4684
网址：www.brightlighting.net

Shanghai Everlasting Glow Technology Co., Ltd.
上海亿光数码科技有限公司
上海市平凉路720号2楼
邮编：200082
电话：021-6589 8640
传真：021-6589 8464
网址：www.segt.com.cn

South China House of Technology Consultants Ltd.
南中国科技顾问有限公司
Unit 1303-04, Block B,Sea View Estate, 2-14 Watson Road, North Point, Hong Kong
电话：+852-2590 6808
传真：+852-2590 6383
电邮：audiovisual@schot.com
网址：www.schot.com

Xiamen Topstar Co., Ltd.
厦门通士达有限公司
厦门同安区西柯镇通福路777号
邮编：361100
电话：0592-726 3188
传真：0592-726 3288
电邮：cnsales@topstar.com.cn
网址：www.topstar.com.cn

Zhongshan Guzhen Godo Lighting Manufacto
中山市古镇高度灯饰厂
中山市古镇冈东第三工业区利丰街1号
电话：0760-2232 5399
传真：0760-2232 3743
电邮：godolighting@126.com
网址：www.godolighting.com

▼灯光照明
Lightings

Zhongshan Poso Lighting Co., Ltd.
中山品上照明有限公司
广东省中山市小榄镇绩东一裕胜工业区
电话：0760-2213 7776
传真：0760-2213 7771
电邮：poso@posolighting.com
网址：www.posolighting.com

东莞欧雅特电器有限公司
广东省东莞市沙田镇环保工业城永晋集团
电话：0769-8868 7999
传真：0769-8868 5566
电邮：service@alart-lighting.com
网址：www.alart-lighting.com

伊诗邦光电科技（上海）有限公司
上海市青浦区北青公路6588号D2-71
邮编：201706
电话：021-3987 8227
网址：www.espasole.com

大理石
Marbles

Beijing Euro-Asia Runcheng Building Materials Co., Ltd.
北京欧亚润诚建材有限公司
北京市朝阳区十八里店
西联国际石材市场3区D16号
邮编：100023
电话：010-8150 5892
传真：010-8150 5891
电邮：postmaster@rcmarble.com
网址：www.rcmarble.com

Beijing West Couplet HongXing Stone Co., Ltd.
北京市西联宏星石材有限公司
北京市朝阳区西联国际石材市场二区15号
邮编：100023
电话：010-8150 5538
传真：010-8150 5536
电邮：bjhxsc@163.com
网址：www.hongxingstone.com

Chengda Stone Company Limited
福建省泉州市诚达石业有限公司
福建省南安市省新镇扶茂岭工业开发区
邮编：362300
电话：0595-8628 5776
传真：0595-8628 5776
电邮：cd_stone@163.com
网址：www.chengdastone.com

Foshan Goloen Milan Stone Mosaic Company Limited
佛山市金景金米兰石材有限公司
佛山市石湾卫浴城A馆2楼A11-12
电话：0757-8266 7590
传真：0757-8266 7589
电邮：gml@fsgml.com
网址：www.fsgml.com

Fujian Wanlong Stone Co., Ltd.
福建省万隆石业股份有限公司
福建省南安市水头镇福山工业区
电话：0595-8608 1111
传真：0595-8607 5555
电邮：wanlong01@126.com
网址：www.wanlong-stone.com

Guangzhou Lixin Stone Art Co., Ltd.
广州立新石材工艺有限公司
广东省广州市广从一路7号
邮编：510540
电话：020-8605 0073
传真：020-8605 0521
电邮：gz@wayon.com
网址：www.wayon.com

Kangli Stone Co., Ltd.
深圳康利石材有限公司
深圳市布吉镇李朗大道康利石材工业园
电话：0755-2872 5668
传真：0755-2852 5602
电邮：info@kanglistone.com
网址：www.kanglistone.com

Nanan Zongyi Stone Co., Ltd.
南安市宗艺石材有限公司
福建省泉州市官桥镇南联工业区
邮编：362341
电话：0595-8681 5555
传真：0595-8681 5999
电邮：service@zongyi.com.cn
网址：www.zongyi.com.cn

Quanzhou XinYu Stone Industry Co., Ltd.
泉州新宇石业有限公司
福建省南安市水头镇蟠龙工业区
邮编：362342
电话：0595-8609 5333
传真：0595-8609 5898
电邮：china@xinyustone.com
网址：www.xinyustone.com

Rong Hua Fu Quartz Stone
荣华富石英石
广东省云浮市云城区牧羊路103号
邮编：527300
电话：0766-821 1377
传真：0766-821 2655
电邮：rhfstone@163.com
网址：www.ronghuafu.com

Shanghai Min Ren Marble Co., Ltd.
上海铭仁石材有限公司
上海市青浦区凤溪镇嘉松中路3199弄5号
邮编：201705
电话：021-3987 2776
传真：021-3987 2778
电邮：mr@minrenmarble.com
网址：www.minrenmarble.com

Shanghai Wayon Stone Co., Ltd.
上海威洋石材有限公司
上海市嘉定区曹安路4589号
邮编：201804
电话：021-5959 6969
传真：021-5959 6699
电邮：sh@wayon.com
网址：www.wayon.com

Shenzhen Mercury Import & Export Co., Ltd.
深圳市达美科进出口有限公司
广东省深圳市福田区车公庙
天安数码时代A座805室
电话：0755-8329 0759
传真：0755-8329 0761
电邮：ahmet@hiquma.com.cn
网址：www.hiquma.com.cn

TaXing Group
塔星集团
上海市青浦区北青公路5777号
邮编：201706
电话：021-3987 8888
传真：021-3987 8089
电邮：webmaster@taxing.com.cn
网址：www.taxing.com.cn

Tino Stone China Co., Ltd.
帝诺石材（中国）有限公司
上海市淮海西路570号C3座301-302室
邮编：200052
电话：021-6283 6051
传真：021-6283 6031
网址：www.tino.es

Universal Marble & Granite Group Limited
环球石材集团有限公司
广东省东莞市长安镇厦岗管理区
邮编：523873
电话：0769-8554 4338
传真：0769-8532 2098
电邮：sales@umgg.com.cn
网址：www.umgg.biz

Wanlong Stone Shares
福建万龙石业股份
福建省南安市水头镇福建工业区
邮编：362342
电话：0595- 8609 5560
传真：0595-8607 5555
电邮：wanlong@public.xm.fj.com
网址：www.wanlong-stone.com

Yunfu City Jundong Stone Material Co., Ltd.
云浮市骏东石材有限公司
广东省云浮市云城区牧羊工业区
电话：0766-814 0031
传真：0766-814 0833
电邮：yunfuhuxin@163.com
网址：www.yfjundong.com

Yunfu City Yueyun New Stone Materials Co., Ltd.
云浮市粤云新型石材有限公司
广东省云浮市兴云东路108号
邮编：527300
电话：0766-882 2331
传真：0766-882 8813
网址：www.yueyunstone.com

Yunfu Elegance Stone Co., Ltd.
广东云浮市新高雅石材有限公司
广东省云浮初城工业区云浮国际石材城29栋
电话：0766-822 6777
传真：0766-821 6048
电邮：yfgy@21cn.com
网址：www.gystone.com.cn

人造大理石
Marbles,Synthetic

Bestone Artificial Stone Products Co., Ltd.
百斯顿人造石制品有限公司
佛山市顺德区北滘镇黄涌工业区南路10号
邮编：528311
电话：0757-2632 4388
传真：0757-2663 7970
电邮：bestone26600912@163.com
网址：www.china-bestone.com

Chit Shing Marble Co., Ltd.
捷成云石有限公司
广东省深圳市南山区深南大道瑞思中心A座2512室
电话：0755-2690 3060
传真：0755-2690 3062
电邮：chitshingmarble@yahoo.com
网址：www.chitshingmarble.com

Foshan Shunde O'riordan Building Materials Manufacturing Co., Ltd.
佛山市顺德区欧雅典建材制品有限公司
广东省佛山市顺德区勒流龙眼工业区
邮编：528322
电话：0757-2533 9911
传真：0757-2563 2121
电邮：ordan@ordan.com.cn
网址：www.ordan.com.cn

Fuyun Engineered Stone (China) Co., Ltd.
云浮市新富云岗石有限公司
广东省云浮市云城区牧羊工业区
邮编：527300
电话：0766-814 1133
传真：0766-814 1155
电邮：fuyungangshi@126.com
网址：www.fuyunstone.com

Golden Edge Artificial Marbles Co., Ltd.
金角石材有限公司
广东省云浮市云城区腰古镇金角石材厂
电话：0766-851 2999
传真：0766-851 2728
电邮：sales@88stone.com
网址：www.88stone.com

Guangdong Nanhai Opal Industrial Co., Ltd.
广东南海澳宝实业有限公司
佛山市南海区九江镇沙咀半岛工业园（龙高路段）
邮编：528203
电话：0757-8650 6188
传真：0757-8656 1948
电邮：export@gdopal.com
网址：www.gdopal.com

Jiujiang Golden Phoenix Decoration Material Co., Ltd.
九江金凤凰装饰材料有限公司
福建省石狮市石灵路建联花园63-67号
电话：0595-8300 1829
传真：0595-8859 2021
电邮：sales@jj-goldenphoenix.com
网址：www.jj-goldenphoenix.com

Shandong (Weihai) Remkinstone Co., Ltd.
山东（威海）银基建材有限公司
青岛市海尔路182-6号财富大厦1106室
电话：0532-8889 8786
传真：0532-8897 8889
网址：www.remkinstone.com

Shanghai Jixiang Building Materials Group Co., Ltd.
上海吉祥建材集团有限公司
上海市松江区石湖荡镇甘德路260号
邮编：201417
电话：021-5776 6633
传真：021-5784 3509
电邮：zwm@zwm.com.cn
网址：www.zwm.com.cn

Shanghai Min Ren Marble Co., Ltd.
上海铭仁石材有限公司
上海市青浦区凤溪镇嘉松中路3199弄5号
邮编：201705
电话：021-3987 2776
传真：021-3987 2778
电邮：mr@minrenmarble.com
网址：www.minrenmarble.com

Shanghai Supe Construction Materials Co., Ltd.
上海秀珀建材有限公司
上海市唐镇工业区上丰路659号
邮编：201202
电话：021-3382 6971
传真：021-3382 6971
网址：www.hopstone.com

Shanghai Zhongyi Stone Engineering Co., Ltd.
上海中意石材工程有限公司
上海市中山北路814弄18号1001室
邮编：200070
电话：021-6143 5361
传真：021-6143 5363
电邮：tao084@yahoo.com.cn
网址：www.1995zy.com

Sunshine Stone Co., Ltd.
惠安阳光石业
福建泉州惠安县黄塘镇接待工业区
邮编：362101
电话：0595-8732 7772
传真：0595-8730 5599
电邮：sales2@sunshinestone.com.cn
网址：www.ygstone.com

Xinyun Stone (Yunfu) Co., Ltd.
新云石业（云浮）有限公司
广东省云浮市初城工业开发区北二路
邮编：521328
电话：0766-855 7863
传真：0766-855 7123
网址：www.xinyun-stone.com

Yunfu Xinlixin Compound Stone Company Limited
云浮市新丽新岗石发展有限公司
广东省云浮市云城区河口初城工业区北二路
邮编：527328
电话：0766-822 6788
传真：0766-822 6778
电邮：xinlistoneco@163.com
网址：www.xinlico.com

北京创利特鑫公司
北京市大兴区团河工业区8号
电话：010-6128 4618
传真：010-6128 4619
电邮：office@cx-renzaoshi.com
网址：www.cx-renzaoshi.com

北京宏达永康石材加工厂
北京市大兴区瀛海镇北普陀影视城
邮编：100076
电话：010-6791 5923
传真：010-6791 0549
电邮：hdyk264@sina.com
网址：www.bjrzs.com

北京美瑾美家商贸有限公司
北京市大兴区团河南村工业区
电话：010-8360 0797
传真：010-8360 0797
电邮：tyszy01@163.com
网址：www.tyszy.com

北京艺景绿源科技开发有限公司
北京市丰台区科学城海鹰路5号
赛欧孵化广场701室
邮编：100070
电话：010-8368 2361
传真：010-6371 5538
电邮：info@bjyjy.com
网址：www.bjyjy.com

马赛克
Mosaic Tiles

Beijing Bilanxuan Tech. & Trade Co., Ltd.
北京碧澜轩技贸有限公司
北京市大兴区西红门同华南大街2号
邮编：100162
电话：010-5157 8603
传真：010-5157 8604
电邮：aschina@public.bta.net.cn
网址：www.bilanxuan.com.cn

Beijing Euro-Asia Runcheng Building Materials Co., Ltd.
北京欧亚润诚建材有限公司
北京市朝阳区十八里店
西联国际石材市场3区D16号
邮编：100023
电话：010-8150 5892
传真：010-8150 5891
电邮：postmaster@rcmarble.com
网址：www.rcmarble.com

Beijing West Couplet HongXing Stone Co., Ltd.
北京市西联宏星石材有限公司
北京市朝阳区西联国际石材市场二区15号
邮编：100023
电话：010-8150 5538
传真：010-8150 5536
电邮：bjhxsc@163.com
网址：www.hongxingstone.com

Chengdu Jiahong Art Glass Co., Ltd.
成都嘉泓艺术玻璃有限责任公司
四川省成都市青龙街27号铂金大厦1号16层
邮编：610016
电话：028-8628 2831
传真：028-8628 2959
电邮：sales@joyzonemosaic.com
网址：www.joyzonemosaic.com

Chengdu Leifu Art Stone Co., Ltd.
成都磊富艺术石业有限公司
四川省成都市三洞桥街2号华业广场5楼505室
邮编：610031
电话：028-8778 6977
传真：028-8778 8260
电邮：info@leifumosaic.com
网址：www.leifumosaic.com

▼马赛克
Mosaic Tiles

Foshan Babagino Company
佛山市芭芭吉若建材有限公司
佛山市澜石镇海滨东路9号海景大厦2905室
电话：0757-8381 0967
传真：0757-8383 7716
电邮：amingo@babagino.com
网址：www.babagino.com

Foshan Goloen Milan Stone Mosaic Company Limited
佛山市金景金米兰石材有限公司
佛山市石湾卫浴城A馆2楼A11-12
电话：0757-8266 7590
传真：0757-8266 7589
电邮：gml@fsgml.com
网址：www.fsgml.com

Foshan Miao Du Decaale Co., Ltd.
佛山市庙都建材有限公司
广东省佛山市南海区平洲夏南工业区2号
邮编：528251
电话：020-8194 9163
传真：020-8120 0573
网址：www.gzmiaodu.com

Foshan Zhaofengnian Art Mosaic
佛山市兆丰年艺术马赛克
佛山市禅城区南庄镇上元柏朗工业区
邮编：528222
电话：0757-8252 4612
传真：0757-8539 0632
网址：www.zfnian.com

Guangzhou Area Expansion Industrial Co., Ltd.
广州朗域实业有限公司
广州市海珠区新港东路中洲中心南塔A座1801室
电话：020-8923 6700
传真：020-8923 6432*818
网址：www.m-c.cn

Guangzhou Tulip Mosaic Company
广州市番禺区钟村郁金香装饰材料厂
广州市番禺区钟村镇都那村西围工业区厂房1座
电话：020-3463 1016
传真：020-3463 1019
网址：www.tulipmosaic.com

Hangzhou Dongsheng Ceramic Co., Ltd.
杭州东升陶艺有限公司
杭州市半山镇石塘村临半路107号
邮编：310022
电话：0571-8814 0836
传真：0571-8814 0821
网址：www.hsysz.net

Hangzhou Kasaro Decorative Material Co., Ltd.
杭州卡莎罗装饰材料有限公司
浙江省杭州市西湖区三墩镇草鞋桥18号
邮编：310000
电话：0571-8896 8920
传真：0571-8896 8921
网址：www.kasaromosaic.com

Hemei Stones Company
和美石材
河南省镇平县安子营街
邮编：474262
电话：0377-6555 3968
传真：0377-6555 2976
电邮：nyhmsc@126.com
网址：www.nyhmsc.com

Huidong County Wilder Mosaic Factory Co., Ltd.
惠东县威尔德马赛克厂有限公司
广东省惠东县大岭镇沙梨园工业区
邮编：516321
电话：0752-890 2197
传真：0752-890 6708
电邮：wed@glassmosaic.net.cn
网址：www.glassmosaic.net.cn

Jinjiang Jiangxing Building Materials Trading Co., Ltd.
晋江市江兴建材贸易有限公司
福建省晋江市磁灶镇宝洋工业区
邮编：362214
电话：0595-8589 2226
传真：0595-8589 5386
网址：www.jxmosaic.com

Nantong Kingston's Building Materials Manufacturing Co., Ltd.
南通金士顿新型建材制造有限公司
江苏省海门市机电工业园区
电话：0513-8277 6502
传真：0513-8277 6266
网址：www.jinshidun.cc

Rose Art Mosaic Co., Ltd.
开平市玫瑰艺术马赛克有限公司
广东省开平市新昌新堤路50号
邮编：529300
电话：0750-238 5807
传真：0750-221 2537
网址：www.rosemosaic.com

Seed Decorative Material Co., Ltd.
佛山市顺德区赛德装饰材料有限公司
佛山市顺德区北滘镇龙涌新工业区
邮编：528311
电话：0757-2633 6300
传真：0757-2633 6301
电邮：jun@seedmosaic.com
网址：www.seedmosaic.com

Shenzhen Canosa Decoration Material Co., Ltd.
深圳市卡诺莎装饰材料有限公司
深圳市罗湖区宝安北路好百年六楼609、610室
电话：0755-8242 9930
传真：0755-8242 9931
电邮：sales@szcanosa.com
网址：www.szcanosa.com

Shenzhen Emmy Shell Mosaic & Tiles Co., Ltd.
深圳市艾美贝类工艺品有限公司
深圳市龙岗区布吉镇沙湾沙平北路98号
邮编：518000
电话：0755-2560 5690
传真：0755-2560 8260
电邮：sales@szaimei.com
网址：www.szaimei.com

Yixing Gu Jin Mosaic Factory
宜兴市古今马赛克厂
江苏省宜兴市张渚镇工业园区
邮编：214200
电话：0510-8739 7228
传真：0510-8739 7227
网址：www.gjmsk.com

管道防冻
Pipe Freeze Protection

Anhui Anze Electrical Co., Ltd.
安徽安泽电工有限公司
安徽省宁国市经济技术开发区外环南路
邮编：242300
电话：0563-418 7588
传真：0563-418 7577
电邮：ngaz@anze.cn
网址：www.anze.cn

Beijing Lucky Techology Co., Ltd.
北京朗境祥技术有限公司
北京市海淀区太平路25号瑞兴写字楼I-103
邮编：100036
电话：010-6818 7520
传真：010-6816 8260
电邮：lucky0188@163.com
网址：www.langjingxiang.cn

Ensmotin Technology & Trading Co., Ltd.
北京恩斯慕天科贸有限公司
北京市朝阳区万红西街2号燕东大厦A4025
电话：010-8450 5870
传真：010-8450 5228
电邮：esmt_china@126.com
网址：www.esmt-china.com

Heifei Xusheng New Electric Heat Trading Technology Co., Ltd.
合肥市旭升新型电伴热科技有限公司
安徽省合肥市四里河路66号
电话：0551-466 9376
传真：0551-467 6056
电邮：xsdbr@163.com
网址：www.xsdbr.com

Tyco Thermal Controls
泰科热控
上海市宜山路1009号创新大厦20楼
邮编：200233
电话：021-2412 1688
传真：021-5426 2967
网址：www.tycothermal.com

北京恒泰诚业电伴热技术有限公司
北京市丰台区草桥欣园四区19号楼3单元1201室
邮编：100069
电话：010-8397 1046
传真：010-8756 4325
电邮：ljianhui2008@sohu.com
网址：www.bjhtcy.net

北京三恒科贸有限公司
北京市石景山区阜石路166号泽洋大厦505室
邮编：100043
电话：010-8890 9978
传真：010-8890 9982
电邮：shdn@shdn.com.cn
网址：www.shdn.com.cn

汉堡阁电热系统（上海）有限公司
上海市徐汇区田州路159号莲花大厦1002室
电话：021-6091 8996
传真：021-6091 8995
电邮：shanghai@halmburger.cn
网址：www.halmburger.cn

▼管道防冻
Pipe Freeze Protection

河南宝泰实业万家暖智能电地暖营销中心
河南省郑州市紫荆山路60号金成国贸大厦1416室
邮编：450052
电话：0371-6661 6909
电邮：wanjianuan@163.com
网址：www.wanjianuan.com

屋檐及落水管防冻
Roof Gutter and Down Pipe De-icing

Tyco Thermal Controls
泰科热控
上海市宜山路1009号创新大厦20楼
邮编：200233
电话：021-2412 1688
传真：021-5426 2967
网址：www.tycothermal.com

北京三恒科贸有限公司
北京市石景山区阜石路166号泽洋大厦505室
邮编：100043
电话：010-8890 9978
传真：010-8890 9982
电邮：shdn@shdn.com.cn
网址：www.shdn.com.cn

安全设备及用品
Safety Equipment & Products

Assa Abloy Hospitality (Shanghai) Co., Ltd.
亚萨合莱保安系统（上海）有限公司
上海市徐汇区漕溪北路737弄
汇翠花园1号楼2704室
邮编：200030
电话：021-6438 9106
传真：021-6438 9106*101
网址：www.vingcard.com

Hings Plastic & Metal Products Mfy
兴业塑胶五金制品厂
广东省顺德市勒流镇富裕工业区
邮编：528324
电话：0757-2533 2788
传真：0757-2533 2993
电邮：hingspmp@hingsgroup.com
网址：www.hingsgroup.com

Promat (HK) Limited
宝时（香港）有限公司
香港九龙新蒲岗太子道东704号
新时代商业中心901室
电话：+852-2661 2392
传真：+852-2661 2086
电邮：info@promat.hk
网址：www.promat.hk

Shanghai Comgear Technology Co., Ltd.
上海禾聚电子有限公司
上海市浦东新区花木路718弄13号1803室
邮编：201204
电话：021-5045 4185
传真：021-5045 4186
电邮：salessupport@comgear.com.cn
网址：www.comgear.com.cn

天津市鼎日安全科技有限公司
天津市河西区解放南路名仕达花园3-1-101
邮编：300200
电话：022-2831 7687
传真：022-2831 7281
电邮：famous@safety-china.com
网址：www.safety-china.com

桑拿及蒸汽浴
Sauna & Steam Baths

Anhui Saunaking Co., Ltd.
安徽桑乐金股份有限公司
安徽省合肥市高新技术开发区合欢路34号
邮编：230088
电话：0551-235 5421
传真：0551-584 7561
网址：www.saunaking.com.cn

Guangdong LianSheng Pool & Spa Equipments Co., Ltd.
广东联盛泳池水疗设备有限公司
广东省中山市南头镇升辉南工业区建业路16号
邮编：528427
电话：0760-2312 7282
传真：0760-2312 7280
电邮：ymir@spa-ymir.com
网址：www.chinaspa.net.cn

H.Jacuzz Sauna & Swimming Pool Equipment Co., Ltd.
上海豪爵桑拿泳池设备有限公司
上海市沪闵路6666号新梅广场30号101室
邮编：201100
电话：021-3358 0828
传真：021-3358 0828
电邮：haojue.com@263.com
网址：www.haojue1.com

Hotwind Sauna Equipment Co., Ltd.
徐州好温迪桑拿设备有限公司
江苏省徐州市建国西路75号财富广场B座3层
电话：0516-8202 6267
传真：0516-8202 6269
网址：www.hotwindsauna.cn

Shanghai D-L Enterprise Development Co., Ltd.
上海东亚利邦企业发展有限公司
上海市瑞金南路1号海兴广场15楼H座
邮编：200023
电话：021-6418 5035
传真：021-6418 5037
电邮：sales@dongyalibang.com
网址：www.dongyalibang.com

Xuzhou Healthlandsauna Equipment Co., Ltd.
徐州海兰特桑拿设备有限公司
江苏省徐州市淮海西路29号财富大厦16F25室
邮编：221006
电话：0516-8590 2725
传真：0516-8590 2735
电邮：info@healthlandsauna.com
网址：www.healthlandsauna.cn

北京康健碧波休闲设备有限公司
北京市朝阳区十里河精品建材厅1号
邮编：100122
电话：010-8736 5110
传真：010-8736 3687
电邮：kjbibo@163.com
网址：www.kjbibo.com

东莞市龙邦卫浴有限公司
广东省东莞市东坑镇东安路262号
邮编：523459
电话：0769-8386 3528
传真：0769-8388 4627
电邮：km@dgkamon.com
网址：www.kamon.net.cn

深圳市卓先实业有限公司
深圳市龙岗区龙城中路东方明珠城5座1704室
电话：0755-8930 2960
传真：0755-8930 2961
电邮：china02@josensauna.com
网址：www.josensauna.com.cn

指示牌
Signs

Beijing Y.T Jia Mei Hotel Articles Co., Ltd.
北京粤通佳美酒店用品有限公司
北京市朝阳区高碑店新村368号
电话：010-6748 9989
传真：010-8575 0237
电邮：cat9918@163.com
网址：www.bjjdyp.com

Caelum International Ltd.
加隆国际有限公司
深圳市福田保税区桂花路5号西塔4层
邮编：518038
电话：0755-8358 8709
传真：0755-8358 8704
网址：www.caelumint.com
请参阅第375页

Changzhou Chaoyi Decoration Sign Co., Ltd.
常州市超艺标牌有限公司
江苏省常州市武进区牛塘镇青云工业区5号
邮编：213163
电话：0519-8639 6298
传真：0519-8639 6328
电邮：cy@czcybp.com
网址：www.czcybp.com

Changzhou Super Sign Ltd.
常州市超凡标牌有限公司
江苏省常州市牛塘镇湖滨北路315号
邮编：213163
电话：0519-8639 1460
传真：0519-8639 5990
电邮：supersign@cfbp.cn
网址：www.cfbp.cn

Changzhou Tengfei Sign Co., Ltd.
常州市腾飞标牌有限公司
江苏省常州市武进区牛塘镇延政路32号
邮编：213163
电话：0519-8831 6818
传真：0519-8831 6858
电邮：jjk@tengfeisign.net
网址：www.tengfeisign.net

Changzhou Wujin Niutang Yunlong Technice Sign Factory
常州市武进牛塘云龙工艺标牌厂
江苏省常州市武进区牛塘镇湖滨路118号
邮编：213163
电话：0519-8639 6968
传真：0519-8639 8978
电邮：w5889485@126.com
网址：www.winglon.cn

www.caelumint.com
Our effort, your reward
我们的努力，您的回报
Caelum International
Digital Signage Network Provider
Leave your Mark
For All Your Inhouse Digital Signage
& Directional Signage Needs
Contact Caelum Professional' s Today!
如果您对内部数码标牌和指示牌有任何需要，
请立即致电加隆国际的专业人士！
Caelum International is the leading Digital Signage Network Provider, yet a quite achiever.
Caelum International is the specialist of Digital Signage technology, having its own design, development, electronic and software engineers, manufacturing its hardware and software product from the ground floor up through to the deployment of multi-national digital signage networks.
加隆国际是数码标牌网络提供商领先者且已经获得相当的成就。
加隆国际是数码标牌技术方面的专家，从基层的设施到跨国数码标牌网络的部署，拥有自己的设计、开发、电子及软件工程师，并自行制造相关软硬件产品。
China 中国
Four Points Business Offices
West Tower Level 4,
5 Guihua Road Futian Free Trade Zone
Shenzhen, 518038, PRC
Telephone: +86 755 8358 8709
Fax: +86 755 8358 8704
Hong Kong 香港
Two International Finance Centre
Level 19
8 Finance Street Central
Hong Kong, China
Telephone: +852 2251 8887
Fax: +852 2251 8807
Sydney, Australia 澳大利亚，悉尼
Chifley Tower Level 29
2 Chifley Square Sydney
NSW, 2000, Australia
Telephone: +61 2 9375 2388
Fax: +61 2 9375 2121
Perth, Australia 澳大利亚，帕斯
Level 18, 152 – 158,
St George's Terrace
Central Tower,
Perth, Western Australia
Telephone: +61 8 9288 1809
Fax: +61 8 9288 1808
加隆国际有限公司数字标牌网络提供商
Caelum International Digital Signage Network Provider
www.caelumint.com

▼指示牌
Signs

Chengbiao Metal Product Co., Ltd.
佛山市海南承标金属制品有限公司
佛山市海南里水沙涌上沙工业区
邮编：528244
电话：0757-8565 0918
传真：0757-8565 0928
电邮：neng69@21cn.com
网址：www.fscb888.com.cn

Guangzhou South Hotel Articles Co., Ltd.
广州南方酒店用品有限公司
广州市越秀区大沙头二马路44号之二
邮编：510100
电话：020-8388 9640
传真：020-8388 9840
电邮：china-south@vip.163.com
网址：www.china-south.com.cn

Humanbins Hotel Supply Limited
佛山南海优曼酒店用品制造有限公司
广东省佛山市南海区狮山工业园B区科大路3号
邮编：528241
电话：0757-8669 9295
传真：0757-8669 9292
电邮：sales@humanbins.com
网址：www.humanbins.com

Shanghai Wangyong Hotel Supplies Co., ltd.
上海旺勇酒店设备用品有限公司
上海市徐汇区田林路111号
邮编：200233
电话：021-5426 4098
传真：021-5427 0238
电邮：zhanwangyong@126.com
网址：www.shwangyong.com

South China House of Technology Consultants Ltd.
南中国科技顾问有限公司
Unit 1303-04, Block B,Sea View Estate, 2-14 Watson Road, North Point, Hong Kong
电话：+852-2590 6808
传真：+852-2590 6383
电邮：audiovisual@schot.com
网址：www.schot.com

Team International Co.
宏创国际公司
Flat K, 13/F Block 2 Golden Dragon Industrial Centre, 162-170 Tai Lin Pai Road
Kwai Chung, N.T., Hong Kong
电话：+852-2480 0528
传真：+852-2480 0508
电邮：sales@tihk.com
网址：www.tihk.com

北京鑫国发酒店用品厂
北京市朝阳区西大望路甲12号
电话：010-5848 7680
传真：010-8770 0990
电邮：xinguofa168@163.com
网址：www.xinguofa.com

常州市武进区亦心标牌厂
江苏省常州市武进区牛塘镇厚恕肖家村15号
邮编：213163
电话：0519-8639 6626
传真：0519-8639 4626
电邮：yx@yxsign.com
网址：www.yxsign.com

深圳市西利标识设计制作有限公司
深圳市南山区侨香路美景工业苑1栋2楼
邮编：518053
电话：0755-8343 5678
传真：0755-8343 5799
电邮：xili@xilisign.com
网址：www.xilisign.com
请参阅第376页

采光罩及天幕
Skylights & Canopies

Beijing Jd-Rainbow Building Decoration Co., Ltd.
北京江达雷博建筑装饰品有限公司
北京市朝阳区管庄乡郭家场村
邮编：100025
电话：010-6557 8221
传真：010-6557 8223
网址：www.jdrainbow.com

Beijing Kekaidi Science And Technology Co., Ltd.
北京科凯迪科技有限公司
北京市亦庄经济开发区
天华园3里一栋洋房1区1栋118号
邮编：100176
电话：010-6787 6601
传真：010-5131 5158
网址：www.bjkkd.com

Guangzhou Goodsense Decorative Building Materials Co., Ltd.
广州吉鑫祥装饰建材有限公司
广东省广州市白云区太和镇和乐东街3号
邮编：510540
电话：020-8743 9816
传真：020-8743 9813
电邮：export@chinagoodsense.cn
网址：www.chinagoodsense.cn

Shanghai Pingcheng Plastics Co., Ltd.
上海品诚塑胶有限公司
上海市盛龙路799号
邮编：201615
电话：021-3782 0388
传真：021-5695 9308
电邮：mail@pcsj.com.cn
网址：www.pcsj.com.cn

衡水宏盛实业有限公司
河北省衡水市和平西路298号
电话：0318-236 1888
传真：0318-236 1888
电邮：shenlongpc@163.com
网址：www.shenlongpc.com

板岩
Slates

Beijing Xiangyu Stone International Co., Ltd.
北京翔宇八方国际石材有限公司
北京市房山区周口店镇南五公里房易路西侧
邮编：102453
电话：010-6930 9118
传真：010-6139 0617
电邮：chinaslate@188.com
网址：www.stone-xy.com

Foshan Gutenberg Craft Co., Ltd.
佛山市古藤堡工艺有限公司
佛山市南海区里水镇和顺和桂工业园
邮编：528241
电话：0757-8510 1277
传真：0757-8512 2844
网址：www.fsgtb.com

Liuhe Stone Co., Ltd.
六合石材有限公司
北京市房山区周口店石材园
电话：0312-822 5625
传真：0312-881 6625
网址：www.liuhestone.com

Shanghai Ape Stone Co., Ltd.
上海古猿人石材有限公司
上海市浦东新区世纪大道1500号东方大厦701室
邮编：200122
电话：021-5058 8111
传真：021-5058 2228
电邮：apestone@vip.163.com
网址：www.apestone.com

地面融雪
Snow Melting

DCR Union (Beijing) Electron & Equipment Co., Ltd.
狄诺合众（北京）电子设备有限公司
北京市顺义区天竺出口加工区
邮编：101312
电话：010-8041 1358
传真：010-8041 1809
电邮：dcr-china@hotmail.com
网址：www.un-dn.com

Tyco Thermal Controls
泰科热控
上海市宜山路1009号创新大厦20楼
邮编：200233
电话：021-2412 1688
传真：021-5426 2967
网址：www.tycothermal.com

北京恒泰诚业电伴热技术有限公司
北京市丰台区草桥欣园四区19号楼3单元1201室
邮编：100069
电话：010-8397 1046
传真：010-8756 4325
电邮：ljianhui2008@sohu.com
网址：www.bjhtcy.net

北京三恒科贸有限公司
北京市石景山区阜石路166号泽洋大厦505室
邮编：100043
电话：010-8890 9978
传真：010-8890 9982
电邮：shdn@shdn.com.cn
网址：www.shdn.com.cn

汉堡阁电热系统（上海）有限公司
上海市徐汇区田州路159号莲花大厦1002室
电话：021-6091 8996
传真：021-6091 8995
电邮：shanghai@halmburger.cn
网址：www.halmburger.cn

软件系统开发及服务
Software System Development & Service

Amtt Digital
安美数字
北京市西城区西直门外大街1号楼(T3)20层B4-5室
邮编：100044
电话：010-5830 5488
传真：010-5830 5300
网址：www.amttgroup.com

Caelum International Ltd.
加隆国际有限公司
深圳市福田保税区桂花路5号西塔4层
邮编：518038
电话：0755-8358 8709
传真：0755-8358 8704
网址：www.caelumint.com
请参阅第375页

Changzhou Bonwin Technology Co., Ltd.
常州市邦威电子科技有限公司
江苏省常州市高新科技园2号楼A座5楼
邮编：213022
电话：0519-8519 9118
传真：0519-8512 9611
电邮：bonwin@126.com
网址：www.bonwin.com

Dataprep Technologies Pte Ltd.
新加坡数据软件科技有限公司
33 Ubi Avenve 3#08-29, Vertes, 408868, Singapore
电话：+65-6509 9153
传真：+65-6509 9154
电邮：sales@dptechnologies.sg
网址：www.dptechnologies.sg

Empire Software Enterprise Co., Ltd.
广州宇盛计算机软件有限公司
广州省广州市番禺区大石南大路187号B座4楼
邮编：511430
电话：020-3923 4301
传真：020-3923 4300
电邮：empire_pos@auphandining.com.cn
网址：www.auphandining.com.cn

Finove Networks Co., Ltd.
上海雅朴网络科技有限公司
上海市张江高科园区祖冲之路887弄72号楼307室
邮编：201203
电话：021-5108 2076
传真：021-5027 6007
电邮：market@finove.com
网址：www.finove.com

Guangzhou Himasoft Tech Co., Ltd.
广州市黑马软件科技有限公司
广州市天河南二路宏发大厦7楼
邮编：510620
电话：020-8759 5514
传真：020-8759 5514*888
网址：www.himasoft.com

Hangzhou HaiHeng Computer Technology Co., Ltd.
杭州海亨计算机科技有限公司
浙江省杭州市滨江区聚工路23号4F
邮编：310051
电话：0571-8668 0389
传真：0571-8668 9619
电邮：hhstech@163.com
网址：www.hhstech.com

Lead Phoenix Electronic Technology (Xiamen) Co., Ltd.
立烽电子科技（厦门）有限公司
厦门市火炬高新区创业园伟业楼S501室
邮编：361006
电话：0592-573 5979
传真：0592-573 5970
网址：www.leadai.com

Next Generation Technologies (Shanghai) Pte Ltd.
捷网信息科技（上海）有限公司
上海市天山路600弄2号楼捷运大厦5C
邮编：200051
电话：021-5206 1992
传真：021-5206 1968
电邮：info@ngwt.com
网址：www.ngwt.com

Shanghai Goodly Electronic Co., Ltd.
上海工理电子有限公司
上海市桂平路680号34幢2层
邮编：200233
电话：021-6495 4368
传真：021-6495 1706
电邮：market@gl200.com
网址：www.gl200.com

Shanghai Weihe Information Technology Co., Ltd.
上海微和信息技术有限公司
上海市北京东路668号科技京城西楼8F
邮编：200001
电话：021-5186 0855
传真：021-5308 1021
电邮：sales@weihesoft.com
网址：www.weihesoft.com

Shenzhen Baopeng Intelligent Technology Co., Ltd.
深圳市宝鹏智能科技有限公司
广东省深圳市龙岗区龙岗街道办
电话：0755-8429 7005
传真：0755-8482 8483
电邮：webmaster@bpscn.com
网址：www.bpscn.com

Sovell Technology Development Co., Ltd.
杭州雄伟科技开发有限公司
浙江省杭州市滨江区滨康路669号
远方科技大厦10楼
邮编：310053
电话：0571-8533 0909
传真：0571-8533 0918
电邮：info@sovell.com.cn
网址：www.sovell.com.cn

音响系统
Sound Systems

Beijing Modern Sound Electronic System Engineering Co., Ltd.
北京现代之声电子系统工程有限责任公司
北京市海淀区西三环北路50号
豪柏大厦C1座1501室
邮编：100044
电话：010-8847 1155
传真：010-5272 2150
电邮：xdzs@263.net
网址：www.xdzs.com.cn

Leader Radio Technologies (Shanghai) Limited
赋信（上海）贸易有限公司
上海市普陀区西康路1018号元茂金豪大厦1010室
邮编：200060
电话：021-5155 2786
传真：021-5155 2785
电邮：info@leaderradio.cn
网址：www.leaderradio.cn

Philips (China) Investment Co., Ltd.
飞利浦（中国）投资有限公司
上海市嘉定区马陆镇沪宜公路1805号
邮编：201801
电话：021-5915 5149
传真：021-5915 9727
网址：www.philips.com.cn

QiaoDeng Video & Audio Equipments Co., Ltd.
深圳市乔登影音器材有限公司
广州市深圳市福田保税区长平商务大厦1501室
邮编：518034
电话：0755-8254 2009
传真：0755-8254 2013
网址：www.qiaodeng.net

Shenzhen Dnets Technology Co., Ltd.
深圳市唐诺科技有限公司
深圳市罗湖区笋岗东路百汇大厦南座11H
邮编：518010
电话：0755-2559 1128
传真：0755-2558 8008
电邮：service@dnets.com.cn
网址：www.dnets.com.cn

Sony (China) Limited
索尼中国有限公司
上海市卢湾区湖滨路222号企业天地一号8楼
邮编：200021
电话：021-6121 6908
网址：www.sony.com.cn

Suntol Technology Company Limited
新涛科技有限公司
珠海市香洲银桦路100号
邮编：519000
电话：0756-211 8001
传真：0756-211 8003
网址：www.2121211.cn

TOA China Limited
提讴艾（上海）电器有限公司
上海市南京西路1038号梅龙镇广场3002室
邮编：200041
电话：021-6272 2584
传真：021-6217 6579
电邮：sales@toachina.com.cn
网址：www.toachina.com.cn

▼音响系统
Sound Systems

北京市奥太电气有限公司
北京市西城区西四北二条21号
计华商务楼303、305室
邮编：100034
电话：010-6653 0863
电邮：bjgbs@yahoo.com.cn
网址：www.bjaotai.com.cn

广州市威尔逊声光像艺术工程有限公司
广州市天河软件园建中路59号西座首层
邮编：510665
电话：020-8555 0050
传真：020-8555 2253*609
电邮：master@v-rshine.com
网址：www.v-rshine.com

南京罗曼音视频系统有限公司
江苏省南京市华海大厦605室
邮编：210000
电话：025-8335 8166
传真：025-8335 8166
网址：www.goodav.cn

SPA设备及用品 SPA Equipment & Supplies

Active Lifestyle (China) Ltd.
奥力来康体设备有限公司
北京市朝阳区朝阳门北大街乙12号天辰大厦608室
邮编：100020
电话：010-6551 6091
传真：010-6551 6095
电邮：activechina@vip.sina.com
网址：www.active.cn

Amersports Shanghai
亚玛芬体育用品贸易（上海）有限公司
上海市浦东新区花园石桥路66号
东亚银行金融大厦6楼602室
邮编：200120
电话：021-5116 5288
传真：021-5116 5299
网址：www.precor.com.cn

BH China Co., Ltd.
钜勋健身器材（上海）有限公司
上海市普陀区真南路822弄455支弄68号
邮编：200331
电话：021-5284 6694
传真：021-5284 6814
电邮：info@i-bh.cn
网址：www.i-bh.cn

Beijing Bibo Water Facilities Factory
北京市碧波水处理设备厂
北京市通州区南大街122号
邮编：101100
电话：010-8409 4311
传真：010-8409 8811
电邮：bjbibo@263.net
网址：www.bibo.net.cn

Equip Asia Limited
依贵雅贸易有限公司
908-909 Kowloon Centre, 29-39 Ashley Rd, TST, Hong Kong
电话：+852-2838 8989
传真：+852-2838 2933
电邮：info@equipasia.com
网址：www.equipasia.com

Guangdong LianSheng Pool & Spa Equipments Co., Ltd.
广东联盛泳池水疗设备有限公司
广东省中山市南头镇升辉南工业区建业路16号
邮编：528427
电话：0760-2312 7282
传真：0760-2312 7280
电邮：ymir@spa-ymir.com
网址：www.chinaspa.net.cn

Kung-sheung International Group
工商国际集团
香港铜锣湾威非路18号万国宝通中心7楼701室
电话：+852-2511 8338
传真：+852-2507 5690
电邮：info@kung-sheung.com
网址：www.kung-sheung.com

Mpeiria
香港中环摆花街1号一号广场7楼701室
电话：+852-2522 7908
传真：+852-2522 7909
网址：www.mpeiria.com

Shanghai D-L Enterprise Development Co., Ltd.
上海东亚利邦企业发展有限公司
上海市瑞金南路1号海兴广场15楼H座
邮编：200023
电话：021-6418 5035
传真：021-6418 5037
电邮：sales@dongyalibang.com
网址：www.dongyalibang.com

Shanghai Ganbor Industrial Co., Ltd.
上海感博实业有限公司
上海市徐汇区吴兴路277号308室
电话：021-6473 9097
传真：021-6415 2161
网址：www.ganbor.com
请参阅第425页

Shanghai Yuankuang Health Engineering Equipment Co., Ltd.
上海远旷康体设备工程有限工程
上海市杨浦区黄兴路1号中通大厦1316室
邮编：200090
电话：021-5580 6108
传真：021-6543 5029
电邮：shyuankuang@126.com
网址：www.yuankuang.com.cn

Suzhou Industrial Park JiaJian Technology Trading Company
苏州佳健科技贸易有限公司
江苏省苏州市东环路1408号东环时代广场701室
邮编：215021
电话：0512-6917 9068
传真：0512-6917 9058
电邮：sales@massothermie.cn
网址：www.massothermie.cn

Technogym (Shanghai) Int'l Trading Co., Ltd.
泰诺健（上海）国际贸易有限公司
上海市静安区延平路98号B栋101室
邮编：200042
电话：021-5175 9833
传真：021-5888 6950
电邮：sales_china@technogym.com
网址：www.technogym.com

广州昆特商贸有限公司
广东省广州市越秀区寺右二横路13号
金霞大厦508室
电话：020-6128 9119
传真：020-6128 9117
网址：www.brandaroma.com

不锈钢制品 Stainless Steel Products

Anhui Gongwa Kitchen Environment Science & Technology Co., Ltd.
安徽港华节能环保科技有限公司
安徽省合肥市双凤开发区金华路与凤锦路路口62号
邮编：230031
电话：0551-639 3366
传真：0551-639 3399
电邮：service@gongwa.com
网址：www.gongwa.com

Beijing Y.T Jia Mei Hotel Articles Co., Ltd.
北京粤通佳美酒店用品有限公司
北京市朝阳区高碑店新村368号
电话：010-6748 9989
传真：010-8575 0237
电邮：cat9918@163.com
网址：www.bjjdyp.com

Beijing Yongjiuliang Stainless Co., Ltd.
北京永久亮不锈钢制品有限责任公司
北京市丰台区木樨园珠江骏景南区603
电话：010-6335 1858
传真：010-6333 9009
网址：www.yjlbxg.com

Dongnan Metals Appliance Company Ltd.
鹤山市东南金属制品有限公司
广东省鹤山市共和工业西区
邮编：529728
电话：0750-830 3133
传真：0750-830 3833
电邮：jmlhsdnjs@21cn.com
网址：www.dn-kitchenware.com

Dongnan Stainless Steel Kitchenware Company Jiangmen
江门市东南不锈钢厨具制造有限公司
广东省江门市杜阮镇双楼工业区5号厂房
邮编：529075
电话：0750-365 6211
传真：0750-365 6211
电邮：dn@jmdongnan.com
网址：www.jmdongnan.com

Equip-master Hotel Equipment Co., Ltd.
马思特酒店设备有限公司
广东省江门市新会区江会路东甲村北中围工业区
邮编：529100
电话：0750-662 0012
传真：0750-662 0013
电邮：equip-master@163.com
网址：www.equip-master.com

▼不锈钢制品
Stainless Steel Products

Foshan Guangneng Kitware Co., Ltd.
佛山市光能厨具有限公司
佛山市顺德区陈村镇岗北工业区伟业大道15号
电话：0757-2330 9370
传真：0757-2210 0008
网址：www.china-gn.cn

Guangzhou Hird Kitchen Equipment Co., Ltd.
广州和依德厨具有限公司
广州市番禺区沙头街小平工业区银平路141号
电话：020-6194 5671
传真：020-6194 5677
电邮：sales@hird.cn
网址：www.hird.cn

Jiangmen Harvest Kitchenware Co., Ltd.
江门市联丰厨具有限公司
广东省江门市西环路325号
（天朗花园）之四202室
邮编：529000
电话：0750-366 6312
传真：0750-366 6310
电邮：info@jmharvest.cn
网址：www.jmharvest.cn

Junpin Metal Products Co., Ltd.
佛山市俊品金属制品有限公司
广东省佛山市高明区明城镇七路33号
电话：0757-8893 0933
传真：0757-8893 0838
电邮：jpm168@126.com
网址：www.junpin168.com

Rui Bao Stainless Steel And Hardware Manufacturer
广州市珠海区瑞宝不锈钢五金制品厂
广州市珠海区广州大道南上涌商业街18号
邮编：511430
电话：020-3993 7541
传真：020-3993 7546
电邮：market@gzruibao.com
网址：www.gzruibao.com

Shandong Conect Kitchen Equipment Co., Ltd.
山东康耐厨业有限公司
山东省博兴县幸福工业园
电话：0543-261 6777
传真：0543-261 6666
电邮：sdkncy@sdkncy.com
网址：www.sdkncy.com

Shenzhen Yuxing Industry Co., Ltd.
深圳市裕兴实业有限公司
深圳市宝安区观澜街道牛湖石二工业区石新路83号
邮编：518110
电话：0755-2808 5626
传真：0755-8291 4902
网址：www.szyuxing.net

Sunnex Metal Products (Shenzhen) Ltd.
日升五金制品（深圳）有限公司
深圳市盐田区沙头角深沙路东和工业大厦A座二楼
邮编：518081
电话：0755-2555 1458
传真：0755-2535 7498
电邮：sales@sunnexchina.com
网址：www.sunnexchina.com

广东省江门市荷塘华美不锈钢制品厂
广东省江门市蓬江区荷塘高村顺成围工业区
邮编：529095
电话：0750-371 3898
传真：0750-3706 6181
电邮：jm-huamei@126..com
网址：www.jm-huamei.com

广州合口美家居用品开发有限公司
广东省广州天河区体育东路118号财富广场1002室
邮编：510610
电话：020-3835 8553
传真：020-3835 8557
电邮：inquiry@hekoumei.cn
网址：www.hekoumei.cn

上海宏仕达厨房设备有限公司
上海市南汇区沪南公路4390弄6号
电话：021-6812 6088
传真：021-6812 6188
电邮：webmaster@shhsd.com
网址：www.shhsd.com

仓储设备
Storage Equipment

Emerson Trading (Shanghai) Co., Ltd.
艾默生贸易（上海）有限公司
上海市虹梅路1801号凯科国际大厦11楼
邮编：200233
电话：021-3395 0000
传真：021-3367 8123
网址：www.metro.com

Huning Pallets Co.
显兴卡板有限公司
香港九龙油塘茶果岭道428号
荣山工业大厦四楼D室
电话：+852-2815 4488
传真：+852-2815 7766
请参阅第381页

惠而康塑胶有限公司
广东省佛山市顺德区乐从镇良教工业区
电话：0757-2836 7878
传真：0757-2885 3162
电邮：info@chinalanying.com
网址：www.chinawelcan.com

泳池设备
Swimming Pool Equipment

Heatwave Swimming Pool & Sauna Equipment Engineering Co., Ltd.
热浪游泳池桑拿设备工程有限公司
深圳市罗湖区笋岗东路12号中民时代广场B座11D
电话：0755-8248 5088
传真：0755-8244 8544
电邮：4006808155@163.com
网址：www.saunapoolspa.com

New Century Pool Satuma Sport Fallow Equipment (China) Co., Ltd.
新世纪（中国）泳池桑拿休闲设备有限公司
广州市东风西增埗路58-60号
邮编：510165
电话：020-8179 1978
网址：www.newpool.cn

Ocean Leisure International
北京大海休闲国际水处理有限公司
北京市经济技术开发区马驹桥镇样本42-2-502
邮编：101102
电话：010-6050 3776
传真：010-6050 2650
电邮：beijingdhtx@163.com
网址：www.dhtx-pool.cn

Shijiazhuang Xinda Health & Leisure Equipments Co., Ltd.
石家庄信达康体休闲设备有限公司
河北省石家庄市谈固北街青年路18号
邮编：050000
电话：0311-8511 2929
传真：0311-8508 2924
电邮：xd0311@163.com
网址：www.xdsnsb.cn

北京康健碧波休闲设备有限公司
北京市朝阳区十里河精品建材厅1号
邮编：100122
电话：010-8736 5110
传真：010-8736 3687
电邮：kjbibo@163.com
网址：www.kjbibo.com

海南沃野环境设备工程有限公司
海南省海口市国贸大道3号
国际贸易商务大厦c座1604
邮编：570125
电话：0898-6676 0122
传真：0898-3636 8802
电邮：woyegs@163.com
网址：www.woyegs.com

上海康乾泳池技术有限公司
上海市真光路1473弄胜益商务中心706室
电话：021-5279 0861
传真：021-5279 0831
网址：www.kq-group.com

上海远亚水处理设备有限公司
上海市虹梅南路986号
掘金大厦306室（近莘朱路）
邮编：201100
电话：021-6173 3596
传真：021-6173 3597
电邮：lypeng@yuanya.com.cn
网址：www.yuanya.com.cn

深圳市财升桑拿泳池设备有限公司
广东省深圳市龙岗区布吉镇
沙塘布城科技园36号2楼201室
邮编：518114
电话：0755-2888 5129
传真：0755-2857 0718
电邮：superbar88@163.com
网址：www.caisheng88.com

顯 興 卡 板 公 司
HUNING PALLETS CO.

倉庫設備總匯 • A Warehouse Equipment Center

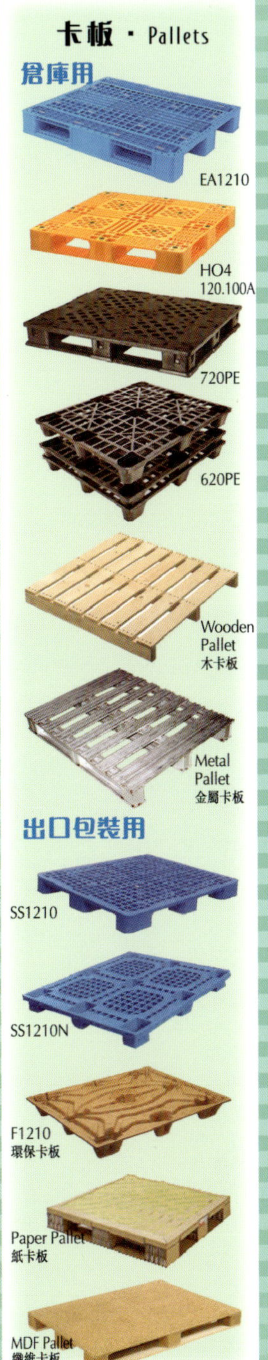

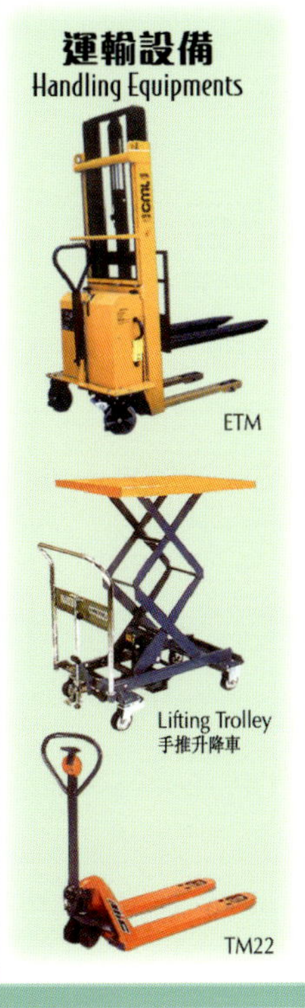

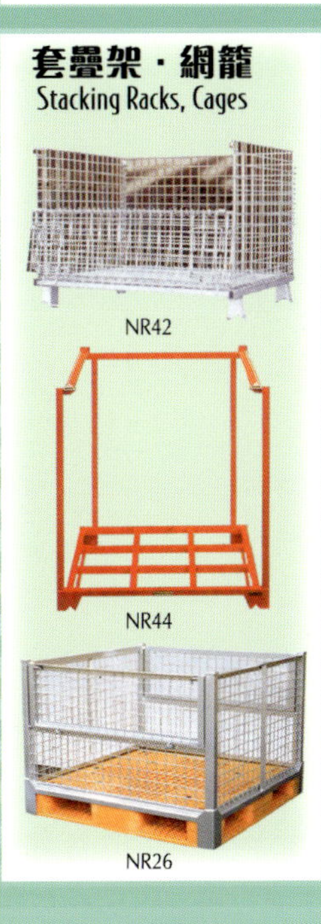

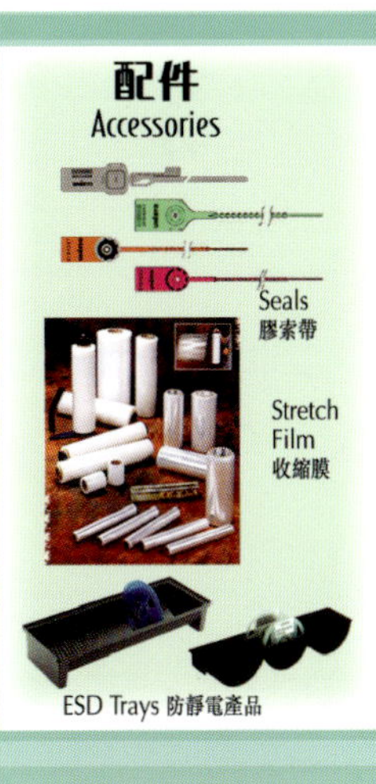

專營倉庫設備
倉庫及出口用卡板
訂造籠車 · 膠箱
設計 · 安裝貨架
自動化貯存系統
中港兩地可交貨

香港办事处 **Hong Kong Office:**
香港九龙油塘茶果岭道428号荣山工业大厦四楼D室
4D Wing Shan Industrial Building, 428 Cha Kwo Ling Road, Yau Tong, Kowloon, Hong Kong
Tel 电话：（852）2815 4488 Fax 传真：（852）2815 7766

东莞办事处 **Dongguan Office:**
Tel 电话：（0769）8630 3626 Fax 传真：（0769）8630 3626

上海办事处 **Shanghai Office:**
Tel 电话：（021）3424 1136 Fax 传真：（021）3424 3418

產品繁多 未能盡錄 **查詢 Enquiry : (852) 2815 4488**

电讯设备及供应
Telecommunication Equipment & Supplies

AEI Communications Corp
台湾新北市汐止区新台五路一段106号16楼
电话：+886(2)-2696 2665
传真：+886(2)-2696 2667
网址：wwww.aeicommunications.com

Guangzhou Kinhao Hotel Appliances Co., Ltd.
广州市健浩电子有限公司
广州市番禺区大石街道南大公路鸿图工业园A2栋
邮编：511430
电话：020-3993 1999
传真：020-3998 1333
网址：www.kinhao.com

Kingtel Information Techlonogy Co., Ltd.
广陵（中国）电子有限公司
广东省惠州市惠台工业区和畅东四路6号
邮编：516006
电话：0752-585 6801
传真：0752-585 6855
网址：www.sela68.com

Media-go Engineering Ltd.
美歌工程有限公司
25/F Westin Centre, 26 Hung To Road, Kwun Tong, Kowloon, Hong Kong
电话：+852-2797 8128
传真：+852-2790 5732
电邮：mediago@mediago.com.hk
网址：www.mediago.com.hk

Multi Business Machines Co., Ltd.
深圳市明捷商用电器有限公司
深圳市福田保税区桂花路5号
福朋喜来登酒店西塔6层
电话：0755-8297 5297
传真：0755-8297 5296
网址：www.chinambm.cn

Nationtel Telecommunications (Shenzhen) Co., Ltd.
深圳市耐施得科技有限公司
深圳市龙岗区平湖上木古平新北路29号
达尔讯科技园1栋4层
邮编：518111
电话：0755-2502 3339
传真：0755-8240 9919
电邮：nationtel@163.com
网址：www.sz3l.com.cn

Shandong Bittel Electronics Co., Ltd.
山东比特电子工业有限公司
山东省日照市日照北路1号
邮编：276800
电话：0633-221 2188
传真：0633-221 2132
电邮：sales@bittel.com.cn
网址：www.bittelcom.com

Shenzhen Cotell Technology Co., Ltd.
深圳肯特科技有限公司
深圳市罗湖区红缕北路中民时代广场B座21楼
邮编：518000
电话：0755-8885 9898
传真：0755-8885 9899
电邮：sales@cotell.cn
网址：www.cotell.com.cn

Shenzhen Kingint Communication Technology Co., Ltd.
深圳市肯天通信技术有限公司
广东省深圳市福永立新南路宝德工业中心4楼
邮编：518103
电话：0755-3393 9299
传真：0755-2606 6679
电邮：sales@kingint.cn
网址：www.kingint.cn

Zhuhai Huawang Communication Equipment Co., Ltd.
珠海华网通信设备有限公司
广东省珠海市南屏科技园屏东二路2号
邮编：519060
电话：0756-881 8081
传真：0756-867 7000
电邮：sales@hwtel.com
网址：www.hwtel.com

美爵信达科技有限公司
（CetisGroup.com）
北京市朝阳区东三环中路9号富尔大厦26层
邮编：100020
电话：010-8591 1289
传真：010-8591 1925
网址：www.aegistelematrix.cn
请参阅第383页、酒店工程及用品书隔页底页

电视机
Television

Hanser Mirror Defogster Ltd.
Room 918-919 Goldfield Industrial Centre, No.1 Sui Wo Road, Shatin, Hong Kong
电话：+852-2601 1506
传真：+852-2601 9951
电邮：info@defogster.com
网址：www.defogster.com

Huipu Electronic (Shenzhen) Co., Ltd.
惠浦电子（深圳）有限公司
深圳市宝安区福永镇凤凰村第四工业区惠浦工业园
邮编：518103
电话：0755-2959 8888
传真：0755-2959 8980
电邮：hr@huipu.com.cn
网址：www.huipu.com.cn

Media-go Engineering Ltd.
美歌工程有限公司
25/F Westin Centre, 26 Hung To Road, Kwun Tong, Kowloon, Hong Kong
电话：+852-2797 8128
传真：+852-2790 5732
电邮：mediago@mediago.com.hk
网址：www.mediago.com.hk

Multi Business Machines Co., Ltd.
深圳市明捷商用电器有限公司
深圳市福田保税区桂花路5号
福朋喜来登酒店西塔6层
电话：0755-8297 5297
传真：0755-8297 5296
网址：www.chinambm.cn

Samsung
三星（中国）投资有限公司
上海市徐汇区虹桥路355号
邮编：200336
电话：021-5464 4777
网址：www.samsung.com.cn

Shenzhen Suprl Industrial Co., Ltd.
深圳市秀波实业有限公司
深圳市南山区西丽镇珠光北路142号
众冠红花岭工业西区二栋3-4楼
邮编：518055
电话：0755-8623 8881
传真：0755-8623 8880
电邮：suprl@suprl.com
网址：www.suprl.com

Sichuan Changhong Electronics System Co., Ltd.
四川长虹电子系统有限公司上海办事处
上海市闸北区中山北路835号上海长虹大厦
邮编：200070
电话：021-5662 5359
传真：021-5662 5359
电邮：wangzhe@changhong.com
网址：www.changhongdianzi.com

South China House of Technology Consultants Ltd.
南中国科技顾问有限公司
Unit 1303-04, Block B,Sea View Estate, 2-14 Watson Road, North Point, Hong Kong
电话：+852-2590 6808
传真：+852-2590 6383
电邮：audiovisual@schot.com
网址：www.schot.com

青岛海尔电子有限公司
山东省青岛市海尔路1号海尔工业园内
邮编：266101
电话：0532-8893 7400
传真：0532-8893 7402
网址：www.haier.com

电视投影器
Video Projectors

Benq
明基
江苏省苏州市新区狮山路268号
邮编：215011
电话：0512-6807 8800
传真：0512-6809 7010
电邮：webmaster_china@benq.com.cn
网址：www.benq.com.cn

Foshan Wabon Electronic Technology Co., Ltd.
佛山市伟邦电子科技有限公司
佛山市南海区桂城深海路17号
佛山瀚天科技城A区四楼一区、二区
邮编：528200
电话：0757-8101 9918
传真：0757-8101 9909
电邮：chinawabon@gmail.com
网址：www.wabon.com.cn

Hitachi
日立（中国）有限公司
北京市朝阳区东三环北路5号北京发展大厦18层
邮编：100004
电话：010-6590 8111
传真：010-6590 8110
网址：www.hitachi.com.cn

Honghe Technology Group
鸿合科技
北京市海淀区上地信息产业基地3街9号
嘉华大厦C座11层
邮编：100085
电话：010-6296 3388
传真：010-6296 8116
电邮：service@honghe-tech.com
网址：www.honghe-tech.com

▼电视投影器
Video Projectors

Infocus
富视科技集团广州市慕迪科技有限公司
广东省广州市中山大道20号明轩1903室
邮编：510620
电话：020-6113 5787
传真：020-6128 6218
电邮：info@projector-china.com.cn
网址：www.projector-china.com.cn

Lenovo
联想集团有限公司
北京市海淀区上地创业路6号
邮编：100085
电话：010-5886 8888
网址：www.lenovo.com.cn

Panasonic Corporation of China
松下电器（中国）有限公司
北京市朝阳区景华南街5号
远洋·光华国际C座5层
邮编：100020
电话：010-6562 6688
网址：www.panasonic.com.cn

Samsung
三星（中国）投资有限公司
上海市徐汇区虹桥路355号
邮编：200336
电话：021-5464 4777
网址：www.samsung.com.cn

Sanyo Electric Co., Ltd.
三洋电机（中国）有限公司
北京市朝阳门外大街18号丰联广场28楼
邮编：100020
电话：010-6588 1501
传真：010-6588 1505
网址：www.cn.sanyo.com

Shanghai Trufeel Technology Co., Ltd.
上海卓飞科技有限公司
上海市长宁区天山支路168号401室
邮编：200051
电话：021-6233 4791
传真：021-6274 9666
网址：www.avin.cn

South China House of Technology Consultants Ltd.
南中国科技顾问有限公司
Unit 1303-04, Block B,Sea View Estate, 2-14 Watson Road, North Point, Hong Kong
电话：+852-2590 6808
传真：+852-2590 6383
电邮：audiovisual@schot.com
网址：www.schot.com

ViewSonic Inc.
优派显示设备国际贸易（上海）有限公司
上海市大连路950号海上海新城9层
邮编：200092
电话：021-6501 9777
传真：021-6237 5373
网址：www.viewsonic.com.cn

夏普商贸（中国）有限公司
上海市黄浦区延安东路550号海洋大厦27-29楼
邮编：200001
电话：021-6104 8888
传真：021-6106 6000
网址：www.sharp.cn

热水器
Water Heaters

A.O. Smit (China) Water Heater Co., Ltd.
艾欧史密斯（中国）热水器有限公司
江苏省南京市经济技术开发区尧新大道336号
邮编：210038
电话：025-8580 1000
传真：025-8580 3100
电邮：info@aosmith.com.cn
网址：www.aosmith.com.cn

Fabri-Techinc Engineering & Trading Co., Ltd.
飞达工程贸易有限公司
17/F Wing Wah Industrial Building, 677 King's Road, North Point, Hong Kong
电话：+852-2815 8388
传真：+852-2815 3223
电邮：enquiry@fabri-technic.com
网址：www.fabri-technic.com

Shanghai Shenyin Group
上海申银集团
上海市黄渡工业园区春雨路336号
邮编：201804
电话：021-5608 1702
传真：021-6661 0622
电邮：rb@shenyin.com
网址：www.shenyinrb.com

Shanghai Shenhua Solar Energy Science & Technology Co., Ltd.
上海申花光能科技有限公司
上海市浦东新区康桥路628号
邮编：201315
电话：021-5812 5332
传真：021-5812 5581
电邮：shsh@shenhua-cn.com
网址：www.shenhua-cn.com

Xiamen Gujia Energy Technology Co., Ltd.
厦门市谷佳能源科技有限公司
厦门市夏禾路1226号
邮编：361012
电话：0592-221 4707
传真：0592-558 8783
网址：www.hotwater.cn

Zhuhai Boka Cool Source Equipment Co., Ltd.
珠海博佳冷源设备有限公司
珠海市高新区创新海岸科技5路1号
邮编：519085
电话：0756-380 3688
传真：0756-339 1668
电邮：zhuhai@boka.com.cn
网址：www.boka.com.cn

瑞美（中国）热水器有限公司
四川省成都市新都工业开发区南一路东段
邮编：610500
电话：028-8396 8311
传真：028-8396 8317
网址：www.rheemchina.com

威能（北京）供暖设备有限公司
北京市朝阳区建国门外大街
甲6号A座SK大厦17层
电话：010-6563 0667
电邮：info@vaillant.com.cn
网址：www.vaillant.com.cn

净水系统
Water Purification Systems

3M China
3M中国有限公司
上海市兴义路8号万都大厦38层
邮编：200336
电话：021-6275 3535
传真：021-6219 0698
网址：www.3m.com.cn

Beijing Bibo Water Facilities Factory
北京市碧波水处理设备厂
北京市通州区南大街122号
邮编：101100
电话：010-8409 4311
传真：010-8409 8811
电邮：bjbibo@263.net
网址：www.bibo.net.cn

GZ Linghe Filter Equipment Co., Ltd.
广州市菱和过滤设备有限公司
广东省广州市江燕路
电话：020-8900 8725
传真：020-8900 8906
电邮：gzlinghe@188.com
网址：www.gzlinghe.com.cn

Mitsubishi Rayon (Shanghai) Co., Ltd.
三菱丽阳（上海）管理有限公司
上海市遵义路107号安泰大楼1601室
邮编：200051
电话：021-6237 5868
传真：021-6237 5832
网址：www.mrc.co.jp

Paragon Water (Xiamen) Corp Ltd.
百诺肯净水设备（厦门）有限公司
厦门现代物流园区长虹路33号
象屿工业厂房八层B1单元
邮编：200041
电话：0952-602 1767
传真：0952-602 1766
网址：www.paragonwater.com.cn

Pentair Water
滨特尔贸易（上海）有限公司
上海市延安西路1118号龙之梦大厦21楼
邮编：200052
电话：021-3211 4588
传真：021-3211 4580
网址：www.pentairwater.cn

Shanghai Canature Environmental Products Co., Ltd.
上海开能环保设备股份有限公司
上海市浦东新区川大路518号
邮编：201200
电话：021-5859 9999
传真：021-5859 9977
网址：www.canature.com

Xiamen Gujia Energy Technology Co., Ltd.
厦门市谷佳能源科技有限公司
厦门市夏禾路1226号
邮编：361012
电话：0592-2214 707
传真：0592-5588 783
网址：www.hotwater.cn

北京和龙春雨环保科技有限公司
北京市西四环郑常庄大成路6号院
大成时代中心1012室
电话：010-6867 0329
传真：010-6867 8927
网址：www.bjchunyu.com

防滑垫
Anti-Slip Mats

Beijing Kadi Weiye Decoration Co., Ltd.
北京德雅伟业商贸有限公司
北京市朝阳区八里庄西里远洋国际D座501室
邮编：100025
电话：010-5908 1197
传真：0101-5908 1179
电邮：kd@bjkadi.com
网址：www.bjkadi.com

Dongguan Guanghaida Rubber Plastic Co., Ltd.
东莞广海大橡塑科技有限公司
广东省东莞市樟木头镇
百果洞百达工业区盘龙路8号
邮编：523638
电话：0769-8713 3338
传真：0769-8202 2610
电邮：guanghai2002@21cn.com
网址：www.szghd.com

Ming Fai Industrial (Shenzhen) Co., Ltd.
明辉实业（深圳）有限公司
深圳市龙岗区平湖白坭坑明辉工业城
邮编：518111
电话：0755-2880 2888
传真：0755-8466 2990*7
电邮：marketing@mingfaigroup.com
网址：www.mingfaigroup.com
请参阅第427页

Rismat International Company Limited
丽施美国际有限公司
上海市凯旋北路1299号4楼
邮编：200063
电话：021-3126 1933
传真：021-2301 0003
电邮：rismat.shanghai@rismat.net
网址：www.rismat.net

Shanghai Richor Hotel Environment Service Co., Ltd.
上海誉成酒店环境服务有限公司
上海市徐汇区桂江路168号（中房园艺院内）
邮编：200233
电话：021-5477 1933
传真：021-5477 1455
电邮：info@ycmat.com
网址：www.ycmat.com

Zhejiang Hua Da Hotel Equipment Co., Ltd.
浙江华大酒店用品有限公司
浙江台州市玉环龙王工业区
邮编：317600
电话：0576-8724 3882
传真：0576-8720 9488
电邮：cnhd@hdpo.com
网址：www.hdpo.com

玉环大华塑胶酒店用品有限公司
浙江省台州市玉环县楚门镇城郊巷38-1号
邮编：317605
电话：0576-8744 8556
传真：0576-8744 8973

玉环连天酒店用品有限公司
浙江省台州市玉环县机电工业区
（黄泥坎加油站斜对面）
邮编：317600
电话：0576-8728 6808
传真：0576-8728 6882
电邮：ltjdyp@126.com
网址：www.tzlantian.com

浴袍
Bathrobes

Foshan Nanzhuang Hengan Knitting Factory Co., Ltd.
佛山市南庄恒安制造厂有限公司
佛山市禅城区南庄镇樵乐东路79号
电话：0757-8201 6768
传真：0757-8201 6768
电邮：heng-an-sales@163.com
网址：www.hha-hoteltex.com

Huai Qin Kang Weaving Co., Ltd.
淮安沁康织造有限公司
江苏省淮安市楚州区河北新民街77号
邮编：223200
电话：0517-8585 6177
传真：0517-8585 6199
网址：www.qinkang.net.cn

Huaian Chuzhou Qiqi Textile Co., Ltd.
淮安楚州区奇祺纺织厂
江苏省淮安市楚州区华亭路19-41号
邮编：223200
电话：0517-8585 8728
传真：0517-8596 0949
电邮：jsqqfz@yahoo.com.cn
网址：www.jsqqfz.com

Huaian Lianlida Manufactory Co., Ltd.
淮安联利达织造有限公司
上海市交通路4703弄6号1205室
邮编：200333
电话：021-5635 1753
传真：021-5635 1735
电邮：ytm@lianlida.cn
网址：www.lianlida.cn

Huaian Xinhaixin Towel Factory
江苏省淮安市心海心毛巾厂
江苏省淮安市楚州区华亭路77号
邮编：223200
电话：0517-8591 0680
传真：0517-8591 0687
电邮：master@xinhaixin.com
网址：www.xinhaixin.com

Jiangsu Canasin Weaving Co., Ltd.
江苏康乃馨织造有限公司
江苏省淮安市楚州经济开发区铁云路8号
邮编：223200
电话：0517-8520 6966
传真：0517-8520 6922
电邮：market@canasin.com
网址：www.canasin.com

Ming Fai Industrial (Shenzhen) Co., Ltd.
明辉实业（深圳）有限公司
深圳市龙岗区平湖白坭坑明辉工业城
邮编：518111
电话：0755-2880 2888
传真：0755-8466 2990*7
电邮：marketing@mingfaigroup.com
网址：www.mingfaigroup.com
请参阅第427页

Nantong Dongyi Textile Co., Ltd.
南通市鼎益纺织有限公司
江苏省南通市通启路598号
邮编：226014
电话：0513-8526 1182
传真：0513-8526 6054
电邮：sml@ntdxmj.com
网址：www.ntdxmj.com

Ningbo Taointex Co., Ltd.
宁波市道盈国际贸易有限公司
浙江省宁波市海曙区苍松路151号天海大厦6楼
邮编：311510
电话：0574-8713 3444
传真：0574-8716 1533
网址：www.taointex.com

Shanghai Chunhui Tour Articles Factory
上海春晖旅游用品厂
上海市嘉定区南翔镇顺达路300弄53号
邮编：201802
电话：021-6989 0588
传真：021-6989 0589
电邮：ly@chun-hui.com
网址：www.chun-hui.com

Shenzhen Damei Hotel Supplies Co., Ltd.
深圳市达美酒店配套用品有限公司
广东省深圳市罗湖区布吉路1021号
农产品天乐大厦丰乐园大酒店4楼
邮编：518019
电话：0755-2585 4218
传真：0755-2585 4255
电邮：818@szdamei.com
网址：www.szdamei.com

卫浴设备及配件
Bathroom Fixtures & Accessories

American Standard (China) Co., Ltd.
美标（中国）有限公司
上海市田林路487号宝石园24号楼
邮编：200233
电话：021-3395 2888
传真：021-3367 4255
电邮：sales@americanstandard.com.cn
网址：www.americanstandard.com.cn

Annwa Ceramic Sanitary Ware Co., Ltd.
佛山市高明安华陶瓷洁具有限公司
广东省佛山市高明沧江工业园区
邮编：528511
电话：0757-8851 0390
传真：0757-8851 0190
网址：www.annwa.com.cn

Appollo (China) Co., Ltd.
阿波罗（中国）有限公司
广州经济技术开发区永和经济区黄旗山路19号
邮编：510623
电话：020-2885 5882
传真：020-2885 5992
电邮：business@appollo.cn
网址：www.china-apollo.com

Atget Decoration & Hardware Co., Ltd.
广州市雅之杰装饰五金有限公司
广州市荔湾区龙津西路172号之2首层、二层
邮编：510150
电话：020-8102 8098
传真：020-8103 8982
电邮：atget@atgetco.com
网址：www.atgetco.com
请参阅第388页

Boloni
博洛尼家居用品（北京）有限公司
北京市朝阳区育慧里11号
邮编：100101
电话：010-5134 8888
传真：010-5134 8810
电邮：hui@kebao.cn
网址：www.boloni.com.cn

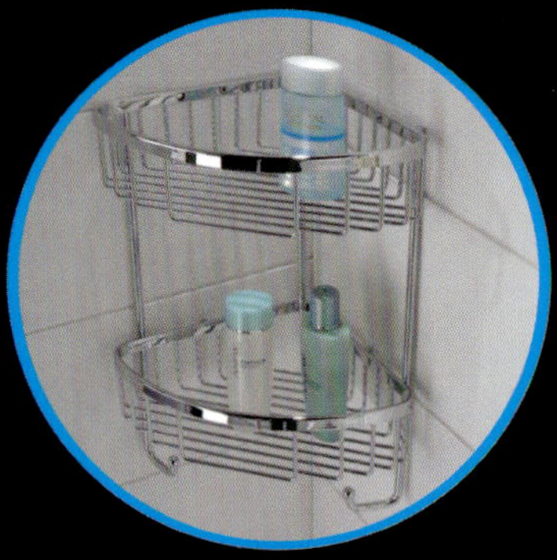

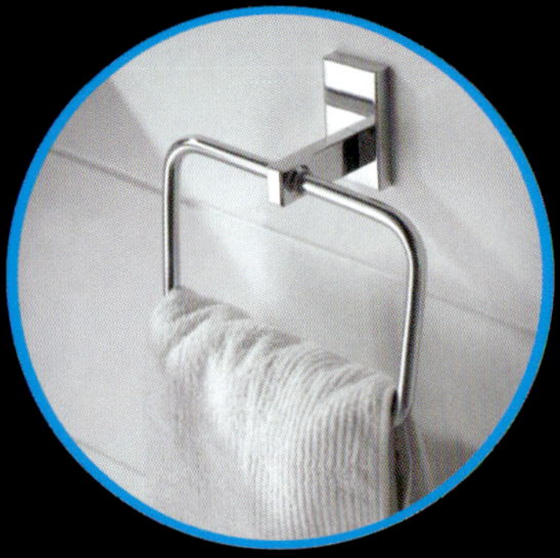

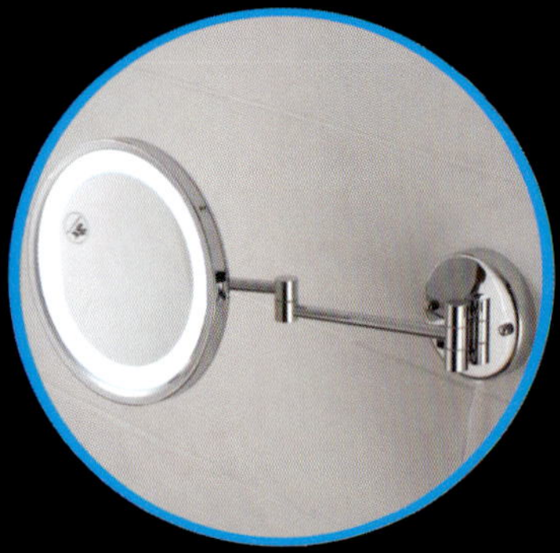

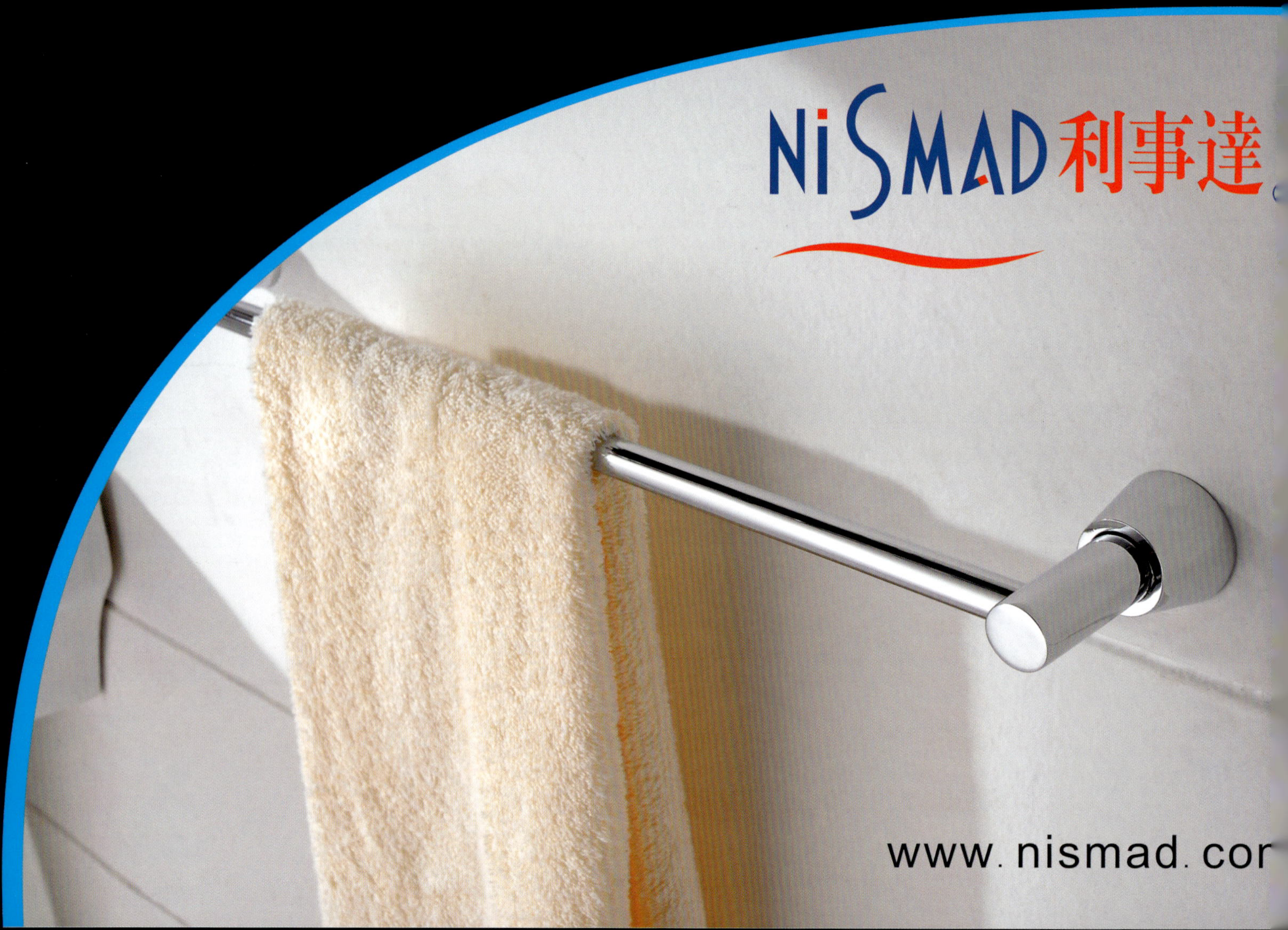
NiSMAD利事達
www. nismad. cor

▼卫浴设备及配件
Bathroom Fixtures & Accessories

Bravat (Guangzhou) Plumbing Industrial Co., Ltd.
贝朗（广州）卫浴器材有限公司
广州市番禺区市桥镇小平工业区福平路二街6号
邮编：511490
电话：020-3480 2916
传真：020-3480 2936
电邮：bravat@bravat.com.cn
网址：www.bravat.com

Eago sanitary ware co., Ltd.
佛山市南海益高卫浴有限公司
广东佛山市南海区小塘狮岭工业开发区
电话：0757-8663 2966
传真：0757-8663 2278
电邮：eagocn@yahoo.com.cn
网址：www.eago.com.cn

Elite Sanitary Ware Co., Ltd.
伊丽卫浴设备有限公司
佛山市高明区富湾镇荷富工业区
邮编：528500
电话：0757-8614 5555
传真：0757-8614 5166
网址：www.top-elite.com

Ellin China
伊翎卫浴（意大利）国际投资公司
上海市普陀区中江路879弄28-205
邮编：200333
电话：021-5107 7728
传真：021-5107 7738
电邮：raymondliu@ellin.com.cn
网址：www.ellin.com.cn

Foshan City Faenza Sanitary Ware Co., Ltd.
佛山市法恩洁具有限公司
广东省佛山市高明沧江工业园
电话：0757-8862 8788
传真：0757-8851 0161
电邮：sale@faenza.com.cn
网址：www.faenza.com.cn

Foshan MICAWA Ceramics Co., Ltd.
佛山美加华陶瓷有限公司
广东省佛山市三水区三水大道南82号
邮编：528131
电话：0757-8756 3886
传真：0757-8751 2305
网址：www.micawa.com

Guangdong Archie Hardware Co., Ltd.
广东雅洁五金有限公司
广东省佛山市南海区大沥长虹岭工业园长岗北路
邮编：528231
电话：0757-8552 3938
传真：0757-8556 6268
电邮：archie@archie.sina.net
网址：www.archie.com.cn

Guangdong Hegii Sanitary Ware Co., Ltd.
广东恒洁卫浴有限公司
佛山市禅城区季华四路意美家卫浴世界24栋
邮编：528031
电话：0757-8226 1083
传真：0757-8226 9083
电邮：hegii@hegii.com
网址：www.hegii.com

Guangdong Heshan Andeli Sanitary Ware Co., Ltd.
广东鹤山市安得利卫浴有限公司
广东省鹤山市址山镇人民北路19号
邮编：529729
电话：0750-865 0888
传真：0750-865 0555
电邮：larsd@163.com
网址：www.larsd.com

Hangzhou Da'ou Metal Handicrafts Co., Ltd.
杭州达欧五金工艺品有限公司
杭州经济技术开发区省军区农副业基地2-97号
电话：0571-8580 9736
传真：0571-8580 9731
网址：www.daougy.com.cn

Hanser Mirror Defogster Ltd.
Room 918-919 Goldfield Industrial Centre, No.1 Sui Wo Road, Shatin, Hong Kong
电话：+852-2601 1506
传真：+852-2601 9951
电邮：info@defogster.com
网址：www.defogster.com

Hocheng (China) Co., Ltd.
和成（中国）有限公司
上海闸北区虬江路1538号和成大楼
邮编：200336
电话：021-6628 6111
传真：021-6628 7898
网址：www.hcg.com.cn

Inax (China) Investment Co., Ltd.
伊奈（中国）投资有限公司
上海市西藏南路218号永银大厦704室
电话：021-6334 3366
传真：021-6473 2360
电邮：sales@inax.com.cn
网址：www.inax.com.cn

Jomoo Group Co., Ltd.
九牧集团有限公司
福建省南安市仑仓镇登峰工业区28号
邮编：362304
电话：0595-8614 9999
传真：0595-8614 2998
电邮：webmaster@jomoo.com.cn
网址：www.jomoo.com.cn

Kohler China Investment Co., Ltd.
科勒（中国）投资有限公司
上海市闸北区江场三路158号
邮编：200436
电话：021-2606 2000
传真：021-6107 8900
网址：www.kohler.com.cn

Kon Sanitary Fittings (Shanghai) Co., Ltd.
上海柯井卫浴设备有限公司
上海市沪闵路8075号虹梅商务大厦539室
邮编：200233
电话：021-5117 1788
传真：021-5117 1789
电邮：freeman-fang@kon.com.cn
网址：www.kon.com.cn

Main Plan Ltd.
敏宝有限公司
9/F, Yau Lee Centre, No.45 Hoi Yuen Road, Kwun Tong, Kowloon, Hong Kong
电话：+852-2698 9233
传真：+852-2690 0585
电邮：general@mainplan.com.hk
网址：www.mainplan.com.hk

Nismad Bathroom Accessories (Shenzhen) Co., Ltd.
利事达卫浴制品（深圳）有限公司
深圳市龙岗区坪山街道办六联洋母账村安得路16号
电话：0755-2517 0910
传真：0755-2517 0920
电邮：nismad@nismad.com
网址：www.nismad.com
请参阅第386、387页

Paja Ceramic Industry Co., Ltd.
鹏佳陶瓷实业有限公司
广东潮州市火车站展宏路中段
邮编：521031
电话：0768-299 3808
传真：0768-299 3809
电邮：sale@paja.cn
网址：www.slom.cc

Peixing Ceramics Making Co., Ltd.
佛山市培兴陶瓷制作有限公司
潮州市古乡镇古乌工业区
电话：0768-683 8429
传真：0768-683 3229
电邮：china@peixing.com
网址：www.peixing.com

Roca (China) Ltd.
乐家（中国）有限公司
上海市徐汇区漕溪北路396号
汇智大厦裙楼503-505室
邮编：200030
电话：021-3368 8822
传真：021-3368 8299
网址：www.roca.cn

Ruian Dulaweite Sanitary Fitting Co., Ltd.
瑞安市杜拉维特卫浴有限公司
温州市平阳县万全轻工基地家具园万盛路17号
电话：0577-6317 8777
传真：0577-6317 8779
电邮：cvs@cvs.com.cn
网址：www.cvs.com.cn

Shanghai Baum Building Material Co., Ltd.
上海宝默建材有限公司
上海市静安区余姚路292号
邮编：200041
电话：021-6218 5528
传真：021-6218 5560
电邮：jojo_lau@yahoo.cn
网址：www.china-baum.com

Shaoxing Faber Sanitary Facillity Co., Ltd.
绍兴市法贝卫浴洁具有限公司
浙江省新昌澄潭工业区
邮编：312530
电话：0575-8605 0022
传真：0575-8605 8800
电邮：sxfaber@163.com
网址：www.faber.com.cn

Shenzhen Hava Industrial Co., Ltd.
深圳市华亿达实业有限公司
深圳市南山区南园村工业区南新路德馨街18-20号
电话：0755-2644 7740
传真：0755-2644 7419
电邮：info@havagroup.com
网址：www.havagroup.com

▼卫浴设备及配件 Bathroom Fixtures & Accessories

Speakman Company
美国舒波曼公司
北京市朝阳区望京西路48号
金隅国际大厦C座2105室
电话：010-8477 5228
传真：010-8477 5176
网址：www.speakmancompany.com.cn

Suzhou Industrial Park Cozy Sanitary Wares Equipment Co., Ltd.
苏州工业园区科逸卫浴设备有限公司
江苏省苏州工业园区唯亭望江路189号
邮编：215132
电话：0512-6299 0758
传真：0512-6299 0759
电邮：info@chinacozy.com
网址：www.chinacozy.com

Tangshan Huida Ceramic (Group) Co. Ltd.
唐山惠达陶瓷（集团）股份有限公司
河北省唐山市丰南区惠达陶瓷城
邮编：063307
电话：0315-852 3618
传真：0315-852 2827
电邮：huida@heinfo.net
网址：www.huidagroup.com

Team International Co.
宏创国际公司
Flat K, 13/F Block 2 Golden Dragon Industrial Centre, 162-170 Tai Lin Pai Road, Kwai Chung, N. T., Hong Kong
电话：+852-2480 0528
传真：+852-2480 0508
电邮：sales@tihk.com
网址：www.tihk.com

Wenzhou Dili Weiss Induction Sanitary Ware Co., Ltd.
温州帝威斯感应洁具有限公司
浙江省温州市龙湾海城工业区工贸路65号
电话：0577-8523 8788
传真：0577-8522 9996
电邮：office@tweis.com
网址：www.tweis.com

Wenzhou Shenyi Hardware Product Factory
温州市神意五金制品厂
温州市欧海区慈湖北村宅新路11号
邮编：325000
电话：0577-8676 9670
传真：0577-8676 9670
电邮：info@sealily-cn.com
网址：www.sealily-cn.com

XinLe Bathroom Products (Foshan) Co., Ltd.
新乐卫浴（佛山）有限公司
广东佛山市禅城区石湾来长岗鹰卫浴总部大楼
电话：0757-8266 2211
传真：0757-8266 2233
电邮：info@ying-sw.com
网址：www.ying-sw.com

Yatin Bath Art Co., Ltd.
浙江雅鼎卫浴股份有限公司
杭州建德市雅鼎路777号
邮编：311607
电话：0571-6409 7766
传真：0571-6409 7799
电邮：service@yatin.com.cn
网址：www.yatin.com.cn

Zhejiang Risheng Sanitary Ware Co., Ltd.
浙江日升卫浴洁具有限公司
浙江省平阳县万全家具生产基地B14-B15（万达路388号）
邮编：325409
电话：0577-6377 6377
传真：0577-6377 6999
电邮：info@argentcrystal.com
网址：www.argentcrystal.com

Zhejiang TianLang Sanitary Ware Co., Ltd.
浙江天朗卫浴有限公司
温州市航标路工业区27号
电话：0577-8835 7862
传真：0577-8835 7861
电邮：tian-lang@vip.sina.com
网址：www.tian-lang.com

艾利秀贸易（上海）有限公司
上海市浦东新区商城路887号
波特营C3幢4楼B-09室
邮编：200120
电话：021-5876 0151
传真：021-5876 0192
网址：www.aliseo.de
请参阅第389页

帝朗卫浴（广州）有限公司
广东省广州市越秀区东风中路318号嘉业大厦8楼
邮编：510045
电话：020-8329 3188
传真：020-8329 3198
网址：www.mplcn.com

东莞市龙邦卫浴有限公司
广东省东莞市东坑镇东安路262号
邮编：523459
电话：0769-8386 3528
传真：0769-8388 4627
电邮：km@dgkamon.com
网址：www.kamon.net.cn

乔登卫浴（江门）有限公司
广东省江门市二合山工业区永盛路148号
电话：0750-350 2188
传真：0750-350 2181
网址：www.joden.com.cn

床上用品及床垫 Beddings & Mattresses

Anhui Honren Co. (Group) Ltd.
安徽鸿润（集团）股份有限公司
安徽省桐城市经济技术开发区鸿润国际工业园
邮编：231400
电话：0556-686 8655
传真：0556-620 3401
电邮：honren@honren.cn
网址：www.honren.com.cn

Anhui Xiazhen Down Co., Ltd.
安徽霞珍羽绒股份有限公司
安徽省桐城市桐安南路988号
电话：0556-613 0160
传真：0556-613 3839
电邮：ahxz@ahxz.com.cn
网址：www.ahxz.com.cn

Beijing Mingye Hotel Supplies Co., Ltd.
北京明业酒店用品有限公司
北京市朝阳区十八里店吕家营中街东头
邮编：100023
电话：010-8769 6616
传真：010-8769 1567
电邮：001@bmoye.com
网址：www.bmoye.com

Beijing Zhongyali Hotel Suppliers Co., Ltd.
北京中亚丽酒店用品有限公司
北京市大兴区旧宫三工业区6号
邮编：100076
电话：010-8791 3349
传真：010-8791 3545
电邮：zhongyali@zhongyail.com
网址：www.zhongyali.com

China Crown Textile Co., Ltd.
上海中冠纺织品有限公司
上海市延安西路728号华敏翰尊国际8楼K座
邮编：200050
电话：021-5237 8666
传真：021-6233 5932
电邮：tony@cctex.com.cn
网址：www.cctex.com.cn

DaYi Bed (Shanghai) Co., Ltd.
大亿床业（上海）有限公司
上海市闵行区浦江镇江月路1500号
邮编：201114
电话：021-5433 3592
传真：021-5433 2685
网址：www.dayibed.com
请参阅第394、395页

De Rucci Beddings Co., Ltd.
慕思寝室用品有限公司
广东省东莞市厚街镇双岗上环工业区
电话：0769-8505 8288
传真：0769-8505 8188
电邮：china@derucci.com
网址：www.derucci.com
请参阅第4、5、392、393页

Dongguan Senlai Trade Co., Ltd.
东莞森莱贸易有限公司
广州市天河区东圃镇新塘村九社工业区
邮编：510660
电话：020-8237 3099
传真：020-8234 9786
电邮：market@sheweedare.com
网址：www.sheweedare.com

Dunlopillo (Shenzhen) Ltd. Shanghai Branch
邓禄普家具（深圳）有限公司上海分公司
上海市闵行区吴中路1100号3号楼
天弘商务楼206室
邮编：201103
电话：021-6406 0372
传真：021-5102 6216
网址：www.dunlopilloworld.com

England Bedding King Bedding Group (China) Ltd.
英国卧皇寝具集团（中国）有限公司
东莞市厚街镇桥头第三工业区博览大道桥头路段
邮编：523950
电话：0769-8169 0666
传真：0769-8589 7936
电邮：donbao@126.com
网址：www.donbao.com.cn

Enlanda
爱蒙床垫
广东省惠州市大亚湾经济技术开发区
西区敏华工业城
电话：0752-528 2559
电邮：hotel-china@enlanda.com
网址：www.enlanda.com
请参阅第397页、封底

DAYI
dayibed
大亿床业

H

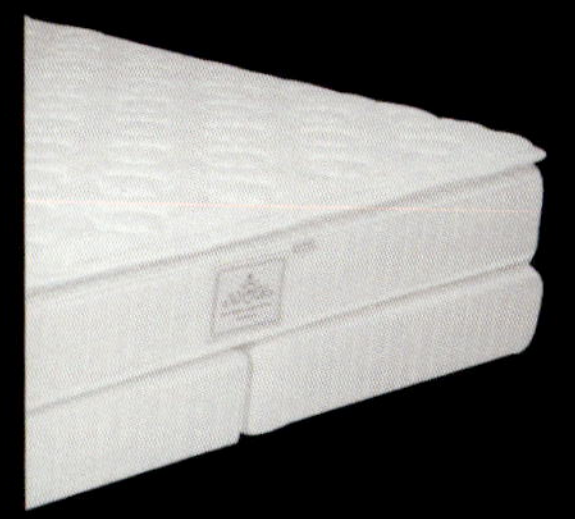

幻知曲床垫系列

幻知曲床垫系列，每款都为客人提供恰到好处的完美承托，让宾客拥有安逸舒适的睡眠。

幻知曲弹簧床架

电幻知曲弹簧床架，有不同弹簧结构可选择，每款床架配有烘干白松木床底框，经久耐用。平均分散上部压力，高品质黑色塑钢床脚及脚轮，美观耐用。万象脚轮也让房务部的同仁移动床垫更加轻松。

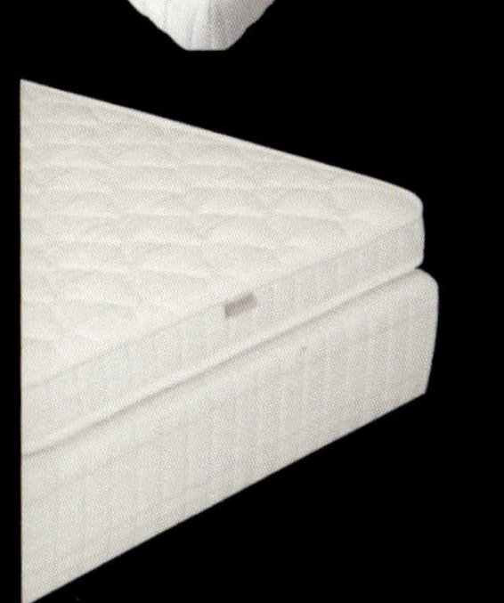

幻知曲薄垫系列

幻知曲薄垫系列，严选高品质的原材料，可放在任何普通床垫上使用，增加原床垫的舒适度，也可以单独当做床榻使用。

幻知曲保洁垫系列

幻知曲保洁垫系列，具有防水、透气、保洁的功能。也有专为高级酒店双拼床垫研发设计的多功能保洁垫，除了解决两张单人床合并后中间缝系的问题，还兼具保洁垫功效。

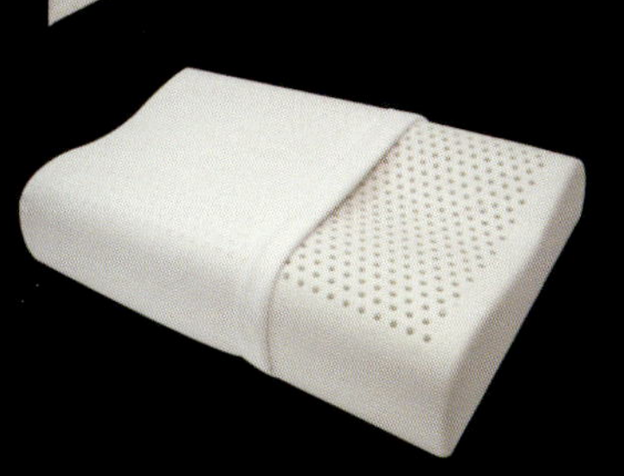

幻知曲枕头系列

幻知曲枕头系列，枕心都采用天然、环保、无毒的Reverie幻知曲天然乳胶，具有防螨抗菌的特性。

量身定作

我们的专业团队会依每个客户的需求，提供专属合适的产品。

独立筒弹簧，互不干扰，独立支撑。

软硬绵毡搭配组合，增加床垫的耐用度及避免身体直接接触弹簧。

性价比高的缇花布，透气排汗针织布，都具阻燃效果。

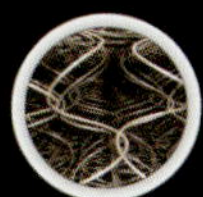
一线钢弹簧，弹簧覆盖率高，弹性及支撑性佳。

高密度或高弹性泡绵，为床垫带来不同的舒适度。

天然乳胶，防螨抗菌。

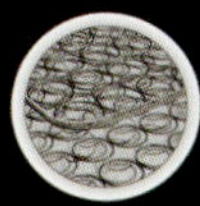
直立弹簧，低干扰，高支撑。

温感记忆绵，随温度变化，记忆人体睡姿，真正服贴人体曲线。

透气绵层，柔软舒适。

卓越的优质睡眠方案提供商

Solutions Provider of Luxury Living

AM01

深圳市雅棉居饰品有限公司

SHENZHEN A-MAIN DECORATIONS CO.,LTD.

地址:中国深圳市笋岗东路宝安广场A栋6

Add:A block 6 baoan square sungang east road.shenzhen china

Tel:+86-755-25161599 Fax:+86-755-25161566

E-mail:info@bedding-cn.com

www.bedding-cn.com www.bedding.en.alibaba.com

全球五星六星级
The Preferred Choice for Global Five & Six Star Hotel
酒店配套专家
运时通家具集团成立于1973年，迄今已有38年历史. 中国总厂面积达15万m²，年产床垫突破100万张，总投资规模超过6亿人民币，为亚太地区最现代化之床垫生产厂商。
运时通是生产床垫、沙发、家具的「全家具制造商」。提供酒店、楼盘、别墅等业者各种家具相关之需求。我们的定位是全方位配套专家，从企划、图纸设计、试做、成品、到交货，每一环节皆经过细部管理。达成适时、适地、适质、和适量，以确保酒店业务成功开幕。
我们的酒店客户，遍布美国、日本、中国大陆、台湾，我们也积极参加中东杜拜、上海及美国酒店专业展。由于我们的努力，广受五、六星级酒店的肯定，被誉为「酒店配套专家」。
Stylution Group was established in 1973. At present, the history of our company is 38 years.The head factory in China is located at Dalingshan Town, Baihuadong Village,which size is 150,000 square meters and the quantity of output is 1 million pieces every year. Moreover,our total investment amount is over than 600 million RMB dollars. Thus,Stylution is the most modernized mattress manufacturer in Asia Pacific.
Stylution is a total furniture manufacturer for the production of mattresses, upholstered furniture and case goods. We supply to Five & Six star Hotels including planning, designing,testing,finishing and delivering under intergrated management. We guarantee just on time,place,quality to meet the deadline of the opening of each new hotel.
亚太家协名誉会长
陈燕木
Jack Chen
诚意推荐
restonic
SUPPORTING DREAMS
Musterring
德國美得麗名床
Musterring
德國美得麗沙發
荷蘭皇家歐品
auping
美國席樂頓名床
STYLUTION
SLEEP THERAPY
DORMIREST
BEDDING PLAZA
床的帝国
STYLUTION

▼床上用品及床垫
Beddings & Mattresses

Eurasia Mattress & Furniture Co., Ltd.
欧亚床垫家具有限公司
广东省广州市万福路133号
邮编：510360
电话：020-8336 7870
传真：020-8338 3599
电邮：marketing@suibao.com
网址：www.suibao.com

Foshan Haima Furniture Co., Ltd.
佛山市海马家具有限公司
佛山市南海区九江镇沙头工业园建业二路
邮编：528200
电话：0757-8690 7222
传真：0757-8690 7111
电邮：sales@hkhaima.com
网址：www.hkhaima.com

Goldsun Home Textiles Inc
江苏金太阳卧室用品有限公司
江苏省通州市川港志浩工业园区金太阳大厦
邮编：226000
电话：0513-8634 4671
传真：0513-8680 1071
电邮：gyw@goldsun.cn
网址：www.goldsun.cn

Guangdong Meige Furniture
广东美阁家具
广东省佛山市顺德区龙江镇涌口工业区优越路
邮编：528318
电话：0757-2322 8712
传真：0757-2387 0718
电邮：mg9988@163.com
网址：www.meige-china.com

Guangzhou Memo's Bedding Co., Ltd.
广州美梦思床具有限公司
广东省佛山市顺德区龙江镇旺岗联新南路7号
邮编：528319
电话：0757-2363 9388
传真：0757-2322 0295
电邮：sell@memos.com.cn
网址：www.memos.com.cn

Guangzhou Meishi Textile Co., Ltd.
广州市美诗纺织品有限公司
广州市番禺区大石镇迎宾路涌口工业区289号
电话：020-3478 5715
传真：020-3478 6431
电邮：jieliya168@yahoo.com.cn
网址：www.meishi-gz.com

H&H Textile & Garments Co., Ltd.
南京辉恒纺织服装有限公司
南京市太平南路333号金陵御景园5楼
邮编：210002
电话：025-8453 7868
传真：025-8453 7888
电邮：mike@hnhtex.com
网址：www.hnhtex.com

Hangzhou Tianzi Household Textile Co., Ltd.
杭州天姿家用纺织品有限公司
浙江省杭州市余杭区乔司工业西区66号
邮编：311101
电话：0571-8619 3698
传真：0571-8619 3393
网址：www.hztzjf.en.alibaba.com

Hefei Yaohai Furniture Production Co., Ltd.
合肥瑶海家具制造有限公司
合肥市瑶海工业园
电话：0551-445 6007
传真：0551-421 2228
电邮：yhjj@yaohaijiaju.cn
网址：www.yaohaijiaju.cn

Hongkong Martha International Down & Textile Products (Guangdong) Co., Ltd.
香港玛莎羽绒（广东）有限公司
佛山市禅城区南庄镇吉利工业园
电话：0757-8532 2999
传真：0757-8532 2111
电邮：martha@martha-hk.com
网址：www.martha-hk.com

Huaian Lianlida Manufactory Co., Ltd.
淮安联利达织造有限公司
上海市交通路4703弄6号1205室
邮编：200333
电话：021-5635 1753
传真：021-5635 1735
电邮：ytm@lianlida.cn
网址：www.lianlida.cn

Hubei Lianle Bedding Mattress Group Co., Ltd.
湖北联乐床具集团有限公司
湖北省武汉市武昌区友谊大道水厂南路联乐工业园
邮编：430063
电话：027-8656 8008
传真：027-8656 7741
电邮：lianle@lianle.com.cn
网址：www.lianle.com.cn

▼床上用品及床垫
Beddings & Mattresses

Jiangsu Bosslong Textile Weaving Co., Ltd.
江苏南通宝仕龙纺织有限公司
江苏省南通华能路288号
邮编：226003
电话：0513-8556 0888
传真：0513-8556 0626

King Koil (Shanghai) Sleep System Co., Ltd.
金可儿（上海）床具有限公司
上海市徐汇区漕溪北路375号
中金国际广场C座13楼B座
邮编：200030
电话：021-6085 1788
传真：021-6085 1758
电邮：sales@kingkoil.com.cn
网址：www.kingkoil.com.cn

King Long Textile Ltd.
敬朗纺织有限公司
Room 5, 15/F, BlockB, Tung Chun Ind, Bldg
11-13 Tai Yuen Street, KwaiChung
N.T., Hong Kong
电话：+852-2695 7621
传真：+852-2699 5538
电邮：wendy@kinglongtex.com
网址：www.kinglongtextile.com.hk

Maxsun Industrial Development Co., Ltd.
佛山市美神实业发展有限公司
广东省佛山市顺德区龙江镇
旺岗工业开发区内108号
邮编：528319
电话：0757-2388 2268
传真：0757-2388 2260
电邮：service@gdmaxsun.com
网址：www.gdmaxsun.com

Ming Fai Industrial (Shenzhen) Co., Ltd.
明辉实业（深圳）有限公司
深圳市龙岗区平湖白坭坑明辉工业城
邮编：518111
电话：0755-2880 2888
传真：0755-8466 2990*7
电邮：marketing@mingfaigroup.com
网址：www.mingfaigroup.com
请参阅第427页

Nantong City Huadong Textiles Co., Ltd.
南通市华东纺织装饰配套用品厂
江苏省南通市九圩港大桥东首
邮编：226003
电话：0513-8556 0964
传真：0513-8556 2518
电邮：huadongzzm@163.com
网址：www.huadong-tex.com

Nantong Gold Sufang Textile Co., Ltd.
南通金苏纺织造有限公司
江苏省南通市通州张芝山镇工业园区中区
邮编：226015
电话：0513-8631 1444
传真：0513-8631 6444
电邮：cnsufang@163.com
网址：www.cnsufang.com

Nantong Red-Golden Top Hotel Supplies Factory
南通红金顶宾馆酒店用品厂
江苏省南通市通州市张芝山镇民安市场东侧
邮编：226314
电话：0513-8634 0499
传真：0513-8634 0399
电邮：nthjd@126.com
网址：www.nthjd.com

Nantong Smbore Textile Co., Ltd.
南通圣宝莱纺织品有限公司
江苏省通州市先锋镇十六里墩工业园
邮编：226316
电话：0513-8667 6933
传真：0513-8667 6711
电邮：hwnj@163.com
网址：www.smbore.com

Nantong Xinjiyuan Hotel Supplies Co., Ltd.
南通市新纪元宾馆用品有限公司
江苏省南通市星明路20号
邮编：226007
电话：0513-8525 8111
传真：0513-8522 4421
电邮：xjy@xjytextile.com
网址：www.xjytextile.com

Nantong YaoGao Textile Co., Ltd.
南通雅高纺织有限公司
江苏省南通市姜灶镇温州路98号
邮编：226006
电话：0513-8633 0000
传真：0513-8160 2098
网址：www.ntyagao.com

Nantong Youmian Haochen Textile Co., Ltd.
南通优棉濠晨纺织品有限公司
江苏省南通市通州川港工业园F区
邮编：226000
电话：0513-8632 0188
传真：0513-8680 2026
电邮：newcon@shum.cn
网址：www.shum.cn

Ningbo Mengshen Mattress Machinery Co., Ltd.
宁波梦神床垫机械有限公司
浙江省宁波市兴甬路165号
邮编：315020
电话：0574-8762 7235
传真：0574-8762 7265
电邮：webmaster@mengshenmattress.com
网址：www.mengshenmattress.com
请参阅第400页

Pacific Coast Feather Company
派赛菲特（上海）商贸有些公司
上海市徐汇区淮海中路1045号
淮海国际广场1602室
邮编：200031
电话：021-6472 2261
传真：021-6472 2260
电邮：infoap@pcf.com
网址：www.pcint.com

Royal Compressed Mattress
佛山市迈吉斯床业有限公司
广东省佛山市里水镇
和顺和桂工业园B区顺展北路1号
邮编：528241
电话：0757-8512 2799
传真：0757-8512 2700
电邮：guh@vip.163.com
网址：www.royalmattress.cn

Sealy Trading (Shanghai) Co., Ltd.
丝涟贸易（上海）有限公司
上海市威海路511号2107室
邮编：200041
电话：021-5213 3821
传真：021-5213 3782
网址：www.sealychina.com.cn

Shanghai Huasheng Textile Decoration Co., Ltd.
上海华晟纺织装饰实业有限公司
上海市宣化路299弄2号15D
邮编：200050
电话：021-6240 8070
传真：021-6240 8071
电邮：hs@huashenglinen.com
网址：www.huashenglinen.com

Shanghai Kormat International Trade Co., Ltd.
上海科唛国际贸易有限公司
上海闵行区浦泉路399弄35号
邮编：201114
电话：021-2428 4650
传真：021-2428 4650*8012
电邮：zhangjie@coco-mat.com.cn
网址：www.coco-mat.com

Shaoxing Swanisland Furniture Co., Ltd.
绍兴市天鹅岛家具有限公司
绍兴市灵芝工业区
邮编：312001
电话：0575-8517 3966
传真：0575-8516 4555
电邮：ted@tianedao.com
网址：www.chinahotelbed.com

ShareWatt Hotels Linens & Amenities Inc.
南通开发区翔华纺织品有限公司
江苏省南通市经济技术开发区花园港路88号
邮编：226010
电话：0513-8598 0088
传真：0513-8598 0099
电邮：info@xianghuatex.com
网址：www.xianghuatex.com

Amain 雅棉

Shenzhen A-main Decorations Co., Ltd.
深圳市雅棉居饰品有限公司
广东省深圳市罗湖区笋岗东路宝安广场A栋6楼
邮编：518025
电话：0755-2516 1599
传真：0755-2516 1566
电邮：info@bedding-cn.com
网址：www.bedding-cn.com
业务范围：
深圳市雅棉居饰品有限公司——中国卓越的优质睡眠方案提供商。
设计生产中国最奢华的酒店床上用品、毛巾、浴袍等。
雅棉使用世界最先进的印染技术，以天然的原料来设计生产环保的产品。是行业中目前唯一使用自有品牌实现在国际市场自主销售的公司。产品50%销往北美、欧洲、中东海湾各国东南亚各国及香港、澳门等地。
雅棉公司的产品经美国F.D.A注册
获得欧洲oeko-tex100绿色纺织品环保标准的认证
获得UKSA质量管理体系的认证和ISO9000的质量体系认证
获得广东省著名商标
请参阅第396页

▼床上用品及床垫
Beddings & Mattresses

Shenzhen Ai Di Furniture Co., Ltd.
深圳市爱的家具有限公司
深圳市坪山新区金碧路309号爱的家具工业园
邮编：518118
电话：0755-2882 0303
传真：0755-2882 0131
电邮：aidi@szaidi.cn
网址：www.szaidi.cn

Shenzhen Airland Furniture Ltd.
深圳雅兰家具有限公司
深圳市龙岗区丹竹头工业区
邮编：518114
电话：0755-2874 9388
传真：0755-2874 9399
网址：www.airland.com

Shenzhen Damei Hotel Supplies Co., Ltd.
深圳市达美酒店配套用品有限公司
广东省深圳市罗湖区布吉路1021号
农产品天乐大厦丰乐园大酒店4楼
邮编：518019
电话：0755-2585 4218
传真：0755-2585 4255
电邮：818@szdamei.com
网址：www.szdamei.com

Shenzhen Fuanna Bedding Co., Ltd.
富安娜家饰用品有限公司
深圳市南山区南油工业区南光路富安娜工业大厦
邮编：518000
电话：0755-2605 5333
传真：0755-2605 5116
电邮：administrator@fuanna.com.cn
网址：www.fuanna.com.cn

Silentnight (Shanghai) Co., Ltd.
上海赛林娜家具有限公司
上海市斜土路2601号嘉汇广场T2座15楼A室
邮编：200030
电话：021-6426 2332
传真：021-6426 1661
电邮：luli@silentnight.com.cn
网址：www.silentnight.com.cn

Simmons Bedding Company
上海席梦思床褥家具销售有限公司
上海市淮海中路222号力宝广场505室
邮编：200021
电话：021-6248 2233
传真：021-6248 0322
电邮：enquiry@simmons.cn
网址：www.simmons.cn

Standard Fiber (Shanghai) Co., Ltd.
世安达纤维（上海）有限公司
上海市淮海中路300号香港新世界大厦1501室
邮编：200021
电话：021-6335 5666
传真：021-3366 2790
网址：www.standardfiber.com

Stylution Int'l (China) Corp.
运时通（中国）家具有限公司
广东省东莞市大岭山镇百花洞村
厚大公路侧（百花洞工业区）
电话：0769-8335 8888
传真：0769-8563 7077
网址：www.beddingplaza.com
请参阅第398、399页

Tongzhou Jincheng Textile Co., Ltd.
通州市锦成纺织饰品厂
江苏省通州市金河镇光河村工业园区188号
邮编：226300
电话：0513-8602 3066
传真：0513-8654 2768
网址：www.jctex.cn.alibaba.com

XiLinMen Furniture Co., Ltd.
喜临门家具股份有限公司
浙江省绍兴市二环北路一号喜临门工业园区
邮编：312001
电话：0575-8515 1888
传真：0575-8516 0798
网址：www.chinabed.com

Zhejiang North Swan Holding Co., Ltd.
浙江北天鹅股份有限公司
杭州市萧山经济技术开发区桥南区块虹迪路58号
邮编：311232
电话：0571-8269 8999
传真：0571-8269 8877
网址：www.tx-zj.com

北京经开万佳国际酒店用品市场
北京市朝阳区南四环东路十八里店
南桥吕家营商业街1号
邮编：100023
电话：010-8769 8883
传真：010-8769 7773
网址：www.bjjkwj.com

北京依丽兰家具有限公司
北京市大兴区西红门镇金大路36号
电话：010-6029 5296
传真：010-6029 5297
电邮：en-land@163.com
网址：www.enleen.com.cn

深圳瑞歌家具有限公司
深圳市宝安三十一区公园路966号
电话：0755-2944 2296
传真：0755-2823 3825
网址：www.szvico.com

深圳市恒安辉纺织有限公司
深圳市宝安区沙井镇衙边学子围第三工业区
邮编：518104
电话：0755-2722 2406
传真：0755-2722 2293
电邮：hah88218687@126.com
网址：www.henganhui.com

清洁承包商
Cleaning Contractors

Beijing Europe and Asia Valuable Clean Service Limited Company
北京欧亚洁保洁服务有限公司
北京市海淀区钢院附中
邮编：100083
电话：010-6235 0546
传真：010-6235 0546
网址：www.bjoyj.com

Beijing Mintaiclean Service Co., Ltd.
北京民泰保洁服务有限公司
北京市海淀区紫竹院路88号紫竹花园
邮编：100089
电话：010-6843 1450
传真：010-6843 1495
电邮：mtclean@163.com
网址：www.mtclean.cn

Polyclean Stone & Marble Care Ltd.
玛斯域云石护理有限公司
Room 808, Opulent Commercial Building, 402-406 Hennessy Road, Wanchai, Hong Kong
电话：+852-2572 3601
传真：+852-2836 0972
电邮：info@polycleancare.com
网址：www.polycleancare.com

Shanghai Lanyun Cleaning Co., Ltd.
上海蓝云保洁有限公司
上海市宝山区月罗路569号
邮编：200941
电话：021-5619 3309
传真：021-5664 9705
电邮：lybjxxbs@online.sh.cn
网址：www.lybj.com.cn

Shanghai Saiqing Environmental Technology Co., Ltd.
上海赛晴环境科技有限公司
上海市金沙江路33号1702室
电话：021-5108 6682
传真：021-5221 0626
电邮：mail@qqbbjj.com
网址：www.qqbbjj.com

Shanghai Shenjie Cleaning Management Co., Ltd.
上海申杰保洁管理有限公司
上海市合肥路271号
电话：021-5383 2757
传真：021-6373 2651
网址：www.shenjie-sh.com

北京东源欣捷清洁用品有限公司
北京市紫南家园东振兴纸箱厂院内
邮编：100023
电话：010-5203 0599
传真：010-8735 5653
电邮：dyxjclean@sina.com
网址：www.dyxj-clean.com

上海金曼保洁服务有限公司
上海市闵行区新镇路603弄29号
电话：021-6475 5881
传真：021-5401 0561
电邮：jinman88@126.com
网址：www.jinmanbaojie.cn

上海世新清洗服务有限公司
上海市闵行区虹中路515号
邮编：200000
电话：021-6401 2810
传真：021-6406 5617
电邮：sxqingxi@yahoo.com.cn
网址：www.shsxqingxi.com

上海宇辰保洁服务有限公司
上海市经高路58弄20号101室
邮编：200317
电话：021-5868 3235
传真：021-6897 9203
电邮：liuxin@shyuchen.com
网址：www.shyuchen.com

上海至诚环境服务有限公司
上海市浦东新区浦东南路1525号3楼
电话：021-5831 4561
传真：021-5820 8401
网址：www.sh-rec.com

清洁设备
Cleaning Equipment

3M China
3M 中国有限公司
上海市兴义路8号万都大厦38层
邮编：200336
电话：021-6275 3535
传真：021-6219 0698
网址：www.3m.com.cn

Beijing Aoshijie Cleaning Equipment Co., Ltd.
北京奥仕洁清洁设备有限公司
北京市南四环东路88号院内
邮编：100176
电话：010-8586 0551
传真：010-8586 2006
网址：www.bjaoshijie.com

Beijing Cabao Cleaning Equipment Co., Ltd.
北京凯堡清洁设备有限公司
北京市经济技术开发区宏达北路16号
邮编：100176
电话：010-6788 1578
传真：010-6788 1594
电邮：market@cabao.com.cn
网址：www.cabao.com.cn

Beijing Clean-King Cleaning Equipment Co., Ltd.
北京健力清洁设备公司
北京市海淀区皂君庙路5号卉园大楼319室
邮编：100081
电话：010-6214 3806
传真：010-6219 4630
电邮：king@clean-king.com.cn
网址：www.cleanking.com.cn

Beijing Irea Trade Development Co., Ltd.
北京伊瑞商贸发展有限公司
北京市丰台区南方庄1号安富大厦801室
邮编：100078
电话：010-6765 5427
传真：010-6765 5427
电邮：irea@irea.com.cn
网址：www.irea.com.cn

CT Corporation Ltd.
佛山市施达清洁设备有限公司
佛山市南海区里水镇
和顺和桂工业园二期顺展北路3号
邮编：528241
电话：0757-8511 5988
传真：0757-8511 6889
电邮：seal@ct-corp.cn
网址：www.ct-corp.cn

Dincher Cleaning Equipment Co., Ltd.
德高洁清洁设备有限公司
北京市东城区北三环东路37号
华世隆国际商务楼B座302室
邮编：100029
电话：010-6443 7473
传真：010-6443 7334
电邮：beijing@digcher.com
网址：www.digcher.com

Dongguan Klenco Cleaning Products Co., Ltd.
东莞格兰高清洁用品有限公司
东莞市塘厦镇莆心湖管理区中心一路21号
邮编：523719
电话：0769-8791 2118
传真：0769-8772 5507
电邮：info@klenco-china.com
网址：www.klenco-china.com

FSI Cleaning Equipment (Guangzhou) Co., Ltd.
广州市法莎清洁设备有限公司
广州市珠海区广州大道南448号财智大厦501室
邮编：510000
电话：020-8422 3845
传真：020-3432 3098
电邮：fsi@fsicn.com
网址：www.fsicn.com

Folks Hydraulics Company O/B Heavy Win Limited
Flat No. 13, 2/F., Tower B, New Trade Plaza 6 On Ping Street, Shatin, Hong Kong
电话：+852-2649 9282
传真：+852-2648 8616
电邮：folks@folks.com.hk
网址：www.folks.com.hk

Gadlee Green Cleaning Equipment Co., Ltd.
嘉得力环保设备有限公司
佛山市南海区桂城东平路翰天科技城A座1-2层
邮编：528000
电话：0757-8101 9199
传真：0757-8212 8900
电邮：gadlee@gadlee.com
网址：www.gadlee.com

Gaojie Clean-Tec Professional Equipment Co., Ltd.
高洁清洁设备有限公司
广东省东莞市莞城旗峰路129号
邮编：523000
电话：0769-2220 7076
传真：0769-2266 3633
电邮：info@gao-jie.com.cn
网址：www.gao-jie.com.cn

Guangzhou Chaobao Cleaning Co., Ltd.
广州市超宝清洁用品公司
广州市白云区江高镇神山工业园
邮编：510460
电话：020-8606 2288
传真：020-8606 3886
电邮：chaobao@china-chaobao.com
网址：www.china-chaobao.com

Hako (China) Co., Ltd.
哈高（中国）有限公司
山东省青岛市城阳区丹山工业园秦家小水西侧
邮编：266107
电话：0532-8965 5980
传真：0532-8965 5985
网址：www.hako.com

Hefei Gaomei Cleaning Equipment Co., Ltd.
合肥高美清洁设备有限责任公司
合肥市包河工业园葛大店产业园6号厂房
（纬五路与经七路交叉口）
电话：0551-512 4259
传真：0551-512 4259*806
电邮：chinagaomei@126.com
网址：www.china-gaomei.com

Karcher (Shanghai) Cleaning Systems Co., Ltd.
凯驰（上海）清洁系统有限公司
上海市浦东新区金桥路1398号金台大厦8楼
邮编：200136
电话：021-5076 8018
传真：021-5076 8903
电邮：marketing@karcher.cn
网址：www.karcher.cn
请参阅第404、405页、封面

Kingsunc Cleaning Equipment (Suzhou) Co., Ltd.
金日清洁设备（苏州）有限公司
苏州市高新区向阳路89号
邮编：215011
电话：0512-6616 2852
传真：0512-6825 8350
电邮：cleanwill@cleanwill.com
网址：www.cleanwill.com

Nilfisk-Advance Cleaning Equipment (Shanghai) Co., Ltd.
力奇先进清洁设备（上海）有限公司
上海市莘庄工业园区银都路4189号
邮编：201108
电话：021-5483 2751
传真：021-5483 2703
网址：www.nilfisk-advance.com.cn

Ohnit Environmental Electron (Shanghai) Co., Ltd.
奥奈特环保电子上海有限公司
上海市虹口区欧阳路568号卢迅大厦6B
邮编：200081
电话：021-5666 0986
传真：021-5666 3062
网址：www.ohnit.net

Polyclean Stone & Marble Care Ltd.
玛斯域云石护理有限公司
Room 808, Opulent Commercial Building, 402-406 Hennessy Road, Wanchai, Hong Kong
电话：+852-2572 3601
传真：+852-2836 0972
电邮：info@polycleancare.com
网址：www.polycleancare.com

Shanghai Comstar GE Co., Ltd.
上海神鹰康星化工有限公司
上海市漕宝路86号光大会展中心F座2605室
邮编：200235
电话：021-6432 5685
传真：021-6432 5633
电邮：market@comstarproducts.com.cn
网址：www.comstarproducts.com.cn

Shanghai EMC Equipment & Supplies Co., Ltd.
上海意美清洁器材有限公司
上海市金钟路658号6-2号2楼
邮编：200335
电话：021-6145 7200
传真：021-6145 7201
电邮：info@emclean.cn
网址：www.emclean.cn

Shanghai Hannover International Tradw Co., Ltd.
上海汉诺威国际贸易有限公司
上海市嘉定区黄渡工业园区杨林路676号
邮编：201804
电话：021-6992 2108
传真：021-6992 2106
电邮：patrickwang@shannover.com
网址：www.shannover.com

Shanghai Honyee Cleanning Equipment Ltd.
上海汉英清洁机械有限公司
上海市松江区九亭镇九新公路599号（近富田路）
电话：021-5485 2222
传真：021-6270 1605
电邮：info@honyee.com.cn
网址：www.honyee.com.cn

Icapsol——地毯清洁方法新突破

德国凯驰，最新推出Icapsol地毯污垢结晶技术，使用凯驰专用设备，通过其滚刷带动，将结晶液喷洒在地毯纤维表面，使污垢结晶，从地毯上剥离，快速的维护清洁（20-120分钟后，地毯即可重新投入使用），让客户耳目一新！

德国凯驰

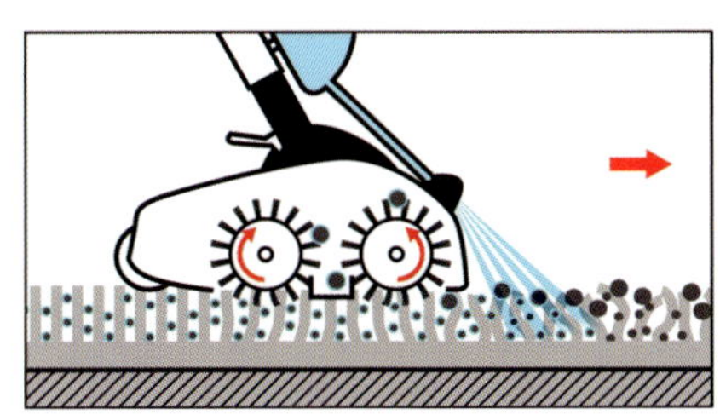

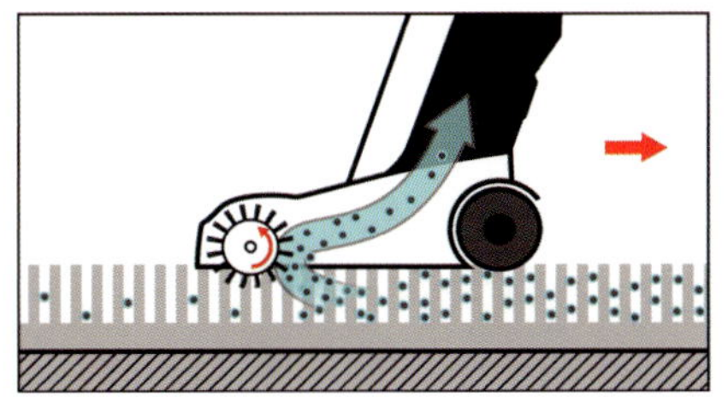

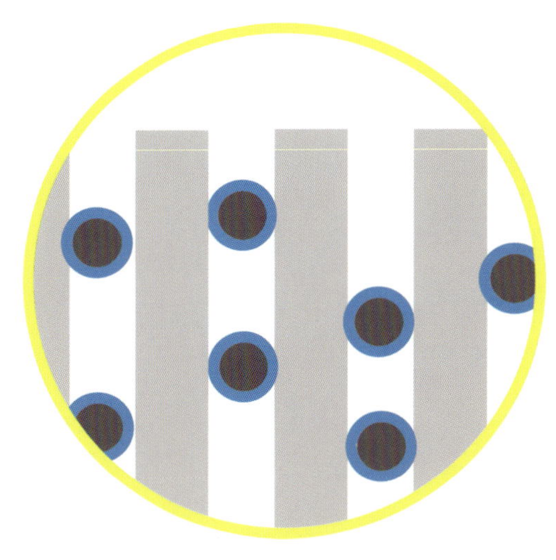

操作步骤：

■　浓度为6%的凯驰结晶液通过凯驰BRS 43/500 C系列清洁设备均匀的喷洒在地毯上。

■　清洁剂与地毯纤维充分接触并发生反应，形成包裹污垢的结晶体，根据地毯污染程度不同，清洁剂用量一般在50—250ml/㎡。

■　待地毯完全干透后，利用凯驰CV系列的带滚刷的直立式吸尘器，将包裹着污物的结晶体吸走。

结晶液
RM 768

地毯清洗机
BRS 43/500 C

德国凯驰集团中国管理中心
凯驰（上海）清洁系统有限公司
www.karcher.cn

上海总部
电话：021-50768018
传真：021-50768903
邮箱：info@karcher.cn

北京分公司
电话：010-87951930
传真：010-87952891
邮箱：kbj@karcher.cn

深圳分公司
电话：0755-83890247
传真：0755-83481239
邮箱：ksz@karcher.cn

成都分公司
电话：028-86008441
传真：028-86008440
邮箱：ksz@karcher.cn

▼清洁设备
Cleaning Equipment

Shanghai New Gaga Trading Co., Ltd.
上海欣芝商贸有限公司
上海市松江区九亭镇朱金公路675号1号楼3楼
邮编：201106
电话：021-6220 9090
传真：021-6220 6000
网址：www.newgaga.com

Shanghai Rongye Cleaning Equipment Co., Ltd.
上海容业清洁设备有限公司
上海市徐汇区沪闵路9512弄9号101室
邮编：200235
电话：021-6475 6182
传真：021-6475 2780*812
电邮：sh-rongye@163.com
网址：www.shrongye.com

Shanghai Shannover Machinery & Equipment Technology Co., Ltd.
上海水威机械设备技术有限公司
上海市嘉定区黄渡工业园区杨林路676号
邮编：201804
电话：021-6992 2108
传真：021-6992 2106
网址：www.shannover.com

Shanghai Shengji Wenshan Cleaning Equipment Co., Ltd.
上海盛吉文善清洁设备有限公司
上海市浦东新区耀华路215号2号楼307室
邮编：200126
电话：021-5119 9703
传真：021-6089 7367
电邮：sjwsclean@126.com
网址：www.sjwsclean.com

Shanghai Xin Mei Hao Cleaning Equipment Sales & Service Co., Ltd.
上海新美好清洁设备销售服务有限公司
上海市莘建东路58弄
绿地蓝海科技岛C座709-711室
邮编：201100
电话：021-5417 6217
传真：021-5417 6163
网址：www.shhost.com

Shanghai Yuli Machinery & Technology Development Co., Ltd.
上海御力机械科技发展有限公司
上海市松江区九亭镇茂联路390号3栋
电话：021-6763 9308
传真：021-6763 9366
电邮：yuli@51stonecare.com
网址：www.mendel.cn

Shenyang Wanjie Clean Equipment Co., Ltd.
沈阳万洁清洁机械有限公司
沈阳市和平区南京南街1甲联营物业大厦13层
邮编：110001
电话：024-2328 6223
传真：024-2328 6401
电邮：wanjie@sywanjie.com
网址：www.sywanjie.com

Sui Hing Cleaning Supplies Co., Ltd.
兆兴清洁用品有限公司
东莞市南城区胜和大朗街商业大厦首8楼
邮编：523000
电话：0769-2241 8231
传真：0769-2241 8143
电邮：sales@suihing.com.cn
网址：www.suihing.com.cn

Tennant Cleaning Systems & Equipment (Shanghai) Co., Ltd.
坦能清洁系统设备（上海）有限公司
上海市青浦区工业园区天盈路66号3号楼
邮编：201700
电话：021-6922 5333
传真：021-6922 5262
网址：www.tennantco.com.cn
请参阅第406页

Universal Electrical Machine Works Co., Ltd.
北京电星舒利电器有限公司
北京市朝阳区曙光西里甲6号
时间国际H座北楼608室
邮编：100028
电话：010-8444 0016
传真：010-8444 0019
电邮：starmix@starmix.com.cn
网址：www.starmix.com.cn

Wuhu Airuite Environmental Protection Technology Co., Ltd.
芜湖爱瑞特环保科技有限公司
安徽省芜湖市繁昌经济开发区
邮编：241200
电话：0553-771 1080
传真：0553-771 1789
电邮：airuite@sina.com
网址：www.airuite.com

Zhejiang Kingwash Electromachinery Co., Ltd.
浙江清化机电有限公司
浙江省台州市路桥区金清镇卷桥工业区
邮编：318058
电话：0576-8271 3389
传真：0576-8271 3398
电邮：sales@kingwash.com.cn
网址：www.tzqh.com

Zhejiang Xinchang Bigyao Power Tool Co., Ltd.
浙江新昌别克跃电动工具有限公司
浙江省新昌县城关镇孟家工业区
邮编：312500
电话：0571-8886 6300
传真：0571-8805 6011
电邮：bigyao@bigyao.com
网址：www.bigyao.com

Zhuhai Junming Co., Ltd.
珠海市钧铭有限公司
珠海市南屏科技工业园屏西5路3号首层
邮编：519060
电话：0756-881 5995
传真：0756-881 5997
电邮：web81@junming.com
网址：www.junming.com

广州裕菖贸易有限公司
广州市番禺区大石沙溪四村东街二巷10号
邮编：514000
电话：020-3450 8253
传真：020-3470 7568
电邮：gz-sales01@fellowyc.com.tw
网址：www.vac-clean.com

纽卫贸易（上海）有限公司
上海市淮海西路570号红坊D栋4楼
邮编：200052
电话：021-2208 5000
传真：021-5230 3517
电邮：info.rcppanchina@newellco.com
网址：www.rcpworksmarter.com

清洁用品
Cleaning Supplies

Beijing Sino-Us Global Cleaning Products Co., Ltd.
北京中美环宇清洁用品有限公司
北京市通州工业园18号
电话：010-5842 5896
传真：0110-5233 5311
电邮：bjzmhy@163.com
网址：www.bjzmhy.cn

Beijing Zhongke AoJie Technology Co., Ltd.
北京中科奥洁科技有限公司
北京市回龙观二拨子工业园北区西路3号院
邮编：102208
电话：010-8271 1337
传真：010-5278 8439
电邮：aojie-fx@263.net
网址：www.zkaj888.com

Binhui Articles For Tourism Co., Ltd.
汕头市彬辉旅游用品有限公司
广东省汕头市潮南区峡山拱上工业区
邮编：515144
电话：0754-8792 9559
传真：0754-8792 8549
电邮：binhui@stbinhui.com.cn
网址：www.stbinhui.com.cn

Chuangdian (H.K) Sanitary Wares
香港创点卫浴精品公司
广东省东莞市凤岗镇南岸工业区
邮编：512708
电话：0769-3889 5818
传真：0769-8207 2027
网址：www.hkcd.cn

Dalian Xin Jian Hai Hotel Supplies & Trade Co.
大连新建海酒店用品贸易行
大连市沙河口区星海广场B3区一品星海6-3-1
电话：0411-8480 5299
传真：0411-8480 4111
电邮：xinjianhai@hotmail.com
网址：www.china-xjh.com

Gadlee Green Cleaning Equipment Co., Ltd.
嘉得力环保设备有限公司
佛山市南海区桂城东平路瀚天科技城A座1-2层
邮编：528000
电话：0757-8101 9199
传真：0757-8212 8900
电邮：gadlee@gadlee.com
网址：www.gadlee.com

Guangzhou Chaobao Cleaning Co., Ltd.
广州市超宝清洁用品公司
广州市白云区江高镇神山工业园
邮编：510460
电话：020-8606 2288
传真：020-8606 3886
电邮：chaobao@china-chaobao.com
网址：www.china-chaobao.com

Johnsondiversey Trading (Shanghai) Co., Ltd.
庄臣泰华施贸易（上海）有限公司
上海市浦东新区福山路455号3楼
邮编：200031
电话：021-5050 9900
传真：021-5050 9911
网址：www.johnsondiversey.com.cn

▼清洁用品
Cleaning Supplies

SCA Asia Pacific
爱生雅亚太区集团
上海市闵行区浦东陈行路1958号
邮编：201114
电话：021-5433 5200
传真：021-5433 3916
电邮：info@sca.com
网址：www.sca.com

请参阅第227页、
厨房、餐厅及酒吧设备书隔页底页

Shanghai Chunhui Tour Articles Factory
上海春晖旅游用品厂
上海市嘉定区南翔镇顺达路300弄53号
邮编：201802
电话：021-6989 0588
传真：021-6989 0589
电邮：ly@chun-hui.com
网址：www.chun-hui.com

Shanghai Hanyang Cleansing Supplies Co., Ltd.
上海瀚洋清洁用品有限公司
上海市莲花南路588弄26号101室
邮编：201104
电话：021-5439 1156
传真：021-5439 1154
网址：www.hyqjyp.com

Shanghai Jiasheng Products Co., Ltd.
上海佳升日用品有限公司
上海市东方路1363号12D
邮编：200127
电话：021-5089 0438
传真：021-5089 0483
网址：www.setbest.com

Shanghai Progent Trading Company Limited
上海普进贸易有限公司
上海市天山路600弄2号楼8楼B、C座
邮编：200051
电话：021-6229 1331
传真：021-5253 0419
电邮：jinqi-pg@suo-ma.com
网址：www.suo-ma.com

Shanghai Whitecat Special Chemicals Co., Ltd.
上海白猫专用化学品有限公司
上海市龙吴路2451号
邮编：200231
电话：021-5482 0020
传真：021-5482 5830
网址：http://whitecatsp-com.idealbiz.com.cn

Sui Hing Cleaning Supplies Co., Ltd.
兆兴清洁用品有限公司
东莞市南城区胜和大朗街商业大厦首8楼
邮编：523000
电话：0769-2241 8231
传真：0769-2241 8143
电邮：sales@suihing.com.cn
网址：www.suihing.com.cn

Sun Shine Fine Chemical Group
北京日光精细（集团）公司
北京市大兴区安定镇安福路1号
邮编：102607
电话：010-8791 0102
传真：010-8791 8078
电邮：bjrgjx@163.com
网址：www.bjrg59.com

Yafeng Sunshine Biotechnology (Beijing) Co., Ltd.
亚峰阳光（北京）生物科技有限公司
北京市西城区白云路1号1405室
邮编：100825
电话：010-6851 9731
传真：010-6858 9064
网址：www.yfsunshine.com

Zhongshan Aoson Fine Chemicals Co., Ltd.
中山市澳臣精细化工实业有限公司
广东省中山市东升镇白鲤工业园
邮编：528412
电话：0760-8850 8797
传真：0760-8850 8505
电邮：aochen_china@163.com
网址：www.aochenoson.com

Zhuhai Junming Co., Ltd.
珠海市钧铭有限公司
珠海市南屏科技工业园屏西5路3号首层
邮编：519060
电话：0756-881 5995
传真：0756-881 5997
电邮：web81@junming.com
网址：www.junming.com

淋浴房
Cubicles-Shower

Cixi Zhongbiao Sanitary Wares Co., Ltd.
慈溪市中标洁具有限公司
浙江省慈溪市长河塘湾工业开发区
邮编：315326
电话：0574-6342 0882
传真：0574-6342 0378
电邮：info@chinajieju.com
网址：www.chinajieju.com

Guangdong Foshan Wen Long Chen Ware Factory
广东佛山市文隆晨洁具厂
广东省佛山市南海区大沥沥西工业区
邮编：528000
电话：0757-8118 5966
传真：0757-8118 5977
网址：www.san-best.com

Guangzhou Lucky Dragon Defend Bath Equipment Co., Ltd.
佛山市吉祥龙卫浴有限公司
佛山市里水镇西线路甘蕉工业区
电话：0757-8565 2069
传真：0757-8565 2066
电邮：sale@gzluckydragon.com
网址：www.gzluckydragon.com

Guangzhou Monalisa Sanitary Ware Co., Ltd.
广州蒙娜丽莎洁具有限公司
广东省广州市花都区花东镇
华侨经济开发区蒙娜丽莎路1号
邮编：510896
电话：020-2860 7788
传真：020-2860 7711
电邮：sales@monalisa.cn
网址：www.monalisa.cn

Hangzhou Constar Sanitary Ware Co., Ltd.
杭州康斯达卫浴有限公司
浙江省杭州市萧山区河庄镇向红村
邮编：311222
电话：0571-8298 4988
传真：0571-8298 4788
电邮：sales@hzksd.cn
网址：www.hzksd.cn

Hangzhou Junlilai Ndustries Co., Ltd.
杭州君利莱实业有限公司
浙江省杭州市萧山区党山井岭路北
邮编：311245
电话：0571-8252 3325
传真：0571-8253 3693
电邮：hzjunlilai@junlilai.com.cn
网址：www.junlilai.com.cn

Ideal Sanitary Ware Co., Ltd.
佛山市理想卫浴有限公司
广东省佛山市南海区大沥镇沥北湖马工业区
邮编：528231
电话：0757-8550 0121
传真：0757-8550 8121
电邮：sales@china-ideal.com
网址：www.china-ideal.com

Oblong International Group (Germany) Co., Ltd.
浙江欧波朗洁具有限公司
温州市新城大道中兴大厦8F
邮编：325000
电话：0577-8891 4578
传真：0577-8892 0498
电邮：oblong@oblong.cn
网址：www.oblong.cn

Shanghai Libi Sanitary Ware Co., Ltd.
上海利比浴室设备有限公司
上海市金山区吕巷工业园区P座
邮编：201517
电话：021-5737 5500
传真：021-5737 5511
电邮：libi@libi.cn
网址：www.libi.cn

客房物料
Guestroom Supplies

Beijing Na Yuan Hotel Articles Co., Ltd.
北京纳源酒店用品有限公司
北京朝阳区亚运村安慧东里17号A318
邮编：100101
电话：010-8039 2670
传真：010-6491 8455
电邮：nayuan1111@126.com
网址：www.nayuan.net

Beijing Tokenism Trading Co., Ltd.
北京汤嘉今悦贸易有限公司
北京市马家堡西路32号5D902室
邮编：100068
电话：010-6754 8688/8788/8988
传真：010-8750 7596
电邮：tokenism@163.com
网址：www.tokenism.cn

请参阅第411页、封底里

Guangdong Kinphon Hotel Supplies Co., Ltd.
广州市健峰酒店用品有限公司
广州市番禺区大石街南公路鸿图工业园A2栋
邮编：511430
电话：020-3993 1999
传真：020-3998 1333
网址：www.kinhao.com

B289 iPod/iphone/收音电子闹钟 Stereo Clock Radio for any iPods

- 数码座式iPod播放
- iPod/iPhone/USB/MP3/MP4等多媒体播放
- 数字FM收音机88–108MHz
- 红外线遥控功能
- 闹铃功能
- 收音频率和时间显示12/24小时制
- 双声道音频输出

B288–B iPod/iphone/收音电子闹钟

Stereo Clock Radio for any iPods

B285 iPod/收音电子闹钟 Stereo Clock Radio for any iPods

Features

- Stereo Clock Radio for any iPod with a dock connector
- Digital FM radio with alarm function, and Snooze button
- Wake and sleep to your iPod, radio or alarm
- Featured with Clock backup function by batteries
- High fidelity sound quality from 10Wx2 and two 2.5" drivers
- Docking Station for power recharging
- Inserts provided for different generations iPod
- Full function remote controls iPod, radio and alarm function
- Aux input for portable audio player like MP3 or laptop
- Video output for iPod connection to TV

Model No.

· Output Power	10Wx2
· Driver	2.5" x2
· Product Dimension (HWD) mm	80 x 300 x 200
· GiftBox Dimension (HWD) mm	300 x 338 x 115
· Master Box Dimension (4pcs/box)	352 x 490 x 324
· Container Loading 20/40/HQ	2000 / 4140 / 4856

Features

- 3 Inserts for iPod in different sizes
- DC adaptor (12V / 2.5A)
- Remote control with battery
- 1 x video & audio cable

上海柏意酒店设备用品制造有限公司

Shanghai Baye Hotel Equipment Manufacture Co.,Ltd

FACTORY ADD: LANE 4755 ZHONG CHUN ST.QING CHUN INDUSTRIAL ZONE,XINZHUANG MING HANG DISTRICT. SHANGHAI,CHINA.

TEL: 86-21-64938170 64938817 64938610 FAX: 86-21-64936044

E-mail: shbaye_2000@126.com

www.shbaye.cn

WORLDNET CHINA LIMITED

滙邦中國有限公司

Flatware	桌面就餐用具
Holloware	名師設計的餐桌器皿
Chinaware	中西餐瓷器
Glassware	水晶及玻璃杯瓶系列
Buffetware	自助餐設備及電磁爐
Banqueting Equipment	活動跳舞板、活動舞臺、可摺疊餐桌等宴會設備
Kitchen Utensils	西廚的烹調炊具及糕點制作器具
Rooms Equipment	客房設備
Luggage Handling Equipment	行李車及行李架
Linen Equipment	客房整理車及毛巾被單運輸車
In-room Telephone	專業酒店客房臥室及浴室使用電話

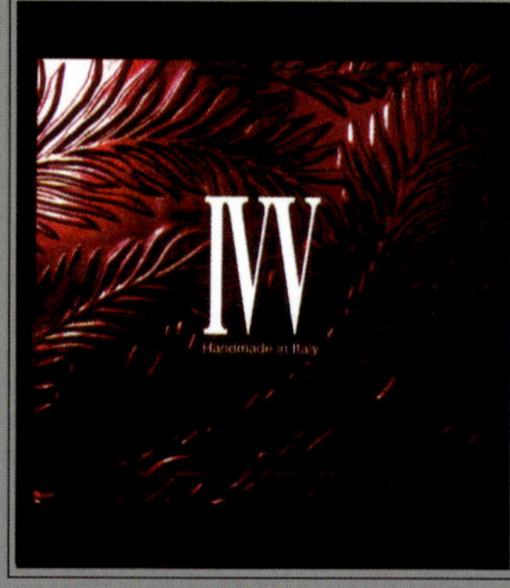

Electrical hairdryers
手提干发器
Electrical kettles
电热水壶
Modern and slim design free-standing and wall-mounted cosmetic mirrors
款式新颖设计特式座台及挂墙美容镜
Bathroom mechanical and electronic scales
外形美观的机械及电子浴室磅
Mobile sleepers (additional beds) and rollaway beds
竖立式及摺合式加床
Induction ovens - stand-alone and table-mounted models
电磁炉 – 独立型和桌面陷入型
Chairs, dance floors, portable stages, banqueting and room service facilities
宴会厅椅子、活动跳舞板、活动舞台、可摺叠餐桌和房膳设备
Luggage trolleys and racks, maid carts, restocking carts, linen and stewarding equipment
行李车、行李架、客房整理车、毛巾被单运输车、服务及管事部设备

Carolyn 卡洛琳 客房精品

Worldnet's Hall of Fame

Wastebaskets, trays, boxes, shower curtains, bathroom accessories, etc. made of all materials
单独或综合不同材质生產的垃圾桶、托盘、储物盒、浴帘、浴室用品等
PVC/PU/Genuine leather wastebaskets, stationery trays, shoe boxes, blanket boxes, etc. items
真皮仿皮産品
Wooden hangers, shoe horns, shoe trees, cloth brushes, etc. wardrobe items
木制衣架、鞋拔、鞋撑、衣刷等衣橱用品
Flower vases, ashtrays, tumblers, wine glasses, mugs, cups and saucers
花瓶、烟缸、客房威士忌杯（可作漱口杯用）、酒杯、咖啡茶杯连碟
Linen baskets and other rattanware
布草篮及其他藤器産品

EC 系列産品 Products

Emergency torches ("EC-Torch")
带夜光标志应急手电筒
Ironing stations equipped with TKE-Irons (or EC-Irons) and organisers ("EC-Press/TKE-Iron")
"烫易"系列烫衣组合（其中包豁烫衣板、电熨斗和挂架）
Electronic room safes ("EC-Safe")
简单易用的精钢电子保险箱
Minibar in absorption system for guestrooms ("EC-Fridge")
酒店客房免压缩机小型电冰箱

Kahn 卡恩

餐飲桌面用具、自動餐設備及西餐刀、炊具
Professional Buffetware, Tabletop and Kitchen Items

Deluxe and fashionable stainless steel flatware
高級時尚西餐餐飲桌面用具
World class holloware and tabletop service equipment
世界級餐飲桌面用具及服務器皿
Fine bone china, traditional chinaware and chopsticks
帶東方味道的高級中、西餐瓷器及筷子
Glass products
玻璃器皿
Stainless steel ice buckets with tongs
不銹鋼冰桶連夾
Stainless steel pots and pans
不銹鋼煮食器皿
Stainless steel wastebasket and bathroom accessories
不銹鋼垃圾桶及浴室用器皿
Knife sets, can openers and kitchen utensils
刀具、開瓶器及西餐炊具
Buffet serviceware
高級自助餐展示設備

Professional Electronic Appliances
专业客房电子産品

Mechanical and electronic clocks
机械及电子座台闹鍾
MP3, CD, iPod, etc. electronic appliances
MP3, CD, iPod 等电子産品

汇邦中国
专业呈献
Worldnet's Hall of Fame

香港總公司：香港葵興華星街8–10號華達工業中心B座7字樓5室
Unit 5, 7th Floor, Block B, Wah Tat Industrial Centre, 8–10 Wah Sing Street,Kwai Hing, Hong Ko
電話：(852) 2420 1039　傳真：(852) 2481 8303　電郵：hkho@worldnetcn.com

中國總公司：上海市靜安區余姚路288號匯智創意園一號樓518室
Unit 518, Block 1, HZCY Building, 288 Yu Yao Road, Shanghai 200040, China
電話：021–62329899　傳真：021–62328488　電郵：sho@worldnetcn.com

MARQUIS SERIES

Polygon

MUSE™
12:08

VS®
SASSOON
沙宣

tokenism™

tokenism™

Dellware®

Smelt

EMBARK

YADA

▼客房物料
Guestroom Supplies

Guangzhou South Hotel Articles Co., Ltd.
广州南方酒店用品有限公司
广州市越秀区大沙头二马路44号之二
邮编：510100
电话：020-8388 9640
传真：020-8388 9840
电邮：china-south@vip.163.com
网址：www.china-south.com.cn

Guangzhou Songfa Hotel Equipment Co., Ltd.
广州松发酒店设备用品有限公司
广州市荔湾区东沙开发区荷景路31号
电话：020-2239 9188
传真：020-2239 9132
网址：www.songfa.cn
请参阅第43页

Hangzhou Binli Hotel Supplies Co., Ltd.
杭州宾利酒店用品有限公司
浙江省杭州市机场路313号花园工业园内中心大楼
邮编：310017
电话：0571-8688 1237
传真：0571-8645 5799
电邮：zjbinli555@126.com
网址：www.zjbinli.com

Hangzhou Keepall Electric Co., Ltd.
杭州科佰电器有限公司
浙江省杭州市留下联胜路13号
邮编：310023
电话：0571-8873 9556
传真：0571-8873 9557
电邮：keepallec@sina.com

Ming Fai Industrial (Shenzhen) Co., Ltd.
明辉实业（深圳）有限公司
深圳市龙岗区平湖白坭坑明辉工业城
邮编：518111
电话：0755-2880 2888
传真：0755-8466 2990*7
电邮：marketing@mingfaigroup.com
网址：www.mingfaigroup.com
请参阅第427页

Ningbo Beilun Walla Electric Appliance Co., Ltd.
宁波北仑华勒电器有限公司
宁波市北仑区明州路500号太平洋国际大厦606室
邮编：315800
电话：0574-8683 1112
传真：0574-8683 1113
电邮：phileyu@walla-hotel.com
网址：www.walla-hotel.com

Royal Pacific Corp
瑞尔普斯菲克有限公司
广东省深圳市宝安区民治街梅龙路
南贤商业广场A1003室
邮编：518129
电话：0755-8178 7646
传真：0755-2927 5900
电邮：yangjiaqi@royalpacific-usa.com
网址：www.royalpacificchina.com

Shanghai Baye Hotel Equipment Manufacture Co., Ltd.
上海柏意酒店设备用品制造有限公司
上海市闵行区莘庄镇青春工业区
中春路4755弄金顾路88号
邮编：201100
电话：021-6493 8170
传真：021-6493 6044
电邮：shbaye_2000@126.com
网址：www.shbaye.cn
请参阅第409页、酒店工程及用品书隔页面页

Shanghai Charn-go Hotel Utensils Co., Ltd.
上海畅高酒店用品有限公司
上海市万航渡路623弄85号建华大厦6楼
邮编：200042
电话：021-6230 1823
传真：021-6249 7960
电邮：charn-go@126.com
请参阅第37页

Taizhou Pingxiao Hotel Articles Co., Ltd.
台州平小酒店用品有限公司
浙江省台州市玉环县坎门镇建州路100号
邮编：317602
电话：0576-8750 7618
传真：0576-8755 7658
电邮：pingxiao@pingxiao.net
网址：www.pingxiao.net

Uni-Sec (Ningbo Hi-Tech Park) Hotel Equipment Co., Ltd.
宁波高新区宁润赛克酒店设备有限公司
浙江省宁波高新区丁香路118号二号楼
邮编：315000
电话：0574-8788 9051
传真：0574-8788 9071
电邮：info@uni-sec.com
网址：www.uni-sec.com

Worldnet China Limited
汇邦中国有限公司
上海市静安区余姚路288号
汇智创意园一号楼518号
邮编：200040
电话：021-6232 9899
传真：021-6232 8488
电邮：sho@worldnetcn.com
网址：www.worldnetcn.com
请参阅第410页

Zhejiang Hua Da Hotel Equipment Co., Ltd.
浙江华大酒店用品有限公司
浙江台州市玉环龙王工业区
邮编：317600
电话：0576-8724 3882
传真：0576-8720 9488
电邮：cnhd@hdpo.com
网址：www.hdpo.com

Zhejiang WuGu Industries Co., Ltd.
浙江五谷实业有限公司
浙江省余姚市丈亭台商投资园区
电话：0574-6299 8803
传真：0574-6299 8899
电邮：sho@hwugu.com
网址：www.hwugu.com
请参阅第201页

艾利秀贸易（上海）有限公司
上海市浦东新区商城路887号
波特营C3幢4楼B-09室
邮编：200120
电话：021-5876 0151
传真：021-5876 0192
网址：www.aliseo.de
请参阅第389页

北京鑫国发酒店用品厂
北京市朝阳区西大望路甲12号
电话：010-5848 7680
传真：010-8770 0990
电邮：xinguofa168@163.com
网址：www.xinguofa.com

北京庄园酒店用品有限公司
北京市昌平区天通苑西三区23号楼401室
邮编：102218
电话：010-6411 8552
传真：010-6411 9833
电邮：zhuangyuanstaff@126.com
网址：www.bjzhuangyuan.com

杭州萧山信诚酒店设备商行
浙江省杭州市萧山区商业城建材市场4B-11号
邮编：311208
电话：0571-8275 2700
传真：0571-8275 2385
电邮：xincheng@xcgf.com
网址：www.xcgf.com

杭州鑫众酒店用品有限公司
杭州市上城区陶瓷品市场7厅2楼27-31号
邮编：310008
电话：0571-8658 5058
传真：0571-8608 2281
网址：www.hzxz0571.com

吹发器
Hair Dryers

Beijing Tokenism Trading Co., Ltd.
北京汤嘉今悦贸易有限公司
北京市马家堡西路32号5D902室
邮编：100068
电话：010-6754 8688/8788/8988
传真：010-8750 7596
电邮：tokenism@163.com
网址：www.tokenism.cn
请参阅第411页、封底里

Guangdong Kinphon Hotel Supplies Co., Ltd.
广州市健峰酒店用品有限公司
广州市番禺区大石街南公路鸿图工业园A2栋
邮编：511430
电话：020-3993 1999
传真：020-3998 1333
网址：www.kinhao.com

Guangzhou Kinhao Hotel Appliances Co., Ltd.
广州市健浩电子有限公司
广州市番禺区大石街道南大公路鸿图工业园A2栋
邮编：511430
电话：020-3993 1999
传真：020-3998 1333
网址：www.kinhao.com

▼吹发器
Hair Dryers

Jiangmen Ayt Electrical Appliance Co., Ltd.
江门市爱威特电器有限公司
广东省江门市麻三平顶山工业园
电话：0750-386 2211
传真：0750-337 8788
电邮：ayt@vip.163.com
网址：www.aytcn.com

Shenzhen Aolq Electronic Co., Ltd.
深圳市奥力奇电子有限公司
深圳市坪山镇沙博新村老围1号
邮编：518112
电话：0755-8992 4300
传真：0755-8992 4302
网址：www.szaolq.com

Shenzhen Svavo Bathroom Products Co., Ltd.
深圳市瑞沃卫浴制品有限公司
深圳市龙岗区坪山街道沙博新屋工业区4号厂房
邮编：518118
电话：0755-8992 8993
传真：0755-8992 8986
电邮：rw@svavo.cn
网址：www.svavo.cn

Shenzhen Upin Sanitary Products Co., Ltd.
深圳市优品清洁用品有限公司
广东省广州市海珠区土华村越和华工工业园B31C
邮编：510288
电话：020-8961 9105
传真：020-8961 9470
电邮：szupin@163.com
网址：www.szupin.com

Universal Electrical Machine Works Co., Ltd.
北京电星舒利电器有限公司
北京市朝阳区曙光西里甲6号
时间国际H座北楼608室
邮编：100028
电话：010-8444 0016
传真：010-8444 0019
电邮：starmix@starmix.com.cn
网址：www.starmix.com.cn

Zhejiang Hua Da Hotel Equipment Co., Ltd.
浙江华大酒店用品有限公司
浙江台州市玉环龙王工业区
邮编：317600
电话：0576-8724 3882
传真：0576-8720 9488
电邮：cnhd@hdpo.com
网址：www.hdpo.com

德国伟嘉
深圳市宝安区沙井街道办
黄埔第二工业区嘉华电器厂
邮编：518125
电话：0755-2742 0040
传真：0755-2742 7605
电邮：wik@wik.com.cn
网址：www.wik.com.cn

干手器
Hand Dryers

Beijing Toms Hardware Co., Ltd.
北京汤姆斯五金有限公司
北京市丰台区南三环中路70号1幢B-802室
邮编：100075
电话：010-8368 6099
传真：010-8368 6453
电邮：tmswj88@sina.com
网址：www.tms88.com

Chuangdian (H.K) Sanitary Wares
香港创点卫浴精品公司
广东省东莞市凤岗镇南岸工业区
邮编：512708
电话：0769-3889 5818
传真：0769-8207 2027
网址：www.hkcd.cn

Fuzhou Zhirong Reaction Equipment Co., Ltd.
福州志荣感应设备有限公司
福建省福州市金山工业区
浦上片台江园百花洲路30号
邮编：350008
电话：0591-8385 0111
传真：0591-8385 5399
电邮：zilong@zilong.com.cn
网址：www.zilong.com.cn

Gibo (Fuzhou) Induction Equipment Co., Ltd.
福州洁博利感应设备有限公司
福建省福州市浦上工业园B区54栋
邮编：350002
电话：0591-8806 6000
传真：0591-8806 5595
电邮：sales@gibo.com.cn
网址：www.gibo.com.cn

Halo Building Materials Inc.
上海华轮建筑材料有限公司
上海市卢湾区徐家汇路378号A栋502-503室
邮编：200025
电话：021-6385 1077
传真：021-5101 0317
电邮：hualun@halochina.com
网址：www.easyheat.com.cn

Jiangmen Ayt Electrical Appliance Co., Ltd.
江门市爱威特电器有限公司
广东省江门市麻三平顶山工业园
电话：0750-386 2211
传真：0750-337 8788
电邮：ayt@vip.163.com
网址：www.aytcn.com

Royal Pacific Corp
瑞尔普斯菲克有限公司
广东省深圳市宝安区民治街梅龙路
南贤商业广场A1003室
邮编：518129
电话：0755-8178 7646
传真：0755-2927 5900
电邮：yangjiaqi@royalpacific-usa.com
网址：www.royalpacificchina.com

Ruian Cheng Long Electrical Equipment Ltd.
瑞安市成龙电器有限公司
浙江省瑞安市塘下镇场桥浦兴街11号
邮编：325205
电话：0577-6526 2611
传真：0577-6526 2198
电邮：zjcldz@alibaba.com.cn
网址：www.racldq.cn

Shanghai Cont Environment Protection Technology Company
上海康特环保科技发展有限公司
上海市浦东金桥出口加工区金皖路389号708室
邮编：201206
电话：021-3872 0362
传真：021-3872 0360
电邮：cont@cont.net.cn
网址：www.cont.net.cn

Shenzhen Aolq Electronic Co., Ltd.
深圳市奥力奇电子有限公司
深圳市坪山镇沙博新村老围1号
邮编：518112
电话：0755-8992 4300
传真：0755-8992 4302
网址：www.szaolq.com

Shenzhen Svavo Bathroom Products Co., Ltd.
深圳市瑞沃卫浴制品有限公司
深圳市龙岗区坪山街道沙博新屋工业区4号厂房
邮编：518118
电话：0755-8992 8993
传真：0755-8992 8986
电邮：rw@svavo.cn
网址：www.svavo.cn

Shenzhen Upin Sanitary Products Co., Ltd.
深圳市优品清洁用品有限公司
广东省广州市海珠区土华村越和华工工业园B31C
邮编：510288
电话：020-8961 9105
传真：020-8961 9470
电邮：szupin@163.com
网址：www.szupin.com

Taishan Jieda Electrical Appliances Co., Ltd.
台山捷达电器制品有限公司
广东省台山市大江工业南区
邮编：529261
电话：0750-543 8296
传真：0750-543 8139
电邮：xinda8@tsjieda.cn
网址：www.tsjieda.cn

Universal Electrical Machine Works Co., Ltd.
北京电星舒利电器有限公司
北京市朝阳区曙光西里甲6号
时间国际H座北楼608室
邮编：100028
电话：010-8444 0016
传真：010-8444 0019
电邮：starmix@starmix.com.cn
网址：www.starmix.com.cn

Wenzhou Huipu Electric Appliance Co., Ltd.
温州市慧普电器有限公司
浙江省温州市瓯海区慈湖路256号
邮编：325014
电话：0577-8608 9289
传真：0577-8608 9282
电邮：info@zjhuipu.com
网址：www.zjhuipu.com

洗衣设备 Laundry Equipment

Castic-Smp
深圳中施机械设备有限公司
深圳市宝安区观澜镇观光路
美泰科技园1号厂房南座3楼
邮编：518057
电话：0755-2663 9451
传真：0755-2663 2860
电邮：info@casitc-smp.com.cn
网址：www.castic-smp.com

Foshan Guohang Laundry Equipment Co., Ltd.
佛山国航洗衣设备有限公司
佛山市文华中路深村南西工业区
邮编：528041
电话：0757-8381 8225
传真：0757-8381 0337
电邮：guohang@fsguohang.cn
网址：www.fsguohang.cn

Shanghai Brocade Laundry Service Co., Ltd.
上海邦纳洗衣服务有限公司
上海市浦东金湘路345号同华大厦1322室
电话：021-5169 6688
传真：021-5138 6366
电邮：brocade@brocade.net.cn
网址：www.brocade.net.cn

Shanghai Denwise Laundry Equipment Co., Ltd.
上海丹威洗衣设备有限公司
上海市虹口区广中路562号东广大厦12F
邮编：200083
电话：021-3603 0531
传真：021-3603 0530
网址：www.denwise.com

Shanghai Gep Laundry Co., Ltd.
上海绿环洗染有限公司
上海市浦东新区浦东大道2000号
阳光世界大厦21楼D座
邮编：200135
电话：021-5852 8888
传真：021-6855 6990
电邮：gep@gep.net.cn
网址：www.58528888.com

Shanghai VIA Trade Co., Ltd.
上海灏胜贸易有限公司
上海市东方路1361号10楼A座
邮编：200127
电话：021-5094 2122
传真：021-5094 2132
电邮：info@via-trade.com
网址：www.via-trade.com

Shanghai Zhongshi Machinery Co., Ltd.
上海中施机械设备有限公司
上海市徐汇区漕东支路1-5号凯翔商务中心201室
邮编：200233
电话：021-6484 5425
传真：021-6408 9423

Shenzhen Lisite Electronic and Science Co., Ltd.
深圳市利思特电子科技有限公司
深圳市南山区南海大道4050号上汽大厦1103室
邮编：518052
电话：0755-8325 0428
传真：0755-2650 4028
电邮：stoney@szlst.cn
网址：www.szlst.cn

布草 Linens

Beijing Na Yuan Hotel Articles Co., Ltd.
北京纳源酒店用品有限公司
北京朝阳区亚运村安慧东里17号A318
邮编：100101
电话：010-8039 2670
传真：010-6491 8455
电邮：nayuan1111@126.com
网址：www.nayuan.net

Beijing ShunJiaRun Textile Co., Ltd.
北京顺嘉润纺织品有限公司
北京市顺义区后沙峪镇铁匠营村铁兴西街22号
邮编：101318
电话：010-8049 7496
传真：010-8049 7488
网址：www.shunjiarun.cn

Beijing Tientrust Hotel Supplest Hotel Supplies Co., Ltd.
北京天亚信嘉酒店用品有限公司
北京市朝阳区王四营乡官庄568号
邮编：100023
电话：010-5139 6596
传真：010-5139 6595
电邮：tyxj@vip.sohu.com
网址：www.tientrust.com

Eliya Hotel Linen Co., Ltd.
依莱雅布草有限公司
广州市番禺区沙溪国际酒店用品城F区126-127号
邮编：511430
电话：020-2262 0015
传真：020-2262 1077
电邮：eliyahl@yahoo.cn
网址：www.eliyacn.com

▼布草
Linens

Foshan Nanhai Huaxing Sleave Weaving Factory
广东省南海华兴丝绵织厂
广东省佛山市南海区丹灶镇塱心上尧工业区
邮编：528216
电话：0757-8544 0122
传真：0757-8541 2128
电邮：weave@weave.cn
网址：www.weave.cn

Foshan Nanzhuang Hengan Knitting Factory Co., Ltd.
佛山市南庄恒安制造厂有限公司
佛山市禅城区南庄镇樵乐东路79号
电话：0757-8201 6768
传真：0757-8201 6768
电邮：heng-an-sales@163.com
网址：www.hha-hoteltex.com

Fushan Furniture Co., Ltd.
富山家具有限公司
广东省佛山市顺德区龙江镇龙峰大道25号
邮编：528319
电话：0757-2388 9269
传真：0757-2322 6908
网址：www.fushan.com.cn

Guangdong Renel Industry Development Co., Ltd.
广东如蕾尔实业发展有限公司
广东省肇庆市高新区文德三街道7号
邮编：526238
电话：0758-362 6685
传真：0758-362 6686
电邮：renel@renelcn.com
网址：www.renelcn.com

Guangzhou Seechin Hotel Supplies Production Co., Ltd.
广州鑫铖酒店用品制造有限公司
广州市白云区均禾街石马村新石路16号
邮编：510430
电话：020-8661 3491
传真：020-8661 3428
电邮：seechin-008@163.com
网址：www.seechin.com.cn

Guangzhou Songfa Hotel Equipment Co., Ltd.
广州松发酒店设备用品有限公司
广州市荔湾区东沙开发区荷景路31号
电话：020-2239 9188
传真：020-2239 9132
网址：www.songfa.cn
请参阅第43页

Hangzhou Tianzi Household Textile Co., Ltd.
杭州天姿家用纺织品有限公司
浙江省杭州市余杭区乔司工业西区66号
邮编：311101
电话：0571-8619 3698
传真：0571-8619 3393
网址：www.hztzjf.en.alibaba.com

Hangzhou Vatican Rain Home Textile Co., Ltd.
杭州梵雨家纺有限公司
杭州市萧山区通惠中路塘湾村
邮编：311200
电话：0571-8258 0009
传真：0571-8256 0007
电邮：jfliu0001@126.com
网址：www.fyjf.com

Jiangsu Canasin Weaving Co., Ltd.
江苏康乃馨织造有限公司
江苏省淮安市楚州经济开发区铁云路8号
邮编：223200
电话：0517-8520 6966
传真：0517-8520 6922
电邮：market@canasin.com
网址：www.canasin.com

Jin Yuan Decorative Articles Manufacturing Factory
大连锦源装饰用品有限公司
辽宁省大连市金州区后石工业园区
邮编：116000
电话：0411-8430 5430
传真：0411-8435 4545
电邮：bosoo@china.com
网址：www.bosoo.com.cn

Ming Fai Industrial (Shenzhen) Co., Ltd.
明辉实业（深圳）有限公司
深圳市龙岗区平湖白坭坑明辉工业城
邮编：518111
电话：0755-2880 2888
传真：0755-8466 2990*7
电邮：marketing@mingfaigroup.com
网址：www.mingfaigroup.com
请参阅第427页

Nantong Red-Golden Top Hotel Supplies Factory
南通红金顶宾馆酒店用品厂
江苏省南通市通州市张芝山镇民安市场东侧
邮编：226314
电话：0513-8634 0499
传真：0513-8634 0399
电邮：nthjd@126.com
网址：www.nthjd.com

Nantong Sidefu Textile Decoration Co., Ltd.
南通斯得福纺织装饰有限公司
江苏省南通市永兴路52号
邮编：226005
电话：0513-8356 8888
传真：0513-8356 8600
电邮：sidefu@public.nt.js.cn
网址：www.sidefu-china.com

Nantong YaoGao Textile Co., Ltd.
南通雅高纺织品有限公司
江苏省南通市姜灶镇温州路98号
邮编：226006
电话：0513-8633 0000
传真：0513-8160 2098
网址：www.ntyagao.com

Shanghai Deyi Hotel Articles Manufacture Co., Ltd.
上海德义酒店用品制造有限公司
上海市民星路201号20号楼
邮编：200433
电话：021-5169 9518
传真：021-5126 2385
网址：www.sh-dy.com
请参阅第414页

Wallyjade Hotel Appliance Factory
北京威尔金顿酒店用品厂
北京市大兴区北臧经济开发区
邮编：102609
电话：010-6125 2575
传真：010-6125 2577
电邮：bjwallyjade@163.com
网址：www.wallyjade.com

Weihai SiWei Textile Co., Ltd.
威海思维纺织有限公司
山东省威海羊亭玉林工业园5号
邮编：264205
电话：0631-576 9675
传真：0631-576 9677
网址：www.swtextile.com

Wuhan Eastern Clean Delicate Hotel Supplies Ltd.
武汉东方洁丽酒店用品有限公司
武汉市江岸区永清街常阳永清城1栋2单元2101室
电话：027-8683 1987
传真：027-5148 8396
网址：www.east-clean.com

佛山市西樵雄胜酒店用品厂
广东省佛山市南海区西樵镇民乐丝织三厂2号楼
邮编：528211
电话：0757-8681 2113
传真：0757-8125 2952
电邮：xs_weave@126.com
网址：www.xs-weave.com

淮安市京华康织造厂
江苏省淮安市清浦区黄码乡工业集中园区
电话：0517-8388 4909
传真：0517-8388 4819
网址：www.jsjhkzz.com

南通市雨楼宾馆纺织用品厂
江苏省南通市三星工业园区
邮编：226112
电话：0513-8233 3281
传真：0513-8233 3280
网址：www.nt-yl.com

深圳市汇庭芳酒店用品有限公司
广东省深圳市宝安区西乡镇
鹤洲村安乐工业园2号楼7A
邮编：518102
电话：0755-2998 0658
传真：0755-2998 0629
电邮：szhtf@126.com
网址：www.szhtf.com

小冰箱 Mini-Bars

Aoyagi (H.K.) Ltd.
香港青柳有限公司
香港九龙观塘开源道72号溢财中心5楼A室
电话：+852-2368 0021
传真：+852-2368 2011
电邮：info@aoyagihk.com.hk
网址：www.aoyagihk.com.hk

Beijing Tokenism Trading Co., Ltd.
北京汤嘉今悦贸易有限公司
北京市马家堡西路32号5D902室
邮编：100068
电话：010-6754 8688/8788/8988
传真：010-8750 7596
电邮：tokenism@163.com
网址：www.tokenism.cn
请参阅第411页、封底里

Colku Industrial Co., Ltd.
佛山市三水歌谷电器有限公司
佛山市三水乐平中心科技工业园B区84号
电话：0757-8736 3068
传真：0757-8736 3067
电邮：colku@colku.com
网址：www.colku.com

Dometic Group Asia Pacific
多美达集团
北京市海淀区西三环北路72号
世纪经贸大厦B座1807室
电话：010-8882 5696
传真：010-8882 5695
电邮：joyce.cheng@dometic.cn
网址：www.dometic.com
请参阅第417页

Gelin Electric Appliance Co., Ltd.
江苏格林电器有限公司
江苏省常熟市虞山工业园汇峰路2号
邮编：215500
电话：0512-5284 7692
传真：0512-5284 8283
电邮：gldq@gelin.com.cn
网址：www.gelin.com.cn

Guangdong Fuxin Electronic Technology Co., Ltd.
广东富信电子科技有限公司
广东省佛山市顺德区容桂高黎高新区科苑3路20号
邮编：528306
电话：0757-2881 5536
传真：0757-2880 3301
电邮：info@fuxin-cn.com
网址：www.fuxin-cn.com

Guangdong Xingxing Refrigeration Equipment Co., Ltd.
广东星星制冷设备有限公司
广东省佛山市三水区乐平镇
南边工业开发区南丰大道
邮编：528135
电话：0757-8732 3866
传真：0757-8732 3855
网址：www.gdxingxing.com

Hangzhou East Electric Appliance Co., Ltd.
杭州伊思特电器有限公司
湖州市德清县越镇禹西港村九里岗
邮编：311102
电话：0572-846 9125
传真：0571-846 9019
电邮：east-asia@vip.163.com
网址：www.minibars.cn

Hangzhou Kalifon Stainless Steel Kitchen Equipment Co., Ltd.
杭州凯利不锈钢厨房设备有限公司
杭州市经济技术开发区16号大街8号
邮编：310018
电话：0571-8671 6016
传真：0571-8671 6018
网址：www.kalifon.com

Homesun Electric Appliance Co., Ltd.
佛山市顺德区奥达信电器有限公司
广东省佛山市顺德区大良新辉路18号
（五沙工业区）
邮编：528333
电话：0757-2832 6808
传真：0757-2839 3788
电邮：lap@homesunproducts.com
网址：www.homesunproducts.com

Huzhou Tengyun Refrigeration Equipment Co., Ltd.
湖州腾云制冷设备有限公司
浙江省德清县乾元镇东郊路7号
邮编：313216
电话：0572-831 3129
传真：0572-842 9010
电邮：tengyun@hztengyun.cn
网址：www.hztengyun.cn

Jiaxing Yongxin Electron Co., Ltd.
嘉兴市永信电子有限公司
浙江省嘉兴市乍浦经济开发区雅山西路329号
邮编：314201
电话：0573-8558 2611
传真：0573-8558 2677
电邮：sales@cn-grl.com
网址：www.cn-grl.com

Multi Business Machines Co., Ltd.
深圳市明捷商用电器有限公司
深圳市福田保税区桂花路5号
福田喜来登酒店西塔6层
电话：0755-8297 5297
传真：0755-8297 5296
网址：www.chinambm.cn

Shenzhen Hoowell Technology Development Co., Ltd.
深圳市弘维科技开发有限公司
深圳市南山区高新园南区深港产学研基地西座
电话：0755-8612 4495
传真：0755-8612 4495
电邮：joan@hoowell.com
网址：www.hoowell.com

青岛海尔电子有限公司
山东省青岛市海尔路1号海尔工业园内
邮编：266101
电话：0532-8893 7400
传真：0532-8893 7402
网址：www.haier.com

深圳市捷力翔科技有限公司
深圳市宝安区龙华民治樟坑三区18号
保险箱销售中心
电话：0755-8354 9535
传真：0755-8354 9500
电邮：earrydeng@163.com
网址：www.jeshine.com

镜子 Mirrors

Beijing Tokenism Trading Co., Ltd.
北京汤嘉今悦贸易有限公司
北京市马家堡西路32号5D902室
邮编：100068
电话：010-6754 8688/8788/8988
传真：010-8750 7596
电邮：tokenism@163.com
网址：www.tokenism.cn
请参阅第411页、封底里

Beijing Zhongda Lantian Glass Company
北京中大蓝天玻璃有限公司
北京市丰台区花乡羊坊村623号
邮编：100070
电话：010-8370 2663
传真：010-8370 2828
电邮：info@bjlt-glass.com
网址：www.bjlt-glass.com

Fujian Kedah Sanitary Ware Co., Ltd.
福建南安市科迪卫浴有限公司
福建省南安市东田镇望珠工业区
邮编：362303
电话：0595-8621 8668
传真：0595-8621 9668
电邮：kedahco@yahoo.com.cn
网址：www.kedah.cn

Hangzhou Junlilai Ndustries Co., Ltd.
杭州君利莱实业有限公司
浙江省杭州市萧山区党山井岭路北
邮编：311245
电话：0571-8252 3325
传真：0571-8253 3693
电邮：hzjunlilai@junlilai.com.cn
网址：www.junlilai.com.cn

Heding Mirror Industry Co., Ltd.
温州合鼎镜业有限公司
浙江省瑞安市塘下山官工业厂区繁华路23-1号
邮编：325000
电话：0577-8551 0807
传真：0577-8892 5999
电邮：heding@hedingmirror.com
网址：www.hedingmirror.com

Imeiss Building Materials Co., Ltd.
佛山市意美斯洁具建材有限公司
佛山市禅城区南庄镇紫洞路段禅高区紫南开发区
邮编：528061
电话：0757-8531 8398
传真：0757-8538 5608
电邮：imeiss@imeiss.com
网址：www.imeiss.cn

Ming Fai Industrial (Shenzhen) Co., Ltd.
明辉实业（深圳）有限公司
深圳市龙岗区平湖白坭坑明辉工业城
邮编：518111
电话：0755-2880 2888
传真：0755-8466 2990*7
电邮：marketing@mingfaigroup.com
网址：www.mingfaigroup.com
请参阅第427页

SZ. Casa.diorr Furniture Co., Ltd.
深圳市卡莎迪奥家具饰品有限公司
深圳市罗湖区梅园路艺展中心A座5011、5026
电话：0755-8247 9037
传真：0755-8247 9037
电邮：vddesign@126.com
网址：www.casadior.net

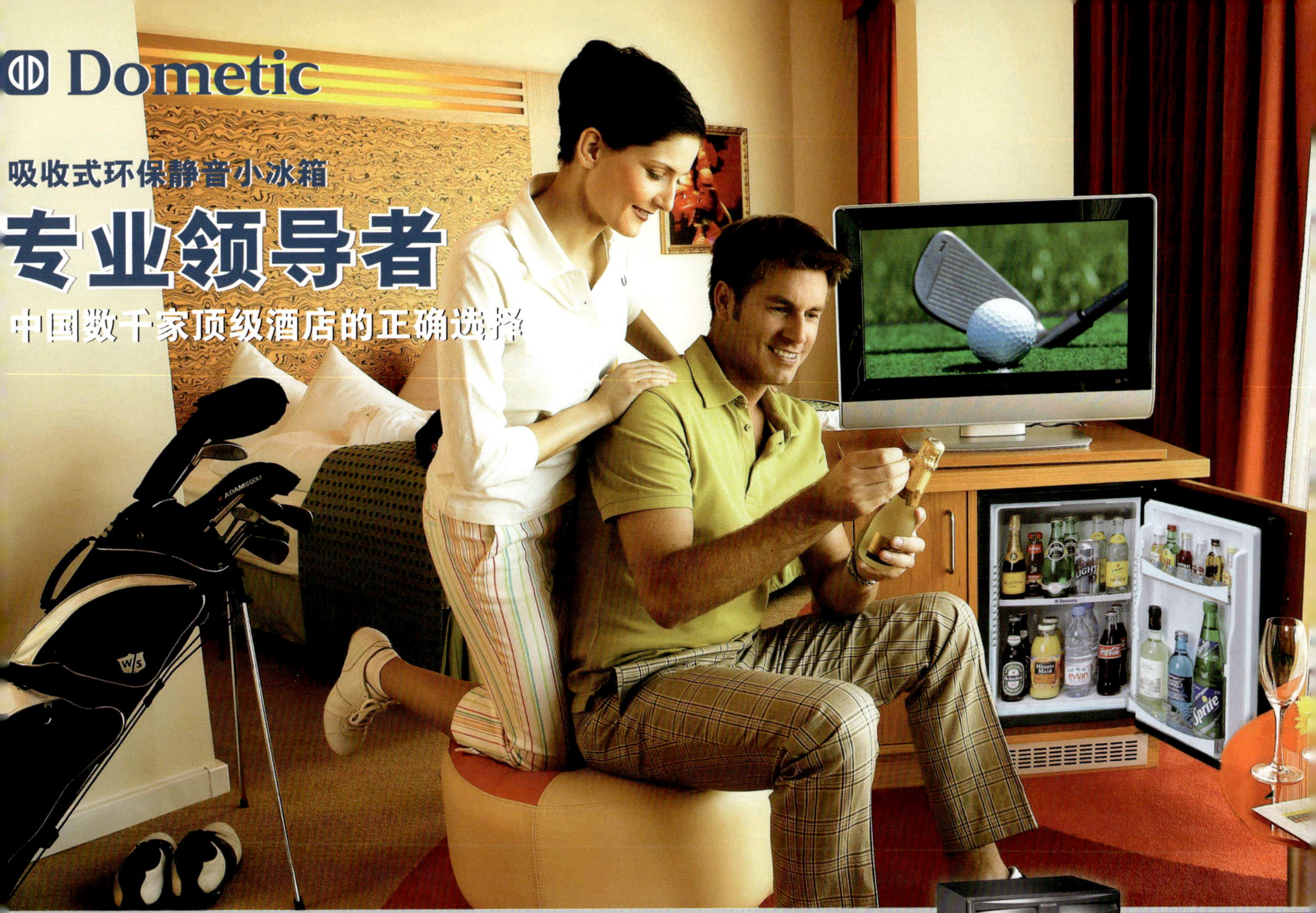

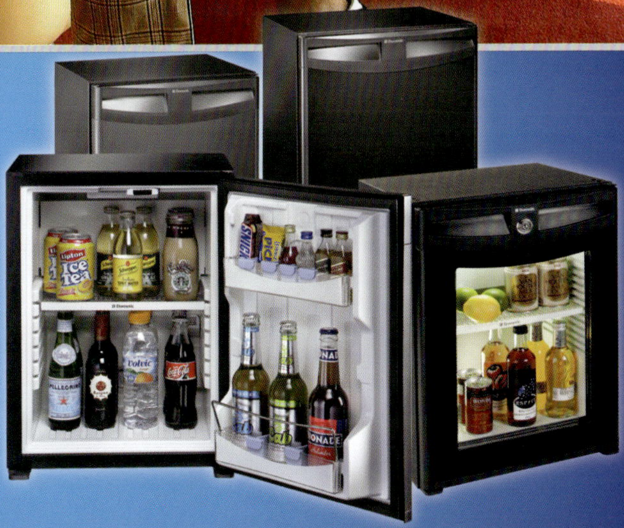

多美达冰箱是全球最畅销的客房冰箱，在制冷技术领域拥有超过80年的设计和研发经验，由于采用了吸收式制冷技术，冰箱在制冷过程中处于完全静音状态，令您的客人免受噪音的干扰，更与众不同的是，多美达吸收式客房冰箱将会让您的投资得到更高的回报，因为众多客户证实她确实是一款优质的小冰箱。

The Dometic RH 440 LD is the world's best-selling mini-Bar. And there are many good reasons why. More than 80 years of experience in refrigeration technologies is just one. Thanks to absorption cooling, the RH 440 LD is noiseless in operation – leaving your guests undisturbed. Moreover, it provides maximum reliability and the longest life time when compared with other absorption mini-bars available in the market. And all these at the lowest energy consumption – a significant cost factor for hotels. All in all, the Dometic RH 440 LD is an investment that pays back. Convince yourself of the very favourable price/performance ratio of this mini-Bar!

我们的客户
遍布全球
Our customers around the world

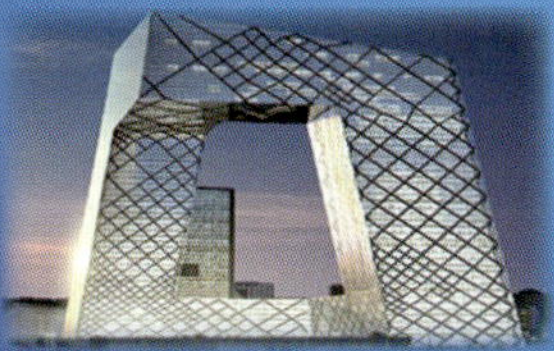

中央电视台新址
CCTV

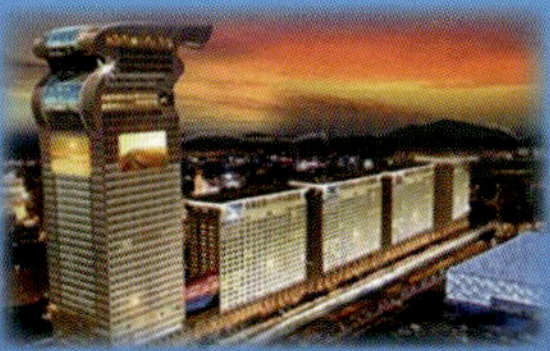

盘古七星级酒店
Pangu seven-star hotel

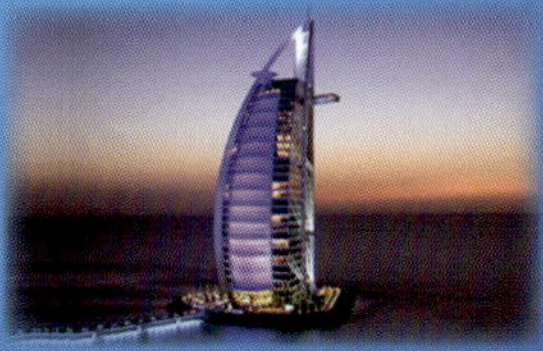

迪拜帆船酒店
Burj Al Arab Hotel Dubai

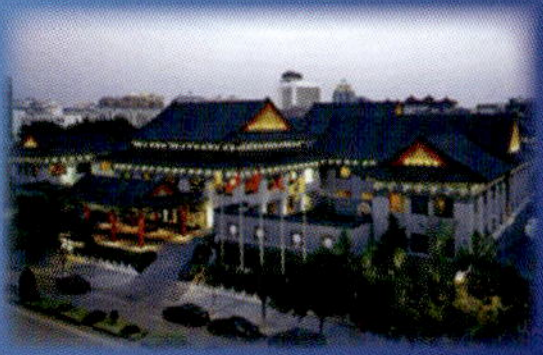

北京香港马会会所
Beijing Hong Kong Jockey Club

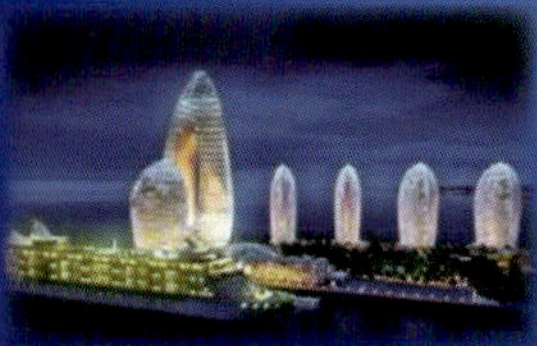

三亚凤凰岛
Phoenix Island Sanya

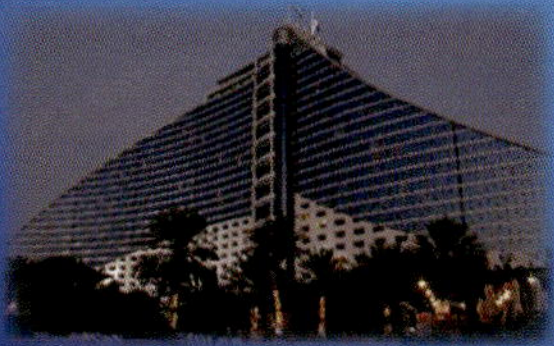

迪拜海滩酒店
Dubai Jumeirah beach hotel

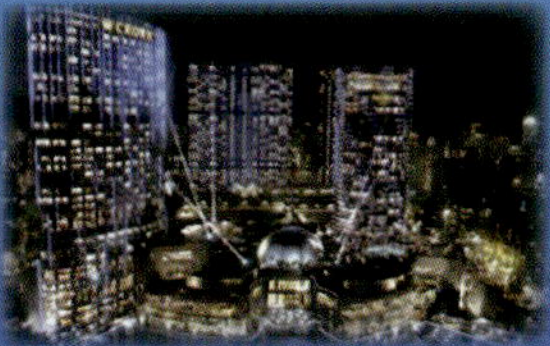

澳门梦之城
City of Dreams Macau

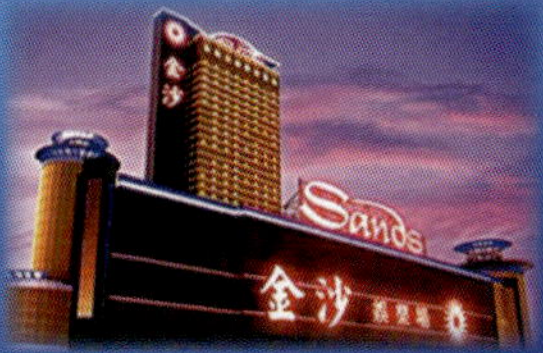

澳门金沙娱乐城
Sands Macao

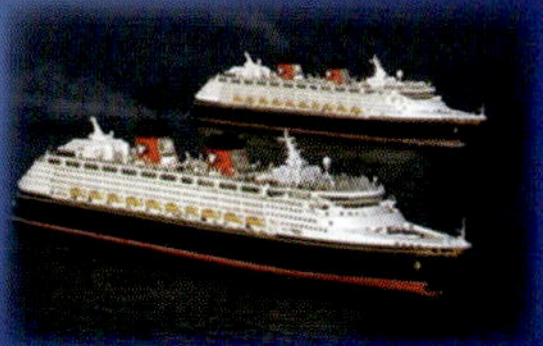

迪士尼豪华游轮
Disney Cruise

酒店客房冰箱专业制造者 · 顶级游艇冰箱 · 豪华车载冰箱 · 酒店专用 冰箱 保险箱

地址：北京市海淀区西三环北路72号
世纪经贸大厦B座1807室
电话：010-88825696 88825698
传真：010-88825695
网址：www.dometic.com
邮箱：joyce.cheng@dometic.cn

▼镜子 Mirrors

Shenzhen Dilang Health Bath Building Materials Co., Ltd.
深圳迪朗卫浴建材有限公司
深圳市罗湖区翠竹路1189号D栋1-102室
邮编：518020
电话：0755-2553 3758
传真：0755-2561 5189
电邮：shaopinghong@126.com
网址：www.dilang2000.com

Shenzhen Jiezhiyang Glass Co., Ltd.
深圳市杰之洋玻璃有限公司
深圳市宝安区送岗街道燕川社区红湖路104号1栋
邮编：518105
电话：0755-8885 9158
传真：0755-2716 4302
电邮：salescn@jzyglass.com
网址：www.lassglass.com

Uni-Sec (Ningbo Hi-Tech Park) Hotel Equipment Co., Ltd.
宁波高新区宁润赛克酒店设备有限公司
浙江省宁波高新区丁香路118号二号楼
邮编：315000
电话：0574-8788 9051
传真：0574-8788 9071
电邮：info@uni-sec.com
网址：www.uni-sec.com

Wenzhou Feilang Glass Mirror Co., Ltd.
温州市飞郎镜业有限公司
温州市龙湾区天河工业区
邮编：325055
电话：0577-8683 2966
传真：0577-8683 2977
电邮：feilang@glassmirror.cn
网址：www.glassmirror.cn

聚乙烯袋 Polythene Bags Manufacturers

Binhui Articles For Tourism Co., Ltd.
汕头市彬辉旅游用品有限公司
广东省汕头市潮南区峡山拱上工业区
邮编：515144
电话：0754-8792 9559
传真：0754-8792 8549
电邮：binhui@stbinhui.com.cn
网址：www.stbinhui.com.cn

Guangzhou Hengfeng Plastic Packing Factory
广州恒丰塑料包装厂
广东省广州市白云区
均禾街清湖一社苏元庄大街18号
电话：020-8601 7917
传真：020-8601 7512
电邮：gzhengfeng@vip.sohu.net
网址：www.gzhengfeng.com

Guangzhou Sanda Plastic Package Company
广州三达塑业包装有限公司
广州市海珠区新滘南路北山村桥头大街228号
邮编：510320
电话：020-3408 7888
传真：020-3408 7776
电邮：xsb@san-da.com
网址：www.san-da.com

Laizhoushi Zhongxin Packing Co., Ltd.
莱州市众鑫包装有限公司
山东省莱州市文峰路仲家洼子村
邮编：261400
电话：0535-228 5558
传真：0535-221 3607
电邮：zxbz@sd-sy.com
网址：www.zx-bz.com

Shanghai Sam Enviroment Protection Co., Ltd.
上海山姆环保设备有限公司
上海市浦东浙桥路277号碧云国际2909室
邮编：201206
电话：021-5032 9599
传真：021-5032 9668
电邮：sam@sam-sh.com
网址：www.sam-sh.com

广州番禺大石胶袋厂有限公司
广东省广州市番禺区钟村镇长江数码花园
邮编：511495
电话：020-8451 6166
传真：020-8451 6166
电邮：shaozhch@yahoo.com.cn

保险箱 Safes

Assa Abloy Hospitality (Shanghai) Co., Ltd.
亚萨合莱保安系统（上海）有限公司
上海市徐汇区漕溪北路737弄
汇翠花园1号楼2704室
邮编：200030
电话：021-6438 9106
传真：021-6438 9106*101
网址：www.vingcard.com

Beijing Tokenism Trading Co., Ltd.
北京汤嘉今悦贸易有限公司
北京市马家堡西路32号5D902室
邮编：100068
电话：010-6754 8688/8788/8988
传真：010-8750 7596
电邮：tokenism@163.com
网址：www.tokenism.cn
请参阅第411页、封底里

Dometic Group Asia Pacific
多美达集团
北京市海淀区西三环北路72号
世纪经贸大厦B座1807室
电话：010-8882 5696
传真：010-8882 5695
电邮：joyce.cheng@dometic.cn
网址：www.dometic.com
请参阅第417页

Guangdong BE-Tech Security Systems Co., Ltd.
广东必达保安系统有限公司
广东省佛山市顺德高新区（容桂）
科技产业园科苑三路17号
邮编：528306
电话：0757-2830 8833
传真：0757-2830 8823
电邮：info@be-tech.com.cn
网址：www.be-tech.com.cn

Guangdong Kinphon Hotel Supplies Co., Ltd.
广州市健峰酒店用品有限公司
广州市番禺区大石街南公路鸿图工业园A2栋
邮编：511430
电话：020-3993 1999
传真：020-3998 1333
网址：www.kinhao.com

Guangzhou Elite Electronic Co., Ltd.
常州市爱莱特电子有限公司
江苏省常州市钟楼开发区梅花路12-2号
邮编：213023
电话：0519-8686 7388
传真：0519-8801 1021*8020
电邮：sales@elitelock.com
网址：www.elitelock.com

Guangzhou Kinhao Hotel Appliances Co., Ltd.
广州市健浩电子有限公司
广州市番禺区大石街道南大公路鸿图工业园A2栋
邮编：511430
电话：020-3993 1999
传真：020-3998 1333
网址：www.kinhao.com

Guangzhou Machine Electricity Equipments Factory
广州市白云区私密保机电设备厂
广东省广州市石井镇大朗村大朗南路六社工业区
邮编：510430
电话：020-8607 4197
传真：020-8607 4896
电邮：gzxingmao@126.com
网址：www.smbsafe.com

Ming Fai Industrial (Shenzhen) Co., Ltd.
明辉实业（深圳）有限公司
深圳市龙岗区平湖白坭坑明辉工业城
邮编：518111
电话：0755-2880 2888
传真：0755-8466 2990*7
电邮：marketing@mingfaigroup.com
网址：www.mingfaigroup.com
请参阅第427页

Ningbo Haishu Weidun Electronic Technology Co., Ltd.
宁波市海曙威盾电子技术有限公司
浙江省宁波市江东科技园区
邮编：315000
电话：0574-6685 5780
传真：0574-8766 6173
电邮：xinjite@yahoo.com.cn
网址：www.wd018.com

Ningbo Kingmark Safes Co., Ltd.
宁波金标保险箱有限公司
宁波市鄞州工业园区
电话：0574-8748 4395
传真：0574-8746 9569
电邮：kingmarksafes@163.com
网址：www.kmsafes.com

Ningbo Sagasafe Electronic Co., Ltd.
宁波市东英禾电子有限公司
浙江省宁波市鄞州区望春工业园区杉杉路151号
邮编：315143
电话：0574-2883 3332
传真：0574-2883 3311
电邮：sales.china@sagasafe.com
网址：www.saga-safe.com

Ningbo Yada Safe Equipment Manufacturing Co., Ltd.
宁波亚大安全设备制造有限公司
浙江省余姚市经济开发区南区鸿运路10号
邮编：315403
电话：0574-6277 8819
传真：0574-6277 7052
电邮：market@yadasafe.com
网址：www.yadasafe.com

Qnn Safe Manufacturing Co., Ltd.
佛山市顺德区安能保险柜制造有限公司
广东省佛山市顺德区大良街道德翔路8号
邮编：528300
电话：0757-2230 8180
传真：0757-2230 8266
电邮：sale13@qnn.com.cn
网址：www.qnn.com.cn

THE SAFE SYSTEM FOR HOTEL ROOMS

Customer desire of the best facilities,stay environment and service from hotel according to rapid development of today's technology. Hotel's operation purpose is to supply customer with best condition of stay environment and facilities while seek to beneficial. Furthermore, create a high efficiency working environment is the heart of hotel management, and a perfect hotel control management system are representing a type of scientific management method,it is must be included in today's hotels.

Elegant star™ Series

The Top-Open Safe

E-safe is design to match the special requirement of today's hotel management,and it is attractive design,easy control,high safety,and in advance of manage, E-safe aim to be the "private butler" of ever hotel's customer, and reflect the high class of hotel service.Furthermore,professional and excellent customer service also supply hotel with full confidence of product quality, thus, E-safe brand be widely accepted by almost international hotel group.

Safe star™ Series

The Digital Safe

▼保险箱
Safes

Safeking Hospitality (Shanghai) Co., Ltd.
上海瑞际酒店设备有限公司
上海市松江工业区松胜路238号3号厂房
邮编：201102
电话：021-5774 5673
传真：021-5774 5275
电邮：safeking_market@163.com
网址：www.safeking.org

Safewell Equipment Ltd.
盛威安全设备有限公司
Flat 01-02，13/F Kwai Cheong Centre, 50 Kwai Cheong Road, Kwai Chung，N.T., Hong Kong
电话：+852-2312 6338
传真：+852-2367 8849
电邮：sales@safewellsafe.com
网址：www.safewellsafe.com

Shanghai ChiXing Hotel Device Co., Ltd.
上海赤星酒店设备有限公司
上海市松江区沪松公路2511弄610-611号
邮编：201601
电话：021-6776 9039
传真：021-6776 9038
电邮：lixusafe@163.com
网址：www.csafebox.cn

Shanghai T&K Industry Co., Ltd.
上海唐年实业有限公司
上海市闵行区梅富路85号A座
邮编：201100
电话：021-5109 6877
传真：021-5440 8867
电邮：esafeintl@163.com
网址：www.esafeindustry.com
请参阅本第419页

Shanghai Zhengxin Safeboxand Cupboard Co., Ltd.
上海正新保险箱柜有限公司
上海市蒙自路364号
邮编：200023
电话：021-6305 7487
传真：021-6304 9495
网址：www.shzhengx.com

Shenzhen Lisite Electronic and Science Co., Ltd.
深圳市利思特电子科技有限公司
深圳市南山区南海大道4050号上汽大厦1103室
邮编：518052
电话：0755-8325 0428
传真：0755-2650 4028
电邮：stoney@szlst.cn
网址：www.szlst.cn

Shenzhen Tongchuangxinjia Science Technology Co., Ltd.
深圳市同创新佳科技有限公司
深圳市龙岗区龙岗街道办同乐社区水田路20号C栋
邮编：518116
电话：0755-2807 2722
传真：0755-2807 2922
电邮：locstar@locstar.com
网址：www.locstar.com

深圳市捷力翔科技有限公司
深圳市宝安区龙华民治樟坑三区18号
保险箱销售中心
电话：0755-8354 9535
传真：0755-8354 9500
电邮：earrydeng@163.com
网址：www.jeshine.com

花洒
Shower Mixers

Aqualem Bathroom Tech Limited
开平炫牌卫浴有限公司
广东开平市水口镇后溪开发区18号
邮编：529321
电话：0750-272 1133
传真：0750-272 1100
电邮：aqualem@yahoo.com.cn
网址：www.aqualem.com

Ateck (Xiamen) Showers Co., Ltd.
伟特（厦门）淋浴设备有限公司
厦门市湖里区殿前街道高殿村前社二号厂房
邮编：361006
电话：0592-520 2288
传真：0592-520 7999
电邮：sales@ateckshowers.com
网址：www.agreat.com.tw

Cixi Changhe Jiayi Sanitary Utensil Factory
慈溪市长河镇佳义洁具厂
浙江省慈溪市长河镇沧田工业区
邮编：315326
电话：0574-6340 9598
传真：0574-6340 6152
电邮：jiayi@jiayi-nb.com
网址：www.jiayi-nb.com

Grohe (Shanghai) Sanitary Products Co., Ltd.
高仪（上海）卫生洁具有限公司
上海市黄陂北路227号中区广场605-610室
邮编：200003
电话：021-6375 8878
传真：021-6375 8665
网址：www.grohe.com.cn
请参阅第322、323页

Hansgrohe Sanitary Products (Shanghai) Co., Ltd.
汉斯格雅卫浴产品（上海）有限公司
上海市松江工业区东部新区申港路2999号
邮编：201611
电话：021-3774 2200
传真：021-3774 2202
电邮：info@hansgrohe.com.cn
网址：www.hansgrohe.com.cn

Xianwei Metals & Plastic Products Co., Ltd.
显威五金塑料制品有限公司
佛山市南海区西樵镇海舟工业区三乡路
邮编：528211
电话：0757-8681 6168
传真：0757-8681 6668
电邮：admin@chinaxianwei.com
网址：www.chinaxianwei.com

帝朗卫浴（广州）有限公司
广东省广州市越秀区东风中路318号嘉业大厦8楼
邮编：510045
电话：020-8329 3188
传真：020-8329 3198
网址：www.mplcn.com

毛巾
Towels

Beijing Huamei Household Textiles Technical Co., Ltd.
北京华美家纺科技有限公司
北京市大兴区西红门福伟路1条3号
邮编：100022
电话：010-5128 6786
传真：010-5238 3606
电邮：muxianwei@126.com
网址：www.muxianwei.com

Foshan Nanhai Huaxing Sleave Weaving Factory
广东省南海华兴丝绵织厂
广东省佛山市南海区丹灶镇塱心上尧工业区
邮编：528216
电话：0757-8544 0122
传真：0757-8541 2128
电邮：weave@weave.cn
网址：www.weave.cn

Foshan Nanzhuang Hengan Knitting Factory Co., Ltd.
佛山市南庄恒安制造厂有限公司
佛山市禅城区南庄镇樵乐东路79号
电话：0757-8201 6768
传真：0757-8201 6768
电邮：heng-an-sales@163.com
网址：www.hha-hoteltex.com

Huai Qin Kang Weaving Co., Ltd.
淮安沁康织造有限公司
江苏省淮安市楚州区河北新民街77号
邮编：223200
电话：0517-8585 6177
传真：0517-8585 6199
网址：www.qinkang.net.cn

Huaian Baiyunjin Weave Co., Ltd.
淮安白云锦织造有限公司
江苏省淮安市楚州区经济开发区铁云路3号
邮编：223200
电话：0517-8537 0660
传真：0517-8588 8658
电邮：byj3325718@126.com
网址：www.byjzz.com

Huaian Caihongfei Towel Factory
淮安市彩虹飞毛巾厂
江苏省淮安市楚州区友谊西路28号
邮编：223200
电话：0517-8582 9133
传真：0517-8580 9233
电邮：web@caihongfei.cn
网址：www.caihongfei.cn

Huaian Chuzhou Qiqi Textile Co., Ltd.
淮安楚州区奇祺纺织厂
江苏省淮安市楚州区华亭路19-41号
邮编：223200
电话：0517-8585 8728
传真：0517-8596 0949
电邮：jsqqfz@yahoo.com.cn
网址：www.jsqqfz.com

Huaian Huayu Towel Co., Ltd.
淮安华宇毛巾有限公司
淮安市楚州区淮城镇古河堤路25号
邮编：223200
电话：0517-8599 7306
传真：0517-8599 8484
电邮：hy5997306@126.com
网址：www.huayumj.com

Huaian Kangte Towel Co., Ltd.
淮安市康特毛巾有限公司
江苏省淮安市楚州区友谊桥西首
邮编：223200
电话：0517-8599 7283
传真：0517-8599 8005
电邮：kt@jscom
网址：www.jskt.com

▼毛巾
Towels

Huaian Mengfeisi Towel Co., Ltd.
淮安市梦妃丝毛巾有限公司
江苏省淮安市楚州区河下城河新街29号
邮编：223200
电话：0517-8582 6388
传真：0517-8582 6386
电邮：mfs@hamfs.com
网址：www.hamfs.com

Huaian Xinhaixin Towel Factory
江苏省淮安市心海心毛巾厂
江苏省淮安市楚州区华亭路77号
邮编：223200
电话：0517-8591 0680
传真：0517-8591 0687
电邮：master@xinhaixin.com
网址：www.xinhaixin.com

Jiangsu Bosslong Textile Weaving Co., Ltd.
江苏南通宝仕龙纺织有限公司
江苏省南通华能路288号
邮编：226003
电话：0513-8556 0888
传真：0513-8556 0626

Jiangsu Canasin Weaving Co., Ltd.
江苏康乃馨织造有限公司
江苏省淮安市楚州经济开发区铁云路8号
邮编：223200
电话：0517-8520 6966
传真：0517-8520 6922
电邮：market@canasin.com
网址：www.canasin.com

Jiangsu Huaian Yizhou Towel Co., Ltd.
淮安市一洲毛巾有限公司
江苏省淮安市楚州经济开发区汪延珍路46号
邮编：223200
电话：0517-8592 6455
传真：0517-8591 9346
网址：www.hayzmj.com.cn

Jiangsu Huaian Tengyu Towel Factory
淮安市腾誉毛巾厂
江苏省淮安市楚州区镇淮楼西路68号
邮编：223200
电话：0517-8588 8926
传真：0517-8588 8938
电邮：js.tengyu@yahoo.com.cn
网址：www.jstengyu.com

Ming Fai Industrial (Shenzhen) Co., Ltd.
明辉实业（深圳）有限公司
深圳市龙岗区平湖白坭坑明辉工业城
邮编：518111
电话：0755-2880 2888
传真：0755-8466 2990*7
电邮：marketing@mingfaigroup.com
网址：www.mingfaigroup.com
请参阅第427页

Nantong Fumei Guesthouse Spinning and Weaving Decoration Co., Ltd.
南通富美宾馆纺织装饰用品有限公司
江苏省南通市城港路华能路口18号
邮编：226003
电话：0513-8556 6860
传真：0513-8556 6860
电邮：ntfm168@163.com
网址：www.ntfumei.com

Nantong No.3 Towel Factory
南通市第三毛巾厂有限公司
江苏省南通市城港路高墩圩桥北首
邮编：226003
电话：0513-8563 0581
传真：0513-8563 0620
电邮：ntsmj@pub.nt.jsinfo.net
网址：www.ntsmj.com

Qingdao Weimay Textile Co., Ltd.
青岛唯美纺织有限公司
山东省青岛市市南区香港中路32号27层
邮编：266071
电话：0532-8079 3158
传真：0532-8384 7637
网址：www.wemaytextile.com

Shanghai Diyi Hotel Supplies Maintenance Factory
上海地一酒店用品厂
上海市青浦工业园区崧复路1590号
邮编：201706
电话：021-5986 8719
传真：021-5986 8720
网址：www.shdyjd.cn

Shanghai Huasheng Textile Decoration Co., Ltd.
上海华晟纺织装饰实业有限公司
上海市宣化路299弄2号15D
邮编：200050
电话：021-6240 8070
传真：021-6240 8071
电邮：hs@huashenglinen.com
网址：www.huashenglinen.com

Shanghai Meijiajing Hotel Supplies Co., Ltd.
上海美加净宾馆用品有限公司
上海市陕西北路1283弄9号2203室
邮编：200060
电话：021-6298 8696
传真：021-6215 2333
网址：www.sh-zyc.com

手推车及餐车
Trolleys & Carts

Beijing Na Yuan Hotel Articles Co., Ltd.
北京纳源酒店用品有限公司
北京朝阳区亚运村安慧东里17号A318
邮编：100101
电话：010-8039 2670
传真：010-6491 8455
电邮：nayuan1111@126.com
网址：www.nayuan.net

Cambro Manufacturing Company
惠州勘宝商业有限公司
广东省惠州市麦地路一号风尚国际18楼A座
邮编：516001
电话：0752-238 7033
传真：0752-238 7019
网址：www.cambro.com

Casifit Metal Products Company
广州裕捷鑫金属制品有限公司
广州市海珠区昌岗中路172号星都酒店大厦
邮编：510288
电话：020-8426 4890
传真：020-8426 4802
电邮：info@casifit.com
网址：www.casifit.com

Guangzhou Jiangnan Metal Product Industry Co., Ltd.
广州江南金属制品实业有限公司
广东省广州市白云区石井街大冈西街35号
邮编：510430
电话：020-8641 6868
传真：020-8641 8678
电邮：jiangnan_gz@163.com
网址：www.gzsteel.com.cn

Guangzhou Sherebo Hotel Products Manufacturer
广州市瑞瑜宝酒店用品厂
广东省广州市花都区迎宾大道
西毕村路口西侧圆玄道观向西200米
邮编：510800
电话：020-6186 7066
传真：020-6186 7070
电邮：sale@sherebo.com
网址：www.sherebo.com

Guangzhou South Hotel Articles Co., Ltd.
广州南方酒店用品有限公司
广州市越秀区大沙头二马路44号之二
邮编：510100
电话：020-8388 9640
传真：020-8388 9840
电邮：china-south@vip.163.com
网址：www.china-south.com.cn

Humanbins Hotel Supply Limited
佛山南海优曼酒店用品制造有限公司
广东省佛山市南海区狮山工业园B区科大路3号
邮编：528241
电话：0757-8669 9295
传真：0757-8669 9292
电邮：sales@humanbins.com
网址：www.humanbins.com

Shanghai Jinxin Metal Decoration Co., Ltd.
上海金鑫金属装饰有限公司
上海市中兴路457号13楼D座
邮编：200071
电话：021-6364 5612
传真：021-5632 5377
网址：www.shjinxin.net

Shanghai Le Crown Hotel Supplies Co., Ltd.
上海乐冠酒店用品有限公司
上海市昭化路508弄50号1511室
邮编：200050
电话：021-6240 2475
传真：021-6240 2476
电邮：doro_business@163.com
网址：www.leguanchina.com

Suzhou Dongfeng Stainless Steel Products Factory
苏州市东风不锈钢制品厂
江苏省苏州市相城开发区88号
邮编：215100
电话：0512-6757 1801
传真：0512-6751 8003
电邮：szeastwlnd@126.com
网址：www.sz-eastwind.com

Xin Qiao Hotel Supplies Factory
广州市新桥酒店用品厂
广州市荔湾区东沙街环翠南路工业区二期15号
邮编：510385
电话：020-8161 0650
传真：020-8161 0670
网址：www.gzxq.com

制服 Uniforms

Antonhill Co., Ltd.
安翘有限公司
香港新界葵涌葵德街15-33号
葵德工业中心2座2楼B室
电话：+852-2541 4177
传真：+852-2544 5797
电邮：info@antonhill.com.hk
网址：www.antonhill.com.hk
请参阅第423页

Baijiayang-Unifrm
广州市百佳洋服饰有限公司
广东省广州市天河区中山大道棠下经济开发区
六社大地工业区D栋4楼
电话：020-3832 4727
传真：020-3832 4717
电邮：baijiayang@126.com
网址：www.baijiayang.com

Beijing Duomilai Garments & Attire Co., Ltd.
北京多米来服装服饰有限责任公司
北京市海淀区清河小营西小口科贸仓库
邮编：100085
电话：010-8293 1040
传真：010-8293 2833
网址：www.checkedout.cn

Beijing Golden Jiayi Clothing Co., Ltd.
北京金色佳艺服装服饰有限公司
北京市丰台区光彩路72号世华水岸C4一单元701
邮编：100075
电话：010-8787 4085
传真：010-8787 5226
电邮：bjjsjyfs@yahoo.com.cn
网址：www.jsjyfz.com

Beijing Mountian Fashion Co., Ltd.
北京曼亭服装有限责任公司
北京市朝阳区
南磨房世纪东方嘉园206号楼5单元201、101室
邮编：100023
电话：010-5126 0198
传真：010-8735 3929
电邮：bjmtfz@126.com
网址：www.bjmanting.com

C & F
无锡创潮服饰设计有限公司
江苏省无锡市扬名产业园B区85号
邮编：214000
电话：0510-8100 3522
传真：0510-8101 7040
电邮：apple32943@sina.com
网址：www.creatfashion.com

Oree Enterprise Co Limited
欧里优商贸（上海）有限公司
上海市卢湾区雁荡路107号雁荡大厦14G
邮编：200020
电话：021-6372 5487
传真：021-6372 4421
电邮：sales@oree.com.cn
网址：www.foodwearcollection.com
请参阅本页上图

Shanghai Fengyan Uniform Co., Ltd.
上海丰彦服饰有限公司
上海市普陀区怒江北路449弄8号C7号楼2F
邮编：200333
电话：021-5265 7259
传真：021-6265 7989
电邮：fengyanfushi@163.com
网址：www.shfengyan.com

▼制服
Uniforms

Shanghai HongLu Fashion Co., Ltd.
上海红鹭服饰有限公司
上海市嘉定区曹安公路4282号10号楼
邮编：200127
电话：021-6959 2985
传真：021-6959 2986*605
电邮：sales@honglu-sh.com
网址：www.honglu-sh.com

Shanghai Ji Zun Uniform
上海吉尊服饰有限公司
上海市怒江北路561弄1号楼3楼
邮编：200233
电话：021-5280 6550
传真：021-5250 1428
电邮：sales@jzuniform.com
网址：www.jzuniform.com

Shanghai Jijia Uniform Co., Ltd.
上海积佳制服有限公司
上海市四川北路1851号11楼1101室
邮编：200081
电话：021-5105 3105
传真：021-5105 3101
电邮：qh1851@qh1851.com
网址：www.qh1851.com

Shanghai LiQiao Garment Co., Ltd.
上海丽巧服饰有限公司
上海市普陀区真南路1111号5号楼804室
邮编：200333
电话：021-6608 1171
13061785188
传真：021-6250 1497
电邮：liqiao5188@126.com
网址：www.shliqiao.com
请参阅第422页

Shanghai Qiantian Uniform Co., Ltd.
上海千田服饰有限公司
上海市虹口区凉城路1319号2号楼2F
邮编：200434
电话：021-6545 6877
传真：021-6592 8706
电邮：qiantianfushi@163.com
网址：www.qiantianfhi.com

Splendid Time Fashion (Hangzhou) Co., Ltd.
杭州流金岁月服饰有限公司
浙江省杭州市江干区丁桥同协路28号
邮编：310021
电话：0571-8816 0666
传真：0571-8609 9835
电邮：info@s-tchina.com
网址：www.s-tchina.com

Tang Dynasty Clothing Business & Trade Co., Ltd.
唐成服装商贸有限公司
武汉市江汉区新华下路17号5楼
邮编：430000
电话：027-8574 5909
传真：027-8578 8569
电邮：tchengzf@tcdynasty.com
网址：www.tcdynasty.com

Tianjin Century Jinding Apparel Co., Ltd.
天津市世纪金鼎服饰有限公司
天津市河西区泰山路6号
邮编：300211
电话：022-2813 7067
传真：022-2813 7068
电邮：webmaster@jd-uniform.com
网址：www.jd-uniform.com

Wuxi Seven Star Kirin Uniform Co., Ltd.
七星锦麟（无锡）服装有限公司
江苏省无锡市运河东路150号园园工业小区
邮编：214000
电话：0510-8281 2608
传真：0510-8281 2308
电邮：girinuniform2000@yahoo.com.cn
网址：www.jdzf.net

Wuxi YiMengDu Dress Co., Ltd.
无锡依梦都服饰有限公司
江苏省无锡市东北塘石新路100号金鹰工业园16-2
邮编：214007
电话：0510-8240 9188
传真：0510-8240 8266
电邮：yimengdoufuzhuang@163.com
网址：www.sharlin.net

上海金霏服饰有限公司
上海市闸北区光复路1号老四行创意园区602室
邮编：200070
电话：021-6380 8557
传真：021-6487 6029
电邮：market@better-u.cn
网址：www.better-u.cn

卫生便利用品
Washroom Supplies

ADA Far East Limited
香港九龙观塘海滨道123号
九仓电讯广场COL大厦12楼1208室
电话：+852-3915 1000
传真：+852-3909 4500
电邮：info@hk.ada-cosmetics.com
网址：www.ada-cosmetics.com
请参阅第426页

Beijing Zhongyali Hotel Suppliers Co., Ltd.
北京中亚丽酒店用品有限公司
北京市大兴区旧宫三工业区6号
邮编：100076
电话：010-8791 3349
传真：010-8791 3545
电邮：zhongyali@zhongyail.com
网址：www.zhongyali.com

Big-J Hygiene Corporation
上海必洁卫生洁具有限公司
上海市徐汇区钦州路785弄4号1楼
邮编：200233
电话：021-5497 2785
传真：021-5497 2787
网址：www.big-j.com.cn

Chongqing LuoLaiYa Hotel Article Co., Ltd.
重庆罗来雅酒店用品有限公司
重庆市丰都三合镇平都大道西段26号
邮编：408200
电话：023-7060 5111
传真：023-8661 5331
电邮：lly2002@126.com
网址：www.lly-cn.com

Daxiyang Hotel Thing Industry Ltd.
大西洋酒店用品实业公司
广州市广州大道洛溪大桥北西侧
南天国际酒店用品市场（星级街）51栋26-29号
邮编：510208
电话：020-3417 1712
传真：020-3417 1712
电邮：a93559@163.com
网址：www.daxy.cn

Dongxing Hotel Supplies Co., Ltd.
汕头市东兴酒店用品有限公司
广东省汕头市泰山路西92号
邮编：515065
电话：0754-8833 5898
传真：0754-8833 7888
电邮：dongxing@st-dongxing.com
网址：www.st-dongxing.com

Foshan Bada Daily & Chemical Co., Ltd.
佛山市八达日用化工用品有限公司
广东省佛山市禅城区南庄镇
吉利工业园新源三路49号
邮编：528061
电话：0757-8533 3373
传真：0757-8533 8692
电邮：sale@bada-gd.com
网址：www.bada-gd.com

Hangzhou Hengyi Hotel Supplies Co., Ltd.
杭州恒溢酒店设备有限公司
浙江省杭州市杭海路1177号海富大厦402室
邮编：310019
电话：0571-8670 0967
传真：0571-8670 0997
电邮：hengyi1688@tom.com
网址：www.hzborun.com

Hanview Amenities Manufacturing (Guangzhou) Ltd.
广州亨咏旅游制品有限公司
广东省广州市黄埔区大沙东路362号
邮编：510725
电话：020-8238 0038
传真：020-8238 2925
电邮：hanview@hanview.com
网址：www.hanview.com

Ihotel Guest Amenities Co., Ltd.
扬州市易德酒店用品有限公司
江苏省扬州市文昌路18号118栋
邮编：225003
电话：0514-8582 8119
传真：0514-8582 3277
电邮：sun@ihtl.cc
网址：www.ihtl.cc

Jiangsu Soho International Group Yangzhou Co., Ltd.
江苏苏豪国际集团扬州有限公司
江苏省扬州市文汇西路303号西城上筑4号楼8楼
邮编：225001
电话：0514-8510 3088
传真：0514-8555 9289
电邮：tony@yzsoho.com
网址：www.chinahotelamenities.com

L'ORCHIDEE
LEONARD

LEONARD

LEONARD

RANCE

Ugo Vanelli

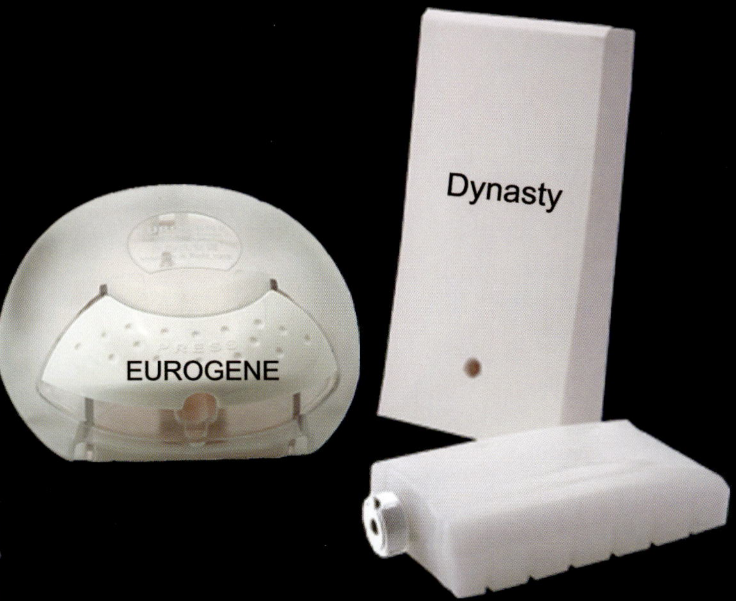
Dynasty
EUROGENE

Ugo Vanelli

Nobility

▼卫生便利用品 Washroom Supplies

Jiangsu XinHeYuan Plastic Daily Chemical Co., Ltd.
江苏鑫禾缘塑胶日化有限公司
江苏省扬州市邗江区杭集工业园翟庄路
邮编：225111
电话：0514-8749 8195
传真：0514-8749 1068
电邮：eison@hotelamenity.cn
网址：www.hotelamenity.cn

LMZ (Yangzhou) Hotel Supplies Co., Ltd.
两面针（扬州）酒店用品有限公司
扬州市邗江区杭集工业园利民路26号
邮编：225111
电话：0514-8749 5555
传真：0514-8749 5005
网址：www.yzlmz.com

Ming Fai Industrial (Shenzhen) Co., Ltd.
明辉实业（深圳）有限公司
深圳市龙岗区平湖白坭坑明辉工业城
邮编：518111
电话：0755-2880 2888
传真：0755-8466 2990*7
电邮：marketing@mingfaigroup.com
网址：www.mingfaigroup.com
请参阅第427页

New West Hotel Necessities Co., Ltd.
新西方酒店用品有限公司
佛山市南海区西樵镇海舟汇泉科技工业园B区
邮编：528211
电话：0757-8682 3417
传真：0757-8682 3553
电邮：sales@newwest.com.hk
网址：www.newwest.com.hk

Shanghai Chaojie Travel Articles Co., Ltd.
上海超洁旅游用品有限公司
上海市中山北路585号508室
邮编：200070
电话：021-6660 0421
传真：021-6654 1717
网址：www.superclean.sh.cn

Shanghai Chunhui Tour Articles Factory
上海春晖旅游用品厂
上海市嘉定区南翔镇顺达路300弄53号
邮编：201802
电话：021-6989 0588
传真：021-6989 0589
电邮：ly@chun-hui.com
网址：www.chun-hui.com

Shanghai Duo Lian Duo Int'l Co., Ltd.
上海朵莲朵贸易有限公司
上海市徐汇区平江路236号2楼202室
电话：021-6312 5678
电邮：info@dap.com.tw
网址：www.dpdap.com
请参阅第38页

Shanghai Ganbor Industrial Co., Ltd.
上海感博实业有限公司
上海市徐汇区吴兴路277号308室
电话：021-6473 9097
传真：021-6415 2161
网址：www.ganbor.com
请参阅第425页

Shanghai Meijiajing Hotel Supplies Co., Ltd.
上海美加净宾馆用品有限公司
上海市陕西北路1283弄9号2203室
邮编：200060
电话：021-6298 8696
传真：021-6215 2333
网址：www.sh-zyc.com

Shanghai Miyako Co., Ltd.
上海乐采卫生用品有限公司
上海市卢湾区打浦路1号金玉兰广场西峰1509室
邮编：200023
电话：021-5396 0291
传真：021-5396 0230
网址：www.miyako-sh.com

Shanghai Pulv Hotel Producis Co., Ltd.
上海浦旅酒店用品有限公司
上海市浦东新区川沙镇妙境路880号
邮编：201200
电话：021-5892 8000
传真：021-5898 7861
网址：www.pdhotel.com

Shanghai Shangteng Tourist Prouist Products
上海尚腾旅游用品有限公司
上海市普陀区华池路58弄
新体育广场1号楼1035室
邮编：200061
电话：021-5187 5093
传真：021-5187 5093*103
网址：www.shangteng9588.com

Shantou Jiayong Industrial Co., Ltd.
汕头市佳永实业有限公司
汕头市潮南区司马浦仙港佳永大厦
邮编：515149
电话：0754-8773 2601
传真：0754-8772 3832
电邮：serve@jiayong-cn.com
网址：www.jiayong-cn.com

Shantou Jingang Traveling Articles Co., Ltd.
汕头市金港实业有限公司
广东省汕头市潮南区仙港工业区金港大厦
邮编：515149
电话：0754-8771 2888
传真：0754-8771 2999
电邮：jingang@stjg.cn
网址：www.stjg.cn

Shantou Kidley Cosmetic Factory Co., Ltd.
汕头奇丽化妆品厂有限公司
汕头市大学路叠金工业区四路前段
邮编：515021
电话：0754-8251 1985
传真：0754-8252 9600
电邮：kidley@kidley.net
网址：www.kidley.net

Shantou Kte Hotel Amenities (Indusrtial) Co., Ltd.
凯特尔旅游用品有限公司
广东省汕头市潮南区峡山拱上工业区
电话：0754-777 1390
传真：0754-779 1390
电邮：sales@86kte.com
网址：www.86kte.com

Shantou Lianda Tourism Industry Co., Ltd.
汕头市莲达旅游用品实业有限公司
广东省汕头市潮南区峡山莲塘工业区
邮编：515144
电话：0754-8778 8399
传真：0754-8779 8844
电邮：lianda@vip.163.com
网址：www.gd-lianda.com

Shenzhen Samsan Hotel Necessities Co., Ltd.
深圳森绅酒店用品有限公司
深圳市深南中路3037号南光捷佳大厦802室
电话：0755-8398 1919
传真：0755-8398 1929
电邮：sales@samsam.com.cn
网址：www.samsam.com.cn

Xiamen Wing Technology Co., Ltd.
厦门卫鹰科技有限公司
厦门市枋湖东路（北段）297号
禾山工商所大院二、三层
邮编：361009
电话：0592-551 3572
传真：0592-551 1562
电邮：wing@china-wing.com
网址：www.china-wing.com

Yangzhou Mingchi Hotel Products Factory
扬州明驰旅游用品厂
江苏省扬州市杭集镇曙光路中段
邮编：225111
电话：0514-8749 8478
传真：0514-8749 8476
电邮：info@yzmingchi.com
网址：www.yzmingchi.com

Yangzhou Pengyou Tourism Supplies Factory
扬州市鹏友旅游用品厂
江苏省扬州市杭集镇利民路20号
邮编：225111
电话：0514-8727 1502
传真：0514-8727 0585
电邮：pengyou1301@yahoo.com.cn
网址：www.yzpyly.com

Yangzhou Yongchun Tourism Products Factory
扬州市永春旅游用品厂
扬州市宁通高速公路杭集出口处
邮编：225111
电话：0514-8727 1356
传真：0514-8727 1356
电邮：yzdwz@china-yongchun.com
网址：www.china-yongchun.com

Yongzhou Toflight Traveling Articles Co., Ltd.
扬州特富莱旅游用品有限公司
浙江省扬州市杭集通州路25号
邮编：225111
电话：0514-8749 9660
传真：0514-8749 9758
电邮：info@toflight.com.cn
网址：www.toflight.com.cn

汕头市潮南区雅兴旅游用品厂
广东省汕头市潮南区峡山环美路北67号
电话：0754-8790 1232
传真：0754-8790 4621
网址：www.styaxing.com

扬州市邗江骋宇旅游用品厂
扬州市邗江区杭集伟业大道锦园路13号
邮编：225111
电话：0514-8727 2468
传真：0514-8727 9278
网址：www.yz-cy.net

餐饮连锁及加盟
Chain Stores and Franchise

Hop Hing Food Group
合兴餐饮集团
北京市东城区北京站街18号
邮编：100005
电话：010-6522 5588
传真：010-6522 2325
电邮：contactus@hophingfood.com
网址：www.hophingfood.com

Inner Mongolia Xiao Wei Yang Catering Fanchise Co., Ltd.
内蒙古小尾羊餐饮连锁股份有限公司
内蒙古包头市青山区装备制造园区小尾羊路1号
邮编：014030
电话：0472-698 0859
传真：0472-698 0777
电邮：chs@xwy.cc
网址：www.nmxwy.com

Kungfu Catering Management Co., Ltd.
真功夫餐饮管理有限公司
广州市天河区体育西路109号
高盛大厦16楼CD单元
邮编：510620
电话：020-3879 2912
传真：020-3879 2952
电邮：cs@zkungfu.com
网址：www.zkungfu.com

Shanghai Iceason Food Co., Ltd.
上海仟果企业管理有限公司
上海市通北路400号
邮编：200082
电话：021-6535 1973
传真：021-6541 1395
网址：www.iceason.com

Tommyboy Food Service Management Co., Ltd.
汤米男孩餐饮管理有限公司
广东省东莞市南城区亨美水濂澎洞工业B区
邮编：523947
电话：0769-8591 9922
传真：0769-8508 9316
电邮：tommyboy-cafe@163.com
网址：www.tommyboycafe.com

两岸咖啡
浙江省杭州市中山北路631号晶晖商务大楼4楼
电话：0571-8580 0711
传真：0571-8580 0608
电邮：jiameng@liangan.com.cn
网址：www.liangan.cn

上海上岛餐饮连锁经营管理有限公司
上海市静安区大沽路396号2楼
电话：021-6340 1966
传真：021-6340 1877
网址：www.ubccn.com

上海一茶一坐餐饮有限公司
上海市漕河泾开发区内田林路398号一楼D室
邮编：200233
电话：021-5464 9520
传真：021-5490 2520
电邮：teaman@chamate.cn
网址：www.chamate.cn

深圳市禾绿餐饮管理有限公司
广东省深圳市罗湖区罗沙路长岭村工业大厦7楼
电话：0755-2577 3839
传真：0755-2577 3889
电邮：hl@hlsushi.com.cn
网址：www.hlsushi.com.cn

外墙清洁服务
Cleaning External Walls Services

Beijing Haohaobaojie Co., Ltd.
北京好好保洁服务有限公司
北京市朝阳区太阳宫路芍药居甲2号
邮编：100029
电话：010-8462 4621
传真：010-8462 4621
网址：www.hhbaojie.cn

Shanghai Kaixin Cleaning Inc.
上海凯欣保洁有限公司
上海市上中西路1689号
邮编：200230
电话：021-5429 4135
传真：021-5429 4135
电邮：www54294135@163.com
网址：www.hyl-clean.cn

Shanghai Yixuan Clean Co., Ltd.
上海逸轩保洁有限公司
上海市虹口区汶水东路510弄30号
邮编：200083
电话：021-6544 4054
传真：021-6531 2933
电邮：xion.gkan@163.com
网址：www.sh-yixuan.cn

Shanghai Yuanyao Cleaning Server Co., Ltd.
上海远耀清洁服务有限公司
上海市金台路161弄
电话：021-5075 8706
传真：021-5865 0312
电邮：13052231710@133sh.com
网址：www.yuanyao.cn

北京东源欣捷清洁用品有限公司
北京市紫南家园东振兴纸箱厂院内
邮编：100023
电话：010-5203 0599
传真：010-8735 5653
电邮：dyxjclean@sina.com
网址：www.dyxj-clean.com

北京华清伟业保洁服务有限公司
北京市海淀区西三旗建材城西一里1号楼后排附院
电话：010-5725 3689
网址：www.cnclean.net

上海立保清洗服务有限公司
上海市巨峰路399弄47号601室
电话：021-5026 1394
电邮：zhang@shlibao.com.cn
网址：www.shlibao.com.cn

上海至诚环境服务有限公司
上海市浦东新区浦东南路1525号3楼
电话：021-5831 4561
传真：021-5820 8401
网址：www.sh-rec.com

上海致洁保洁服务公司
上海市龙吴路2388弄42号101室
电话：021-6496 4748
传真：021-5435 6116
电邮：shclean@sogou.com
网址：www.cleansh.net

防火测试及顾问公司
Fire Safety Testing & Consultants

Beijing Zhongjiadacheng Fire Technology Co., Ltd.
北京中加大成消防科技有限公司
北京市丰台南三环东路6号嘉业大厦B座16层
邮编：100075
电话：010-6760 7099
传真：010-8787 7646
电邮：bjzjdcxf@163.com
网址：www.bjxfgc.com

Guangzhou Sunho Fire Test Techology Co., Ltd.
广州新禾防火测试技术有限公司
广州市海珠区赤岗西路328号
邮编：510310
电话：020-2237 7587
传真：020-2237 7568
电邮：sales@sunho.cc
网址：www.sunho.cc

Warringtonefire Research (Asia-Pacific) Ltd.
威灵顿消防集团
Unit 2009 Level 20, Millennium City 2, 378 Kwun Tong Road, Kwun Tong, Kowloon, Hong Kong
电话：+852-2851 8976
传真：+852-2851 3282
电邮：info@wfrc.com.hk
网址：www.wfrc.com.hk

北京国安防火保安有限公司
北京市经济技术开发区成寿寺威仪路6号
邮编：100164
电话：010-6761 2605
传真：010-6769 3955
电邮：guoanqingxi@126.com
网址：www.gahztcqqx.com

园艺服务
Gardening Services

Shanghai Dalong Green Project Co., Ltd.
上海大龙绿化工程有限公司
上海市宝山区沙浦路128弄42号503室
邮编：201906
电话：021-3631 3253
传真：021-6616 5296
电邮：shdalong@126.com
网址：www.dalonglvhua.com

北京桂合园艺绿化有限公司
北京市丰台区黄土岗兴隆花木场
邮编：100070
电话：010-8618 8942
传真：010-8618 8942
电邮：guiheyy@163.com
网址：www.guiheyyom

柳州市云龙花卉园艺部
广西省柳州市东环路金东花市B区7、8号
邮编：545001
电话：0772-269 0915
电邮：wyl612188@sina.com
网址：www.lzylyy.com

厦门欣桐苑园艺有限公司
厦门市乌石浦二里19号201室
邮编：361000
电话：0592-552 8537
电邮：xthuahui@163.com
网址：www.xthuahui.com

上海舍真园林景观工程有限公司
上海市新金桥路828号3号楼2楼
邮编：201206
电话：021-5169 6149
传真：021-5169 6149*2
电邮：shezhen168@yahoo.com.cn
网址：www.shezhen.com

杀虫服务
Insecticidal Services

Beijing Bangjieshi Pest Management Co., Ltd.
北京邦洁士有害生物防治技术有限公司
北京丰台区东铁匠营顺一条8号大陆写字楼288B室
邮编：100079
电话：010-5846 0322
传真：010-6764 4439
电邮：pco@bjs008.com
网址：www.bjs008.com

Beijing Chubaidi Insecticide Serving Co., Ltd.
北京除百敌杀虫服务有限公司
北京市朝阳区劲松南路1号海文大厦646室
邮编：100021
电话：010-6779 4106
传真：010-6779 4106
电邮：cbdpco@163.com
网址：www.chubaidi.com

Beijing Mintaiclean Service Co., Ltd.
北京民泰保洁服务有限公司
北京市海淀区紫竹院路88号紫竹花园
邮编：100089
电话：010-6843 1450
传真：010-6843 1495
电邮：mtclean@163.com
网址：www.mtclean.cn

Green Harbour, Service of Ecolab
15/F Lu Plaza, 2 Wing Yip Street, Kwun Tong, Kowloon, Hong Kong
电话：+852-2341 4202
传真：+852-2763 5576
电邮：sales@ecolab.com.hk
网址：www.ecolab.com

Guangzhou Lifeme Trade Co., Ltd.
广州耐芙美贸易有限公司
广东省广州市海珠区南大干围38号
南华西第五工业区10号楼6楼东南面
邮编：510288
电话：020-3189 4644
传真：020-3417 1680
电邮：sammi@lifeme.com.cn
网址：www.lifeme.com.cn

Shanghai ZhengXin Environmental Potection Science and Co., Ltd.
上海正欣环保科技有限公司
上海市周家嘴路1683弄30号405室
电话：021-3126 8223
传真：021-5102 6160
电邮：pco163@126.com
网址：www.zxcdc.com

东莞市高力杀虫服务有限公司
东莞市莞城红山路15巷1号
电话：0769-2247 1708
传真：0769-2247 1531
电邮：gaoli@dg-gaoli.com
网址：www.dg-gaoli.com

富力杀虫有限公司
香港北角英皇道625号13楼1301室
电话：+852-2590 0355
传真：+852-2590 0255
网址：www.ghgroup.com.hk

金恒益杀虫服务有限公司
北京丰台区刘家窑北里13号北侧平房
邮编：100075
电话：010-8729 9829
电邮：tyh_ruizhaolong@163.com
网址：www.jhysc.com

宁波市海曙益民杀虫服务部
浙江省宁波市冷静街67号
电话：0574-8729 7022
传真：0574-8729 7022
网址：www.nbpmp.com

上海史伟莎清洁灭虫服务有限公司
上海市闵行区莲花路1733号华纳商务中心612室
电话：400 888 6869
电邮：info@swisher-sh.com
网址：www.swisher.com.hk

包装服务
Packaging Services

Hong Kong International Printing & Pakaging Fair
快捷包装有限公司
香港新界荃湾白田坝街23-39号
长丰工业大厦5楼501A室
电话：+852-2412 2581
传真：+852-2411 3260
电邮：quickpack@quickpack.com.hk
网址：www.quickpack.com.hk

Shanghai Shanyi Enterprise Co., Ltd.
上海山一企业有限公司
上海市漕宝路82号光大国际会展中心E座12楼
邮编：200235
电话：021-6432 5470
传真：021-6432 5978
电邮：export@shanyi-jrx.com
网址：www.shanyi-jrx.com

工程项目管理及顾问
Project And Construction Management Consultancy

Confluence Project Management Pte Ltd.
上海市南京西路1266号恒隆广场1座39楼
邮编：200040
电话：021-6103 8598
传真：021-6103 8597
电邮：contact@confluencepm.com
网址：www.confluencepm.com

Shenzhen Boarton Hotel Management Co., Ltd.
深圳市泊顿酒店管理有限公司
广东省深圳市红荔西路7002号
第一世界广场B座7D
邮编：518034
电话：0755-8305 8820
传真：0755-8305 8812
电邮：boarton@163.com
网址：www.boarton.com

梦中的洗碗机 – 温特豪德台下式洗碗机UC系列

温特豪德新型台下式洗碗机可以满足您所有的愿望，因为每一个酒吧或餐厅，从洗涤物到餐厅规模，都有他自己的特点和要求。新的UC系列的创新概念让这一切成为现实，在每个领域里都发挥最完美的性能：

最大的操作简单化

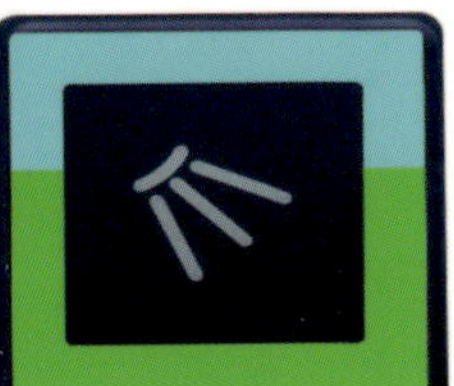

触摸屏设计
- 简单的单键式控制：无需语言，带过程指示功能
- 三个洗涤程序，简单选择
- 自我清洗程序
- 内置操作手册和洗涤小贴士
- 保养提醒
- 错误显示

最完美的洗涤效果

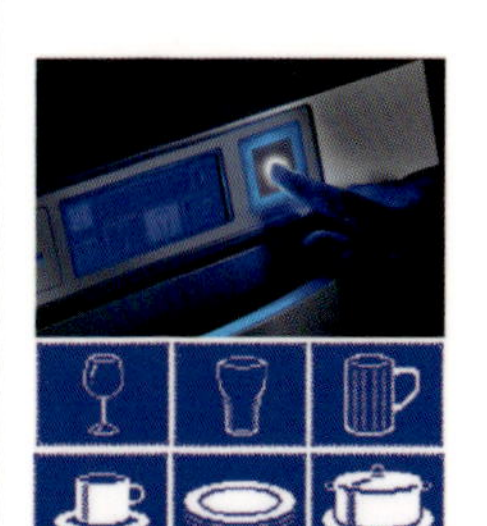

可调的程序：标准和个性化
- 新的UC系列能完成用户的不同愿望。我们都知道不同的餐厅会有不同的洗涤要求，简单地选择适合的图标。
- 新的UC系列，根据洗涤物的类型及污垢程度，选择适合的洗涤程序，进而自动调节影响洗涤效果的四大要素。即使默认的程序要求，也可以通过触摸屏进行简单设置。
- 三种标准的洗涤程序：碗碟、玻璃杯、多功能

最大的维修方便性

新的UC的触摸屏设计 – 最简单的方式调试和维修机器
- 触摸屏，对于员工来说，是操作界面；对于管理人员来说，是获 取卫生日志、监控洗碗机工作的途径；对于工程师来说，则是进行调试、故障判断和维修最便捷的方法。
- 这款新型设计的触摸屏，能满足每一个愿望，并在最快的时间内诊断并修正错误。

最高的经济效率性

节约能源，节省成本
- 节能系列(选配)：机器顶部配置热回收装置，将排出的水蒸汽，用来预热冷的进水，一年可以节省3000度左右的电，前期投入在两年内收回，被排出的蒸汽控制在最小量，改善厨房吧台环境，尤其适合在拥挤狭小的酒吧间里使用。
- 经济程序(标配)：每个程序都有自己的经济程序，通过延长洗涤时 间，降低水压、清洁剂和催干剂的用量，达到节省能源，每个洗涤过程可以节能16%。

联系方式：021-51511310　　传真号码：021-51511950
地　　址：上海市闵行区申旺路5号　　更多详情请与我们联系……

展览会 Exhibitions

日期 Date	展览会名称 Exhibition Name	城市 City	页码 Page Number
2011.09/05-09	The 26th International Famous Furniture Fair (Dongguan) 第26届国际名家具（东莞）展览会	Dongguan 东莞	432
2011.09/14-17	The 17th China International Furniture Expo 第十七届中国国际家具展览会	Shanghai 上海	434、435
2011.09/15-17	ECO Lifestyles 2011 上海国际生态生活方式展览会	Shanghai 上海	433
2011.09/22-24	Sweets & Snacks China 2011 2011中国糖果文化节	Shanghai 上海	436
2011.09/27-29	The 10th China International Exhibition On Housing Industry 第十届中国国际住宅产业博览会	Beijing 北京	437
2011.10/20-22	FruVeg Expo 2011 上海世界果蔬展览会	Shanghai 上海	438
2011.11/08-10	China (Shanghai) International Hospitality Equipment & Supply Soureing Fair 中国（上海）国际酒店设备及用品采购交易会	Shanghai 上海	440、441
2011.11/10-12	Wine & Gourmet ADIS 2011 亚洲美食佳酿暨酒店及餐饮设备展	Macau 澳门	439
2011.11/16-18	The 15th International Exhibition for Food, Drink, Hospitality, Foodservice, Bakery & Retail Industries 第十五届国际食品、饮料、酒店设备、餐饮设备、烘焙及零售设备供应服务展览会	Shanghai 上海	442、443
2011.11/23-25	The 7th International Hotel Expo 2011 第七届国际酒店展2011	Macau 澳门	444、445
2011.12/08-10	18th Guangzhou Hotel Equipment and Supply Exhibition 第十八届广州酒店用品展览会	Guangzhou 广州	446
2012.03/05-08	19th China International Building Decorations and Building Materials Exposition 第十九届中国（北京）国际建筑装饰及材料博览会	Beijing 北京	448
2012.03/05-08	13th China (Shanghai) International Wallpaper & Decorative Textile Exposition 第十三届中国（北京）国际墙纸布艺博览会	Beijing 北京	449
2012.03/18-20	29th China International Furniture Fair (Guangzhou) 第二十九届中国广州国际家具博览会（民用家具展）	Guangzhou 广州	447
2012.03/27-30	29th China International Furniture Fair (Guangzhou) - Office Show 第二十九届中国广州国际家具博览会（办公环境展）	Guangzhou 广州	450
2012.04/09-12	The 13th China Clean Expo 第十三届中国清洁博览会	Shanghai 上海	451
2012.04/09-12	Hotelex + Design & Deco China 2012 第21届上海国际酒店用品、酒店建筑设计、陶瓷卫浴与建材、清洁、照明、家具系列配套博览会	Shanghai 上海	452、453
2012.04/09-12	Expo Build China 2012 第二十届中国国际建筑装饰展览会	Shanghai 上海	454
2012.04/09-12	Ceramics, Tile & Sanitary Ware China 2012 第十三届中国国际建筑陶瓷及卫浴科技精品展览会	Shanghai 上海	455
2012.04/17-20	Wine & Spirits Asia (WSA) 2012 第12届国际葡萄酒及烈酒展览会	Singapore 新加坡	456
2012.04/17-20	Food & Hotel Asia (FHA) 2012	Singapore 新加坡	457
2012/05	The 13th Xi'an International Hospitality Equipment & Supplies Fair 第十三届西安国际酒店设备及用品展览会	Xi'an 西安	458
2012.05/09-11	SIAL 2012 第十三届中国国际食品和饮料展览会	Shanghai 上海	459
2012.05/23-26	Kitchen & Bath China 2012 第17届中国国际厨房、卫浴设施展览会	Shanghai 上海	460
2012.05/23-26	International Building & Construction Trade Fair 2012 第17届中国国际建筑贸易博览会	Shanghai 上海	461
2012.06/28-30	The 10th International Hospitality Equipment & Supplies Fair, Guangzhou China 第十届广州国际酒店设备及用品展览会	Guangzhou 广州	462

电子辐射

大气污染

低碳育儿

绿色电器

化学毒素

净化水质

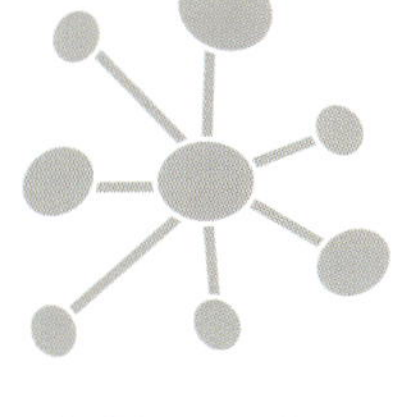
转基因食品

噪音污染

废品回收

绿色家居

药品危害

危险电器

低碳出行

健康饮食

你想选择怎样的生活？

打造你的生态之家：

- LOHAS一站式居家体验馆
- 80年代怀旧主题馆
- 健康母婴生活馆
- 家庭休闲体验馆
- 零碳生活设计展

ECO Lifestyles 2011
上海国际生态生活方式展览会
www.ecolifestyles.cn
上海世博主题馆
2011.9.15-17

承办方： 

协办方： 

官方合作媒体：   

海外合作组织：   

乐活行业合作研究机构：现代传播乐活研究机构

作为继美国高点家具展，意大利米兰家具展之后跻身世界三大家具展览会之一的中国国际家具展览会每年9月以逾2000家参展企业之众在中国上海拉开帷幕，为您呈现涵盖家具业内各大领域的展品。展会同期还将举办中国国际办公家具展览会、中国国际家居饰品布艺及灯饰展览会、中国国际橱柜展览会、中国国际家具生产设备及原辅材料展览会以及中国国际家具配件及材料精品展。2011年第十七届中国国际家具展览会将于9月14日–17日在上海新国际博览中心举办。

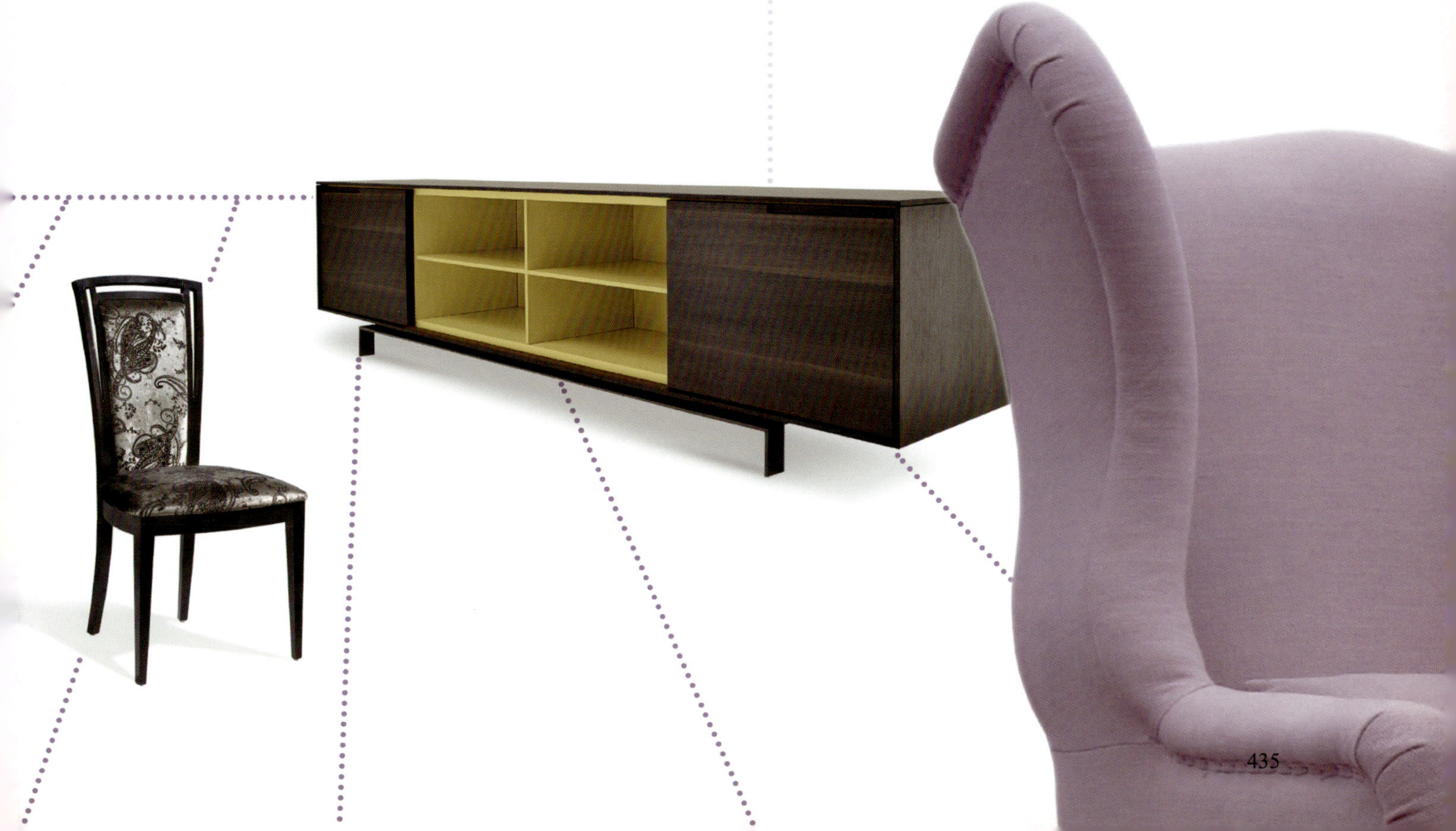

力邀酒店开发商、酒店管理公司、酒店设计公司、专业采购决策者
打造酒店业最高端精品展

精彩的现场活动
Events & attractions

"10+10"闭门峰会
10 plus 10 Closed-door Summit

酒店样板房展示
Hotel Sample Room Display

现场体验区
On-site Experience

买家专区
Tailored business match between buyers and suppliers

高峰论坛
Industry Forum

展品分类
Exhibits categories

食品与饮料
Food & beverage

烹饪与餐饮
Catering & kitchen equipment

放松与休闲
Fitness & leisure

连锁与管理
Hotel Franchise & Management

装饰与设计
Decorative arts & design

工程与信息
Facilities & hotel IT

清洁与养护
Cleaning & maintenance

国际展区
International pavilion

往届参展商
Previous Exhibitors

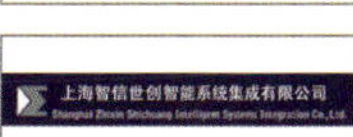

The 7th International Hotel Expo 2011

(Equipment & Supplies, Audio & Lighting, Entertainment Performance, Decoration Materials, Food & Beverage, Hotel Operations & Management)

第七届国际酒店展 2011

（设备、用品、灯光、音响、娱乐表演、装饰材料、餐饮及酒店经营）

2011. 11. 23 - 25

Cotai Strip® CotaiExpo™ (The Venetian Macao)
路氹金光大道® 金光会展™ (澳门威尼斯人会展中心)

Concurrent Activities同场精彩活动:

- ★ Asian Hotel General Managers Forum
  亚洲地区酒店总经理高峰论坛
- ★ Seminar on Co-operation between Hotels & SMEs
  酒店业与中、小企业合作研讨会
- ★ Business Matching
  商业配对
- ★ The Best Hotel Furniture Suppliers Election
  金牌酒店家具供应商选举
- ★ Macau Int'l Lotus Cup Hotel Furniture Design Competition
  荷花杯酒店家具设计大赛
- ★ Coffee Culture Workshop
  咖啡文化工作坊
- ★ Lotus Cup PRD The Best Coffee Enterprises
  荷花杯珠三角最佳咖啡企业
- ★ Spa & Wellness Forum
  水疗及养生论坛
- ★ Cooking Demonstration
  烹调示范

…and many more 及更多

◆ Approval Authority / 批准单位
中国国际贸易促进委员会
◆ Sponsors / 主办单位
中国国际展览中心集团公司
中国建筑装饰协会
◆ Organizer / 承办单位
北京中装华港建筑科技展览有限公司
◆ Chief Strategy-cooperated Media
首席战略合作媒体
2012年3月5日-8日
Mar.5th-8th,2012
13th China (Shanghai) International Wallpaper & Decorative Textile Exposition
第十三届中国(北京)国际墙纸布艺博览会
13th China (Shanghai) International Home Textile & Interior Decorations Exposition
第十三届中国(北京)国际家居软装饰博览会
新国展 & 老国展
两馆同期联展 精彩不容错过
China International Exhibition Center,Beijing
北京.中国国际展览中心[老馆]
[北京.朝阳区北三环东路6号]
China International Exhibition Center [New Venue],Beijing
北京.中国国际展览中心[新馆]
[北京.顺义天竺裕翔路88号]
Exhibition Scale / 展会规模
Show area / 展览面积 / 160,000 平方米
No. of Booths / 展位数量 / 8000 余个
No. of Exhibitors / 参展企业 / 2000 余家
No. of Visitors(2011) / 上届观众 / 180,000 人次
始终·被·模仿 & 从未·被·超越
Always Been Imitated, Never Been Exceeded
Contact information / 展会联络:
北京中装华港建筑科技展览有限公司
China B & D Exhibition Co.,Ltd.
Address / 地址:
Rm.388,4F,Hall 1,CIEC, No.6 East Beisanhuan Road,Beijing
北京市朝阳区北三环东路 6 号中国国际展览中心一号馆四层 388 室
Official Website / 官方网站: Http: www.build-decor.com
Tel / 电 话: +86(0)10-84600901 / 0903
Fax / 传 真: +86(0)10-84600910
E-mail / 邮 箱: zhanlan0906@sina.com
Guangzhou Office / 广州办事处
Tel / 电 话: +86(0)20-34318225
Fax / 传 真: +86(0)20-34318227
E-mail / 邮 箱: qianmin521@126.com
LOVE WALLPAPER ENJOY LIFE
全球年度顶级墙纸盛宴
Top Global Wallpaper Exposition
HOMEDECOR CHINA
CHINA WALLPAPER

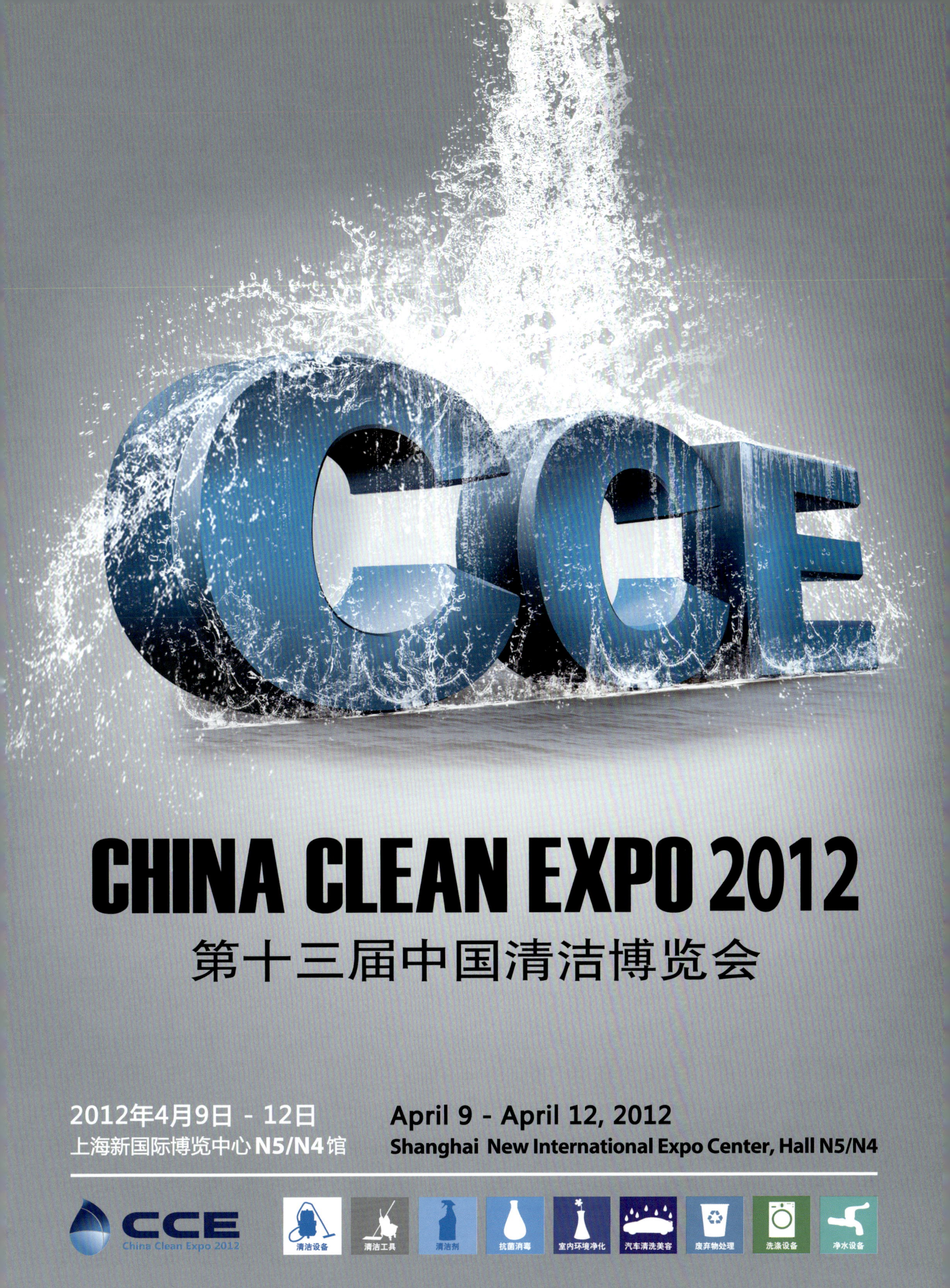

CCE
China Clean Expo 2012

清洁设备

清洁工具

清洁剂

抗菌消毒

室内环境净化

汽车清洗美容

废弃物处理

洗涤设备

净水设备

第十三届中国国际建筑陶瓷
及卫浴科技精品展览会
CERAMICS
CHINA
Ceramics, Tile & Sanitary Ware China 2012
www.ceramics-china.cn
2012年4月9日－12日　上海新国际博览中心（龙阳路2345号）
亚洲第一大建陶行业盛会！
同期举办
2012中国国际马赛克、装饰艺术砖及石材展览会
2012中国国际建筑装饰展览会
2012 国际精品设计展
主办单位：中国建筑卫生陶瓷协会　上海博华国际展览有限公司
86-21-64371178　ceramics@ubmsinoexpo.com
HDD Hotelex+Design&Deco
200,000 平米 sqms
2,200 供应商 exhibitors
100,000 观众 visitors